D1569572

The French Tradition and the Literature of Medieval England

The French presence in English literary history in the centuries following the Conquest has to some extent been glossed over or treated as an interlude. During this period, roughly 1100–1420, French, like Latin, was the language of the educated; in the courts of England, and for nobles, clerics, and the rising commercial elements, communication was multilingual.

In his ground-breaking study, William Calin explores this era of medieval English literature and culture in relation to its distinctly French influences and contemporaries. He examines the Anglo-Norman contribution to medieval literature, concentrating on romance and hagiography; the great continental French texts, such as *Prose Lancelot* and the *Romance of the Rose*, which had a dominant role in shaping literature in English; and the English response to the French cultural world – the two 'modes' in English where the French presence was most significant: court poetry (Chaucer, Gower, Hoccleve) and Middle English romance.

This book is grounded in French sources both well known and relatively obscure. Translations of the Old French make *The French Tradition and the Literature of Medieval England* accessible to scholars and students of Medieval English, comparatists, and historians, as well as those proficient in French. Calin develops a synthesis of medieval French and English literature that will be especially useful for classroom study.

WILLIAM CALIN is a graduate research professor in the Department of Romance Languages at the University of Florida, Gainesville.

WILLIAM CALIN

The French Tradition and the Literature of Medieval England

UNIVERSITY OF TORONTO PRESS
Toronto Buffalo London

Toronto Buffalo London
Printed in Canada

ISBN 0-8020-0565-9 (cloth)
ISBN 0-8020-7202-X (paper)

Printed on acid-free paper

Canadian Cataloguing in Publication Data

Calin, William
The French tradition and the literature of medieval England

(University of Toronto romance series)
Includes bibliographical references and index.
ISBN 0-8020-0565-9 (bound) ISBN 0-8020-7202-X (pbk.)

1. English literature – Middle English, 1100–1500 – History and criticism.
2. English literature – French influences.
3. Anglo-Norman literature – History and criticism.
4. French literature – To 1500 – History and criticism.
I. Title. II Series.

PR128.C35 1994 820.9′001 C94-930359-3

Contents

Preface

For three hundred years after the Conquest French was the language of the upper classes in England – the language of the court, international commerce, law and administration, and, along with Latin, of belles-lettres. The most important vernacular literature produced in England between 1100 and 1350 was in French; writing in English, up to 1500 and beyond, was bathed in a French ambiance and looked to the French in addition to the Latin for order and inspiration.

All this is known; it has long become a scholarly cliché. Nevertheless, earlier generations of scholars in English studies, working within their own domain and producing, I may add, the finest corpus of practical criticism of medieval texts anywhere in the world, were inevitably too busy to attend to the French sphere, or they treated French texts largely as sources for Chaucer and Malory. Similarly, the great books in Anglo-Norman were neglected by specialists in Old French; they have been scrupulously edited and their literary history determined but have not, for the most part, been studied within a critical framework. The same is true for a number of great works produced on the Continent.

In more recent years, major studies by Anglicists have broken new ground and opened up new vistas (among others, Vinaver 1947, Muscatine 1957, Wimsatt 1968, 1991, Benson 1976, Crane 1986). Much of the spadework has also been done; the microanalysis, the minute comparison of French and English texts, is exemplary. Unfortunately, given the functioning of highly specialized scholarship in our universities, it takes time for a major shift in consciousness to reach all people in the profession.

It is still the fact today that, for a number of historians and literary people, the French phase in English literary history is glossed over or treated as an interlude. There are many who still refer to Chaucer's French *Roman de Renart* and fabliau sources as international beast fables or international comic tales, and to the French sources of English metrical romance as popular romance or legend or folk tradition. A number of studies still comment on the creative genius and conscious artistry of an English text when it is a direct translation or adaptation of a French text. It is also inevitable that currents in scholarly research come and go and that the 'French Chaucer' will give way to an 'English Chaucer' or an 'Italian Chaucer.' And it is by no means uncommon to find students of Chaucer, Gower, Lydgate, or Middle English in general, who refer to their author(s) as having, in his (their) best work, moved away from rigid French allegory or facile French courtliness or superficial French conventionality, toward a deepened, more genuine, more authentic consciousness and sense of the work of art. This artistic consciousness, encompassing a grander view of man's freedom and dignity and a new, exalted idea of classical Antiquity, is often then ascribed to the influence of Italy, or even to the presence in fourteenth- and fifteenth-century England of something akin to the Renaissance.

Here the question of aesthetic value-judgment enters in. The great French texts of the Middle Ages do not, as a matter of course, form part of the English-speaking nations' canon of world literature. With the exception of Villon, and perhaps *La Chanson de Roland* and Chrétien, the student of English literature does not hold books written in Old French in the same esteem as he does the Greek and Roman classics, or for that matter the Italian classics of the trecento. Therefore, until recent times Anglicists have treated a topic such as 'Chaucer and Machaut' or 'Malory and the *Prose Lancelot*' quite differently from the way they treat, say, 'Chaucer and Boccaccio' or 'Gower and Ovid.' When the French books are compared to those of a major English author, it is assumed that the English text is central, and the French text functions in relation to it. This way of viewing things, the 'great books approach' or the 'Whig school of literary history,' is itself a product of the action of historical forces in the late nineteenth and early twentieth century;[1] it has changed in recent years, partly as a result of France's own revaluation of her medieval heritage and partly because scholars in French studies have laboured to bring into the canon the entire range of texts from the *Song of Roland* to the end of the fifteenth century. Nevertheless, old ideas die hard. Here also, the consciousness of a new generation of Anglicists and of Old French scholars has not necessarily reached the profession as a whole.

For these reasons and others, I believe that the question of the French Middle Ages and medieval English literature needs to be reconsidered; indeed the time is ripe for a synthesis or, if the term 'synthesis' is inappropriate and unfeasible in less than ten volumes, for a study in some depth in a few of the more significant problem areas. I propose four such areas.

The first concerns Anglo-Norman. I should like to indicate the distinctive features of the Anglo-Norman contribution to medieval literature. In my opinion, it is not primarily historical, didactic, or religious, but narrative. Therefore the two principal 'imaginative' genres are explored: romance and hagiography. Following Legge's (1963) example, I consider Anglo-Norman to comprise all literature written in the French language in England or for the use of an English (francophone) patron or public and so Marie de France, Beroul, and Wace are included. The consecrated authors of romance – Marie, Beroul, and Thomas – have long been enshrined in the medieval canon. I endeavour to indicate some of the reasons why their works are literary masterpieces and what they have contributed to the medieval mindset. I am also concerned with the avenues that Anglo-Norman romance took after the 'classical generation': mannered, sophisticated wit and artistic self-consciousness, in *Ipomedon*; the extremes of sentiment and the implications of extreme sentiment in an idyllic romance structure, in *Amadas et Ydoine*; story-telling and adventure for their own sake combined with English national spirit in an ancestral-baronial romance, *Gui de Warewic*.

The other genre presented here is sacred biography. Saints' lives, a neglected genre in French medieval studies, manifest in traditional, conventional, and archetypal terms fascinating patterns of narrative and of imagery, and a no less fascinating world-view. Particularly important is the fact that the Anglo-Norman achievement extends beyond the third quarter of the twelfth century and beyond Arthurian romance and Breton lay.

The second section treats major continental French texts that were translated, adapted, or imitated by English writers, and which thus played a dominant role in shaping Middle English literature. Some of them contributed 'myths' that were later to occupy a significant place in English culture. Some of these books are well known to medievalists, others await serious critical scrutiny. The reason for devoting space to the analysis of continental French books is three-fold. I wish to emphasize the fact that writers in English were never restricted to 'their own' Anglo-Norman insular tradition in the past but, on the contrary, were always aware of the latest developments on the Continent in the present. They were truly international and contemporary in taste and culture. Shifts in taste on the Continent explain otherwise paradoxical directions taken in Middle English – romance, in verse and in prose, was oriented toward the *Lancelot-Grail* in prose, not Chrétien de Troyes; Chaucer and Gower were shaped by Machaut and Froissart, not Chrétien nor the early trouvères. The standing of these French books today and how today's French medievalists interpret them can help relate them to the English because the way we read Digulleville or Machaut or the *Prose Lancelot* helps determine how we read Chaucer, Gower, and Malory. In sum, I wish to show that a number of crucial developments in Middle and Early Modern English – great mythical figures such as Auberon, Lancelot, and Arthur; the narrative technique of interlace; the mode of allegory, sacred and secular; literature as irony and satire or as disjunction and deferral; the dream vision and *dit amoureux*; the self-conscious pseudo-autobiographical narrator; the historical ideal of English chivalry and heroism – are derived from continental French masterpieces.

I then propose to deal with the English response to and assimilation of the Anglo-Norman and continental French cultural world. The third section focuses on the summit of medieval English literature in the French style – the court poetry of Chaucer, Gower, and Hoccleve. In the Chaucer chapter I shall concentrate on structure, narrative technique, irony, and intertextuality, both in dream poems and in six of the *Canterbury Tales*. The French influence was pervasive throughout Chaucer's career. John Gower is especially interesting as a native Englishman who composed two important books, *Mirour de l'Omme* and *Cinkante Balades*, in French, and his *Confessio Amantis* in English. The majority of scholars treat Gower as an avowedly Christian author, working within the penitential tradition; I read him from a French perspective, as a secular, courtly writer, full of comic brio, the follower of Jean de Meun and Guillaume de Machaut. Thomas Hoccleve, relatively neglected in English studies, is, in my opinion, a major poet in that same secular, courtly tradition beginning with *Le Roman de la Rose*. Throughout I make the point that the English poets adopt themes, motifs, conventions, and genres from the French; much of what marks Chaucer and Gower as innovators in English is also to be found in the works of their French predecessors. There is then, continuing the work of the predecessors, a complex, dynamic, sophisticated English tradition in the secular courtly mode.

The last portion of my book is devoted to the phenomenon of translation-adaptation in English romance. Applying the findings of Michel Huby (1968, 1984) on Hohenstaufen Germany, I try to dispel misconceptions concerning the social and aesthetic function of the genre due in part to what I should call an incomplete appreciation of the French romance tradition. Middle English romance ought not to be condemned vis-à-vis an abstract model of romance based on, for instance, Chrétien de Troyes because, among other things, French romance itself evolved in the thirteenth century in a manner parallel to the one the English romances generally took; besides, English romances often correspond to French romances and *chansons de geste*. Both languages have masterworks different from but not necessarily inferior to Chrétien. Secondly, the English romancers, faced with a French text, did not create their own philosophy or world-view. They were 'courtly adapters' or 'courtly translators,' concerned with adhering to the precepts of *amplificatio* and *abbreviatio*, and with the idea of making their version of the French source more courtly and chivalrous and even more the exemplar of courtly ideals.

After theoretical considerations, I examine a number of English verse narratives as discrete works of art from an archetypal and myth criticism perspective, concentrating on romance narrative structure. This section then proceeds to a brief analysis of the English adoption of a new, fashionable current of French literature in the second half of the fifteenth century – prose romance – and of the impact of the new fashion on Caxton and Malory. *Le Morte Darthur* can also be envisaged fruitfully within the tradition of courtly adaptation, performing in prose what Malory's predecessors did in verse.

Such a book, even extending to six hundred pages, inevitably proves to be incomplete. I had to limit myself; therefore, important areas – satiric and religious allegory (Langland, the *Pearl*-poet), Lydgate, the late courtly lyric, and the theatre – will not be covered. Also, for reasons of space, except for the Malory section, I stop at approximately 1420. The shape that the French presence and the imitation of French will take after that date is by then determined. Also, without adhering to Huizinga's (1924) misleading notion of decline or waning, I recognize that the English poets of the fifteenth century are not quite of the same rank as the Ricardians. Finally, I should explain that, for reasons of clarity, I group the French and English books separately. This is because I do not propose the microanalysis of English texts and their French sources. It has been done by a number of scholars. Instead, I am concerned with broader issues of genre, mode, structure, and style.

Among the issues I implicitly and explicitly address are the following: Which French genres and modes were the most popular in England, and why? What shifts in taste can be observed over the centuries, and what are the shifts from insular to continental fashion? What are the goals and uses of translation-adaptation at the time? Which characteristics in outlook, ideology, structure, and style did the English borrow from their Francophone (insular and continental) predecessors and contemporaries? Are there verifiable divergences in temperament between the French and the English? the Anglo-Normans and the English?

I concentrate on the close reading of texts (practical criticism) that can lead to theoretical and cultural considerations of a more general nature. I hope to show the pervasiveness of the Anglo-Norman and continental presence from 1066 to the fifteenth century, and to show that it shaped the English court poem in its entirety, providing the climate for Chaucer's best books and also for those of Gower and Hoccleve. In addition, the writers of English romance, in verse and in prose, from *King Horn* and *Floris and Blauncheflur* to *Le Morte Darthur,* worked entirely in the French tradition and benefited totally from it. The French legacy casts new light on the English modes, genres, and texts. There are other implications as well. Much of traditional, medieval English culture – chivalry, courtesy, courtly love, and clerical urbanity – is of international and more specifically French origin. Much of what we in America rightly consider to be the foundations of modern Western civilization comes from the Middle Ages, from a burst of creativity in France and England, an 'Anglo-French Connection' made up of nobles and clerics who spoke the same international language and inhabited the same international world.

Acknowledgments

Some pages in this book were published previously. They are taken from material that appeared in *The Legacy of Chrétien de Troyes II* (Amsterdam: Rodopi, 1988); *French Review* 62 (1988–9); *Continuations* (Birmingham: Summa, 1989); *Fifteenth-Century Studies* 17 (1990); *Mediaevalia* 16 (1992); *In Honor of Hans-Erich Keller* (Kalamazoo: Western Michigan University, 1993); *The Shaping of Text* (Lewisburg: Bucknell University Press, 1993); and my *A Muse for Heroes* (University of Toronto Press, 1983).

The research and writing were aided by a Fulbright Travel Grant (1982), a Fulbright Senior Research Grant for France and the United Kingdom (1987–8), and a National Endowment for the Humanities Fellowship for Independent Study and Research (1984–5). I also benefited from being appointed Visiting Professor at the University of Poitiers (1982, 1984) and Visiting Fellow of Clare Hall, Cambridge (1984–5). I thank the Council for International Exchange of Scholars, the National Endowment for the Humanities, the Centre d'Etudes Supérieures de Civilisation Médiévale, and Clare Hall. The University of Florida provided superb working conditions and major financial support.

Françoise Calin (University of Oregon) offered encouragement and instilled common sense, from beginning to end; her counsel was invaluable. My former student, Caroline Jewers (University of Kansas) read the manuscript and proposed emendations with wit and brio, improving its style and substance. So also did the anonymous referees for the University of Toronto Press, and my copy-editor, Miriam Skey, of the Records of Early English Drama (University of Toronto). I am grateful to Alexandra Johnston, who served on the University of

Toronto Press Manuscript Committee; and to my research assistants at the University of Florida: Sylvia Newman, Renée Jourdenais, and Tonhu Hoang.

It was a special pleasure to work with Ron Schoeffel, Editor-in-Chief, Anne Forte, Managing Editor, and Miriam Skey, who are the exemplars of their domain.

I thank them all.

The French Tradition and the Literature of Medieval England

Introduction

French was for three centuries after 1066 the language of the upper classes in England. Or was it? In recent years a fascinating controversy has surfaced concerning who actually spoke French and for how long, a controversy little known outside specialized circles of philologists and historians of the language.

According to the old view, argued most vigorously by Legge (1941–2, 1950, 1980), French was used not only in any number of areas – informal correspondence, semi-formal and formal official correspondence, wills, deeds, writs, petitions, bills, proclamations, epitaphs, Privy Seal and Signet documents, the baronial courts, diplomacy, mercantile and municipal laws, merchant guilds' ordinances, land and sea commerce, and discussion, conversation, and instruction in the cloisters – but also, in the twelfth and thirteenth centuries, French became a true vernacular in the Kingdom of England. This means that French would have penetrated widely and deeply into the lower strata of society, that nearly everyone was, during this period, bilingual to some extent, and that nearly everyone had some fluency in French, a tongue that, more than English, played the role of insular *lingua franca*.

A number of specialists, however, contest the theory (especially Rothwell 1968, 1975–6, 1983, 1985 and Short 1979–80). According to the revisionists the masses of the English people remained largely monolingual, and the nobles and the high clergy, originally Francophone, soon became bilingual. Furthermore, by the thirteenth century and perhaps as early as the end of the twelfth century, French ceased to be the mother tongue even of the nobles. It became, for everyone, an acquired language not used in everyday life. The major pieces of documentation supporting this hypothesis are the following: evidence from men of letters, in Latin, that Englishmen of good family went abroad or undertook special studies to learn French; evidence from sources on the Continent and in England that the French spoken in England (Marlborough French, 'Gallicum Merleburgae') was subject to mockery, for its morphology, syntax, and lexicon as well as the pronunciation; a whole corpus of texts – word-lists, grammars, conversation books – that appeared in England to teach the French language, using as the language of reference Latin or English; apologies from Anglo-Norman authors, going back to the 1160s, for their inadequate command of French; and finally, church writings confirming that both Latin and French were elite tongues not normally understood by the faithful.

In my opinion, the evidence on both sides is, as always in matters of controversy, subject to interpretation. Was the spate of language books in thirteenth- and fourteenth-century England a sign that everyone needed to learn French? or that the middle classes and some county families were eager to rise socially? or that people felt insecure in their vernacular vis-à-vis the French of Paris, now become an international standard? Indeed, did the aristocracy cease to speak French as a native tongue or did they accept the Parisian judgment that insular speech lacked the elegance and refinement of the standard? In other words, did they wish to learn French or to unlearn Anglo-Norman? If in Froissart's day the English commissioners claimed not to understand the 'franceis de France,' should we take their reticence at face value? Or are they not shrewdly stalling for time and playing a diplomatic game?

Rothwell's revisionist interpretation is very convincing. I believe that he and his colleagues read the evidence with more rigour and, unlike the older school, are more likely to distinguish between writing and speaking and between a mother tongue and an acquired language. I agree with the conclusions that French never made great headway with the masses of the people and that, even with the upper and educated elites, French was a living language primarily in the southern half of England and those occasional towns, such as York, that housed civil servants from London. Geographical closeness to London and the seat of government or to foreign commerce (Southampton, Dover) are the keys to prevalence of French. In addition, the uniformity of the French spoken in England, in contrast to the diversity of the English dialects, is clear evidence that the language was not a true vernacular in all classes. If it had been a true vernacular for a good two centuries, we would be informed of the particular evolution of London French, Southampton French, Oxford French, etc. As it is, we are not.

However, I am not convinced that, for the upper classes and educated elites, French was always an acquired language. The influx of continental Francophones throughout the Middle Ages caused social tensions and political resentment. They also brought native-speaking competence. The exchange of children between courts in a general Francophone ambiance would also contribute to language use (Legge 1980). That Anglo-Normans apologized for the quality of their French, and that continental Frenchmen mocked the English, proves only that the Parisian standard was in the process of asserting its hegemony against the insular language but also against Picard French and Occitan. In modern times also, central French writers have mocked the *patois* and French-speakers from Gascony or Alsace or Canada. Richter (1979) offers some fascinating statistics concerning evidence given for the proposed canonization of Bishop Thomas Cantilupe, after the year 1300; of the clerks, one-half testified in Latin, one-half in French; lay people from the town testified one-half in French and one-half in English; lay people from the country testified ninety per cent in English.

Rothwell (1985, 1985–6) himself insists that, unlike Latin, French remained a vital, living language and the most current medium of communication in the upper echelons of society. He also reminds us of the extraordinary, native-like command of a complex linguistic system in the major writers such as Grosseteste. Instead of the analogy of immigrant tongues failing to survive in today's England, we might offer the picture of English in India, where, acquired for many, native for some, the extremes of dialect development juxtapose with the most elegant Oxonian and where diglossia is a more or less general rule. Perhaps for Anglo-Norman also, centuries ago, whether the language was native or acquired is indeed less important than its functioning in society. This was probably a process of diglossia where the learned, refined French would dominate in literature, the schools, the court, the law, administration, commerce, and the cloister and the familiar English would prevail in the home, in the tavern, on the road, and on the farm.

In addition, it is the revisionists who insist that after 1204 we must not consider Anglo-Norman to be dead and degenerate. It was specifically in these later Middle Ages that French replaced Latin as a language of record and a great, vital language of culture. French proved to be a rich, complex medium adequate for the needs of a complex civilization and for the expression of ideas in science, medicine, history, agriculture, the law, administration, devotion, and theology. The very language books written in England – Walter of Bibbesworth's *Tretiz de langage; Nominale; Femina; Tractatus orthographiae; Orthographia gallica; Donait françois;* and the various 'Manieres de langage' – that testify to the decline of French as a widespread natural vernacular also testify to the high esteem in which it was held; like Latin, French was studied, glossed, and taught in the schools, especially in Oxford. Throughout Western Europe French became the principal non-classical vehicle of cultural ideas and of belles-lettres. In these domains Anglo-Norman went hand-in-hand with, and often preceded, central French.

Whatever the linguistic condition of French in the British Isles, spoken or written, native or acquired, in the twelfth century or the fourteenth, the facts of French literary presence and dominance are unquestionable. Let us consider the manuscript situation and the question of patronage.

We have relatively good knowledge concerning monastic libraries in England (Blaess 1957, 1973; Wilson 1958). Some six thousand manuscripts are extant, along with fifty-eight catalogues and one hundred sixty-eight lists of 'books on loan,' donations, or partial inventories. In general, the vast majority of manuscripts are in Latin and, as to be expected, there is a strong preponderance of religious texts over the secular. However, second only to Latin, ahead of all other languages, ancient and modern, stands the French corpus. Forty-one monastic libraries are known to have contained books in French. In first place by far were the Benedictines, followed by the Austin Canons and the Cistercians. Sometimes *chansons de geste* and romances were to be found alongside the usual devotional and didactic books, psalters, and chronicles. Although the French literary presence in the cloisters is especially frequent in the fourteenth century when the impact of epic, romance, and chronicle is felt, French manuscripts are also listed in the earlier centuries and, again, in the fifteenth.

One of the most famous donations of books occurred in 1305 when Guy de Beauchamp, Earl of Warwick, gave some forty volumes in French to the Cistercian abbey of Bordesley in Worcestershire. He gave none in English. This donation, which includes a good number of texts in secular narrative (epic, romance, history), tells us that the holdings in the monasteries were determined by bequests and donations as well as by the religious' own interests; it also tells us about the culture and taste of the English aristocracy that made the bequests.

We know that, of the one hundred sixty 'libri diversi' issued and/or received under Edward II and the young Edward III, fifty-nine were 'libri de romanciis' (Vale 1982). A large number of French books were issued to Queen Isabella in 1327. Quite a bit of controversy has developed over the library of Richard II. However, Green (1976) is very convincing when he argues that Richard inherited some fourteen French books from Edward III and that eleven of them were pawned or sold. Only three were recovered, although Richard both received and donated other French books in his lifetime. One such occasion was in 1395 when Froissart presented the monarch with a luxurious copy of his works in verse.

The library of Thomas Woodstock, Duke of Gloucester, was confiscated in 1397. It included twenty-five volumes in Latin, three in English, and forty-eight in French; there was a rich, varied selection of French works, sacred and secular. Eleanor de Bohun, Duchess of Gloucester, bequeathed a number of primarily religious volumes – a few in Latin, the majority in French, and none in English. The inventory of Sir Simon Burley, executed in 1388, includes one book in Latin, one in English, and nineteen in French; of the nineteen, eight volumes were devoted to narrative fiction. Duke Humphrey of Gloucester, famous for his 'humanist' collection in Latin, also had books in French and apparently preferred to read his Latin in French translation. John of Bedford acquired Charles V's famous library in France, though it was dispersed after his death. Finally, Edward IV is known for his strong Burgundian taste, stimulated by exile in Bruges as the guest of Louis de Gruthuyse; his stay led to the acquisition of a number of elegant, expensive French manuscripts which helped shape the literary interests of a generation. In general, after 1200, the English monarchs and magnates, except for Gloucester and Bedford, were less cultured and less book-conscious than their immediate contemporaries on the Continent. However, whatever their culture and consciousness, as far as we can tell, their libraries had a very large, often dominant, French orientation; also, like the cloisters, they had few or no English volumes at all.

Again, without having the same wide cultural interests as their equivalents on the Continent, the English aristocracy and monarchy played a role in encouraging and patronizing letters in French (Legge 1963, Salter 1988). Some tried their own hand. King Richard the Lion-Hearted is credited with the composition of two lyrics in French and Occitan; Edward II authored a fifteen-stanza *complainte* after his deposition, a song of sorrow and repentance. Charles d'Orléans' friend,

William de la Pole, Duke of Suffolk, may have composed the seven French courtly lyrics attributed to him. Sir John Montagu, Earl of Salisbury, did write some French poems, praised by Christine de Pizan, which, unfortunately, are not extant. More important than this is the major devotional work in prose by Henry of Grosmont, first Duke of Lancaster, the very gifted *Livre de Seyntz Medicines.* In the fifteenth century a number of English noblemen turned to translating from French into English: Sir Richard Roos worked on Alain Chartier's *Belle Dame sans mercy;* Edward, Duke of York's *The Master of Game* is a version of Gaston de Foix's *Livre de la Chasse;* Sir Gilbert Hay translated from French books; Anthony Woodville, Earl of Rivers, translated Chartier and Christine de Pizan, and his books were printed by Caxton. Caxton also published, as we well know, Sir Thomas Malory's *translatio* of French Arthurian romance. There are a number of other literate gentlemen of the period, for example, Sir Robert Shottesbrook, who translated Laurent d'Orléans' *Somme le roi.*

The English upper classes maintained close contact with continental French aristocrats and continental French writers, a number of whom spent time in England, sometimes but not necessarily under the patronage of an English lord. In the twelfth century, of course, Marie de France dwelt in England, although under what conditions we do not know. So did the Norman Guillaume le Clerc, and the author of the *Life* of William Marshall. Guernes de Pont-Sainte-Maxence, author of a famous life of St Thomas à Becket, visited the island; so, probably, did Beroul, and perhaps also Chrétien de Troyes and some troubadours; however we cannot be certain. By the age of Edward III, we find the poet and composer Jean de la Motte installed in England for a number of years, along with Jean Froissart, both as clients of Queen Isabella. Under the auspices of King John II, taken prisoner at Poitiers, we find Gace de la Buigne, who began his *Roman des Deduits* in England. Also in residence during the Chaucer years was Oton de Granson. And, in the fifteenth century, we must not forget the most distinguished of captives, the prince-poet Charles d'Orléans. All these figures had an impact on insular writing in French and in English; they all contributed to the fruitful cultural interchange between the two kingdoms and the two languages.

Even during the decline of Anglo-Norman, kings of England took an interest in French literature. Books were dedicated to them, and they commissioned other books or the translation of books (especially of Guillaume de Digulleville). Henry IV tried to persuade Christine de Pizan to come to his court; the Duke of Bedford purchased Charles

V's library and, had he lived, would have prevented its dispersal. Lydgate is perhaps the leading exemplar of what I mean – a major English poet commissioned by generations of English royalty and high aristocracy, active primarily in adapting from the French. And, at least in the domain of music, the cultural relations were reciprocal; because of Bedford's regency, major English musicians – Dunstable, John Pyamour, Robert Morton, and Walter Frye – worked in Paris and later in Burgundy, and made settings for French as well as Latin texts (see Wilkins 1983).

I have touched upon only a few areas. Even so cursory an overview indicates to how great an extent French was perceived as the language of lay culture, and French literature as a natural prerogative of the English upper classes. It made up part of an international feudal-chivalric-courtly civilization in which the English naturally and automatically participated and which was *theirs*.

In this discussion I have referred for the most part to the later Middle Ages, when French was an acquired language of prestige and culture, and its impact upon the English vernacular was very important. In the twelfth century, the years included in the reigns of Henry I, Stephen, Henry II, Richard I, and John, we find a quite different situation altogether (cf. Bezzola 1960–3). The Norman and Angevin monarchs were truly Frenchmen as well as Englishmen, and more occupied with their French holdings and French concerns than their insular ones. Their courts attracted a mixture of races and peoples: English, Welsh, Norman-French, Angevin-French, speakers of Occitan from Poitou and Aquitaine, and many more. In contrast to the Capetian kings of France, at this early period not especially oriented toward culture and the life of the mind, the Norman and Plantagenet kings and queens of England presided over an extraordinary renaissance in letters, both sacred and secular, in Latin, French, and Occitan. It is true, we must avoid the sometimes excessive adulation of an Eleanor of Aquitaine, which has led enthusiasts to ascribe to her personal patronage almost all the great secular writing of the century. Distinctions have to be made when texts are dedicated or offered to a (potential? real?) patron or when a later text claims that 'X' was written for 'Y' or when, in the course of a work, author 'W' (gratuitously? with patronage as a goal? in the actual service of his patron?) praises monarch 'Z.' Bearing all this in mind, it is nonetheless a fact that, in the course of the century, a number of major literary modes were cultivated within first the Norman and then the Plantagenet domain, the 'espace Plantagenêt.' These include

1. History in Latin. The *Historia Normannorum* by William of Jumièges and the *Gesta Wilhelmi Conquistoris* by William of Poitiers were composed for the Conqueror. A far greater school of historical writing surfaced in the succeeding century, the luminaries all from England: William of Malmesbury, Henry of Huntingdon, Roger of Hoveden, and William of Newburgh.

2. Belles-lettres and Ideas in Latin. In this category should be ranged a number of writers and intellectual figures, the majority of whom come from the island kingdom: John of Salisbury, Gerald of Wales, Walter Map, and Peter of Blois; and on the more technical side (science, law, administration), Adelard of Bath, Richard Fitzneale, Ranulf of Glanville, Gervase of Tilbury, and Aelred of Rievaulx.

3. Latin Poetry. Here we find three great poets from the Continent, with connections to the English royal house: Marbod of Rennes, Hildebert of Lavardin, and Baudri of Bourgueil. Later, in the time of Henry II, two epic poets appear, Walter of Châtillon and Joseph of Exeter.

4. Troubadour Poetry. Some one hundred and thirty poets of Occitan flourished in the 'espace Plantagenêt.' A number of the very greatest – Bernart de Ventadorn, Bertran de Born, Guiraut de Bornelh, Peire Vidal, Gaucelm Faidit, Folquet de Marselha, and the Monk of Montaudon – had relations with King Richard I, Geoffrey of Brittany, the 'Young King,' and/or Queen Eleanor.

5. History in French. After books in Latin come chronicles and history in French concerned with the Norman, British, and English past: Gaimar, *Estorie des Engleis*; Wace, *Roman de Brut* and *Roman de Rou*; Benoît, *Chronique des ducs de Normandie*; Jordan Fantosme, *Chronique*.

6. Romance in French: Matter of Rome. In the Plantagenet region, probably under the auspices of Henry and Eleanor, came into being the first great classicizing endeavour in modern Western culture, the romance adaptations of books from Antiquity: *Le Roman de Thèbes*, *Le Roman d'Eneas*, Benoît's *Roman de Troie*, and the Alexander romances.

7. Romance in French: Matter of Britain. At the same time and at the same courts, occurred the creation of the great new Arthurian myth, derived from (pseudo)history – Geoffrey of Monmouth's *Historia* and Wace's *Brut* – and also from Celtic folklore. These texts include Marie de France's *Lais* and the first great Tristan romances by Beroul and Thomas. They and the Matter of Rome were to give rise, in turn, to a flowering of romance on the Continent and in England, that was to last into the thirteenth century.

This literary flowering, in all its varied modes and genres, is associated, first of all, with the kings and queens of England, almost all of whom played a role in the patronage nexus: William the Conqueror; Henry I, Maud, and Adeliza; Stephen and the Empress Maud; Henry II, Eleanor, and the Young King; and Richard I. A number of great barons also served as patrons as did several princes of the Church. It is the Anglo-Norman families – the Lovels, the Bigods, the Beauchamps – who probably launched the Matter of England ancestral or baronial romances, conceived to enhance the Norman line by associating it with semifictional great figures of the national past. And the monasteries were particularly important as nurturing sources for literature, in French as well as in Latin.

The result was a new literature giving voice to new ways of looking at the world. It marked the flowering of vernacular, courtly, personal, and secular literature in juxtaposition to the Latin, learned, public, and sacred. Just as the Norman and Angevin kings encouraged the new myths of King Arthur and British history to counter the Capetian monarchs with their Carolingian myths and French history, so also they aided the growth of a new secular humanism, grounded in the ideals of *urbanitas* and *dulcedo*, of *fin' amor* and *curteisie*, and of *chevalerie* and *clergie*, all contributing to a *translatio imperii et studii* that would celebrate feats in arms and piety, of course, but also civility, the polishing of manners, beneficent emulation, a renewed bond with Antiquity, and the rise of the individual. This would culminate in the ideal of the lettered prince, master of *fortitudo et sapientia*, and of the new writer, a clerkly narrator figure who participates in the world of *curteisie* and, by his presence and his writing, makes it live. This is perhaps the major contribution of vernacular culture to the Middle Ages, in England and in all of Europe.

The impact on English of all these developments is enormous. First of all, there is the influence of French on the language. It is well known that the English vocabulary was immeasurably enriched by borrowing from French in the areas of government and administration, the Church, the law, the army and navy, fashion, cuisine and social life, art, learning, and medicine. Some ten thousand French words were taken over in the Middle Ages; three quarters of them have survived to our day. Less publicized is the effect of accelerated drift due to linguistic interference, the acceleration of 'natural' evolution in the language caused by the presence of French and the consequent absence of a scribal or aristocratic class that could have slowed the evolution.

Therefore, we find in English the loss of inflections and of grammatical gender, compensated by a relatively fixed word order. We find idioms and syntactical innovations that are the result of contact with French; we also find that the auxiliaries, pronouns, conjunctions, and prepositions of Germanic origin now function in the English sentence à la française. Orr (1962) lists the following areas he ascribes to French influence: formal and semantic fusion, homonymic and paronymic perturbations, affinities and innovations of structure, syntactical affinities and/or innovations, parallels in phraseology and semantics, and proverbs and proverbial sayings.

The impact of French was equally great in the domain of metre and versification. The vast majority of Middle English poets chose verse-forms of French origin over the Anglo-Saxon alliterative line. These were, for the most part, either rhyming couplets corresponding to the French octosyllabics, decasyllabics, and Alexandrines, or identical, recurring stanzas in rhyme, also of French origin. Unlike continental French, Anglo-Norman metre appears to have been as much accentual as syllabic, with regular recurrence of beat and an irregular syllabic count. This pattern was then adopted in English. The adoption of a more-or-less iambic line, roughly determined by stress but also by syllabification plus rhyme, was as revolutionary in a Germanic tongue as the imposition of the Greek non-rhyming quantitive meter on early Latin.

Grosso modo, English had survived as the spoken language of the English people, the upper as well as the lower orders, but in a state of diglossia vis-à-vis Latin and French. English had no prestige. For a long time, it was not considered worthy of literary cultivation and was not cultivated. This means, Blake (1977) has observed, that, as a literary language, English was copied only for local use; therefore educated Englishmen as a whole would be more familiar with the French version of a text than with its English translation. English audiences were disparate and dispersed, rendering intertextual allusion in English difficult. The dispersal also meant that a number of writers might be adapting the same French text at the same time. English had become a number of competing spoken dialects. There was no literary standard, and the dialectical diversity of English was constantly contrasted with the perceived unity and fixity of Anglo-Norman.

English authors were, of course, aware of their vernacular's seeming lack of tradition, precision, and literary weight. To counter these obstacles, they turned to French and Latin, to translate from the noble tongues and to adopt their lexicon, transferring their prestige to English. A translation from the French, with a Frenchified vocabulary in the French style, would make the colloquial vernacular more learned and more dignified.

Chaucer and Gower in particular, having decided that English was the appropriate language for serious writing by Englishmen, applied French standards to their English. They defended and illustrated the mother tongue by transmitting to it a French lexicon, French courtly style, rhetoric, and, of course, rhyme and metre. One might even say that the rise of a courtly and 'classical' English in the second half of the fourteenth century followed upon the disappearance of Anglo-Norman in its customary functions and that because Anglo-Norman no longer functioned as a vital speech of the courts, the English poets decided that English would.

Although English style and diction were Frenchified in all areas and all genres, it can be maintained that the French literary impact was greatest in courtly and aristocratic literature, whereas the monastic and more ostentatiously Christian works turned toward Latin antecedents. There was also a continuous tradition in the written vernacular of chronicle, satire, disputation, pulpit oratory, and devotional prose that bridged the gap from Old to Middle English and had a significant impact on the evolution of literature in the later Middle Ages.

The French influence appears everywhere. One of the most popular and prevalent literary genres in Middle English is romance. The word 'romance' means, originally and for much of the period, a French book or a narrative taken from a French book or in the French style. The vast majority of verse romances are French translations or adaptations, and the others indeed reflect the French style. Virtually all the prose romances are taken from French originals.

On the whole, the love visions (dream visions, love poems) in the courtly mode, practised by Chaucer, Gower, Hoccleve, and Lydgate, among others, are not translations. They are more likely to be original creations, in the modern sense. However, if anything, these poems of the court are even more in the French mode, mirroring, exemplifying, and cultivating the themes, images, motifs, narrative techniques, and stylistic registers to be found in similar contemporary works composed on the Continent, their sources and inspiration.

These are the two modes where French impact was the greatest. However, the French presence was felt in other areas such as the secular lyric, specifically love poems which adopted continental stanzaic forms, rhyme, and metre, and the themes and motifs of *fin' amor*; the few fabliaux that were composed in English, Chaucer's being the most famous; the domain of fable and beast epic, where *Le Roman de Renart* and French fable collections exerted their sway; and the writing of history, where Layamon rewrote Wace, and others rewrote Langtoft, Trevet, the *Brut d'Engleterre*, and eventually even Froissart.

By the fifteenth century English was established as a worthy medium for literary endeavour, and Chaucer and Gower were recognized as appropriate models for imitation. Still, instead of decreasing, the French influence maintained its full impact. Lydgate, portraying himself as Chaucer's disciple and heir, strove to assert the status of English and to extend its range by turning again to French and Latin, illustrating English through his own French-Latin transmission, which often assumed the form of translation-adaptation. The majority of Lydgate's central works are translations or adaptations from French sources or from the Latin where a French version was also used. These include *Reason and Sensuality, Troy Book, Siege of Thebes, Pilgrimage of the Life of Man, Danse Macabre, Fall of Princes*, and even one or two saints' lives.

This brings us to the question of the French presence in English sacred letters. French is second to Latin, often a distant second. Richard Rolle, Walter Hilton, Julian of Norwich, Nicholas Love, and Margery Kempe all wrote in English, some of them wrote in Latin, and none in French. They are not part of a French tradition. John Trevisa translated only from Latin. Although English sermons quote from or cite French, theirs also was an English and Latin heritage. So too for Wyclif and the Wycliffite Bible, glosses, sermons, and tracts.

On the other hand, we know that medical prose and cynegetic books are grounded in French as are other scientific genres. Translations from the Latin often were facilitated by versions in French, when the latter were available; this was true for Boethius, the *Legenda Aurea*, and the *Secreta secretorum*, among many examples. Most important of all was the flood of devotional literature in French that came into being after the Fourth Lateran Council of 1215. English versions of Anglo-Norman books (St Edmund's *Mirure de Seinte Eglise*, Grosseteste's *Chasteau d'Amours*, and William of Waddington's *Manuel des Pechiés*) and of books in Central French (Marguerite Porete's *Le Mirouer des simples ames*, Frère Laurent's *Somme le roi*, Jacques Legrand's *Livre de Bonnes Moeurs*, and *Li douze services de tribulaccioun*) had a powerful impact upon writing in English and upon medieval English culture in the broadest sense of the term.

Whether sacred or secular, the French impact is greater than one simply of translation and imitation. Burrow (1971) made a major step in characterizing the nature of English literature in the Ricardian age. What I find fascinating is that so many of his observations and categories are equally valid for French literature, whether of the fourteenth century or from earlier periods. Typical of the poets of Charles V and Charles VI would be the oblique simplicity of the I-narrator; a loose-woven, open texture; the undercutting of the exemplary and the process of exemplifying; an unheroic image of man; humour and a larger view of life; accommodation and detachment. Some of these are also found in works of the twelfth and thirteenth centuries. Specific to the earlier French tradition is a simple, conventional, and in some sense oral idiom and rhetoric; verse narrative and the joy of story-telling; and the omnipresence of exemplification. It would appear that the most vital parameters of the Ricardian mind-set come from contact with the dominant francophone culture.

It is very important to realize that there was a shift in aesthetic taste and fashion in continental French literature *c.* 1300, that writers in English were aware of the shift, and that one element in their originality was their capacity to juxtapose or fuse the Frenchness of the past and the Frenchness of the present. English romancers largely worked in the old courtly tradition, Chaucer and his circle largely in the new one. This is not a judgment of quality. The *Gawain*-poet and Malory were as magnificent writers in their oldfashionedness as were Chaucer and Gower in their newfangledness. Furthermore, the time lag was not the same in all genres; romances such as *Havelok, Horn, Amis and Amiloun,* and *Floris and Blauncheflur* followed upon the French with a half-century's delay, more or less; Malory with two centuries and a half. Chaucer transmitted Machaut and Froissart immediately, but the fabliaux, *Roman de Renart,* and for that matter the Breton lay with almost the same belatedness as in Malory. Unlike the others, Chaucer was capable of appropriating almost the entire tradition and making it live again in his verse. He benefited especially from belatedness, from the time lag, both long and short, that was endemic to all English creators vis-à-vis their French models.

Burrow (1982) quite rightly defines the Middle English period (1100–1500) as the age of French influence and predominance. The French contribution was, of course, not limited to language and literature; it was equally decisive in architecture, music, philosophy, church governance, the law, and administration – almost all areas of culture. Furthermore, although the French presence was felt most decisively and for the longest duration in England, it was not limited to the British Isles. In the Low Countries, Germany, Italy, Spain, Portugal, and for that matter in Palestine, we find the comparable phenomenon of French books and the aristocratic, courtly ideal of *chevalerie* and *clergie*. The civilizing process, in the terms of Norbert Elias (1939G, 1969G), had begun and it was an international, European phenomenon.

Meanwhile, in England, as in other lands, this proved to be the decisive formative period for what was to become modern English language, literature, and culture. First in French and then in English, literature spoke to the new *curteisie* and *urbanitas*. (John Gower, a master in both tongues, marks the divide). It taught a lesson of chivalry, courtliness, heroism, and piety that has characterized the Middle Ages in our consciousness ever since. For the English, and the French, this was truly a 'Channel culture,' elaborated by people on both shores, at first in the common language and always with the common ideals of secular and Christian humanism, which were to pervade our civilization for centuries and which live on today.

PART ONE

Anglo-Norman Narrative

Introduction

One finds quite often in scholarly writing, even today, the idea that the Anglo-Normans were a grave, sober, practical, brutal, pious, and unimaginative people, and that their literature correspondingly manifests traits of gravity, seriousness, didacticism, and religion; above all that it is not a literature of poetry and the imagination. This is a cultural stereotype, perhaps even a racial one, that originated in the nineteenth century when English philology and English literary history were struggling to find their place as academic disciplines; at this time jingoistic nationalism accompanied the rise of modern language studies.

It is true that, quantitatively, the greatest number of folio pages in the Anglo-Norman corpus are devoted to pious, didactic works of various provenance, especially after the Fourth Lateran Council of 1215. However, such was also the case on the Continent; for that matter, an equivalent phenomenon occurred during the centuries of the Renaissance and of classicism in both France and England. Put simply, the enormous production in medieval French and post-medieval French and English has permitted specialists to concentrate on 'literature of the imagination' (poetry, theatre, fiction) to the relative exclusion of the by far greater portion of the corpus. Because of the much smaller total corpus in Anglo-Norman and the extraordinary diligence of Anglo-Norman scholars, we can benefit from one of the most accurate total characterizations of any world literature. This characterization, however, should not draw us into making misleading claims for the uniqueness of Anglo-Norman vis-à-vis continental French or Middle English.

Another claim has been made, quite justified in my opinion, as to the 'précocité' of Anglo-Norman literature compared to Central French (Legge 1965), and similar to the 'précocité' of the Occitan troubadours. The pioneering spirit of Anglo-Norman concentrated on certain genres and modes, as did the troubadours. In England we find the earliest (and only) manuscripts of a number of classical Central French *chansons de geste* (see below, p. 126), and the first French texts ascribed to specific authors. Among the French literary genres first cultivated in Anglo-Norman are Bible translation, hagiography, the miracle, the chronicle, theatre, science, biography, and, I should add, the narrative *lai*, and perhaps the romance.

This flowering of early literature is to be ascribed in part to the subsidization of vernacular letters both by the cloisters and by the high aristocracy, especially great ladies with culture. It is also possible that, since French was associated with the Norman conquerors, the writers who chose French as their medium of expression were of a higher social class than on the Continent. The precocity of Anglo-Norman literature may also have been inspired by a tradition of chronicle, hagiography, and religious prose in the English vernacular, which is one legacy from the pre-Conquest culture of Anglo-Saxon England. At any rate, the outpouring both of sacred and secular literature – saints' lives and miracles, chronicles, lays, and romances – forms part and parcel of the twelfth-century Renaissance, the extraordinary cultural vitality that, throughout the century and across the entire 'espace normand' and/or 'espace Plantagenêt,' marks the reigns of the Norman and Angevin monarchs.

This said, it would be a terrible mistake to neglect Anglo-Norman writing after 1180 or 1204, when continental French caught up with insular French and when French became, for so many Francophone inhabitants of England, an acquired not a native language. After the 'classical generation' (Marie, Thomas, Clemence of Barking), masterpieces were produced in England as they were on the Continent after Chrétien; the very late twelfth and the entire thirteenth centuries witness new orientations and developments. The very important genre of the ancestral or baronial romance, for instance – the exaltation in French of native English heroes in a romance context – is largely a thirteenth-century phenomenon. Furthermore, it is in the thirteenth century that French, insular and continental, most surely attains recognition as a medium of culture different from but not inferior to the Latin of the schools.

In my opinion, the most exciting phenomenon in Anglo-Norman is the flowering of narrative. Great narrative is the enduring Anglo-Norman legacy both to subsequent writing in English and to world culture as a whole. The three major genres are romance, sacred biography, and chronicle. The historical tradition and medieval historiography are topics that have been treated elsewhere; chronicle also takes us outside the domain of imaginative literature. I shall therefore focus on Anglo-Norman romance and hagiography.

Romance and the saint's life – these are fascinating medieval genres that explore to the fullest medieval narrative structures and literary archetypes. Tristan and Isolt, Amadas and Ydoine, Ami and Amile, Havelok, Horn, Guy of Warwick, Bevis of Hampton, and Fulk Fitz Warren – these are among the great mythical figures cultivated by Anglo-Norman writers; some were invented by them. The martyrs and confessors – Lawrence, Margaret, Catherine, Giles, and Mary of Egypt, among so many others – are also great mythical figures, exemplifying their own version of heroism and manifesting their own archetypal power. It is these two narrative genres, I believe, that gave Anglo-Norman letters so much of its radiance, dynamism, imagination, mythic power, and, above all, poetry. They also helped codify the kind of literary patterns and archetypes that would go on to inform so much subsequent literature, in England and throughout Europe.

I. Romance

1. Marie de France

Among the vernacular writers associated with the court of Henry II and Eleanor of Aquitaine – a circle that includes Wace, Benoît de Sainte-Maure, Beroul, Thomas, Bernart de Ventadorn, and Bertran de Born, to cite the most eminent – Marie stands out. We know practically nothing about her except that she came from France or the Ile de France, that she lived and wrote in England, and that she frequented royalty. She proves to be, without doubt, the most accomplished woman writer of the Middle Ages in the West.

Marie's opus comprises three sorts of texts: a collection of fables, probably translated from the Latin and close in sense and style to the standard Latin fable books; a version of *St Patrick's Purgatory*, also translated from Latin; and twelve Arthurian *lais* (narrative short stories or nouvelles) in verse. The *lais* are Marie de France's most significant, original contribution to letters. They treat a variety of subjects and themes, united by a common preoccupation with *fin' amor*; all but one are associated with the supernatural and permeated with Celtic romance motifs. A number of the lays are moderately long and can be considered a version of Arthurian romance in miniature; others, briefer, treat one episode only and rely for their effect on the literary amplification of a single image or symbol. Due to constraints of space, I shall limit my reading of Marie to four representative lays, two from each category.

Lanval

For the medieval public *Lanval* was Marie's greatest success, extant in the largest number of manuscripts and in the most foreign translations and adaptations, including three versions in English. The story can be considered a courtly romance in miniature. The hero, a knight at King Arthur's court, leaves on an adventure and is loved by a fay from the Other World. However, when Arthur's queen tries to seduce him, Lanval breaks the one condition the fay had set to their love, secrecy. Under pressure, he boasts of the existence and supreme beauty of his lady, saying that the lowest of her servant girls are superior to the queen. As a result, the latter accuses the youth of having made advances to her and of having insulted her, and the fay abandons him. Lanval is tried, defenceless. Only at the last minute do the fay and her court come to Carlisle to exonerate him from the queen's accusation, proving that his boast was justified. Acquitted, Lanval follows his fay to Avalon, in the Other World.

Marie's *lai* can be deemed representative of the literature of Arthurian romance and *fin' amor.* The hero loves a lady of much higher status, who dominates him. He is faithful to her at all costs. Love is the central motivating force in his life. And the issue of *mezura* – moderation and self-control – is evidenced in the discretion (*celar*) central to the narrative. In a sense, *Lanval* illustrates and justifies the directive to be found in Andreas Capellanus' *Tractatus de amore.* 'Amor raro consuevit durare vulgatus' [Love does not usually survive being noised abroad] (Walsh 1982G: 282–3).[2] No less significant are the Arthurian motifs: the hero who leaves the court and undergoes an adventure; a fay from the Other World, with magic powers, who attracts and seduces a mortal but who also imposes a *geis* or prohibition; and judgment before King Arthur's court followed by a happy ending, the final voyage to fairy land in the Other World.

Like Chrétien de Troyes, Marie twists traditional motifs to scrutinize contemporary literary doctrine. She also uses the traditional motifs, shaping them for her own purposes, to create her own unique vision of the world and her own unique work of art. Thus, in Marie's text, the great lady makes the advances and takes the young man to her bed on the spot. As in Chrétien, the action centres on their relationship after it is consummated, not on the episodes that lead up to consummation.

Secondly, *Lanval* concerns the relationship only. Though we are told of the hero's 'valur' and 'prüesce' (21–2), we never see them. We never see him in battle. The only adventure that comes to him (*ad-venire*) is a fair maiden offering her love, and he lives and dies for her (not for prowess or the reputation of prowess). Ultimately, it is she who rescues him; he rescues nobody. Furthermore, once accused by the queen and imprisoned, Lanval can only sigh, weep, and contemplate suicide. He weeps much in the course of the narrative and is easily discouraged; he is an emotional person, living on nerves and sentiment, speaking and acting little. The key words to describe him, repeated obsessively, are 'pensif' and 'dolent.' As such, as a literary type, Lanval resembles Thomas's Tristan and anticipates the protagonist of idyllic romance, Amadas for example, or Aucassin.

In a tale of love, in the twelfth century, Marie de France focuses on her protagonist's inner state – his feelings, scruples, emotions, and his sensitivity to himself and to the beloved. This is an inner-directed tale concerning an inner-directed man. From a medieval and modern perspective, Lanval is more 'feminine' than the usual hero of narrative: Roland, Guillaume, and Raoul; Tristan, Lancelot, Gauvain, and Perceval. Is it his very innerness and weakness that attracts the fay, making him lovable to her? Is his very existence not a critique of the court-war society in which he dwells?

From the beginning, Lanval is portrayed as an outsider to the Arthurian world, a stranger and an exile far from his own land:

> Fiz a rei fu de haut parage,
> Mes luin ert de sun heritage ...
> Hume estrange descunseillez
> Mut est dolent en autre tere,
> Quant il ne seit u sucurs quere. (27–8, 36–8)

He was the son of a king of noble birth, but far from his inheritance ... a stranger bereft of advice can be very downcast in another land when he does not know where to seek help. (Burgess and Busby, p. 73)

Above all, he has no inheritance; he is unendowed in lands and women. The fay also voyages from her land. She comes near Carlisle only on account of him (110–12). They meet at the conventional frontier between everyday existence and the Other World – flowing water – neither in her realm nor his, but, above all, not at Arthur's court. In the end, Lanval will achieve happiness – he will cease to be an exile and he will find his true kingdom – by fleeing with the fay to her supernatural realm. Significantly, the protagonist's true kingdom is associated with love and with the Other World; it is not to be found in the 'real world,' the war-law-court existence of King Arthur and his knights.

On his road from exile to the kingdom, Lanval encounters two women and two worlds: his mistress, queen of the fays; and his seducer-accuser, queen of King Arthur's court. From beginning to end the Arthurian experience proves disastrous to Lanval. First, Arthur forgets him, while the others keep silent. There is no justice, and the outsider, who is poor and desperately in need of reward, is not rewarded. Later, once his libidinal and financial needs have been satisfied, the situation worsens. Wealthy, happy, capable of dispensing gifts and patronage in his own right ('riches duns,' 'granz honurs,' 209, 212), Lanval attracts the queen's notice. He is now subject to her authority, and her attention proves to be far more dangerous than her husband's distraction. She acts out of lust and pride, not love. He is attacked, pressured, symbolically raped or castrated (accused of being a sodomite), and then accused of the very sins of which the queen is guilty. The queen's slander and the rigid, cumbersome court procedure bring the youth to the edge of dishonour. The Arthurian court is profoundly unfair, unjust, and corrupt, a world of calumny and adultery.

In contrast, the fay represents a better, finer world: one in which natural affection and genuine passion are freely expressed, in contrast to the lust and hypocrisy of the court; one in which love takes precedence over war and law, or, rather, where the law of love is finer, more subtle, and more discriminating than the law of kings and queens; one in which imagery of the pavilion, fine clothes, and gentle viands are contrasted to the Arthurian stone prison and stone block of marble ('perrun').

Lanval is offered two roads, two worlds, and two kingdoms, embodied in two women. Although he spurns the Arthurian queen's advances, symbolically he does take both roads and try both kingdoms. In his growth experience, perhaps it is necessary for him to test the court both when he is poor and when he is covered with wealth, to realize that on both occasions he is alone. Perhaps he can only truly know which world is better after he has tried both. Furthermore, the two worlds and the two life experiences are intimately bound. The fay chooses Lanval no doubt because of his 'virtue,' the quality of character which has been revealed and has made a name for him at court. And it is his success with the fay – the libidinal joy radiating from him and the prestige of the riches with which she has endowed him – that distinguish Lanval in the queen's eyes.

In the end and only in the end, the two worlds are brought together. The fay comes to confront the queen and to vindicate her lover. Preceded by four of her maids-in-waiting – each of them also more beautiful than the queen – in a three-part climax she conquers the Arthurian court and triumphs not only over her lustful, adulterous rival but also over the Arthurian world of arms, law, and feudal justice. Three times a train of women – maids-in-waiting or the fay herself – disrupts the trial; they disrupt men's speech by their actions and men's logic by their radiant physical beauty. However, although she clears him from the queen's accusation, the fay does not pardon Lanval from having broken her tabu – the tabu of secrecy – nor does she claim him as her lover. She does not speak to him at all.

In the end, it is Lanval who forces the issue; climbing on a 'perrun' next to the castle, he leaps onto the fay's horse as she rides out and, grasping her in his arms, lets her take him where she wills. The fay and her suite return to Avalon; Lanval is never heard from again:

Lanval esteit munté desus.
Quant la pucele ist fors a l'us,
Sur le palefrei detriers li
De plain eslais Lanval sailli.
Od li s'en vait en Avalun ...
La fu ravi li dameiseaus.
Nul hum n'en oï plus parler ... (637–41, 644–5)

Lanval mounted it and when the maiden came through the door, he leapt in a single bound onto the palfrey behind her. He went with her to Avalon ... Thither the young man was borne and no one has heard any more about him. (p. 81)

Thus the passive youth, who had sinned by excess of speech ('vantance'), for the first time commits a physical act, literally a leap of faith. He knows and then he acts. His leap of faith commits him not only to the fay but to her kingdom, the Other World. Lanval renounces King Arthur, his wife, their court, and their world; he voluntarily forsakes the king's service, choosing the very sentence of exile that was his had he been convicted in the trial. For the first time, he truly makes a decision on his own; it is his will to decide, his will to act, and his coming to maturity that force the issue in the fay's eyes. Thus for the first time he masters her and wills her to take him with her to her realm, forever.

Lanval chooses the fay over Arthur's queen and, implicitly, over Arthur. The sensitive, passive, weeping, feminine youth renounces a male, feudal, collective, closed, war-oriented society in favour of a female, courtly, individualized community open to love and dreams. The fay brought only women with her to Carlisle; in terms of the diegesis, Lanval is, to the best of the audience's knowledge, the only male in the fairy world, just as Guinevere is the only prominent woman in the Arthurian world. Lanval, a man rescued by a woman, chooses the feminine, the erotic, the irrational, the other; the author presumably approves of his choice.

On the one hand, the hero's evolution and his choice can be envisaged as stages in a process of growth. The adolescent discovers his first love, rebels against a *pater durus* and a no less *mater dura* and, as an adult, leaves them for his new home. He is initiated by a fay into the mysteries of Eros and the still greater mysteries of her sacred realm, Avalon. He integrates the anima into his own personality and successfully achieves individuation. Yet, from another vantage point, although Lanval's choice proves to be an excellent solution for himself as an individual and an excellent means for Marie de France to end her tale, it in no way resolves the problem of corruption and calumny in the courtly world. Marie's criticism of the Arthurian court is penetrating and absolute; Lanval's escape does nothing to bring about reform.

That is the crux of the problem. Lanval's choice is to escape, to abandon the real world in favour of a fairy realm, to die upon the point of capital judgment, and to be reborn in the Other World. If he be reborn. After all, the Celtic Other World is also, in part, the realm of the dead, and in the medieval world-view, as in Freud's, Eros is ever allied to Thanatos. One theme in the literature of the age is the assimilation of masculinity to light, life, and reason, whereas the feminine is associated with darkness, death, and the irrational. By choosing woman and giving himself to a mother surrogate, Lanval receives ultimate nurture and protection in stasis; he symbolically embraces death. He also embraces the irrational, that is, the world of dreams. For the medieval public as for us, the Isle of Avalon in particular and fairy realms in general are a wish-fulfilment fantasy that corrects the inequities of everyday life. Within the fiction of *Lanval*, the hero's adventures – meeting the fay, revelling in love and wealth, and escaping death – provide consolation for his poverty, loneliness, and profound alienation in waking reality. All that happens to Lanval from the moment he dismounts, releases his steed, and lies down to rest in the field near Carlisle is on one level a dream.

Nonetheless, dreams and escape, fantasy and wish-fulfilment, cannot provide an answer to social problems. (On these problems, Ribard 1978 and Rieger 1979 offer a sociocritical reading of Marie.) They presumably solve an individual's dilemma by drawing forth the innerness, sensitivity, and imagination latent in him from the beginning. They also solve a literary dilemma. Lanval's adventures provide wish-fulfilment and escape for him within the diegesis, also for the implied audience extradiegetically. His imagination functions within the plot as the author's functions outside it. Presumably the implied audience will undergo a growth experience and a moment of comprehension on a large scale, similar to Lanval's on his scale. The plot of *Lanval* is the perfect objective correlative of the *lai* genre and of the functioning of artistic creativity; the hero's imagination mirrors the author's imagination, his dream her dream, his comprehension her comprehension, his life the functioning and creating of her work of art.

Yonec

A comparable situation is evoked in Marie's lay *Yonec*. The 'message' of the tale is more overt, and yet Marie elaborates the narrative in a more complex manner. The title figure, Yonec, is revealed to be the protagonist of the classical 'family romance.' He discovers that his putative father is not his real father. On the contrary, his mother's husband slew the real father, Muldumarec, a fairy prince from the Other World. At the moment of his death, the father bestowed on the mother a magic ring and gave her, reserved for Yonec, his sword which will serve as a recognition token. Discovering Muldumarec's tomb enlightens Yonec and precipitates the crisis. With his father's sword, Yonec slays the false father and, his mother having expired, reunites her with Muldumarec in his tomb. Then he inherits his father's kingdom.

Marie has described a classical case of oedipal conflict, resolved in the most flagrant of wish-fulfilment fantasies. The youth, upon reaching manhood, is enabled to slay his putative father with no sense of guilt, for the latter is not his real father. Furthermore, Yonec and the real father are more noble and more powerful than the murderer for they are semi-divine. Potential oedipal conflict with Muldumarec is allayed since Yonec acts upon realizing that his own father is dead, and decapitates (castrates) the false father. Thus Yonec takes his mother's side; he protects her in his father's name and on his father's behalf, employing his father's sword; he wields a phallic weapon in his father's stead, in complicity with him, having licitly become (replaced) him.

Oedipal guilt is further allayed by the mother's immediate demise; Yonec restores her to the father and cleanses himself of sin by uniting them, both dead. He then proceeds to become a king, attaining sovereignty and wielding his sword, freed from both parents, in full maturity.

The *Yonec* story may have been derived from an oral source related to Celtic folklore, if Marie had a source. We do not know. From a literary perspective, we do know that Yonec's story – his growth to maturity – did not interest Marie for its own sake. She uses the young man as a pretext; her real interest focuses not on Yonec but on his parents, especially the mother. The family romance by its very nature concerns the hero's genealogy, his real as opposed to putative parents; Yonec himself might have approved the notion that his glory and his innocence are best stated by recounting the glory and innocence of his progenitors – his mother and her supernatural lover, the bird-prince Muldumarec. Nonetheless, by devoting some three quarters of the narrative to the parents, and by narrating their love from the Lady's point of view, the author makes the audience concentrate on and empathize with the Lady. Indeed, her son's story (his growth and his triumph) are included in her story and made to seem the final increment in her own development.

The Lady, like the son and like Lanval, undergoes a maturation process linked to wish-fulfilment fantasy. Indeed, her fantasy parallels Lanval's more closely than Yonec's does. Lanval's oedipal struggle, tragedy, and triumph, through the aid of an otherworldly lover, correspond to her Electra-complex struggle, tragedy, and triumph. Locked in a stone prison by an old man (her husband) and an old woman (his sister), both authority figures in dominance over her, she is rendered sexually alone, sterile, and frigid. She loses her once-famed beauty. The wall in the stone tower with its narrow aperture is a symbolic metaphor for her frigid body and frustrated libido; she is reduced to symbolic darkness and death.

Then, in immediate response to a prayer for sexual liberation grounded in desire, the fantasy is actualized:

> Quant ele ot faite pleinte issi,
> L'umbre d'un grant oisel choisi
> Par mi une estreite fenestre. (105–7)

Having lamented thus, she noticed the shadow of a large bird through a narrow window. (p. 87)

In the form of a great hawk, Muldumarec soars into her chamber, becomes a supremely handsome man, proves his Christian orthodoxy, and makes love to the affection-starved Lady. As was the case for Lanval and his fay, Yonec's father will come to the Lady upon her wish. Last of all, he confesses that she is the only woman that he has ever loved; therefore he is also a virgin. The form he adopts is significant. He is said to be a 'ostur' or hawk, one of the noblest of birds, prized in the sport of falconry. An aristocratic hawk for an aristocratic pastime, aggressive, martial, but well-trained and obedient, Mudumarec assumes the guise of ideal male sexuality. Birds are intimately involved in the literature of *fin' amor.* Soaring into the sky, freed from material bonds, the bird symbolized liberty, a natural, good life, spirituality, and the positive aspects of Eros. Muldumarec evokes the rebirth of life in springtime, the light of the sun, and triumph over death. And he represents triumphal, potent desire, male libido, soaring in flight. In opposition to the wicked parental authority figures, he makes the Lady a whole woman.

As proof of her flowering womanhood, the Lady radiates joy, the radiance of a successful sexual experience:

> Pur la grant joie u ele fu,
> Que ot suvent pur veer sun dru,
> Esteit tut sis semblanz changez. (225–7)

The great joy she often experienced on seeing her lover caused her appearance to alter. (p. 89)

Unknowingly, she commits an indiscretion (unconcious 'vantance' through unconscious 'sous-conversation') which alerts the husband and leads to his discovery of her secret. When the blocking *durus pater* figure places prongs, sharpened like razors, at the window, he not only slays the bird man, but symbolically he castrates him; he destroys the power of love and the power of the Lady's dream desire, the very existence of her new-found animus. Thus he also violates her.

When Muldumarec leaves her, wounded unto death, the Lady commits an act of folly; she leaps from the window some twenty feet to the earth. By a miracle comparable to the one that granted her erotic prayer in the first place, she is saved. She then follows the traces of Muldumarec's blood into his magic kingdom, inhabited by no living soul. He entered her chamber of love; now she penetrates to his chamber of death, achieves a final apotheosis with him, and receives the gift of the ring and the sword. She also receives the gift of his son, for it was in her tower, at her lover's slaying, that she discovered he would live on in the person of their child. The Lady succeeds in integrating the animus. After the wounding of Muldumarec she attains a new state of freedom and awareness and dares to leap into the unknown, to commit herself – like Lanval – in a way inconceivable in her earlier life. From enclosed space, she discovers the open road. She descends into and through a hill and then rises into the Silver City. The Lady literally undergoes a death-rebirth experience, communing with her dying lover in his Other World city of the invisible, and then returning to her home to give birth to new life. She also has plunged into her unconscious, and upon her return becomes a mother, the guardian of the couple's honour and eventually their revenge. The magic ring keeps the secret that her body language was unable to. By magic and by ruse, she who once was the slave of her lord and master, becomes his master, awaiting the day of judgment. He who once was the master of illusion and reality falls prey to illusion and forgets reality. For her son the Lady brings back the feminine ring of protection and the masculine sword of prowess and sovereignty; together they embody her completed, total self. She has arrived at consciousness, understanding, and individuation.

It is she who tells her story to Yonec, and makes him act:

> 'Beaus fiz,' fet ele, 'avez oï
> Cum Deus nus ad mené ici!
> C'est vostre pere que ici gist,
> Que cist villarz a tort ocist.
> Or vus comant e rent s'espee:
> Jeo l'ai asez lung tens gardee.' (527–32)

'Fair son, you have heard how God has brought us here! It is your father who lies here, whom this old man unjustly killed. Now I commend and hand over to you his sword, for I have kept it long enough.' (p. 93)

After having heard old tales of adventure in the past and listened to Muldumarec's prophecy of events in the future, the Lady becomes an author figure in turn, and Yonec is now, in the present, her reader or audience. She causes him to do things, she acts upon him. Furthermore, by recounting her 'adventure,' she produces the first version of what will become Marie's lay, and her oral narrative serves as a *mise en abyme* [interior duplicator] for Marie's total work of art.[3]

From another perspective, Yonec, as the Lady's son, is a projection of her. Although her love and lover are dead, they live on in the son. Eros leads to Thanatos, for both Muldumarec and his beloved move from a bed to a bier, and the tale is brought to its end at a tomb. The husband's tower and the Lover's city both culminate in the stone of the tomb. The Lady dies but her son lives on. He takes up his father's sword and slays the slayer. He embodies his mother's thirst for freedom and joy as much as he embodies his father's virile sovereignty. He *is* the totality and the future that they wanted to be but could not. Muldumarec and the Lady are united in the grave, and yet they both live on in their triumphal son, master of the ring and the sword, the anima and the animus, the lord of their city and the titular hero of their story.

Chevrefoil

Among Marie's briefer *lais* probably the best known and certainly the most studied by scholars is *Chevrefoil*. *Chevrefoil* recounts an episode from the Tristan legend, one event in the lives of Tristan and Isolt. Tristan has been exiled from court. Desperate to see his beloved, he hears that she will be riding out and decides to wait near a spot where her suite will pass. To capture her attention, he cuts down a hazel tree, splits and squares the wood, inscribes a message on it, and thrusts it into the ground where the queen will see it. Isolt does see it, dismounts, and leaves her escort for a brief tryst with her lover. Then, to commemorate their meeting, Tristan composes a new *lai*.

A vast corpus of scholarship has been devoted to what Tristan carved on the wooden stake, and what role the stake plays in the narrative. Following Spitzer (1946–7) and Verhuyck (1982), my opinion is that, with his knife, Tristan carved on the wood only his name: 'De sun cutel escrit sun nun' (54). A longer text would be cumbersome to inscribe, impossible for Isolt to read as she ambled down the path on her mount, and unlikely to be kept hidden from her retinue. However, Tristan does send Isolt a message; he communicates with her, and on several levels. According to the common medieval Christian understanding of allegory, a literal or surface meaning, the bark or cortex, opens up to reveal a deeper, symbolic truth, the kernel or nucleus. How appropriate then that Tristan in the diegesis, and, behind him, his author Marie de France, should have chosen carving on a hazel tree to embody concretely these levels of reading, both bark and kernel, cortex and nucleus.

The cortex can be explained as a relatively simple form of communication, the equivalent of a semantic sign. The split, trimmed piece of wood, with the word 'Tristan' carved on it, states simply the following: 'I Tristan did this. I am here. I am waiting for you. Stop and look for me. Come.' As a sign, it functions as visual communication that will lead to a more fruitful verbal, and then tactile communication – verbal exchange and tactile union. The word and its message are concrete, external, and eminently practical. They require no reflection, meditation, or understanding – because Isolt has no time for reflection or meditation; she must stop the procession and find an excuse to leave her party before they have wandered too far down the road. And because, as we are told (57–8), the lovers have met this way once before, we know that this is not the first time that Tristan has done this. Furthermore, having been informed in advance, Isolt is on the lookout for a squared, trimmed piece of wood. When she perceives the sign, she apprehends its message immediately and, quasi-automatically, responds to it.

On another level, we have to deal with the nucleus, a deeper, symbolic truth. This deeper level is evoked when Marie refers to the 'summe de l'escrit' (61), the quintessence of the writing, either inscribed on the staff or implied by Tristan in some other manner. They are like the hazel tree and the honeysuckle vine; separated, neither can live. 'Bele amie, si est de nus: / Ne vus sanz mei, ne mei sanz vus!' (77–8) ['Sweet love, so it is with us; without me you cannot survive, nor I without you' (p.110)].

The cortex is grounded in a metaphor derived from a folk belief that has an objective foundation in nature. The honeysuckle vine twined around a hazel tree will flourish as will the tree, the two in a state of symbiosis; ripped from it, the honeysuckle will die and, its bark lacerated, so will the tree. Tristan and Isolt, and/or the love of Tristan and Isolt, and/or all love will flourish when the lovers are together; forced apart, they (it) will die. Marie makes a powerful, bittersweet commentary on their story. They have been separated. Tristan longs for a rendezvous. They do meet, but their encounter is agonizingly brief. In the end the lovers part again, in the hope that soon Isolt can bring about an accommodation with King Mark that will recall Tristan to court. Yet Marie could count on her audience's knowledge of the intertextual, extradiegetic context, which she herself evokes plaintively; the Tristan legend ends in the death of the lovers. Their only union is the grave. The forest is only an interlude, of quasi-pastoral innocence, before the lovers have to face civilization and the world of the court. The lay itself, like the Tristan legend in its totality, is made up of a sequence of alternating moments of joy and sadness, exaltation and misery, life and death. It functions as a self-conscious fragment that is part of and contributes to the total corpus. Such is the story of Tristan and Isolt; such is the nature of love.

The natural metaphor or objective correlative of the tree and vine functions on several levels. On the one hand, because this exquisite love corresponds to a phenomenon in the natural world, it lends their passion qualities of naturalness, simplicity, innocence, and beauty. The 'green world,' in the twelfth century as in ours, called up a vision of the primeval. Vegetable growth symbolizes fecundity and life; the *fin' amor* between Tristan and Isolt contributes to their fecundity, life, innocence, and beauty. It is their only fecundity, life, innocence, and beauty.

Extensive Freudian theorizing is scarcely necessary to justify our position that, in the hazel-honeysuckle symbiosis, the hazel tree represents Tristan the male, and the honeysuckle vine Isolt the woman. The tree stands forth, erect, solid, phallic; the vine twines around it, enclosing, engulfing, female. Tristan works upon the tree, inscribes it with his name, and places it on the path where he would stand if he dared. It is, so to speak, his totem. And the vine is significant by its absence. Split and pared, the staff was once a living tree. Now alone, without Isolt, calling for Isolt, it is dead. The staff and Tristan evoke male presence and reality; the vine and Isolt female absence and dream, the dream of male desire.

Last of all, their moment together is a moment of destiny, compressed, crystalized, and intensely inner, a moment of revelation and ecstasy. The realization of the truth of love, of the symbol and its meaning, is also revelation and ecstasy. Even though the sign of recognition was employed before, it is only now that Isolt discovers and comprehends Tristan's message concerning the eternal nature of love. Communication becomes initiation.

Theirs is a crystallization of love and understanding about love – not only love but the poetry of love. Tristan's staff is inscribed with his name in writing, in 'letters.' Nature is allied with culture and is improved upon by culture. The writing on the staff contributes to the sign and to the symbol. As a symbol the staff cum writing offers a message, an idea. Tristan is the teacher, Isolt the student; he the author, she the reader. It is the realization, the distillation of his idea – in the end expressed through the medium of his speaking voice – in her consciousness that constitutes the precious instant of love. Furthermore, Tristan's idea of their love as the hazel and honeysuckle is expressed in verse; it is a sort of poem on Tristan and Isolt at the center of Marie's lay of the honeysuckle, about Tristan and Isolt. Then, Tristan's name and the symbol-message are later expanded into a genuine poetic text. At the end of the lay, because of his joy at their meeting, because of what he wrote to her (the name, the message), because she said it, and because he wishes to commemorate their speech, Tristan composes a lay, called 'Chevrefoil':

> Pur la joie qu'il ot eüe
> De s'amie qu'il ot veüe
> E pur ceo k'il aveit escrit,
> Si cum la reïne l'ot dit,
> Pur les paroles remembrer,
> Tristram, ki bien saveit harper,
> En aveit fet un nuvel lai ...
> Chevrefoil le nument Franceis. (107–13, 116)

On account of the joy he had experienced from the sight of his beloved and because of what he had written, Tristram, a skilful harpist, in order to record his words (as the queen had said he should), used them to create a new lay .... the French [call it] *Chevrefoil.* (p. 110)

Whatever the words or speech referred to – Tristan's message understood and repeated to him by Isolt? Isolt's assurance that he will return to court? Isolt's ordering him to write? Their words of joy at the reunion? – we find that Tristan's name, his message, and his symbol generate a poem, and the poem generates, or rather is, Marie de France's *lai*. So we have a text within a text within a text. Tristan's purported lay functions both as an authority and as a source for Marie's 'real' lay that contains or reconstructs it. Marie's lay tells of its own purported coming into being and celebrates its genesis as well – the creation and interpretation of the work of art as *mise en abyme* which it celebrates and without which it cannot exist. Creation and exegesis, writing and reading, art and gloss, lie at the centre of Marie's poem. The poem is an act of love, caused by an act of love (Tristan's poem and Isolt's speech, Tristan the writer and Isolt the reader). Since the hazel staff stood alone on the road, Tristan the poet, in love, devoted to it, creates a text called 'Chevrefoil,' the name of which is Isolt alone. Marie, whose call for communication parallels Isolt's call, respects his wishes. This is the woman's text, *Chevrefoil.*

Laüstic

Marie's *Laüstic*, like *Chevrefoil*, portrays tragic love through the literary elaboration of a symbol, the symbol once again serving as *mise en abyme* not only for the essence of love but also for the creative process in general and the creation of this lay in particular. As with *Chevrefoil* and the first section of *Yonec*, there are three characters: husband, wife, and lover. The Lady is married to a Knight; she falls in love with the knight next door. The Lady and the Lover cannot indulge in physical intimacy since, like Pyramus and Thisbe, they are separated by stone – the walls of their respective houses. They can go to the window, look at, and speak to each other. Then, at night, when speech is impossible, they can gaze at the moon and at each other. The husband questions his wife as to why she rises in the middle of the night. She says she cannot sleep because of the song of the nightingale, which she loves more than anything else. He captures the little bird and kills it, ordering her to bed. The Lady then sends the nightingale's body to her beloved with its story; he constructs a precious coffer for it and carries it with him ever after.

The title figure of this story is the nightingale. It can be deemed the protagonist. After all, the people do little or nothing; their lives remain largely stationary in the course of the narrative; the little bird alone undergoes transformation. The only action of the poem, the unique 'aventure' (1, 134, 147, 157) to which Marie alludes, comprises its death and the disposition of its remains. And the nightingale is the only subject of discourse reported directly.

The 'laüstic' is the dominant image in the text, the arch-image; it is a complex, multivocal symbol that has to be interpreted on at least three levels, corresponding to the three stages in its existence. Alive, the nightingale serves as an excuse for the Lady to stand at the window and gaze at the Lover. The little bird functions as a mediator, indeed a go-between (*internuntius*). When the nightingale sings, the Lady and the Lover presumably meditate on each other and commune through the nightingale's song. Because they are unable to speak, the nightingale helps them communicate spiritually. It sings for them. Traditionally in the Middle Ages, especially in the lyric, singing birds evoke springtime, renewal, *fin' amor*, and the joy and the pain of a beautiful, spiritual love. The couple are performing as models of *fin' amor* – their passion is secret and illicit, adulterous but pure; their sentiments are noble, exalted, and altruistic. The nightingale then stands for their love, the love that the world ought to have honoured. In addition, because the little bird sings at night and they listen to him at night in the light of the moon, we realize that love involves the nocturnal, feminine, unconscious, 'lunatic' side of the human condition in contrast to the bright sun of man's reason and law. Finally, because the bird sings in a sense on behalf of the Lover and his Lady, we associate *fin' amor* with artistic creation and with the song of a lover who creates from desire.

The Knight's act of violence, trapping and killing the nightingale, corresponds to the husband's deed of violence in slaying Muldumarec, to the queen's undermining Lanval's love, and to the separation of Tristan and Isolt. The dead little bird symbolizes the fragility and evanescence of *fin' amor,* the fact that the joy of love will end in tragedy. The husband has succeeded; the joy of love ('delit') is dead.

In spatial terms, Marie's text focuses first on the town, then on the two houses, and finally on the Lady's chamber. Space becomes more and more restrictive and oppressive. The Lady is contained, enclosed, smothered inside the room by her husband, who wishes to limit her even more to his bed. For her, the stone walls that enclose her and prevent her from contacting the Lover are a prison, as much a prison as the husband's tower in *Yonec.* The Knight's bed must embody an even more oppressive captivity, that of the *debitum conjugale.* Therefore, for her and for Yonec's mother, freedom and salvation are represented by the window, the opening to another world; this is the Other World of *fin' amor* portrayed by flowers in the spring, nighttime and the moon, love, tenderness, mystery, and the world of dreams. In response the Knight sets traps, nets, snares, and birdlime. He traps the nightingale and he traps the Lady. The slaughter of the nightingale closes the window and extinguishes the dream. The Lady's prison now becomes absolute. When the Knight traps the bird, wrings its neck, and tosses it, bloody, on his wife's chemise, he commits an act of violence. To the extent that the singing, soaring nightingale symbolizes the phallic male libido and the desire of a singing lover-poet, then the husband has symbolically castrated his wife's lover or, at least, love. However, the act of violence he commits – flinging the little bird's corpse at his wife, bloodying her gown and mocking her with sarcasm – is violence against her, a form of rape:

A sun seignur l'ad demandé,
E il l'ocist par engresté;
Le col li rumpt a ses deus meins –
De ceo fist il que trop vileins –

Sur la dame le cors geta,
Se que sun chainse ensanglanta
Un poi desur le piz devant. (113–19)

She asked her husband for the bird, but he killed it out of spite, breaking its neck wickedly with his two hands. He threw the body at the lady, so that the front of her tunic was bespattered with blood, just on her breast. (p. 95)

After all, the nightingale became the image of unhappy love in the West because of Ovid's recounting the legend of Philomela, a Greek myth of violence and rape. The husband's killing and his symbolic rape of his wife are powerful with overtones of incompatible sexuality; the husband triumphantly and brutally makes her return to the bed which she is so desperate to escape.

In Ovid, Philomela communicates with Procne by means of a tapestry that recounts her story. The nightingale was the means by which the lovers communicated. Even after its death and the death of their hope for continued contact, Marie's Lady renews communication with her neighbour one last time, by sending him the nightingale wrapped up in a delicate velvet cloth, 'A or brusdé e tut escrit' (136) [embroidered in gold and covered in designs, p. 96], on which she has 'written' her story, her 'aventure,' so that, even though she can no longer go to the window, the Lover will not think that she has forsaken him of her own will. The Lover then places his beloved's gift in the little coffer made of precious metals and jewels. The dead little bird, enveloped in precious cloth, housed in a precious box, a 'chasse' (155), resembles not so much a corpse in a coffin as a saint's relic in a shrine. The nightingale is a martyr to love in the cult of *fin' amor.* Imagery of the Church is employed to indicate how pure and innocent and holy the couple's love was; and that it lives on, surviving the present, eternal because its memory is eternal. Like Tristan and Isolt in the grave, the lovers are united forever, the phallic bird prepared by the woman, in a vaginal coffer made by the man. Thus is their desire sublimated and transformed into stasis.

The Lady and the Lover, by embroidering the cloth and making the reliquary, themselves forge the symbol of their love. In Ovid, Philomela was metamorphosed into the nightingale; in Marie a nightingale is metamorphosed into the symbol. It exists as a symbol only because they have explained and enshrined it. Indeed, their symbol concerns the nature of symbols and their work of commemoration tells of the nature of memory. The precious, embroidered cloth and coffer are works of art. These works of art, a concrete realization of male-female union, conceived in reverence and carried out in beauty, reflect not only their love but Marie de France's poem. The Lady's embroidery, 'tut escrit,' gives rise to Marie's text, also 'tut escrit.' The reliquary survives the present; so will Marie's lay. Marie's lay tells how the cloth and shrine came into being, just as they tell how the love came into being. The works of art, containing the Lady's first telling of the story, are artifacts *en abyme* reflecting the aesthetic as well as the artistic problematic of the lay as a whole. Marie's *Laüstic* encloses the coffer which encloses the embroidered cloth which encloses the 'laüstic.' And the coffer cum nightingale in microcosm represents the same delicate work of the spirit as does Marie's text as a macrocosm. Like *Chevrefoil*, *Laüstic* is a metatext, a self-reflexive work of art that recounts its own genesis, a work of artistic creation that treats the problem of artistic creation.

Like Chrétien de Troyes, Marie de France has created a unique synthesis of poetry and counterpoetry. The counterpoetry is represented by her deft, probing analysis of human relations: love and jealousy in the courtly world, the power of sexuality, and courtly social and psychological dilemmas. The poetry is embodied in romance motifs derived from a fictional, legendary Celtic Other World; they suffuse Marie's texts with mystery and charm, and powerful images. These symbols illuminate her 'Problem-Märchen' (as Spitzer 1930 called them) and confer meaning and beauty on otherwise mundane events. Above all, Marie's characters undergo an illumination, a crystallization, of love and of the human condition. They discover the joy, the power, and the fragility of *fin' amor*; they experience the inherently evanescent, therefore tragic quality of love. They discover that people are doomed by fate, that they suffer, that love also is doomed (for it leads to separation and death), and that the only compensation for humans is to be resigned and to understand. Another compensation is the power of imagination and dreams, for resignation rules but does not smother passion and poetry. Through the power of imagining and dreaming, these characters attain a measure of wholeness in the Self, even in sadness and death, by integrating the Other (anima, animus) and recognizing its value. Marie's sympathy, generosity, and pity vis-à-vis love's victims is exemplary and total. Finally, we must not forget Marie's metatextuality: her lays, concerned with remembering and commemorating old stories, tell how they themselves came into being; her characters are writers and readers, singers and audience, telling their own tales as they love and tell of love, and telling of the creation of their tales and of the lays that contain them. In some cases, the work itself becomes the protagonist of its own text. No early medieval vernacular poet is so self-conscious, so metatextual, and so modern, as Marie de France.

In a well-known prologue to her *Lais*, Marie states the goal and functioning of her art (consult Hunt 1974, Pickens 1978, and Dragonetti 1986). Elaborating the standard exordium-topoi of medieval rhetoric, she seeks to mould the implied reader's norms and beliefs and to establish a bridge between her text and the reader, thus winning his favourable disposition (*captatio benevolentiae*). Marie exalts tradition, authority from the past, and the Ancients' writing in Latin, and emphasizes the virtues inherent in teaching and learning; it is the writer's duty to increase understanding and the reader's duty to learn. This monument to high artistic self-consciousness, grounded in the tradition of grammatical studies and secular humanism, according to Hunt, is then followed by a sequence of texts in the vernacular elaborated in a mode of high art, courtly and learned, full of classical allusion and based on sources in Latin. Like Chrétien and Thomas, Marie is a student of Ovid in this, her century, the *aetas Ovidiana*. The presence of Ovid weighs heavier and is more easily identifiable than hypothetical Celtic sources.

Marie of course cites Breton 'lais' that commemorated the 'aventures' of which she speaks, and that she merely retells in her 'contes.' Such a stance is one additional manifestation of *captatio benevolentiae*, a modesty-topos, a way of grounding her tales in the Arthurian world, claiming authority (authenticity) from it; it is also her way of assimilating her beloved Bretons to 'li auncïen' in their 'tens ancïenur,' granting veracity, dignity, and beauty to her tales even though they are not Greek or Roman. It is possible that Marie heard some of her stories from oral legends in Welsh; these legends may have been associated with lyric poems (*'lais'*) also in Welsh. It is more likely that Marie learned the motifs independently, from Geoffrey of Monmouth and Wace, among others, and that she made up the stories herself. For a number of specialists, the narrative Breton *lai* is Marie's invention, a genre created by her. Whether or not this extreme formulation is true, Marie did recast Celtic legend in line with her own, learned reading of Ovid. The recasting, and the resultant synthesis, may well represent the revival of a specifically insular literary tradition, as well as the best way of interesting continental writers and a continental public in insular doings. In the *lai* genre Marie achieved an acme of perfection unique in her age. Other anonymous lays were based upon hers, following in her traces on both sides of the Channel, but never with comparable mastery. It is because of her that the word 'lai' ('lay') came to mean, in French and later in English, a brief romantic narrative, just as in later centuries writers were to translate Marie into English, imitate her, and perpetuate her genre in the English vernacular.

2. *Le Roman de Tristan*

The love of Tristan and Isolt has become one of the great myths of literature. Originally independent from the Arthurian nexus (Lancelot and Guinevere, the Holy Grail), it was later gathered into the Arthurian world in the *Prose Tristan* and in Malory, but it also had its own modern resurgence in Wagner's *Tristan und Isolde,* a work as universal in our time as any French book was seven or eight centuries ago. In France, Joseph Bédier's version – perhaps the greatest 'translation' ever performed by an academic – had tremendous impact as did Denis de Rougemont's vision of courtly love, based largely on Wagner and Bédier. Wagner, Bédier, and de Rougemont are at the origin of much contemporary meditation on medieval myth in general, and Tristan and Isolt in particular.

There is a general Tristan and Isolt myth, made up from a number of divergent texts from different centuries. One has the right to generalize on the myth, but we should always be aware of the specificity, the unique individuality of the texts that contribute to it and without which there would be no myth. As it happens, the two earliest romances of Tristan are closely associated with England. Beroul was a Norman who displayed knowledge of Cornwall and probably wrote for an Anglo-Norman public; Thomas was most definitely an Anglo-Norman, perhaps the greatest writer from Great Britain who ever composed in the French tongue. The romances by these men, even though they have come down to us in fragments, are supremely powerful and beautiful; they are truly 'medieval classics' in a way few texts can claim to be.

Beroul

Traditionally Beroul's *Tristan* is labelled 'popular' or 'common' in opposition to the allegedly more 'courtly' version by Thomas. The words 'popular' and 'common' are revealing, not for the essence of Beroul's text but for scholars' sense of disarray when confronted by a romance which differs so strikingly from what they have come to expect as medieval.

A first, perhaps simplistic but by no means trivial question, concerns ethical norms. What are the author's intentions vis-à-vis his characters? What is his moral and ethical judgment? And how and why does he manipulate the implied audience to share his beliefs? In the extant portion of Beroul's romance, which recounts the lovers' adventures during a period of life at court before Tristan's exile to Brittany, Isolt is wedded to King Mark, and the lovers commit terrible deeds from a normal medieval perspective. In their continued and continual indulgence in sexual passion, they are guilty of fornication (one of the seven capital sins), adultery (breaking one of the Ten Commandments), feudal treachery (Mark is Tristan's lord), treason (he is Tristan's king), and incest (he is Tristan's uncle). They also commit murder, slaying their adversaries without warning. Furthermore, to maintain secrecy, Tristan and Isolt construct an elaborate web of lying and deceit for the purpose of misleading the king. The king's advisers, on the other hand – Frocin, Godoine, and Ganelon – tell the truth, warning him about the danger and dishonour threatening him; they are on his side, acting on his behalf.

Nonetheless, as Vàrvaro (1963) has argued, Beroul does all he can to exalt the lovers and to denigrate the counsellors. In the guise of implied author and narrating persona, he speaks out, encouraging the lovers and cursing the barons. This active authorial voice increases tension and drama, underscores key moments in the plot, and helps bridge the gap between characters and audience by manipulating the implied audience's response to the plot and characters and making it react the way he wants. Similarly, Beroul employs a version of Greek chorus by stating the sentiments of King Arthur and his knights, the subjects of King Mark, including the poor people ('la povre gent,' 913), and describing how they react to events. It goes without saying that the Narrator and his chorus respond identically. They express total solidarity with the lovers. Tristan and Isolt are golden; beloved of God and man, they can do no wrong. The sympathy they evoke, in suffering and in joy, in defeat and in victory, is absolute. In contrast, the advisers are designated most often as 'felon' and 'losengeor,' traitors and sowers of discord, and are heartily despised by all concerned. The authorial voice and the chorus take sides with commitment and enthusiasm.

It would also appear, though to a lesser extent, that God himself sides with the fornicators and adulterers. Tristan escapes from his jailers by a miraculous leap from the chapel, a leap he and others consider to be a judgment from God. He slays one of the felons after a prayer to God to aid him. Also, Isolt triumphs in a *judicium Dei*, by swearing a false or 'tricky' oath (*juramentum dolosum*) on sacred relics. If God disapproves, we have no way of knowing it. He certainly does not intervene against the lovers. They invoke him and invariably win. Furthermore, the lovers and the Narrator enjoy the situation immensely, savouring every drop of their ethically ambiguous drink.

There is a tendancy in scholarly circles to justify the moral stance that Beroul appears to take, that is, to harmonize it with what we know to be traditional Christian and feudal ethics. According to scholars, perhaps the lovers are guiltless in intent if not in act, since their passion is the result of the love potion drunk on board ship. They do not wish King Mark harm; indeed thay are concerned about his reputation. Conversely, the accusers act from the basest of motives. They do not love Mark or serve him well. They are envious of Tristan's prowess and jealous of his happiness. Tristan and Isolt function as magnets, attracting wicked impulses: jealousy, envy, greed, and hatred. It can even be maintained that King Mark, by his very credulousness and weakness, inconsistency and indecision, deserves all that he gets and more. Perhaps, indeed, Mark's behaviour is the ethical and epistemological focus of the story. The king and his advisers are the exemplars of a shame culture, obsessed with external appearance and the letter of the law, in antithesis to the lovers who are conscious of inner feelings and responsibility, subjective and problematic, exemplars of a new guilt culture. Pehaps, as Hunt (1977) argues persuasively, Beroul's ethical vision rejoins an Abelardian current. Perhaps Beroul wished to separate judgment from appearance and intention from external action.

Much of this is true and helpful to our understanding of the text. I also believe that it would be a mistake to veil or underestimate the brutality and violence, the 'shock component.' It is not just that Beroul recognizes the power, complexity, and mystery of passion and feels pity for the lovers, or that he respects their courage and vitality even when they are in the wrong. For Beroul, Tristan and Isolt are never in the wrong. For Beroul, love is the dominant, liberating force in the natural world, the source and embodiment of life. Love is good because it is love. Love is innocent because it is love. The values of Eros – in this case, a version of *fin' amor* however we define it – take precedence over the values of all other calls, duties, and mind-sets, including the feudal and the ecclesiastical, including community and marriage. The fact that Tristan cuckolds his uncle, lord, and king, and that he commits fornication and adultery is irrelevant; love is love, and love comes first. Indeed, there is some question whether fornication and adultery enter into Beroul's mind-set at all, except as arguments used by the blocking figures. Except in the mouth of the hermit Ogrin, an unusually obtuse blocking figure, the word 'pechié' can be interpreted systematically to mean 'misfortune' or 'error' but not 'sin' (see Caulkins 1971–2, also Ollier 1990), and 'repentir' to mean 'regrets,' not 'repentance,' both terms referring to a social not an ethical condition.

In addition, Beroul treats his characters and his plot in a manner that we have come to associate with melodrama. Tristan and Isolt are Beroul's heroes. They wear white. The 'felons,' and to some extent King Mark, are the villains because they are opposed to the heroes. They wear black. The lovers can only do right because they are heroes. Indeed, whatever they do is considered good because it is they who do it. In this fictional world, good is defined as that which the heroes do or which contributes to their good, and evil is defined as that which is performed by their adversaries or which harms them. The same acts, such as deception, violence, treachery, when committed by the lovers are good, and when committed by their enemies are bad. Such are the ethical norms in this fictional world.

Trickery and deception are to be found at the centre of Beroul's *Tristan*. Along with the opposition of appearance and reality, they contribute to an imaginative structure unique in medieval letters prior to the era of Jean de Meun. In the very first episode that has survived, Mark hides in a tree to spy on the lovers during one of their evening rendezvous. Isolt, however, spies out his shadow and begins a bogus dialogue with Tristan, insisting that they must never talk again and he must never again sollicit such an interview:

> 'Sire Tristran, por Deu le roi,
> Si grant pechié avez de moi,
> Qui me mandez a itel ore! ...
> Par Deu, qui l'air fist et la mer,
> Ne me mandez nule foiz mais;
> Je vos di bien, Tristran, a fais,
> Certes, je n'i vendroie mie.' (5–7, 16–19)

'Tristan, for God's sake, it is very wrong of you to send for me at such a time! ... For the sake of the Lord who created all things, never send for me again. I am sorry to say this, Tristan, but I am sure I should not dare to come.' (Fedrick, p. 48)

Tristan understands the ruse. Both lovers give the impression of being totally loyal to Mark, innocent of wrongdoing, and the victims of slander. Tristan even begs Isolt to speak on his behalf to her husband, which she refuses to do.

Here the irony proves to be double, even triple. Mark goes out at night in order to see and hear the truth. He sees and hears apparent facts and comes away from his adventure with the true discovery that he has been deceived. Unfortunately for him, he believes he has been deceived by the felons, whereas in fact the deceivers are Tristan and Isolt. Isolt sees Mark's shadow, draws the appropriate conclusion, and invents a tissue of lies, of illusion. Mark then takes her illusion, her lies, for the truth; he takes appearance for reality. Ironically, when Isolt apparently declines Tristan's request to speak on his behalf to Mark, they both have been doing just that. In fact, Mark is the spectator at a scene from a little play, acted by the lovers and directed by Isolt, the purpose of which is to manipulate him. It succeeds totally. We the implied audience understand this because we also are spectators at the same play or rather the larger play containing Isolt; a play of which the director is Beroul. We see what Mark sees but we also see how he sees and how others see and manipulate him. Mark has only one perspective, his own; he is rightly suspicious of it and of all evidence that comes to his purview; hence his eternal vacillation. He can never distinguish properly between 'veoir' and 'savoir.' The lovers, on the other hand, are actors not spectators, and masters of deception and ruse; they live for ruse as much as for their love.

This is one lesson to be drawn from Isolt's even grander theatrical performance, her *judicium Dei* at the Mal Pas. Isolt offers a compurgation or 'deraisne' to exonerate herself from all present and future accusations of adultery. She makes the banished Tristan disguise himself as a leper and a beggar. The leprosy is an ironic metaphor for Tristan's libidinal potency and a no less ironic recall of the lepers to whom Mark had entrusted his wife. The wife, as queen, in her regal potency, arranges for the new leper to carry her over the ford on his shoulders. She then swears an oath of her own formulation, a *juramentum dolosum* (cf. Jonin 1958a), in which she proclaims that no man has ever been inside her thighs other than her husband King Mark and, of course, the beggar who carried her over the ford; these two she exempts from her oath:

> 'Or escoutez que je ci jure ...
> Q'entre mes cuises n'entra home,
> Fors le ladre qui fist soi some,

Qui me porta outre les guez,
Et li rois Marc mes esposez;
Ces deus ost de mon soirement.' (4199, 4205–9)

Isolt does tell the truth, with an aura of precision meant to convince sceptics. Her intent, however, is to deceive, and she succeeds magnificently. King Arthur and his court are manipulated as grossly as is Mark. Once again external illusion is taken for a deeper, moral or ethical reality, and reality is distorted by illusion. Once again, but this time in the grand manner, Isolt puts on a spectacle for others; she functions as the director and Tristan as her chief actor. And this time the lovers triumph over their adversaries in a joyful, carnival-like manner, laughing at them and revelling when Tristan as the helpful beggar delivers a speech to Mark full of sexual double-entendre and when he insults the felons or lets them fall into the mire 'by accident.'

We the extradiegetic spectators see far more than do Isolt's diegetic witnesses or spies or judges. On the contrary, we are made aware of the lovers' guilt at the very moment they proclaim most resolutely and cynically their innocence, and when they lie about the past, the present, and the future. We understand the cynical semantic games that Isolt plays when she swears that she loves only the man who had her as a virgin:

'Mais Dex plevis ma loiauté,
Qui sor mon cors mete flaele,
S'onques fors cil qui m'ot pucele
Out m'amistié encor nul jor!' (22–5)

'But before God I swear I have been loyal: may He scourge me if anyone has ever had my love except the man who had me as a maiden.' (p. 48)

Mark thinks she alludes to him; everyone else knows she means Tristan. Later she plays on the words 'vilanie' (34) and 'seignor' (38) again to baffle him. There is as much disparity between their lying speech and truth as there is between Mark's false perceptions and the same truth.

It would be a mistake, however, to assume that Beroul's universe is uniquely one of knaves who manipulate fools and of masters who manipulate slaves. Tristan and Isolt, though to a much lesser extent than their king, are subject to the capriciousness of appearances, illusion, and incorrect interpretations. A cogent example is provided by the scene in the Forest of Morois; Mark discovers the lovers asleep and decides not to harm them but, before leaving, he exchanges his sword for Tristan's and his ring for Isolt's, and places his glove on the branch of a tree to protect her from being awakened by the sun's rays. I am convinced that both he and the lovers equally misinterpret the visual evidence presented to them. King Mark, observing his wife and his nephew asleep with clothes on, a sword between their bodies, and their mouths separated, arrives at the false conclusion that they are innocent and have not been lovers, whereas in fact the clues prove only that they have most probably not made love that day. His manipulation of sword, ring, and glove, and the fact that he does not slay the couple in their sleep, indicate not indecision but that he pities them and also, probably, retains some very real affection for them. He wishes to communicate and to re-establish relations with them. Tristan and Isolt, however, realizing from the instant they awaken that the king has been present and knows where they are, leap to the equally false conclusion that he has gone to seek his men, that they are in mortal danger, and that they must run away in fright (2095–100).

Both the lovers and their blocking figure are offered concrete evidence, which they misread. To some extent Beroul's Tristan romance is a romance of interpretation, a text in which the characters are compelled again and again to distinguish illusion from reality and to read the signs presented to them; we the implied audience, even though we are aware of much that the characters do not know, are also compelled to interpret the characters' motivation and to reach ethical or moral conclusions concerning them and their actions. The difficulty in interpretation is one of the principal themes working within it. And the characters – King Mark, King Arthur, but also the lovers – are readers; they play a readerly role in the diegesis comparable to ours on the outside.

To the extent that Tristan and Isolt are, on the whole, successful readers and their adversaries are not, derives largely from the fact that they force the action and present the evidence. In other words, they – especially Isolt – function as writers and compel the others to read them. In so doing, they employ occasionally a written text – Ogrin's subtly deceiving, subtly lying letter to Mark – but, more often, oral speech, comparable to a written work of literature read aloud. Tristan and Isolt are intelligent enough to employ speech on two or three levels, seriously and ironically, to deceive others while picking up each other's signals at once. Language cements them as a working unit just as it isolates their enemies. The spoken word and the intellect behind it, creativity in disguise and ruse, play acting and play direction – all triumph in a world previously subject only to force and the law, literally applied. In this sense, the word becomes as subversive of the old order as the desire that it reflects and that gives it being.

Tristan used to be part of their world, indeed its finest flower and exemplar. He was the hero, the warrior beyond compare, who slew the Morholt, committed other great deeds in Mark's name, and gave him a bride. He was the quest hero, the master of *aventure*. But, once he drinks the love potion (a feminine image of water) in a boat on the open sea (another feminine image of water) his prowess ceases to function. Now he is ruled by desire. The desire is all-powerful and never-ending because of the tabu (Isolt belongs to Mark), and so Tristan triumphs again and again, sometimes committing acts of violence, and yet never attaining final victories. There is no finality and he has nowhere to go. Each ruse leads only to other ruses. The plot line resembles that of *Le Roman de Renart* or the fabliau. The chief difference lies in the fact that, whereas in fabliaux and the beast epic, the final comic twist often demands that the husband be made aware of his cuckolding, such is never the case in *Le Roman de Tristan*. The implied audience, informed by the narrator-implied author, is made aware of the total situation, including the cuckolding. So too are Tristan and Isolt. But Mark and Arthur never are allowed comparable insight. For the deception to continue, for episode to follow episode in a sequence sufficient to make up an epic narrative, the victims have always to be kept in the dark, even as they always lose to the heroes.

Winning consistently through ruse, Tristan and Isolt function as trickster heroes (compare Regalado 1976 and Blakeslee 1989), who triumph over their adversaries through ingenuity and artifice; they are geniuses at manipulation and deception and lie for the sheer pleasure of it, for their joy in *gaudium* and *jocum*. On at least two occasions – the episode of the tree, and Isolt's oath at the ford – the lovers' little play is far more elaborate than would be necessary to attain their ends. They risk all by daring their blind and deaf adversaries to see and hear. In this sense the play of the game and the victory of wit and will over blind force become more important than desire itself.

On the other hand, it is no less a fact that ruse, play, will, and wit are all products of desire; they come into being because of it and owe their existence to it. Beroul's text celebrates the triumph of desire and an impenitent, erotic fantasy. From a Freudian perspective, Beroul's Tristan story re-enacts the Oedipus complex in its totality. The young Tristan slays hostile father adversaries; he also supplants his surrogate father, the king. The surrogate father is sometimes hostile and sometimes kind but in any case manifests the negative qualities that Tristan could only resent in his real father. In the woman's world, on a boat on the open sea, Tristan drinks a woman's drink, the love filter. His id rebels and his ego awakens. He commits the oedipal incest; indeed he fulfills the ultimate oedipal dream of enjoying the mother figure virgin before she is possessed by the father. At court and later in the dark forest (another image of woman as the wild, the primitive, and yet also a refuge), Tristan combines the pleasure principle and the reality principle. Although the lovers do suffer in the forest and ultimately comprehend they cannot function alienated from society, the forest is a locus where their desire can run free; it is authentic nature in contrast to the culture of slander and hypocrisy at court. Whatever the laws of society, Tristan braves them with impunity and without remorse. His id and his libido triumph in a feast of desire, with the full potency of the word, in an atmosphere of transgression and joy. There is an aura of carnival, in Bakhtin's (1968G) sense of the term, about the jokes of the leper and the trial of the queen at Mal Pas. Mark is insulted, and the felons are tossed into slime and eventually slain.

This is the release of tension through desire and violence, Eros and Thanatos. Tristan loves Isolt and he slays the felons; he indulges his passion and his will for vengeance. Governal presents one dead felon's head, Tristan another's shorn hair as a trophy. The heroes express joy. There are no moral or religious scruples in this world of the passions, instinctual survival, deceit, violence, desire, and the all-triumphal id. Nothing restrains transgression and the flouting of traditional order as the lovers live their fantasy in Beroul's rich, powerful fantasy world.

Thomas

Beroul's tone – of triumphant Eros, trickery, and transgression – may have been conditioned in part by the fact that the extant portion of his *Tristan* treats a period when the lovers are together in Cornwall, under the watchful eyes of King Mark or briefly separated but eager to be reunited, in spite of the husband's still watchful eyes. But for the occasional exception, the Thomas fragments recount different events later in the story, with Tristan in exile in Brittany, cut off from his beloved. Even so, Thomas's tone, his emphasis, and his obsessions are so different from Beroul's that we recognize two divergent literary temperaments, each treating a traditional narrative in his own way, each arriving at the creation of a distinct literary world.

Beroul is 'realistic' in his portrayal of deception and violence, brutality and desire. Thomas is no less realistic but in other ways. The fragments of his text that have survived – some 3200 octosyllables – contain 500 lines of inner monologue, 900 lines of inner dialogue, and 350 lines of authorial analysis. The psychology of the individual lover and the abstract, philosophical analysis of the nature of love make up the larger portion of the romance. Thomas's discussion of 'voleir,' 'desir,' and 'raisun' is of clerical origin and more than a little clerical in its rhetorical and intellectual structure. Considering the later evolution of the novel in France, from *La Princesse de Clèves* through Marivaux, Laclos, Stendhal, and Flaubert, to Proust, no medieval writer appears to be so prescient and so French as this unknown Anglo-Norman, Thomas of England.

On the one hand, Thomas, in his own voice as implied author and through the voice of his protagonist Tristan, scrutinizes the nature of *fin' amor.* With extraordinary insight, Tristan muses on the fragility of love and on how it can be uprooted through external events (separation) or internal weakness (jealousy). He discovers how exceptional passion proves to be yet also how harmful. Among the problems analysed are the relationship of love to marriage and of love to pleasure. We are made aware (as never before in Beroul and Chrétien) of the corporeal, physical nature of *fin' amor,* of desire and jealousy, and of passion that involves the body as well as the spirit; in an adulterous triangle such as Tristan, Isolt, and Mark (or Lancelot, Guinevere, and Arthur), people are not disembodied spirits or libidos.

Thus one of the greatest romances of *fin' amor* undermines the idealism of courtly love. The crucial moment is Tristan's extended inner monologue-dialogue resulting in his decision to wed Isolt of the White Hands, the daughter of King Hoël of Brittany. Tristan convinces himself that his beloved, Isolt of Ireland, happily installed as Mark's queen, has now forgotten him because, among other reasons, she is being made love to continually by her husband, and she enjoys it, sharing his 'buen,' 'deduit,' and 'joie,' her 'desir' and 'delit' with the present 'seignur' triumphing easily over 'amur' for the absent 'ami':

> 'Pur vostre cors su jo em paine,
> li reis sa joie en vos maine,
> sun deduit maine e sun buen,
> ço que mien fu ore est suen ...

Sa [Isolt's] grant belté pas nel requirt,
ne sa nature pas n'i afirt,
quant de lui ad sun desir,
que pur altre deive languir.
Tant se deit deliter al rei
oblier deit l'amur de mei;
en sun seignur tant deliter
que sun ami deit oblier.
E quei li valt ore m'amur
emvers le delit sun seignur?' (69–72, 151–60)

'My body aches for yours, while the king takes his pleasure with you: he has his pleasure and delight, what once was mine is now his. ... her great beauty makes it unnecessary (nor is it within her nature), for her to pine away for another when she fulfills all her desires with him. She should find such pleasures with the king as to forget her love for me; find such pleasures with her husband as to forget her lover. What is my love to her now, compared to the pleasure she finds with her lord?' (Gregory, pp. 7, 11)

The reasons for which Tristan decides to marry the second Isolt are the following: he wants to imitate Isolt of Ireland by making love to another person; he wants to discover how Mark feels, making love regularly to *an* Isolt; and he thinks that if, through sustained intercourse, Isolt of Ireland has forgotten him, he will be able to forget her. Thomas probes the reality of *fin' amor*, grounded in obstacle and sometimes in adultery, and, by so doing, reveals pitilessly the foibles of his protagonist. From a medieval courtly perspective and from a modern one, Tristan is guilty of lack of trust in his beloved; a good courtly lover would never suspect Isolt of forgetting him or of infidelity in her heart. His jealousy of the imposed physical bond between Isolt and her husband (the *debitum conjugale*) is unworthy. Even worse, he himself can be accused of fickleness and of more than a little Sartrean bad faith. Although obsessed with what goes on in Mark's bed, Tristan is self-centered, wallowing in his own egotism, grounded in *En soi* or *Pour soi*, as he blames others for his own anxiety or depression. Furthermore, since he is attracted by Isolt of the White Hands, by her 'belté' as well as her name and availability, we can ask whether all this inner probing and anxiety-ridden introspection does not unconsciously mask and buttress awakening desire for the new Isolt.

On the wedding night, Tristan notices the ring on his finger, a ring belonging to Isolt of Ireland, placed there by her at the moment of their leave-taking. This ring functions not only as a recognition token and as a token of fidelity but it also symbolizes spiritual marriage. Because of it, Tristan cannot love another. The ring is Isolt, her presence in Tristan and her power over him. Like Isolt, a sorceress and a sorceress's daughter, it casts a spell over the exiled knight, preventing him from consummating his marriage. He is literally made impotent by the ring that encircles his finger. Torn between 'voleir' and 'poeir,' between 'voleir' and 'desir,' desiring Isolt of Brittany but unwilling and unable to make love to her, ironically and unconsciously Tristan attains his end. Truly guilty of madness ('derverie' and 'fol corage'), he discovers exactly how miserable Mark and Isolt are and comes to share their misery to the full. And he drags an innocent person into the quagmire, an act that will undo him in turn.

If, then, Beroul's romance embodies a joyful, triumphant, wish-fulfilment explosion of the liberated id in conjunction with the awakened ego, in Thomas the superego (remorse, regrets, anxiety) and the castrating Mother prove to be all-powerful. The ego, facing the loss of a love object (in this case the oedipal surrogate mother), is unable to transfer its desire to another and proceed beyond the oedipal stage. Tristan remains emotionally a child; indeed he regresses into masochism, punishing himself with the new marriage and his incapacity to consummate it. Ego loss and identification with the love object (Isolt of Ireland) plus an inferiority complex vis-à-vis the Oedipal Father (Mark) cause him to wish to *become* Isolt (or Mark) by wedding the second Isolt. Impotence in the face of his bride is one form of self-instigated punishment. Later, Tristan will be mortally wounded by the husband of another man's mistress (a man also called Tristan), a surrogate for King Mark (symbolic oedipal castration) and slain, as it were, by his frustrated, vengeful bride. Transgressing a libidinal tabu proves fatal. The superego (the ocean, the winds) opposes the lovers, and their only union is a moving but mortal *Liebestod*.

It goes without saying that Thomas's universe is one of suffering and pain. Larmat (1979) has shown that the key terms in his vocabulary, repeated incessantly, are 'mal,' 'dolur,' 'peine,' 'anguise,' 'plaindre,' and 'plurer'; also 'pitet,' 'irur,' 'tristur,' 'languir,' 'murir,' 'perir,' 'dehait,' 'ahan,' 'mesaise.' 'Amur' rhymes with 'dolur' and 'haür'; 'pesance' rhymes with 'desevrance' and 'desturbance.' Words evoking a more pleasurable semantic field refer inevitably to the past or to the experience of others, especially in jealous anxiety fantasies. If Beroul can be considered, to some small extent, the Corneille of early romance, Thomas anticipates Racine. Each of his characters stands alone, separated from the others by a wall, internalizing his or her anguish, incapable of resolving it through verbal communication, and incapable even of expressing it. The 'peine' and 'dolur' are meditated upon, in rhetorical, sonorous verse, the rough twelfth-century equivalent of Racine, Chénier, Hugo, and Aragon.

Tristan, the slayer of the Morholt in the legend, Beroul's active trickster, in the Thomas fragments is rendered totally passive, enclosed, and melancholic, enduring his *tristitia*: sadness, sloth, melancholia, and insanity. Rendered impotent by Isolt of Ireland's ring, he explains to Isolt of the White Hands that a wound prevents him from consummating their marriage. He who slew dragons and giants will soon be wounded by a jealous husband in turn, and then restricted to his bed where the second Isolt will successfully plot his demise. In Thomas, as in Wagner, Eros is allied to Thanatos. To the extent that women are responsible for the one, they also contribute to the other. True, Isolt the Queen loves her knight and comes to him over the seas. Nonetheless, she, her mother, her servant Brangain, and her rival are all, in one way or another, sorceresses, magicians, and wielders of power over men, whom they subdue and humiliate.

The lovers' separation occurs in space and time. Thomas makes us conscious (as Beroul never does and as the authors of *chansons de geste* seldom do) of the discontinuity between past and present and the crucial change that individuals undergo in the course of time. Tristan is painfully aware that because of duration, in Andreas Capellanus' terms, 'Amor enim semper minuitur vel augetur' [Love always waxes or wanes] (Walsh 1982G: 36–7). The past is associated with love, life, communication, togetherness, and joy; the present with forgetting, death, separation, loneliness, and misery. Unhappily for Tristan, joy in the past can be invoked only through dreams, meditation, and memory. Wretchedness in the present *is* reality. Furthermore, joy in the past is assimilated to Cornwall, wretchedness in the present to Brittany. Except for the brief adventure of a brief rendezvous, Tristan dwells now in Brittany and cannot return to Cornwall. Isolt the Queen and Isolt of the White Hands reside each in her own land. Tristan is obliged to remain with the wrong Isolt, and when Isolt of Ireland comes to heal his wounds, she arrives too late. As we have seen, the characters are isolated psychologically and existentially.

Whereas in Beroul, the lovers communicate successfully and spy out the ruses that their adversaries invent to confound them, here Isolt the Queen is kept in ignorance of Tristan's deeds abroad; Brangain is misled concerning Kaherdin's heroism; Isolt and Brangain quarrel, each blaming the other and each blaming Tristan, for non-existent faults. Each lover converses with himself or with figments of the Other in his (her) imagination but never with the Other present. Nor does Tristan ever communicate with the other Isolt, his bride. Had he done so, the disaster might have been averted. As it is, the lover addresses directly, with tenderness and passion, neither his wife nor his mistress, but his mistress's statue, built by himself in a grotto. Such discourse has limited practical use. On the contrary, when Tristan does address his wife concerning the boat on the ocean, Isolt of the White Hands, who has successfully spied out his secret unknown to him (she is a much better spy than Mark, Ogrin, and the felons in Beroul), commits a dark deed. An ironic, substitute Isolt, she ironically substitutes the sail, that is, she lies about the colour (changing it from white to black) and intentionally gives her husband the false impression that Isolt of Ireland has not come to cure him, with catastrophic results; his last thoughts are that she abandoned him: 'Quant a moi ne volez venir ... N'avez pité de ma langur' (3033, 3037). ['Since you have no wish to come to me ... You take no pity on me in my languor' (p. 155)].

The white (or black) sail is but one of several images in Thomas's romance, arch-images of power and beauty that function ambiguously in the narrative and are subject to ambiguous, multivocal interpretation. The white sail signals presence, healing, purity, goodness, and life; physically it brings Isolt to Tristan. Yet, in the second Isolt's mouth, from Tristan's perspective, the sail becomes falsely black, and it falsely signals absence, illness, deceit, evil, and death. Yet, because of the second Isolt, the false symbolism of evil, absence, and death proves to be true, for the ship indeed fails to bring Isolt in time. The tragic myth of Aegeus and Theseus is consciously re-enacted by the clerk Thomas in his modern, tragic story of Tristan and Isolt.

If the sail fails to communicate and unite the lovers, this is because of deceit on the part of Isolt of the White Hands, but also because the ocean and the winds do not function as they ought. Tristan and Isolt drank their 'lovendrinc' in a boat on the open sea. The sea is the archetype of the eternal mother, the *Ewig-Weibliche*, feminine generative and natural power, the irrational, the unconscious, the explosive, superhuman form of Eros. Yet, although the sea brings Tristan to Isolt in Ireland, and Tristan to Isolt in Cornwall, it fails to bring Isolt to Tristan in Brittany. The magician, daughter of a magician, mistress of magic potions, cannot control the winds or the sea. The sea unites and separates; it ebbs and flows, like the eternal nature it is; it grants life and love yet also death, *amor* and *mort*.

Finally, we find Tristan's only personal contribution to his universe, the Hall of Images (studied by Polak 1970, Ferrante 1979, and Grigsby 1980). In the cave Tristan has carved sculptures of Isolt, and also of Brangain, Mark, and himself. He is wont to converse with Isolt's statue, kissing it when he is in a good mood and berating it when he is not. From one perspective, this situation can be considered the nadir in the young man's emotional life. He regresses to living only in the past, unable to cope with the present. He regresses to narcissism, living only in his dream world of fantasms, unable to cope with reality. All the youth's libido is occupied in discoursing with an inanimate object, a fetish object that has replaced the real Isolt or her namesake, the Breton Isolt, in his mind. It is clear that Tristan embraces the statue in place of his wife, the flesh-and-blood woman whom he cannot or will not embrace. Also, Tristan clothes the statue, embellishes it, speaks to it, and adores it. He treats it the way Pygmalion treated his statue – a parody of the devotion the Christian offers to the Virgin Mary. His behaviour becomes, in the world of Venus, a dark parody of worship, an act of idolatry; the Hall of Images, a hidden cave, is shown to be a dark parody of the Church.

On the other hand, Tristan in his cave may have found a productive, functioning, organic, albeit temporary, resolution to his problem. He enters the cave (a feminine image, symbolic of the womb, the unconscious, the creative female Eros) and in it he creates works of art. The 'images' may be false, but Tristan is so great an artist that they appear true in Kaherdin's eyes. It is when Kaherdin beholds the statues that he discovers the truth about his sister's marriage with Tristan and why Tristan loves so powerfully Isolt the Queen. Tristan does place his ring on the statue's finger; he loves the statue (his memory, his vision of Isolt) in a way that is not absurd or ridiculous. We gaze at the depths of his passion in awe, not mockery. And we admire his greatness as a creator – here as a sculptor and earlier as a poet and composer. The Cornish knight, famous throughout the world for his artistic accomplishments as well as for prowess and love, after having seduced Isolt of the White Hands by his singing, later transmutes suffering into art. For good or ill, Tristan lives life as an artist. He creates, performs, teaches, and manipulates others and plays the poet's role vis-à-vis the audiences in his world: his wife, his brother-in-law, his absent mistress, and his statues. A melancholic lover cast down by an excess of black bile, wallowing in *tristitia*, Tristan is also inspired to create. In his creativity and deep, subtle, tortured, psychological introspection, he is an author figure in the diegesis who reflects the preoccupations, needs, and triumphs of his creator, the extradiegetic implied author Thomas. In his Hall of Images Tristan is at his best; here he is most active, most authentic, and perhaps most fulfilled. The Hall of Images is a *mise en abyme* for the problems – of communication, time, and love – and structures that are *Le Roman de Tristan* as a whole.

Nonetheless, whatever Tristan's victory and consolation in the cave, the statues are not living beings. In Thomas death is not a sign of the tricksters' mastery over their adversaries, as in Beroul. It is indeed the outcome of deception and revenge, and yet it is inflicted on the lovers, not by them. Tristan's wounds from battle with a jealous husband; a storm at sea and the subsequent calm; Isolt of Brittany's hurt and jealousy; the white sails interpreted as black – these are the links in a chain, the wheels and pistons in an infernal machine, that bring the lovers to their doom. At the same time the links and the wheels are somehow insignificant, mere earthly manifestations of a supreme, supernatural destiny. Tristan and Isolt, the archetypal lovers of their age, are brought to death by their love. It is their destiny to love and to die; their love is death, and their death is love. As Tristan explains to Kaherdin:

> 'El beivre fud la nostre mort ...
> a tel ure duné nus fu,
> a nostre mort l'avum beü.' (2495, 2497–8)

'Our death lay in that potion ... those were the circumstances under which it was given, that we drank with it our death.' (p. 129)

The potion, 'lovendrinc,' is also a 'poison,' in the modern as well as the medieval sense of the term. The fluid potion, created by women, embodying the passion of the Eternal Woman, drunk on the open sea, leads to death on cold dry land, with the sea, in storm and in calm, now conspiring against the lovers. Kariado, the protagonist's rival in Cornwall, rightly associates the lovers with death, and Tristan falls, fighting in the name of love for another Tristan, a lover like himself, bearing his name. Eros leads to Thanatos; Eros is Thanatos, as if it were only in death that love can be itself and fulfil its destiny.

As in Marie's lay, neither lover can survive isolated from the other. Tristan falls, and Isolt perishes immediately thereafter:

> 'Amis Tristran, quant mort vus vei,
> par raisun vivre puis ne dei.
> Mort estes pur la meie amur,
> e jo muer, amis, de tendrur ...
> Pur mei avez perdu la vie,
> E jo frai cum veraie amie,
> Pur vos voil murir ensement.' (3083–6, 3111–13)

'Tristram my love, now that I see you dead, I have no reason for living any more. You are dead through love for me, and I die too, my love, out of grief. ... You have lost your life on my account, so I shall do as a true lover should: I will die likewise for you.' (pp. 157, 159)

Neither speaks of an afterlife, in heaven or hell, or of salvation and its opposite. Neither confesses his sins or requests the last rites. Neither is conscious of a Christian cosmos or a Christian world-view.

For all the demystification of the protagonists' moral character and for all the demystification of *fin' amor,* both lovers, in their *Liebestod,* achieve a dignity and nobility rare in literature. Theirs is a magnificent human tragedy that purges pity and terror in the audience and grants catharsis. Before the supreme mystery of Eros man stands in silence and in wonder. In this tragic vision, life can be horrifying, and yet the power of love remains supreme, and *fin' amor* – the love of princes – retains its goodness and beauty, a goodness and beauty beyond mortal ken, and beyond the power of the grave. In this, Thomas reveals himself to be as subversive of the established order as Beroul is. Both men, in divergent ways with divergent temperaments, place the call of love above all other calls, including feudal law, personal honour, and Christian faith. The one, in his comedy of joyful transgression, the other in his tragedy of suffering and death, both claim a new absolute in literature and in life; it is the claim for passion, for human values, and for the art that makes the claims and gives them being. From this comes one of the great modern myths in literature.

3. *Ipomedon*

Marie, Beroul, Thomas, and the greatest romancer of the age, Chrétien de Troyes, as well as a number of other figures – Wace, Benoît de

Sainte-Maure, and Gautier d'Arras – form a 'classical generation' that bursts upon the scene with a splendour unique in medieval letters. Their contribution to Western culture, by 'inventing' the courtly romance genre and by raising it to a level of artistic perfection, is incalculable.

It is also true, though less well known even in medievalist circles, that courtly narrative continued to flourish after Chrétien de Troyes, during the last years of the twelfth century and well on into the thirteenth, and that romance masterpieces were produced in French for a hundred years after the great classical generation. Although the delicate balance of forces embodied in the work of Marie, Chrétien, and Thomas is perhaps lost to their successors, their themes are developed by a host of narrators, often with brilliant success. The Anglo-Norman courts participated in the process of continuation, elaboration, and re-creation, contributing a number of *romans* and *lais* of notable quality. Limits of space allow me only to explore a few byways in this rich land of fiction. I shall treat three texts representing independent intertextual responses to the masterpieces of the earlier age. Hue de Rotelande's *Ipomedon* is an exercise in urbane wit and cynical undermining. *Amadas et Ydoine* achieves an extraordinary balance of idyllic, tender love and paradoxical frenzy in excess. Finally, *Gui de Warewic* embodies the *roman d'aventures*, of particular insular importance because the hero of adventures is an Englishman and the romance text exalts the national past in a subgenre unique to England.

It can be claimed that Hue de Rotelande ranks second only to Thomas as a writer of Anglo-Norman romance. A Norman-Welsh cleric like Gerald of Wales and Walter Map, he was born at Rhuddlan, dwelt at Credenhill near Hereford, and wrote for Gilbert Fitz-Baderon, Lord of Monmouth. His masterpiece, *Ipomedon*, and its sequel, *Protheselaus*, date from the 1180s. *Ipomedon* gave rise to three separate translations or adaptations in Middle English. It was apparently known by Wolfram von Eschenbach and, either in its original form or in one of the English versions, was most likely the principal source for the tale of 'Gareth of Orkney' in *Le Morte Darthur.*

The plot is relatively simple. The princess of Calabria vows to marry only the greatest knight in the world – hence her name, La Fière. Ipomedon, son of the king of Apulia, visits her court incognito and serves her as a page. They fall in love. However, La Fière rebuffs the youth because he does not enjoy a reputation for valour. Ipomedon leaves in despair and sets out to win a name. He returns twice to Calabria to protect La Fière from having a husband imposed on her.

Hue de Rotelande elaborates the Three Day Tournament motif; disguised as a knight-in-waiting to the Queen of Sicily, Ipomedon triumphs in the tourney, each day wearing different-coloured armor and accessories. Hue then exploits the tradition of the Fair Unknown.[4] Disguised as a madman, Ipomedon volunteers to defend La Fière; even though rebuffed mercilessly by her messenger and confidante, Ismeine, he eventually convinces the latter of his worth. In the end the youth overcomes all obstacles, weds his princess, and is crowned king of Apulia.

In spite of its non-Arthurian setting and the absence of faerie, *Ipomedon* follows in the wake of Beroul, Thomas, and Chrétien de Troyes. The court situation in Sicily – a benevolent but passive king; a beautifully regal queen to whom several knights pay court, but who falls passionately in love with the hero; the king's nephew, who becomes the hero's best friend; and the braggart, boastful seneschal punished for his wicked tongue – parallels the Arthurian nexus in Logres and (sans nephew) the Mark, Isolt, Cariados triad in Cornwall. From Chrétien, Beroul, and Thomas Hue de Roteland takes a number of other motifs, including the Three Day Tourney, love sickness, the proud maiden, the 'forthputting damsel,' a spritely, witty suivante, and a faithful older tutor.

We can begin to understand *Ipomedon* by placing the poem in its literary context, the 1180s, when Beroul, Thomas, but above all Chrétien de Troyes had enlarged the horizon of expectations of the public for the new literary genre, romance. Arthurian in theme and motif, Italo-Byzantine in names and locale, this 'hybrid' grows in Chrétien's field, under his shade, and serves as an imitation but also a parody; it becomes a homage to and a critique of the texts of the Master. Thus Hue follows in Chrétien's wake and yet dares to scrutinize the romance conventions that Chrétien helped to elaborate. Hanning (1974) and Spensley (1974) argue for a pattern of growth in the hero and a purposive, serious, organic narrative structure. Agreeing with much of what they say, I would like to envisage Hue's text from a somewhat different perspective.

One aspect of my investigation focuses on the protagonist's attitude after victory in the tournament and his decision not to wed La Fière and not to govern his kingdom but to continue a life of adventure:

> 'Nel ferai pas uncor, amis,
> Ainz m'en irrai quere mun pris,
> Jombles hom sui e bacheler,

> De femme aveir ne dei haster;
> Li jomble ki trop ço desirent,
> Se un en amende, mil empirent.' (6647–52)
> ... Ne volt mie curuner sei
> E si lur ad ben dit purquei,
> Ke il volt uncor de terre en terre
> Aler ses aventures quere,
> Kar, deske il curunez serreit
> A enur fere nel purreit. (7219–24)

'I will not yet marry, dear friend; on the contrary, I will set out in quest of renown. I am a young man, not married and not established; I should not haste for a wife: of the young who want this too badly, for each who improves a thousand worsen. ... ' He does not at all wish to be crowned and has told them precisely why: that he still seeks to wander from one realm to another in quest of adventures, for if he were to be crowned, he could no longer perform deeds of honour.

'Pris,' 'aventures,' and 'enur' form part of the dialectic elaborated by Chrétien in *Erec et Enide* and *Yvain*. Unlike Beroul, Thomas, and Marie, Chrétien investigates the relationship between *militia* and *amor* (prowess and love). These two elements give meaning to existence and are spurs to perfection in courtly man; a knight cannot expect to attain plenitude in the hierarchy until he performs deeds in arms and is loved by a great lady. In addition, the two forces depend on each other, each reinforcing the other. A hero achieves the greatest feats only at the goading of Eros, and he will be rewarded only because he has succeeded in martial pursuits. However, love can also undermine war, as war can undermine love, because, in a paradoxical world similar to Corneille's, neither passion nor prowess is determined once and for all as essence. Each must be reaffirmed within a state of existential contingency. Furthermore, Chrétien does not allow the tension between *militia* and *amor* to be resolved in a wish-fulfilment fantasy world of adultery where a not overly dangerous husband and his obtuse retinue provide the obstacle that reinforces *fin' amor*, and where the lover is compelled to leave the court, thereby winning martial renown. He prefers to scrutinize marriage as a solution to the courtly dilemma, a socially productive compromise between 'amor' and 'reison.' And where Erec and Enide or Yvain and Laudine are married to each other, the built-in obstacles of adultery necessarily cease to function. The couple must invent new ones in order, through their own will, to surpass themselves. The danger of 'recreantise' remains ever present.

Despite obvious similarities, the situation elaborated by Hue de Rotelande differs from the one in *Erec* or *Yvain*. Chrétien's protagonists are never offered a crown early in their careers. Young Ipomedon spurns his father's kingdom and a girl he has not yet married, on the pretext that he likes adventures and that one should not marry young. Following Köhler (1956G), I propose that, whereas Chrétien de Troyes arrives at a kind of synthesis, wherein love and prowess reinforce each other and in which the private life (*fin' amor*) and the public life (chivalry) contribute to the establishment of an ideal *ordo* where the aspirations of the petty nobility are given free reign, in the period following Chrétien the synthesis breaks down, and the old *ordo* loses its ideological hold on the public. As early as 1180, *Ipomedon* embodies a post-Chrétien response, an optimistic fiction (the *roman d'aventures*) in which the private and public domains are now separate and the various characters undergo no inner development. Unlike Chrétien's knights-errant, Hue's protagonist does not grow in the course of the action, physically, socially, or spiritually. Nor is he guilty of a flaw or lack for which he must do penance and that he will eventually transcend. In contrast to Perceval the Welshman, for instance, he does not become great nor, until the end, is he recognized to be so. His virtues are present from the beginning. He displays them in disguise, for the inherent joy of display. And his arrested development in psychology and ethics corresponds to a comparable lack of evolution in social obligations. Ipomedon has fallen in love but does not want marriage or a kingdom. He has no public life. In his own words, he is a 'jombles hom' and a 'bacheler'; in Duby's (1964G) words he is a *juvenis* and will remain one as long as he can. Significantly, Hue de Rotelande tells of a conflict between a young knight, Dryas, who loves feats in arms and defends La Fière's right to dispose of her person as she chooses, and Amphion, who is wise ('saive') but old, dislikes war, and wishes to marry off the princess against her will. The author's position is clear; in the tourney his protagonist rescues Dryas and slays Amphion. Love, freedom, and adventure, associated with youth and war, stand in opposition to the constraints of society, assimilated to old age. The *juvenis* seeks at all costs to avoid responsibility, to avoid becoming a *senior*, and to avoid growing old, presumably with the author's and public's approbation.

In Chrétien, as five centuries later in Corneille, *militia* supports *amor*, and *amor* provides inspiration for *militia*. Erec, Alexandre, Cligés, Lancelot, and Yvain succeed in Eros because they are the best knights in the world, and they become and/or remain the best because they are cherished by the likes of Enide, Soredamors, Fenice, Guinevere, and

Laudine and because of their ability to commit themselves to a lady in the most absolute way. However, *militia* and *amor* each is in a state of flux, rising or falling; when a knight's prowess (that is, in a shame culture, his reputation for prowess) begins to decline, the love of an Enide and a Laudine declines with it. Hence the need for Erec or Yvain to seek new adventures and to maintain or increase his reputation for valour; this is the only way, in this aristocratic, military universe, to maintain the love of his wife. Hue de Rotelande pushes the Chrétien formulation to its logical, therefore absurd, conclusion. No matter what triumphs Ipomedon has obtained – winning the tourney, rescuing the King of France, slaying the invader Léonin – how can he be sure that he is the best knight in the world, or that he is worthy of La Fière, or that she will not break her oath to marry him? Following chivalric precept to the letter, Ipomedon can go on forever and commit a quasi-infinite series of exploits, never stopping to wed the woman he loves and who loves him.

Perhaps La Fière then was at fault in seeking to keep herself for the best, in declaring,

> Ke ja mes seignur ne prendreit
> Ne espuseie ne sereit,
> Ne pur rei ne pur homme,
> Mes ke cil fust sire de Rome
> E de tuz les reines del mund
> E de tuz les hommes ke sunt,
> Si il ne fust chivaler si pruz
> Ke il as armes venquit tuz,
> Ke en totes terres ou entrast
> Le los e le pris en portast. (123–32)

That she would never take a husband and be wed: neither to king nor to king's vassal even if he were the lord of Rome and of all kingdoms and peoples on earth, unless he were a knight of such prowess that he vanquished all in feats of arms and that, in all the realms where he travelled, he won the highest praise and renown.

The vow makes explicit what is implicit in Chrétien in the consciousness and behaviour of his heroines. Nonetheless, the Narrator as implied author and, later on, La Fière herself condemns her vow in the strongest possible terms. In fact, everyone denounces her for being proud ('fere' and 'orgoillose'). Her purported 'orgoil' and 'folie' are one of the leitmotivs of the romance; indeed, they give the princess her name.

La Fière is condemned not only for spurning love but, above all, for assimilating it to *militia*, thus making it depend uniquely upon martial accomplishment and, by so doing, for acting in bad faith, since she will succumb to a man apparently lacking such accomplishment. Ipomedon appears before her and before the Queen of Sicily incognito. He is courtly, elegant, a superb hunter, and ravishingly handsome. However, he appears to be 'cuars' (521), that is, he does not choose to perform feats of prowess. Several times it is suggested that, if only he were valorous, La Fière and the queen would seek him out; in time this 'bel malveis' (fair coward) is loved by both of them. And they love him most of all for his beauty; for, as the narrator states, love seeks only its pleasure, and good jousting occurs in bed: 'Amur ne quert fors sun delit, / Mult valt le juster enz el lit' (4313–14). Hue de Rotelande here contrasts 'delit' with 'los' and 'pris,' setting off *militia* against *amor*. In real life, as opposed to chivalric notions found in books, women love men for the same reasons that men love women, for 'belté' and 'curteisie.' Therefore, thickness of biceps is not the unique nor even the most important secondary sexual characteristic of the male. In addition, is not La Fière's problem also a literary one of generic confusion? She is something like a *chanson de geste* heroine dropped into a *roman courtois*; she judges her romance suitor by epic standards, comically expecting him to be Roland.

Ipomedon's commitment to the pleasures of the hunt should be interpreted in this context. Both in Calabria and in Sicily he allegedly performs outstanding feats with game in the woods while other men spend their time in the lists. La Fière becomes enamoured upon observing the youth's competence in felling and dressing a stag. And, in his role of 'bel malveis,' he mocks the tourney, claiming it isn't safe – one can get hurt – and he boasts of the prowess of his hunting dogs, Baucan, Ridel, and Baailemunt.

In the Middle Ages the chase can be interpreted as a symbol of vanity and idolatry or as behaviour in opposition to or in competition with the erotic. However, imagery of the chase, as of falconry, was also assimilated to the noblest impulses of *fin' amor*, and in later centuries the 'hunt of love' became a familiar theme in the *dit amoureux*. Although *Ipomedon* in no way evokes the chase as leading to supernatural exploits in the *forest aventureuse*, it does partake of the Hunt of Venus, which that goddess recommends to Adonis in the *Metamorphoses*. In the context of Hue's romance, it is the ideal pastime for lovers and exponents of 'curteisie,' the appropriate 'service' for one who calls himself the queen's lover, 'dru la reine.' This hunt of Venus, in which Ipomedon bags venison, is opposed to the hard hunt of wild boars or fierce men, in which the victor wins horses and trophies. For Hue, the chase functions as a game; it is an artificial structure that parodies the tourney (itself a game) and real war. The protagonist's prowess in the woods (the realm of nature as opposed to culture, and of darkness and the unconscious as opposed to the harsh light of social intercourse in hall and on the field) is considered antisocial behaviour. Indeed it is, to the extent that it undermines the 'rules of the game' elaborated by a court society for hall and field. Thus Hue exploits the chase, in its amatory aspects, in order to mock the tourney and a society which measures human value according to tourney rankings.

Finally, the author undermines *fin' amor* and the courtly by playing with the notions of wisdom and folly – wisdom ('sens,' 'reison') is assimilated to 'curteisie,' and folly ('folie') is envisaged both as foolishness and insanity. In Chrétien, and for that matter in the *Prose Lancelot* and *Prose Tristan*, a great lover is, at one time in his life, driven mad by love. Madness is an experience he must undergo; in the case of Yvain, it is the just punishment for a sin against *fin' amor.* The protagonist's goal is attainment of wisdom along with sovereignty. Yet the greatest of lovers, a Lancelot or a Tristan, will always sacrifice 'reison' to 'amor.' Theirs is a holy madness, sacred to the new cult of Eros of which they are high priests and in which ladies are venerated like goddesses.

With regard to the veneration of ladies in a cult of *fin' amor,* Ipomedon and his author remain agnostic. Although La Fière is 'saive' and acts 'sagement' to institute the tourney in which her lover will have the opportunity to win her hand, on the whole she, her confidante Ismeine, and the queen are repeatedly guilty of 'folie.' The Narrator himself says they are foolish to misjudge Ipomedon, to scorn him, and to make exorbitant demands in matters of the heart. Then their 'folie' increases, for they do go mad (metaphorically) upon discovering their folly, and upon falling in love. The most extreme case is Ismeine who admits, at some length, that she is madder than the presumed madman she adores, and insane because she adores him (9123–48).

In contrast, the young man, although he does cherish La Fière, is not at all 'fol.' His 'sens' and 'curteisie' are evident when he serves La Fière and the queen incognito, playing the fool, and later when he disguises himself as a mad knight in order to combat Léonin. Ipomedon's strength lies in his 'engin' [wit, intelligence, cunning, artifice] (7748, 7756) (see Hanning 1974), his capacity to counterfeit madness and drive others crazy while himself remaining sane; thus through intelligence and will power, lucidity and self-control, he masters others instead of being mastered by them.

'Engin' is embodied in manipulation and deceit. Before the action begins, Ipomedon's mother gave birth secretly and devised a ring token so that her offspring one day would be recognized. With Ismeine's connivance, La Fière convinces her lord, the King of Sicily, to authorize a tournament, thus giving her time to find Ipomedon and preventing the barons from imposing on her a husband. Later, Ismeine selfishly withholds key information from her mistress in order to further her own designs on the unknown mad knight. In the practice of deception, La Fière resembles Isolt and Laudine, and Ismeine recalls Brangain and Lunette. However, these examples pale before the career of Ipomedon, trickster hero par excellence, multiple trickster through multiple disguise. Ipomedon, prince of Apulia, (1) serves La Fière as a page, incognito. (2) He commits feats of arms all over Europe, incognito. (3) He serves the Queen of Sicily as a gentleman-in-waiting, incognito, (4) pretending to be a coward interested only in the chase, while (5) he wins first prize in the tourney on each of three successive days, incognito, where (6) dressed in three different suits of armour, he makes people believe that he is three distinct men. (7) Ipomedon defends the King of France against invasion and rebellion, incognito. (8) He returns to Sicily, disguised as a mad knight, incognito, (9) in order to assume La Fière's defence against Léonin, incognito. In the process, (10) he defends Ismeine and allows her to fall in love with him, incognito. Finally, he wears armour of the same colour as Léonin, which permits him (11) to convince people that he is not the knight who rescued Ismeine, and (12) to claim in Léonin's voice that Léonin won. As a result of this, (13) he duels almost to the death with his comrade and brother Capaneus, since the latter also has come to protect La Fière and believes his adversary to be the hated invader.

It goes without saying that the triumph of a lowly boy later discovered to be a prince and the triumph of a modest prince who chooses to conceal his identity are staples of romance. Nonetheless, there are staples and staples, conventions and conventions. *Ipomedon* contains more incidents of disguise than almost all other medieval romances. These disguises are not all necessary to the plot. Indeed, some complicate it beyond measure and, in the process, bring about the deaths of innocent people.

Why is Ipomedon obsessed with disguise? Or, rather, why does Hue de Rotelande endow his protagonist with this obsession? First of all, as in Beroul, for the sheer fun of it. Ipomedon and, presumably, his author-creator enjoy deceiving, tricking, and manipulating others because thus the protagonist proves his superiority in 'sens' and 'curteisie'; this is his function as a trickster hero, and it is what he loves best. Just as Ipomedon prefers adventure to marriage, so, we come to realize, he prefers disguise to all other manifestations of adventure, including feats in arms, even though disguise demands anonymity and therefore results in a relative, provisional decrease in 'los' and 'pris.'

At the same time Ipomedon and his author undermine the notion of chivalry elaborated by Chrétien de Troyes. The central role of prowess or of reputation for prowess and the central role of passionate love, *fin' amor*, are both held up to ridicule. Hue de Rotelande emphasizes throughout the distinction between appearance and reality, *être* and *paraître*. Losers ground their lives in appearance only, whether social, intellectual, or ideological; they perceive externals reflecting an artificial code of chivalry in books. Winners, on the other hand, are aware of both illusion and reality, books and life, for they see beyond the mask and can unmask liars and hypocrites or themselves don a mask at will. Indeed, the hero dons a mask for the specific purpose of unmasking the others.

Furthermore, Ipomedon and his author are aware of the comic potentialities latent in manipulation and disguise; disguise is intrinsically amusing. The medieval public found *travestissement*, which brings about change from a higher to a lower social class – an epic or romance hero transformed into a merchant, cleric, monk, jongleur, leper, fool, or woman – funny in principle. On the one hand, the courtiers within the story laugh at the fair coward and the knight-jester as fools who try to live an aristocratic life and apparently fail. However, the audience outside the story, along with Ipomedon himself, laugh not at Ipomedon but with him, at the courtiers, who perceive only surfaces and cannot recognize a true aristocrat when they see one. They not he, in Bergsonian terms (1950G), are guilty of imposing 'du mécanique sur du vivant'; they, and especially La Fière and Ismeine, pay allegiance to what has become a rigid, mechanical, artificial code of chivalry, not to the supple reality of people with bodies living in the real world. Ipomedon is the puppet master who manipulates the others, his puppets; he rolls the snowball which engulfs them; they, not he, repeatedly, ridiculously, mechanically respond to the same stimuli like the Bergsonian jack-in-the-box. (On three successive days a great knight, a tall dark stranger, triumphs in the tourney. On three successive evenings he announces to La Fière his identity. On none of the three days does she suspect who the winner really is. She is not very clever.) It is they, guilty of antisocial behavior (La Fière's vow impedes normal exogamic marriage and the natural, day-to-day functioning of her kingdom), who have to be corrected through laughter.

It is surely no coincidence that the Narrator indulges in a series of antifeminist asides concerning woman's fickleness and the sex's inherent, essential proclivity to deceit (a few examples: 1911–24, 2139–50, 2576–82, 8651–66); his protagonist in large measure corrects women, deceiving the deceivers. Although La Fière's oath is directed against marriage, in practical terms her 'orgoil' frustrates and humiliates the barons who would like to order her life and the young men who come to claim her hand. Her insistance on knightly prowess as a precondition for expressing or even feeling sentiments of Eros humiliates Ipomedon and Jason in their male pride, both martial and phallic. Nor is it an accident that the people who ridicule the disguised 'bel malveis' for his 'malveisté' are primarily the ladies-in-waiting on the Queen of Sicily, just as it is Ismeine who manifests the most virulent rage at the idea of the mad knight protecting anyone. The motif of their *gabs* (mockery) directed against a man reverberates through the romance. So does its punishment, for Ipomedon's revenge is to trick, deceive, and manipulate the women who have mocked him and to mock them in turn, in a more subtle, complex, and decisively cruel manner. Hue de Rotelande's solution is to have each of the three ladies (La Fière, the Queen, Ismeine) fall in love with the protagonist and to become aware of her passion at just the moment when, because of her mockery or her lack of faith in him, it has become impossible for her to win him. Ismeine offers herself like a Saracen princess in *chansons de geste* to the alleged fool who, playing the role of madman to the hilt, discourages her advances by biting her hand, causing her to spend a sleepless night torn by desire for his magnificent body. It is significant that, whereas women lust after him, Ipomedon, in opposition to Lancelot, Tristan, Yvain, and Lanval, can willingly forgo enjoying his lady's favours. Although he loves La Fière, her physical person makes little demand on him. He really prefers other things. Therefore, women are subject to him, and not he to them. We witness here, and elsewhere in *Ipomedon*, the reversal of *fin' amor* – a masculine wish-fulfilment fantasy in which the male hero wins the War of the Sexes, wiping out the opposition. He defeats men in battle with his strong right arm; he defeats women in hall and bower with his supple, ingenious brain. His will triumphs over theirs, on their terrain, in a universe of tension and downright hostility between the sexes, latent in the romances of Chrétien de Troyes but never exploited by him to the same extent.

I wish to emphasize the specifically verbal, intellectual aspect of Ipomedon's 'sens.' People guilty of bad speech – the ladies who mock; La Fière and Ismeine, who insult; the Queen's suitors, 'vanteürs de dames,' who boast – are punished. The punisher never boasts and never speaks out of turn. He maintains self-control, power of the will, silence, and what the author calls 'bel teisir' (2630) (a variation on the 'bel mentir' in Beroul?), one element of his 'engin' and of his 'curteisie.' At the same time, under the dictates of will and reason, he uses speech himself and triumphs by manipulating verbal signs at pleasure. Ipomedon's ultimate discomfiture of the others derives from his capacity to disguise himself and the truth behind a mask, and then to declare the truth – vaunting the prowess of his white, red, and black animals after the tournament; and claiming, as a madman, that he is a great warrior and beloved of the Queen and of La Fière – when no one will believe him. Language is one of the means that brings about comic victory and is one form that his victory adopts; it mediates between the hero and his society just as it distances him from it. The hero wins in the game of war and also in the game of life; he is a master of clerical *sapientia* as well as of knightly *fortitudo* and the career of this Norman-Italian knight with a Greek name can be deemed one more example of *translatio studii* in addition to *imperii*. Moreover, given his functions as theatre director, actor in disguise, and inventor of fictions, is Ipomedon not also, in his own way, an author figure, one who manipulates and pleases his public? He wins the approbation and love of his audience of women – he who is so intellectual, and they so merely physical. (For a convergent reading, Krueger 1990.)

Hence the validity of the notion that he is a wish-fulfilment alter ego of his creator, Hue de Rotelande. Hue or, rather, the Narrator as implied author, in his prologue, contrasts 'sens' and 'folie.' Both can be heard in old stories telling of 'aventures / Ke avyndrent a l'ancien tens' (5–6) [adventures that occurred in bygone times]. Furthermore, exploiting a rhetorical commonplace, the Narrator accuses those learned men of folly (madness) who keep their wisdom to themselves instead of imparting it to the world (13–16). On another occasion, he claims never to lie; that is, he explains, he lies only a little, like Walter Map (7175–88). However, Hue commits his first bare-faced lie in the prologue when he posits a classical text in Latin as source, which he allegedly translates into French, apologizing for the fact that he cannot retain in the vernacular all the Latin cases and tenses:

Ne di pas qe il bien ne dit
Cil qi en latin l'ad descrit,
Mes plus i ad leis ke lettrez;
Si li latin n'est translatez
Gaires n'i erent entendanz;
Por ceo voil dire en romanz
A plus brefment que jeo savrai,
Si entendrunt e clerc e lai.
Hue de Rotelande nus dit,
Ky cest' estorie nous descrit,
Ky de latin velt romanz fere
Ne lui deit l'em a mal retrere
S'il ne poet tuz ses cas garder,
De tut en tut les tens former ... (25–38)

I do not claim that he who first set it down in Latin didn't write well, only that there are more lay people than learned. If the Latin is not translated, they will scarcely comprehend it; therefore I wish to narrate in the vernacular as tersely as I know how, so that clerks and lay people will understand. Hue de Rotelande, who sets down this narrative, tells us that we ought not hold it against a man who seeks to turn Latin into French if he is not able to retain all the Latin cases and to construct the verb tenses in their totality.

This statement we know to be false, as we do his other claim in the epilogue that *Le Roman de Thèbes* was taken from the 'estorie' that he has just made (10541–2) and is, therefore, its sequel. On the contrary, *Ipomedon* is pure fiction. As a man, the Narrator makes no boast concerning prowess in arms but he does parody Thomas's address to good lovers in the *Tristan* (3124–43), claiming, as a clerk of love, that he has the power to absolve or excommunicate sinners against *fin' amor*. He then adds, as his last word in the romance, the *conclusio* that if a lady or maiden does not believe him, she may visit his cottage in Credenhill; before she leaves he will show her his charter and register her therein, and it will surely cause her no great harm if his seal is affixed to her rump:

A Credehulle a ma meisun
Chartre ai de l'absoluciun;
Se il i ad dame u pucele
U riche vedve u dameisele
Ne voille creire ke jo l'ai,
Venge la, jo li musterai;

> Ainz ke d'iloc s'en seit turné
> La chartre li ert enbrevé,
> E ço n'ert pas trop grant damages
> Se li seaus li pent as nages. (10571–80)

After all, he is a cleric not a knight! And, as a clerk, the Narrator-implied author seeks to manipulate his implied audience by means of *captatio benevolentiae*. He will win its approbation by praising himself or by a display of mock humility, by lauding his purported source, the classical book, as *auctoritas*, and by claiming to conserve the memory of past deeds and to propagate 'sens,' thus to benefit humanity by his service of *translatio*. The act of writing becomes his priestly service and act of faith in 'clergie'; he helps regain dignity and authority for the vernacular by positing a classical authority and by translating it as a clerkly task. And as a courtier and lover, a clerk and a scholar, he has the right to praise and blame, to manage the story and to comment on it, to mediate, and to serve as a bridge between the story ('estorie') and its audience. Yet this very conscious, overt mediating creates distance and emphasizes mediation and thus estrangement. For the implied author also manipulates his audience by undermining as well as exalting the clerkly-narrator tradition derived from Thomas, Chrétien, and their predecessors, by lying and admitting he is a liar, by claiming to be a clerk of love as well as learning and emphasizing the phallic prerogatives of his clerkship. Although the theme of cynical amorous deception comes from the predecessors, especially Beroul, Hue, in contrast to Marie, Beroul, and Thomas, undermines and denigrates aesthetically, plays with the plot and its conventions, and exploits 'engin' as author just as his hero does, mocking and triumphing over his audience in the same way that Ipomedon does over his lady friends at court. *Ipomedon* as a romance is a masterpiece of trickery and disguise that recounts the hero Ipomedon's victories in trickery and disguise. The 'sens' and 'engin' displayed by the hero are one element in a literary structure of 'sens' and 'engin' due to his creator. And the evident martial and amorous exploits of the one are mirrored by the hoped for amorous and intellectual exploits of the other. In narrative technique as well as in other aspects of the text Hue de Rotelande, in the 1180s, exalts and undermines the tradition of romance as he knew it, the legacy of the 'classical generation.' This was his contribution to the evolution of courtly narrative in the post-Chrétien era, to be followed by Jean Renart and the author of *Aucassin et Nicolette*, among others. Yet his witty, cynical, sophisticated text, neglected for so long, can stand on its own as one of the summits of the medieval romance tradition and as one of the great Anglo-Norman contributions to medieval culture.

4. *Amadas et Ydoine*

Amadas et Ydoine was written between 1190 and 1220, perhaps earlier. Considerable fragments have survived in two Anglo-Norman manuscripts, and a complete version in a Picard manuscript from Arras can be dated 1288. It is agreed that the original text was Anglo-Norman; the Picard copy represents a later redaction, a conscious rewriting in line with continental taste (Le Gentil 1950).

In its day this romance was relatively well known, at least by name, especially in England. It is cited in lists of famous lovers or stories of love: in two French works, four in Dutch, and seven in English, including two romances – *Emaré* and *Sir Degrevant* – and Gower's *Confessio Amantis*. Also a copy was bequeathed by Guy Beauchamp to Bordesley Abbey in 1361. Finally, through the English connection, *Amadas* had an impact on the Icelandic saga.

Ydoine is daughter to the Duke of Burgundy, Amadas the son of the duke's seneschal. Ydoine sends her suitor out into the world to win martial renown. When the duke marries his daughter to someone else, the Count of Nevers, Amadas falls into madness. However, with the assistance of three sorceresses, Ydoine manages to conserve her virginity. The countess eventually cures the young man of his insanity, and he rescues her after she has been abducted by a demon. Ydoine then arranges for her marriage to be annulled so that she can wed her true love.

Amadas et Ydoine differs markedly from the sort of narrative we find in Thomas and Chrétien, in Beroul and Hue de Rotelande. In my opinion, this text partakes of a special mode or subgenre within the tradition that has been called the idyllic romance. The chief representatives of this mode are *Floire et Blancheflor, Galeran de Bretagne, L'Escoufle* by Jean Renart, and the deservedly famous *Aucassin et Nicolette*.

Our Anglo-Norman-Picard romance shares with the other idyllic stories a non-military, non-adulterous, and non-hierarchical erotic relationship. Except for tourneys, rapidly 'told' but never 'shown,' and except for the duel with Ydoine's abductor, Amadas performs no martial feats. Like Lanval and Thomas's Tristan, he is a hero of love, not war. Indeed, once the youth and maiden avow passion for each other, it alone dominates their lives. This reciprocal desire reduces the sexual differences between them. On the contrary, Amadas, like Aucassin, Guillaume, and Galeran, becomes passive, and like Blancheflor, Aelis, and Nicolette, Ydoine assumes the active role in bringing about a happy ending.

In an idyllic romance love is the centre of the universe, the unique motivating force behind the action. Here love is inscribed in the title and in the protagonist's name – Amadas, the lover; his essence and existence is determined by his name. Others mock him in his name as 'Amadas, le fin amoureus' (98) [Amadas the Perfect Lover (Arthur, p. 22)] and 'Le fin amoureus Amadas' (100) [The Perfect Lover Amadas (p. 22)]; unbeknownst to them, the youth's 'aventure' (233), the adventure of his life, will indeed be to fall in love.

However, the *Amadas* trouvère differs from other romancers by taking a number of love conventions literally, and pushing them to their extreme limits, exploring what they imply, both as fact and as metaphor. One such convention or metaphor is the Malady of Heroes, love sickness. This is a constant motif in medieval letters, originating in Ovid. Amadas falls ill three times: first when desire for Ydoine, Cupid's flame, seizes him; secondly, when Ydoine's imminent marriage is announced; thirdly, when he discovers that she has been kidnapped. Especially on the first occasion, he undergoes the standard Ovidian symptoms: pallor, trembling, sighing, weeping, swooning, unwillingness to speak or take nourishment, and a wasting away. Each time that he offers his suit to Ydoine and she refuses, his illness increases and he wastes away still more. This process of physical and psychological decline occupies some two and a half years. It goes without saying that the only 'mire' capable of curing the patient is Ydoine herself, who does so (once she also has been wounded by Cupid's shot) by returning his love or, on the second occasion, by pronouncing her name along with his.

On the second occasion Amadas's illness proceeds immediately to its logical terminus, insanity (also an Ovidian motif). A comic theme in *Ipomedon*, here it is treated more seriously and with greater complexity. To love, happily or unhappily, is to participate in the irrational, in a 'folie' that is both folly and madness. Hearing that his beloved will wed, the youth immediately and instantaneously endures 'fine fole caleur,' 'droite derverie,' and 'fine foursenerie' (1794–6) [true insanity (p. 47)] and dashes off into the wilds like a werewolf. Eventually, we find him in Lucca, Italy, where as love's jester he provides the daily afternoon distraction. Naked, he leads a parade up the high street pursued by the rabble of the town, who mock him and beat him without pity.

Amadas's first madness, manifest during his apparently unsuccessful suit to win Ydoine, is of a different, more problematic order. At first, insanity is a metaphor or a rationalization to explain the fact that he dares to love the duke's daughter and to tell her that he loves her. Both the youth and the maiden agree that his outrage ('outrage') is a manifestation of 'folage,' 'rage,' and 'derverie.' Ydoine tosses at him the following epithets: 'Leciere outrequidiés, / Gars anïeus, fox assotiés!' (736–7) ['You outrageous lecher ... troublesome boy, stupid fool!' (p. 32)]. These insults, which cover the semantic fields of folly and foolhardiness as well as of lechery and churlishness, allude to the loss of reason in social life presumed endemic in a low-class churlish lecher. Social irrationality has a cause – love itself. Therefore, we are not surprised to discover that, in the course of his wooing, Amadas really goes mad; he falls into physical 'derverie' and 'folie' as a result of Ydoine's constant refusals. On the other hand, insane or not, he indulges in *fin' amor* casuistry, reasoning subtly in the following terms: rather than simply waste away in foolish passion without doing anything about it, would it not be better for him to plead his cause one more time? Would it not be madness for him not to entreat the maiden one more time?

> Que langui a trop longement
> Par fol corage et par folie ...
> Pour fol se tient au departir
> Qu'il ne requiert plus d'une fois
> La pucele ... (627–8, 635–7)

Love madness becomes problematic indeed. Amadas is love's fool.

Insanity is intimately associated with those subject to Venus and also born under the sign of Saturn, the Greater Infortune; for them love manifests itself as an explosion of black bile (melancholia) or of choler (frenzy). Love violates the rational code of society; to feel it and to express it goes against the code and becomes a concrete manifestation of folly. Amadas becomes society's fool, a jester in Ydoine's court or on the streets of Lucca. Yet, in the court of Venus, this madness is a sacred madness, a higher wisdom; Amadas's *sancta stultitia* is a form of martyrdom; it is the greatest humiliation for a *miles* and a rational male who ought to occupy a high place. Such is his sacrifice for truly the highest of all goods – to abandon all; to become the lowest of the low for the highest of the high. For, from the vantage point of Eros, acts or attitudes that block love's progress are foolish, and all that contributes to love is sane, healthy, and full of good sense.

As we know from other texts, especially *Le Roman de Tristan*, the bond between Eros and Thanatos is a constant in medieval literature. For the people of the Middle Ages, insanity was considered a form of death because the madman was dead to social life and because the demise of the mind is the worst of all possible ends. Since man is a mortal animal, and since reason is the quality which distinguishes him from all other creatures (except the angels) and therefore is the essence of his manhood, insanity is perceived as the equivalent of death. How appropriate then that Amadas's fit of madness in Lucca does render him dead to the world and that Ydoine, by ending his mental alienation, restores him to life and to society, the rebirth heralded by a purifying, healing bath.

Earlier, at the Duke of Burgundy's court, Amadas was again close to death. Yet here, as with his insanity, death is problematic and the trouvère explores the ambiguities inherent in our conceptualization of it. If love leads to illness, the latter can be mortal. The true lover, when his passion is not reciprocated, finds himself on the point of dying. Furthermore, in his despair, the lover will wish he were dead and will contemplate suicide as an avenue of escape. This does not prevent Amadas from employing traditional male seduction arguments in the face of a recalcitrant female: If you do not respond favourably to my petition, I shall perish. You will be responsible for my death. Not only that. The youth also justifies to himself still another declaration on the grounds that, if he kills himself or perishes from love madness, he will be damned; much better for him to try once more to seduce Ydoine. When she then has him killed, as she has threatened, at least there will be hope for the salvation of his soul (933–55). To some extent, Amadas reasons in good faith; to some extent he is inauthentic and grasping at straws, rationalizing his repeated efforts at seduction with one object in mind – winning Ydoine. Similarly, the author explores with sympathy but also with amused detachment the youth's will to Eros and to Thanatos, as he explores the concrete and metaphorical connotations of death. In this romance, death is concrete and metaphorical often at the same time.

In the second half of the narrative, after the lovers have been reunited, a stranger Knight abducts Ydoine. She is recovered but then falls ill (not love sickness this time) and apparently dies. In the middle of the night, Amadas and the stranger fight a duel for Ydoine's corpse, as if she were a living damsel. Inspired by the sight of her tomb, Amadas wins and succeeds in breaking the enchantment. The couple then proceed to a happy ending.

Our strange Knight is a standard motif in Celtic folklore, the fairy prince from the Other World. Within Celtic legend, the Other World constituted a realm of the dead as well as of the fays. And in *Amadas et Ydoine* the death theme is pervasive. The Knight, called a 'maufé,' is himself immortal but associated with death. He makes Ydoine appear to die and has power over her when she is in a death-like trance. He comes to her at night, spirits her away in her coffin, and, like a vampire or an evil spirit, must not be surprised by the dawn. Whether Satanic devil or Celtic fay, this black Knight is the concrete embodiment of death. Nevertheless, Amadas rescues Ydoine from death, the peril to the body ('Venue estes de mort a vie,' 6576 ['you have returned from death to life' (p. 116)]; 'Car vous m'avés de mort garie,' 6708 ['for you have saved me from death' (p. 117)]), as she rescued him from madness, the death of the spirit. In what is truly 'aventure fiere' (4733) they each return from their respective Other Worlds; both of them conquer insanity and death, coming to maturity, after which the youth and maiden are allowed to wed and to exert sovereignty. (For a Jungian reading of the text, see Aubailly 1986, 'Préface.')

Fundamental aspects of love are thus scrutinized as concrete behaviour and literary convention. They are shown to be illusion or reality, illusion and reality, in sequence or at the same time. In addition, this ambiguous, paradoxical reality and our perception of it are shaped by Ydoine at her will for Ydoine, like Isolt, is a master manipulator; she masks her feelings and her inner reality while causing other people to act in ways that serve her ends. For example, hearing that her beloved is playing the village idiot in Lucca, she convinces her husband to allow her to go on a pilgrimage to Rome. Stopping off at Lucca, she veils her anguish – she is 'sage' and will not reveal her 'rage' – then, at night, she finds the sleeping Amadas, cures him, and arranges for his purportedly coincidental arrival in town. Afterwards, she manipulates her counsellors into advising her to retain him in the vicinity, under her auspices and at her expense, while she continues on the pilgrimage. Ydoine actively engineers her spectacle of wit – the dashing Amadas returning from a crusade; the embarrassed Ydoine seeking counsel from her men – which corresponds to, and is in antithesis with, Amadas's passive spectacle of madness as he is chased through the streets by the town rabble.

Two other performances are more significant still in their scrutiny of appearance and reality, truth and deception, and the functioning of sickness, insanity, and death. To preserve her virginity, Ydoine has three witches work on her prospective husband, the Count of Nevers.

These mad creatures, 'dervees,' are also full of 'sens.' They come to the man at night pretending to be the three Fates and announce to him that Ydoine is tabu, will never know love, and if he forces her he will die:

> 'Je vous voel de la mort garir.
> Vous volés Ydoine espouser,
> La fille au duc, o le vis cler;
> Mais saciés bien, se la prenés,
> Vous estes mors et afolés.
> Ja ne l'avrés despucelee
> Ausi tost que par destinee
> Ne muiriés a mult grant dolor
> Et a martire et a tristrour.' (2286–94)

'I want to save you from death. You want to marry the Duke's daughter, Ydoine with the fair complexion, but you must know that if you marry her you are ruined and dead! As soon as you have deflowered her you are destined to die in great sorrow, torture, and suffering.' (p. 54)

They lie to the count and commit 'mençongne' (2266), 'par felounie' (2209), so that Ydoine may remain true to Amadas. Significantly, the witches do not employ supernatural enchantments or transform the physical world. Although, like Beroul's Isolt, they lie and create an illusion, from another perspective they only offer reality to the count; that is he sees three women talking among themselves and to him. If he makes the error of taking their speech literally and then acts on it, that is his responsibility. Their intimidation of the count, and his willingness to be intimidated, is psychological in essence, not physical or metaphysical. This is true even though the count does go insane, in some sense of the term (he is 'tresafolé,' 2156, and in 'folour,' 2322), and may well risk death were he in fact to possess his bride.

The bride rises to the occasion in a most ingenious manner. With 'voisdie' (cunning) she pretends to be ill and her proclaimed illness, compounded by the count's, assures her of a sound sleep on their wedding night. Thus she claims to be ill but is healthy; the count appears to be healthy, yet inside he is ill. On the other hand, pale and discoloured (2404), suffering from psychological ills and, like her husband, very afraid (he dreads death, she dreads defloration), the countess soon declines physically and manifests all the symptoms of love sickness for Amadas that Amadas endured earlier for her (2549–68).

When Ydoine appears to be dying in Lucca, she confesses to her suitor that, before making his acquaintance, she for seven years had been the mistress of three of her cousins and had had three babies by them; urged on by Satan, she slew them at birth. If this were true, she would be guilty of lechery, infidelity, incest, and infanticide. The young countess claims that her appearance of virginity was a ruse to deceive others, but now she willingly unmasks in order to reveal reality to Amadas. In fact, just the opposite is true. She was chaste and is chaste. Her alleged lie in the past is true, her alleged confession of truth in the present is a lie. Paradoxically, Ydoine tells this lie, which ought to destroy her reputation for fidelity and Amadas's love for her, out of 'Estrange loiauté d'amour' (4959) [a strange act of devotion (p. 93)] and 'fine loiauté d'amie' (4964) [pure loyalty in any mistress (p. 93)] for him. The reasoning is the following: if she dies pure in his eyes, he also will perish from love sickness or even commit suicide, 'a derverie' (5236). Because of the horrible story she has now told him, his life will be spared. He will not cease to love her, but, since he is her unique confessor, he must live on to offer prayers and alms in her name in order to preserve her soul from hell. Part of the irony derives from the fact that, unbeknownst to Ydoine, she is not on the point of dying but is indeed menaced by a demon from hell. And it is true that her confession (her total sacrifice of self and honour) is as much an 'aventure' as the kidnapping and subsequent rescue.

As a result of all this, Amadas, the 'fin amoureus,' in a state of libidinal exaltation, remains committed to Ydoine and her love, regardless of illusion and reality. He believes in her troth, and the truth of her words. In spite of her 'pecié,' the truth of which he accepts, he loves her, will obey her and will stay alive to pray for her soul. He accepts the fact that she is dead, and yet he refuses to leave her coffin; he remains there literally to ward off any devils that may turn up looking for her soul. When the 'estrange cevalier' (5770), having lied about Ydoine's death, also lies claiming she was his mistress and that she betrayed Amadas with him, Amadas refuses to believe him. He refuses to accept 'reality' – Ydoine's state of infidelity, 'proved' by the concrete evidence of the ring, Amadas's ring, that the Knight plausibly declares Ydoine had given to him as a token of her love. As it turns out, Amadas is right not to accept such evidence or such reality. Ydoine lied; the Knight also lied. She is not dead and she has not been untrue to him. The real is false and, because of his boldness, Amadas makes the ideal real.

Such distinctions are crucial in a text that scrutinizes appearance and reality and that exalts romantic idealized love yet also insists upon natural cause and effect, upon life in the concrete world of everyday, as opposed to enchantment (even to the Christian supernatural). Ydoine, in a series of invented Christian visions and in her dramatized recounting of them to the court, resembles the three sorceresses who also invent a story and put on a play. Perhaps they, as women, using the physical weapons of women (speech, psychology, and the body) have to be distinguished from the 'maufé,' a male employing knowledge of the supernatural and masculine force and effecting metaphysical transformation. Ydoine and the magicians are authors, actresses, and theatre directors, manipulating their male audiences in a good cause. And when Amadas, the man, is rendered irrational and impotent because of Eros, the woman assumes power and employs reason in his stead. The women are good because they hurt no one, because they believe in sacrifice, and because they work on behalf of love. The Knight is evil because he willingly hurts others, thinks only of himself, and opposes true love. The women win, and he loses.

We now perhaps are in a position to appreciate the ironies inherent in the Narrator's fascinating tirades against women, 3568–656 and 7037–97. In two approximately equal passages the Narrator denounces women for their power and proclivity to trick and deceive, to turn wise men into fools and fools into sages, and to be disloyal at whim; he exculpates good women in general and Ydoine in particular, commending her for her loyalty and for following reason and right and thus not adhering to her nature as a woman. Clerical clichés! Yet it is obvious to the implied twelfth-century audience and to the real author that this is a half truth at best and that the entire romance text of *Amadas et Ydoine* proves it. Yes, Ydoine has been loyal, but she has used all the ruse, trickery, deception, even 'ingremance' (3586) and the capacity to 'enfantosmer' (7044) denounced in others. Never does she adhere so well to her feminine nature as when she purportedly surpasses it. Furthermore, indeed she has embodied 'raison' and 'droiture,' but reason and law in a particular sense, i.e., in the name of love against the reason and law of family, marriage, and church. By her very unpredictability, is not Ydoine typically a woman? And does not her active, obtrusive, intelligent domination of the narrative and her function as 'sujet actant,' not 'objet,' 'destinateur,' or 'destinataire,'[5] make her story a text strongly in praise of woman and of *fin' amor*? It is then fitting that directly after his second antifeminist tirade, the implied author makes his retraction and invokes 'Le bien, la francise et l'ounour' (7089) [virtue, nobility and honour (p. 123)], also to be found in women. In addition, whatever he says, he admires their ruses and their wisdom. After all, he has created them. So, as a maker of attacks and of palinodes, this early trouvère anticipates the greatest makers of attacks and palinodes, Jean de Meun, Machaut, and Chaucer.

In the end, through Ydoine's careful machinations, the marriage is annulled and Amadas weds his lady. Then, their parents gracefully dispatched, the couple obtains sovereignty as Duke and Duchess of Burgundy. A cliché denouement. Yet the ending is, in its way, of the utmost significance. Ydoine succeeds not only in marrying her beloved; she also succeeds in imposing her will totally. She never had to yield her body to the count, whom she does not love; nor did she ever yield her body illicitly, before their wedding, to Amadas, whom she does love. She neither indulges in adultery nor submits to marital rape, 'point de folor' (6955). In other words, the young woman remains pure throughout. She maintains social respectabilty and moral integrity, external and internal honour. In both a shame and a guilt culture she is exalted. Thus she 'improves' upon her two chief forbears in the hoaxed husband line – Thomas's Isolt and Chrétien's Fenice. The trouvère can be said to have consciously authored an anti-*Tristan* and an anti-*Cligés* or, if you prefer, a hyper-*Tristan* and a hyper-*Cligés*. Furthermore, although some scholars consider the Count of Nevers to play a ridiculous role, I propose that, unlike Isolt's husband the king and Fenice's husband the emperor, this husband gets off easily. He is kind, understanding, and supportive of Ydoine. Therefore, after the annulment ('Par conscïence et par raison,' 7325 [reasonably and in good conscience (p. 126)]) he is allowed to wed the young daughter of the Count of Poitiers. Both couples live happily ever after.

The trouvère adheres to a tradition that dates back to Roman comedy, in which one blocking figure plays the role of scapegoat (the Black Knight?), but, overall, the society of law opposing the young lovers is reformed, not overthrown; the parent or authority figures are converted, not defeated, and at least two couples are united in a denouement of festivity and social integration. The trouvère also seeks to provide ideals for irreproachable courtly conduct in order that the social code and its external forms be respected. This must take place and yet, at the same time, allow love – *fin' amor* – to flourish and to triumph, in all its pathological manifestations of desire and melodramatic extremes of sentiment.

Sentiment, desire, and social conformity – these are juxtaposed, balanced, and fused, more or less harmoniously in a fascinating romance text in which ambiguity is the rule and paradox the norm. By the beginning of the thirteenth century, we find in literature something comparable to post-classical mannerism, with the play with forms and the pushing of convention to its logical extremes. And we find something comparable to post-Romantic Biedermeier, a world-view in which sentiment, domestic tranquillity, social order, and happiness stake their claim to a place in the universe. The medieval aristocracy also had its yearning for young love, a happy ending, the art of play, and the play of art.

5. *Gui de Warewic*

One of the most interesting categories of Anglo-Norman romance includes texts that have specifically English heroes. *Horn*, *Haveloc*, *Guillaume d'Angleterre*, *Waldef*, *Fergus*, *Boeve de Haumtone*, *Fouke Fitz Warin*, and *Gui de Warewic* are the major works included in the subgenre. According to Legge's (1963) theory, these are ancestral romances, composed for the great Norman families recently established in England, families that sought roots and a sense of legitimacy in their new home and had a very real interest in, and nostalgia for, its historical past. Poets would take old stories or bits and pieces of old fictions and elaborate them into extended new fictions, with a local setting and with the protagonists identified with figures, real or imagined, associated with the lineage in question.

According to S. Crane's (1986) theory, these are feudal or baronial romances and not particularly ancestral at all; they exalt the Anglo-Norman aristocracy as a whole, offering an idealized vision of the baronry and upholding seigneurial privilege. The two theories are not mutually exclusive; both contribute to our understanding of the texts. In any case, these are narratives composed in French by Anglo-Norman poets for their patrons, the Anglo-Norman nobility, recounting the careers of English (insular) protagonists. Significantly, two of the protagonists – Guy of Warwick and Bevis of Hampton – obtained both insular and continental fame. They were then adopted as national heroes by the native English population and became figures of legend in England, whose fame endured over the centuries until almost the present day.

Gui de Warewic was written roughly between 1232 and 1242, perhaps by a canon of Oseney to flatter Thomas, Earl of Warwick, heir to the d'Oilli lands. The d'Oillis of Wallingford were constables of Oxford and founders and patrons of the Abbey. Guy's name is taken from Wigod of Wallingford, Edward the Confessor's cupbearer, and some of his exploits resemble those of Brian Fitzcount, who defended Wallingford in 1139. Two Anglo-Norman versions of the story have survived, represented by five manuscripts each. They gave rise to a fifteenth-century prose *Rommant de Guy de Warwick et de Heralt d'Ardenne* (which may go back to an early fourteenth-century original), also written with an English bias; contained in two manuscripts, with at least two others non-extant, it in turn gave rise to two printed editions in the sixteenth century. A play, which dramatized one episode from the legend, can be dated 1536–50. Meanwhile, the original *Gui de Warewic* was translated at least four times into Middle English. R. Crane (1915) observes that Guy's story in general, and his great duel with Colebrant in particular, deemed to be part of English history, was included in four Latin chronicles from the late Middle Ages and a host of sixteenth-century histories in English. The printed version of the story was reissued throughout the sixteenth century, for it had already become a popular boyhood classic for the upper classes, concerning a national and local hero. New versions appeared from 1590 to 1710, including a play by Day and Dekker, poems and histories in verse, and eventually chapbooks in prose. By this time, the text appealed above all to the lower classes. However, rescued by eighteenth-century antiquarians, Guy then became the delight of nineteenth-century children's literature. All in all, no single Anglo-Norman book can be said to have had so great an impact on the English consciousness and the English national character as did *Gui de Warewic*.

The standard view on *Gui* is to divide the romance into two parts, the first courtly, the second religious. Gui falls in love with Félice, daughter to the Count of Warwick. At her impulse and to win her hand, he voyages on the Continent and commits deeds of valour. Then he returns home and weds her, only to discover that he has forgotten God. In order to honour God and to expiate his sins, the protagonist leaves his wife and sets out as a poor pilgrim. In the course of his travels, Gui commits other deeds of valour, culminating in his patriotic defeat of the invading giant Colebrant. Gui then retires to a hermitage and dies in the odour of sainthood.

To some extent the courtly, and the sacred even more, contribute to the action and to the 'literary reality' that is *Gui de Warewic*. No less important (S. Crane's 1986 reading) is the political and social message, an ideology oriented toward the baronry. With a double withdrawal and double return, the author upholds baronial rights, the claims of the nobility to land and lineage, in a relatively unproblematic society where class division was less overt than on the Continent. However, I am convinced that *fin' amor*, the political, and the sacred also serve as pretexts for the telling of deeds of adventure.

Admittedly, the narrative begins just like *Amadas et Ydoine*, with Gui desperately in love, ill from love, daring finally to broach his suit, and ordered by his lady, the count's daughter, to seek martial renown. The martial renown attained, Gui returns to wed his beloved, who is urged by her father to accept the young hero because, among other things, he has spurned so many offers from princesses in order to remain loyal to her. Gui himself proclaims that he has committed all his feats in arms for her.

In point of fact, the situation is totally different. In his first major tournament Gui receives the prize from Blancheflur, the emperor's daughter, along with her love, 'Od tut iço sa driuerie' (941). The youth accepts with alacrity: 'E sa druerie volenters recoil, / Sun chevaler tut dis estre voil' (947–8) [He takes her love with pleasure, he wishes to be her knight always]. Still more significant is the episode where the Emperor of Constantinople offers his daughter, Laurette, to the English hero. We soon discover that she is known to be his 'amie' (3238) and that Gui treats her as such: 'Gui la prist, si la beisa, / Par grant amur a lui parla' (3247–8) [Gui held her, and kissed her; he spoke to her moved by much love]. The father offers her in marriage; the prospective son-in-law accepts; it is only on their wedding day that, in a scene taken from Thomas's *Tristan*, Gui, for the first time, remembers Félice (4231–40) and invents a pretext to postpone the ceremony. Finally, we ought not to forget that Gui's real marriage lasts a full fifty days and no more. After less than two months, he converts and sets out on further adventures.

Adventure is the purpose of his travels; he goes forth to win 'los' and 'pris' in arms and never to be 'pereçus': to commit deeds of prowess in youth so that in old age he can hold honour, reputation, and fame, because of those past deeds. From Normandy to Lombardy, from the Empire to Constantinople, then back to Lorraine, Gui wins tourneys, defends besieged cities, and rescues unjustly imprisoned warriors. He runs to fight and fights to the death all over the western world (for some seven thousand lines and over a period of years) without any thought of his beloved pining away for him in Warwick. After his marriage and conversion, he will do the same. One grand love story does occur during those early days, with a young lover abducting his beloved and escaping to avoid an angry father and an angrier fiancé. But the protagonists of this tale are Tierri de Guarmeise, Gui's best friend, and Tierri's beloved, Osille. Aside from winning imperial 'amies' as trophies, Gui's chief contact with women is to bring together Tierri and Osille. The most moving episodes in the whole narrative recount, in moving detail, recognition and separation between Gui and his male friends, Tierri and Heralt. The lines of affection, as in early *chansons de geste*, are from comrade to comrade or youth to tutor, not man to woman. And the story line of wars and battles is pure *chanson de geste*.

Perhaps because of the *chanson de geste* character of this text, a better case can be made for the religious, didactic, and penitential elements in the second half which, in fact, determine the thrust of the narrative taken as a whole. Intelligent, perceptive studies of the English *Guy* by Schelp (1967), Richmond (1975), and Hopkins (1990) support a Christian reading. After all, Gui does spend years clothed in rags, unkempt, unrecognizable, travelling through the world as a pilgrim, doing penance for his sins. He serves the Lord as he had served men, with virile, Christian heroism. In the end, he passes away gently, at peace with God. Meanwhile Félice, who in a magnificent scene had opposed his conversion, follows him into the devout life and into a good death. The didactic, exemplary nature of Gui's career and his total heroism no doubt contributed to the Guy legend in the Middle Ages and to medievalists' appreciation of the story today.

However, once again, I cannot help wondering if the hero's sudden conversion, like his sudden falling in love, does not function primarily as a device to (re)launch the narrative and force the protagonist to set out on further adventures. Like it or not, although we are told that Gui visits shrines and holy places and that more than once he wends his way to Jerusalem, we never see him at his devotions. Gui's function in the narrative is to fight and to fight often. He fights as the supreme warrior Guy of Warwick who he once was. Furthermore, his battles are not uniquely Christian. He begins by intervening in a Saracen civil war (admittedly at the behest of a Christian captive prince). Although the winning side, his side, will now be friendly to Christians, Islam does not collapse at the behest of Gui's strong right arm. He then undergoes a second series of adventures, intervening in imperial politics and aiding his old friend Tierri against the wicked Pavia family. Furthermore, at one point, Heralt and Gui's son Reinbrun take opposite sides in a Saracen civil war, recognize each other, and sail off together with the emir's blessing.

The battles and duels of the second half do not differ in any fundamental way from those of the first half. Both before and after the protagonist's marriage and conversion, good defeats evil. Good equals Gui and his friends. Evil equals Lombards and some Germans, Lorrainers, Danes, and Saracens indiscriminately. The trouvère was influenced by texts such as *Le Moniage Guillaume*, Old French epics in which a great hero, Guillaume d'Orange, becomes a monk and yet returns to the world in order to fight more fights and win more battles. Even here, it is the fighting and the battles that count. And Gui's pilgrim incognito serves as an excellent narrative device that creates tension and suspense. Will the threatened good people find a champion in time? And will they recognize the champion once they have found him?

It is difficult to speak of growth and evolution or even of politics in a text that contains so little description, dialogue, and psychological or ideological analysis. After seven hundred and fifty lines of Part I Gui is a great warrior; after even fewer lines of Part II he is a great warrior-pilgrim. And that is that. The story simply recounts his exploits. It concentrates upon action and episode, upon the statement and restatement, the doing and redoing, of traditional epic and romance narrative elements.

Curiously, themes and motifs are introduced only to be dropped prior to literary amplification. Given the rapidity of such appearance and disappearance and the rapidity of the plot in general, much of the narrative may well appear unmotivated and capricious from a Chrétien de Troyes perspective. Gui's loyal followers, Thoralt and Orri, who might have made up a group of supporters, are killed off in the first ambush. Gui's friends, the Constable Reiner and Duke Seguin of Louvain, marry ladies we have never heard of and then disappear from the story. In Byzantium, following in the traces of Chrétien's Yvain, Gui rescues a lion from a dragon and the lion becomes his pet. However, before adventures with the lion are allowed to occur, a treacherous steward slays it. Later on, both Gui and his Saracen adversary Amorant are presented with magical arms and armour. These objects serve no role in the plot, given that the duel between the champions occurs in the traditional manner, as a test of skill and endurance with conventional weapons. Similarly, the brusqueness of certain speeches such as Gui's farewell to his parents

> 'Bel pere, a Deu vus comant,
> E ma mere ensement;
> Aler m'en voil erralment.' (1162–4)

'Dear father, and mother too, I bid you farewell; I am leaving immediately.'

or the Emperor's marrying off his daughter to Gui

> 'Gui, d'icest di en trente jurz,
> Faire vus voldrai mult granz honurs:
> Ma fille doner vus voldrai,
> En mun corage purpensé l'ai.
> – Sire, fait il, vostre merci!
> Bel m'est, si ben vus ai servi.' (4103–8)

'Gui, one month from today I intend to set you up magnificently; I plan to give you my daughter. I have reflected on it; it is my intention.' – 'Sire,' he says, 'Thank you! If I have properly served you, then it is pleasing to me.'

can be justified in psychological terms. Yet it is equally possible that psychology was of no interest to our trouvère. He wanted to launch Gui on his career by having him leave England and to continue his career by having him leave Constantinople. Speech and motivation are the least of his concerns.

The themes and motifs are legion; they reflect a mass of conventional material to be found in all *chansons de geste* and *romans courtois*. However, larger patterns emerge. Part I contains the following episodes: fighting a tourney; escaping an ambush by Otto; helping Seguin of Louvain against the German Emperor; helping the Emperor of Constantinople against Saracens; helping Tierri of Guarmeise against Otto; hunting a boar; and helping the King of England against a dragon. With the exception of the wild boar (a bit of adventure relief), these episodes build up to a climax. The crusade, the comrade, and the homeland offer arenas for action. Gui wins renown defeating Saracens in exotic, far-off climes in the name of Christianity; he defeats his arch-enemy, the treacherous Otto, in the name of friendship; he defeats a dragon in the name of something like patriotism.

A comparable pattern evolves in Part II. Once again, Gui first delivers Christian captives, Jonas of Durazzo and his sons, by participating in a Muslim civil war; he then rescues Tierri a second time, on this occasion from the machinations of Otto's nephew, Bérard; finally, he defends England a second time, from an invading army of Danes and their champion Colebrant. The three increments, in ascending order, are, as before, the crusade, the comrade, and the homeland.

In both parts of the romance, Gui sets out from England, endures adventures all over the world, arrives in far-away places in the East (Byzantium or Africa), and then returns to the point of departure. His wanderings form a double circle. However, in terms of difficulty and of symbolic importance, his adventures are not cyclical but linear; they build to a climax. Gui's most significant exploits are not associated with Saracens and the crusade, but with Germany and Italy, with feudal rivalry and friendship, and above all with the state of England. Paradoxically, for one of the greatest of Christian heroes, the crusade serves as a springboard to further adventures and exploits; paradoxically, for one of the greatest travellers in literature, the ultimate adventures and exploits occur at home.

In addition, within these concentric structural circles, we find a single pattern repeated incessantly. The dominant schema of Part I is the siege, in a context of battle. Gui hastens to defend an unjustly besieged baron, he leads a victorious sortie, and he launches a series of engagements as both sides muster reinforcements. The dominant schema of Part II is the single combat, in a context of justice. An accused victim searches all of Europe for a champion, Gui. He discovers the pilgrim Gui, who, unrecognized, volunteers to replace the sought-after Englishman, and vanquishes his adversary in the equivalent of a *judicium Dei*. These themes, amplified and embellished, create a rhythm and texture of their own and attain quasi-archetypal power. It is this quality of archetype that may have constituted much of the attraction of *Gui de Warewic* for the medieval public.

As I said before, whereas an earlier generation arrives at a kind of synthesis wherein love and prowess reinforce each other in establishing the ideal, in succeeding generations the synthesis breaks down. One alternative dominates Hue de Rotelande's era and the following century, and that is an optimistic fiction (the *roman d'aventures*) in which the public and private domains are largely separate and the protagonist undergoes no inner development. Among the characteristics of such fiction are an imposed series of happy endings, an idealized oedipal pattern of displaced wish-fulfilment (the *juvenis* triumphing over the *senior*), and a preference for marriage at court as opposed to adulterous trysts with a fay.

These thirteenth-century romances, in England and on the Continent, are in no way problematic. They avoid posing serious ideological or ethical questions, and idealism and abnegation are significant by their absence. On the contrary, they revel in marvels and adventures, rapidity of incident, a reasonable dosage of sex (or, at least, of rescuing damsels in distress), and, once again, the happy ending. In such texts, especially in *chansons de geste*, neither king nor captain is now to be blamed, since guilt is projected onto scapegoats: inner scapegoats, such as wicked stewards or a lineage of traitors, who play the role of evil counsellors; or external scapegoats, merchants and/or Saracens who kidnap. The action, launched by these embodiments of evil, permits the innocent protagonist to lead a life of adventure and to acquire the highest reputation for prowess. In both epic and romance the ultimate is to tell a story and to entertain the public, not to instruct it. Thirteenth-century narrative literature has become the recounting of adventures, and favourite plot increments are repeated again and again for the sheer pleasure of story-telling. At its worst, it is what Curtius (1960G) has called 'Unterhaltungsliteratur' in the manner of Dumas and Sardou (for our generation, say, television serials and science fiction in the cinema), produced to satisfy the public's craving for distraction; at its best, it is the no less popular but highly literary and powerfully archetypal legend of Guy of Warwick.

Chansons de geste and *romans courtois* evolve in the same direction in the course of the thirteenth century. In addition, a case can be made that the distinction between *chanson de geste* and *roman courtois*, valid on one level, is exaggerated on another. In the English tradition, 'Charlemagne romances' exist alongside 'Arthurian romances.' In the German tradition *Nationalepik* exists alongside *höfische Epik*. From the perspective of world literature as a whole, classical and modern, medieval verse narrative (French narrative at any rate) provides the medieval equivalent of epic and was always considered against the backdrop of Virgil and Ovid.[6] This is also true for Anglo-Norman England. Two of the major ancestral romances, *Horn* and *Boeve de Haumtone*, were composed in 'epic' laisses; the other, our text, in 'romance' couplets. All contain a plethora of *chanson de geste* as well as *roman courtois* themes and motifs. *Gui de Warewic*, in its narrative structure, is a thirteenth-century *chanson de geste* in all but verse form. Perhaps this can help explain the absence of original *chanson de geste* creativity in England. The Old French epic was associated with Charlemagne and Capetian dynastic claims. The Anglo-Norman English asserted their claims, explicitly or implicitly, either in the King Arthur stories or in their ancestral-baronial romances, the latter meant to be epic in tone, style, subject matter, and even national aspiration. Texts such as *Haveloc*, *Horn*, and the stories of Fulk, Bevis, and Guy, even though they concentrate so much on the diegesis, do exalt the Anglo-Norman aristocracy in its military and chivalric essence, and exalt its legendary past too. Perhaps they are the Anglo-Norman epic.

II. *Vitae*

As stated earlier in this book, I do not agree with the characterization of the Anglo-Normans and their literature as grave, practical, and didactic vis-à-vis their brothers and cousins on the Continent and the native Anglo-Saxon population. Nonetheless, it is true that perhaps the most successful literary genre cultivated by the French in England, after romance, was the saint's life. The two narrative forms developed concurrently with more than a little cross influence.

Some two hundred and forty verse lives in Old French have survived, devoted to one hundred and one saints. Of the two hundred and fifty extant manuscripts, over one hundred are Anglo-Norman. Almost one half of the thirteenth-century texts and two-thirds of the twelfth-century ones are of insular provenance. Hagiography was therefore a particularly English or Anglo-Norman preoccupation. Along with some other genres – biblical translations, miracles of the Virgin, and the sacred drama – it was first cultivated in the vernacular in England and can be cited as evidence for the precedence or 'précocité' of Anglo-Norman culture. Among the reasons cited by Legge (1950, 1975) for this 'précocité,' in its distinctively clerical manifestation, are the presence in Anglo-Norman England of vernacular writers of higher social class than on the Continent (in other words, members of the nobility were more likely to want to write, and to write in French); the conjunction of worldly-oriented clerics and a sophisticated, urbane baronry; the direct patronage of the vernacular arts by monasteries, great ladies, and the royal family; and the influence of the Orders, in particular, houses of the Benedictines, Austin Canons, and Franciscans. It is a fact that a number of important men (public figures, ecclesiastics, and intellectuals) chose French as well as Latin as their medium of expression: Matthew Paris, John Pecham Archbishop of Canterbury, St Edmund of Abington, and the philosopher Robert Grosseteste. It is also of some significance that we find the same aristocratic and learned or semi-learned public, including women, for both the courtly and the sacred; the Orders catered to the upper classes, the same classes that promoted French secular writings. To this we can add the example of literature in the Anglo-Saxon vernacular, a tradition that surely encouraged the Anglo-Norman baronry and clergy to attempt the same in their vernacular, including the genre of sacred biography.

Hagiography has been a relatively neglected subject in French literary studies. This is the case in part because the medieval texts are highly stylized, for the most part translations, and, of course, unabashedly Christian, whereas academic critics in France, since the heyday of the Third Republic, have traditionally been Paris-centred, secularist, and strongly influenced by the Romantic notion of originality. With a more recent critical orientation, it is now possible not only to shed light on a crucially important facet of Anglo-Norman culture but also to restore to its rightful place one of the major literary genres in the tradition of the West.

There are two categories of saints represented in vernacular texts of the age. The martyr is a spiritual warrior who confronts the pagan world, breaks its idols, and converts others through his exemplary death; the confessor is an ascetic who flees the world, pagan or Christian, escapes to the desert, and converts others through his exemplary life. The categories correspond to distinct chronological stages in the history of the Church: the period of persecutions, and then later, after Constantine, the period of consolidation. The two categories are different as literature, having assumed distinct literary structures and appealing to their public in divergent ways. Of the two, by far the more popular, enshrining the most famous saints, is the legend of martyrs.

Saint Lawrence

An excellent example of the martyr legend is *La Vie de saint Laurent*, 1140–70, one of the earliest Anglo-Norman *vitae* and the oldest version of the story in French. Saint Lawrence is a genuinely historical figure, although specialists in the historicity of saints' lives claim that the legend of his martyrdom is spurious. The story tells of Decius Caesar who wishes to impound Christian gold. Before his own martyrdom, Pope Sixtus confides this gold to the care of archdeacon Lawrence, who in turn distributes it to the poor. Ordered by Decius to hand over the treasure, to betray the identity of the remaining Christians in Rome, and to adore pagan gods, Lawrence refuses. He is tortured and dies a martyr.

Iconographically, Saint Lawrence, patron of the poor, is traditionally depicted with a gridiron but also with a purse or cup filled with gold. Gold and treasure form perhaps the dominant pattern of imagery in the narrative. As archdeacon and financial officer of the diocese, Lawrence's ecclesiastical duties include management of the resources. Lawrence does not guard the treasure; instead he invests it by releasing it as alms to the poor. Arrested and ordered to produce his treasure, Lawrence gathers the *pauperi* and shows them to Caesar. Furious, Caesar has Lawrence tortured. The debate between the two turns on the semantic fields pertaining to the word 'treasure.' 'Don't count on your treasure to get you out of this!' states the emperor. 'Indeed I do,' replies Lawrence. 'Give me your treasure!' demands the tyrant. 'I can't; it is in heaven!' replies Lawrence (596–609). While in prison, Lawrence offers to show Hippolytus, his jailor, 'les tresors' (327) and eternal life, if the latter will believe in Christ; he subsequently baptizes the man.

If the pagans are so eager to seize Christian treasure, it is partly out of greed – the capital sin of *avaritia* grounded in *cupiditas* – but also because they must have gold and silver to construct their idols. Sixtus himself is offered great wealth if he will worship the gods but he refuses, pointing out that they are not alive; they are only gold (179–83). Prior to his execution, Sixtus calls upon the idol in the Temple of Mars, 'Ymage qui n'os ne [ne] veiz, / Tu qui la fole gent deceiz' (211–12) ['You, statue, who neither hear nor see, you who deceive the foolish crowd'] to fall, and by divine power much of the structure does. It is not surprising, then, that a good portion of the verbal dispute between Decius and Lawrence concerns the relative value of the idols, of gods, and of God, always expressed through the metaphor of treasure. Lawrence wins the argument (convincing his implied extradiegetic audience if not the real Caesar inside the narrative) by insisting that the gods are not gods at all but things created by men, whereas God, the God of the Church, is a creator. He has created the men who in turn create the idols that pagans foolishly presume to be gods. In reply, Decius accuses Lawrence of being a sorcerer or of having rapport with demons, false gods who sustain him with their voices and who enable him to resist torture without suffering pain. From all this, and from Lawrence's own allusion to demons inspiring the Romans, it becomes apparent that the contest of pagan and Christian, or of idol and icon, in fact masks the cosmic war between Satan and God. Satan stands behind idol worship and, implicitly, induces the pagans into error and vice, indeed into damnation, by inciting the Romans to persecute the Christian minority, the righteous remnant, under their sway.

In the Prologue to his text the anonymous clerkly narrator, as implied author, condemns the world and its riches, elaborating rhetorically the *contemptus mundi* topos yet also preparing us for his spiritual discussion of treasure and gold. Gold as the object of earthly desire and of pagan worship is the most concrete possible manifestation of the *vanitas vanitatum*. Sixtus and, above all, Lawrence understand that real treasure is people not gold, the Christian faithful, the *pauperi* to whom are promised the Kingdom of Heaven. Lawrence gives away what he has received, casts his bread onto the waters, and is rewarded tenfold by the metaphorical multiplication of the loaves, the multiple conversion of good pagans to the Church. Just as earthly gold both embodies and is a lure for *cupiditas*, the fountain of vices that transcends mere avarice, so its antitype, *caritas*, stands not only for good works, specifically generosity to the poor, but also the love of God and of one's neighbour. Decius Caesar is a creature of the ego, of absolute selfishness and self-centredness. In contrast, Lawrence thinks always of others: of his spiritual father, Sixtus; of the Church in his charge; and of the living Christ and his Father, creator of heaven and earth. Decius seeks to grasp, keep, and exploit; he fails. Lawrence seeks to give and to exchange (love, salvation, spiritual treasure); he succeeds. For the only genuine treasure is spiritual gold, the truth of God's Word, the *verbum in principio* stored in his realm, the eternal heaven.

For this reason, Decius' threats of death and Lawrence's obliviousness to them take on particular significance. Sixtus rightly exhorts his flock to imitate Christ by dying for him. Sixtus practices what he preaches; so does Lawrence. Both attain eternal life because of their manner of death, whereas not only are the idols lifeless but Decius the tyrant endures a living death awaiting his merited eternal damnation. Finally, by having Sixtus, the 'father,' predict his 'son' Lawrence's death in three days time, the text induces the implied audience to behold typologically in Lawrence a Christ figure in his death and life, and in Sixtus a figure either of God the Father or John the Baptist, depending on one's reading of the allegory.

Just as Christ was persecuted by his tormentors – with the crown of thorns, the sponge of vinegar, the lance in the side, and finally crucifixion – so too Lawrence imitates and postfigures him in his own passion. Particularly striking about his *vita* (and a number of others) is the variety and complexity of physical torture of the body prior to decapitation. The pagans beat Lawrence, first with branches of wild, thorny roses and later with cudgels; they burn his flesh to the bone with hot sheets of metal; they strike his feet with straps or clubs embedded with nails; they place him on a rack; they smash his teeth and mouth with stones; and, finally, they literally roast him on a grill of iron.

Saint Lawrence with his grill is the favourite iconographical representation of a figure who became the patron of all who work with fire: cooks, bakers, glass-makers, fire-fighters, etc. Because of the grill, the *vita* employs a variety of flesh and meat imagery, for the characters unknowingly anticipate the denouement long before it takes place. During the verbal confrontations, Lawrence assures Decius that the torments he endures for God are 'douce viande' (555). Decius' savage response expands the metaphor:

> 'Quant torment t'est douce viande,
> Ou sunt dunc li escumengé,
> Li fol crestien renoié?
> Di ou il sunt, enseigne les moi!
> Ferei les venir manger o tei
> La viande que loes tant.' (557–62)

'Since torture is to you choice meat, where are then the anathematized ones, the mad Christian turncoats? Tell me where they are, show them to me! I will make them come dine with you on the meat you praise so highly.'

Lawrence replies, 'They do not want your food' (565). Although Decius is unaware of the fact, Lawrence is making a traditional Christian statement on earthly as opposed to spiritual food: Man cannot live by bread alone. He also informs Decius that 'li premiers fruiz' (494), 'la pome' (502) [the first fruit, the apple], in the Garden of Eden and its tree (498) gave us death, whereas the Holy Rood grants us the fruit of life incarnate in the flesh of a man, 'vie en la char de homme' (503), and he who ingests it will live in the glory of paradise. This fruit, this flesh, is Our Lord's body on the cross and the bread of the eucharist, the flesh of the Agnus Dei devoured during the Mass. Therefore, after Lawrence's death Hippolytus takes his flesh and annoints it with spices, buries it, and mourns over it for three days. Then the disciples sing the Mass, and Justin offers the Corpus Christi (939). Lawrence imitates Christ in his flesh, and his flesh, like Christ's, like the wafer of the Mass, will be distributed as Lawrence distributes the treasure of the Church; it will multiply in the people who are members of Christ, the flesh of the Church.

Lawrence's flesh, beaten, broken, and ultimately grilled, is (to employ a Lévi-Strauss metaphor) good nature (the raw) degraded by false culture (the cooked). It is also living humanity torn by machines, by hard cutting objects: cudgels, nails, plates, stones, a rack, and a grill. Soft living matter is pierced, lacerated, and burned by dead wood, metal, and stone, by the Bachelardian hard earth of the will.[7] The inhuman, dead tyrant exerts his will on the living lambs of God's flesh. Also, twice Lawrence is made to see the instruments of his torture, a means of intimidation almost as literally nerve-racking as the torture itself. The way the author portrays the episodes of Lawrence's torture in their concrete detail, by means of which he and the implied audience in some sense relish the scenes of torture, reveals an element of latent sado-masochism; there is an identification with the saint, grounded in empathy and pity, but also an identification with the tyrant, the sinner, whom all of us, sinners, resemble and who, in his excess of sinful violence, mirrors our violent excess of sin. On both levels a tragic or, if you prefer, melodramatic catharsis will function. Cazelles (1982) and Hyun (1983–4) have proposed, from a Girardian point of view (cf. Girard 1972G, 1978G), that in the *vitae* a scapegoat is substituted for all other victims, past and present. The archetypal sacrificial victim becomes the focus for communal violence; violence is allayed through violence, whether perpetrated by the torturer or suffered by the victim. Society purges itself through the ritual of sacrifice, and the sacrifice as well as the act of violence are rendered sacred. With this act of sacred violence, the need for violence will then cease in the new Christian community of peace.

Whatever our response to *le girardisme*, it is certain that Lawrence is meant to be considered a hero. He, like Sixtus, is heroic in his deeds of combating and destroying idols. He is even more heroic as a victim and martyr. As with the protagonists of Baroque epic (D'Aubigné, Saint-Amant), this is a Christian heroism of patience, endurance, and passive suffering as opposed to martial conquest. The true Christian hero imitates Christ on the cross. The true martyr is a soldier in Christ's army, a *miles Christi* successfully confronting, resisting, and overcoming his earthly self and the earthly institutions of a corrupt, fallen society. Thus the deacon triumphs over the Caesar, *ecclesia* over *militia*, and the slave, following the Prince of Peace who freed slaves, overcomes his torturers and masters.

As we have seen, Decius Caesar has Lawrence beaten in the mouth and in the teeth by stones. This particular torture is the penultimate, directly preceding the ordeal of the grill. Well might the pagan wish to silence the Christian, to close his mouth with stone just as he opens his body with metal. Lawrence's victory is symbolized by his famous retort to the torture of the grill: 'Wretch, turn me over; eat from this side, it's well done':

> 'Chaitif, l'altre part car tornez;
> Mangez deça, quit est assez!' (896–7)

The retort is an example of Curtius' (1948G) Kitchen Humour, so prevalent in the Middle Ages, employed here in a sacred context with sacred irony. It underscores the antithesis of which I have spoken all along: nature versus culture, humans versus things, flesh versus the spirit, earthly food versus God's eucharist, false gold versus genuine treasure. Decius has a flawed sense of reality. Lawrence, on the other hand, perceives the truth. He is able to use figurative or metaphoric language, taking the pagan's limited speech and turning it upside down. Finally, this last scene reveals the extent to which Caesar's apparent physical triumph (the grill, torture, and death) is countermanded and surpassed by the saint's spiritual victory (suffering, eternal life, and speech). Before the torture begins, Decius and Lawrence indulge in a lengthy verbal confrontation, in which the Roman seeks to convince or coerce the Christian to hand over his treasure but which soon evolves into a *disputatio* over their respective faiths. The issues raised in the debate – treasure, idols and idol worship, creatures and their creator – are then concretized in Lawrence's life as a saint and in his martyrdom, and in the sacred biography which recounts it. The debate is not external, extraneous discourse; it mirrors the issues raised by the text, within the text, and thus is, in the modern sense of the term, a *mise en abyme* of the narrative taken as a whole.

It is true that in the terms of the debate itself, Lawrence does not convince Decius Caesar. Decius, his provost Valerian, and the emperor remain obdurate to the end. Two disparate worlds collide: Christianity and pagandom, icon and idol, God and Satan. There can be no communication between them. However, Lawrence succeeds very well in communicating with individual pagans, whom he converts – hence Decius' eagerness to break his mouth. Before his confrontation with Decius, Lawrence restores sight to a man gone blind in prison. As a result, the prisoner, Lucillus, requests baptism. Others convert with him; Lawrence's fame extends to the mass of captives; even his jailer, Hippolytus, converts. The Romans are especially moved by the sight of an angel who tends Lawrence's wounds. A distinction is established between those who have ears to hear and eyes to see, and those who do not: those who see the angel and have been granted spiritual sight, and those who see only the light of burning sheets of metal and are spiritually blind; those who speak or hear the Word, and those who are spiritually deaf.

In the Prologue to the *vita*, the implied author, exploiting conventional humility-topoi, requests that his text be corrected and improved. He also asks his implied readers to pray with him so that he may complete his task and so that God may grant him grace. Then, in the Conclusion, he urges us to pray to Lawrence that he assist us in our search for salvation. The implied author imitates the saint in humility, in prayer, and in his use of speech. He urges us to do the same. Indeed, he identifies with his public, the Church faithful in quest of grace and salvation, who seek to imitate Lawrence and Christ. Thus is established a complex nexus of voices and bonds from the implied reader to the implied author to Lawrence to God: a golden chain of mediators. The goal is grace, perfection, and salvation. The means are mediation, imitation, and use of the word. The word is speech, intercession, and prayer effected in the *vita* and from the telling of the *vita*. Speech forms a bond of communication among the community of the faithful, the Church – *clerici* not *milites*, men of the word not the sword. This is because, on all levels, saints, potential saints, and repentant sinners, the living and the dead, the Church Militant and the Church Triumphant, listen to the word because it reflects the Word – God's power, wisdom, and love that created the universe in the beginning, as a book, and that created his Book, Scripture, that contains the universe, including Saint Lawrence and his story.

Saint Margaret

Saint Margaret of Antioch's story is also, according to the specialists, a legend (fable, fiction) of Greek origin. It would appear that the veneration of Saint Margaret was stronger in England than in France. Over two hundred pre-Reformation churches were dedicated to her and, of the fourteen versions of her legend in Old French verse –

there are eighteen in prose – one-half (counting Wace) are Anglo-Norman. Of all these, *La Vie de sainte Marguerite* by Wace, which survives in three manuscripts, is the oldest. Although Wace is properly speaking a continental Norman, born in Jersey but raised in Caen, he deserves, like Beroul and Marie de France, to figure in the Anglo-Norman canon.[8] He earns this place because of his lifelong service to Henry II and the Angevin House and because of his crucially important adaptation of Geoffrey of Monmouth, *Le Roman de Brut*, as well as his own *Roman de Rou*, both designed to recount British history and exalt the Anglo-Norman ruling class. The life of Saint Margaret may well be his first work and, dated by Keller (Wace, *La Vie* 1990) between 1130 and 1140, has to be considered one of the earliest sacred biographies in French.

The story is simple. Margaret, having promised her virginity to God, refuses the advances of Olybrius, the pagan provost of Antioch. He jails her. In her prison cell Margaret is attacked, then devoured by a dragon. She makes the sign of the cross, the dragon bursts open, and the maiden is released, only to discover a demon, bound hand and foot, who confesses his secrets to her. Olybrius, his further propositions spurned, eventually beheads the martyr.

As with Saint Lawrence, speech plays a crucial role in Margaret's career. She debates with Olybrius at various times in the narrative. She refuses his sexual offers, including marriage, because she has already consecrated herself to virginity and will not break her pledge. Indeed, Margaret prays incessantly. It is as a direct result of one of her supplications that she is spared death from drowning. It is in response to an invocation to God, who has dominion over the four elements and the abyss and who harrowed hell and bound Satan (319–28), that she is delivered from the beast's maw. One of Margaret's most significant signs of victory is her ability to force the bound demon, the dragon's brother, to reveal to her not only his name, but also information about hell. Saint Margaret's last prayer, prior to her decapitation, asks salvation for those who read her life, build her church, and invoke her name. The martyr's discourse is then answered by the song of angels come to escort her soul to paradise. Immediately thereafter she does save one man, a certain Theodimus, who aided her in prison and buries her remains; it is he, an eyewitness, who will write her life.

In Margaret's case, unlike Lawrence, the verbal 'agon,' whether with the demon or with Olybrius, occurs after the physical 'agon' with the dragon. On the other hand, Margaret does presumably convince the extradiegetic audience long before she confronts her persecutor; she also converts masses of pagans. As in the story of Lawrence and more explicitly, a complex nexus of communication is established; there is speech, intercession, prayer, writing, and reading, between God, Saint Margaret, her spectator-witnesses, and her alleged author, Theodimus, in the early Church; and between God, Theodimus, Wace, and their audience in the twelfth century. Speech gives rise to further acts that give rise to further speech that gives rise to acts that give rise to a book that in turn gives rise to acts and speech across space and time, in the communion of saints and the body of the Church.

Unlike Lawrence, Margaret does not triumph uniquely through speech nor by manifesting qualities of submission, endurance, and passive resistance. On the contrary, her heroism is concretely active. When the black dragon, fire bursting from its mouth and a dagger in its claw, assaults and devours her, Margaret slays it. She then conquers a demon, bound and shackled before her, and she triumphantly places her foot on his head. Her hand, making the sign of the cross, causes the dragon to burst open; her foot tortures the demon. Resembling Saint George as well as Tristan, Lancelot, Yvain, and Gauvain, Margaret is a slayer of dragons and a conqueror of devils, in imitation of Christ. We are told that Margaret is held for three days in her prison cell, and we see her devoured by the dragon. Typologically she postfigures Christ the Martyr, who was entombed for three days, and Christ the Warrior, who harrowed hell between Good Friday and Easter Sunday. It is hardly coincidental that Margaret, threatened by the dragon, evokes the Christ who broke into hell and bound Satan, 'Infer brisas, Sathan lias' (324), to help her. Thus, in *La Vie de sainte Marguerite*, we find explicitly what was implicit in *La Vie de saint Laurent* – behind pagan provosts and Caesars stand Satan and the host of fallen angels. These devils are responsible for idols and idol-worship; they are also responsible for the persecution of Christian martyrs. It is their task to tempt and defeat if possible the fledgling Church. Therefore, victories over Caesar and his pagans are also triumphs over the powers of hell.

In this struggle between God and Satan, or heaven and hell, it is appropriate that the metaphor most closely associated with Margaret is the dove and that, in a metaphoric or iconographic sense, it is the dove who vanquishes the dragon. Dreading torture, Margaret begs help from 'La columbe do ciel' (245) [the heavenly dove]. After her victory she gives thanks to God for having sent the dove (351–4). Later, she physically beholds Christ's cross and the dove, who speaks to her (389–92). Still later, the dove returns with a crown of gold in its beak to save Margaret from death by water, and descends from heaven at her final passing, upon which the saint's soul ascends in the form of a dove (715–17). As Margaret herself observes, the dove who succours her is the Holy Ghost:

> 'La colonbe est del ciel venue
> Que por confort ai atendue,
> C'est Saint Espir que j'atendoie,
> Que jo sor toutes riens voloie.' (351–4)

'The dove, whose solace I awaited, came from heaven; it is the Holy Ghost whom I expected, whom I wished for over all other beings.'

The Holy Spirit is one with God and Christ; he is God's voice and the manifestation of his love. Hence the appropriateness of the dove as the protective force and identifiable icon for this victory of a martyr and a woman.

Margaret's femininity is central to her *vita*. The bound dragon groans that, miserable wretch that he is, his shame would be so much lessened had he been vanquished by a man of war, not a virgin, a mere girl:

> 'Las moi! caitis maleüré,
> Une virge m'a sormonté!
> Se uns proudome vencu m'eust
> Assés menre honte me fust.' (447–50)

It is as a woman, with the humility of a woman (Margaret insists several times that she is God's servant, like Mary, *ancilla Dei*) that she conquers Satan's pride and forces unwilling humility onto the demon. Frail, an orphan, she defeats a pair of powerful devils reinforced by the hosts of darkness. A shepherdess from the country, imitating the Shepherd of Men, she bests the city of hell and its earthly antitype, the corrupt Roman empire.

Finally, it is in her chastity, the purity of a spotless maiden, that Saint Margaret resists the male libido directed against her. Olybrius desires her; he is willing to make her his concubine or even his wife, depending on the girl's social condition:

> Par ses chevaliers li manda
> Que sa moillier de li feroit,
> Se ele france feme estoit;

> Et se ele ert altrui ancele,
> Por ço qu'ele ert et gente et bele,
> En sognantage la tendroit,
> Del sien a grant plenté aroit. (98–104)

He sent his knights to inform her that, if she were a freewoman, he would make her his wife; and, because she was both beautiful and of great worth, if she were someone's slave, he would keep her as his concubine, and she would possess an abundance of his riches.

However, Olybrius insists that Margaret bow down before his idols. Known as a persecutor of Christians, he represents idolatry as well as lechery. It was in response to the persecutions that Margaret offered her 'casteé' (79) to God. Threatened by Olybrius, she states again and again that her choice is that of the soul over the body, the spirit over the flesh, and it is because of this that she accepts, indeed welcomes, torture and death. Furthermore, we are told in so many words that the demon, in the form of a dragon, sought to defile Margaret's virginity and that it is her virginity, in addition to her prayers and the sign of the cross, that destroys him and humbles his brother. Under these conditions it is not fanciful to propose a Freudian reading of the dragon: black, flames spurting from its maw, and with a dagger grasped in its talon, it embodies aggressive male libido, the *luxuria* that Satan hopes will consume Margaret. This is a sexual onslaught from hell, demonic rape. She resists the onslaught; the dragon fails and expires. It fails because Margaret has chosen to sacrifice the pleasures of the world and her body to greater joys of the soul in the afterlife (269–70). The sacrifice is symbolized by the flagellation she endures prior to imprisonment. This initiation, a sacrifice of blood, is the spiritual gift of her maidenhood to God in heaven. Henceforth, the dove will respond to her prayer and she will overcome whatever ordeals the Enemy has in store for her. In addition, the blood of Margaret's flagellation anticipates the blood of five thousand pagans, converted by her and on her behalf, whom Olybrius orders to be beheaded. They endure a good baptism of blood: 'Mult orent bon baptisement / Del sanc dont il erent sanglant' (585–6). So also does Saint Margaret, who will be beheaded shortly afterwards.

Like Saint Lawrence and to greater effect, given her status as a woman, Margaret chooses God the heavenly Father over the world and her earthly father, virginity over a 'normal' sex life and family, and ecclesiastical over lay values. She will not inherit her father's goods

(55–6) nor will she wed and bear children. Yet Margaret also proclaims, in her own voice, that she is to be the patron saint of expectant mothers and of mothers in labour. Is this because she was engulfed by the dragon but then was coughed up, as an infant comes out of its mother's womb? Of course, but also because Margaret is a spiritual mother to the five thousand converted during her lifetime and to countless numbers of the faithful after her death. Chaste death gives rise to the life of the soul and to the multiplication of Christian lay people, children in the spirit. The divine genealogy takes precedence over human genealogy, just as the communion of saints takes priority over secular kinship. Margaret, a woman, the patron saint of babies and mothers, educated by her nurse, creates her personal line of descent, scale of values, estate, and kingdom, that resist fire and water and are more powerful, more lasting, than the virile, martial empire of Rome.

One of the saint's icons, derived etymologically from her name, is the pearl, a precious stone that, according to the lapidaries, cures illness and symbolizes purity. Because Margaret and her pearl are humble and chaste, they cure (save) those who have faith. Like the other Gem of Gems (Mary), Margaret is a virgin and a mother (spiritually a mother although physically a virgin) and *mediatrix* because she is both. Like the other Gem of Gems, she conquers the Serpent and succours fallen womankind, Ave redeeming Eva.

The pearl shines brightly; it is white in its perfection, as opposed to the black dragon. It shines in its virtue (purity, humility), as opposed to the pride and lust of demons. Margaret's is the sheen, sparkle, and joy so important to a medieval aesthetic based on light, which projects reason, virtue, beauty, harmony, and order. These qualities are also invoked by the pearl's perfect circular shape, which is also embodied in the crown of gold brought to the saint by her dove. Roundness corresponds to light, and light to roundness. As Montgomery (1977) has demonstrated, the story of Margaret's life can be envisaged as a frame structure, the centre of which – an incident that occurs spatially in her enclosed prison cell – is her victory over demons. This is a private inner triumph witnessed only by the Holy Ghost but preceded and followed by public confrontations, verbal and physical. The extreme outer framework of the story includes Olybrius' proposal of marriage in the beginning and his order for decapitation in the end. From this perspective, the prison cell becomes an inner sanctum, a point of epiphany, the locus of combat between heaven and hell, and a sacred locus where the saint's holiness is tested and revealed. Margaret defeats the provost in verbal battle, she defeats the demons that assault her body, she endures torture and death, and she converts thousands. In this sense hers is a linear as well as a circular tale, one in which she does not evolve but her sanctity is sequentially revealed to God and to men and celebrated by them, with the results in communication and mediation that constitute the communion of saints.

Saint Catherine

Saint Catherine of Alexandria first appears in a Greek text of the ninth century. According to the scholars, her life is as legendary as the life of Saint Margaret. Like Margaret of Antioch, she is to be counted among the most revered of Christian saints. Of the eight rhymed versions of her biography in medieval French, the oldest (1175–1200) is by the Anglo-Norman nun Clemence of Barking, who probably also composed a *Vie d'Edouard le Confesseur*. Clemence and Marie de France are the most important women writers in French prior to Christine de Pizan, whose career bridges the end of the fourteenth century.

According to the story, during the last persecutions Catherine attempts to persuade the emperor, Maxentius, of the justness of the Christian cause; she urges him to cease compelling his subjects to sacrifice to pagan gods. Catherine is forced into a formal philosophical *disputatio* with fifty of the greatest Roman 'clers.' She argues them into submission, and they convert. The scholars are martyred. Catherine also is tortured, including torture on the wheel. Out of empathy for her, numbers of pagans convert, including her jailors and the empress. In the end, Maxentius has her decapitated.

The sexual aspects of the diegesis are still more prominent than was the case for Saint Margaret. Catherine is the object of erotic prey and erotic competition. Seduced by her beauty, Maxentius insistently asks Catherine to be his mistress, and then, after the empress has expired, to become his bride and empress of Rome. She refuses him on the grounds that she has an 'ami,' Christ in heaven. Her joy (a *gaudium amoris* greater than *fin' amor*) derives from the fact that she is 'la Deu amie' [God's beloved], for their covenant is 'Que amie sui e il amant' (1360) [that I am his beloved and he my lover]. Furthermore, she is, in a very real sense, his fiancée, since an angel has promised her she will dwell with her 'espus' (582) in the afterlife, and Catherine herself refers to Christ more than once as her husband, 'le mien espus' (1357, 2616). (By the early fifteenth century the betrothal ring was included in Catherine's iconography.)

As if this were not enough, Maxentius not only fails to win Catherine, but he also loses his wife. The saint convinces the empress to convert to Christianity, for in Christ she also will have another 'ami' (2283), a better love and better husband and, in his heaven, a better kingdom than her pagan spouse can offer her on earth:

'Reine, fait ele, bele amie,
Mun Deu a ses noces t'envie ...
Ne dutez pas l'empereur,
N'aiez mais desir de s'amur.
S'amur est fraille e decevable,
E sa poesté trespassable.' (1633–4; 1641–4)

'Queen,' she says, 'dear friend, my God invites you to his wedding ... Do not dread the emperor; desire his love no longer. His love is weak and deceptive, and his power ephemeral.'

Maxentius is as furious at his wife's sexual betrayal as he is at Catherine's sexual resistance. He envisages other wives similarly deceiving their husbands. And, as we have seen, the Catherine who refuses his lecherous advances is not beyond seducing others; she employs her tongue and brains to win over the empress and her goodness and beauty to win over the jailers.

The issue is a sexual battle between the earthly suitor and the divine spouse. The battlefield is the mind and body of the virgin Christian girl. The emperor falls in love with her, but she is already occupied by another. The other is more powerful than he is, offering a greater kingdom and a deeper love. The spirit triumphs over the flesh, on the flesh's own grounds.

Not that the flesh (the pagan tyrant) gives up so easily. Frustrated libido and thwarted desire express themselves in violence and a sadistic will to dominate and mutilate. Sexuality and violence, Eros and Thanatos, are linked in this pagan, non-spiritual obsession with the body; flesh if it cannot be enjoyed will be obliterated. Therefore Maxentius has his wife's breasts pierced and pulled out; he orders Catherine, after she is flagellated, to be tormented on wheels and racks studded with nails and knives. The wheel, along with the sword of her decapitation, is her icon, and she has become the patron saint of all who use wheels in their trades: carters, millers, spinners, etc. The torture (real with the queen, projected with the saint) of these two ladies is by no means an anomaly. In the brief *vitae* composed by the

Anglo-Norman Nicole Bozon alone, we find comparable tortures inflicted on Saints Agatha, Agnes, Christina, and Juliana.

On the one hand, the pagan worshipper of idols, in his pride, ugliness, and lechery, lusts after the Christian's physical and spiritual 'belté.' Because of her resistance, he succeeds only in torturing and dismembering her, trying to extirpate all that makes her beautiful and a woman. Doing this, he is a monster and the servant of Satan, his machines invented by the Enemy. However, from another perspective, the church fathers distrusted the female body because they were attracted to the body as well as repelled by it, and repelled especially because of its attraction. Like the Roman emperor, they were willing to destroy what they could not enjoy. Catherine, like Agatha, Agnes, Christina, and Juliana, possessing a woman's body, *fax Satani*, is redeemed by the loss of her body, by its sacrifice and purification. Because her female sexuality is impure, Catherine, like Margaret, consciously, willingly, and joyfully sacrifices it. The libidinal pagan assault, the metaphoric rape of the flesh, is the necessary prerequisite to liberation of the spirit, the soul's marriage in heaven.

As a sign of purification, upon decapitation, the ultimate, successful violation and dismemberment of her body, milk flows from Catherine's veins in place of blood, just as, later, holy oil will seep from her tomb on Mt Sinai. The milk is an image of food, of spiritual nurture. It is the feminine equivalent of God's blood, the cup of wine ('calix sanguinis mei') of the Mass. Just as Catherine's jailers feed her out of pity, she assures them that her divine spouse offers heavenly viands. As she demonstrates to the pagan scholars, Christ on the cross substituted his 'froit' for the evil fruit, the 'pume' (1000) that caused the Fall of Adam. The milk is also an image of maternity for Catherine became the patron saint of wet-nurses. A virgin, wed only to Christ, she is transformed into a spiritual mother to the thousands who convert because of her mutilated body, unfit for generating desire or children but all the more capable of instilling charity.

Catherine's milk is the equivalent of Christ's blood; her speech, prayer, and homilies also function to imitate Christ. Margaret's symbolic victory was, in the guise of a *miles*, to slay the dragon. For Catherine, on the other hand, the crucial confrontation and triumph is a theological debate with Maxentius and the fifty scholars ('clers,' 'maistres') he summons to oppose her. In this she acts in the guise of a *clericus*. It is no less certain, however, that Catherine commits an act of heroism in her role of 'plaideresse' [female advocate], advancing to join battle with the pagans. The outcome, her 'victorie' (577), is one of the spirit – bloodless, on God's side. As a direct result of Catherine's 'raisun' (her powers of reasoning and discourse) and by her 'verté' the fifty doctors are first convinced and then converted to Christianity. Infuriated, Maxentius condemns them to be burned alive, a fate that Catherine proclaims to be a baptism of fire and gift of the Holy Spirit, the wisdom of the Word appropriate to scholars:

> 'Seignurs, fait ele, n'aiez pour.
> Cunfortez vus el criatur,
> E del baptesme, ço vus pri,
> N'en aiez dute, mi chier ami.
> El sanc Deu estes tuit lavé
> E par sa mort regeneré.
> Par la flame que ci veez,
> Le seint espirt recevrez.' (1139–46)

'My lords,' she says, 'do not fear. Take comfort in the creator and in your baptism, I beg you. Doubt not, my dear friends, you are washed in God's blood and reborn in his death. You will receive the Holy Spirit through the fire that you here behold.'

Therefore a book forms part of Catherine's traditional iconography, and she becomes the patron saint of clerks.

More than others, Saint Catherine is a 'plaideresse,' one who uses her powers of speech. She speaks to and converts her jailers, the empress, the emperor's chief of staff Porphyrius, and, of course, the fifty doctors. She speaks to God and to angels in her prayers. Her prayers, like her exhortations and her *disputatio*, are models of eloquence. Perhaps Catherine's most important prayer is the request that Christ grant her powers of speech for the upcoming confrontation when she offers combat in his name to illustrate his right by the force of his truth, for as he himself said to his disciples 'Buche te dunrai e science / E parler par sapience' (543–4) ['I shall give you a mouth with which to speak, knowledge, and discourse in accordance with wisdom'].

As in the case of Saint Margaret, the vanquished scholars are ashamed to yield to a mere 'femme' (1062), even worse a 'pucele tendre' (1065). The triumph of the 'pucele' is all the more miraculous, given that she is a woman. Despite her womanhood, Catherine acts like a man; she conquers clerks as a clerk, dominating them and the spectators by her beauty and goodness but, even more, by her power of logic, quick wit, and agile tongue. As much as any figure in literature, she partakes of the topos *puella senex*, a woman with the beauty of a young girl and the wisdom of a sage. Implicitly, marginally, imitating Catherine and seeking to partake of a comparable topos, stands the author, Clemence of Barking, like the subject of her *vita* a woman, a mere religious in a convent, but one who knows Latin and recognizes, in the Prologue, her clerical, rhetorical duty not only to seek her own salvation but to tell Catherine's story for the benefit of others.

The paradox inherent in Catherine – a girl, triumphing in the domain of 'raisun' over fifty qualified men – is mirrored in the reasoning she puts forward to defend Christianity and to overthrow idol-worship. A master, she employs all three elements or registers of classical rhetoric: demonstrative (arguments in praise of God), judicial (arguments to prove his existence), and deliberative (arguments to persuade her audience to act and to convert). The central issue of the debate is the Incarnation and the Resurrection – how Christ can be god and man at the same time, how, if he is god, he died and, if he is man, he was reborn. Catherine, accused of speaking against 'nature' (799) and 'raisun' (800), explicates the Christian paradox. From a theological perspective, the classic distinction is made between God's substance as god and the human person, one of three, he chooses to embody. Furthermore, she says, being omnipotent, by his very godhood, God has the power to do whatever he wants; his actions are not inhibited by our perceptions of nature and reason. Secondly, from an empirical or historical perspective, invoking textual authority, Catherine cites as proof of the death and rebirth of God (1) the eyewitness evidence of the Gospels; (2) the historical evidence, also from the Gospels, of Christ's miracles and specifically of Christ's raising Lazarus from the dead (if he resurrected Lazarus, he can resurrect himself); and (3) the evidence of prophecy of events in sacred history from pagan sources such as Plato and the Sybilline oracles. Finally, from a symbolic or typological perspective, Catherine demonstrates how, since man fell through the sin of eating the fruit from the forbidden tree and was condemned to death for it, ontologically it is appropriate that we be redeemed by a god-man who suffers death on a tree and substitutes the fruit of that tree, his body, for the wicked fruit offered by Satan and thus conquers the power of death for himself and for all humankind.

Catherine's paradox mirrors the central issue that faces mankind – a matter literally of life and death. Christ conquered death and died for life, to grant life. Hence it is absurd to worship lifeless idols and to sacrifice living animals to them, for birds and dogs will not respect a mere statue but defile it. The idols are dead; they were created by mere men who are alive and were created by God. 'How ridiculous it is,' says Catherine, 'to adore dead created beings, or even the sun and moon, and not God.' How appropriate that she should have become also the patron saint of the dying. 'Of course the tyrant can slay my body,' says Catherine, 'but not my soul; he has no power over that which shall be reborn in the afterlife (1929–32). In this I shall imitate God and repay the offering – of body, blood and life – he made for me. The pagan, however, like his gods, will die forever.'

It is on these terms that Catherine deals with Adam's 'folur' (706) and with the 'folie' and 'errur' of the pagans, and she substitutes for them her 'raisun,' 'verrur,' and 'verté.' Just as the Old Adam (*vetus homo*) is redeemed but also replaced by the Christ of the New Covenant (*homo novus*), so also old pagan 'clers' are redeemed and give way to the 'pucele tendre.' On several occasions she comments that she was raised in a pagan (Graeco-Roman) culture but has since abandoned it for the truth revealed by her new 'Maistres' (381) and 'ami' (386). Catherine's victory reflects the historical evolution/revolution on our planet caused by the Advent – the Old Covenant gives way to the New and the Roman Empire gives way to the *pax Christiana* which derives its authority from the *civitas Dei*. Representing her Church, Catherine is meek, humble, and chaste; she disputes with love not war, the word not the sword. Unlike Margaret, her first and most important 'agon' is verbal, intellectual, and spiritual; only later does she conquer death in the flesh, represented by her icons, the wheel of torture and the sword of decapitation.

As a conqueror of death, Catherine is offered the crown of martyrdom she will wear in heaven. Actually, the wheel of physical torture, destroyed at her prayer, is, symbolically and iconographically, transformed into her spiritual crown. The empress also, in a vision, beholds Catherine placing on her head the new crown, an act which later occurs in reality. The crown, for the afterlife, is superior to the crowns of this world. A king's daughter, who in charity gave away her family treasure, wins spiritual treasure – souls – for the Church; she who imitated the Blessed Virgin Mary, *regina coeli*, is rewarded with the only sovereignty that endures, her own spiritual crown as the bride of her divine spouse, the Lord of all that was, is, and ever shall be.

Saint Giles

It would appear that the life of Saint Giles is as spurious as those of the other saints I discuss in this chapter. His *vita* was authored by a monk of St-Gille-en-Provence during the tenth century, when the monastery was contending with the Bishop of Nîmes; it ought to be considered one among several forged documents highlighting that contest. For a variety of reasons, Giles became one of the more favoured medieval Christian saints: he is the patron of Toulouse, Nîmes, Nuremberg, and Edinburgh, and had some one hundred and sixty churches and twenty-four hospitals dedicated to him in pre-Reformation England.

La Vie de saint Gilles by Guillaume de Berneville (1170–1200) is generally considered to be, from a literary perspective, the best *vita* in Old French. Gnädinger (1972) rightly considers this text to be a masterpiece. The author is perhaps Willelmus de Bernewell, who was elected prior of the monastery of St Giles at Barnwell in Cambridgeshire in 1213. His text was adapted into German and perhaps also, with a version from the *Legenda Aurea*, into English by Lydgate.

According to scholars, unlike most of the vernacular *vitae* which are more or less direct translations from the Latin, Guillaume de Berneville amplifies the original, making it more 'realistic' and more lifelike. He adds picturesque descriptions, rhetorical monologues, sharp, witty, dramatic dialogues, and mimetic portraits of contemporary life, especially sea travel and the chase. As an exponent of French *curteisie*, he also delves into his hero's inner existence, more than is usually the case in contemporary hagiography.

Saint Giles is presented as a youth from an aristocratic Greek family who abandons all for the ascetic life. After a series of adventures, he is shipwrecked near Marseille and becomes a famous hermit, performing miracles. Eventually he consents to become the abbot of a new, austere monastery in Provence and, with celestial aid, confesses Charlemagne, convincing him to avow his great hidden sin. After a final pilgrimage to Rome and the gift to his monastery of the doors of St Peter's, Giles dies in the odour of sanctity.

This hero of sacred biography embodies perfectly the ascetic or confessor type as opposed to the virgin and martyr. Unlike the Lawrences, Margarets, and Catherines, he flees the world instead of confronting it. Yet, his withdrawal is not limited to a single action; because, in fact, people seek him out and he flees again and again, his fleeing entails activity. Therefore Giles participates in the active life; his *fuga mundi* leads to the *vita activa* as well as the *vita contemplativa*, and his story proves to be at least as exciting as those of the passive heroes of martyrdom.

The original *vita* dates from the tenth century and thus antedates vernacular romance by two hundred years. Hagiography influenced *chanson de geste* and *roman courtois* more than they shaped it. However, by the end of the twelfth century the two great modes of narrative – secular and sacred – were on a par, and it is certain that the authors of saints' lives, and their audience, knew courtly fiction and had their horizon of expectations extended by it. The courtly presence is evident in Guillaume de Berneville's sacred fiction, in the nature of his additions to the Latin source. Because Saint Giles is a wilfully holy aristocrat, his career becomes, in part, a sacred parody of the career of the secular romance hero, and his life a sacred antiromance.

Like the traditional epic-romance protagonist, Giles is of noble blood, handsome, rich, and well educated. Yet, as a boy, he refuses to play with other little boys: 'Sa vie esteit espiritel' (82) [he lived the spiritual life]. Instead, he hears Mass, studies, and delivers a spirited lecture to his father on charity and the Last Judgment; he also performs a small miracle. This is a very special *puer senex*.

Largesse forms an inherent part of the aristocratic code. Giles surpasses the expected norms of largesse when, after his parents die, he gives away all he has – lands, honour, wealth, everything – and chooses holy *paupertas* for his lord (3) (not his secular master of course, but Christ the Lord of Hosts). While others eat, drink, sleep, and gorge themselves, Giles survives on herbs and roots. He refuses food and the care of his body. He stays awake and prays, in Greece and with Charlemagne in Orleans; he also refuses sex. Urged by his people to be a good knight and marry, Giles demurs. His refusal is not the antierotic and hypercynegetic stance of a Guigemar (Marie de France's hero, who learns to cherish love and a lady). Giles points out that he already loves a 'dameisele, / Si est uncor virgene e pucele' (351–2) ['young lady who is still virgin and a maiden'], and that he will presently make a decision concerning her. The 'pucele' presumably is the Blessed Virgin Mary, and Giles voluntarily adopts sacred folly in preference to the secular wisdom of his class. Whereas great knights in song and story win a bride at the end of their career, as reward and recompense, Giles renounces his before he sets out; indeed his act of renunciation is his first adventure, the first ordeal that will reveal his potentiality for greatness. As a clerk and the embodiment of *ecclesia*, Giles repudiates the knightly code; he will disrupt the family line and dissipate the family inheritance, leaving no feudal 'heir' for his 'honur.' He freely chooses spiritual purity over love and marriage, and the spiritual family of God over his own carnal lineage. Lineage and the fief, *fin' amor* and the *geste*, give way to Christian conduct outside the norms of feudal society. Last but not least, Giles continues to flee from recognition, fame, and honour, even in his new sacred career. Humility, indeed anonymity, are preferred to the sense of honour and respect inherent in the martial code. Non-recognition, non-existence, the state of shame and/or folly, the very death in life that form the nadir in the careers of Lancelot or Yvain, become Giles's most sought-after, most deeply appreciated norm of living:

> 'Le los del siecle est trespassant:
> Trop s'i delitent li alquant;
> Jo ne m'i quer ren deliter,
> Meis guerpir le e esluigner.' (535–8)

'Renown in the world is ephemeral: a number of people delight in it far too much. I do not seek such delight, only to avoid it and ward it off.'

For all that, because of his desire to avoid fame and to escape from the people who flock to behold him, Giles, like his romance brothers, undergoes a physical quest in space. He crosses sea and land, voyaging steadily to the West. As his first 'aventure' (387), while still in Greece he cures a man from snake bite; thus in his own way he defeats the Serpent and slays the Dragon, but in the manner of Saint Margaret or Saint George, not that of Lancelot, Tristan, and Yvain. Although Giles's departure from home is portrayed in terms of escape or flight, he does undergo a quest, on sea and on land. A storm at sea threatens shipwreck, a common romance motif; Giles calms the waters and saves the ship. He experiences adventure on an island, his first encounter with a hermit and his first initiation into the contemplative life. Later, in Provence, he twice sets off alone into the dark forest and on the first occasion it is an archetypally savage region inhabited by wild beasts (1232–8). Giles strives to escape the accolades of those who seek him out; he also desires, in more positive terms, wisdom and holiness; hence he decides to travel to Rome or to encounter Caesarius of Arles. His is a quest for perfection, insight, and Christian initiation. And it results in a pattern of withdrawal and return, of death and rebirth, that partakes of the archetypal career of the hero central to our Western cultural myths.

On his quest Giles enters into a relationship of holy *amicitia* with the men he comes across: the Bishop of Arles, King Flovent, Emperor Charlemagne, and, especially, the two hermits. The first, encountered on an island, struggles in combat with Satan; Giles will aid him with his prayers. With the second, Fredemius, Giles dwells on a rock for two years. They share the same chaste, holy life; they love each other; they work miracles together. The ultimate separation of the two 'compaignun' recalls the separation of the great secular epic comrades: Roland and Oliver, Ami and Amile, Guy and Tierri.

Giles's deepest emotional friendship occurs with a creature from the realm of nature, a doe, which he encounters during his sojourn as a hermit. Indeed, the Giles-doe couple partakes of a form of *amor* or *caritas* as well as *amicitia*. Giles sets off into the deep woods where he finds a natural grotto inside a grove, alongside a fountain. Here he can lead a life of solitude in a sacred version of *locus amoenus*. As a *locus amoenus*, this setting is meant to recall symbolically our spiritual paradise. It is an earthly symbol for the celestial garden, in antithesis to the evocation of the gardens of love in profane lyric and romance. In an example of secular *contrafactum*, it is plausible, according to Lewes (1978), that Thomas was inspired (from the Latin) by Giles's grotto when he imagined Tristan's Hall of Images.

It is then to the grotto and to Giles that a mother doe comes rushing, to nourish him with its milk. There is a tradition in hagiography of the saint meeting animals in the desert, the saint transforming wild beasts, the beast humanized, the beast granting assistance to the saint, or the saint acting like a beast out of sacred *humilitas*. There is a comparable tradition in romance, the most famous examples being Yvain and his lion, imitated in a number of texts including *Gui de Warewic*. There is also the tradition of a knight wounding a stag or doe and paying for his crime (Guigemar, St Eustachius, and St Julian). Here, in place of the lion (St Jerome, Yvain) we find a feminine, nourishing doe, and Giles treats the doe with love and understanding. Indeed, the doe is evoked in all but erotic terminology:

> Gros out le piz e plein de leit:
> As pez Gire se veit gesir,
> Presente sei de lui servir. (1514–16)

Her breast was large and heavy with milk: she throws herself at Giles's feet; she offers herself to serve him.

Domestic intimacy develops between them, and Giles treats the doe with charming familiarity in what is indeed a family situation:

> Ben sout ke ele esteit chascée;
> Il l'ad chosée e chastiée,

> Dit ke veit trop luinz el desert:
> Mal est bailli si il la pert. (1731–4)

He knew well that she was subject to the chase. He scolded and chastized her, saying that she strays too far into the desert; should he lose her he would be in a bad way.

To King Flovent, the hunter, it appears to be a 'chose faée' (1780), the magic beast in a magical Other World.

Giles's great deed of charity is to protect the doe and eventually to be wounded by an arrow in its stead. It is this episode that made him the patron saint of archers, nursing mothers, the timid and the fearful; a wounded doe and an arrow are included in his iconography. From a Christian perspective, the doe's milk symbolizes God's spiritual food, the grace (*dulcedo, suavitas*) offered to the Christian soul. By choosing to be wounded in place of the doe, Giles imitates Christ also wounded, in place of mankind. This is an act of *caritas* like God's charity. This is also an act of chivalry, a sacred chivalry that defends the weak and the helpless from that aristocratic class given over to the pleasures of the chase, in which Giles was born and which he renounced. Dwelling in a cave and nourished by the milk of a doe, Giles has attained a state of security and repose associated with the mother. He then chooses, as a man, to be substituted for the mother, to shed his blood in exchange for the doe's milk, and to become a weak, helpless creature, feminized, in order to lead his life of Christian charity.

But then, at the moment of his discovery by king and bishop, the wounded hermit returns to the public life and becomes a leader of men. First Giles is named abbot of a newly founded monastery. Then he is called to Orleans to confess Charlemagne. Finally, he voyages to Rome to ensure the future of his house. All three acts are performed in the service of the community; all three grant to Giles a measure of sovereignty.

It is obvious that the saint's sovereignty, the end of his quest, is spiritual in nature, not chivalric, and that he is a hero of the Church of Christ, not of the warriors and princes in this world. He points out to Charlemagne that even though he is a victor on the field of battle, yet he is not capable of conquering Satan or his own self (2877–86). Giles, of course, does have that power and uses it. When Charlemagne refuses to confess his sin orally, God sends a letter, a written document recounting the sin, to Giles, who reads it aloud to the emperor. Charles will do all he can for the monastery as will Flovent, but this is not enough. Giles quite properly seeks the support of a greater monarch, Christ's own Vicar in Rome, whose word and whose writing alone can ensure the health of the community. Then, when Giles dies, angels come to take his soul to heaven. Clerks see the angels and hear their 'chant' and 'melodie' (3733). This is told and translated by the canon, Guillaume de Berneville.

Giles begins his quest in Greece and ends it in Rome. He who founded his community, a spiritual family of brothers, attains communion with the spiritual father ('apostoile') of all men. The culmination of the quest occurs in the earthly Rome, a prefiguration of the *civitas Dei*, where the Pope offers to Giles and his monastery the doors of his church, St Peter's, an earthly metaphor for the *portae coeli*, which miraculously, according to God's will, float over the waters to Provence. Giles and his doors undergo the same voyage, the same *peregrinatio*, from East to West, a *translatio studii et sacerdotii* that reaches its final stage when Giles's soul is taken through the real gates of Saint Peter into his real kingdom of heaven; and when, still further in the West, a canon in the priory of St Giles in Cambridgeshire translates and transmits Giles's life to the French-speaking English flock under his jurisdiction, in his own land.

Saint Mary of Egypt

The female version of the confessor or ascetic is less common than the male. It is also less common than the female martyr. This is, no doubt, the case for a variety of historical reasons, including the fact that the public found passive women martyrs a more appropriate subject for devotion and for narrative than their active hermit sisters. Technically, a woman saint can be a virgin, a martyr, a queen, and a repentant sinner but not, strictly speaking, a confessor. The most notable example of the pseudo-confessor (female ascetic) is Mary of Egypt. I shall treat *La Vie de sainte Marie l'Egyptienne* very briefly because Dembowski (1981) has demonstrated that there is no compelling reason to believe that the best and oldest redaction is ultimately of Anglo-Norman origin. (On this text, Cazelles 1979–80, Robertson 1980, and Dembowski 1983.)

Mary's story is that of a repentant prostitute; she is a lover and destroyer of men who sees the light and, for many, many years, dwells in the desert, expiating the seventeen years she had spent wallowing in lust. Whereas Giles is innocent and mortifies his flesh out of love of God and contempt for the things of this world, and whereas Margaret and Catherine remain pure in spite of their woman's nature, Mary is guilty of the worst sins of the flesh and is responsible for the deaths of young men, who kill themselves for her. Like Giles, she travels over water and land, voyaging however to the East not the West, and her trip over water (the feminine element) is the high point in her career of sin, as she corrupts all the men on shipboard, passengers and crew. Yet her retreat into the desert, across the Jordan, is one of penance and expiation, a spiritual quest to the Other World in search of death and rebirth. She mortifies the body that was the cause and the means of her fall. Her false, worldly beauty is transformed into the physical ugliness of a peasant or an animal; this is also the beginning of true spiritual beauty. As a metaphor for this transformation, she survives, nourished on the barest minimum and food from angels. For the first time in her life, having conquered sensuality, Mary comes to know love – the fraternal charity that unites her to the holy monk Zosimus. She is old and very ugly; so presumably is Zosimus. A rich friendship, Christian *amicitia – caritas* – grows between them; each begs the other's benediction, and they arrange a spiritual rendezvous in the wilderness. This is the sacred antitype of a prostitute's lust and of chivalric *fin' amor*.

Mary, a mere woman, knows the dogmas of the faith and manifests grace and ascetic fervour. She prophesies Zosimus' illness and her own death. She is the subject of an angelic letter, informing Zosimus of her name and ordering him to bury her, even though angels with swords had forbidden her to enter church on the Feast of the Ascension. On the one hand, Mary is the antitype of the Mother of God, impure in antithesis to the latter's virginity and sterile in antithesis to her fecundity. Yet they bear the same name and, like Mary Magdalene, Mary of Egypt can be redeemed; she is an Eva capable of salvation through the mediation and the femininity of Ave. Mary of Egypt's prayer to the image of Mary the Virgin in Canaan is the first step in her process of conversion, expiation and salvation. The end result is that her body, like her soul, is redeemed; she expires nude and her flesh is preserved awaiting Christian burial by Zosimus. Because of ascetic and doctrinal fervour, she transcends her state and becomes one with Zosimus, worthy to be a member of his fraternal community. She is a true servant of Christ, in the spirit and the communion of saints.

In the prologues and epilogues to the Anglo-Norman and French *vitae* we find a consistent pattern: the implied authors state that the purpose of their work is to edify the implied readers, causing them to emulate the saint whose life the text recounts. Often the epilogue will evoke the saint's good offices vis-à-vis the author and his public. Writing a saint's life is in and of itself a devotional act done in God's name and to his glory, for the only appropriate, worthy use of one's talent is to praise God. One praises God by translating from the Latin and helping the ignorant lay people, the *illiterati* (therefore the *pauperi*), in their quest for God. These texts are consciously didactic and religious. Yet they are also consciously literary. They proclaim the existence of what Uitti (1975) calls the clerkly narrator figure, whose values and purpose are served through his literary creation; this is also an act of *translatio*, translating and transmitting the culture, wisdom, and holiness, that which is read (*legenda*) in the liturgy, from Latin into French, from the past into the present, from East to West, and from clerical to lay people. Thus is established a professional credo, a duty, and an authority for writing; as a manifestation of medieval Christian humanism, this will have its impact on the newly emerging secular humanism embodied in *chansons de geste* and *romans courtois*.

From a formal perspective, sacred biography resembles epic, romance, and chronicle but has its own fund of themes and motifs of Latin church origin (a number of which are derived from the romances of late Antiquity in Greek). Hagiography can be perceived as containing archetypal epic or romance heroes who function in a supernatural universe. The relations between sacred biography and romance are fascinating (Hurley 1975, Legge 1975, Dembowski 1976, Lewes, 1978). As I see it, in both genres we find a lone protagonist at odds with the community, adventures, heroism, a quest, and a death-rebirth experience. Unlike romance, heroes of sainthood remain humble in our world, attaining power and fame after death in another kingdom. Their movement is not from the forest to acclamation at court but from the court to obscurity in the forest. They are sought by others instead of seeking them, and they renounce a spouse in the beginning in place of winning one in the end. Although theirs is a spiritual quest for knowledge, love, and God, they do not grow more holy in the course of the narrative; instead, they are holy from the beginning and are slowly and surely recognized to be so. Theirs are stories of revelation and recognition, as their sanctity is discovered by the community and as it propels them to the inevitable outcome: in the private sphere, death in God from martyrdom or renunciation; in the public sphere, an example and a lesson for all men.

Among the fundamental structures of the *vita* are two features: the agon, a conflict in which the saint is defeated physically but triumphs spiritually; and the quest, a *peregrinatio* in which the saint flees those who seek him (persecutors or disciples) but attains the kingdom of heaven and also attains or creates a new sacred community of converts. Both the struggle and the quest are paradoxical, given the norms of classical and medieval epic. Theirs is the 'absurd' of the Christian faith – 'credo quia absurdum.' The leap of faith demands the ever-present, ever-intervening deity, for the hopes and fears of the community are projected onto supernatural power in a supernatural kingdom. As Heffernan (1988) has proposed, God breaks into time and history, making his grace, his power, and himself present in his saints. From the audience's perspective, the supernatural is recuperated, integrated, and understood in our world. The stance of the public vis-à-vis the saint is, even more than in the case of an epic or romance protagonist, one of admiration and astonishment. The hagiographic figure, celebrated not analyzed, embodies an ideal of perfection which, *in parvo,* we strive to emulate. Even more, this ideal is a reality of power that can intercede on our behalf with the deity. Miracles and martyrdom testify to God's power to conquer Satan and spare the saint, and also to the saint's power, because of Christ's presence in him and in his relics, to spare us. Hagiography shows how holiness becomes manifest in our world of sin, how virtue can be made visible to mere mortals, and how, in a spirit of celebration, the saint can redeem mankind through communication, by using his powers of intercession.

The saint's life is a story perhaps with historical foundation and embellished by the popular imagination and/or by clerical amplification of the popular imagination, 'un texte popularisant.'[9] The authors have taken a fund of common themes and motifs and elaborated them in a process of condensation, displacement, projection, and crystallization. The *vita* is the typical, highly stylized representation of one reality, the saintly. Even more than other medieval genres, it typifies a classical-Christian aesthetic of theme and register, of archetype and convention, in which the author seeks not to express his originality but to work within the tradition, manipulating and developing the given register and partaking of the given conventions, in the spirit of *translatio* and *imitatio.*[10]

Among other things, the modern world is obsessed with verifiable, empirical, historical veracity. As a result of this obsession, saints' legends have been demystified, and some of Christendom's greatest figures, including Margaret and Catherine, have been removed from the calendar. In the Middle Ages and in the Baroque age people readily believed in a Christian reality of the marvelous: heaven had primacy over earth, symbolic structures over mundane representation, and the celebration of virtue over the authentification of facts. They cared more about goodness, usefulness, beauty, and moral and aesthetic truth in a neoplatonic world-vision than about truth as fact in our empirical sense of the term. In other words, hagiography is one of a number of kinds of writing to be subsumed under the category of rhetoric for the purpose of edification and persuading to the Good. To persuade to the Good, one celebrates virtue and seeks to instil it. The guarantee of the saint's life - if one were needed - lies in the fact that the hagiographic protagonist is holy; therefore, his holiness ensures that his character and deeds are holy - exemplary, appropriate, and ethically authentic. Both sacred biography and history are fine writing; they take Latin books about the past which illustrate a pattern of figurative typology that explains that past and relate it to the present: 'Omnia autem probate, quod bonum est tenete' (I Thess. 5: 21). Whatever the historical reality behind the *vitae*, they defend and illustrate the essence of historical Christianity, the moral ideal and the aesthetic beauty of the early Church and men's early faith. That essence is a message, an ideal, and a beauty which people also crave today.

Conclusion

Anglo-Norman romance had a powerful impact upon romance writing in Middle English. Vernacular English poets relied upon continental as well as insular French models, to be sure; nonetheless, the vast majority of Anglo-Norman texts were translated or freely adapted, a number of them in several versions. The English romancers may well have turned to insular French sources first, especially when they celebrated insular heroes. It has also been proposed that the English romancers adopted the ideological message and the spirit of their Anglo-Norman predecessors (Crane 1986).

The texts I have discussed in this section are representative of the corpus as a whole. Marie de France's legacy in the English vernacular includes a *Lai le Freine* and three versions of *Lanval*, the two most important being a relatively faithful translation, *Sir Landevale* (early fourteenth century), and a much freer adaptation of the story, Thomas Chestre's *Sir Launfal* (later fourteenth century). Although Beroul and Thomas were to be supplanted by the *Prose Tristan*, we have from the late thirteenth century a 'reduction' of Thomas, *Sir Tristrem*, that retains the plot and concentrates on its quotient of adventure. *Amadas et Ydoine* was not adapted into English, although the romance and its hero are cited more often in England than in France, and one Englishman borrowed the famous lover's name for his otherwise unrelated tale of *Sir Amadace*. On the other hand, the fourteenth and fifteenth centuries have bequeathed to us three versions of *Ipomedon* (a faithful, sophisticated translation, *Ipomadon*; a much briefer *Lyfe of Ipomydon*; and an *Ipomedon* in prose) and four versions, complete or in fragments, of *Gui de Warewic*, one in tail rhyme, the others in couplets.

The significance of Anglo-Norman romance extends well beyond the question of its use as source material by later writers, in English and in other languages. The artistic achievements of these early poets and their contribution to world literature are of the first importance.

Marie de France probably invented the narrative Breton lay; she was among the first to elaborate Arthurian myth in the vernacular. Above all, she created masterpieces in terms of psychological analysis, *fin' amor*, symbolism, archetypal narrative, and metafiction treating its own coming into being as art.

Beroul's and Thomas's are the first surviving Tristan romances; the two trouvères are also creators of a great world myth. Each, in his way, subverts contemporary ideals of feudalism and church hegemony. Beroul's world-vision of triumphant passion, of violence, transgression, and deceit and Thomas's world-vision of destructive passion, of jealousy, loneliness, and death – these also are unique in the Middle Ages, and a unique gift to our civilization.

After this first generation of writers, the romance mode is explored and amplified in a variety of ways that can be thought of as early mannerism. Hue de Rotelande's *Ipomedon* appears to be simply an adventure story restating the topoi to be found in Chrétien de Troyes. In fact, *Ipomedon* mocks and undermines the traditional ideals of chivalry and *fin' amor* in a witty, sophisticated text where the protagonist is a trickster hero and author figure who manipulates the other characters and, in so doing, mirrors his witty, sophisticated, manipulative, intrusive author Hue de Rotelande.

Amadas et Ydoine partakes of the idyllic romance structure. The poet explores fictional conventions in which *omnia vincit Amor*, and it is the unmarried heroine, the girl, who assumes the role of protagonist and actant, dominating the plot. The author plays with the idea of the girl as heroine and trickster with a number of standard motifs of *fin' amor* – love sickness, madness, and death – which he turns upside down and pushes to their extreme limits.

Gui de Warewic is the most notable of the ancestral or baronial romances. A good half-dozen Anglo-Norman poets, perhaps acting under the patronage of local magnates, exalted fictional English heroes presumed to be the ancestors of the magnates and whose lives embody the values of the baronry. *Gui de Warewic* recounts the hero's feats in arms and his adventures as a pilgrim. Military prowess coincides with spiritual strength in defining the insular public's notion of rights of inheritance, rights to land, and rights to a place in the hierarchy, but above all serves as a pretext for the telling of great deeds.

In contrast to the romances which demonstrate such extraordinary powers of innovation, the saint's life is a genre grounded in conventionality. Also in contrast to the romances, Anglo-Norman *vitae* had a relatively small impact on sacred biography in English. The number and popularity of *vitae* in French surely encouraged Englishmen to write *vitae* in their own tongue; this said, English writers for the most part turned to the original Latin versions of hagiographic narratives, not the French translations. It has been said that Guillaume de Berneville may have influenced Lydgate's *Legend of Saint Giles*: the matter is far from certain, and research in this area needs to be done. Compared to epic and romance, hagiography still is a neglected topic.

For all the inherently restrictive parameters of the genre, the Anglo-Norman *vitae* offer fascinating patterns of imagery and a fascinating narrative structure. The stories of martyrs (the *Lives* of Lawrence, Margaret, and Catherine) reveal a pattern of physical and verbal struggle between the mighty pagan torturer and his weak Christian victim. Opposition is established between master and slave, gold and food, blood and milk, death and life, flesh and spirit, harsh instruments of torture and soft human bodies, force and the word, man and woman. The passive, enduring victim is often a woman or a man who acts like a woman. Christian paradox justifies how a mere 'pucele' can conquer a dragon in combat or fifty clerks in argument. Because of the paradox, the chaste maiden weds Christ, becomes a mother of thousands of converts and, with her spouse and her heavenly crown, upsets the earthly and satanic powers arrayed against her.

The stories of confessors (the *Lives* of Giles and Mary of Egypt), on the other hand, revolve around a man or, in an exception, a woman who acts like a man. The confessor goes on a quest into the desert; he flees the world in order to discover finer *amicitia* and a more worthy community under sacred auspices. He also commits his own deeds of *fortitudo* and achieves the highest *sapientia* through sacrifice and renunciation. These *vitae*, like the biographies of the martyrs, reveal powerfully archetypal narrative structures, with intertextual reference to other texts and to the genre as a whole. Hagiography, like romance, has its own aura and its own vital typology; the heroism of the sacred is as stylized and as awe-inspiring, in literary and in human terms, as is secular heroism.

The two genres have influenced each other ever since the Hellenistic age. By the twelfth and thirteenth centuries, we find romancers adapting for secular purposes a number of crucial sacred themes, including, among others, the spiritual quest for love, knowledge, and God, the idea and ideal of initiation, and the clerkly narrator figure as implied author. The hagiographers not only borrow from secular narrative a penchant for description, monologue, dialogue, and even a version of 'curteisie,' they also pay romance the compliment of condemnation, intentionally slanting their themes, motifs, and conscious ideology in terms of antiromance. *Gui de Warewic* is truly an 'exemplary romance' that combines elements of heroism and hagiography, of prowess, courtesy, and piety; on a different register, from the opposite perspective, so also does *La Vie de saint Gilles*.

The result is two powerful literary modes, each with its own intertextual matrix and conventional imagery. Both modes give expression to the deepest sentiments of the age. They explore the farthest reaches of the human condition and the highest stretches of the imagination. They are profoundly archetypal in essence; romance and *vita* helped shape new myths that have enriched the Western consciousness ever since.

PART TWO

The Continental French Legacy

Introduction

Most histories of English literature do not pay special attention to the Anglo-Norman phenomenon. A number that do work around the fact that, after all, the central focus of literature in French was located on the Continent. However, aristocratic and royal patrons of literature in English, and authors practising the English vernacular, were as aware of what was being written in France as they were of French literary practice closer to home. French writers were invited to England; French manuscripts were collected on the Continent; continental books were read and translated. The very fact that Englishmen, whether of Norman or Anglo-Saxon extraction, tended to regard their own French – Anglo-Norman French – as being linguistically inferior to the standard of Paris or Chartres or Blois, and that they sent their sons abroad for the linguistic experience, reinforces my point that the people in England, to the extent they were Francophone (whether by birth or by acquisition), formed part of a European cultural matrix that was never limited to the British Isles. It is significant that of the two earliest English verse romances – *King Horn* and *Floris and Blauncheflur* – one is the adaptation of an Anglo-Norman ancestral romance celebrating a native English hero and the other the translation of a central French idyllic romance with no English ties at all. For the verse romance, for the devotional treatise, and for other genres, the central French impact will rival the Anglo-Norman. For the later courtly tradition in the Chaucerian vein, for sacred allegory, and for prose romance, the continental impact will dominate. It is impossible to measure the French presence in Middle English letters without taking into account the entire tradition, from all the regions of *langue d'oil*.

Once this is recognized, other problems arise. Some accounts of the Middle Ages in English discuss French books up to the *Romance of the Rose*: the *Song of Roland*, Wace, Marie, Chrétien, and, of course, Guillaume de Lorris and Jean de Meun. These studies, concerned primarily with English literature, naturally enough treat the preceding French and Anglo-Norman tradition as background for Chaucer, the Alliterative Revival, and Malory. The immediate French contemporaries of Chaucer and Langland inevitably attract less notice. An unintentional side effect of this phenomenon (which itself can be ascribed to what has been called Whig literary history) would be the impression that French ceased to be of major importance once English reappeared.

However, it is not fair to blame Anglicists (of the past) alone for the phenomenon. Specialists in medieval French studies for generations were subject to Romantic literary history – the assumption that, in the Middle Ages, the truly great works are the oldest because they are the purest, the most authentic, and the closest to the *Geist*. Therefore, general studies on French literature cited, for the Middle Ages, *Roland*, Chrétien, and perhaps *Tristan*, and then jumped to Villon. The period from 1200 to 1450 was considered one of decline because it was *literary* and did not reflect the qualities that scholars thought they saw and wanted to see in the earliest texts. Late *chansons de geste*, late *romans courtois*, and late poets such as Machaut were not studied seriously until the 1960s. The first serious, modern scholarly edition of the *Prose Lancelot* dates from 1978–83; there is still no serious, modern scholarly edition of Guillaume de Digulleville. It is a fact that many a French literary history or general survey of literature, to this day, refers only in passing and, at best, with measured praise to the later Middle Ages.

One can hardly blame Anglicists for taking French literature as Frenchmen gave it to them. The result, however, can lead to historical and critical distortion. Distortion in history occurs when scholars do not take into account the passing of generations and the change in literary taste; for example, Chaucer knew and had a high opinion of late medieval French books but the Whig and the Romantic critics tend to ignore this fact. It is perhaps a mistake to look for Chaucer's Arthurian allusions in Chrétien when it is almost certain that Chaucer, like everyone else in his century, and Malory's, received his French Arthurian education from the *Prose Lancelot*. It is perhaps a mistake to compare Chaucer only to Guillaume de Lorris and Jean de Meun when he also knew and made major intertextual use of Machaut and Froissart. Distortion in criticism occurs when English professors give French books the same aesthetic valuation that Romance philologists gave them a generation or a century ago and, therefore, are not loath to demonstrating Chaucer's superiority over the entire French court tradition or Malory's superiority over the entire *Prose Lancelot* and *Prose Tristan*.

In this section I discuss seven French books: a comic-adventure epic, *Huon de Bordeaux*; the greatest of the romance cycles, the *Prose Lancelot*; the most important of the dream-vision allegories, *Le Roman de la Rose*; the major sacred allegories of the time, Guillaume de Digulleville's *Pèlerinage de la Vie humaine* and *Pèlerinage de l'Ame*; four of Guillaume de Machaut's sophisticated, self-referential tales of love; Froissart's *Chroniques* of the French and English wars; and Alain Chartier's court debate poem, *La Belle Dame sans mercy*, that rounds out the centuries' discussion of *fin' amor*. The seven works extend from 1210 to 1425, covering the epoch of French literature that once was neglected by scholars. It is the literature of this period that offered the richest legacy to writing in English. Some of these books will be little known to many Anglicists; a few of them may be little known to Romance scholars. They all had a powerful impact upon English writing in the Middle Ages and the Renaissance and upon the overall development of English culture. Among the elements in this tradition bequeathed to the English are great myths of love and heroism, the interlace technique of adventure romance, the allegorical personification technique, the mode of the first-person dream vision, courtly sophistication and metatextual self-referentiality, disjunction and deferral, and the notion of chivalry as part of history, contributing to the national myth.

I propose to examine the seven books from a modern critical perspective, using approaches that correspond to and reflect the kinds of reading proposed by the medieval French critics since the 1960s. It is this more modern scrutiny and revaluation of French literature that corresponds to the comparable scrutiny and revaluation in Middle English. I wish to make the claim that much of what traditional Anglicists considered to be Chaucer's or Malory's originality vis-à-vis the French was instead a direct borrowing from the continental tradition. It is my belief that the characteristic traits, the modes, and the mind-set of the Ricardian Age do reflect, because they are derived from, centuries of literate Frenchness, just as so much of the English romance world, including Malory, also reflects, because it is derived from, centuries of literate Frenchness. Outlook, ideology, structure, style, and myth are transmitted as they are translated, adapted, amplified, and elaborated by writers in English. Not only French courtliness but the entire medieval French secular world is Englished; it forms an integral part of the historic European totality.

1. *Huon de Bordeaux*

One of the most fascinating anomalies of both Anglo-Norman and Middle English literature is the absence of epic, epic in the tradition of *chanson de geste*. It is true that a number of the oldest and greatest French *chansons* – *Roland* (in its first version), *Guillaume*, *Gormond et Isembard*, and *Le Pèlerinage de Charlemagne* – survive only in single Anglo-Norman manuscripts. This proves that, in twelfth- and thirteenth-century England, a public existed for *chansons de geste*, a conservative public that esteemed texts gone out of fashion on the Continent. Still, of the seventy-five to one hundred extant *chansons*, none is of specifically Anglo-Norman provenance, composed by an Anglo-Norman trouvère. In addition, the genre had relatively little impact in Middle English. A few adaptations, mostly of second-rate texts, were produced, that today are called 'Charlemagne romances,' one among a number of subdivisions in the over-all category 'romance.' The leading importer of Charlemagne romance was Caxton, following a Burgundian trend, at the very end of the medieval era.

This phenomenon can perhaps be accounted for (1) because the *chanson de geste* is an old genre, its high point in France extending from 1100 to 1230, so that by the time Englishmen began to write seriously in English on a large scale it had passed from vogue; and (2) because the genre was associated with the aspirations and dynastic claims of the French royal family, whereas the competing Norman and Plantagenet dynasties encouraged a radically different subject matter and literary mode. Thus the 'Matter of France' was embodied in French epic. The 'Matter of Britain,' specifically the legend of King Arthur, was embodied in French, Anglo-Norman, and, later, English romance.

Finally, as we have seen, the 'Matter of England' or ancestral romance, sometimes composed in the *chanson de geste* style (irregular monorhymed laisses), told the deeds of great English heroes, the putative ancestors of the Anglo-Norman baronry, and reflected their hopes and aspirations. This ancestral romance mode fulfilled the need for epic; indeed it was the epic par excellence of the Anglo-Normans. English writers then adapted these texts into English. They also created other works that can be called epic, that fulfilled their need for stories of heroism, such as Layamon's *Brut* and the alliterative *Morte Arthure*.

However, one French *chanson de geste* had a lasting impact on English literary culture – the great thirteenth-century text, *Huon de Bordeaux* (1212–29). This masterpiece gave rise to five sequels in the *chanson de geste* format, all preserved in a manuscript dated 1311: *Esclarmonde*, *Clarisse et Florent*, *Yde et Olive*, *La Chanson de Godin*, and *Le Roman d'Auberon*. *Le Roman d'Auberon* serves as a prologue to the cycle; it treats the genealogy and early history of the king of the fairies, associating him with Judas Maccabaeus, Saint George, and the Flight into Egypt. The original *Huon de Bordeaux* and the first sequels were then adapted into Alexandrines. A prose *Huon* from 1454 or 1455, printed in 1513, went through eleven sixteenth-century editions. It gave rise to the popular chapbook version of the Bibliothèque Bleue, which led in turn to the Comte de Tressan's treatment in *Corps d'Extraits de Romans de chevalerie* (1782). These various *rifacimenti* concentrate on episode, adventure, war, love, and, above all, the supernatural.

It is the Michel le Noir prose edition of *Huon de Bordeaux* (1513) that was turned into English prose, probably between 1517 and 1520, by Sir John Bourchier, second Lord Berners, who also translated Froissart and *Le petit Artus de Bretagne*. *The Boke of Duke Huon of Burdeux* was published in 1534, perhaps earlier, with two later editions coming out in 1570 and 1601. Berners's version, which has been called the last English book of the Middle Ages, ensured Huon and Auberon a long vogue in high and then popular culture in England, although the principal characters and their story had already made an impact in the two previous centuries. For at least one hundred years Duke Huon was included among the Worthies of History. It is to Berners's version that Spenser alludes in the *Faerie Queene*. It is from Berners, and therefore from *Huon de Bordeaux* (and perhaps from a contemporary Elizabethan play, non-extant), that Shakespeare took his Oberon, king of the fairies, in *A Midsummer Night's Dream*, and made of him one of the great mythical characters in literaure. Because the *Huon* epic is relatively little known to Anglicists, or even to medieval French scholars, I shall devote a chapter to the study of this poem, one of the seminal texts of its age.

Exiled from France by Charlemagne and accompanied by a small troop of followers, Huon travels to Rome and Jerusalem and then, against good advice, traverses a forest inhabited by the redoubtable fairy king, Auberon. Contrary to expectations, Auberon befriends Huon, offers him magic gifts, and swears to come to his assistance when necessary. Huon then undergoes a series of adventures culminating in his challenge to the emir of Babylon. Imprisoned by the emir, Gaudisse, he is succoured by Gaudisse's daughter, Esclarmonde. The youth eventually triumphs over the Saracens (with the help of Auberon's army) and takes Esclarmonde home to be his bride. After further adventures – a storm at sea, seizure by pirates, and further battles with Saracen armies – Huon, Esclarmonde, and their band escape to France with a treasure. Further acts of treachery give rise to further adventures before the inevitable happy ending.

Rossi (1975) has shown that *La Chanson de Huon de Bordeaux* has a tangible political dimension. The first and last sections of the poem make up a frame narrative that treats the theme of royal injustice. Huon the good vassal is badly treated by the emperor, who is associated with and influenced by several villains: the traitor Amauri, Charles's weakling son Charlot, and Huon's own brother Gérard. 'Malvais iretier' are contrasted with Huon, the exemplar of a good son and heir. The king acts from the worst of motives: avarice, jealousy, envy, flattery, and drunkenness. It is possible that one reason for the story's popularity in England was this conflict between a Francophone baron and a French king, between Bordeaux and Paris, with implicit reference to the contemporary, historical resistance of Aquitaine and Bordeaux to French hegemony for three full centuries.

Although these political episodes are of interest in their own right, and the poet and his public were concerned with such issues, structurally the disinheriting-treason material serves as a frame for the quest. The fundamental structural increment of the narrative is the romance quest (also an epic quest), which provides an excuse for adventure. More than once Huon rejects the suggestion that he adhere to his mission. On the contrary, he says, he has come to the Orient for the sake of adventure, and it will have priority:

> – 'Sire, dist Hues ...
> Jou ne lairoie por vo grant disnité
> Que jou ne voise le gaiant visiter;

Car por çou vin ge de France le rené,
Por aventures et enquerre et trover.' (4617; 4619–22)

– 'Sire Geriaumes, dist Huelins li frans,
Por l'amor Dieu, c'alés vous dementant?
Tres puis cele eure de France fui tornant,
Si m'aït Dix, n'aloië el querant
Fors aventures, ce saciés vraiemant.' (4716–20)

'Sire,' said Huon, ... 'for all your great power, I will not fail to go visit the giant; for that is why I came from the kingdom of France, to seek and find adventures.' ... 'Sir Gériaume,' said the noble Huelin, 'for the love of God, why are you lamenting? Know this in truth: since that hour I left France, so help me God, I have sought nothing but adventures.'

Once the youth leaves Jerusalem, he enters an exotic, magical realm which bears little resemblance to the real world of the thirteenth century. Great cities, vast armies, uncountable riches, and wonders of all kinds appear along Huon's route. The trouvère creates a stylized, highly evocative portrait of the East, a pagan (Muslim) world replete with elements of the supernatural. *Huon de Bordeaux* is drenched in the marvellous; the supernatural has become natural and appears to be the only possible way of life. It is this omnipresence of the supernatural, of *chanson de geste* faerie, added to the dazzle, sheen, and riches of the Orient, that so impress Huon the protagonist and his audience.

Huon's career illustrates, more than that of any other French epic hero, the archetypes of romance and the stylized quest pattern of withdrawal and return that is traditional to heroic-romantic literature everywhere. Like the Anglo-Norman saints, Huon crosses sea and land. He traverses a desert, and on more than one occasion his road leads through a 'bos.' Auberon's power extends over one of these forests; he himself is perhaps derived from or partakes of the Merlin Sylvester figure. The dark forest embodies for Huon, as for medieval man generally, the deepest elements of adventure and of the unconscious, to be resisted and to be overcome.

Water barriers also must be crossed; feminine symbols, they stand for the mystery of primeval nature. On his return voyage across the Mediterranean, Huon's boat capsizes during a storm and more than once he is left naked and abandoned, 'Tout aussi nu comme au jor qu'il fu nés' (6841, repeated seven other times) [as naked as the day he was born]. As a 'sauvages hom' (7196), a wild man and an outcast, Huon experiences a symbolic death and rebirth. The young hero risks dying through immersion and expects to perish, but survives to participate in a new life.

It is significant that to the extent to which Huon's adventures are inherently sexual in nature, they lend themselves to a Jungian or Freudian reading. The adversaries are demonic figures: Oede the renegade, who violates the laws of hospitality and family; ogres such as the giant Orgueilleux and his brother Agrapart, cannibals kin to devils in hell; and the pagan emirs Gaudisse and Yvorin. These are hostile father figures, competing masculine adversaries, who dwell in threatening castles or towers. All three of the towers (Tormont, Dunostre, and Babylon) serve as jails with dungeons where good people languish. Dunostre and Babylon assume the form of a maze or labyrinth, surrounding an inner sanctum redolent with the mysteries which Huon must penetrate. They are defended by serpents or serpent figures such as the sword-wielding automatons that guard Dunostre. At Babylon custom declares that a French, Christian visitor will have one hand severed at the first bridge, the other at the second, a foot at the third, and his remaining foot at the fourth, whereupon guards will carry him before Gaudisse to be decapitated. This sadistic castration imagery is repeated on the Christian side, given that Huon was sent to the Orient specifically to slay the first knight he beholds at the emir's table, to kiss Gaudisse's daughter three times, and to bring back a hoard of treasure including a thousand maidens plus hairs from the pagan monarch's beard and his four molar teeth (2364–70).

It is most important that Huon is aided in his quest by his followers, by helpful nature figures, by talismans (one of which, a magic horn, has phallic overtones), by his goodness and valour, and also by the beautiful maidens whose path he crosses. These maidens – Sebile, Esclarmonde, and Yvorin's daughter – all Ariadne figures, seduced by his skill in arms and by his beauty, help him defeat the ogre. Significantly, Sebile is Orgueilleux's prisoner, prize, and perhaps mistress; and Esclarmonde and Yvorin's daughter (otherwise nameless) owe filial hommage and affection to the emirs who oppose the youth. Therefore, in all three cases the girl betrays her father, master, or lover in favour of the handsome stranger. In all three Huon defeats the adversary in war and in love; indeed his erotic victory precedes and is responsible for his victory in arms. This is the archetypal male wish-fulfilment fantasy where an anima figure helps him defeat an ogre and then offers herself as his prize.

In love as in war, Huon defeats old men. He wins the affection of beautiful maidens and survives. To do so he must defy the Saracen potentates who guard them. Despite their jailers, however, the young women aid Huon in fulfilling his quest. The four greybeards (three emirs and a giant), whatever their function in the narrative, are father or husband surrogates; Huon then plays the role of a young lover who opposes their will and wins the maiden(s) for himself. Denying the sexual repression promulgated in a male world, he successfully harmonizes the demands of the pleasure and reality principles. The id frees itself from the superego, the sons from their fathers, and the weak from the strong. Huon comes alive in the more feminine world of the East (forest, ocean, prison, and maze), a world of sensuality and luxury; he dies and is reborn to beautiful women who rightly prefer him to the stern *duri patres* ruling their lives. Thus youth triumphs over age and nature has its way, as in so much of world literature, ancient, medieval, and modern.

From an English perspective, most important is the role played by Auberon, king of the fairies, as Huon's protector and mentor. He is the major factor in Huon's success and, aesthetically speaking, the most striking character in the poem, destined to acquire greater fame than the young duke himself. Since Auberon's father was Julius Caesar and his mother was Morgan la Fée, he partakes of the classical and Arthurian world, inheriting the power and wisdom of both. He appears to be all but freed from the limits of mortality; he is a practitioner of white magic who serves God's will, possesses the secrets of heaven, and is assured one day of sitting next to God:

> 'De paradis sai jou tous les secrés
> Et oi les angles la sus u ciel canter,
> Nen viellirai ja mais en mon aé,
> Et ens la fin, quant je vaurai finer,
> Aveuqes Dieu est mes sieges posés.' (3579–83)

'I know all the secrets of paradise and I hear the angels sing up there in heaven. I shall never grow old and, at the end of my span, whenever I wish to pass away, my throne is waiting, next to God.'

As a non-hostile divine agent acting on the hero's behalf, an outside dispenser of justice who rectifies the evil perpetrated by villains (Frye's 1957G archetype of the wise old man with magical powers), he symbolizes the benign, protective force of destiny. Archetypally, the gifts of power and wisdom are accompanied by a corresponding mutilation – Auberon is a 'nains bocerés' [hunchbacked dwarf]. Yet he also possesses beauty equal to the sun's; he is a light and sun figure blessing and making fecund all he touches.

It will not surprise anyone that Huon, an orphan who has lost his real father and has been betrayed by Charlemagne, should be, symbolically at least, searching for a father substitute. Given that Auberon, presumably unmarried and childless, has equal need of a son and heir, it is natural that, at the denouement, Huon becomes Auberon's child, joins his family, and will inherit his fairy kingdom. He will replace his new father and presumably become a father in turn (as he does in the sequels). Huon chooses Auberon, a 'good father,' over Charlemagne, a 'bad father.' Auberon, the judge of Gaudisse and Charlemagne, who brings an army to overthrow them, is the supernatural father surrogate his predestined child has been seeking. Therefore, the story of Auberon and Huon becomes one of initiation and the succession of male generations, from father to son.

The symbolic father-son relationship between Auberon and Huon also helps explain the contention, competition, and latent hostility that surfaces between them. On seven occasions Huon consciously and wilfully defies his mentor. Auberon ordered Huon not to summon him with the magic horn except in an emergency; Huon blows the horn to test it. He commands Huon not to visit the renegade Oede at Tormont; the youth goes there intentionally. A second time Huon sends for Auberon when not in mortal danger. Again Auberon begs his disciple not to seek a fight with Orgueilleux; Huon visits Dunostre with a view to challenging him. The fairy king tells him never to lie; in Babylon Huon declares he is a Saracen. He forbids the boy to sleep with Esclarmonde before their marriage; Huon rapes her on the ship returning to France. Finally, the paladin once again sends for help when not in mortal danger and once again lies.

This said, we have no reason to doubt that the audience's sympathy and empathy remain with the Duke of Bordeaux throughout the story of his career. Like Tristan and Ipomedon, he can do no wrong, and those who oppose him are at fault. His goodness is absolute, a given of the plot and not open to discussion. This is shown by the fact that Huon himself never expresses regrets or remorse over his actions; he simply refuses to accept Auberon's value-judgments or to play the game according to Auberon's rules.

Secondly, since the youth has suffered from the power exerted over him by bad father surrogates such as Charlemagne and Gaudisse, he has reached a point where he refuses to obey the good father surrogate as well. Why should Huon obey one father figure, Auberon, when the others have been so cruel to him? In essence, he calls into question all parental authority, whatever domination is placed upon him. Expelled from France and the French feudal world, in the fantasy world of the Orient he calls into question the feudal hierarchy and the values it upholds (Adler 1963, Calin 1966, Rossi 1975). To the extent that Auberon, as a symbolic master and a father, represents hierarchy and wields power, Huon calls him into question also. At the heart of the Oedipus complex lies the struggle between son and father, between symbolic id and symbolic superego. Benevolent as Auberon is, from Huon's perspective the king of the fairies embodies the superego; he is a blocking figure, one seeking to control, channel, and impede the youth's vital spirits. As such, he is overthrown.

One aspect of Huon's character is his humanity which breaks through the conventional trappings of the epic and romance protagonist. Thus are to be explained traits of character both physical and unheroic. The youth suffers from bouts of hunger and is driven to excess because of his appetite for wine. Secondly, on more than one occasion he manifests fear; indeed he lies and transgresses out of cowardice. Huon is also prone to tears. He weeps throughout the diegesis at every moment of crisis. Although weeping (symptomatic of a passionate, even violent emotive life) was typical of the feudal period, Huon, like Lanval, cries too much; and fear, natural to an ordinary mortal, is unworthy in a hero of his grandeur.

Finally, whereas Auberon and Huon's tutor Gériaume, both older men, take a conservative, puritanical stand toward the duke's relationship with Esclarmonde, forbidding the couple to make love before they wed, Huon reacts to sex differently. Desiring Esclarmonde on the boat, he takes her in spite of the greybeards, exulting in his passion and its fulfilment. On a desert island he encourages his fiancée to make love again:

> 'Acolons nous, se morrons plus soef;
> Tristrans morut por bele Iseut amer,
> Si ferons nous, moi et vous, en non Dé.' (6848–50)

'Let us embrace, we will die more sweetly. Tristan died for love of fair Isolt; we shall do the same, you and I, in God's name.'

Then, after they have been reunited, Huon must be separated from Esclarmonde the one night they spend in an abbey. If they slept together, says the narrator, Huon would surely have had his will of her and profaned the holy place.

Huon's humanity, his physicality manifest in body, desire, and fear, his dependence on physical comfort, his impetuosity, foolhardy courage, forgetfulness, naïve boasting, and even his weeping are associated with youth. He is a child, an 'enfes,' the 'baceler,' the 'petit orfenin'; the above are all manifestations of childishness ('grant enfanche,' 2671), traits ascribed to the young and forgiven all the more readily because so often in literature and in real life *jovens* sets the standards for society as a whole; the admirable traits in a child – purity, generosity, and enthusiasm – more than offset the liabilities. As Johnson (1975) observes, the 'enfes' is thus assimilated even to Abel and Jesus.

The young Duke of Bordeaux refuses to live up to an artificial, social code imposed on him from the outside; he refuses to live up to a code of literature. Starving as an inner discipline, confronting death as a proof of heroism, and declining with ascetic contempt the gift of a Saracen princess – this is the stereotyped, expected behaviour of characters in a book, of paladins in *chansons de geste*. Yet, as a guide to conduct and behaviour, they mean nothing to Huon. He will not be forced by an artificial literary doctrine beyond the bounds of human nature. The youth refuses to place himself in situations normal for a hero of romance but in conflict with everyday common sense. The poet mocks literary conventions; he contrasts the animal vitality of everyday life to the rigid conventions in the city of books.

Like Chrétien de Troyes's *Cligés* and Hue de Rotelande's *Ipomedon*, *Huon de Bordeaux* is a text that exalts chivalry and undermines it at the same time. There is heroism and romance in this poem, and also comedy. The hero's physicality underscores the Bergsonian contrast between the ideal and the actual, between man's intellectual pretensions and the physical elements that also make up the human condition. According to Bergson (1950G: 39), 'Est comique tout incident qui appelle notre attention sur le physique d'une personne alors que le moral est en cause.'

A second Bergsonian element is repetition. As we saw, on seven occasions Huon defies his master. He reacts like an automaton opposing whatever counsel Auberon offers, however logical, and opposing whatever command Auberon utters, however peremptory. A humorous effect is created by the element of repetition, central to the notion of 'raideur mécanique.' Bergson's image of the jack-in-the-box is appropriate to this context.

Although the comic aspect of Huon's persona is brought out most clearly in his rapport with Auberon, the latter does not exist merely as a foil. How often he is obstructed and baffled by Huon! Yet, though blustering with rage and indignation, each time he forgives the prodigal son. The comic element in his nature springs from a tension between fierceness and good nature, blindness and lucidity, the righteous condemnation of a judge and the loving forgiveness of a father. He acts and reacts, back and forth, also like a jack-in-the-box.

Auberon and Huon, each a comic character in his own right, interact to form a comic pair. Repeatedly Auberon will be angry at his protégé. He will rage against the paladin's folly, in his presence or from a distance. Huon, fully aware of Auberon's wrath and his own guilt, becomes terribly afraid. Then, moved by the pitiful condition into which the youth has fallen, Auberon will take pity on him, restoring him to favour and giving him another chance. But, as Huon gains confidence in himself, he ceases to dread Auberon. In response to Auberon's affection he demonstrates indifference and a stronger chafing at his master's domination. When, in order to assert independence, Huon defies the magician, this act unleashes rage and his own misfortune. Both characters return to the point from which they began, and the action is launched once again. The inner pattern of the narrative is thus circular; the increments, repeated and extended, make up *Huon*'s total comic structure.

The structure is rendered so inevitable because it follows directly from the two main characters' personality traits and from the initial situation in which the trouvère placed them. Neither can exist without the other. Auberon is a great king but childless and seemingly friendless. He seeks affection and an heir, someone on whom to bestow his favour. He chooses Huon by chance, without the latter's deserving such good fortune. Huon, on the other hand, is an orphan who has been disinherited. He has already been mistreated by one father surrogate (the king) and must defy and conquer another (the emir). He is proud and independent, a young rebel lacking altruism, concerned only with his personal love of adventure and quest for glory. Auberon should be the dominant figure in their relationship, since he possesses the riches, wisdom, and power without which Huon cannot survive. Nevertheless, the king of the fairies is disempowered by the very emotional involvement with a youth who, indifferent, defies his patron, knowing he will be forgiven in the end. Huon is the master; he knows it and acts on it. The author has constructed a parody on the traditional familial relationship; the father suffers at the son's hands and is held up to ridicule by the son. The insolence with which Huon treats his benefactor is different in style, but not in kind, from that of *Le Roman de Renart* and the earthiest of fabliaux.

For all the rigidity and repetition manifested by patron and protégé independently, and by the two of them as a team, the comedy in this text is not uniquely Bergsonian; a Bergsonian analysis alone will not account for its literary reality. Huon is the image of freedom and animal vitality, and of quick wits triumphing over custom and inertia. By refusing to obey, he acts far more authentically than his entourage. He denies oedipal guilt and any form of predetermined ethical conduct. He acts freely and naturally in the face of literary constraint or conventional artifice, constraint and artifice that embody the Bergsonian 'raideur mécanique' more than he does. Furthermore, although he and Auberon appear to lack the resilience of human nature at its best, the public sympathizes with their changeability because it sets into relief the conflict of words and deeds, theory and practice, intellectual construct and empirical reality; and because, unlike literary stereotypes, genuine human beings do, at one time or another, act in a humorous, that is, unnatural manner. Comedy often requires distance, a lack of emotional involvement from the public. But no less often the public, while recognizing a man's foibles, will also empathize, even identify with him, seeing themselves and all of humanity in him. For these reasons, in a Dickensian rather than Molièresque mode, we laugh as much with Huon and Auberon as we do at them, sympathizing and empathizing with them, sharing their joy and freedom, their rage and rebellion, their heroic strength and their all too human, too lovable, less than heroic weakness.

Huon's quest anticipates the career of the *pícaro* as well as it parallels the voyage of the Arthurian knight. These French pilgrims to the Orient are aided by supernatural beings from a fairy land; they also get out of more than one scrape by their quick wits and agile tongues. Huon exploits Auberon's magical gifts and undermines them at the same time. Failing to heed his mentor's advice, he achieves a victory all the more spectacular. And his 'foleté' adds salt to the recital of his exploits. Perhaps he is a 'fool,' but an invincible one, committed to festivity and the affirmation of life; he is a trickster hero and a sacred fool, sacred to the extent that he is protected by the supernatural and that he serves as a moral barometer by means of which we judge the world.

Comic catharsis is achieved by sympathy and ridicule instead of pity or terror; here sympathy plays at least as great a role as its companion. The protagonist is a heroic, Christian adolescent. Although he is guilty of 'foleté' and 'desmesure,' we laugh at these faults. The young duke triumphs over his world and the public triumphs with him. The comedy in *Huon de Bordeaux* is one of rapidity, enthusiasm, and love. The heroism and the comedy express a sense of the richness and beauty of life, and the closeness of poet and public to the realities of existence. Humour and romance both contribute to an aesthetic of joy, the conversion of the *senex iratus* to the values of youth, and the triumph of youth and of reformed age through adventure and laughter. Sin and death are overcome. Mankind endures.

Sir John Bourchier, who adapted the expanded *Huon*, was one of a number of English noblemen eager to translate from the French in the late medieval, Burgundian age. Lord Rivers and Sir Thomas Malory are other notable examples. The last of the great medieval translators, Berners chose high courtly French romance and chronicle, the genres most appropriate as models for the English literary revival of his day. He shifted some discourse from indirect to direct and other discourse from direct to indirect; he deleted some repetitions and battle descriptions, adding moral or didactic material. All in all, following medieval practice, Berners as a translator is most accurate and faithful to the original.

Like the other translators, he was concerned with the moral and didactic facets of his *oeuvre*, and with how belles-lettres could contribute to civic life in the community. Even more, Berners loved a good story. His work, as Lewis has said (1954: 149-56), blends the fantasy of vital legend with homely, realistic detail. His is a work and a world of pure myth, story-telling, and youthful élan. As such, it reproduces much of the archetypal spirit of the original. Above all, Berners equalled Malory in his capacity to transmit the French legacy of heroism, chivalry, and romance to an English public that would make it totally its own.

2. *The Prose Lancelot*

Marie de France, Beroul, Thomas, and Chrétien de Troyes had some influence on medieval literature in English. Two of Marie's *lais* (*Lanval* and *Fresne*) were adapted into Middle English, as were Thomas's *Tristan* and Chrétien's *Yvain*, and probably also the *Conte du Graal*. Nonetheless, the impact of the great early classics in Old French verse proved to be no greater than that of their successors. The unknown poets of *Floire et Blancheflor*, *Partonopeus de Blois*, and *Guillaume de Palerne*, for example, were as well and as assiduously translated as Marie and Chrétien. The Anglo-Norman verse romance and works in the ancestral or baronial tradition such as *Ipomedon*, *Gui de Warewic*, and *Boeve de Haumtone* also found a place, at least as great as that of Marie, Thomas, and Chrétien.

One explanation for this state of affairs is the fact that in the twelfth and thirteenth centuries relatively little was written in English. The literate clergy and aristocracy read and wrote Latin and French. By the fourteenth and fifteenth centuries, when a public for texts in English came into being and when texts were provided for them, the tradition of French verse romance now covered at least two centuries. In addition, the pre-eminence modern scholars (rightly or wrongly) grant to the generation of 1150–80 does not reflect the aesthetic response of either francophones or anglophones in the 1350s. The English translator or adapter had a mass of romance material from over two centuries to choose from. He took material from continental and Anglo-Norman sources without prejudice, but he leaned toward narratives whose subject matter related to his own land, England, and to English heroes.

More important is the fact that by 1350, or for that matter by 1250, prose had displaced verse as the natural medium for French romance. (The two modes did coexist for a good century, however.) Beroul and Thomas survive in fragments and Chrétien in a handful of manuscripts, yet the *Prose Lancelot* and the *Prose Tristan* survive literally in the hundreds. This was also the state of affairs for up-to-date readers of French in England. When Chaucer and Gower allude to Lancelot or Tristan, they allude to the prose cycles of the thirteenth century, not the verse classics of the twelfth, which had gone out of fashion. Then, a century later, when Malory provides England with her greatest Arthurian text, one that would maintain the Arthurian myth in England for centuries and make it part of English history, he naturally translated sections of the French *Prose Lancelot* and *Prose Tristan*. Similarly, Caxton reinvigorated English with a dozen translations of heroic narrative, all taken from French prose.

In France the shift from verse to prose occurred at the beginning of the thirteenth century, in England at the end of the fifteenth. French prose is associated with texts in Latin – with the writing of history, and with Holy Scripture. The use of prose implies, under the influence of history and chronicle, a quest for truth or the illusion of a quest for truth, and a quest for the sacred, the desire to enrich the world of chivalry by superimposing on it the universe of Christian faith. The shift from verse to prose, coinciding with the constitution of epic cycles, even the cycle of the beast epic (*Le Roman de Renart*), also brings in its wake the lengthening of narrative. Stories of medium length become interminable; they concern not a few feats of valour but a hero's lifetime or the feats of a group of heroes or exploits that cover generations. Because of the historical and biblical impulse, the author also scrutinizes the beginnings of the dynasty or the kingdom.

The *Prose Lancelot*, c.1210–c.1240, is the first and the best of the great prose romance cycles.[11] Its survival in hundreds of manuscripts and dozens of printed editions and its impact, through translation and adaptation, in England, Germany, Italy, Spain, and Portugal make it the most important single romance of the Middle Ages. There are three principal sections: the gigantic *Lancelot propre*, recounting the story of the fall of Lancelot's parents, his education, and above all his exploits in the service of King Arthur and his passion for Queen Guinevere; *La Queste del saint Graal*, telling of the quest for the Holy Grail by King Arthur's knights, culminating in the mystical death and apocalyptic victory of Galahad; and *La Mort le roi Artu*, treating the decline and fall of

Arthurian chivalry and the destruction of Arthur, Guinevere, and Lancelot. Later were added, in typical medieval fashion, sections meant to precede the main narrative; they recount the origins and fill in whatever had been 'left out' of the original story: an *Estoire* concerning the origins and history of the Grail from the days of Joseph of Arimathea; a *Merlin* concerning the birth of Arthur and his coming to power; and a *Suite du Merlin* concerning the early history of Arthur's realm up to the arrival of Lancelot. The *Estoire* and the *Suite du Merlin* are perhaps of doubtful literary value, compared to the rest. However, all six branches of the Cycle contributed to disseminating the ideals of chivalry and the glory of King Arthur. A good dozen Middle English romances are partially or entirely dependent on sections of the French *Prose Lancelot*. These include some relatively mediocre texts and also masterpieces in the line of *Morte Arthure* and *Le Morte Darthur*. Of all foreign romances, the *Prose Lancelot* had the most decisive impact on the evolution of romance in English.

A question that has preoccupied scholars for almost a century concerns the relative unity of the *Prose Lancelot* as a whole. Opinions remain divided. My own conviction, rejoining that of Lot (1918) and Micha (1976, 1987), states that the *Lancelot propre*, the *Queste*, and *La Mort Artu* do evidence a coherence, unity, and purposefulness of subject matter, theme, motif, and design; they are quite possibly the work of one writer.[12] The grand design treats the rise and fall of the Arthurian kingdom, with its power and glory grounded in the person and career of Lancelot. Lancelot is the hero from beginning to end, and the prose cycle concerns his deeds and prowess, the highest that the secular world can know. Yet because both his prowess and his glory derive from the adulterous passion for Guinevere, they and the Arthurian world are denigrated. The ultimate triumph, the successful quest for the Holy Grail, is achieved not by Lancelot but by his son, Galahad; and eventually the adultery separates Lancelot from Arthur and brings the kingdom to ruin. Magnificent as it is, human glory proves to be sterile, and the Christian ethos of renunciation leading to salvation provides a redeeming counter-ideal or super-ideal. Earthly chivalry is beautiful and essential but eventually yields to the even more beautiful, essential *militia Christi*.

The guiding structural principle of the *Prose Lancelot* is the interlace pattern of narrative; this exploits multiple, varied strains, each developed intermittently, none neglected or forgotten, none developed to the exclusion of the others. Thus the text recounts multiple feats performed by multiple heroes; the story itself is infinitely expandable.

Events occurring long in the past, which apparently drop from sight, prepare the audience for other events, recounted hundreds or perhaps thousands of pages later. Interlace also creates patterns of analogy caused by variation on a theme; the reactions of Lancelot, Gauvain, Bors, and Galahad to the same phenomenon will cause us to reflect on the phenomenon and on the characters who react to it. Structural parallelism by analogy plays as important a role in the *Lancelot* as does empirical cause and effect.

Interlace corresponds to and is in part derived from the practice of medieval rhetoric, a mind-set attuned to *amplificatio, digressio,* and *dilatatio.* In terms of the 'grand design,' it enables the author(s) to fill in the given time frame of the story with narrative so as to 'cover' the two generations and fifty-odd years that extend from Lancelot's infancy to his fathering of Galahad, Galahad's growth to maturity, and the eventual fall. Most of all, interlace permits, even demands, that the author(s) concentrate on the narrative. Multiple story lines and heroes and the breaking of each line in turn effectively prohibits psychological analysis, social commentary, or even extended patterns of symbolism – traits we have come to expect in the modern novel from Mme de La Fayette to Camus, or for that matter in early medieval verse romance. Given the enormous length of the corpus, it is inevitable that the author draws from a limited fund of conventional themes and motifs. For the medieval public the repetitions and the conventional are considered good in and of themselves and are expected.

The fundamental increment, repeated hundreds of times with variations, is the quest; after being notified of injustice or being defied by an injunction, a lone knight sets out to attain a goal, to right wrongs, and to trangress upon the injunction. In the process he will combat wicked adversaries, make love to or resist the advances of temptresses, and, hopefully, rescue damsels in distress; he will free prisoners, defend the widow and the orphan, and obtain a treasure or prize. The call to adventure takes varied forms. Sometimes it is a threat to King Arthur's court from the hostile outside world – a military invasion (Galehaut) or a solitary, personal act of defiance (Meleagant); then the adventure begins. Sometimes an individual knight or lady seeks redress of wrongs and begs for a volunteer from the Round Table to offer support; and the adventure begins. Or an individual calls for a 'rash boon' from the king or one of his knights; and the adventure begins. Or some trivial flaw in behaviour on Lancelot's part (some break of the courtly code) elicits Guinevere's jealousy and/or wrath, upon which Lancelot flees into exile, perhaps into insanity; and his new adventure begins.

To keep the adventures moving requires a sufficient number of adversaries. With the exception of Galehaut, these are usually dark Shadow figures, evil for the sake of being evil, who slay, pillage, and imprison because it is their nature to do so; and they are sufficiently powerful that only the greatest of Arthur's men – Lancelot, Bors, or Hector – are capable of overcoming them. Then there are the women, also evil and corrupt, who employ feminine wiles, tricks, ruse, and the black arts to harm good people and destroy the *pax arthuriana*. The most notorious of these are Morgan la Fée, who imprisons Lancelot by sorcery on three occasions but fails to seduce him; and Camille and the False Guinevere, who each bewitch Arthur and do indeed seduce him.

The genius of the *Prose Lancelot*, the only way interlace can work and the adventures multiply and be perpetuated, lies in the device of multiple heroes. The quests are undertaken not by one protagonist or, at the most, two, as in Chrétien de Troyes, but by five, ten, fifteen, or thirty men and, for the quest of the Grail, all the knights of the Round Table. Lancelot is the hero, the protagonist of his Cycle; but so also, on another level, is Arthurian chivalry embodied in all King Arthur's knights. This permits marvellous complications. The weaker knights, even relatively strong figures such as Saigremor, Yvain, Agloval, and eventually Gauvain himself, will be defeated and imprisoned, permitting the very greatest – Lancelot and his cousins, and finally his son – to rescue them, thus performing the greatest feats of all. The greatest knights are those who seek, find, and deliver from captivity those who are lost, imprisoned, and sought after. They are also the ones about whose exploits 'li contes' [the story, the account] tells the most; they occupy the greatest diegetic space and time.

Since, for the purposes of narrative, these worthies ride about the countryside with visor down and change or exchange their armour-cum-heraldic devices at the slightest provocation, friends often fight each other by mistake, almost to the death. Great knights will don neutral armour to test their greatness or to assist Arthur's adversaries in a tourney or (as with Lancelot) to keep their private life secret. As if this were not enough, when we may have tired of the old warriors, new recruits arrive at King Arthur's court and set about their careers: Yvain, Clarence, Lyonel, Bors, Dodinel, Saigremor, Agloval, Agravain, Guerrehet, Gaheriet, and finally Galahad.

The knights of the Round Table manifest an extraordinary sense of solidarity in arms. Whenever one of the great knights has disappeared – Gauvain, Lancelot, Gauvain a second time, and Hector – the others (five, ten, or thirty) vow to go on a quest until they find him. The situation is complicated by the fact that the great knight in question may well be as mobile and as active on his own as those who are in the process of seeking him. Furthermore, since each man quests alone, by the time Knight 'A' has been found, rescued, or healed, Knights 'D' and 'H' will have probably disappeared. Therefore, a new quest is launched in order to find them. By the time 'D' and 'H' have been restored to the community, 'B', 'F', and 'K' will have disappeared. 'A', 'D', and 'H' may well be reinvolved on the quest, eventually to become lost a second time. Therefore and in any case, unless the others choose to do so, as, for example, at the end of *La Queste del saint Graal*, there is no compelling reason for all of King Arthur's knights to dine with him at the Round Table, safe and sound, at any one time ever. Concern for the missing is as great a motivation for continuing the action as the intrusion of a friendly (weak) or hostile (strong) outsider or the granting of a rash boon.

The interlace and the motif of the quest grant the *Prose Lancelot* an extraordinary sense of space. King Arthur's court is the centre; it is a nucleus of civilization, generosity, and law, an island of love, joy, and fellowship, the centre from which knights set out and to which they must return, where their deeds are recorded, their presence essential, and their absence a cause for dread. At the centre of this centre stands the focal microcosm of the macrocosmic realm – the Round Table. Yet the centre, the court, is constantly menaced from without, and more than once by hostile giant figures like Caradoc, Meleagant, and Galehaut himself. Civilization must protect itself from barbarism, generosity from greed, altruism from self-centredness. For a (provisory) happy ending, the giants are defeated; Galehaut is converted, becomes one with civilization, and is made one of the Round Table.

To bring this about, however, the knights leave the known centre in favour of the unknown outside; they adventure alone, lost in the dark forest (the 'forest aventureuse') which begins at the gates of Carlisle or Winchester. This indeterminate, infinitely extendable space is defined by the paths that bring a knight into contact with other knights, friendly or hostile, and that bring him to the gates of castles and prisons. These inaccessible, impregnable castles, in the hands of the enemy, are places of no return and must be won or lost forever.

Here, instead of the knight escaping from passive idleness with Arthur and Guinevere and engaged upon limitless, free wandering in a universe of expanding horizons, on the contrary we find the knight making his way through and into narrow spaces, breaking doors, and piercing shields; he is fighting through a maze, from the outside to the inside, or from heights into the lower depths.

Lancelot's capture of the Dolorous Guard is the archetypal episode, repeated by him and others. The aim is to liberate prisoners. The winner frees the prisoners; the loser becomes one himself. Whether in the form of a tower, castle, island, cemetery, tomb, cave, or pavilion, whether an impregnable stronghold or mysterious enclosure, whether ruled over by an ogre or a fay, the locus and the situation are the same. One is either the master of space, free to enter and exit, or a slave, entrapped, immobile, awaiting liberation by another.

No less important is time. We are made aware of duration through the interlace pattern when seemingly insignificant causes give rise to crucial results years and decades later. We observe the steadfastness of an individual state or commitment that acts and reacts, reverberating through the Arthurian world over the years and decades: Lancelot's love, Morgan's hatred, Galehaut's friendship, Merlin's prophecies. The tyranny of time enters into the fabric of the narrative. Knights are expected to return to Camelot or to participate in tournaments on specific days after a fixed duration, and they make herculean efforts to do so. On the other hand, a rash boon or a promise to follow someone in distress (the injunction) will disrupt time as well as space. This is also one of the functions of imprisonment or madness; the captive and the insane cease to exist in time just as, from the perspective of the centre, they are no longer perceivable in space. Finally – this is particularly true for *La Mort Artu* but typical of the Cycle as a whole – people evolve in time; for better or worse they grow. Lancelot and Gauvain are the early heroes, young men proving their manhood; they are young lovers, one faithful, the other a bit of a Casanova. In time they age; Gauvain declines and ceases to be the greatest of knights second only to his friend. New young men – Hector, Lyonel, Bors, Perceval, and finally Galahad – come to the fore. Guinevere ages and with her aging greater passion is unleashed, as well as greater pride, jealousy, and rage. *La Mort Artu* is unique in medieval literature – a narrative of older people, enduring the passions of the old, rigid, fixed in their ways, close to death, and always in antithesis to the generosity, idealism, and élan of their own youth as portrayed in the early sections of the Cycle.

One element of the *Prose Lancelot* is prowess and the other is love, *fin' amor* in all its splendour. If Lancelot is the greatest of knights, it is because of his passion for Guinevere; if he dares to love her and she chooses to love him in return, it is because he is the greatest of knights. *Militia* and *amor* reinforce each other as the foundation stones for this idealized vision of chivalry. The narrative concerns Lancelot and Guinevere as lovers as much as it does Lancelot and the others as warriors. The early books recount his sudden infatuation and the slow, steady, inevitable evolution of the relationship into one of physical passion and adultery; the later books tell the inevitable outcome of passion and adultery.

Lancelot's character and his behaviour as a *fin' aman* also contribute to the elaboration of the narrative. How many times the greatest warrior of his day falls into a trance (is 'esbahis' or 'en oblie'), cut off from the world and deprived of control over his body because he perceives Guinevere (her literally 'ravishing' beauty, the literal dazzle of her gaze), or hears her voice, or makes a fetish of what was once part of her body (strands of blond hair in a comb)! This is a form of madness, comparable to the madness Lancelot falls into when Guinevere manifests anger towards him or orders him from the court. As the greatest of earthly lovers Lancelot is prey to the ecstasy of *fin' amor*, the *sancta stultitia* of the secular religion of desire, which is a parody of Christian mysticism. These fits of madness place the hero in danger; because of them he risks losing his reputation and/or his life. However, the worst never occurs. The trance always ends in action and even greater prowess; the provisionally humiliated Knight of the Cart[13] ever proves to be the Greatest of the Great, not in spite of his total commitment to his Lady and *fin' amor* but because of it.

The *Prose Lancelot*, like the romances of Chrétien, is, in part, anti-Tristan. Lancelot and Guinevere are adulterous, it is true, but the cause of their adultery is praiseworthy (*fin' amor*); its commission is justified in the narrative (King Arthur commits adultery with Camille); and its effect is to enhance the glory of the Arthurian world. The damsels or fays who love Lancelot and hope to seduce him fail in their efforts, failing before the glory and aura of Guinevere. Guinevere's love is the best, even though she is a married woman. This is so because she is the best; also because, in contrast to the early Tristan of Beroul and Thomas, *fin' amor* encourages Lancelot in his devotion to society. Guinevere's lover is always Arthur's best knight, his right hand, his strongest support. He and his kin – Bors, Hector, and Lyonel – with no vassal or blood ties to the king, serve him for a lifetime and are more responsible than anyone for the enhancement, glory, and prestige of his reign.

Lancelot's existence as a lover also makes a statement concerning the nature of the ideal warrior figure. The paradox of chivalry states that the greatest knight is great because of, not in spite of, his passion for a woman and because of the 'feminine' characteristics – madness, irrationality, shyness – that *fin' amor* brings to him. Unlike the others, Lancelot is impeccably chivalrous to all women; women see themselves or their ideal in him and flock selflessly to love and succour him even though he cannot love them in return. Significantly, from birth the hero of love is associated with women, and men are prominent by their absence. Lancelot's real mother, Helaine de Benoyc, offers him princely and saintly lineage, his 'nature.' Then, as an orphan, the boy is raised by the Lady of the Lake; she offers him 'noireture.' His 'education,' manly in all respects, derives from her and from his own exemplary instinctual nature and not from the lessons of a male tutor, the 'maistres' whom he loathes. The Lady of the Lake – Merlin's old mistress, the fay who outwitted him – raises Lancelot maternally, with love and tenderness, in a symbolic Other World of the Mothers, not the Fathers. She, not Merlin, brings him supernatural aid and wise counsel; she, not Merlin and not Arthur, will be his principal adjuvant. She is his surrogate mother, and it is presumably from her as well as from within himself that the youth derives his miraculous power over women, the power to love and be loved. Lancelot then is loved, as if he were the *domna* in a *fin' amor* narrative, by Guinevere, who grants him his sword in war and seduces him in the realm of peace, and by Galehaut, who also loves him and pays court to him as to a woman.

This means that Lancelot, more than the other knights, more perhaps than any other hero in medieval literature, balances the masculine and feminine components of his human nature; he is the greatest of the great because of the fusion of the masculine and feminine – *militia* and *amor*, animus and anima. Separated from his real mother and exposed on the waters, isolated from society and deprived of his name, he is raised beneath the lake in the Other World of the Mothers, a realm of nurturing protection and the unconscious. Then, reborn, he proceeds to the masculine court of King Arthur, the centre and locus of wholeness, where he is still protected and influenced by the Mothers – the Lady of the Lake and Guinevere. Indeed, with the arrival of Lancelot at court, magic power in Logres has shifted from the masculine (Merlin) to the feminine (the Lady of the Lake and Morgan) just as Lancelot the lover himself replaces Merlin the clerk. On his adventures, especially the conquest of the Dolorous Guard, Lancelot undergoes initiation experiences, enters into the maze of love and death, conquers the mysteries, and emerges with the keys to the castle and the discovery of his name. He achieves maturity, fullness, and identity; he dies and is reborn. And by liberating prisoners with his sword and healing the wounded and the disabled, he affirms his pre-eminent male sexuality as well.

Lancelot's sexual initiation and subsequent liaison with Guinevere not only crown his process of maturation and individuation, they are also an oedipal wish-fulfilment fantasy. On the one hand, Arthur has just slept with Camille, committing a transgression against Guinevere (later, he will also prefer the False Guinevere to her), thereby enabling Lancelot to 'replace' him without guilt or remorse. The enemies of the king, including but not limited to Meleagant and Galehaut, can be considered rebellious sons. Meleagant as well as the False Guinevere and Morgan hope to seduce or destroy Guinevere. Sexual guilt is projected onto them. They are evil sons and mothers. With King Arthur unable to defend his wife and his kingdom, it is Lancelot who replaces him, repels the bad son, and chastises the evil mother, thereby winning the approbation and gratitude of his surrogate father and symbolic superego. The guilt-ridden id is projected onto others, enabling the ego to align itself with the superego. As a result, Lancelot can sleep with Guinevere without guilt or shame or one moment of embarrassment before her husband, his lord the king.

Oedipal wish-fulfilment and the triumph of *fin' amor* and of the chivalry with which it is bound – this is one half of the 'world' of the *Prose Lancelot*. The brilliance of the text in its complexity consists of a constant dialogue with and tension between this vision and another one in opposition to it. The author(s) of the Cycle question and undermine the very qualities of love and prowess that they are in the process of exalting. The early books of the Cycle are largely romantic in essence; the questioning and the undermining develop slowly but surely so that, by the end in *La Mort Artu*, it is the tragic vision that dominates. A shift in perspective and in perception takes place as the characters grow older and become more rigid in their behaviour and all the effects of love and prowess (passion and war) come to fruition.

On one level, the conventions of the quest, indispensable to the attainment of glory and to feats of *militia* without which *amor* would be inconceivable (and, incidentally, without which the narrative would grind to a halt), prove to be flawed, giving rise to situations in which justice and morality are degraded, not exalted.

Gauvain's family, sterling knights of the Round Table, act in a manner less noble than do Lancelot's kin, and yet they are Arthur's nephews (one is his son); they embody his values and proclaim his name. Mordred first appears in the plot as a rapist. In a fabliau scene of doubtful taste Guerrehet makes love to a married woman lying in bed with her husband, the lady unaware of the substitution; Guerrehet then proceeds to slay the husband, abduct the wife, slay a knight who seeks to protect the woman, and wound three of her four brothers.

Other knights, acting with the best intentions, cause more harm than good. Yvain unwittingly breaks a tabu, a *costume*. As a result, Mauduit the Giant mutilates Yvain's messenger and goes on a rampage of sadism. The people of the country are furious at Yvain; they curse him and take him prisoner. Even Lancelot, when hospitality is refused him, kills one knight and wounds another. A maiden calls for his assistance; she is slain and then Lancelot slays the slayer. Well and good, but are these deaths necessary? Are they not caused by the intrusion of an Yvain and a Lancelot? By a system that calls for their intrusion? In *La Queste del saint Graal* traditional martial activity is deemed to be murder. Gauvain murders some seventeen times. In *La Mort Artu*, at the battle of Salisbury, the knights all murder each other, the last killing due to King Arthur himself, who slays his son knowingly out of hatred, and his dearest servitor unwittingly out of love.

The major problem, nonetheless, is *fin' amor*. However noble the sentiments shared by Lancelot and Guinevere, they are sentiments of carnal passion embodied in acts of adultery. The couple's tragic fall is anticipated in the tragic story of Galehaut. The 'bad son,' the savage giant from the outside (Baumgartner 1985), the Other World, is conquered and even converted by Lancelot, the 'good son'; Galehaut becomes Lancelot's best friend and a Knight of the Round Table, and helps bring Lancelot and Guinevere together. One of Lancelot's greatest achievements is to conquer such an enemy and to win such a friend. Heroes are measured by the quality of their friends; for each Achilles, Orestes, Aeneas, and Roland there will be a Patroclus, Pylades, Pallas, and Oliver. Galehaut is worthy. The tragedy derives from the fact that he is not just a supernumerary, a faithful friend. He has his own personality, pride, ambition, and, above all, passion. His passion is Lancelot. Without the slightest hint of overt homosexuality, Galehaut *loves*

Lancelot with the same jealousy, tenderness, and all-consuming absorption, the same 'desmesure,' as Guinevere's. Guinevere's *amor* and Galehaut's *amicitia* are depicted in identical terms and manifested in identical behaviour. The world is not large enough for both passions. Although Galehaut effaces himself as best he can, in a universe of disguise, absence, and rumour he is informed of Lancelot's presumed death; then he pines away, suffering from classical love sickness, and himself dies of love.

Galehaut is, after all, Lancelot's double, his alter ego, the Shadow that Lancelot does not successfully integrate; he suffers a magnificent tragic fate that will overcome Lancelot and Guinevere as well, years later. Guinevere indeed becomes as passionate, jealous, and self-absorbed as Galehaut was. For any number of reasons, some justified, most not, she takes out her rage on her lover, exiling him from court and driving him away in despair, sometimes driving him to insanity. One example among many:

> Si erra par la forest .III. jorz an tel manniere sanz boivre et sanz mengier es plus estranges leus qu'il savoit come cil qui ne volsist mie estre conneuz par home qui l'entercast . .VI. jorz fu Lanceloz an tel manniere et fesoit tant duel que ce ert merveille coment il vivoit; si en fist tant dedenz cel terme, a ce qu'il n'avoit qui le confortast, ne ne mengoit ne ne bevoit: si em perdi le sens si outreement qu'il ne savoit qu'il faisoit ne n'encontroit home ne fame a cui il ne se preist ... (*Lancelot* 6, p. 177)

> He wandered thusly in the forest for three days, without food or drink, in the most remote places that he knew of, as one who didn't want at all to be recognized by whomever might come across him. For six days Lancelot remained in this state and endured such pain that it was a miracle how he remained alive. During this period of time his behaviour was so excessive – in that he had no one to console him nor did he eat or drink – that as a result he lost his wits totally to the point of not knowing what he did, and from every man or woman whom he came across he seized, etc.

Neither Galehaut nor Guinevere is to be blamed for the strength of their passion or for a fictional world in which suspicion and jealousy become all but inevitable. The more tragic aspects of the fictional world, seen throughout the *Lancelot*, come to a head in *La Mort Artu*. On the one hand, a series of characters – Guinevere, Lancelot, the Maiden of Escalot, the lady of Beloe, Morgan la Fée, even Mordred – are in love, and their love is all absorbing ('force d'amors') and will brook no resistance. 'Force d'amors' leads to jealousy – amorous, personal, and political. Guinevere is jealous, of course; so also are Arthur, Morgan, even Mordred and Agravain. On the other hand, given the conventions of quest narrative, with Lancelot away from the court on a series of adventures (sometimes intentionally in disguise), and the conventions of *fin' amor*, comprising an adulterous liaison that must be kept secret, rumours inevitably spring up, the same sort that killed Galehaut. The rumours (that Lancelot loves the Maiden of Escalot; that Lancelot doesn't love the Maiden of Escalot) and the evidence (Lancelot's absence from court, a letter of denunciation from Morgan) add fuel to the flames. Everybody is jealous at one time or another; everybody is suspicious. One report will allay Arthur's suspicions but cause Guinevere to fall into a rage of jealousy; another one will allay her fears but then nourish those of her husband.

People fail to communicate in a world of deception, where knights on the road fight with helmets closed and knights and ladies at court speak metaphorically behind another kind of mask. At one point the entire court appears to be aware of the adultery; everyone except Arthur knows, and even Arthur knows in his heart. Yet, somewhat as in Beroul's *Tristan*, all good people desperately try to play the game, to keep the secret, and to maintain illusion, for reasons of personality, friendship, family, and state; but evil characters like Morgan and Agravain seek to rip off the mask and proclaim reality from their own selfish motivations of jealousy, envy, passion, and vengeance. The play between illusion and reality and the tension between good and evil are complex indeed. And the tragedy of *La Mort Artu*, as of the *Prose Lancelot* in its totality, is the slow but inevitable unveiling of the truth – speech from Agravain, speech from Morgan, Lancelot's paintings when he was Morgan's captive, and finally the concrete evidence of Lancelot and Guinevere caught in the queen's chamber, *in flagrante delicto*.

One lesson of *La Mort Artu* and of the *Prose Lancelot* as a whole is that the individual does not stand alone; the actions of all people have a profound impact upon society. The *fin' amor* centred on Lancelot and Guinevere is the spur to action for Lancelot's prowess as a knight, and therefore for the prestige of the Arthurian world. At the same time, the same *fin' amor* undercuts and eventually destroys the society that it raised to glory.

Individual love and individual friendship, when *fin' amor* is involved, enter into conflict with the rights and duties of the family. Lancelot's kin – Bors, Hector, and Lyonel – are eventually forced to choose between him and Guinevere or between him and Arthur. When Guinevere chases Lancelot from her presence, she can no longer count on the support of Bors and the others:

'– Certes, dame, fet Boorz, se chevalier vos faillent, ce n'est mie de merveille, car vos avez failli au meilleur chevalier del monde ... Dame, fet il, ja Dex ne m'aïst, se vos ja en moi trouvez secours; car puis que vos m'avez tolu celui que ge amoie seur touz homes, je ne vos doi pas aidier, mes nuire de tout mon pooir.' (*Mort*, p. 99)

'If knights are failing you, my Lady, it is not surprising,' he replied, 'because you have failed the finest knight in the world.' ... 'My Lady,' he replied, 'God forbid that you receive any help from me, because as you have taken away from me the man I loved above all others, I ought not to help you, but do all I can to harm you.' (Cable, pp. 101–2)

Worse still, in *La Mort Artu*, once the adultery is revealed and Lancelot enters into a state of war with Arthur, the king finds those loyal to Lancelot out of blood ties arrayed against him. The Arthurian universe is now split down the middle.

Meanwhile, for all Gauvain's closeness to Lancelot (but for the Galehaut episode, Gauvain was always Lancelot's closest comrade in arms), Arthur's nephew also owes fealty to the king. Indeed, more than the others he is the extension of Arthur. Gauvain, torn between his two duties, seeks desperately to avoid a rift. However, when in order to rescue Guinevere Lancelot slays two of Gauvain's brothers posted to guard her (again a case of misperceived identity), Gauvain, out of kinship loyalty, himself makes war on Lancelot and spurs Arthur to more severe measures than he otherwise would have taken. Thus what, during the later books of the *Lancelot propre* had been a steadily developing rivalry between the Gaul family headed by Lancelot and the Orkney family headed by Gauvain, now becomes a clan feud that will only be ended with Gauvain's death.

Finally, just as the Arthurian story begins in passion, adultery, and incest (Uther Pendragon seduces the Duke of Cornwall's wife and fathers Arthur; Arthur seduces Lot of Orkney's wife, his sister, and fathers Mordred) so the saga ends in passion, adultery, and incest; the incestuous son, Mordred, falls in love with Guinevere, replaces Arthur, and makes war on him. He would have ravished Guinevere had he the chance. He and Arthur do slay each other, just as Pendragon indirectly slew Cornwall. The oedipal wish-fulfilment fantasy (Lancelot and Guinevere) gives way to an oedipal nightmare (Arthur and Mordred) in part because the entire Arthurian world had its genesis in oedipal nightmares involving Pendragon, Arthur's own father. Pendragon, Arthur, and Lancelot are all punished where they have sinned.

Lancelot and Guinevere implicitly from the beginning, and Arthur and Gauvain explicitly at the end, fail to separate the private and the public; individual pleasure or pain and individual duty or loyalty are not separated from the public weal. A series of wars between Lancelot's people and Arthur's people weakens Arthur to the extent that when he is betrayed by Mordred he no longer has the strength or the following (Lancelot is away and Gauvain is dead) to overcome the traitor. Vassalage, the feudal bond, and kin-right all prove disastrous in the end; they are destructive to the kingdom and to the values it embodies.

Here again the end joins the beginning, and the symbolic structure of the *Prose Lancelot* is shown to be circular as well as linear. The beginning of the *Lancelot propre* depicts how the tyrant Claudas deposes and slays two kings, the fathers of Lancelot, Bors, Lyonel, and Hector. Pharien, the good feudal knight, is torn between divided loyalties – on the one hand to Claudas and on the other to the orphan boys. The emphasis is on politics and disruption, not on *fin' amor.* Young Arthur is criticized because he does not come to the aid of the victims, his vassals:

'–Sire, fait chil, et je vous di que se ne fust une cose, je ne seusse en vous rien que reprendre: ch'est la mort au roi Ban de Benoÿc que vous ne venjastes onques, qui fu mors en la venue de vostre court. Et si est sa feme remese veve desiretee et s'est reubee d'un des plus biax enfans qui onques fust. C'est si laide chose et si vilaine a vostre oels qu'il est mervelle comment vous poés ne osés nul preudomme veoir en mi le vis.' (*Lancelot* 7, p.100)

'Sire,' he said, 'I say to you that, except for one matter, I have nothing to reproach you for: but that one is the death of King Ban of Benoyc, who died in the jurisdiction of your court and whom you never avenged. Furthermore, his wife was left a disinherited widow and had stolen from her one of the most beautiful children who ever lived. This is visibly so vile and ugly an affair that it is a marvel how you dare look a decent man in the face.'

Much later Claudas, out of hatred and fear of the greatest of the victims, Lancelot, himself insults Guinevere and strives to bring the adultery to light. The Arthurians eventually invade Gaul, defeat Claudas, and set matters right. Yet, in the end, a second Claudas,

Claudas's double – Mordred – will come to power. By employing the most subtle political manoeuvring and playing on his subjects' greed and on the letter of the law, he seizes power. This time Arthur and Guinevere do not prevail and the world of chivalry is doomed.

It is for all these reasons that we can speak of a tragic dimension in the *Prose Lancelot*. Tragic because an aura of fatality hangs over Arthurian Britain, with the various peripeteia including the Fall of Arthur prophesied from the beginning. Tragic because the doom comes from within: Pendragon's adultery, Arthur's adultery and incest, and for that matter the adulterous liaisons of Lancelot and Guinevere and of Arthur and Camille or Arthur and the False Guinevere. Tragic because the major characters are aware that they are being punished and that they are doing penance for their faults. Tragic because the narrative tells of flawed human beings tested to the utmost, attaining great heights but also dropping to the depths, falling because of their hubris in war (Galehaut, Gauvain), in friendship (Galehaut), or in love (Lancelot and Guinevere). Lancelot is the greatest of the great in the Arthurian secular world. He is also a tragic hero among other tragic figures because, in the last analysis, the values of Arthur's world – *fin' amor* and chivalry – prove to be inferior to other, higher values.

The other, higher values are those of Christianity, present and implicit throughout the *Prose Lancelot*, predominant and explicit in *La Queste del saint Graal*. Once again all the knights set out, this time on the last and greatest of quests – for the meaning of the Grail. As in the preceding books, there is a herald to adventure, the departure, ordeals, and success or failure, reward or punishment. More than in the preceding books we find the closeness of comrades, the loneliness of the road, the anguish of separation, and the joy of reunion. Also, in this 'romance representation' of Christian mysteries certain traits of the early 'classical' texts by Chrétien and Marie – the supernatural, the Other World, death and rebirth, a sense of *tremendum* and the uncanny – weigh more heavily than in the overtly secular portions of the Cycle. The famous line from Job 7:1, 'Militia est vita hominis super terram,' is taken seriously, in an allegorical narrative meant to infuse Christian values in the secular chivalric aristocracy, and to transform the chivalric mentality into something roughly comparable to the ideal of the Templar and Hospitaller Orders.

Thus, the values of chivalry are surpassed by those of Christ. Gauvain's exploits are condemned as murder. Lancelot is forced to do penance for his sins of the flesh. Humility, gentleness, and above all virginity are exalted; only Galahad, Perceval, and Bors will see the Grail in its splendour. *Fin' amor* is suppressed, and the great ladies and wicked temptresses are replaced by 'prud'oemes,' white monks who guide the knights in their quest and explain the enigmas that they encounter. At the same time, the author(s) maintains pity, compassion, and even admiration for the old values. Lancelot remains the hero. He does not totally fail. He endures penance, learns humility, and, as a flawed human being in a flawed world, attains a partial vision of the mysteries, the vision 'sicut speculum in aenigmate' that is the lot of mortals:

> 'Je ai, fet il, veu si granz merveilles et si granz beneurtez que ma langue nel vos porroit mie descovrir, ne mes cuers meismes nel porroit mie penser, com grant chose ce est. Car ce n'a mie esté chose terriane, mes esperitel. Et se mes granz pechiez et ma grant maleurtez ne fust, j'eusse encor plus veu, se ne fust que je perdi la veue de mes euz et le pooir dou cors, por la grant desloiauté que Diex avoit veue en moi.' (*Queste*, p. 258)

> 'I have seen,' he said, 'such glories and felicity that my tongue could never reveal their magnitude, nor could my heart conceive it. For this was no earthly but a spiritual vision. And but for my grievous sins and my most evil plight I should have seen still more, had I not lost the sight of my eyes and all power over my body, on account of the infamy that God had seen in me.' (Matarasso, p. 264)

Fin' amor and the quest are purified and surpassed but not repudiated. The old aristocracy participates in and partakes of the new mysteries. Their physical prowess is spiritualized and crowned by a new moral and spiritual insight, by a mystical initiation that all of them had, unconsciously perhaps, been seeking from the beginning.

The structure that concretizes the two value systems of the *Prose Lancelot* is the father-son bond between Lancelot and Galahad. Lancelot not only breaks the Seventh Commandment with Guinevere, but he also, unknowingly, fornicates with the daughter of the Grail King. Yet from this pattern of sin will be born the redeemer, a virgin knight who will accomplish what Lancelot cannot. From the beginning Galahad's birth and 'coming' are prophesied; throughout the *Lancelot propre* a number of feats, denied to Lancelot, are reserved for one greater than he, who will be his son. Lancelot himself was baptized 'Galahad' but took the name Lancelot instead. In a sense he ought to have been the Galahad that he is not; he is not because of Guinevere. In another sense he contains Galahad within him and will sire the real Galahad, an act that proves to be his greatest exploit as a knight and his most valuable contribution to the Arthurian world. Lancelot and Galahad are the best, each in his own realm. The one completes and redeems the other in what is both a synthesis and a fusion. Galahad is the actualization of Lancelot's promise. Lancelot's potentiality becomes Galahad's actuality.

The old gives way to the new; the *vetus homo* is redeemed and replaced by a splendid *homo novus*. Galahad is a Christ figure, in both the medieval and modern conceptions of the term. Arriving at court, clad in red, radiant with the spirit, his coming is the coming of the Holy Ghost at Pentecost: as the Spirit, as Christ surrounded by his disciples at the Round Table Galahad appears and then disappears, instilling in them the unalterable will to follow him and seek the Truth. At Corbenic he re-enacts the Last Supper; on the Ship of Solomon he re-enacts the Crucifixion; at Sarras he is imprisoned (the descent to hell) and then crowned (the resurrection); he expires in ecstasy, transported to another world, his own true kingdom. His request –

> 'Et puis qu'il est einsi, biax dolz Sires, que vos m'avez acomplies mes volentez de lessier moi veoir ce que j'ai touz jors desirré, or vos pri ge que vos en cest point ou je sui et en ceste grant joie soffrez que je trespasse de ceste terriene vie en la celestiel.' (*Queste*, p.278)

> 'And since, sweet Lord, Thou hast fulfilled my wish to let me see what I have ever craved, I pray Thee now that in this state Thou suffer me to pass from earthly life to life eternal.' (p. 283) –

is granted.

Fin' amor is not redeemed either by Lancelot or Galahad. Guinevere is not consulted concerning the quest for the Grail; she disappears from the narrative. Perceval is tempted sexually by one of Satan's demons and resists the temptation, but wounds himself in the thigh (symbolic castration) as punishment and penance. The redemption of Eros comes from a woman, to compensate for Lancelot's fall because of a woman (Guinevere). In *La Queste* it is Perceval's sister who knights Galahad as Guinevere had knighted Lancelot; she sacrifices her hair to provide the girdle for his sword; she sacrifices her life's blood to cure a leper maiden. She then is reunited in Sarras with her brother, Perceval, and with her spiritual husband, Galahad. She is a Mary figure, the image of the *femina nova*, the Ave who redeems Eva in the name of a higher, greater love; true virginal charity surpasses and crowns the courtly *passio*.

The feminine element in *La Queste* is most apparent in patterns of imagery, especially the dominant image, the Grail. This cup in earlier texts may have had some connection with Celtic mythology. By the thirteenth century the Grail is assimilated with the cup of the Last Supper, the vessel in which Longinus collected Christ's blood from the wound in his side, and the chalice of the Mass. According to the critics, it represents God, the Trinity, the Grace of the Holy Spirit, the Mystery of the Faith, the Incarnation, and/or the Eucharist. It grants those who behold or partake of it the grace of God, the presence of the Spirit, the *corpus Domini*, and his blood-wine. Symbolically, the Grail, whatever the original Celtic myth, does serve as a source of spiritual food for all who are capable of drinking from it. It is a nurturing, purifying, uplifting feminine image, source of plenty, and contrasts sharply with the swords and lances, especially Excalibur, that have dominated the narrative heretofore. As a *vas electionis* – a vessel, a container – the Holy Grail forms a pattern of imagery with other vessels: Solomon's ship, the Holy Sepulchre, and the human body itself. Vessels can be polluted or pure; Galahad's, Perceval's, and his sister's bodies remain pure and are therefore capable of partaking of the Grail feast. Others, nourished with secular food, are unworthy of an invitation to the banquet.

In *La Queste* wood imagery is second in importance only to the Grail itself. The table of the Last Supper is assimilated to wood and stone: the Holy Sepulchre, the Grail Table, the Round Table of Arthur's court, Solomon's altar, and the altar of the Mass. Galahad says a Holy Mass in Corbenic and expires taking communion before an altar at Sarras. Solomon's ship, which transports our heroes over the seas, is built from the wood of a tree descended directly from the cursed tree in the Garden of Eden but also is an ancestor of the Holy Rood. The ship, constructed in the heyday of the Old Testament, recalls Noah's Ark, the Ark of the Covenant, and the Temple of Solomon, all of which prefigure the Church, of whose body Christ is the head. Galahad reclines in this boat, resembling Christ attached to the cross or any mortal in his coffin. The tree-ship is a symbol of life, growth, refuge, and also of death; yet, it is a holy death that leads to eternal life.

Life in *La Queste* is conceived in terms of light, the triumph of day over darkness and understanding over ignorance. Night equals dread and temptation; day, awakening and joy. Life also is manifest in the community, a chosen group of spiritual comrades – Galahad, Perceval, Perceval's sister, Bors, and for a time Lancelot – and even a spiritual city. The action of *La Queste* shifts from Camelot to Corbenic (Corbenic already plays a role in the *Lancelot propre*) and from Corbenic to Sarras. Sarras is an earthly metaphor for the celestial city, the Church triumphant, the *civitas Dei* that surpasses the capital of what is now a degraded *pax arthuriana*.

In the course of the Grail quest white monks interpret allegorically the adventures that the knights undergo; 'sanblance' [appearance, sign] gives way to 'senefiance' [meaning, interpretation]. The functioning of the allegory is central to our comprehension of the text, as has been argued by Pauphilet (1921), Gilson (1925), Locke (1960), Tuve (1966), Todorov (1969), Matarasso (1979), Bourquin (1981), and de Looze (1985). It is obvious that the implied audience also is meant to read the *Queste* narrative in allegorical terms and to discover its 'senefiance.' The audience undergoes a learning experience; we learn 'senefiance' and learn how to learn 'senefiance' to the same extent as the protagonists in the diegesis. Glosses of events are included in the diegesis along with the events themselves; the speech of interpretation is juxtaposed with the action of heroic deeds. The romance is in part an investigation into how it itself ought to be read by the characters within and the implied audience without.

As Locke (1960), Matarasso (1979), and Burns (1985) have observed, the message is ethical but also historical. An historical and figural bond exists between the Old Testament (Adam, Eve, the Tree, the sword of David, the ship of Solomon), the New Testament (Christ, Mary, the Cross, the Sepulchre, the cup and calix, the table), and the present of King Arthur's day, with Lancelot, Galahad, Perceval's sister, the Grail, the Round Table, and the return of the sword and the ship, and for that matter the cup. All four levels of typological exegesis are possible, including the anagogy of ecstasy in the mysteries of the faith. Old Testament murder, lechery, and sin are redeemed by the New Covenant and the new grace pouring from the cup, the calix, and the Grail. The Old Law foreshadows the New Law, which fulfils the Old. Both Old and New are then postfigured by the more recent history of King Arthur, in which a world fallen through *luxuria* and *ira* can be redeemed by Christ and by the Christ-figure, Galahad, who brings his cup to his allotted seat at his table. Without falling into the Joachimite heresy, the author offers us the possibility of an Age of the Spirit, with Galahad as messiah. This age will not occur. Only Galahad, Perceval, and Perceval's sister are taken directly to God; Bors and Lancelot, each according to his merits, are favored with the vision. The world then returns to its normal state of passion, jealousy, suspicion, and secular bonds of kinship and friendship; and the Arthurian kingdom collapses. The collapse, however, does include a Christian end. With the century played out, Lancelot, Guinevere, Bors, Hector, and Lyonel turn to God and attain personal salvation. They become religious. Even Gauvain is saved. In a fallen world, after the Revelation but before the Second Coming, personal salvation is the only answer to the tragedy of existence. It is the only solution offered by *La Mort Artu*, at the end of the *Lancelot* Cycle.

This heroic, tragic, and Christian narrative is presumed to have an historical basis in the chronicles of Britain and Gaul at the time of the Saxon invasions. Because of typology this relatively 'modern' epoch is made part of world history as a whole – pre-Advent history (the Old Testament), the Coming of Christ (the New Testament), post-Advent history (which contains the centuries extending to the narrative present in the fifth century), and the present of the narration (the thirteenth). Thus the text reflects upon its thirteenth-century present and its own distant origins.

The shift from narrative in verse to narrative in prose reflects the desire to create the illusion of historical and religious authenticity (Latin historiography and the Latin Bible are in prose). Burns (1985) and de Looze (1985) have demonstrated the importance of the theme of writing and the book. The Cycle repeatedly describes its own coming into being. Merlin goes off into the wilds to rejoin his friend Blaise, who takes down in writing the account of the adventures that Merlin tells him orally. Later, the knights of the Round Table return to Camelot and tell the story of their adventures (Lancelot is the most active adventurer and therefore the most prolific teller); these are consigned to writing by King Arthur's clerks. Merlin, Lancelot, and Bors tell the stories of the deeds they have committed; they are both actants and creators.

Finally, *La Queste* and *La Mort Artu* inform us that these texts, originally in the Welsh language, are translated into Latin and then from Latin into French, and that part of the process is due to the noted Norman-Welsh writer of the reign of Henry II, Walter Map:

> Quant il orent mengié, li rois fist avant venir les clers qui metoient en escrit les aventures aus chevaliers de laienz. Et quant Boorz ot contees les aventures del Seint Graal telles come il les avoit veues, si furent mises en escrit et gardees en l'almiere de Salebieres, dont Mestre Gautier Map les trest a fere son livre del Seint Graal por l'amor del roi Henri son seignor, qui fist l'estoire translater de latin en françois. (*Queste*, pp.279–80)

> When they had dined King Arthur summoned his clerks who were keeping a record of all the adventures undergone by the knights of his household. When Bors had related to them the adventures of the Holy Grail as witnessed by himself, they were written down and the record kept in the library at Salisbury, whence Master Walter Map extracted them in order to make his book of the Holy Grail for love of his lord King Henry, who had the story translated from Latin into French. (p. 284)

Therefore, the two greatest of 'British' kings – Arthur and Henry – order the preservation and diffusion of the book of British history. All this, of course, is pure fiction. But it is fiction justifying and exalting a narrative, 'li contes,' that in time assumes and proclaims its own authority as a text; as history, as wisdom, and as writing, it takes over the function of authorship and authentification from the tellers, scribes, and translators who are its purported source.

The *Prose Lancelot* is the coherent, unified masterpiece that some claim Malory wrote; it is the book that Malory did not write but might have written had he lived two centuries earlier and had the English tongue then been a literary medium available to him. The narrative treats the rise and fall of the Arthurian world, concentrating, in spite of the interlace, upon one man, who is, from beginning to end, the hero and protagonist – Lancelot. Unlike the earlier verse romancers – Beroul, Thomas, Chrétien, and Hue de Rotelande – the author(s) of the Cycle see no conflict between *fin' amor* and deeds of prowess. Chivalry includes love and valour, each supportive of the other. In the *Prose Lancelot* the conflict is transferred to a higher level – between secular chivalry, at its best, and another call – another *militia et amor* – the sacred chivalry of God. The two elements are present in the Cycle from the beginning (from Merlin's and Arthur's conceptions) to the end (Lancelot's and Guinevere's deaths). Chivalry is shown to be magnificent yet tragically flawed. The faith embodied in the Grail through Lancelot's promise and Galahad's fulfilment is magnificent yet, in a fallen world, evanescent and limited to only a few. Merlin was conceived by a demon and a virgin; Lancelot, after all he has done, ends his days as a hermit. And we are left with the memory and the record, 'li contes,' of the greatest story of the Middle Ages.

The legacy of the story proved to be far richer and longer lasting in England than in France. There are Middle English verse romances taken, in whole or in part, from books of the grand Cycle: *Arthour and Merlin*, *Joseph of Arimathie*, Lovelich's *Merlin* and *Quest*, *Le Morte Arthur*, and *Morte Arthure*. There are also the prose *Merlin* and the *Works* of Sir Thomas Malory. Romancers, in England as in France, were inspired by a mode and a technique of story-telling using the pattern of interlace. They were inspired by narrative that exalted the interaction of two great ideals, love and chivalry, while at the same time allowing for fruitful conflict between the ideals. Specifically in England, the prose romances perpetuated (for francophones) and helped reveal (for anglophones) a viable tradition of native British heroism and statecraft. It is this legacy of British chivalry and British martial glory that appealed to all writers of English Arthurian romance. To a greater or lesser extent, the English heirs also profited from a dual historical vision. One aspect, found in the *Estoire*, the *Merlin*, and the *Queste*, emphasizes Christian origins and Christian continuity, symbolized by a New Covenant offered by God to his chosen people, extending from Joseph of Arimathea to Merlin, Arthur, and Galahad, that would ennoble and redeem secular chivalry. The other, in the *Queste* and *La Mort Artu*, points to tragic opposition and the ultimate fall of the Arthurian world. The anonymous creator of *Morte Arthure*, Malory, and Caxton would prove to be the writers who best understood the vision of the French prose romances and who would pass that vision on to the modern world.

3. *Le Roman de la Rose*

Le Roman de la Rose by Guillaume de Lorris and Jean de Meun has survived to our century in some three hundred extant manuscripts. It also enjoyed twenty-one printed editions from 1481 to 1538. The *Rose* was translated partially or in toto once in Dutch, twice in Italian, and three times in English. One of the English versions is attributed to Chaucer. The original text was also revised a number of times in French; one of these is a *rifacimento* in prose by Jean Molinet, and another is an edition and modernization by Clément Marot. Jean de Meun and Guillaume de Lorris both influenced Dante, Boccaccio, Machaut, Froissart, and a host of lesser writers. The *Rose* played a dominant role in the literary formation of both Chaucer and Gower. The dominant mode of the later Middle Ages in England was allegory, and it was *Le Roman de la Rose* which shaped the direction that allegory in the vernacular was to take, both secular (Chaucer's dream poems and the *Confessio Amantis*) and sacred (*Piers Plowman* and *Pearl*). Furthermore, Jean de Meun's section became the subject of the first great French literary quarrel, which occurred at the turn of the fourteenth century and engaged such recognized figures as Christine de Pizan, Gerson, Pierre and Gontier Col, and Jean de Montreuil. Jean de Meun proved to be the first recognized *auctor* and *auctoritas* in French literary history, and his book the first true secular classic, glossed, explicated, quoted, indexed, anthologized, and fought over; that is, it was treated as if it were a masterpiece from Antiquity. The total *Roman de la Rose*, containing some 21,750 lines,[14] along with the *Prose Lancelot*, is for the development of both French and English culture the most important works of literature produced during the Middle Ages.

Guillaume de Lorris

Guillaume wrote his *Roman de la Rose*, some 4028 lines, in the early 1220s. A personification allegory, the text is meant to be interpreted on two levels, the literal and the allegorical. *Literaliter*, the Narrator tells how, five years previously, he dreamed that he took a stroll to the Garden of Delight, entered the garden through a narrow wicket guarded by a girl named Oiseuse, and danced with personages named Leece, Beauté, Largesse, Courtoisie, Jeunesse, etc. He gazed into the Fountain of Narcissus, and beheld, reflected in two crystal stones, a rose plot and a rose. He then would have picked the rose but was wounded by the God of Love, who forced the youth to become his vassal and listen to his instruction. Twice the dream protagonist approached the rose and was encouraged by a young man called Bel Accueil and later by Franchise and Pitié, but he was repulsed and sent off in tears by characters named Danger, Honte, Peur, Jalousie, and Male Bouche. Jalousie built a castle around the rose, with Bel Accueil locked in the keep under the surveillance of la Vieille. The text breaks off with plaints of despair from the young man in the dream. The majority of scholars esteem that, for one reason or another, Guillaume de Lorris left his *Roman* incomplete. An excellent case, however, has been made that Guillaume chose to end the *Rose* with the Lover's dream plaint, in which case our reading of the text will inevitably be quite different.[15]

This is the *sensus litteralis*. The *sensus allegoricus* concerns the progress of courtship in the experience of a young man. The youth in the dream (let us call him the Lover) represents the ideal courtly lover. In the course of time we see him wake up to the urgings of nature in springtime, enter courtly society, meet a beautiful girl (let us call her Rose), fall in love with her, discover the reality of love, and then hope to win the girl. During the seduction process the Lover is aided by aspects of the girl's psychology and by a person in the outside world, Ami, his friend or confidant, just as he is repulsed by other aspects of Rose's nature and by persons in her entourage; scandalmongers (Male Bouche), the girl's father or husband (Jalousie), and even an old servant or retainer (la Vieille) exert pressure on her.

There are two allegorical efforts to seduce Rose. On each occasion the Lover tries to go beyond the verbal expression of love to the physical act. First he touches and then he kisses the Rose. It seems likely, according to Friedman (1965–6), that Guillaume's narrative is patterned after the topos of the *gradus amoris* or *quinque lineae amoris* in courtship.

The five stages of love are the following: *visus, alloquium, tactus, osculum* or *basium*, and *totius personae concessio*, the *factum*. The Narrator takes the Lover through the first four steps. Should Guillaume have completed his romance, the 'deed' ought normally to have crowned the final episode. On the other hand, if Lejeune (1973) and Hult (1986) are right and Guillaume chose not to 'complete' the *Rose*, it is because he could or would not impose on his text a denouement of *factum*.

Guillaume de Lorris has constructed a perfectly balanced, structurally coherent allegory; at every point in the narrative, there is a precise, congruent, and logically appropriate connection between the *sensus litteralis* and the *sensus allegoricus*, and the two levels are logical and coherent each on its own terms. It is also true that, at each stage of the narrative, Guillaume uses allegory to teach the nature of love, his ideal of *fin' amor*. Furthermore, given that the Lover evolves in the course of the narrative, that he is lectured to by the God of Love at the center of the diegesis, and that Amor's lecture on the duties of love service and his prediction of the Lover's future plight are taken directly from Ovid (who is the greatest of *magistri amoris*), we perceive that the Lover, Amor's narratee, learns the nature of love as the implied audience does, and that the implied audience learns what the Lover does when he learns it. Indeed, the implied audience learns much more, for it is capable of appreciating the Lover's youthful mistakes. Complicity is established between the older, wiser Narrator and his implied audience vis-à-vis the impetuous courtly wooer.

The *fin' amor* of the troubadours and trouvères, of Chrétien and Thomas, is not meant for everyone. It can flourish only under ideal conditions, in a society of elegance, refinement, and good taste – at the court. In Guillaume de Lorris the court is represented by the Garden of Delight enclosed by high walls, with a narrow wicket and a gatekeeper, Oiseuse (Leisure) (Virgilian *otium*). Oiseuse holds a mirror, which identifies her also with Ovidian Venus. The paintings on the outside of the wall of characters named Haine, Félonie, Envie, Tristesse, etc., and their opposites, characters who dance within, indicate that true love is reserved to an elite group of young people of the highest possible character. As with the *Stilnovisti*, love repairs only to a gentle heart, and determination of virtue (the gentle heart) is a necessary precondition for partaking of *fin' amor*. Necessary but not sufficient. Guillaume's prohibition against Pauvreté and Vileinie (the state of being a peasant) as well as his presentation of Oiseuse mark *fin' amor* also as a characteristic of social class. Only people of birth, breeding, and leisure are capable of indulging in the good life. *Fin' amor* is an aesthetic as well as a libidinal state; it is a luxury that the poor can ill afford and the uneducated cannot comprehend, and it demands a concentration of the faculties and the expenditure of both time and energy that leave no room for other concerns.

Within the garden the Lover meets people who embody the traits he must possess in order to be initiated. These virtues – Beauté, Richesse, Largesse, Franchise, Jeunesse, etc. – are beautiful young girls, whereas the non-love vices are hags. Also, they are 'real people,' alive, vocal, and joyful in harmonious song and dance, whereas the vices are silent, isolated images, mere paintings. Guillaume tells us that, from the perspective of *fin' amor*, non-love is only love distorted or the absence of love; it does not exist. From the perspective of human psychology, young people in love are oblivious to everything but themselves, for, in their state of passion, only they exist.

The Lover gazes into 'la fontaine au bel Narcisus' (1511) [the ... fountain of the fair Narcissus (Dahlberg, p. 51)], perceives the rose garden, and a particularly lovely rose, and yet he is prevented from plucking it by the God of Love, who shoots him full of arrows, seizes him, forces lordship on him, and instructs him. Guillaume de Lorris tells us that love is indeed physical, that the Lover desires his lady, and that the desire is born from acquaintance with her, more specifically from the sight of her beauty. He tells us that acquaintance of beauty and desire precede falling in love. However, he also tells us that *fin' amor*, in its finest, most delicate crystallization, restrains brute desire, makes the Lover timid not aggressive, and causes him pain as well as pleasure.

With the fountain, Guillaume expores playfully the Ovidian and courtly conceit that man falls in love after gazing into a lady's eyes. Whether the fountain refers to the Lover's or to Rose's eyes is less important than the fact that this is the Ovidian fountain of Narcissus, and that the eyes are represented by mirrors which reflect one half of the garden (the rose plot) and also, potentially, he who gazes into them. (The fountain has been analysed by Köhler 1963, Kessler 1982, Hult 1986, and Dornbush 1990.) Thus, beholding beauty in a woman even before he falls in love, opens up a new world to the Lover and brings him knowledge of himself. From a Jungian perspective, the anima projected onto a girl (or a rose) in a dream is an aspect of the dreamer's own psyche. Gazing into the fountain is no doubt the crucial action in the narrative. It creates a break in the Lover's consciousness; it is truly a 'new gaze' and makes him a new man. He was formerly a boy in a dream; he is now truly a Lover. He was formerly an observer of paintings and music; he is now an actor in the drama of life. Because of the fountain, the stasis of lyric is transformed into the duration of romance narrative. Furthermore, because this is Ovid's fountain it serves as a *mise en abyme* for the thirteenth-century narrative structure that contains and proclaims a new *Ars amatoria*, the '*Romanz de la Rose, / ou l'art d'Amors est tote enclose*' (37–8) [Romance of the Rose, in which the whole art of love is contained, p. 31]. Narcissus saw only himself; he was closed to himself, and he died; Guillaume's Lover (the Narrator as Lover in his younger state), in his dream, perceives roses and the Rose, and as he is open to the court and the world he proceeds to live and to learn.

Finally, let us not forget that the Lover's life and his learning process take the form of an initiation. He inhabits an earthly paradise where he communes with a god, accepts him as lord, and receives from him the Ten Commandments of Love while at the same time undergoing *passio* – passion and martyrdom. This is secular love, grounded in desire, but desire displaced and deferred; this love is expressed in spiritual terms as a serious parody and aesthetic pastiche of Christian faith, a second faith open to the secular aristocracy, paralleling the first one, which remains the privilege of 'clergie.'

We must also not forget that the story is a pseudo-autobiography, told from one point of view, the Lover's, and recounted with additional comments from himself as Narrator years later. Therefore, it is reflected through one prism only, his. Rose and her psychology appear in the romance only when he makes contact with her, and her psychological elements are depicted as they appear to him, with his value-judgments imposed on them. Therefore, any changes or evolution in her character – the appearance of new allegories – mean not that her psyche has evolved but that, in the flux of duration, the Lover perceives her to be different. Bel Accueil (Fair Welcome) is conceived as a handsome youth and Danger (Resistance) as a disgusting wretch precisely because this is how the suitor, in the throes of desire, reacts to them. Rose, were she to have a voice and a point of view, would, of course, envisage them in very different terms.

Le Roman de la Rose treats the progress of a total love affair. Adhering to the conventions of *fin' amor*, it is the man who loves first and attacks. However, once he sets out to win tangible favours from Rose, she must inevitably play a more active role herself. He becomes aware of contradictory trends in her conduct towards him and of divergent traits within her. Another self enters the narrative, and the play back and forth between her psyche and his constitutes the action. We perceive her reactions to the Lover and to the people around her, her shifting from 'no' to 'yes' and from 'yes' to 'no.' A case can be made that the poem's décor is transposed from life in general (the river bank) to the court (the garden) to the girl's psyche (the rose plot). The conflict that comprises the drama of the poem occurs within her; her heart is the stage on which the Lover seeks to play a part and where his fate will be determined. Both male and female exist only for Eros – he to pluck the Rose or perish in despair and she to accept or decline being plucked – and yet significantly each treats the other uniquely as a thing, a love object. For the Lover, no doubt also for Rose, the Other exists as a series of distinct entities, each embodying an aspect of character, but the total person is never perceived or even imagined. Neither lover nor beloved ever knows the Other or succeeds in establishing what we would call a meaningful relationship.

It is for all of these reasons that Guillaume de Lorris's vision of *fin' amor* is by no means idyllic. Yes, there are hearts and flowers, birds and bees, and the sweetness and joy of a *locus amoenus* – until the Lover gazes into the fountain, beholds the Other, and encounters for the first time a real girl, his Rose. The Fountain of Narcissus is embellished with patterns of imagery negative as well as positive and with notions threatening as well as cajoling – nets, traps, confinement, pain, and death. As the 'Fontaine d'Amors' brought death to Ovid's hero, here it is the cause for the Narrator's falling into the nets and traps of Amor:

> car Cupido, li filz Venus ...
> et fist ses laz environ tendre
> et ses engins i mist por prendre
> demoiseilles et demoisiaus,
> qu'Amors si ne velt autre oisiaus ...
> que maintenant ou laz cheï
> qui maint home a pris et traï. (1586, 1589–92, 1611–12)

For ... Cupid, son of Venus ... stretched his nets and placed his snares to trap young men and women; for Love wants no other birds. ... for now I have fallen into the snare that has captured and betrayed many a man. (Dahlberg, p. 52)

Eventually, pejorative character traits, painted on the outside wall and banished from the world of the court – Vileinie and Vieillesse, among others – will be manifested in the girl's psyche and in her entourage as qualities like Danger and la Vieille. The God of Love predicts years of misery for the Lover, misery which the Narrator confesses to having endured. The dreaming Lover's diegesis, as we have it, ends with a plaint of despair; has the Narrator enjoyed a better fate in his waking existence? Falling in love leads to conflict, hostility, the building of a metaphorical castle and prison, confrontation, and war.

This is true in part because of the nature of love, which requires two people not one; but two psyches can never be one, in part because, for Guillaume and his medieval public, love cannot exist in a private sphere between two elect souls in the style of Shelley or Hugo. As Tristan and Isolt or Lancelot and Guinevere discovered, love takes place in the world, where lovers must cope with the concrete social reality that surrounds them. The pleasure principle of desiring Rose is counterbalanced by the reality principle embodied in the girl's reticence and by the conventions that the community has evolved to socialize and incorporate the threat provoked by unintegrated *juvenes*. The privileged irresponsibility of childhood, the play and self-absorption represented by Oiseuse and Deduit, have to be surpassed before the Lover can become an integrated, adult member of society. *Fin' amor*, by its very nature, occurs at court. The love affair ultimately is a social act and is meant to contribute to the well-being of an aristocratic caste. To the extent that the Lover evolves successfully, it is in a social sense. A solitary figure in the beginning, he joins a group of dancers in the garden, and later interacts with a host of beings in the vicinity of the rose plot. From passively observing pictures on a wall, he takes part in a dance, undergoes social obligations including becoming vassal to the God of Love, and seeks to alter the garden by plucking one of the roses. A case can be made that all the knowledge the Lover obtains is to be used in society, and that his every act is directed as much to acceptance by society as to winning Rose. Presumably he hopes to establish his identity in the community and, once integrated into it, will contribute to the ordering of a true *curialitas*.

Guillaume's book contains a dream that contains a world. Within the world is to be found a wall, within the wall a garden, within the garden a fountain, and within the fountain circular crystals. Near the fountain lies a rose plot and within the rose plot a rose or, later, encompassing it, a fortress; within the fortress lies a keep, and within the keep Bel Accueil. The Lover, in a state of perpetual desire, penetrates from without to within, from the hideous to the beautiful, from stasis to the dance. The youth's suffering and lyric plaints derive from the courtly lyric; his quest, motion, and ordeals derive from romance. Living with greater and greater intensity, he gives himself utterly to the quest, into his Self and into the community; the quest leads through a labyrinth to the sacred place, the *Rosa rosae*, a paradise surrounded by magical defences and repellant guards, containing warmth, intimacy, festivity, song and dance, but also coldness, distance, dysfunction, and disharmony. The woman is the garden, and the garden a woman; she, circle and center of the circle, in this quasi-anagogical realm, can only be known and enjoyed from within.

In *Le Roman de la Rose* the external world mirrors the Lover's inner state. It is a world of perpetual spring, of tenderness and ecstasy, that corresponds to the troubadour ideal of *jovens*. The Narrator's dream implies nostalgia for a better life, for Eden or a lost Golden Age and, in the form of wish-fulfilment, consecrates his return to innocence, idyllic peace, and the green world.

The imagery reflects this state as Guillaume de Lorris takes the matter of Arthurian romance and turns it inwards; the adventures, the quest, the marvels, the battle of *opposants* and *adjuvants* are now applied to representing the hero's inner self as he learns to love. The Garden of Delight with its river barrier, walls, narrow entrance, pleasance, fountain, and castle is as redolent of myth as the Other World in Chrétien or the *Prose Lancelot*. Among the images that contribute to the numen and the myth are the grove itself as *locus amoenus*, the rose as archetype of woman, and the fountain as the feminine element, with its magical alchemical crystals that reveal wisdom. Finally, we have Cupid's arrows, Venus' torch, Danger's club, and Jalousie's castle; these are images of war, the war of the sexes and the war of sexual intercourse, the inner psychomachia and the outer battle of the wills between man and woman, attacker and defender, victor and vanquished.

We can consider the *locus amoenus* in general and Guillaume de Lorris's Garden of Delight in particular as a feminine landscape. This is soft earth; the dream of refuge and rest and of sensuous well-being evokes nostalgia for the Mother. *Le Roman de la Rose* completes the evolution of the long poem from epic to romance and idyll, from war to love. Light, open fields, and the sword give way to shade, intimacy and flowing water. Male gives way to female. The décor consecrates woman, love, and beauty. The God of Love himself chooses a lady who, more than all others, incarnates the Garden of Delight:

> cele dame avoit non Biautez ...
> el ne fu oscure ne brune,
> mes reluisant come la lune

envers qui les autres estoilles
resemblent petites chandailles.
Tendre ot la char come rosee ... (992, 995–9)

a lady ... whose name ... was Beauty ... neither dark nor brunette, she shone as clear as the moon, to which other stars are like the tiny candles. Her flesh was as tender as dew. ... (p. 44)

Delight gives rise to desire, and then, because it is deferred, to love, the dream, and the poem. As the Lover penetrates to the center of the *hortus conclusus*, it is as if he returns to the womb; he masters the labyrinth of enclosed intimacy that is the nature of the Eternal Feminine and, for man, the only path to fulfilment.

The *Rose* thus is a spiritual journey; it is an initiation into a state of grace, of knowledge of woman and all she can give, of absolute truth, of beauty, and of pleasure. It is this sense of initiation – the waking, the ablutions, the straight and narrow gate, the magic crystals, the wound and symbolic death and rebirth in the service of Amor, the neophyte's commitment to a god, his psychomachia, his struggle to conquer obstacles, his pressing onward toward the inner sanctum – that grants the text its numen. Although *Le Roman de la Rose* is not a Christian poem in any meaningful sense of the term (which does not mean that the author, a clerk, failed to practise his faith), it is a religious text, expounding and exploring the new secular faith of *fin' amor.* The absolute commitment of self to a person and to a scale of values other than those taught in the schools becomes a secular faith and dream that have been one hallmark of the West ever since.

Jean de Meun

In the decade extending approximately from 1264 to 1274 Jean de Meun brought to a conclusion the book he claimed was left unfinished some forty years earlier by Guillaume de Lorris. The length of the *Rose* in its entirety, 17,722 lines added to Guillaume's beginning, tells us much about Jean's intentions and character. Jean de Meun does not merely complete the earlier poem; he grafts a totally original sequel onto it. He uses Guillaume's *Rose* as a foundation on which to build his own mansion.

In terms of the plot, the God of Love comes with his army to succour the forlorn Lover. First, Faux Semblant and Abstinence Contrainte slay Male Bouche, permitting the Lover to speak with Bel Accueil. A pitched battle then takes place between the attackers and the defenders of the castle, ending in a truce. Finally, Venus leads a victorious assault, flinging her torch into the sanctuary; the castle bursts into flames and the Lover wins the Rose, just before waking up from his dream.

This is not much for about 18,000 lines of verse. The truth is, the action slows down considerably. Much of Jean's *Rose* is devoted to speeches: exhortations from Raison and Ami to the Lover, Faux Semblant's confession of his nature to the God of Love, la Vieille's exhortation to Bel Accueil, Nature's confession to Genius, and Genius's exhortation to the army, before the final assault.

The God of Love refers to Jean's book as a *'Miroër aus Amoreus'* (10,621) [*'Mirror for Lovers,'* p. 188], alluding to Guillaume's *'Romanz de la Rose,* / ou l'art d'Amors est tote enclose' (37–8). Thus, Guillaume's *Romanz* has been metamorphosed into a mirror, a *speculum*, an encyclopedia. On the one hand, Jean, like his predecessor, writes of love; he simply interprets the term in a much broader sense. Jean de Meun's text expounds all facets of the subject: good love (sex and reproduction, friendship, justice, the love of one's fellow man, reason, and God) and bad love (passion, enslavement to Fortune and money, hypocrisy, clerical celibacy, and the inauthentic relationships between false friends and false lovers). He treats the *theoretica* (by Amor, Nature, Genius) and the *practica* (by Ami, Faux Semblant, la Vieille) of his *ars*. Gunn (1952) is right when he says that all love, human and divine, is contained in the *Rose*.

On the other hand, Jean transforms Guillaume's narrative and refutes it. Jean's philosophy, art, and vision of the universe are totally different from Guillaume's. It is not just that he treats problems – ethics, economics, cosmology, astrology, optics, alchemy, the University – foreign to Guillaume's world. He also mocks, undermines, and destroys the ideal of *fin' amor* at every turn. Furthermore, the speeches are longer and the style more varied (sometimes more sublime, sometimes more earthy, and always more rhetorical). Guillaume's poetry and delicate allegories give way to virulent satire and burning invective; his sentimentality gives way to sensuous instinct and high intellectual wit. The very nature of allegory has been subverted and transformed, for allegory now functions as a pretext, and an entirely new mode of literature takes its place.

Like Guillaume de Lorris but to a much greater extent, Jean de Meun is a teacher, and his book is a masterpiece of didacticism. Throughout his portion of the romance, the Lover plays the role of student, listening to a series of lectures (in a parody of the school *disputatio*), from a number of figures each seeking to mould the young man (or Bel Accueil) in his image and to inculcate his principles, as *magister* and *auctoritas* to the putative disciple. Jean de Meun also uses these sundry voices and personae to teach the implied audience; and, in his role as implied author, he defends himself and his book because they are didactic and they inculcate truths that ought to be known.

The problem the reader faces, as in Chaucer's *Canterbury Tales*, is to discover the author's message. The difficulty occurs because Jean exploits a narrative technique and control of voice and point of view different from those of earlier writers, in fact, unique in medieval literature.

In Jean's portion of the romance, Amor informs his troops that the youth on whose behalf they are waging war is Guillaume de Lorris, who will begin *Le Roman de la Rose* but leave it incomplete, to be taken up more than forty years later by Jean de Meun:

> Puis vendra Johans Chopinel,
> au cuer jolif, au cors inel,
> qui nestra seur Laire a Meün,
> qui a saoul et a geün
> me servira toute sa vie,
> sanz avarice et sanz envie ...
> Cist avra le romanz si chier
> qu'il le voudra tout parfenir,
> se tens et leus l'en peut venir,
> car quant Guillaumes cessera,
> Jehans le continuera,
> enprés sa mort, que je ne mante,
> anz trespassez plus de .XL. ... (10535–40, 10554–60)

Then will come Jean Chopinel with gay heart and lively body. He will be born at Meung-sur-Loire; he will serve me his whole life ... without avarice or envy. ... He will be so fond of the romance that he will want to finish it right to the end, if time and place can be found. For when Guillaume shall cease, more than forty years after his death – may I not lie – Jean will continue it. ... (pp. 187–8)

The God of Love urges that Lucina preside over this great poet's birth, and Jupiter over his upbringing, for the baby one day will become famous throughout France. Now it is physically impossible that Guillaume de Lorris (as Lover in a dream in a book) dreamed of his own death and that he dreamed that the book he had not yet conceived of writing would be continued by someone else. It is no less impossible that Jean de Meun should have heard story material from Guillaume's purported dream that Guillaume himself did not include in the first 4028 lines of the *Rose*, all this forty years after Guillaume's demise.

Whether Amor is or is not conscious of the fact (it would appear he is), the implied audience is reminded in no uncertain terms that the God of Love, his army, and the Lover-Dreamer are all characters in a book, and that the events they are in the process of 'living' occur years before the author's (their author's) birth. The God of Love makes us aware that the diegesis, of which he is a part, contains two persons – Guillaume de Lorris and Jean de Meun – both of whom will become poets but who are not poets yet, for one is still dreaming the diegesis which he will create five years later, and the other is to be born in the more distant future still. Yet the God of Love and the others only exist because they are characters in a book composed by their future authors. In an extraordinarily modern manipulation of point of view, in a first-person, homodiegetic narrative, Jean undermines with comic brio the privileged experience of the Lover and the privileged voice of the I-narrator (both assimilated in part to the persona of Guillaume de Lorris) and establishes distance between that character as lover and observer and himself as implied author. The Lover is still an active agent in the story, and his participation contributes drama and immediacy, as in all first-person tales. However, since he lacks the author's support, we are expected neither to identify with him nor to espouse his views. He is reliable enough as a narrator (*erzählendes Ich*), but not at all as a character (*erlebendes Ich*). He tells the story accurately but does not control our judgment or mould our beliefs. The point of view is clearly actorial rather than authorial, and so we see beyond him (as a character), and we gain insights into the plot and the doctrinal line that he does not have.

Furthermore, a number of characters deliver speeches containing metadiegetic narrative, which, although filtered through the Lover's consciousness and recounted to us as they were purportedly told to him, are so lengthy that we forget the filtering process and can imagine that the Jealous Husband, Faux Semblant, and Genius address us directly. In episodes that occur during the Lover's absence (la Vieille's lecture to Bel Accueil, Nature's confession to Genius), the presence of the I-narrator is so unobtrusive that we can fall into the illusion that he is an objective omniscient third person, and that the *Roman de La Rose* frame structure is heterodiegetic and what Stanzel (1955G) would call *Auktorialsituation*. Jean de Meun's *Rose* can be considered an outstanding early example of polymodality and of multifocalization: it is a story told by an I-narrator who is at various times hero, witness, or quasi-omniscient outsider (mock-author, scriptor), and at the same time it is a story delegated to a series of secondary I-narrators and focalized through their consciousnesses. Indeed, the poem contains so much dialogue that no genuine internal focalization (in the Lover) is possible. On the contrary these delegated voices provide so much immediacy and drama that the protagonist's own point of view disappears temporarily from the narrative. This means that when the Jealous Husband, for example, perorates for nine hundred lines against womankind, exploiting all the rhetorical verve, vehemence, and vitality of Jean de Meun at his best, the implied reader may well forget that he is a comic character whose absurd ideas are reported as being absurd both by Ami and the Lover-Narrator. On the contrary, for nine hundred lines he is the I-narrator, his is the authorial, privileged voice. For nine hundred lines this empassioned orator has the opportunity to convince the implied audience and to overpower and seduce it under the weight and the power of his discourse.

The problem is, each of the great delegated narrators – Raison, Ami, Faux Semblant, la Vieille, Nature, Genius, as well as le Jaloux – speaks in his own voice, with equal vehemence and authority. We cannot assume that Jean de Meun necessarily agrees with any one over the others. Indeed, lest we yield to the rhetoric, he creates distance and undermines his own delegated voices. First of all, each of the speakers is a comic character in his own right, one at whom the implied audience ought to be laughing. In addition, in terms of argument, each has a proclivity to contradict himself and to invoke authority (texts from the Classics) inappropriate to the point in question and often serving to refute rather than support the speaker's position (this will be imitated brilliantly by Chaucer). Hill (1966–7) and Baumgartner (1974) have shown that Jean de Meun has le Jaloux cite the examples of Lucretia and Heloise that in fact argue against his own denial of freedom to women in matrimony, and he has la Vieille cite Venus, Mars, and Vulcan, as well as Boethius, who in fact argue against her espousal of freedom for women in or out of matrimony. Ami urges absolute liberty for both sexes, and then counsels the Lover how to keep Rose for himself once he has won her. Debating with Raison, the Lover-Narrator himself irrationally refuses speech as communication and poetry; the protagonist of allegory refuses metaphorical discourse. It is no accident that the story of Pygmalion – an episode that crowns the

Roman – can be interpreted *in sensu bono* (the triumph of love and art) and *in sensu malo* (the triumph of narcissism and idolatry), or even that the Lover's final plucking of Rose can be interpreted as an act of triumphant comic phallicism and procreation and as the ultimate reification and degradation of woman and his own Self.

As in real life, no commentator leads us by the hand through *Le Roman de la Rose*, although it is to be hoped that the reader will eventually know more than any of the characters, including the Lover and the Narrator. It is up to the reader to judge each character in turn, as the figure unconsciously reveals his own shortcomings, blatantly holds forth logical inconsistencies, and sophistically misinterprets the very classical *auctores* he cites so badly. It is the reader's job to analyze fact and motivation, cause and effect, and mind and rhetoric, whether he wants to or not. The result, determined by Jean de Meun's narrative technique, is a state of doctrinal indeterminacy in which the Lover as narratee intradiegetically and we the implied audience extradiegetically are offered a sequence of philosophies, doctrines, and worldviews. Although, in the end, the Lover decides, the implied audience is not obliged to confirm his decision. The indeterminacy remains to the end, part and parcel of Jean's text and of a late medieval mentality of which Jean de Meun is the first outstanding master.

Less a matter of indeterminacy is the phenomenology of Jean de Meun's imaginative world, an area in which he is as great an innovator as in narratology. Compared to Guillaume de Lorris, Jean is a master of vulgar speech, material detail, and picaresque naturalism. He shifts our perspective from top to bottom, from rose petals to what they hide, to Bakhtin's (1968G) 'material bodily lower stratum.' A generation defore Dante, and three generations before Chaucer, Jean de Meun juxtaposes high style and low style, *genus grande* and *genus humile*. Scenes, images, and speech once confined to the fabliau are now included in a serious work of art, next to the sublime. Le Jaloux and la Vieille stroll side by side with Dame Raison and Dame Nature. The pilgrims to Canterbury are already present in Jean de Meun's rose garden.

The presence of le Jaloux and la Vieille underscores the role of money in the erotic life. Ami urges the youth to bribe Rose's defenders. 'There were no riches in the Golden Age,' he says, 'but since then we have both gold and kings; nowadays ladies listen to the jingle of coin, not to the roll of fine verses.' The Jealous Husband is a miser, who chastises his wife as much for spending his earnings as for deceiving him, and he is convinced that her lovers sniff about his doorstep for her gold as well as for her body. Faux Semblant is one of a band of wicked friars who amass ill-gotten wealth by begging; they take false vows of poverty, offering spiritual succour only to the rich, who succour them in turn. Finally, la Vieille urges Bel Accueil to prostitute himself, to sell himself to rich men for money and to fleece his lovers and their families without mercy.

In sum, le Jaloux envisages his wife as a thing, as property to be enjoyed and then defended against the outside world. So also for Ami and la Vieille, the opposite sex is an object to be purchased, bartered, or exchanged for money or other commodities. The young Lover and, for that matter, the older Narrator conceive of Rose only as a sex object; indeed, when recounting the story of her defloration, the Narrator discourses in prollepsis on his other, postdream conquests, contrasting the relative merits of young and old roses. The process of reification and of antifeminism is crowned by Jean de Meun's transformation of the woman-rose into a piece of lifeless architecture (the sanctuary), which the Lover pries open with his pilgrim's staff, while alluding to his conquests in gastronomic terms as the courses of a meal or as wide and narrow roads that constitute female topography:

> Quant suis en aucun leu requoi
> et je chemine, je le (mon bourdon) boute
> es fosses ou je ne voi goute
> ausinc con por les guez tanter,
> si que je me puis bien vanter
> que n'i ai garde de naier,
> tant sai bien les guez essaier,
> et fier par rives et par fonz ...
> Mes or lessons ces voies lees
> a ceus qui les vont volantiers;
> et nous les deduisanz santiers,
> non pas les chemins aus charretes,
> mes les jolives santeletes,
> jolif et ranvoisié tenons,
> qui les jolivetez menons. (21370–7, 21398–404)

When, in my travels, I find myself in a remote place, I put it [my staff] into the ditches where I can see nothing, to see if they can be forded. That way, I can congratulate myself that there's no delay [drowning (my translation)] to fear, so well do I know how to deal with the fords, to trust [thrust into (my translation)] the banks and brooks. ... But let us leave these wide roads to those who travel them willingly, and let those of us who lead a light-hearted life

> keep gaily to the seductive bypaths, not the cart roads but the intriguing footpaths. (p. 349)

The Lover does not make love with a woman; he plucks a rose, he opens a reliquary, he crosses a road.

Jean de Meun evokes a world populated by different social classes, all of which are motivated by two and only two forces: lust for flesh and lust for money. The two are conceived in identical terms. Both men and women are victims of the process of reification to which the entire community is subjected; this is a way of life in which property, the profit motive, and the hoarding of riches give men 'mestrise' and in which things take precedence over persons.

More striking is the role the author ascribes to manipulation and duplicity. At the centre of the romance stands Faux Semblant (False Seeming), the archetype of duplicity (Brownlee 1991). This is the most honest of Jean de Meun's tricksters (he confesses his own nature and denounces himself). Because of his virulent condemnation of cheating, he is inconsistent with himself and therefore commits a further act of deception. After the speech is over, Faux Semblant returns to a position of integrity, that is non-integrity, tricking and killing Male Bouche (Evil Tongue, Foul Mouth). The most communicative creature in Jean's poem slays the figural representation of communication. Significantly, Amor and the Lover welcome Faux Semblant into their army. He is a necessary element in the war of the sexes and is as important as Venus herself in forcing the castle to surrender.

Communication (speech) serves to instruct but also to trick. All people can be divided into two classes – knaves and fools, masters and slaves, the deceivers and the deceived. Ami, le Jaloux, la Vieille, Faux Semblant, even Raison and Nature, seek to be masters not slaves, to exploit and not to be exploited. Each is an embodiment of will-to-power with every word and action directed toward triumphing over the Other. This means that the Other is always an object, and the individual's prime concern becomes not to be treated like an object in turn. In the long run, the fundamental issue is one of freedom as opposed to non-freedom and power and domination as opposed to passivity and impotence; only through power and domination do people attain the money and pleasure they crave.

Finally, the beings who inhabit Jean de Meun's world create illusion behind masks; they disguise themselves. Faux Semblant dresses as a pilgrim, and Abstinence Contrainte as a Béguine; Genius plays the role of bishop to exhort Love's army; and the Lover becomes a pilgrim when he is about to force Rose's sanctuary. La Vieille advises a repertory of disguises – changes in dress and the use of cosmetics – to seduce men. 'Clothes do not make the monk,' says Faux Semblant, and the Jealous Husband, who objects to the expense and the obstacle to his libido, claims that his wife's raiment is silk and flowers on top of manure. Yet, between a clothed wife and a naked one, which is reality and which is illusion? Is Pygmalion perhaps wiser than le Jaloux when he dresses up his statue, creating an illusion later transformed into reality? It is not easy for people to distinguish appearance from truth, or the mask from flesh, or the literal bark from an allegorical kernel. Jean's characters discover this; so do his readers.

The author tells us that dissimulation, violence, and evil are part of the human condition (and have been since the end of the Golden Age) and that we must learn to cope with them. Throughout the *Rose* he urges the Lover (the principal inscribed narratee) and the extradiegetic implied audience to go beyond appearances and seek the truth. He holds up to scrutiny commonly accepted ideas about love, money, fortune, kingship, dreams, alchemy, and clerical celibacy. All the delegated voices speak to open our eyes and rip aside the mask of falsehood.

Jean de Meun favours light not darkness; he wants us to raise up the mask, to open the garden, and to peel off clothes and petals, or at least to recognize the fact that masks exist and are as real as the faces they cover. Although art is inferior to nature and optics distort, especially Guillaume de Lorris's 'miroërs perilleus' [perilous mirror], it is possible, in Jean's '*miroër aus Amoreus*,' to strive for truth; this involves not only hoarding a fund of information about the cosmos but also (anticipating a later notion of enlightenment) teaching us to seek truth and avoid appearance and illusion.

Knowledge can then lead to action. Some of Jean's characters remain passive, blind, and impotent. One of these is the Lover himself at the beginning of Jean's section of the *Rose*; there Guillaume's Lover is reduced to despair, on the point of abandoning the rose quest, and unaware of what he really wants from Rose, all because he is a prisoner of the false, artificial conventions of *fin' amor*. Seventeen thousand lines later, whatever may be his cynicism and selfishness the Lover has joined those who are lucid, open to reality, and capable of dealing with it. He recognizes his lustful nature and commits himself to satisfying it. He attains a measure of freedom and participation in the vital force of the universe. He becomes a master not a slave, a free man not a captive, an adult not a boy, and a *doctor amoris* not a pupil.

Having discovered the reality of life, he is able to use deceit for his purposes, and not to be used by it.

In a very real sense of the term Jean de Meun's is a world of comedy. Several of his characters embody the comic archetypes derived from the classics of ancient Rome: Ami the *dolosus servus*, an *eiron* figure of wit and brio; the Jealous Husband the *senex iratus*, an *alazon* obsessed by jealousy and avarice; la Vieille the *vetula*, an old whore who acts as a go-between. The others, of more immediately medieval provenance, are no less obsessed and rigid in their compulsions, whatever they may be. More to the point, the narrative line, such as it is, constitutes the triumph of young desire over old constraint. In spite of the blocking figures, and in spite of *fin' amor* and a castle's walls, Venus's torch wins out, and this medieval Human Comedy ends, as comedies must, in joy and laughter, with the couple packed off to bed.

Oiseuse was Guillaume de Lorris's gatekeeper. In Jean de Meun's section she is replaced, so to speak, by Nature, who labours incessantly, running a never-ending race with Death, to ensure fecundity and the preservation of the human line. She embodies an ideal of activity contrasting with Guillaume's static Garden of Delight. In his turn Genius urges the soldiers in Amor's host to work:

> Saiez es euvres naturex
> plus vistes que nus escurex
> et plus legiers et plus movanz
> que ne peut estre oiseaus ou vanz! ...
> Remuez vos, tripez, sailliez,
> ne vos lessiez pas refredir
> par trop voz mambres antedir!
> Metez touz voz ostiz en euvre:
> assez s'eschaufe qui bien euvre.
>   Arez, por Dieu, baron, arez,
> et voz lignages reparez. (19659–62, 19666–72)

At the works of nature, be quicker than any squirrel, lighter and more mobile than a bird or the wind may be. ... Move, skip, leap; don't let yourself get cold or let your limbs [members (my translation)] become tepid. Put all your tools to work; he who works well keeps warm enough. Plow, for God's sake, my barons, plow and restore your lineages. (p. 324)

Love as ecstasy gives way to love in action.

The poet's vision is elaborated through patterns of imagery. Nature reproduces the species by hammering out individuals at her forge. Genius exhorts the army to make love in terms of phallic metaphor; it is to hammer on anvils, plow fields, and scrape quills on parchment. These 'soldiers' swear fealty on 'relics' (their arrows and other pointed instruments), whereupon the Lover breaks into the sanctuary with his pilgrim's staff. Such blatantly Freudian motifs, corresponding to Bachelard's hard earth of the will, are reinforced by the equally 'masculine' image of the torch; the soldiers swear on torches as well as on arrows, and it is by tossing her firebrand into the fortress that Venus brings victory. Analogous to the Holy Spirit, the spark of fire symbolizes the male seed, striking out against feminine images of fountain, *hortus conclusus*, and enclosed castle. From this torch comes the light that pierces the darkness of courtly obscurantism. Nature and Venus both assume masculine characteristics, as if the notion of sexual and intellectual liberation is perceivable only within a male world-view. This can be explained by Jean's elaboration of the images of the hunt and of the siege, whereby Guillaume de Lorris's *bellum intestinum* is transformed into a battle of cosmic proportions with genuine epic overtones. The war of the sexes proves to be one of Jean's recurring motifs; in la Vieille he has created one of the most dynamic, devouring, castrating women in world literature. Finally, although Guillaume's Garden of Delight has all but disappeared from Jean de Meun's poem, the rose remains. As in Guillaume de Lorris it is an image of Nature's bounty and of the good life. However, Jean also interprets it blatantly, 'vaginally,' as the female sexual organ, to be literally and figuratively deflowered by the pilgrim-Lover's purse and staff (21675–96).

Jean de Meun's world, partially inherited from Guillaume de Lorris, is one of enclosed, compartmentalized space: Rose in her sanctuary, Bel Accueil in la Vieille's tower, Male Bouche and the others guarding the castle, Nature and Genius talking indoors in her chapel, and Fortune's island and the Garden of the Lamb protected within barriers. However, in the course of the poem the walls are broken, the enclosed space opened, and the sanctuary door shattered. The end of the *Rose* is a humorous, perhaps satirical, perhaps profound representation of the sexual act; male and female libido (Amor and Venus) unite to help fecundity triumph. In this wish-fulfilment, allegorical universe Amor, Ami, Faux Semblant, la Vieille, Nature, and Genius are all manifestations of the id. Raison alone represents the superego, and she is vanquished. Although one Terrible Mother (la Vieille) does make an appearance, she embodies an aggressive pleasure principle and sides with the young against their obstructive society. The Father-enemy appears only as a shadowy, ridiculous *gilos*, playing no active role in the narrative. The superego figures are females, whereas the male authorities, Amor and Genius, take the Lover's side. Those who decline to reproduce are threatened with castration, a fate which overcomes Adonis, Abelard, Origen, and Saturn and which ought to overcome more than one friar. When Faux Semblant cuts off Male Bouche's tongue, the latter also pays the price for opposing the vital force of the cosmos.

One aspect of Jean's vision is what appears to be the denigration of the intellectual and artistic pursuits that the goddess Raison embodies. Early in his career the Lover declines her invitation to gloss the poets; he will put aside studies until after he has plucked the Rose. Then, just before the plucking, an older, wiser Narrator proclaims that he prefers his sexual organs to his harp and guitar. On the other hand, since Jean insists that the author and the Lover (a character derived from Guillaume de Lorris) are not identical personages, we have to view with a critical eye everything that the Lover does and that the Narrator says. The *Rose* is a story of language. It is made up of lengthy speeches that replace the narrative plot central to Guillaume de Lorris; Guillaume's erotic diegesis is deferred in favour of discourse, in which the characters communicate with each other intellectually and often recommend rhetoric or sophistry as an arm in the war of seduction. Indeed, Guillaume de Lorris's Lover-narrator is transformed by Jean de Meun into a Lover-narratee; he listens to others, and is a reader of the discourse of others (a discourse created, of course, by Jean de Meun). Furthermore, Jean's work is not only a sequel to but a gloss on the text of his predecessor; Jean includes Guillaume's *Rose* intertextually in *his Rose* in toto as one of the doctrinal positions in a complete *disputatio amoris*. The famous comic debate between Raison and the Lover over 'coilles' [balls] and relics, and whether or not euphemisms are appropriate in erotic discourse (itself an implied criticism of Guillaume's ideal of courtesy) concerns the functioning of language, specifically literary language, in society; so does Jean's denouement, in which an older, wiser lover plucks his rose and seizes his 'relic'; he masters euphemism but for obscene not courtly purposes.

Nor should we forget that Jean cites his literary predecessors over eighty times, alluding to forty-four specific authors and sixty specific exempla (Regalado 1981). By having Amor designate him by name as the favourite of Jupiter, and by having Amor prophesy that he (Jean) will become the finest poet of France, Jean de Meun exalts himself as the creator of *Le Roman de la Rose*. He locates himself, along with Guillaume de Lorris, as an heir to the great legacy of poets in Latin. He even claims the title of erotic Moses or Joshua. Then, in another passage (15105–272), Jean as implied author intervenes obtrusively in the narrative to defend himself against possible charges of misogyny and anticlericalism. Although he assumes a posture of humility ('I only quote the Ancients; I only criticize bad monks'), in realty his apology is an example of ironic 'affected modesty' and serves as a counter-offensive against his enemies, reaffirming his status as poet and satirist and proclaiming his right to seek the truth and tell it as he sees it. Jean de Meun is the first writer of fiction in a modern vernacular to introduce himself into his own story obtrusively and to emphasize the role of the book (his creation) in his own plot. God, creator of the universe, is largely absent, but not Jean de Meun, creator of the book that imitates Nature, who carries out God's work. The book serves to vindicate the Lover's career and prove that his waking up is not an end but a beginning – the beginning of the narrative of the dream. Highly significant is the analogy made by Genius between phallic, procreative desire and the writer's work of striking quill on parchment. This can mean, following Gunn (1952), Poirion (1970), and Payen (1976), that only two successful lovers, fathers, and artists are to be found in the *Rose*: Pygmalion, the creative sculptor, and the Lover become Narrator, the creative poet. It can also mean that the purpose of *Le Roman de la Rose* is not to encourage free love or to condemn it but to play with words, speech, and ideas, and so to argue all sides and create a work of art.

Given that Jean de Meun lashes out at his characters, proclaiming their foibles without mercy, he also portrays them with such gusto and breathes the breath of life into them with such joy that we cannot help being overawed by them and sympathizing with them too. Le Jaloux is a fool, yet we are carried along by his rhetoric; although la Vieille is a knave, we respect her courage, persistance, and indomitable will to power. How can we resist these Faux Semblants and these Reynard the Foxes who are so intelligent and always victorious? Humanity breaks through the mask. We have the right to admire, even to cherish, such magnificent satirical types, trickster heroes and master rhetoricians, vibrant with life and true to the human condition.

The usual distinction between comedy and satire, love and hatred, Horace and Juvenal, is misplaced in the literature of France, especially when we read books like *Le Roman de Renart* and *Le Roman de la Rose*.

Whatever Jean's doctrine, I believe his ultimate purpose is to evoke a comic world. He laughs at everyone and everything – at all the ineptness, cruelty, stupidity, and ruse that make up our lives. He also tells a story in which, owing to quick wit, cynicism, libidinal vitality, and an unconquerable will-to-power – whether for good or ill – the army of Eros, made up of comic tricksters, triumphs over the old law of opposition. Whether for good or ill, the victory of defiant instinct, celebration, youth, and man's healthy animal nature is achieved in a denouement of erotic explosion in which society itself is transformed. Humanism, plenitude, and the exaltation of life are fused with clerical irony and mockery. More than any of his predecessors, Jean de Meun embodies the awaking of humanism, the rebirth of interest in classical Antiquity, the joyful lust for life, and the exaltation of art and the artist that mark the medieval Renaissance twelfth and thirteenth centuries. His *Roman de la Rose* is one of the most extraordinary works in the history of France; in Frye's (1957G) sense of the term it is an anatomy that contains the best of its age.

The legacy of *Le Roman de la Rose* to the subsequent tradition, in France and in England, was immense. To the extent that Lewis (1936) is right and allegory is the dominant mode of the later Middle Ages, that later tradition is derived from Guillaume de Lorris and Jean de Meun. Guillaume de Lorris was the first writer of stature to construct a vernacular allegory. He created a dream vision that is both subjective and objective; it mirrors the dreamer's day residue and also predicts future events while teaching universal truths. His application of personification allegory to the secular, amorous psychology of the individual marks a watershed: he discovered radical new ways of exploring the growth of the individual and the inner workings of the psyche, and of granting deeper levels of meaning to otherwise mundane events. Without Guillaume de Lorris there would have been no Machaut and Froissart, no *Book of the Duchess* and *Parliament of Fowls*, no *Pearl* and no *Patience*.

Jean de Meun's heritage is different. He neglects consistency of allegory and subtle psychological analysis in favor of the big picture – people functioning in society and the fundamental intellectual problems of his age. Jean's *Rose* mushrooms into a summa that includes all of life and all the cosmos. His mode is satiric not idyllic and his discourse is one of invective not narrative. The satire and the comedy attain a unique juxtaposition of low and sublime denunciation. These can then proliferate in the secular domain or they can turn back into the sacred. Jean's inheritors are Digulleville and Langland as well as

Machaut and Chaucer. An additional element of Jean's legacy proves to be the multiplicity of voices contributing to a grand symposium with no overt intellectual closure; closure is ever deferred and life itself perceived to be fragmentation and disjunction, a world where Ami (Pandarus), Faux Semblant (the Pardoner), and la Vieille (Alice of Bath) speak and live on equal terms. In this domain, as in the encyclopedic, the comic, and societal, Jean de Meun's chief heir is Geoffrey Chaucer, and England's *Roman de la Rose* is the *Canterbury Tales.*

4. Guillaume de Digulleville

Guillaume de Digulleville[16] represents an extraordinary anomaly. He was perceived to be a major figure in his own lifetime and for a good century at least after his death, and his impact on late medieval letters, in both France and England, was immense. Yet in modern times and in modern scholarly circles, he has never been taken seriously nor received the scrutiny or the rehabilitation that Machaut and even the grands rhétoriqueurs have come to enjoy. The critical attention paid to him is due almost uniquely to Anglicists, who sought him out because of Lydgate and, more recently, to art historians who recognize the importance of the illuminated Digulleville manuscripts.

A monk in Chaalis, a Cistercian house near Senlis, Digulleville was well-read in French and Latin, and wrote texts in both languages. *Pèlerinage de la Vie humaine*, an allegorical account of the Narrator's spiritual voyage through life, was composed in 1330–2, and then revised and amplified (an additional four thousand lines in French and eleven hundred in Latin) in 1355. *Pèlerinage de l'Ame*, treating the soul's adventures in the afterlife, comes from the years 1355–8; and in 1358 appeared a biography of Christ, the final panel of Digulleville's pilgrimage triptych, *Pèlerinage de Jésus Christ*. Guillaume also composed a briefer text, *Le Roman de la Fleur de lys* (1338), upholding the Valois claim to the throne of France as opposed to the Plantagenets.

Digulleville's opus enjoyed wide popularity and intellectual prestige; it also exerted concrete influence on other writers. We have more than fifty extant manuscripts of the 1330s version of *La Vie humaine* and nine manuscripts or printed editions of the 1355 version. Both redactions and *Pèlerinage de l'Ame* were adapted (revised) into French verse and prose, and into Latin prose. *La Vie humaine* also benefited from translation into modern tongues, including Spanish, German (three versions), and Dutch (three versions) as well as English. The Duke of Bedford, one of Digulleville's staunchest readers, ordered several of these efforts at modernization and/or vulgarization, in both French and English. As is the case for other works discussed in this section, Guillaume's posterity proved to be richer in England than on the Continent. Lydgate translated the 1355 *Vie humaine* into English verse (1426–8); someone else translated the 1330s version faithfully and accurately into English prose (*The Pilgrimage of the Lyfe of the Manhode*: six extant manuscripts). A prose redaction of *L'Ame* dates from 1413; copied in a number of manuscripts, it was later published by Caxton (1483). Chaucer himself translated the famous 'ABC' Prayer to the Virgin from *La Vie humaine*; Hoccleve translated one prayer, perhaps thirteen others, from *L'Ame*. In addition, *Pèlerinage de la Vie humaine* furnishes an inestimable gloss on several of the *Canterbury Tales* as well as the whole idea of the pilgrimage poem. Since Digulleville's masterpiece was the first 'Pilgrimage of Life' book and since it launched the pilgrimage of life subgenre of the sacred allegory, it may even have given Chaucer the idea for his masterpiece. Finally, an English prose rendering was copied and illustrated several times up to the middle of the seventeenth century. *Pèlerinage de la Vie humaine*, in its English or French versions, was the most elaborate and the best pilgrimage of life text prior to Bunyan's *Pilgrim's Progress*. Not only was Digulleville translated by Chaucer, Lydgate and Hoccleve, but his is the first link that leads to John Bunyan, or for that matter to C.S. Lewis.

Pèlerinage de la Vie humaine

Pèlerinage de la Vie humaine recounts in terms of allegory the spiritual journey of an I-narrator from birth to death. The Pilgrim dreams that he beholds in a mirror the New Jerusalem. He meets Grâce Dieu, who invites him to her castle where he listens to speeches by Grâce Dieu, Raison, Nature, Sapience, Aristotle, and Moses. He then sets out on a voyage on which he is attacked by Peresce, Orgueil, Envie, Ire, Avarice, Gloutonnie, and Venus. Having escaped from his foes through the Hedge of Pénitence, after a prayer to the Virgin and the intervention of Grâce Dieu, the Pilgrim falls into the Sea of the World where he avoids Satan's nets, is whisked about by Jeunesse, and falls into the hands of Tribulation. Finally he attains peace and security in the Ship of Religion. There he suffers from Enfermeté and Vieillesse, is comforted by Miséricorde and Pitié, and is wounded by Mort, upon which he wakes up.

It is obvious that the characters the Pilgrim meets, the objects he employs, and the regions through which he voyages are personifications and allegories; furthermore, each stage of his voyage, recounted literally, is meant to be understood on another, allegorical level. Contained within a dream-vision frame, the pilgrimage action is made up primarily of speech (dialogue), motion (the quest or voyage), and confrontation (warfare). In essence, the action with symbolic figures through a symbolic landscape recounts both the Pilgrim's outer, physical, temporal journey from birth to death and his inner, spiritual, timeless journey from the fallen condition of man, *peccatum Adae*, to the redeemed state of the Christian soul *in Christo*. Twice we observe the Pilgrim suffer from spiritual weakness, fall into temptation, and give way to sin, but then he returns to a godly life through understanding and repentance. In the end, the order of the monastic community on the Ship of Religion parallels the exposition of the sacraments in Grâce Dieu's castle in the beginning; these two moments of order in stasis encompass and, ultimately, harmonize the life of chaos in the world inserted between them.

But for a handful of tentative, apologetic caveats, *Pèlerinage de la Vie humaine* has been roundly condemned by the scholars; allegedly, the poem is too dry and intellectual and too verbose; action is replaced by an excess of description and discussion; the conversations are dull and too long; and the action that does occur is absurd from a mimetic perspective and lacks order from a structural one.

Part of the problem derives from the fact that a number of these scholars view Digulleville through the prism of Lydgate's *Pilgrimage of the Life of Man*. Lydgate chose to translate the 1355 redaction which, indeed, is more verbose, more didactic, and duller than the original book from the 1330s. Furthermore, Lydgate's own pedestrian verse (he was far more inspired elsewhere) dampens the flair, the verve, the satirical bite, and the gaiety of Guillaume de Digulleville's style at its best.

In addition, scholars judge the monk of Chaalis not for what he did, but for what they wanted him to do, in the line of Dante and Chaucer, or for that matter Balzac and Dickens. In point of fact, the medieval allegorist begins and ought to begin with abstract concepts which he then conveys in concrete terms. As in *Le Roman de la Rose*, allegory functions on two levels, literal and figurative, vehicle and tenor, signifier and signified. The interpretation of allegory is primarily an intellectual process not a poetical or imaginative one, although good allegory inevitably contains a ration of poetry and imagination. This means that the relationship between tenor and vehicle is precise, logical, fixed, and universal; it also means that the reader-audience's principal task focuses on the intellectual deciphering of the relationship and/or the intellectual judgment of its appropriateness.

In the case of Guillaume de Digulleville, as with all serious medieval and Renaissance allegory including Guillaume de Lorris and Jean de Meun, the text 'produces' a narrative, but the narrative also functions on another level deemed to be more serious, a level of wisdom. The story of the Pilgrim is not meant simply to entertain, nor is the personage to be identified with any one person, historical or imaginary, not even the author. The 'I' is universal, his tale is one of universal growth through life, and at the heart of *La Vie humaine* lies the scrutiny of man's spiritual growth – serious moral and intellectual issues.

Secondly, for people in the Middle Ages the world was a book and books were a world. Both a book and the world were texts to be deciphered; containing all, they were to be explored in their every detail. Treating the entire spiritual life, Digulleville's *Pèlerinage* elaborates on all seven sacraments, all seven deadly sins, all seven cardinal and theological virtues, the creed, and the Mass (cf. Henry 1986b). Hence Digulleville's summa exhibits not only comprehensiveness but also the minuteness of classifications and subdivisions. In this scholastic, late Gothic, mannerist world one can dramatize an idea-become-metaphor (Wrath, Gluttony) or (cf. Blythe 1974) one can depict it by breaking it down into its constituent parts. Description and commentary are not reductive; they are a kind of gloss which, as in *Le Roman de la Rose*, contributes to our understanding and thus to the world book in its totality. It is only through such rigorous order that people could expect both to understand and to resist the chaos of corporeal vice. Furthermore, the medieval reader-audience took pleasure in anticipating the explanation – trying to decipher the meaning of the description before the description is explained – or commenting afterward on its appropriateness. In either case the implied reader-audience participates in the hermeneutic process, learns along with the Pilgrim, judges him, and empathizes with him at the same time.

Pèlerinage de la Vie humaine has an intellectual structure – it discusses the seven sacraments, the seven virtues, and then the seven vices, etc. – as well as a narrative structure, the Pilgrim's voyage through life. Guillaume de Digulleville's chief error, as a writer, may be to have had 'makers of discourse' reveal to the Pilgrim (or in his presence) a vast amount of didactic material before he actually sets out on the quest. For the first five thousand lines the Pilgrim remains largely motionless, observing and listening to what occurs around him but not acting on his own.

Digulleville can be defended on several grounds, however. It is a fact of Christian doctrine that, by the very act of baptism, the Christian becomes a member of the Church and receives God's grace (Grâce Dieu as teacher and guide) and the three theological virtues, faith, hope, and love. He benefits from the seven sacraments and from Holy Mass, all of which occur within the bounds of Ecclesia. This also means that the moral responsibility of the Christian is greater than for other men, for, if he commits vice, it is in the full knowledge of sin. He is expected to know what happens when, as Digulleville explains, the body takes control and overpowers the reasoning faculty. The Christian sins in spite of his reason, God's grace, and his knowledge of the good; appetite corrupts the will, and both appetite and the will corrupt reason.

Digulleville explores the psychology of the Christian soul when struggling with temptation and vice. For many young people, the sacraments and virtue itself appear to be abstractions, learned more or less by rote, whereas vice is another matter; it is immediate, concrete, and very physical, involving a confrontation in and with the world. The first category, mastered by the intellect, is perceived to be verbal; the second, mastering the flesh, is perceived to be physical. The narrative structure, as structure, mirrors the psychological reality it purports to treat.

Furthermore, Guillaume's quintessentially medieval message is that life is a war in which one is continually on the defensive, assaulted by enemies; one's only hope for survival is to resist through the mind, by faith, reason, prayer, and the refusal both of temptation and the gifts of Lady Fortune. This battle of life begins in late adolescence or early manhood. Yet its outcome depends upon the traits of character or the moral instruction the child will have received previously.

Finally, the Pilgrim's relative stillness, seeming impotence, or even stupidity if you will, in the presence of the seven monstrous ladies (the capital Vices) also is meaningful. On the one hand, the Pilgrim is not meant to embody any single mimetic person. He is a universal type, an Every Man or Any Man, an Every Pilgrim, who serves as a bridge between the implied author and his implied reader-audience and, in his ignorance and passivity, helps us become less ignorant and less passive. It is also true that Digulleville wants us to learn that one truly knows vice by participating in it and that the committing of wrong is indissolubly bound to the knowledge of wrong; the two occur simultaneously. The Pilgrim is a dupe; so are we. We all are dupes when confronted with our favourite sins; we all are assaulted and initiated (defiled) in the same way. We learn through experience of good and evil; so does the Pilgrim. And from the perspective of a Cistercian monk, does he not also tell us that authority (speech in Ecclesia) is good, but experience (life in the world) can cause great harm?

Allegory is in essence verbal, for its function is to teach, and the teaching process occurs when the reader discovers or is told both the message to be taught and the functioning of the allegorical process – how he is taught. Thus Jean de Meun's *Roman de la Rose*, containing little narrative action, is devoted largely to speeches by entities who, in the *conflictus amoris*, aim to seduce the Lover and win him and the implied reader to their ways of thinking. Similarly, for all its quite tangible efforts at creating visual effects, Digulleville's *Pèlerinage* is also a poem of speech. As in *Le Roman de la Rose*, the Pilgrim is the provoker of discourse, and the various personifications he encounters, all authority figures *in bono* or *in malo*, are the discoursers. Therefore, the Narrator describes in minute detail the appearance of the characters he, as Pilgrim, encounters, and he recounts in no less detail the dialogues that occur between them or the speeches they deliver directly to him. In his role as Pilgrim he does ask questions, facilitating the speechmaking. However, his most important use of speech is in prayer – appeals to help from God, Grâce Dieu, or Mary – and supplications the Pilgrim makes in dire straights that prove to be his only means of 'salut,' the term to be understood as cure, rescue, and salvation.

Verbal communication is crucial in this didactic text about the nature of good and evil. Good and evil figures – Moses, Grâce Dieu, Miséricorde; Ire, Avarice, Venus – teach the Pilgrim; then the Pilgrim, as Narrator, transformed from a student into a master, teaches his implied audience. Similarly, early in life, as Pilgrim he is a reader, a spectator, and an audience to the texts of others; then, as a writer in turn, as Narrator and implied author he makes us read his text. It contains speech in the form of texts, it is about speech and the textual process, and it tells a story in which speech plays the dominant role whether the Pilgrim wanders on the road or stands immobile in the Castle of Holy Church.

It is significant that *Pèlerinage de la Vie humaine* alludes to a *texte générateur* [textual generator] that functions as a negative *mise en abyme* – *Le Roman de la Rose*. The Pilgrim falls asleep and has his dream vision because he was reading the *Rose* (cf. Badel 1980, Wright 1989):

Une vision veul nuncier
Qui en dormant m'avint l'autrier.
En veillant avoie lëu,
Considere et bien vëu
Le biau roumans de la Rose.
Bien croi que ce fu la chose
Qui plus m'esmut a ce songier
Que ci apres vous vueil nuncier. (7–14)

I want to recount a vision that came to me the other night as I was sleeping. While I was awake, I had read, studied, and looked closely at the beautiful *Romance of the Rose*. I am sure that this was what moved me most to have the dream I will tell you about in a moment. (Clasby, p. 3)

Like Chaucer (here Chaucer undoubtedly imitated him), Digulleville conceives a quite specific narrative and aesthetic structure; reading a book leads to sleep and a dream that leads to the writing of a book. A number of characters in the *Pèlerinage* are derived from or influenced by Jean de Meun: Jean's Raison and Nature reappear in Guillaume's text; they also contribute to the figure of Grâce Dieu. Lorris's Vieillesse and Meun's la Vieille are reincarnate in all seven of the capital sins, including the now degraded lechery embodied in Venus. Like Guillaume de Lorris's Lover, Digulleville's Pilgrim chooses the path of Oiseuse, but this time with disastrous results. And the erotic, obscene phallic satchel and staff with which Jean's Lover pries open the sanctuary are restored to their true Christian function as sacred metaphors in a spiritual quest. Guillaume de Digulleville began intertextually with Guillaume de Lorris and Jean de Meun and yet his purpose is to refute the pre-texts – both Guillaume's *fin' amor* and Jean's *amour libre*. Digulleville pleads for *caritas*. Therefore, his dream, his vision, and his text deny the dream and dream quest of his predecessors, exposing the folly of their desire and the falseness of their discourse.

In so doing, however, Digulleville all but creates an allegorical *contrafactum*; he is writing allegory which is a pseudo-autobiographical dream vision peopled by personifications, and his purpose, literary as well as doctrinal, is to take the now canonical *Roman de la Rose* and recast it in a sacred vein, restoring to allegory its sacred dimension. The literary structure of his *Pèlerinage* is a dream vision. Both the falling asleep (while reading *Le Roman de la Rose*) and the waking up (to the touch of death's scythe in the dream and the tolling of bells outside) are motivated by an external, extradiegetic cause or event. The 'I' is a passive witness (a listener and recorder of discourse) and a traveler (both receptor and actor) who observes and records but who also chooses, seeks, and evolves in the course of the narrative; he chooses roads, he seeks a precious object, and he tells all. After instruction comes the voyage; after *être, agir.* The voyage occurs on land and sea; on land especially it involves psychomachia, a sequence of encounters martial in nature. Finally, the narrative is punctuated by metaphoric death-rebirth experiences: birth, baptism, penitence after defeat by the Vices, penitence again upon entering the Ship of Religion, the last passage, and the presumed crossing to the afterlife.

Before he sets out, the Pilgrim not only listens to other people's *disputationes* and is instructed in speeches directed to him but he also receives important gifts from Grâce Dieu – a suit of armour and the pilgrim's purse and staff. The segments of the suit of armour stand for patience, fortitude, temperance, sobriety, continence, justice, humility, and prudence, and the purse and staff stand for faith and hope. These representations of the cardinal and theological virtues ought to protect Christians from the onslaught of the Evil One and his daughter vices. In strictly literary terms, the suit of armour and the purse and staff will aid the Pilgrim in his two great physical ordeals; they embody or prefigure the ordeals, which also are the two dominant elements of narrative that make up his pilgrimage and the *Pèlerinage* – the psychomachia and the quest.

The Pilgrim's encounter with the deadly sins is portrayed in terms of warfare; the goal of the personified vices is to seize, imprison, wound, and slay the Pilgrim. The imagery can be conceived in negative Bachelardian terms as patterns of hard and soft earth and also of fire.[17] Ire attacks the Pilgrim with a saw, nails, and a scythe, and, resembling a hedgehog, with thorns and nettles; she also employs flame. Venus wields a lance and Avarice, portrayed as a Saracen, employs cutting instruments and a hook. From another perspective, Peresce causes the Pilgrim to fall into her nets and traps; Envie is painted as a ghoul, with serpent, poison, and rot imagery; Avarice sucks one's blood and vitals; Gloutonnie is redolent with garbage and animal lowness, and Venus with cosmetics and garbage. These creatures are depicted as humans (frightful, aged hags) but also as animal or supernatural monsters. Orgueil has a horn on her forehead; daggers strike out from Envie's eyes; Avarice has six arms and hands. Their inhumanity and 'monsterness' is typically medieval and meant to teach a lesson, the same lesson that Dante teaches in Canto 34 of the Inferno where he depicts Satan as a three-headed monster. Dante and Digulleville tell us that there is nothing attractive or glamorous or romantic about vice. Vice is simply the distortion of virtue. All distortion is unnatural, ugly, and monstrous. To commit sin is not lofty nor does it grant pleasure; it is squalid, nauseous, alien, degrading, and mean. For a rational mind platonically attuned to respect for order, proportion, and harmony, and to the equivalence of beauty, truth, and goodness, such representations of vice will automatically evoke a response of disgust and horror. The Pilgrim perceives them as he should, with disgust and horror. Nevertheless, he cannot defend himself, for, out of consideration for his body – the weakness of the flesh – he has been travelling without his suit of armour which had been committed in the baggage train to Memory. The sudden onslaught of the hags does not permit him the leisure to arm; they do not fight chivalrously, as in secular romance. It is only the Pilgrim's satchel – faith – that spares him from immediate extinction and permits him to escape the hags by forcing his body through the Hedge of Penitence onto the right path. In the process he is badly wounded but this is good mortification of the flesh.

Given the tradition of crusade *peregrinatio,* and given Guillaume de Digulleville's desire to write sacred allegory in opposition to secular allegory and romance, it should not surprise us that the quest also employs military imagery and, like *La Queste del saint Graal,* it can be deemed antiromance. In his primeval vision the Pilgrim beholds a castle – the celestial Jerusalem – with people desperately trying to force their way over the walls. At birth he crosses a river into the earthly castle of the Church where priests are armed with swords. The Pilgrim, like Lancelot, Perceval, and Galahad, has a choice of two roads and, like Gauvain, takes the wrong one. Then he swims in the ocean, menaced by Satan's nets and hooks and Tribulation's hammer and tongs; resembling characters in the *Odyssey* and the *Aeneid*, or for that matter *Huon de Bordeaux* and *Le Roman de Tristan*, he risks drowning. He finally is rescued by the Ship of Religion, where he submits to good metal and armour, and good ropes and nets. Pieces from the Pilgrim's old suit of armour are now worn by the allegorical virtues who inhabit the cloister on the ship. His pilgrimage is therefore from a castle to a castle, from birth to death, on the road and sea of life; here he is constantly assaulted and defended militarily and sword, mace, dagger, net, hook, and hammer play as great a role as purse and staff, prayer and supplication.

Well might the Pilgrim be wounded, cut to pieces, held captive in nets and traps, caught on Satan's hook, tangled in weeds, or drowned in the sea. Yet he is saved. The salvation imagery includes the visual and the visionary; the Pilgrim beholds the celestial Jerusalem as in a mirror at the beginning of his dream:

> Avis m'ert si com dormoie
> Que je pelerins estoie
> Qui d'aler estoie excite
> En Jherusalem la cite.
> En un mirour, ce me sembloit,
> Qui sanz mesure grans estoit
> Celle cite aparceue
> Avoie de loing et veue. (35–42)

As I was sleeping, I dreamed I was a pilgrim eager to go to the city of Jerusalem. I saw this city from afar in a mirror that seemed to me large beyond measure. (p. 3)

This reflected image of salvation in a glass darkly (*speculum in aenigmate*) is so powerful that the child ever after seeks the castle he once saw. On the point of dying, he is informed by Grâce Dieu that he now stands at the door of the place he saw mirrored at birth:

> 'Or regarde, së apointie
> Tu es bien et appareillie.
> S'a toi ne tient, tantost verras
> La grant cite ou tendu as.
> Tu es au guichet et a l'uis
> Quë ou mirour piec'a veïs.' (13467–72)

'Now look and see whether you are well prepared and arrayed. If you are, you will soon see the great city you have been heading for. You are at the gate and at the door you saw long ago in the mirror.' (p. 185)

The beginning and the end of the Pilgrim's life (the Narrator's life) are thus joined.

Also crucial to the Pilgrim's progress are a series of nurture images: the river of baptism; healing oils; seed, bread, and milk assimilated to the sacrament of the eucharist; a banquet offered inside Grâce Dieu's castle; and the blood and milk that heal the Pilgrim at the end of his days. Moses, figure of the priest, transforms bread and wine into flesh and blood for the holy meal, a miracle incomprehensible to Nature and to Aristotle. Miséricorde cures the ailing, aged Pilgrim with milk from her breast, the transmuted, redeemed blood Christ shed on the cross. All seven sacraments are depicted as ointments that heal and cure.

Finally, the Pilgrim's prayer to the Virgin is embellished with imagery of light and water. Mary heals, intercedes, and brings life and freedom in terms of carbuncle and milk, for she is a fountain of joy and love, the light of the world and the star of the sea. This pattern – of fountain, milk, seed, bread, wine, precious stones, mirrors, light, city, and castle – can be interpreted as Frye's apocalyptic imagery, that counters and ultimately negates the demonic imagery of cutting metal and rotting garbage. The Pilgrim is cured; he completes his pilgrimage.

The Pilgrim is an Every Man, an Every Pilgrim. He encounters a series of teachers and authority figures, *potentiae animae, in sensu bono* and *in sensu malo*; they are masters of discourse who embody psychic forces within him yet also universal elements of the cosmos. The Pilgrim undergoes purgation and redemption in his encounter with the dark powers, experiencing a spiritual evolution with overtones of ancient ritual and myth. His is the great Quest and the great War, over land and sea, from birth to death, from the castle of baptism to the castle of the afterlife, including five rites of passage and five death and rebirth experiences: birth, baptism, repentance after the seven vices on land, repentance after excesses of youth and tribulation on the sea, and death itself. The Pilgrim attains maturity and becomes a whole, individuated person upon entering the Ship of Religion and choosing one of its towers; he enters a castle (the Cistercian Order) that parallels the castle of Grâce Dieu and prefigures the castle of heaven, the only *locus* he seeks and that is worthy to be sought. It is in part this process of growth and of continual change that gave Digulleville's *Pèlerinage* its vogue in the Middle Ages; this quality of exemplariness and universality can move modern readers as well.

Perhaps still more significant, especially for the modern reader, is the imaginative form the maturation and individuation process takes. Adhering to modern (that is, universal) dream psychology, the Pilgrim is a passive figure who submits to whatever comes his way. What comes his way, in large measure, is sin. And sin is personified always as the feminine in its most squalid, repellant, and ugly form. The capital sins are seven ancient, disgusting hags, who assault the Pilgrim; they seize, wound, and threaten him with their knives, nails, saws, nets, hooks, and traps, and make off with his pilgrim's staff. Guillaume de Digulleville is at his best depicting these horrors in a fictive world in which the ultimate horror is woman, sex, the flesh, and the world. The Pilgrim, in his passivity, stands a slave before these terrifying mistresses, a victim in the grip of these monster torturers; he then masochistically re-enacts and retells his symbolic castration and rape at their hands. A comparable structure is elaborated later when the Pilgrim desperately seeks to keep afloat in the sea; he is threatened by Satan's hook and net, and by the seaweed that drags him down, and also by his fear of drowning which is as great as his earlier fear of bondage. Both times he is drowned-mutilated-castrated because he allowed his undisciplined body to dominate reason and will instead of being dominated by them.

It is true that the Pilgrim escapes. It is true that good allegorical figures – female ones – assist him: Grâce Dieu, Miséricorde, and even Tribulation. Still, the imaginative uniqueness of this strange, powerful work of art is one of disgust and horror, of fear and trembling, and of all-but-useless resistance in the face of overpowering odds; it is a vision of the human condition in its dread of woman and the mother and its horror of the body, typical of one mentality of the age – the early Church and our early culture.

Pèlerinage de l'Ame

I shall devote only a brief note to *Pèlerinage de l'Ame*. As is the case with *Pèlerinage de la Vie humaine*, Digulleville begins with a sequence of speeches and then has the Pilgrim set off on a quest; again, being precedes becoming, *être* precedes *agir*. The speeches, however, are dynamic. They treat what is perhaps the most dramatic and successful section of the text – the trial of the Pilgrim's soul, immediately after death. Christian psychology and Christian responsibility are emphasized in the character Zinderises; she is the worm of conscience and the gnawing consciousness of remorse who testifies against the Pilgrim. The Pilgrim committed sin in spite of her and in spite of his knowledge of good and evil.

Because of God's mercy and pardon from Jesus and Mary, the Pilgrim is condemned only to a thousand years of fire in purgatory. Here, with a guardian angel, he is taken on a tour of hell to observe the tortures of the damned. The cutting, slicing, garbage, and putrefaction imagery and the horror and the terror of the seven capital sins are now applied to tortures inflicted on those who have committed the sins; these poor wretches lose their humanity and, like the seven Vices, become monsters. In this mass of swarming activity, with hooks, forks, and stakes, hordes of demons go about their torturing in an atmosphere of both brutality and chaos. As in *Pèlerinage de la Vie humaine,* the body is punished in its corporeality, with orifices stuffed and glutted, and body parts cooked or weighted down. Everyday domestic objects – knives, hooks, cooking pots – contribute to a more than exemplary dread and anxiety. Resembling the situation in Dante, Lucifer is master of hell yet chained in fire, tortured by his own demons while he tortures his daughter Orgueil in turn. The damned, in their monstrous state – the envious, hanging by their tongues or their eyes; the gluttonous, their bellies cut open while pitch is tossed in – are perceived to be an allegorical statement on the nature of sin and damnation. As in Dante, the punishment fits the crime, and one's status in eternity proves to be the concrete, physical representation of what one has been in life. Sin *is* torture and suffering, before and after death; and sin transforms people into monsters, before and after death.

Three patterns of imagery contrast with Digulleville's sado-masochistic portrayal of hell. One is musical; we hear the poetry and music emitted by angels and souls released from purgatory, who sing lyrics allegedly heard by the Pilgrim in his dream and later written down by the Narrator (but which were of course composed by the author Guillaume de Digulleville himself). Secondly and far more important, Guillaume elaborates an impressive commentary on trees, good and bad, old and new, dry and green, and their fruits, with typological allusions to Eden and Bethlehem or Golgotha, Eve and Mary, Adam and Christ, and the tree of Satan and the Holy Rood. Last of all, the Narrator gives us, at length, a symbolic cosmology grounded in the houses of the Zodiac, the feasts of the liturgical year, the life of Christ, and the joys and sorrows of the Virgin. This portion of the text, typical of the Digulleville of the 1350s, is absent from the 1330s *Pèlerinage de la Vie humaine.*

Guillaume de Digulleville is one of the great masters of sacred literature in the fourteenth century. He channels yet also gives full voice to popular emotionalism – the irrational, mystical mentality of his age, and the irrational, mystical, sado-masochistic mind-set in some members of the Church and its Orders. He partakes of the great archetypes: debate, judgment, war, and quest. More than any vernacular writer of the Middle Ages, he gives expression to the idea that life and death are pilgrimage, that we are strangers and pilgrims in exile on a journey to our celestial home, driven by love and enduring the pain and hardship of thwarted love. The eternal pilgrimage reveals an inner journey of growth, suffering, learning, fall, and eventual redemption. Compared to Jean de Meun or Guillaume de Machaut, Guillaume de Digulleville appears powerfully conservative, a holdover from an earlier age. However, we should think of him also as a radical reformer (radical reactionary), the spokesman for a new age of piety, consciously reacting against *Le Roman de la Rose* and all it stands for, seeking to force his readers into believing better ideas and living a better life. After all, Digulleville is as much an innovator as Jean de Meun and his Pilgrimages are, in their way, allegorical, spiritual epics of the new times, encyclopedic Christian epics of the late Middle Ages; they are as representative of the Middle Ages and of late Gothic as any other author and any other texts.

Digulleville bequeathed to French and English medieval culture a world-vision, a gathering of themes and motifs proper to the literary realization of the vision, and, according to Wenzel (1973), a new literary genre, the pilgrimage of life poem. The war of the vices against the virtues and against man, the pilgrimage of Every Man's life, the moral, didactic exposition of the allegories and the sub-allegories – these will influence literature for over a century. Chaucer, Gower, and Langland are among the writers who benefit from and elaborate on the monk of Chaalis's repudiation of secular belles-lettres and his truculent, grandiose restatement of Christian *veritas* in a changing world.

5. Machaut

Of those who came after the authors of *Le Roman de la Rose*, only Guillaume de Machaut (1300–77) succeeded in renewing the love-allegory genre and illustrating it in a major way. Machaut is best known as one of the greatest composers in the Middle Ages; he was a master of *ars nova* who set to music *ballades, rondeaux, virelais, lais*, and a variety of sacred compositions, including the *Messe de Nostre Dame*. He was also a major lyric poet, who practiced the *forme fixe* genres cited above; and, in the period of his full maturity, extending from 1330 to 1370, he wrote ten long narrative poems or *dits*. In these *dits amoureux*, tales of love, Machaut harmonized the disparate voices of Guillaume de Lorris and Jean de Meun and, particularly in the realm of narrative technique, he made contributions to the development of fiction that can only be appreciated today. Furthermore, he manifested extraordinary self-consciousness and pride in his own function as an artist. Machaut helped launched in France and in England a mode of narrative that treated questions of *fin' amor* – the epitome of elegance, refinement, and stylization – and was to mark almost all court poetry of the later Middle Ages. More particularly, it is in the complex structural modulation of the I-narrative, in the creation of the inept, blundering lover as a hero, and in the realm of artistic self-consciousness that Machaut had an impact across the Channel as one of the major French influences on both Chaucer and Gower. I have chosen to discuss four of his most successful and influential texts.

Remede de Fortune

Remede de Fortune (4298 lines) is a didactic allegory and a poem of love and art. In this text the I-narrator recounts his own story as a lover.

The Lover dreads revealing his feelings to the Lady. He composes a *lai* telling of his love, which falls into the the Lady's hands. Pressed by her into reading it and questioned as to the author, he runs away in confusion to a park where he is comforted by an allegorical figure, Dame Esperence. Then, Hope in his heart, he returns to the Lady, confesses his love and authorship, and is accepted as her 'amis.'

Machaut, in this and other texts, has contributed to the development of an important subgenre of the love allegory – the poem of complaint and comfort. Dame Esperence exhorts the Lover in much the same manner that Lady Philosophy addresses the prisoner in Boethius. Following in the wake of Boethius, Machaut composes his own *remedium Fortunae*. However, he diverges from Boethius in several ways. Concentrating on the problem of love, he is not in the least interested in relating happiness to the Good Life or to God. Esperence consoles the Lover by defending erotic love and assimilating it to friendship. She preaches on how to overcome Fortune and, at the same time, on how to attain one's ends through Fortune. *Fin' amor* is not subject to Fortune. Reason teaches that 'pacience' and, above all, 'souffissance' (moderation) will lead the Lover to happiness. A true lover finds contentment in meditating on his beloved's perfections and will remain happy whether or not she grants his suit, no matter what happens to him or to her. *Remede de Fortune* is a work of high courtly idealism, in which desire, subject to Fortune, is repudiated in favour of hope which is free from sublunar vicissitudes; chaste hope becomes the foundation for both love and happiness; happiness rewards the new style of *fin' amor*, sublimated desire grounded in 'bien de vertu' (Kelly 1978).

It is also a poem of growth and of education, in which the protagonist does not learn passively; he develops dynamically in time. Significantly, he appears as an artificial, inept, fumbling lover who recalls the artificial, inept, fumbling witness of Machaut's own earlier text, *Le Jugement dou Roy de Behaingne*. Cowardice and dread are his most significant traits. However, the education process he undergoes from Esperence causes him to gain confidence in himself and in the world. Unable to adapt to a given situation, he is transformed. He breaks out of the despondent stupor in which he had been wallowing to become a more vibrant, active human being. Then he leaves the garden and returns to society. In the end, an inept, narcissistic, cowardly adolescent is transformed into a relatively mature lover and member of society.

Most important, the Lover is an artist, a poet-musician who, later in life, recounts his own first-person story as the narrator-implied author of *Remede de Fortune*. Furthermore, the narrative contains seven lyrical inserts, a *lay, complainte, chanson roial, baladelle, balade, chanson baladée* or *virelay,* and *rondelet,* ascribed by the Narrator to himself as the Lover or to Esperence.

Remede de Fortune is Machaut's first endeavour at a 'poetic pseudo-autobiography,' that is, a narrative text containing lyrical inserts, the narrative purporting to explain the conditions under which the lyrics were composed. (On this topic, with views similar to mine, see Steinle 1985, Huot 1987, Brownlee 1991, Enders 1992.) It goes without saying that such a poem uses intertextual practice as its very reason for existence.

The narrative tells how the lyrics came into being; the lyrics amplify and exemplify the story told by the narrative. The frame provides the songs with an illusion of authenticity and historical specificity; the songs in turn contribute authenticity to the narrative, and also intensity, lyricism, and passion. They express in the most direct, vibrant terms the state of mind in which the singer finds himself at that instant and the problem he has to resolve. Action is slowed down and we see variety of texture and mode as the literary corpus appears as fragmentation, discontinuity, and diversity. Lyrics and narrative are transformed by contact with each other, the audience is made aware of 'literariness' and the literary process, and the totality of genres is seen to be artistically greater than the sum of its parts.

Of the seven lyrical inserts, the most important is the first one, the *lai* (431–680). I shall concentrate on it. This lyric functions as a *texte générateur.* The *lai* not only plays a crucial role in the narrative but it also launches the narrative; without it there would be no narrative. Only because the Lover has composed a *lai* and because the Lady makes him read it to her is there need for a 'remede de Fortune' and for *Remede de Fortune* answering the need. At first the Lover was in despair because the *lai* forced him to quit the Lady's presence. However, in the end the *lai,* which speaks of the Lover's incapacity to speak, serves as a pretext that will enable him to talk; then both Lover and Lady discuss not love in general but *their* love, in concrete personal terms. The *lai* bridges the gap of silence between them and thus functions as mediator or go-between.

The Lover is a poet-musician, and it is his creation, in song and verse, that voices his love and makes the Lady notice him. He plays the role of writer and composer, while she becomes his reader and audience. It is as an interpreter of texts and behaviour that she discovers him: he is the author; he is an author in love; his love and his texts are directed to her; and the sentiments they express are authentic and adhere to the precepts of *fin' amor*. It is also as a reader and as a mistress that in the end the Lady is to be given *Remede de Fortune*, the book that recounts her role in the love affair that constitutes its plot.

More than other lyrical inserts, the *lai* corresponds to our notion of *mise en abyme*. As a statement of amorous doctrine and depiction of a relationship, the lyric *lai* mirrors perfectly the situation in which Machaut has placed the narrative Lover at that stage in the *dit*. The lyric voice in the *lai* also anticipates communication with the lady – 'Amours' will tell her – that does in fact occur later in the story, brought about by the *lai* itself. The *lai* thus plays a role in its own implied narrative, serving as go-between for a fictional lover and a lady created by or reflected in itself. Also, the message of the *lai* – that a lover should limit his desire and be content with 'souffissance' – anticipates the doctrine that Esperence will set forth once the Lover enters the garden.

Finally, the aesthetic structure of the *lai* (twelve stanzas, each diverging from the others in metre and rhyme scheme except for the first and last, which are the same) reveals a cyclical pattern comparable to the cycles of time and space – the twelve months of the year and the twelve signs of the zodiac. As a total verbal and musical pattern, the *lai*, harmonious and perfect, mirrors in microcosm the harmony of the spheres in its macrocosmic perfection. Furthermore, the circular, recurring *lai* resembles other objects, circular or round *structures en abyme*, to be found elsewhere in *Remede de Fortune*: the round, walled *hortus conclusus* in which the Lover communes with Esperence; the ring she places on his finger; the round song, *rondelet*, sung by the Lover, the last and simplest of the lyrical inserts rejoining the first and most complex. The *lai* and the series of seven lyrics as a whole reproduce the cyclical structure of the *Remede de Fortune* narrative – the story of a lover who withdraws from court and lady, communes with Esperence in solitude, and then, endowed with the gift of wisdom, returns to his beloved and to the community.

The greater number of the remaining lyrics, plus a *priere*, develop from the confrontation between the Lover and Esperence. Most important, two of the texts – the *chanson roial* (1985–2032) and *baladelle* (2857–92) – are placed in Esperence's mouth. This permits Machaut to indulge in playful, sophisticated exaltation of himself as an artist; he has Esperence praise her own purported *chanson* and the Lover-Narrator be so moved by the verse and music of her purported *baladelle* that he concentrates on learning them both by heart.

The lyrics reflect the Lover's state of soul at the moment they are uttered; they also express the doctrine of 'souffissance' that Lady Hope seeks to instil in him and thus contribute to his education. On one level the seven lyrics, illustrating seven genres, provide an *Ars poetica* of contemporary lyrical and musical forms. The teaching of poetry and music, by the implied author to his implied audience outside the text, is allied to the teaching of the nature of love, by Esperence to the Lover within the diegetic narrative, and to the extradiegetic implied audience as well. The harmony and formal perfection of these texts illustrate how to make poems and music. They also serve to console the Lover and teach him how to love.

On the one hand, Esperence ought to be envisaged as a double of the Lady, a surrogate Lady and transference figure. Like the Lady, she is beautiful, blond, radiant with light, semidivine, all-good and all-knowing. Unlike the Lady – here the projection and wish fulfilment enter in – she comes to him, forces communication on him, and offers him symbolic satisfaction of desire, even symbolic marriage. Given that the Lover is the Narrator earlier in life, a maker of lyrics, and eventually, a teller of tales, it is important that Esperence responds to the Lover-Narrator in his artistic function. Significantly, she responds as a reader. She comments on his *lai* and *complainte* accurately and with sympathy. More important still, she joins him in the process of making texts, whereupon the Lover becomes the reader-audience-interpreter of her discourse. This reciprocal interchange in the realm of art mirrors an equivalent collaboration in the erotic sphere that culminates in the midpoint action of Esperence placing a ring (a work of art signifying fidelity, devotion, and harmony) on the Lover's finger (2094–6). The dreaming Lover hopes that these artistic fantasies will ultimately be transformed into a truly amorous interchange with the Lady.

Esperence represents not only a numinous, semidivine allegory and one of the three theological virtues, but she is also a character trait of the Lover's psyche. She embodies the feminine anima, which he must succeed in integrating before the individuation process is complete and he can function as a mature person in society. Indeed, after receiving her ring and gaining Hope, the Lover returns to society, is received into the group, and obtains what appears to be a satisfactory relationship with the Lady. Furthermore, in this one day of passion and metamorphosis, he creates seven texts. The poems are due to the Self and the anima, the male and female principles within him, which, activated in harmony, transform him into a good lover and a productive artist and eventually into the clerkly narrator who, in the present, recounts the entire story.

The last two songs mark the Lover's reception into the community and his new maturity in the ways of love. We are to assume that he succeeds in integrating the public and private spheres of both love and art. Are we to conclude also that the ordering of the lyrics in a linear pattern, beginning with the most complex form, the *lai*, and ending with the simplest one, the *rondelet*, corresponds to a comparable linear ordering of the narrative? This would bring the Lover from ignorance, ineptness, despair, solitude, and failure in love to knowledge, sophistication, hope, a sense of community, and amorous success. On one level and from one vantage point, yes. However, it is also true that the increasing simplicity of the lyrics as verse corresponds to an increasing complexity of the lyrics as music. In musicological terms, the sequence from *lai* to *rondelet* is one of increasing difficulty.

The narrative situation also may prove to be more complex than it first appears. After all, the *rondelet*, composed in a paean of joy, is nonetheless scarcely a song of triumph. Proclaiming the Lover's fidelity, it announces separation not union and prays to God that the Lady remain true:

> 'Dame, mon cuer en vous remaint,
> Comment que de vous me departe.
> De fine amour qui en moy maint,
> Dame, mon cuer en vous remaint.
> Or pri Dieu que li vostres m'aint,
> Sans ce qu'en nulle autre amour parte.
> Dame, mon cuer en vous remaint,
> Comment que de vous me departe.' (4107–14)

'My lady, my heart stays with you, although I myself must leave you. With true love I bear within, my lady, my heart stays with you. Now I pray God that your heart will love me, without being shared with any other. My lady, my heart stays with you, although I myself must leave you.' (Wimsatt and Kibler, pp. 398, 400)

Although he is now at a more advanced stage of the *gradus amoris*, the Lover still must beg; he remains uncertain concerning his love and its future. This last *mise en abyme* in fact anticipates the problem to be considered in the immediately succeeding section of the narrative.

Machaut chooses not to end his tale symmetrically, with the Lover's return to the Lady neatly balancing his earlier withdrawal from her, his declaration of love redeeming the earlier silence, and his success nullifying the earlier failure. On the contrary. After the happy ending,

Machaut adds a final, asymmetrical, decentring episode; the Lover quits the Lady briefly, returns a second time, is torn by jealousy because she treats other suitors more amiably than she does him, but then is mollified by her explanation that she does love him and has acted bizarrely only out of need for courtly discretion.

It is true that the Lady's words are loving and loyal. It is true that the Lover believed her then:

> Si que pour ce je la crëoie,
> Et qu'il m'iert vis qu'en amité
> Me disoit pure verité,
> Que j'estoie en sa bonne grace. (4246–9)

So therefore I believed her and felt that in friendship she told me the unadulterated truth, that I was in her good graces. (p. 406)

The Narrator wants to believe her still (4226–8). Nonetheless, we the audience have cause to question the Lady's good faith and the Lover's good enthusiasm. In this final scene the Lover appears once again in a comic light, his ineptness underscored. Furthermore, the Narrator refers in prolepsis to his (the Lover's) misery at the hands of the Lady, suffering that presumably occurs after the story is ended but before the Narrator has written it down:

> Comment que puis mainte päour,
> Maint dur assaut et maint estour,
> Meinte dolour, meinte morsure
> Et meinte soudeinne pointure,
> Maint grief souspir, mainte hachie
> Et mainte grant merencolie
> M'en ait couvenu soustenir. (4219–25)

Although I later had to bear many fears, many harsh assaults and many attacks, many sorrows, many biting torments and many sudden pangs, many sorrowful sighs, much anguish, and much deep melancholy. (pp. 404, 406)

Remede de Fortune is told entirely from the point of view of the young Lover and the slightly older clerkly Narrator, focalized through their largely identical consciousnesses. We are informed of the Lady's speeches and her acts; we have no reason to doubt the Narrator's accuracy. But we are not informed of her thoughts or sentiments. We do not know them because the Lover and Narrator do not know them. The Lover communicates with Esperence and becomes a reader of Esperence's texts, to his profit and joy. In the end he also enters into an author-reader reciprocal relationship with the Lady, listening to her speeches of love and her explanations for apparent nonlove. This is what he wants, and yet it poses problems. After all, Esperence is the Self; the Lady is the Other. The Lover finds himself in a hermeneutic predicament, obliged not only to make his own texts but to gloss the Other's. He does so with a leap of faith. We the implied audience also are expected to gloss them but not necessarily in the same way that the Lover-Narrator does. Machaut establishes distance between himself and his narrative and lyrical personae just as he establishes distance between them and us. We are conscious of the interpretive dilemma; we can discover the Lover's inadequacies as an interpreter as well as as a suitor. We recognize that, while seemingly proclaiming communication, community, success, and the process of writing, Machaut also makes a place for noncommunication, solitude, failure, and the process of reading. Further, we realize that love and art are more complex than they first appear and that one lesson of intertextuality concerns the reading of texts, interpretation within and without, and a narrative calling upon its characters and upon us to interpret it and them.

Le Jugement dou Roy de Navarre

Sometime after 1349 Machaut wrote *Le Jugement dou Roy de Navarre* (4212 lines). In the *Navarre* Machaut's narrating persona recounts how in springtime, following upon the harsh plague winter, he is accused by Lady Bonneürté and her suite of personifications of having defamed ladies and *fin' amor* in a previous book, *Le Jugement dou Roy de Behaingne*. In the *Behaingne* a court of love had to pronounce on who suffers more, a lady whose lover has died or a knight whose mistress has left him for another man. King John of Bohemia decided in favour of the knight. The decision is now being appealed before a new court and a new judge. This time, the judge – King Charles of Navarre – decides for the lady, and the Narrator is condemned to write a *lai*, a *chanson*, and a *ballade*.

In this text the Narrator is accused not only of having been wrong in the previous poem, but he is also taxed with having spoken against ladies, an act anathema to the God of Love; therefore he has taken a stand both antifeminist and anti-*fin' amor* (3797–804). What does this mean? Bonneürté and the others blame the Narrator-implied author for having the King of Bohemia state that, in matters of love, infidelity is worse than death. What really angers them, however, is the fact that the *Roy de Behaingne* determined that the knight suffered more than the lady, and therefore that a man can love more profoundly than a woman; it is a woman, the knight's mistress, who was guilty of treachery. In the *Roy de Navarre* the death-infidelity issue is quickly forgotten, and from Bonneürté's first speech the trial degenerates into a debate on the respective virtues of men and women; it is a war of the sexes in the tradition of Jean de Meun. The only real question at issue is who loves better, men or women.

It would appear that Machaut has perpetrated heretical writings against women and against *fin' amor,* but that the second *Jugement,* a formal palinode, makes up for the first *Jugement* and restores courtly orthodoxy. In fact, the opposite is the case. From an objective, neutral stance, it is obvious that *Le Jugement dou Roy de Behaingne* is a poem adhering one hundred per cent to courtly tradition and to the principles of *fin' amor.* That the King of Bohemia decides in favor of a man not a woman is, in the context of the *Behaingne,* irrelevant. The ladies of the court, whether in the fictional world of the *Navarre* or in real life, were mistaken when they thought thay saw misogyny in Machaut's poem. However, once they did, Guillaume de Machaut has the opportunity to reconsider the entire business in his own way, following literary norms determined by him alone.

We know nothing of the little event at court that may have caused Machaut to write *Le Jugement dou Roy de Navarre.* Some such court event – discussion, debate, joke, or teasing – most probably did take place. Whether it was serious or play (*jocum curiale*) remains a mystery. However, the event in question must have caused people to reconsider the relationship between ladies and *fin' amor* and between anti-*fin' amor* and antifeminism. And it is manifest that outside the diegetic world of the courts of love no one is obliged to adhere to the value system of *fin' amor.* The poet and at least a section of his public can adhere to a different system with different rules and different icons.

How does Machaut do it? First of all, the Narrator in his role as defendant denounces women in his authorial voice, accusing them of being fickle and hard-hearted. Of course, you can find occasionally a 'loial amie,' he says

> Mais je croy qu'entre cinq cent mil
> N'en seroit pas une trouvée;
> Car tel greinne est trop cler semée. (3106–8)

But I believe that not one such would be found among five hundred thousand, for this seed is too thinly sown. (Palmer, p. 139)

The Narrator loses because he dared stand up to 'dame de si haut pris' (4196) [a lady of such high station (p. 189)], but he never repents or retracts in his own voice. His ideas remain. Subtly, indirectly, the Narrator proclaims his right to tell the truth as he sees it. Also he pokes fun at Bonneürté and her ten followers, who all plead against him. They are comic characters, in the Bergsonian sense, rigid, narrow, obsessed, excessive, and insulting; above all, they talk too much. The Narrator enjoys teasing them until they lose their collective tempers, upon which the misogynist requests that his adversaries be permitted to continue their pleading in unison, to have done more quickly! They do speak all at once, each one in anger, whereupon King Charles smiles and the Narrator rejoices, together in masculine complicity:

> Si firent elles, ce me samble;
> Qu'elles parloient tout ensamble,
> Dont li juges prist a sousrire
> Qui vit que chascune s'aïre.
> Et certes, j'en eus moult grant joie,
> Quant en tel estat les vëoie. (3157–62)

Last of all, Machaut depicts his alter ego, the accused poet, as an inept defendant at court, given to cowardice, snobbery, pedantry, and above all, antifeminism. Guilty of excess, he reacts in a deliciously comic manner to the ladies of the court. Given Jean de Meun's formulation of the problem, ironically it is the ladies who tell classical stories from Antiquity and it is the clerkly Narrator who disregards his own learning and relies upon dubious contemporary anecdotes and his own no less dubious personal experience.

Nevertheless, the Narrator also appeals to our sympathy as he defends himself alone against twelve demigoddesses; after all, he is the hero of the story which concerns him alone as a writer. Here is a text in which the central focus treats a poet writing poetry about the writing of poetry by a poet. The Litigant is accused, condemned, and allowed to repent not as a man, in his alleged function of lover, but as an implied author, in his real function of maker of texts. Machaut depicts an unusually sophisticated view of the writer as the clerkly poetic narrator (author of books), proud of his artistic achievement and yet at the same time capable of mocking himself both as poet and lover. Furthermore, in the course of the *Navarre* the Narrator becomes the antifeminist he is mistakenly accused of having been in the *Behaingne*. Like Jean de Meun vis-à-vis Guillaume de Lorris, Machaut vis-à-vis himself mocks courtliness and mockingly defends himself as a mocker of courtliness. Furthermore, like Jean de Meun, Machaut's narrating persona is a writer, a male author figure indicted for what he has written by female implied readers. Now these great ladies, for all their exalted status, because they are readers, depend on him. Everything in his 'judgment,' including the very existence of his adversaries, flows from him the implied author, the creator of the first *Jugement* as subtext and of the second *Jugement* as intertext.

This takes place due to a very sophisticated employment of narrative technique. *Le Jugement dou Roy de Navarre*, like *Remede de Fortune*, is a homodiegetic narrative with an actorial rather than authorial focalization. The Machaldian 'I' is the center of consciousness and the single focus for the narrative. Indeed, since the mode of the *dit amoureux* is relatively dramatic – the Narrator shows rather than tells; his technique is scenic rather than panoramic; and there is no interference from other, delegated voices as in *Le Roman de la Rose* – Machaut succeeds in creating, up to a point, the illusion of objectivity and impartiality. However, for this very reason the focalization is external to the Narrator's deepest feelings. Like Jean de Meun's protagonist, we recognize him to be obtuse and naive; he is too close to himself as hero and not aware of all the comic overtones in what he says. Specifically, this inept, obtuse, comic Narrator as a narrating voice is reliable enough in his recounting of events; yet he is totally unreliable too in that, in spite of what appears to be his conscious intention, the picture he paints of defeat reveals and at the same time conceals the story of victory – a poet writing poetry in answer to criticism of his poetry – elaborated by the real author.

Even though he identifies with his Narrator, Machaut erects a barrier between himself and his all too human literary creation. He is more sophisticated than his Narrator and his Litigant. From this situation emerges distance and control; the unself-conscious, unobtrusive Narrator is separated from the moderately self-conscious and obtrusive Litigant. Yet both *erlebendes Ich* and *erzählendes Ich* are unaware of the true meaning of their story and are separated from the implied author behind the scenes, who provides support and correction, sympathy for and criticism of, the Narrator and Litigant as hero(es). As in *Le Roman de la Rose*, it then becomes the reader or audience's duty to interpret meaning and to interpret texts, and indeed to judge character, much as the authorities do within the fiction of the book, although in a more sophisticated manner and with better results. And the modern reader will find highly self-conscious texts, metatexts concerned with the nature of writing and with their own textual creation, especially pertinent.

Also like Jean de Meun, Machaut elaborates this particular *dit* in part because he is interested in literature rather than ideas; he wants to create literary characters and a world of comedy. The world is centred upon the fiction of a trial. Machaut follows the workings of the law closely. The author's realistic parody of judicial proceedings contributes a sense of authenticity to *Le Roy de Navarre* but also generates humour because we can never forget that they are so preposterously and obviously a figment of his imagination. We cannot take seriously a trial where both sides indulge in irrelevant casuistry – arguments over who suffers more, Pyramus or Thisbe, Hero or Leander; over who loves more deeply, a person dying from a broken heart or one who has gone insane for the same reason; over whether the insane lover remains perpetually in excruciating torture or suffers only the instant he goes mad. We cannot take seriously a trial where a purportedly fear-striken defendant proclaims it will be good to hear the fine arguments on both sides, at which Bonneürté, the plaintiff, laughs (1083–90), and where the verdict and sentencing also provoke laughter. An absurdly minor point of love casuistry, discussed in a poem at least ten yers old, unleashes a full-fledged legal confrontation before the King of Navarre; the result of this massive trial machinery is to condemn the defendant, a poet, to write more poetry.

Secondly, although the plot of *Le Roy de Navarre* is not based on the romance pattern, the themes of adventure and the chase do contribute to the narrative in a comic register. When the Narrator goes hunting, he is so engrossed that he fails to notice Bonneürté ride by. Hurt by the Narrator's discourtesy, she summons him into her presence and accuses him of having failed to show respect to her as a lady and thus having insulted ladies in general. His action parallels in humorous fashion the more serious affronts he allegedly made as a poet in *Le Roy de Behaingne* and that he will make in the trial scene to come.

The Narrator's participation in the chase is anathema to Bonneürté, for by so doing (like the protagonist of *Ipomedon*) he partakes of a pleasure different from love. He remains ignorant of love and of Bonneürté's presence, enjoying himself fully in a parody of the only true joy a priestess of *fin' amor* can admit. Finally, he dares partake of a court pastime; he, a non-noble, a coward, a poet, and a clerkly narrator opposed to *fin' amor*, presumes to act like a knight and even to defend hare-hunting as a sport in which he can attain honour. Instead of bagging the foundation of *ragoût*, he will discover that he is the hunted not the hunter in a quite different game.

Machaut places his protagonist in a situation which recalls Arthurian romance. The Narrator believes in enchantment, he is concerned for 'onneur,' and he lives a sort of 'queste' with 'aventure' and 'merveille.' In terms of theme and motif, he does encounter Bonneürté as by accident or in some miraculous way and is observed by her, unaware of her presence. For a long time Bonneürté's identity remains hidden from the Narrator and the reader; her name is revealed only at her moment of triumph (3851). She resembles the fairy-queen of the Other World, proud, domineering, and potentially a dangerous enemy. After having endured threats and insults, the hero metaphorically undergoes an ordeal (a parody of sacred combat), expiates his sins, and is delivered from enchantment. The court is free to revel in joy.

In fact, however, the Narrator takes no risks, fights no battles, and has engaged upon no covenant. A mighty hunter of hares, his only prowess is verbal; participation in solitary sport (the hunt) and courtly games (the trial) are ironic parodies of real war. Our hero defends the wrong side and loses. Fair ladies impede rather than assist him; benevolent, supernatural authority figures prove hostile; and his ordeal turns out to be a joke. Once again Machaut demonstrates that men are foolish because they cannot live up to the courtly ideal and that they are naive in seeking to live up to an ideal which itself is untrue to life. Once again we see the hand of a master of comedy.

Structurally, *Le Jugement dou Roy de Navarre* is more complex than *Remede de Fortune*. The major action is preceded by five hundred or so lines that describe the Narrator's experiences during the plague winter of 1349. The function of this seemingly disjunctive material has been studied by Calin (1974), Lanoue (1981), Palmer (1987), and Ehrhart (1992). This section not only constitutes a semirealistic frame set in contrast to the central episode so that the allegorical court of love can be assimilated to a credible context; it also contributes to the narrative as a whole. The calamities striking France in the winter of 1349 – flame, tempest, earthquake, war, and plague – conform to a traditional motif, the universe upside-down (Curtius's [1948G] notion of *verkehrte Welt*). All four elements that man corrupted are now used by the Almighty to scourge him. If the universe has decayed (*mundus senescit*), in an earlier, happier age people lived at peace with God and themselves. 'When I was young,' says the Narrator, 'no such calamities befell' (*Laudatio temporis acti*).

The *mundus senescens* reflects a comparable state within the Narrator. Examples of pathetic fallacy were by no means rare in the Middle Ages. Humankind is guilty of sins against God and nature; the Narrator in his paltry way is guilty of a sin against polite society. We hear repeatedly that the Narrator suffers from melancholia, a condition linked to an excess of black bile in the body under the influence of the Greater Infortune, the planet Saturn, matching autumn or winter in the cycle of the year and old age in man's life. Therefore, the Narrator becomes melancholic in autumn; meditates on the calamities of an old, decaying world set against the times of his youth; and evokes the historical personage Guillaume de Machaut, who was about forty-nine years old when the action of the poem supposedly occurred and later in the story opposes the doctrine of young love espoused by Bonneürté. A melancholic man is presumed antisocial and prone to cowardice and to the sin of *acedia* – especially rampant in those who practice the contemplative life – as much a state of sadness as of sloth. Therefore, the Narrator spends all winter alone, hiding in his cold, gloomy room, dreading the plague and the prospect of defending himself in court. The melancholic Narrator is the central focus of both parts of the *Jugement*, first as an 'objective' person in history and then as a 'subjective' author figure in allegory.

The Narrator seeks refuge from the plague and contests the rules of courtly orthodoxy. Although he compares aspects of the amorous life to imprisonment (1992–3, 2045–62), it is he who has spent the winter in a kind of jail (485). This is an intimate, enclosed, feminine refuge, appropriate to a hunter of hares meditating on death, but not to an insulter of ladies. Then with the coming of spring, the season of love and sunshine, he breaks out of containment within four walls. But he succeeds no better in the world of life than he had in the world of death. Terrified, 'enclosed' at court and again overcome by melancholia, he must defend himself in hostile surroundings. The second captivity is, to be sure, presented ironically, in the comic vein. Because the refuser of festivity remained by himself in winter and then in springtime went hunting alone, he is now forced to share human company. A contrast is drawn between savage, dreary, cold, wintry solitude and the elegant, sunny, warm, springlike court of love in which song, happiness (Bonneürté), and the work of art (*Le Roy de Navarre*) find a place. The court is a good prison, beneficial to the social order and a possible refuge in a world upside-down. And for all its excess and artificiality, love is a powerful force in nature and polite society. Common sense ('mesure' and 'souffissance') urge the poet to avoid hubris and to accept the best the world has to offer, since his place ultimately lies in the world and at the court.

From Parts 1 to 2 winter gives way to spring, isolation to the community, Saturn to Venus, and death to rebirth. With an end to the plague the Narrator hears a fanfare of musical instruments, for men are no longer dying. People celebrate the return of spring with games and pastimes, the hunt, and a mock trial that reflects the archetypal struggle between the old and the new, dying winter and the birth of spring. In this combat the mature, antisocial, melancholic Narrator represents, againt his will perhaps, the old. His aristocratic patrons permit him to enter their society. He serves as a scapegoat, the intruder or killjoy whose presence contributes to the festivities, since he must lose and his views be defeated. Death and the calamities of a *mundus senescens* are overcome at King Charles's court. Spring wins out; the rebel is converted or, at any rate, subdued; and his sentence delivered with laughter and joy.

La Fonteinne amoureuse

La Fonteinne amoureuse (2848 lines), written between 1360 and 1362, is a complaint and comfort poem in the tradition of *Remede de Fortune*. The plot tells how the Narrator-Observer is kept awake at night by plaints from a Knight in a room nearby. The Knight bewails the fact that he must go into exile and that he cannot communicate with his Lady. The next morning the Narrator and the Knight stroll together into a garden where, near a Fountain of Love, they fall asleep and dream that Venus brings the Lady to comfort her suitor. After they wake up, the Knight does cross the sea into exile but with joy in his heart.

Unlike the narrator in *Remede de Fortune*, here the protagonist as lover and the protagonist as poet-musician-narrator are split into distinct personae. The lover is a great prince – the text commemorates the voyage to England by Jean, Duke of Berry, as hostage in 1360 – who desires an unattainable great lady, and his desire exploits the conventional motifs of *fin' amor*. However, the Knight will eventually win his Lady's love and communicate with her, in large measure due to the intervention of other characters, such as the Narrator. As in *Le Jugement dou Roy de Behaingne* and *Le Jugement dou Roy de Navarre*, the Narrator stands on the fringes of the courtly world and the domain of love. He is a witness, literally an eavesdropper, but not a direct participant. Nonetheless, he listens to his princely patron, understands him, advises him, and comforts him. The protagonist is a *miles*, a lover, a master; his friend is a *clericus*, a witness to love, a servant. Because both the Knight and Trojan Paris (described in the dream) are princes of the blood, they adhere to the realm of Venus; she has chosen them because of their nobility. The more humorous and human Narrator, a disciple of Pallas, a professional writer, a cleric, coward, busybody, and snob, serves as a foil to the serious, dignified Knight. Somewhat closer to the average man because of his failings and plebeian extraction, he functions as a bridge from the Knight to the implied audience. Also, the Knight is more than eager to accept the Narrator's offer of friendship for the old poet does console a young prince with the word. The prince needs a poet as confidant and adviser as much as the poet needs him as patron and provider of literary material. Man to man and master to man, a warm, human relationship between the two is established.

What we find here and in other Machaldian texts is a Narrator-witness who mingles with the high aristocracy, is received as a friend and confidant, helps the Knight to express himself, and succeeds in providing comfort, consolation, and understanding. At the bottom of the social scale, a 'povre homme' (1263), he nonetheless participates in courtly doings as a user of words, in part because his patron and master also composes verse. Indeed, the Narrator is first made aware of the Knight's presence as a singer of complaints. Machaut exploits the medieval topos of the patron as source and model and of the patron as poet and participator in the creative process, as it has been analyzed by Kelly (1987). In this process and according to this fiction, the artist – a real or metaphoric cleric – seeks to establish a bond with his secular aristocratic master, the *miles dominans*, through flattery and self-denigration; thus he can achieve through rhetorical manipulation that synthesis of *fortitudo et sapientia*, Mars and Apollo, or *chevalerie et clergie*, which served as a courtly ideal. The speaker is admitted into the company of the high nobility and, because of his tact and wisdom, and their graciousness, permitted to become their friend. The tact, the refinement, and the subtle, elegant human interaction between prince and poet are manifestations of the topos of Horatian friendship that extends in literature from the late Middle Ages to the fall of the ancien régime – from Machaut to Voltaire and, transferred across the Channel, from Chaucer to Pope.

The Knight's problems, however, are not solved or resolved by the Narrator. He is comforted and a happy ending ensured when he and the Narrator together dream of a visit by Venus and the Lady. Venus projects the aura of a Greek goddess and an astrological House. She represents an elemental power of nature, the Eros that moves men's souls; also, in the tradition of Arthurian romance, she is a good fay who aids the hero to win his bride. Venus, the most powerful of the goddesses, promises the Knight happiness. She brings him the Lady who, in her *Confort*, informs him that she shares his love. The Lady is a warm, passionate human being, who desires her sleeping prince and embraces him in a scene both graceful and sensuous:

> Adonq la dame s'abaissa
> Qu'onques pour moy ne le laissa,
> Et plus de cent fois le baisa
> En son dormant;
> Et puis elle le resgarda
> Et de son droit braz l'embrassa
> Et li dist: 'Amis, trai te sa!'
> En sousriant. (2495–502)

Thereupon, the lady leaned over (my presence didn't impede her) and kissed him in his sleep more than a hundred times; then she gazed at him, put her right arm around him, and, smiling, said to him: 'Sweet love, come close!'

The two, Venus and the Lady, like Esperence and the Lady in *Remede de Fortune*, appear as anima figures, images of beauty, harmony, and transcendence. They partake of the great mother and virgin bride archetypes, divine goddess and fairy princess, respectively (1594–5). Like the two mentors in *Remede de Fortune*, they function as teachers. Their lesson is one of restraint, control, and 'souffissance.' The Knight will be separated from his Lady; their desire cannot be consummated. Venus will help him only if he remains chaste in thought and deed. The Knight should not complain to Dame Fortune of his predicament. He shall be happy. Happiness is defined as love for the Other and knowledge that the Other loves him; it is symbolized by his right to keep the Lady's heart and image in his breast.

Venus and the Lady are closely bound to the Knight and the Narrator. Inside the net of Eros are the Knight and the Lady. Although involved, Venus and the Narrator stand outside, as mentors, advisers, and confidants. However, the Narrator is of lower social status than his friend, whereas Venus ranks high above the Lady. Thus Machaut establishes a hierarchical pattern. A poet-cleric on the fringe of society, the Narrator stands at the bottom of the scale but can nevertheless participate in courtly doings, serving his prince. The Knight dominates the world of the court but is a slave to his absent Lady, whereas both he and she are in thrall to Love. In the domain of Eros the conqueror is conquered, and the amorous life (Venus) triumphs over both the active (Juno) and the contemplative (Pallas), over the prince and the poet.

The Knight's consolation and transformation occur while he is asleep. The themes of sleep, insomnia, and dreaming are fundamental to *La Fonteinne amoureuse*. The lover, who suffers from conventional love sickness (one symptom of which is insomnia), stays awake all night delivering the grandiloquent *Complainte de l'Amant*. The Narrator, also a lover and an insomniac, is on the point of falling asleep when he hears noises through the window, takes fright, and eventually copies down the complaint, with the result that he also keeps a vigil from dusk to dawn.

In his complaint the Knight tells the myth of Ceyx and Alcyone, recounting how the God of Sleep and his son Morpheus appear before Alcyone in Ceyx's guise and recount her husband's death. The Knight then prays to Morpheus to grant him sleep, to inform the Lady of his love, and to return with the knowledge of whether or not she loves him in return. The next day he and the Narrator slumber together and, in their dream, Venus and the Lady appear with the news he wishes to hear. After he has awakened, the Knight thanks Venus and Morpheus and promises to make an image of Morpheus in gold on a marble pillar and to build a temple to Morpheus and the God of Sleep. Thus, in the frame narrative both men, suffering from sleeplessness and from love sickness, hear or evoke Ovid's tragic myth of Ceyx and Alcyone, a story of love and sleep. Praying for sleep, they dream; the Narrator dreams of the tragic love of his prince. Sleeplessness, melancholia, and Eros in the frame are linked to the same themes in the dream. *La Fonteinne* tells of myth, dream, and reality, of a story from the Ancients related to concrete experience and to the realm of Morpheus. Morpheus, god of dreams, and the dream itself functioning as reverie, adventure, initiation, and imagination are key structural motifs in Machaut's text.

Machaut's dream visions always mirror the reality of the dream experience in everyday life in what we call modern dream psychology. In the *Fonteinne* dream Venus recounts the wedding of Peleus and Thetis, the Apple of Discord, and the Judgment of Paris, and she refers to the Fall of Troy; then she and the Lady comfort the Knight. This manifest dream content is derived from the dreamers' day residue, including their obsession with love and their respective ladies; they fall asleep near a fountain on which are carved images of the Abduction of Helen and the Trojan War, and they talk of the pagan gods, including Venus, who built the fountain. It is also true that the hero-lover can be considered, to a certain extent, the Narrator's alter ego, on whom he has projected his own wretchedness. By rendering the prince more miserable than himself, the Narrator lightens his own burden. And by consoling the Knight, he creates for himself a measure of hope. The Narrator indulges in wish-fulfilment and releases tension in a fantasy world of dreams.

On the one hand, Machaut makes an effort to give these dreams an aura of the *somnium coeleste;* he supports them with authenticating devices that guarantee the truth of his narrative. Such devices include classical myths presumed to be verifiable – Morpheus in fact appeared to Alcyone and told the truth concerning Ceyx's death; Hecuba dreamed truthfully of giving birth to Paris, who did bring about the destruction of Troy – and a plot increment that has the Narrator and the Knight, upon awakening, perceive on the Knight's finger the Lady's ruby, which in the the dream he received in exchange for his own diamond. On the other hand, by creating believable oneiric psychology Machaut also undermines the dream's authority since, in the Middle Ages, a dream derived from the subject's personal anxieties and reflecting his day residue was an *insomnium* or *somnium animale,* of subjective and, therefore, limited value. The poet recognizes that the stories in *l'Ovide moralisé* need not be taken literally; they are myths. He is aware that Morpheus is a creator of illusion and that Morpheus and his father are themselves creations of an author's imagination. Therefore, although the Narrator and the Knight, as literary characters, more or less believe in the reality of what they experience, the poet as creator knows better. He knows that his own narrating persona is an illusion and that his dream world is no more and no less fictional than the waking one. Thus the literariness of the dream process, the fact that worlds are an artistic construct, is also made manifest.

Machaut concludes his tale with 'Dites moy, fu ce bien songié?' (2848) [Tell me, was this well dreamed? (Meaning, perhaps: Was this dream well told?)]. Several interpretations of this line are possible. I believe that the Narrator-implied author here reveals that the whole poem, or at least all of it but for the introductory scene depicting the Narrator alone in bed at night, was dreamed by the Narrator, and that all the action – including the Knight's complaint, his encounter with the Narrator, and their falling asleep together – makes up the

Narrator's own original dream. In this case the Narrator dreams that he and the Knight are dreaming and that in their dream Venus tells the story of Hecuba's dream. In other words *La Fonteinne amoureuse* contains a dream within a dream within a dream. Furthermore, illusion and reality fuse; dreams are treated as seriously as reality, and reality is portrayed in terms of a dream. By constructing in the Garden of Love a temple to the God of Sleep, the poet in this *Livre de Morpheüs* does indeed anticipate Shakespeare and Calderón, for whom, also, life is a dream and dreams are life. Also, as Morpheus mediates between Ceyx and Alcyone, the Narrator helps to mediate between the Knight and his Lady. Morpheus, the creator of images, is assimilated to the Narrator, a creator of words; and Morpheus as a metaphoric artist parallels the implied author, a metaphoric dreamer.

Venus comes to the Lover. She comes to him in a *locus amoenus* à la Guillaume de Lorris, covered with trees, flowers, and birds, a locus of shade and green grass. This is a feminine décor, a place of security and repose, that evokes our nostalgia for the Mother. In penetrating to the centre of the garden, the Knight masters the labyrinth of enclosed intimacy. And at the centre he finds the Fountain of Love, image of nature's renewal by water, the feminine element, cold and moist, *fons et origo* of desire, nurture, nourishment, purification, and healing.

Equally important, the fountain is a work of art (Calin 1983). It was constructed by Pygmalion. On its basin is chiselled in bas-relief the story of the Abduction of Helen and the Fall of Troy. Nearby stands a column of ivory on which is told the story of Narcissus. The fountain and the column are associated in our mind with the Knight's complaint, a poem recounting another Ovidian tale, the story of Ceyx and Alcyone – a poetic tour de force in fifty stanzas using one hundred distinct rhymes – a work of art attributed to the Knight and praised by the Narrator. As in *Remede de Fortune*, praise of art attributed to one of the literary characters serves as a subtle, witty self-encomium, given that the implied audience is fully aware that the Knight and the Narrator are characters in a work of art created by one man, Guillaume de Machaut, who is responsible for their lyrical impromptus. Here the Narrator-poet lends his craft to the prince, acts as his scribe, and even dreams his dream. In the complaint the Knight compares himself to Pygmalion, who created 'l'image d'ivoire' (963) [the ivory statue] that he later married. This is the same Pygmalion who allegedly built the fountain where the Knight and Narrator attain communion with Venus and the Lady. Pygmalion and Orpheus in Antiquity (Venus mentions that the latter sings his works at the wedding of Peleus and

Thetis), the Knight and the Narrator today – the Narrator a persona for Guillaume de Machaut – are associated in a nexus of artistic creation and aesthetic play.

These works of art are beautiful in and of themselves. They also tell stories and teach wisdom. The stories and the wisdom are in no sense due uniquely to the imagination of the author, Guillaume de Machaut. Just as the *fonteinne amoureuse* is said to be the Fountain of Narcissus that reflects, for good or ill, the images of those who gaze upon it, so too these artifacts, whether poetry, sculpture, or architecture, are derived from an earlier tradition of culture. *La plainte de l'amant* speaks of Ceyx and Alcyone; Venus's 'reconfort' recounts the Wedding of Peleus and Thetis, the Judgment of Paris, and the Trojan War; all are myths taken from the *Metamorphoses* and transmitted by *l'Ovide moralisé*. The Fountain of Love, which itself recounts Ovidian myths, because it is the Fountain of Narcissus, is derived from Ovid and also from *Le Roman de la Rose*. Its purported builder, Pygmalion, is derived from Ovid and also from Jean de Meun. Like *Remede de Fortune, La Fonteinne amoureuse* is a masterpiece of medieval intertextuality. It contains a series of pre-texts existing in Ovid, Guillaume de Lorris, and Jean de Meun. These pre-texts, coming from classical *auctoritates*, bring to Machaut's text intellectual richness, depth, intensity, and an accrued lyricism. The 'borrowings' contribute to the narrative, while the narrative refashions them in its own way on its own terms.

It is obvious that the stories concerning Ceyx and Alcyone, and Paris and Helen, function as *mises en abyme*. They comment and even prefigure the career of the lover in *La Fonteinne amoureuse*, offering the implied reader-audience the possibility of comparing the lover's situation to parallel situations, in song and story. The same is true for the fountain. The Knight and the Narrator appear before the fountain, where they dream of Venus, who tells them stories they saw sculpted on the marble and ivory. Due to her offices, in antithesis to the destiny of Paris of Troy, the Knight's fate proves to be happy, in part because Venus, born from the waves, is associated with a fountain, source of water, feminine element of fecundity and love.

Also, the fountain stands as the formal objective correlative of Machaut's text, *Le Dit de la fonteinne amoureuse*. Located at the centre of the garden and at the midpoint of temporal narration, it is named *'la Fonteinne'*; constructed by Pygmalion, it is described as being perfectly symmetrical – a serpent in gold at its centre with water flowing from the serpent's twelve mouths. Allusions to the zodiac and to alchemical creation is evident. Machaut's poem, also a masterpiece of art and symmetry, reveals a comparable structure. According to the plot, two lonely men meet and attain communion with feminine authority figures, but in the end separate, each drawn to his own destiny; this happens in a fiction in which the Narrator dreams that he and the Knight are in the process of dreaming a dream in which Venus tells them of the dream of Hecuba. A dream within a dream within a dream.

In another sense, the Lover's complaint can be considered a *texte générateur* and the fountain an *objet générateur*, much as we saw the Lover's *lai* to be in *Remede de Fortune*. Because of the complaint, the Narrator becomes aware of the Knight and his fate, is attracted to him, and takes the trouble to make his acquaintance and become his friend. Because of the complaint, which includes a prayer to Morpheus, Venus and the Lady comfort both men in their sleep. Thus the *complainte* is a lyric text that launches the action recounted in the narrative text that contains it.

The same is true for the fountain. Without the fountain the two friends would not have fallen asleep, and Venus would not have come to them bringing comfort and the story of Helen of Troy. In a sense, the Fountain of Love precedes Machaut's *Fonteinne amoureuse*. Historically speaking, the fountain, to be found in the *Metamorphoses*, in the *Roman de la Rose*, and in the *Ovide moralisé*, had existed for over a millenium prior to Machaut's era; it preceded by over a millenium Machaut's decision to create a Knight, a Narrator, and a poem. The intertextual, archetypal fountain is the source, the center, and the title of Machaut's tale. In the last analysis, in this poem of tender, gentle yearning, of fervour and beauty, reverie and desire, it *is* his tale.

Le Voir Dit

According to *Le Voir Dit* (1363–5), a beautiful young girl called Toute-belle sends the Narrator a *rondeau*, in which she offers him her heart. Soon the aging poet and his admirer enter into an amorous correspondence. He visits her more than once and they enjoy physical intimacies. Later, however, the Narrator dreams that Toute-belle's sentiments toward him have changed. Although the lovers continue to write to each other, a harsh winter, the plague, fear of bandits, and gossip concerning the lady cause the Narrator to postpone additional rendezvous. In the end, Toute-belle convinces him of her good will, and in the book's denouement they swear eternal love and plan once more a reunion.

With the title of *Le Voir Dit* (*The True Story*), Machaut makes a claim for authenticity, inviting comparison with romances of his day and with his own previous *dits*, presumed less 'true' than the new one.

The Narrator declares that the *Voir Dit* plot occurred in real life and that he tells of his amours with Toute-belle at her request. She wants everyone to know their story even if her reputation suffers because of it. And to support his claim to authenticity, Machaut includes in the text of his tale the lyric poems and letters in prose that the Narrator and Toute-belle are alleged to have exchanged.

It goes without saying, as in Machaut's earlier *dits* and *Le Roman de la Rose*, that whatever the autobiographical kernel which may have launched the poem, *Le Voir Dit* is a work of the imagination; like *Remede de Fortune* it is a poetic pseudo-autobiography, an account by a poet of his purported love life, containing his own interpolated lyrics and presuming to explain how they came into being. The letters and poems are central to the plot of *Le Voir Dit*. The story exists to set them off and to explain why they were composed. They in turn guarantee the authenticity of the narrative and contribute in complex ways to its elaboration.

As in his earlier tales, Machaut mocks traditional courtly artifice and creates a parody of *fin' amor.* The courtly and the non-courtly, the romantic and the everyday, illusion and reality, the world of books and the world of fourteenth-century Paris, are juxtaposed; one convention is played off against another for literary purposes, to create a mood of laughter and of sophisticated, ironic detachment. The Machaut Narrator is subject to love sickness and melancholia ('Si pris à merencolier ... Si devins merencolieus,' p. 24) repeatedly; as often as Toute-belle cures him, he undergoes a relapse and is put to bed. At the same time, we discover that he suffers from the gout, is several times physically incapacitated, and has lost the sight of an eye for he alludes to himself as 'vostre borgne vallet' (Letter XIII, p. 118). The Narrator's inferiority complex is justified by concrete physical infirmity; their love story concerns a young girl and an old man, a love that has come too late.

Secondly, although the Narrator refers more than once to Tristan, Lancelot, and Arthur of Little Brittany as chivalric and amorous models, he himself proves to be a magnificent coward. On one 'aventure' he dreads encountering bandits and is, in fact, taken prisoner – he is taken, however, by a woman, an allegorical figure, Esperence, whom we last saw in *Remede de Fortune* and whom the Narrator has neglected since – and then he rides home and hides in his chamber. Later in the narrative, the aging clerkly lover is dissuaded from visiting Toute-belle because the weather is bad, bandits are prowling, and the times prove to be too harsh for a young man, not to speak of one with gout. This is all well and good. However, Toute-belle eventually observes that the Narrator also stayed at home in summertime when the roads were open and his health had improved. If she had been in his shoes, she says, she would have acted differently.

By comparing himself to Gauvain, Lancelot, and Tristan, the Narrator reveals how his conduct differs from theirs; in fact he resembles King Arthur and Mark. The Narrator's only adventures are psychological, and his ordeal is merely to face a lady. No father or husband prevents him from loving Toute-belle, and the opposition he must overcome is not the plague, bandits, or cold weather, but his own fear. He himself is old enough to be her father or grandfather. He is the *durus pater*, the superego arousing anxiety in himself, bearing within his own psyche the obstacle to erotic success. Meanwhile, Toute-belle, pleasure principle incarnate, cannot overcome the greybeard's scruples. At his age he still cannot integrate the anima.

If he cannot, it is because he is not a knight; he is only a clerk. The Narrator cuts a ridiculous figure as a lover and devotee of Venus, when he ought to be thinking of another God and another Lady. Unlike Lancelot, Guilhem de Nevers (in the Occitan romance, *Flamenca*), and other heroes of romance who as knights parody or masquerade as clerics, the Narrator is a cleric aping a knight. At the same time, he participates in the knightly erotic life with all the religious fervour of his *clergie*. Thus we see him adore Toute-belle like a goddess, proclaim that she has cured his illness by miracle, and adore the poems, letters, and tokens of love she sends him. He kneels before her portrait as if it were an icon, and we are told that the 'image' heals him and appears in his dreams. Finally, the *clericus amans* undertakes a novena as an excuse to visit Toute-belle; in church he thinks only of her, reads the Hours while waiting for her at a rendezvous, and composes lyrics in her honour instead of performing his devotions. A scholar and poet, the Narrator takes himself seriously as a lover, abandons Reason for Amor, and fails miserably. We discover that the knight-lover and the poet-musician are distinct entities. Any effort to play both roles at the same time results in disaster.

In *Le Voir Dit* the functions of lover and beloved, of knight and lady, are reversed. The Narrator manifests cowardice, prudishness, vacillation, and a quick temper (he resembles Lady Fortune). Toute-belle, on the contrary, makes the advances and gives evidence of pluck and courage. For all her innocence, she appears more experienced in the code of *fin'amor* than her favourite author. He teaches her poetry and music; however she instructs him in love. Wisdom is to be found in the girl, a *puella senex*, not in the distinguished literary figure who, despite his years, acts like a child. The Narrator, clerk that he is, functions as a woman, while Toute-belle assumes the man's role. Thus the clerkly narrator dares to be the hero of his own book, as if he were a prince; he does so but pays the price, assuming the comic mode of a buffoon and ending in failure. The roles of the sexes and of the social orders are held up to scrutiny and mocked in a world where literary clichés are already three centuries old.

The scrutiny and the mockery extend to the narrative itself. More than in *Remede de Fortune* and much more than in *Le Jugement dou Roy de Navarre*, interpreting the diegesis is subject to ambiguity; the implied reader-audience is not told important facets of the 'reality' recounted in the text. When the Narrator comes to say goodbye to Toute-belle (pp.153–63), in a delicious hyper-alba or anti-alba, Venus's cloud descends, physical intimacies take place, and Toute-belle offers the Narrator the symbolic Key to her Treasure. However, the precise nature of these intimacies, specifically whether or not the girl is deflowered, is veiled from us. Similarly, at the denouement although the lovers are reconciled and although the Narrator believes a rendezvous is forthcoming, whether or not he and Toute-belle will, in fact, meet or make love again, and whether or not either really loves the other, is left open to question. He also has to recognize that, during the second half of the tale, what appeared to be a successful accomplishment of *fin' amor*, adhering to the *gradus amoris*, begins to unravel. The second half deconstructs the happy, united love of the first half. Machaut refuses to offer a clear, unambiguous explanation for the estrangement. Why do the lovers not meet again for over two years? Is the trouble due to Toute-belle's fickleness? To the Narrator's cowardice and jealousy? To both at the same time? We do not know.

Perhaps the author wishes us to understand that the concrete physical details of a story – whether the man and woman have intercourse or merely 'pet'; how often they meet and when – are secondary to the nature of the relationship and the characters' perception of it; therefore, given the ambiguity and the decentring inherent in such perceptions, the lovers will never be certain of the relationship any more than the implied reader-audience.

For the Narrator and for Toute-belle, ascertaining the truth is rendered difficult by space and by time. The time recounted in the narrative (*erzählte Zeit*) covers almost three years, from summer's end, 1362, to a moment in the present, after 1 May 1365. We are made aware of the changes of seasons and of a lover's frustration as he goes without word from the beloved. The Narrator insists too much on the theme of metamorphosis in Ovid and the Bible not to be conscious, and to make us conscious, of metamorphosis in his own life; the lovers are separated and communication between them is precarious. Much of the external décor and many of the secondary characters – bandits, storms, winter, the plague, and figures such as Malebouche and Danger – serve one function and that is to keep the Narrator and Toute-belle apart. Space stands between them, limiting perception and preventing understanding.

Toute-belle and the Narrator do communicate by letter. The forty-six prose epistles introduced into the text as a truth claim also contribute to our understanding of the communication problem. A person's letters are an artificial, semi-literary projection of himself. The lover-clerk who once intentionally tampers with the truth (p. 313) can never be certain that the girl's missives are sincere; nor can she count on his. Furthermore, by the time one of them reads the other's letter, it no longer necessarily reflects the writer's sentiments or how their situation has evolved in the interval. Although the lovers also communicate in their sleep, the Narrator does not believe his dreams to be infallible, for he declares: 'Car clerement vi que mon songe / N'avoit riens de vray fors mensonge' (p. 233) [For I saw clearly that there was nothing true in my dream – except for the lies]. Dreams, letters, lyric poetry, even the portrait are mediators; they help the lovers to maintain contact; nonetheless, objects, even objects of art or the process of imagination (the dream), contain no guarantee of empirical, factual validity. The Narrator and Toute-belle each is aware of his own sentiments but can never 'prehend' the other's. Neither, of course, can the reader.

For the first time in the history of French fiction the limited perspective of the homodiegetic narrator plays a crucially important role in the plot. Machaut makes us aware of how much an 'I' can know outside his own purview. The *erzählendes Ich* is not necessarily reliable; nor are we obligated to accept without question his interpretation of events. We have the right to disagree with him. We know the Narrator's opinion but not that of Guillaume de Machaut, the author, for whom the *erlebendes Ich* is a literary character the same as Toute-belle. This blurring of focus is the key to the tale's structure. Illusion is taken for reality, and reality for illusion. Truth can be revealed through appearance (a dream), or, on the other hand, a lie is told in seemingly truthful terms and given the authenticity of a dream vision. Narrative omniscience is out of place in a story that reveals the Narrator-hero's lack of omniscience. In *Le Voir Dit* (*The True Story*) neither the protagonist nor the implied reader-audience ever succeeds in unravelling the *Voir Dit* mystery.

One thing is certain, however; knowing no more than the Narrator, at least we perceive his weakness and vacillation. We do not see the reality behind Toute-belle's mask, but we do recognize that it is a mask and that her suitor is incapable of distinguishing between it and reality. The Narrator's tragedy lies not in the Other but in himself, and the ultimate truth of *The True Story* concerns not his external amours with another, over which he agonizes, but his inner self, of which he is almost totally oblivious. In this sense the implied reader discovers a truth the Narrator never dreamed of and arrives at knowledge far beyond his.

The *erlebendes Ich* of *Le Voir Dit* is a fictional character once removed, a narrated self who exists in words, not historical fact; he has been created not only by Guillaume de Machaut but by his other half, himself at a somewhat later stage in life, the *erzählendes Ich* who composes their story. By sending her portions of the book as they are completed, the Narrator seeks to mould Toute-belle's interpretation of the events he has just lived. The same is true for Toute-belle and the Narrator as poets and correspondents; the lyrics and prose epistles are written specifically for their narratees – the Other in the love relation – and for the diegetic inscribed public, friends and courtiers in the region, to create a calculated effect on them. The entire book assumes the existence of intradiegetic implied readers called upon to witness the fictional selves of the purported authors: Toute-belle, the Narrator as *actant*, and the Narrator as *scripteur*.

Each seeks to impose his own vision of the self on the other and on the public through works of art. Communication in *Le Voir Dit* is embodied largely in the written word – songs, prose letters, and the True Story that the Narrator is supposed to be composing. In spite of his age, ill health, and loss of an eye, Machaut's protagonist attracts Toute-belle because of his reputation as a writer and composer. Throughout the story she sends to him for lyrics and declares that she adores reading them and will learn them by heart. He then goes along with her game by composing songs in her praise. The Narrator also agrees, though with misgivings, to transcribe the whole of their affair in his book. Toute-belle not only sacrifices her honour and defies convention for the sake of fame, but she succeeds in her objective. Diegetically, she becomes known in society as the Narrator's muse;

in the extradiegetic world of the history of French letters, like Délie and Cassandre, Elvire and Eva, she is known today because she was a fictional woman beloved of a poet in a work of art.

The Narrator is a lover and a poet, a lover because he is a poet and vice versa. Poems, letters, and the tale itself (their story in the making) bring the Narrator and his beloved together. They are perhaps the only mediators in an affair that otherwise would never have come into being and that is kept alive only in poetry. They also generate the plot; they are the chief increments in a narrative whose prime reality is the subtexts and how the characters interpret them. It is not surprising then that Machaut's hero does not succeed as a lover. He tells stories and draws conclusions but he does not act to win his lady, as a young suitor must. Significantly, he flees Toute-belle, preferring the world of books and his bookish vision of the *domna* to concrete experience of the real girl; his knowledge of her is derived from the act of reading – her poems, her letters. In a sense he creates her as a work of art in his imagination, whether it be the fetish of her portrait or her actual presence as a literary character. For good or ill, both lovers envisage the Other exclusively as writer and reader; for them, the book replaces the bed. The Narrator would never have had a chance with Toute-belle had he not been a great poet, but the absence of concrete human experience, *sub specie Veneris*, implicit in the clerical life, condemns him to failure.

In compensation for his failure as a lover, the Narrator's status as an artist is never left in doubt. He is conscious of his pre-eminence as a poet and more than once brings off a tour de force, answering Toute-belle's songs in their own rhyme scheme and composing impromptu lyrics to illustrate intense emotional states or crucial moments in the liaison as they occur; the most extraordinary of these is the *virelai* he creates at the very moment he enjoys Toute-belle in bed. At that moment artistic prowess supplements, supplants, and perhaps compensates for the absence of phallic prowess. On her side, Toute-belle also develops into a poetess. She learns to answer his poems following his rhyme scheme and to compose *rondeaux* in moments of intense emotion. Approximately one half of the *Voir Dit* lyrics form 'duets,' companion pieces in which one of the lovers answers and imitates the other. There is a direct analogy between art and desire. However, in the comic world of *Le Voir Dit* the two calls become disjunct, from a pedagogical perspective as well as others. It can be said that Toute-belle turns out better as a poet than the Narrator as a lover.

She improves in the one realm while he falters in the other; and, to give him his due, he is a more successful *maistre* of letters than she is an instructress in the ways of Eros.

The protagonists collaborate on their story, *Le Voir Dit*; in the second half especially, the writing of *Le Voir Dit* becomes the subject of *Le Voir Dit*, the poem making itself. The Narrator ceases largely to be a lover; his life as a writer increases. For the Narrator, as for Toute-belle, their secular opus partakes of much of the symbolism the Medievals ascribed to the Book of God and the Book of Nature; it is a world and comes to make up their world. Toute-belle delares that her greatest pleasure lies in reading parts of it as it comes into being; she is urged to assume some editorial control in its elaboration; and her love is nourished by the book and by her own role in its elaboration. At the end, although the future of his relationship remains uncertain, the Narrator has the book to fall back on; he will complete the history of their amours. It exists, when all else proves to be illusion. This man, who loves his craft more than his lady and who perceives his lady in terms of his craft, sublimates an impossible desire for her by creating *Le Voir Dit*. The two reconcile not to make love but to make the book. As Apollo kills Coronis but their son, Aesculapius, is saved, the Narrator's love eventually dies but his creation, the book, will live on. Ultimately, art triumphs over existence because the latter, as Machaut's protagonists live it, has no meaning or permanence apart from art. Literature creates life, not the opposite, and the Narrator-implied author creates the characters of his story, including himself. In our modern sense of the terms, Machaut's opus in general and *Le Voir Dit* in particular are truly self-reflexive and metatextual. It is not coincidental that the book appears in the title; it is the archimage which dominates a poem that refers to and is justified only by itself.

Le Voir Dit is the most complex of Machaut's tales. The three literary genres and styles contained in it – lyrics, octosyllabic narrative, and prose epistles – can recount the same incident three times. Continually juxtaposed, they interrupt narrative continuity and create an aura of fragmentation and of extreme literariness undermining the truth they purport to make (cf. Calin 1974, Brownlee 1984, Cerquiglini 1985, Boulton 1989, 1990, Sturges 1991). Furthermore, as in our best contemporary fiction, the reader has to interpret the situation at any given moment without help from the author. This, along with the incomplete ending, gives the poem an aura of truth, as is so often the case in real life. The plot is open, not closed; the characters live on; and their problems persist, not to be resolved by a fortuitous marriage or death.

Machaut also anticipates the novel and the more fashionable criticism of our age by creating the illusion that his book takes shape as the characters live it, that they create their own story, and that the work of art itself becomes a living organism, free from convention and an author's will. Yet such is not the case in Machaut's world any more than in Gide's and Sartre's. An author does shape his characters; he adheres to or rebels against literary conventions; he constructs a narrative. The contrast between the authenticity of artistic creation and the illusion of realism, and the contrast between the ideal of *fin' amor* and the reality of a young girl and an old man are central to the structure and vision of Machaut's True Story.

Machaut's greatest triumph as a poet may well be the new literary type he made his own – the inept, blundering narrator who is also an inept, blundering lover. This pseudo-autobiographical character is prone to cowardice, sloth, snobbery, misogyny, and pedantry. Guilty of excess, unable to cope with everyday social life, and obsessed by his failings, he acts in a delightfully comic manner, in contrast to the elegant regulars of the court. For the first time in French literature the fool has become a protagonist in a serious work of art.

Sometimes in Machaut a lover recounts his experiences directly; sometimes they are told by a witness observer. The Narrator may participate actively in the story or withdraw from it; he can be reliable or unreliable, omniscient or in error. By playing with point of view and illusion-reality, Guillaume pioneered the development of a more sophisticated narrative technique. These themes enter into the structure of his finest tales, giving them a complexity seldom equalled in early fiction.

Finally, he manifests extraordinary self-consciousness and pride in his own function as a poet; he reveals a sense of the dignity and importance of his vocation, by, among other things, making the craft of writing the subject of writing. According to Brownlee (1984), we find a 'poëte,' replacing the trouvère; as such he combines the roles of first-person lover-hero of lyric, clerkly narrator of romance, and scribal editor organizing codices; he resembles the classical *auctores*.[18]

All of these developments were to have a profound influence upon Guillaume's most gifted successors: Froissart, Christine de Pizan, and Chartier in France; Chaucer, Gower, and Hoccleve in England. *The Book of the Duchess*, *The Prologue to the Legend of Good Women*, and *Confessio Amantis* derive much of their structure, imagery, and tone from the works of the Champenois master. The Machaldian presence is to be felt throughout Chaucer's career, in the early love visions but also in the independent lyrics, *Troilus and Criseyde*, the *Merchant's Tale*, and the *Manciple's Tale*. No one, not even Jean de Meun, had a greater impact shaping the Ricardian poets and their sensibility.

From Machaut the Ricardians and their successors took much: a fund of themes and motifs; the Boethian poem of (amorous) complaint and comfort; an aura of court refinement and elegance, of beautiful people discoursing on love and love casuistry in a beautiful setting; the give and take of a new social bond between the clerkly author figure and his high aristocratic patron; the humour and the reflexivity of the author figure; and a gently ironic vision of love, life and art, illusion and reality, dream vision and waking perception. These contribute to the formulation of a new, late medieval world-view and artistic consciousness that constitute perhaps the apex of the Franco-English cross-channel high court culture.

6. Froissart

Of the continental authors who visited Great Britain and actually dwelt there for a time, none is more important than Jean Froissart. A native of Hainault, he served Philippa, Edward III's beloved queen, from 1361 to 1366 and again in 1367 and 1368. Being Philippa's 'secretary' may simply have meant a sinecure for the recognized, rising court poet. During this period Jean made friends and did extensive travelling, including a six-month's voyage to Scotland, where he spent fifteen weeks in the entourage of the French-speaking King David II.

That he knew Chaucer is probable but by no means a certainty. They frequented the same court circles; Geoffrey was indeed influenced by several of Jean's *dits amoureux*. However, in all the *Chroniques* Froissart alludes to Chaucer only once, as one of the English commissioners who in 1377 were negotiating a royal French marriage. Upon Froissart's return to England in 1395, the only old friend with whom he renewed acquaintance was Sir Richard Stury.

At any event, Froissart always treasured his British memories; they constituted the joy of his youth and the nostalgia of his old age. Scotland provided the backdrop for his Arthurian verse romance *Meliador*. The splendour and glory of the English nobility and the éclat of English chivalry are some of the leading themes of *Les Chroniques*. Perhaps they are the impulse that caused Froissart to become the greatest chronicler of his age. The return in 1395 can be envisaged as Froissart's last effort to gather material and to recapture the old spirit of chivalry as well as the memories of his youth. Even the relatively hostile reaction to the English people, recognizable in Jean's later work, is a tribute to the ideal England, for he considered the commons to be responsible for the overthrow in 1399 of Richard II, great grandson of the revered queen of his early days.

Jean Froissart's opus includes a number of quite original *pastourelles* and a series of *dits amoureux* in the tradition of Machaut. These tales of love, for the most part written in England, carry further the Machaldian experiments in narrative technique and the Machaldian self-consciousness. *Le Paradis d'Amour* and *Le Bleu Chevalier* influenced *The Book of the Duchess* and lines and tags from Froissart appear throughout the Chaucerian corpus.

His masterpiece, however, and the work which had the greatest impact upon French and English culture lies in the domain of non-fictional prose – *Les Chroniques*. Froissart's history mushroomed into one of the most imposing monuments of the Middle Ages. The equivalent of some 13,000 pages, it is divided into four books that recount the wars between France and England from 1325 to 1400, from the beginnings of strife to the fall of Richard II and the Plantagenet line. It is with *Les Chroniques* that Froissart elaborates new, late medieval myths and also brings to the domain of historical writing the insights into story-telling and the complexity of narrative structure that he learned from Machaut and from his own practice in the *dit amoureux*.

Froissart's fame as an historian eventually eclipsed his poetic renown. A tribute to his glory came through a negative compliment – the seizure in 1381 by the Duke of Anjou of a *Chroniques* manuscript deemed too favourable to the English. Thirty-two beautifully illustrated medieval codices and at least ten printed editions from 1495 to 1520 testify to Froissart's success, as do twelve editions of a Latin abridgment, and translations into English and Dutch. It is the version (1523–5) by Lord Berners, the translator of *Huon de Bordeaux*, that preserved in English the epic of fourteenth-century historical chivalry in the same manner that Malory recaptured in English the epic of thirteenth-century romance chivalry. During the age of the *Prose Lancelot*, the *Prose Tristan*, and the prose Froissart, Englishmen of quality read the texts in the original. Malory and Berners, the great translators, ensured that the medieval aristocratic heritage would not be lost with the end of bilingualism.

Berners, like Malory, avoided the ornate, aureate style in favour of a more simple range of expression, *genus medium*, perfectly adapted to the original. Like Froissart and Malory, Berners, in his Prefaces, insists upon the importance of great deeds in bearing witness to a reign or an age and in encouraging emulation in subsequent generations. According to Berners, the writing of History, which recounts those great deeds, will immortalize them and will cause all people to lead better lives:

> The most profytable thyng in this worlde for the instytution of the humayne lyfe is hystorie ... But above all thynges, wherby mans welthe ryseth, speciall laude and praise ought to be gyven to historie: it is the keper of suche thinges as have ben vertuously done, and the wytnesse of yvell dedes: and by the benefite of hystorie all noble, highe, and vertuous actes be immortall ... What knowlege shulde we have of auncyent thynges past, and historie were nat? whiche is the testymony therof, the lyght of trouthe, the maystres of the lyfe humayne, the presydent of remembraunce, and the messanger of antiquyte. (I: 4–5)

Froissart, Englished by Berners, became a staple of English historiography. Included in the major chronicles, including Holinshead, he influenced, directly or indirectly, anonymous Elizabethan chronicle plays and Shakespeare's *Richard II*. Later, in French or in English, *Les Chroniques* received the praise of La Curne de Sainte-Palaye, Gray, Scott, Southey, Hazlitt, Chateaubriand, Mérimée, and Morris. Up until quite recent times Froissart was the best known and the most widely read French writer in England. A modern Plutarch in the fourteenth century, he served to instill in the young and to remind the old of the myth of English chivalry, the joys of chivalric adventure, and the English vision of national history in the Middle Ages.

Les Chroniques are immense and the problems faced by Froissart scholars are of comparable magnitude. The official Société de l'Histoire de France edition, begun in 1869, now totalling fifteen volumes, has just reached Book 4 of *Les Chroniques*. Volume 15 stops at the year 1389. Froissart himself composed at least three (five, according to Palmer [*Froissart* 1981: 9]) redactions of the First Book and relied upon two written sources, Jean le Bel and Chandos Herald. Recent scholarship calls into question the accepted order and chronology of these redactions. It is possible that all extant versions of Book 1 date from later than was previously thought, or that some or all of them were subject to scribal interference, or that Froissart never revised his text in a formal manner but simply composed new versions altogether. Did Froissart conceive of new versions superseding older ones? Or did he simply offer alternate redactions? Were the materials put together from different manuscripts or notebooks by him or by others? I cannot determine with confidence the evolution of Froissart's use of sources, his political opinions, and his art in Book 1. What we can probably agree upon is that Jean improved as an historian and as a writer over time, and that Books 2, 3, and 4, and the final partial redaction of Book 1 in the Rome manuscript, see him at his best. We must not forget, however, that it is Book 1, in its simpler, more naive form, that consecrated for Lord Berners and for us the vision of Froissart given to posterity. This Froissart is as living and vital as the other, and cannot be forgotten.

Due in part to the popular redactions of Book 1 but also to a modern-oriented reading of *Les Chroniques* as a whole, the favourite author of Scott and Mérimée has been criticized by professional academic historians for a number of reasons. It is said, by scholars of impeccable credentials, Palmer and his colleagues (*Froissart* 1981), that Froissart consistently gets the names, dates, and places wrong (the worst example being his inability to distinguish Galicia from León); this is because he relies almost exclusively on oral testimony and has no critical sense or capacity for nuance. Nor does he seek to verify his informants' reports. There have been other criticisms: Jean is concerned only with war and chivalry, thus giving us the impression that Europe lived only for war and chivalry; he fails to see the social and economic fabric of his age and the true causes of events, the inner truth of history; he emits no judgments and offers no lesson or grand design; finally, he has contempt for the masses of the people and, in contrast to other historians including his predecessor Jean le Bel, blackens the peasants in order to create a melodrama of autocracy.

I am a literary person, not an historian. I recognize that historians have the right to ask different questions from a chronicler of reality, such as Froissart, than from a creator of fiction such as Chrétien de Troyes. It is eminently fair for historians to determine which documents from the fourteenth century are the most reliable in helping us to reconstitute the *histoire événementielle* of the age. On the other hand, from a literary perspective, we judge the great historians of the past – Herodotus and Thucydides, Livy and Tacitus, Froissart and Commines, Voltaire and Gibbon, Macaulay, Carlyle, and Michelet – on their accomplishments as writers; we value their vision of the world and the mythical universe they have created, not the extent to which they conform to present-day standards of academic scholarship. For example, it has been a generation now since any literary critic of consequence has praised or blamed medieval trouvères on the basis of their similarity or dissimilarity to Balzac or Flaubert. The peculiar non-mimetic narrative techniques of, say, Beroul, Jean de Meun, and Guillaume de Machaut expand the parameters of our conception of narrative fiction and of narratology. The same ought to be true for history.

In my opinion, part of the problem derives from the fact that certain modern philosophies of history – Whig history and its French Third

Republic secularist equivalent, or for that matter the Marxist and Annales schools – are as culturally determined, ideological, and biased as was Froissart's aristocratic historiography of high chivalry. Modern historians politically on the Left are sympathetic to the masses of the people and work on social and economic problems. For them it is almost a cliché that a decadent French upper class was responsible for Crécy and Poitiers, and that decadent English kings and counsellors were responsible for allowing the French to recover what they had lost. Froissart, in contrast, was a conscious conservative-reactionary fascinated by the high and low aristocracy in arms. Is he more prejudiced, referring openly to the Jacques as 'meschans gens,' than Marie-Thérèse de Medeiros (1979), who alludes to Froissart ironically as 'le bon chânoine'? Perhaps war indeed was the dominant feature of life in the fourteenth century. Perhaps the values of the feudal aristocracy were then and are still today one of the great contributions of medieval France to the spirit of mankind. Perhaps the idea of the decadence of the medieval aristocracy is a Whig–Third Republic myth. I do not know. What I propose is that Froissart has a vision of history and a literary and historical grand design. It is not for me to agree or disagree but simply to observe that it is ideological and literary, just as the ideological discourse of Voltaire and Michelet, or of Le Roy Ladurie. For historians and critics interested in the mind-sets of people from the past, no work offers a richer mine to explore than *Les Chroniques*.

Froissart's is a world of war – of heroism and deeds in arms. In the Prologue (Book 1, First public redaction, revised) he speaks of 'proèce,' the subject of his work. 'Many marvels in the military sphere have occurred in our age,' says the author. 'Young "bacelers" should imitate their predecessors, be active, and win glory.' Froissart alludes to the three Orders: knights fight, the people speak of their deeds, and clerks write them down:

> Li vaillant homme traveillent leurs membres en armes, pour avancier leurs corps et acroistre leur honneur. Li peuples parolle, recorde et devise de leurs estas, et de leur fortune. Li aucun clerch escrisent et registrent leurs avenues et baceleries. (I: 5)

> Men of valour weary their limbs in feats of arms, in order to put themselves forward physically and to increase their honour. The people speak of, relate, and discuss the warriors' situation and destiny. Some who are clerks write down and record their encounters and their exploits.

Clerks register feats of war from the present or past in order to keep their memory alive and to encourage young knights in the present to continue the tradition in the future. The great deeds of the present form part of a pattern of history, from past to present to future; the *translatio imperii* passes from East to West, from the Chaldeans and Hebrews to France, and now, perhaps, to England.

'Deeds in arms' means battles, and Froissart excels in the great set-pieces such as the English or English-supported victories at Crécy, Poitiers, Nájera, and Aljubarrota; the naval battles of Sluys and La Rochelle; Ghent's triumph over Bruges at Beverhoutsveld and France's triumph over Ghent at Roosebeke. We follow the careers of the princes, the captains, the rebels, and the bandit chieftains: Edward III, the Black Prince, Du Guesclin, Cliçon, Chandos, Knolles, Jean de Hainaut, Walter de Mauny, Van Artevelde, and Aymerigot Marcès. Froissart is a master of vivacity, colour, vibrant images, and fine speeches. His forte is what great men say and do, the drama of the moment. With these he reconstitutes the flavour of war and concretizes the aristocratic values of the age: valour, victory, and glory.

The author of *Meliador* is as much a writer of romance as a chronicler of events. He exaggerates. The great scenes are literary scenes, redolent with ceremony, melodrama, spectacle, laughter, and tears; they are aspects of the sublime à la Huizinga. Whatever we think of Huizinga as an historian, his view of the Middle Ages will help us to understand Froissart's vision of his own era. The bloody, sordid, sadistic executions of Edward II and Hugh Despenser; the glorious weddings of King John of Portugal to John of Gaunt's daughter Philippa, and of Charles VI to Isabeau de Bavière; the hommage proffered by Edward to Philip VI; Isabeau's grand entry into Paris; the confrontations to the death between Richard II and Wat Tyler or between Gaston Phoebus and his son – these are spectacles with speech and gesture, plays put on for public entertainment, and quasi-ritual acts. Whether they actually occurred or were perceived to have occurred in this manner by the participants is problematic. Froissart, however, envisions them and recreates them in the grand manner for his readers and for posterity.

One of the most famous scenes tells the story of the Burgesses of Calais. After stylized, rhetorical pleading by Walter de Mauny and others, King Edward consents not to massacre all the inhabitants of the captured town, but only six of the burgesses at his pleasure. Six do volunteer, in an ambiance of pity, tears, and melodramatic spectacle. They leave the town and form a procession to Edward's camp, unarmed, barefoot, and with ropes hanging from their necks. Mauny, followed by the pregnant Queen Philippa, plead for mercy on their knees. Only then does the implacable Edward grant it, tears flowing from his eyes also. The spectacle of the burgesses' procession, beheld by the English and the French, the pleading and speeches heard by the English and by the burgesses, the rhetoric and tears, and finally the symbolism of justice yielding to mercy as a surrogate to God the Father is swayed by a surrogate to the Blessed Virgin Mary – all this makes the scene one of the greatest and most quintessential in *Les Chroniques*.

Warfare in Froissart is enriched by a patina of gallantry and courtesy. Froissart's characters try to live up to the standards of the *Prose Lancelot*; often they succeed. Some will commit deeds in arms for their ladies. Others, including the supremely eminent Edward III and Gaston Phoebus, will grant a 'rash boon' to a 'damsel in distress' that will cost them military or financial profit. Jean de Hainaut, who helps punish Edward II and restores Queen Isabel and her son, does so in an aura of romance, as if he were rescuing a princess persecuted by an ogre. Similarly, Jean de Carrouze avenges his wife's dishonour on Jacques le Gris; he fights for her to the death in the style of Lancelot. Froissart also blackens the rebellion of the Jacquerie by inventing his own little courtly myth – the Duchesses of Normandy and Orleans in Meaux, threatened by animal-like peasants with rape in mind, are rescued by the Count of Foix and the Captal of Buch who, returning from a pilgrimage, intervene in order to save them.

Chivalry is not limited to the amorous; on the contrary, some of the most touching *beaux gestes* occur between comrades in arms or between adversaries. At Crécy King Edward declines to rejoin the Black Prince in the front lines in order that all the glory will fall to his son. At Poitiers the Prince shows extreme courtesy to his prisoner, King John of France, offering John the prize for valour on the French side and serving his captive at table. In 1360 an English captain, mining beneath a French castle, with 'courtoisie' and 'gentillèce' calls for a truce and shows his sappers' work to the defenders, permitting them to surrender before he literally collapses their walls. Later, during one of the Duke of Anjou's campaigns to capture Italian lands claimed by his family, his enemy, the Count of Savoy, beheads a magician who had offered use of occult powers to betray Anjou's castle.

Froissart relates how the 'gentils homs' follow the precepts of 'onneur,' 'gentillèce,' and 'courtoisie' in holding to the rules and playing the game. After all, these men, who sought 'aventures' and 'renommée,' formed an international aristocratic elite in which bonds of friendship and potlatch rituals of generosity took precedence over national and dynastic hostility.

However, in Froissart's book not all is chivalry and roses. At Crécy, after the rhetoric and the generosity comes the slaughter. No quarter is given – except for affluent prisoners – on the day of the battle and the following day, a Sunday; on that Sunday innocent bystanders from Beauvais and Rouen are cut down, including an archbishop and the Prieur de France, and the stragglers. The dead are honoured, and then all the land in the direction of the sea is put to the flame. Edward does finally show mercy to the six burgesses of Calais; still, the inhabitants are forced into exile to be replaced by Englishmen from England. Violence and extremes in emotion contribute to the late medieval world-view; they also constitute part of the reality of war in all times and places.

Froissart's protagonists try to act like Lancelot and Arthur, Roland and Charlemagne. However, in his day the conditions of war were quite different from when the *Song of Roland* and the *Prose Lancelot* were written. Or rather, the conditions of war differ inevitably from reality to romance. For one thing, the massed battle of Crécy or Poitiers and the staged duel or joust (Le combat des Trente) are rare exceptions. For the most part, Froissart describes one army, the stronger one, wandering around the countryside, seeking to capture castles belonging to the weaker army. As in the century of Condé, Turenne, and Vauban, the attack and defence of strongpoints proves to be far more important than mass movement across the plain. The operation of the various siege machines, the attack and counterattack of the engines, or the burrowing and counterburrowing by sappers is not the least intriguing facet of Froissart's art of war. One example among many is the great siege of Aquillon in 1346 with bridges built, destroyed, rebuilt, and redestroyed; twelve siege engines are brought forward by the attackers but six of them are demolished by machines from the castle; then an assault is made by enormous siege towers on boats which are demolished by the defenders' catapults.

Froissart's is a war of ruse as well as of force. He differs from trouvères of *geste* and of *romans* in that for him the intelligent, clever outwitting of an opponent is always subject to praise. We find infinite variations on several themes: warriors disguised as women or monks, sneaking inside the walls of a town; cattle or merchants or a petty contingent dangled in front a castle, causing the defenders to rush out and then find themselves overwhelmed by a superior force lying in ambush, or find the walls scaled and the citadel seized in their absence. Froissart also recounts more sophisticated ruses, an especially amusing one concerning the Rochelois who in 1372 trick an English captain, 'qui n'estoit mies trop soutieulz,' by delivering to him a counterfeit written order from Edward III calling for a muster of the troops to be followed by payment of back wages. Poor Philip Mansel, who didn't know how to read (or didn't know how to read French) and who wanted his pay so badly that he fell for the ruse, opened the gates, and lost the castle of Saintes. Thus the *engin* of some romance heroes in the sphere of love becomes a standard component of all soldiers in a more 'modern' war setting.

When armies were not besieging castles, they pillaged, burned, and destroyed the countryside. War is depicted as an endless series of brief forays, brutal and self-serving. After all, seizure of gold, silver, and other goods, including people to be held for ransom, was an accepted means of waging war and of enriching warriors. Even worse than the regular armies are the mercenaries, on both sides, who, during periods of truce, having nowhere to go and no recourse at hand, become private Free Companies and pillage, burn, and destroy on their own, seizing and selling castles, towns, and people. These are the ones who, according to Froissart, 'avoient apris à pillier' and, as a result, 'telz manières de gens persevèrent en leur mauvaisté et fisent depuis moult de mauls ou dit royaume' (VI: 60) [had learned how to pillage ... such kinds of soldiers persevered in their wickedness and since that time did much harm to the said kingdom]. Nonetheless, the same Froissart who scorned and feared the freebooters admired the Bascot de Mauléon and even Eustache d'Aubrécicourt for their élan, skill, and success.

Add to this the changing fortunes of war and the fact that, as fortunes shift, captains and bandits switch camps at will. Throughout the century the Gascons were divided, with castles on both sides, and people changed allegiance whenever it was politic to do so. The same became true in the North, especially during the French *reconquista* of the 1370s when, in Normandy or Poitou or the Limousin, towns and castles faced each other, some 'French,' some 'English,' with families divided or the lord taking one side and his vassals the other, or burghers eager to yield when the garrison held out. The epitome is probably to be found in the Ile de France, during the year or two after the battle of Poitiers, when the following military entities were making their presence felt: three official armed factions – the French, the English, and the troops of Charles, King of Navarre; the Companies of mercenary bandits more or less allied to each one; and the rebel bands of Etienne Marcel and the Jacques. The only word to describe the situation is absolute chaos. Towns survive, when they survive, by private contract; they hire their own mercenaries, freebooters or regular troops and pay them to protect the town against any and all comers. And any and all did come. This is not the world of Roland and Huon de Bordeaux or of Lancelot and Tristan. This is the horror of war in its physical concreteness. Froissart does not veil the chaos and the horror. He presents them graphically, without hypocrisy.

Thus, for Froissart, war is inevitable; it is a way of life, *the* way of life for the nobility, and, win or lose, a man of war accepts his fate, and war goes on. This does not mean that Jean was unaware of or insensitive to the plight of civilians. He pities the poor and states in no uncertain terms that they pay for the follies of the rich. He also sympathizes with the inhabitants of 'gras pays,' rich, fertile lands that have not known strife – Normandy in 1346 and central Languedoc in 1355 – and are suddenly subject to invasion. The case of Languedoc is exemplary; the people simply do not know how to defend themselves. Their goods are taken and often their lives as well, 'dont ce fu pités.' Froissart is aware that the hostility of the English yeomanry to Jean de Hainaut in 1326 and the hostility of the Scots to Jean de Vienne in 1385 can be traced to culture shock and the extreme poverty of the local population; he also tells us that, during preparations for the invasion of England in 1386, the peasants in the region of Sluyse suffered more from their 'defenders' (the French army waiting to debark) than from any English incursion. He emphasizes that it was the little men, the soldiers of low rank, who were never paid.

Although *Les Chroniques* do not take the same side in the class struggle as do most Parisian professors, their author is conscious of the struggle and analyzes it keenly. Among his best pages are those devoted to the Flemish burgher wars. He shows how a feud between two family chieftains – Jan Hyoens and Gijsbrecht Mayhuus – eventually stirs up the city of Ghent, the county of Flanders, and all of northern Europe. Inside Ghent one side cultivates the lower orders, the other appeals to the count. The patricians sympathize with the count but fear for their lives and fail to act in time. Since the count is a vassal of France, Van Artevelde, now the champion of the small traders and the urban riff-raff, develops into quite a demagogue. Brutality, intimidation, and personal vendettas become an everyday occurrence. The divisions that plague Ghent spread to the vassal and sister towns. Meanwhile, everyone keeps his eyes on Flanders. According to Froissart, if Van Artevelde and the downtrodden are allowed to succeed, all of Europe will burst into flame. Already in England 'gloutons,' 'maleoites gens,' and 'folles gens' [scoundrels, accursed people, and crazy people] are on the march. Already the commons rebel in Paris and Rouen. No ransom and no quarter are taken in this war. Yet, for all his passionate defense of hierarchy and order, the chronicler does portray Van Artevelde in magnificent colours; he grants him oratorical speeches and theatrical gestures of defiance, and he recounts the victory of the Ghentish phalanx at Beverhoutsveld with as much power and excitement as he does its destruction at Roosebeke.

According to a number of scholars, including Archambault (1974), Froissart creates his 'world' by showing us what people see and say, concentrating on instant progression in time and space; his is a text of surfaces and of discontinuity, with no sense of duration, consciousness, ultimate purpose, or the inner development of personality.

This is part of the literary reality of *Les Chroniques*, but not all of it. It is also a fact that, as Froissart ages and *Les Chroniques* mature into the later Books and last redaction of the First Book, we also perceive an historian who analyses, speculates, and proposes causes and explanations; he provides what we have come to consider a more modern type of historiography. In Froissart's own words:

> Se je disoie: 'Ainsi et ainsi en avint en ce temps,' sans ouvrir ne esclarcir la matere qui fut grande et grosse et orrible et bien taillie d'aler malement, ce seroit cronique non pas historiée, et se m'en passeroie bien se je vouloie; or ne m'en vueille pas passer que je n'esclarcisse tout le fait ou cas que Dieu m'en a donné le sens, le temps, le memoire, et le loisir de cronissier et historier tout au long de la matiere. (XIII: 222)

> If I said, 'Thusly and thusly it happened at that time,' without disclosing and elucidating the subject matter, which was important, weighty, horrible, and destined to end badly, it would be a chronicle and not history. If I wanted to, I could easily avoid doing this. However, I do not wish to elude explaining every action or event for which God has given me the intellect, time, memory, and leisure so to chronicle and to write history all through the material.

Especially in the Rome manuscript (the final version of Book 1) we see an author distancing himself from his characters and their ideals; he is more skeptical of prowess and glory and more cynical vis-à-vis the façade of chivalry. If the early Froissart is a writer of romance, the later one assumes all but a novelistic pose. Figures such as Robert d'Artois or Jean de Brabant now are undermined (cf. Diller 1984).

Their personal, egotistical, Byzantine attitude toward the great events of the day, and their cynical manipulation of these events, enter into the telling of history.

Secondly, whatever we think of his politics and whatever errors Froissart makes in the microtext (and they are legion), it can be maintained that in the macrotext he is a great historian and he is right about many things. The nature of medieval warfare; the victories and defeats; the flights and panic; the technology of siege engines and the new canon; the functioning of transport, provisions, and the budget; realities of climate and terrain; tactics and the conduct of warfare (chivalric, popular, and guerilla) – in all this 'le bon chânoine' not only expresses medieval mentalities but he also presents a picture that, to the extent we believe in objective reality, we can accept as objectively real.

Finally, it may well be that, in the long run, Froissart's very 'surface phenomenology,' and his neutrality and distance vis-à-vis the events he recounts give his account an objectivity and a subtlety (he will not blame John the Good in order to praise Charles the Wise, nor will he praise Edward III in order to blame Richard II). Contrast this with more partisan readings of the same people and events – by not only Voltaire and Michelet but also Perroy and Calmette. The later accounts may well appear crude and extreme in comparison.

Something roughly the same is true for the depiction of character. Froissart's method, *grosso modo*, is that of the *chanson de geste*, whose authors sing of a man's words and deeds, his speeches and actions. Analysis is left to the implied audience which, assuming it has ears to hear, will make the appropriate deductions. Take as example Edward the Black Prince. Over thousands of pages, Froissart depicts his glorious rise and tragic fall: the bravery, gallantry, and élan; victory in the greatest battles of his century at Crécy, Poitiers, and Nájera, making him the most renowned captain in the world and a Tenth Worthy in his own lifetime; then the heat of Castile, dropsy, the retreat, lack of funds, taxation of the Gascon vassals, rebellion, the beginnings of defeat, cruelty in defeat, débâcle, and death. Fortune's wheel turns and we witness the tragic fall of the mighty: Louis de Mâle, Charles VI, Richard II, and many others. At a particular point in *Les Chroniques* the champions, the indomitable English captains of the early wars, die off one by one: Audley, Chandos, the son of the Black Prince, his great father, the great father's father King Edward, and finally the Captal de Buch.

The passing of generations contributes to a vision of the world and a sense of destiny. The old heroes die out. They are replaced either by weaklings and misfits or by a new breed of warriors who are outsiders or interlopers, highly successful but with different values and a different world-view. Henry Trastámara overthrows Peter the Cruel; King John defeats the Castilians and secures the throne of Portugal; Bertrand du Guesclin becomes the finest captain of France and is named constable. The problem is, the first two are bastards and the third is a member of the petty nobility. All three are worthy men but, in terms of the old feudal order, illegitimate, as Froissart repeatedly informs us. For all their greatness, they undermine the old order. Froissart also knows that a more serious, concrete, and menacing threat to order comes from other interlopers and outsiders – Wat Tyler and Philip van Artevelde. The new good order, grounded in *sapientia* as opposed to *fortitudo*, is symbolized by the conduct of war rightly attributed to Du Guesclin and Charles V. For example, in 1373–4 the Duke of Lancaster and the Duke of Brittany lead an expedition through France. They seek another pitched battle. However Charles the Wise does not wish his men to fight and be subject to the chances of war (VIII: 155). Du Guesclin, Cliçon, and the Duke of Anjou agree. The English ride at will. Nonetheless they are harried by the French using guerilla tactics on their flanks and rear. The new methods work perfectly. In Auvergne the English suffer from hunger and the cold, whereas the French live 'grassement' in the towns, behind stone walls. The English end up losing their supplies and baggage train. They fall sick and crawl, bedraggled, into Bordeaux. Then, in the spring, Anjou, Du Guesclin, and Cliçon, rested, lead a counterattack into the Gascon regions and succeed in capturing forty towns plus the stronghold of Lourdes.

Froissart neither approves nor disapproves. He recognizes the Treaty of Brétigny to be unjust, and he knows that it is wrong and dangerous to force provinces loyal to Paris to swear fealty to London. In the 1390s he will come to loath the fickleness and greed of the English commons. Yet, as Fortune's wheel turns, for every gain there is loss and for every loss there is gain. The Prince, Chandos, Derby, the Captal, Audley – what great captains they were! What great deeds they committed! Of all men, the Count of Foix stands out as Froissart's personal favourite, his model for the public life. Except for the sin of wrath, Gaston Phoebus, who never loses, does synthesize *fortitudo* and *sapientia*, English valour and French prudence; this makes him an ideal prince and the ideal neutral force, neither Plantagenet nor Valois, in the Pyrenees. Let us not forget that Gaston Phoebus, the warrior and judge, is also a writer; he is the author of an important treatise on venery, perhaps the first book written in French by a native-speaking Occitanian. Similarly, for what it is worth, Froissart the writer, the clerk, the witness, the master of *sapientia*, undertook voyage after voyage, and quest after quest, to seek the truth and to emulate, in his book, the greatness in *fortitudo* of his heroes, the subjects of his book.

Froissart succeeds in part because of the interlace structure of narrative that he inherited both from the chronicle genre of his day and from romances such as the *Prose Lancelot*. Interlace implies multiple, varied strains of narrative, developed intermittently, none neglected or forgotten and none overdone. In Froissart's case a theatre of war (a campaign or series of campaigns in a particular geographical region) becomes the narrative kernel, rather than, as in the romances, the exploits of a single knight or a group of knights. So, for example, in volume 4 of the Société de l'Histoire de France edition, the reader takes the following journey: Calais, Aquitaine, Scotland, Calais, Flanders, Brittany, Calais, the ocean (for naval battles), Paris (for political intrigue), Poitou, Brittany, Calais, Paris, England, Scotland, Aquitaine, and Normandy.

What are the implications of the interlace technique? *Les Chroniques* recount many actions committed by many heroes. No one person can claim the role of protagonist, and no one person approaches even the centrality of a Lancelot or Tristan in the romance cycles. What counts is the story, the events of the wars. Hence, the episodic and discontinuous are the norm and even have a certain universal import; history is a series of unrelated individual events. Stendhal envisaged war in these terms. So in a way does Froissart.

Also, as in the prose romance cycles, once a history begins it is infinitely expandable; the only reason for an ending is either the cessation of war or the author's death. Froissart does not ordinarily seek vulgar effects of suspense. Still, it takes years and volumes for events to work out, and the results are prepared long in advance. The proud, wilful mistreatment by a Valois king of one of his barons – Robert of Artois, or Godfrey of Harcourt – may seem trivial enough at the time. Yet Froissart both shows and tells us that such a hasty act of injustice can have far-reaching consequences when, for decades, the victim, his family, and his descendants support the Plantagenet claimant and help open up new fronts for his campaign. Similarly, King

Edward's decision to second the Count of Montfort's claim to the Duchy of Brittany, apparently a brilliant strategic coup that opened for him a beach-head onto the continent, proves disastrous in the long run. The Montfort family remain as 'bons Anglois' as they dare. However, the Bretons eventually force their dukes to offer homage to the Valois king. And it is these pro-Valois Bretons, 'bons François' – Du Guesclin and Cliçon with their vassals and mercenaries – who provide the élan to repel the Plantagenets from France. Froissart shows us how the mercenaries create problems during times of truce. To get rid of the Companies, the French have the brilliant idea of sending them to Spain to help Henry of Trastámara overthrow Peter the Cruel. The Black Prince rises to the bait and supports Peter. He wins a great victory at Nájera. But then the heat of the Castilian summer and Peter's avarice set in motion a mechanism that slowly, inevitably leads to the Prince's death and to the reduction of all the English conquests ratified by the Treaty of Brétigny. The repercussion of events is recognized thousands of pages after the beginnings. This is the essence of the interlace structure.

Interlace, by concentrating on the episodic and the discontinuous, works upon a limited corpus of conventional themes and motifs. Again and again castles are attacked and defended, troops ambushed, prisoners ransomed, and cities taken. The repetitions of the conventional are of course considered to be good in and of themselves, fulfilling the expectations of the medieval public. Also, as themes and motifs vary, the contrast shapes our understanding of the narrative and of history. The Black Prince was generous at Poitiers but ruthless twenty years later at Limoges; after twenty years the Plantagenets now are losing, the Prince is dying, and the very flow of history has changed. So too for variations on the theme of wise counsel. In Spain the French knights, because of their fame as great warriors (derived more from epic and romance than from historical reality?), determine the tactics of a particular battle. On one occasion, in spite of all they ought to have learned at Crécy and Poitiers, they decide on the old cavalry charge; the result is Aljubarrota. The second time they promulgate the Du Guesclin method of withdrawal and scorched earth. This time they win.

Even more than in the *Prose Lancelot,* interlace gives the reader a sense of expanding horizons. The wars concern the Plantagenets and the Valois, francophone claimants to the throne of France, centred, respectively, in London and Paris. To understand the causes of the wars Froissart, following Jean le Bel, takes us to Scotland. Ambassadors negotiate, and the first campaign is launched in the Low Countries. Then Brittany becomes involved. Then the South – first Gascony and then the Limousin, Auvergne, and Languedoc. Then Spain. Then Portugal. Also, whenever a throne becomes vacant, or whenever a dispute occurs over inheritance, the Plantagenets and the Valois choose opposite sides, and a new front opens up. The chronicler makes us aware of difference in these remote locales: the cold of Scotland, the heat of Castile and León, and the poverty of the masses in both lands. He also shows us the strategic relationship between these strands. Neither camp can concentrate a powerful army on all fronts. Each camp tries to disconcert the other. John of Gaunt, having married one of Peter the Cruel's daughters, became a claimant to the throne of Castile. He was not unhappy, Froissart tells us, when in 1383 the Bishop of Norwich's 'crusade' in Flanders failed, because Norwich had diverted attention from Gaunt's ambitions (XI: 152). By 1385 Jean de Vienne joined the Scots in an incursion into Northern England, and plans were afoot to invade by sea from the Low Countries. Although the incursion was a failure and the invasion never took place, the English felt obliged to keep a sizable force at home on defence. As a result, dozens of castles fell in the South of France, and John of Gaunt received even less support in his Spanish adventures.

In Book 3 the interlace structure is modified in a highly significant manner. In the prologue Froissart makes the usual statements concerning his work as an historian. However, he then proceeds to explain that although peace had been made in Flanders in 1385, given that the wars continue elsewhere, it became his duty not to be 'oiseux' but to find out the truth, 'pour savoir la verité des lointaines marches' (XII: 2). Accuracy in history would also be a work of art, 'bonne et juste narration' (4) that he would 'esclarcir par bel langaige' (3) [in order to discover the truth about the distant border lands ... good and just telling ... make clear through fine speech]. Therefore, even though he had already travelled to England, Scotland, and Brittany, in 1388 he sets out on his longest, most romantic voyage to the court of Gaston Phoebus, Count of Foix, in order to enrich his chronicle with more accurate data concerning Spain, Portugal, and the south of France.

Froissart does describe the events in Spain. Before this, however, heterodiegetic narrative becomes, for a time, homodiegetic; the narrator talks about himself as an author figure – an historian figure if you wish. He describes how he travelled to Béarn, what he saw of Count Gaston Phoebus and his court, and how he heard of the materials that shall be included in *Les Chroniques*. The most striking example of this is the famous autobiographical or pseudo-autobiographical account of his trip on horseback from Pamiers to Foix, accompanied by a local informant, Sir Espan du Lion. Froissart recounts the alleged conversation between Espan and himself en route. This conversation contains the early history of the region, and in particular the count's exploits as Espan tells them to Froissart. The narrative structure now is based neither on chronology of events nor coherence of theme. Instead, the castles and towns along the road either solicit a question from Froissart or remind Espan of a story. Espan delivers his answer or his story, which is history; Froissart purportedly takes notes at their halts on the road:

> Des paroles que messire Espaeng de Lyon me comptoit estoie tout rafreschi, car elles me venoient grandement à plaisance et toutes très bien les retenoie, et si tost que aux hostelz, sur le chemin que nous fesismes ensamble, descendu estoie, je les escripsoie, fust de soir ou de matin, pour avoir en tou[t] temps advenir mieulx la memoire, car il n'est si juste retenue que cest d'escriture ... (XII: 65)

> I was totally revived by the words that Sir Espan du Lion told me, for they gave me great delight and I retained them all so well that, as soon as I stopped at the hostels located on the road the two of us took, I would write them down, morning or night, always the better to refresh my memory, for there is no truer retention than in writing.

He later incorporates the material into his book in the same order. The narrative structure is topographical; it follows the road. It is psychological; it adheres to the order of Espan's stories as they occur to him or as he chooses to tell them. It is historiographical; it depicts how an historian, in this case a very special variety of author figure, discovers, collects, and ultimately composes his material, transposing it into a book.

One function of the new pattern is to guarantee authenticity; it is a truth claim. Past history is made by copying the books of past historians. For contemporary history you usually have to rely upon living memory and oral testimony. Furthermore, for medieval historians as for medieval writers of fiction, the crucial distinction was not between true and false but between authorized and apocryphal. The existence of an Espan du Lion grants Froissart his credentials, guaranteeing that he is *authenticus* and *approbatus*.

In addition, the stories chosen by Froissart, following a certain order, lead to a climax just as the horseback ride leads to a goal (the castle of Foix). The goal of the narrative proves to be the central story – the most important event, which Espan du Lion consistently and insistently refuses to tell. This event, when it is finally revealed to Froissart at Foix, and by Froissart to his readers, is the climax – the story of how Gaston Phoebus slew his son and thus, for all his greatness, manifests a fatal flaw (wrath); he will die without a direct heir, a *mise en abyme* that reflects the thematics and problematics of the entire history of the age recounted in *Les Chroniques*.[19]

It is obvious that all this is literature. Froissart never simply wrote up the notes from his diary. That is the fiction of authenticity he wishes to impress on us. In fact, some of Espan's anecdotes are left out, others adhere too well to the topographical-voyage scheme, and the whole pattern builds up too perfectly to an equestrian and literary climax. Froissart, the clerk, writing of arms, in time becomes a kind of quest-hero in turn, like the great knights of the past about whom he read, and like the great knights of the present about whom he writes. He will not be negligent, 'oiseux,' 'pareceus,' or 'recreant.' He will seek out the truth, just as they seek out glory. He will visit Foix and discover the count's secret in the same way that Lancelot visits and discovers the Dolorous Guard and that Galahad visits and discovers the City of Sarras.

As if once were not enough (is once ever enough for Lancelot and Galahad?), the same Froissart, having heard at Foix the Castilian version of events, will travel to Zeeland in 1390 to seek out a Portuguese informant, Joao Fernandes Pacheco, to hear the other side. Pacheco recounts the rise of King John and the great victory of Aljubarrota. However, the high point of his account is of a different quest – the voyage of Portuguese ambassadors to England where Pacheco's hero, the chief ambassador, Lourenço Anes Fogaça, retells the events of Aljubarrota to the Duke of Lancaster and his court. Fogaça is a model hero, a Portuguese version of the Count of Foix. And Froissart plays with a *tiroir* or Chinese Box structure: as implied author telling us, Espan du Lion telling him, and Gaston de Foix telling Espan; again he tells us how Pacheco told him, how Fogaça told Lancaster, how a herald told Fogaça, etc, etc, ... Instead of the dream within the dream à la Machaut, this is a story or testimony within a story within a story. In terms of *mise en abyme*, John of Gaunt, as listener-reader, plays the same role inside the *tiroir* that Froissart plays outside, whereas Fogaça, of course, as teller-writer, plays the same role as Pacheco.

The literariness or, given that all medieval literature was read, chanted, or sung aloud, the oralo-literariness of this process is striking. Froissart goes to Gaston Phoebus' court as an historian in search of history and as a poet possessed of poems. Every night, as a writer, he reads aloud to the assembled court passages from his romance *Meliador*. During the day, as reader-audience, he listens to accounts of the wars from Espan du Lion, the Bascot de Mauléon, and Gaston Phoebus himself. Under different circumstances, he listens to Joao Fernandes Pacheco. He takes notes and, at some later time, either writes up his history as a writer writing or dictates it to a secretary as a writer reciting. The final *Chroniques* will then be read aloud anywhere in Europe; among the listeners will prove to be some of the very participants involved in the narrative. This pattern resembles the Arthurian one where Lancelot, Gauvain, and Bors tell their exploits at court, or Merlin tells his to Blaise; clerks or Blaise write them down; eventually they are transformed into Latin and then French. Froissart however never hides behind *li contes*. It is always he at the centre; he has sought out his heroes (an Arthurian clerk interviewing Lancelot on the road?) and he then tells all, in his own name.

As an historian and writer, Froissart cannot function without the tellers, his informants. Within the narrative, however, they are diegetic characters as much as the warriors, whose exploits they recount. Indeed, quite often the hero is his own informant. Therefore, they exist in Froissart's book for him and because of him. And they know it; they come to him to be tellers, and thus to be included in the Book. Whether he intended it or not, Froissart not only depends on his informants, but he also amplifies their exploits in his narrative. If we hear a great deal concerning some men and little or nothing about others equally important, it is because the first category is made up of those who told Froissart what they did, and so he writes what they told and what they did.

The Espan du Lion-Pacheco method contributes one additional structural innovation. The chronology of interlace is broken. Espan will reveal events that go back in time to the 1360s. The Bascot de Mauléon recounts his career since Poitiers (1356). Furthermore, Froissart had already given accounts of events in Spain, Portugal, and Occitania through the year 1381. Now, with new, vital, more accurate information, he retells some of the same events, including Aljubarrota. Although he does 'correct' himself, the chronicler does not choose to rewrite his chronicle, integrating the new material in a more complete, synthetic totality. Instead he reports the same events from a different perspective, in a different form. Once again it is fragmentation but not the fragmentation of interlace; instead it is the repeated, multiple, juxtaposed but non-integrated representation of the same. The unique focus of the narrative becomes the implied author's consciousness; it concerns his changing perspective and evolving knowledge and how he changes and learns; it reveals the phenomenology of his fragmented, juxtaposed, non-synthetic mental self. Is this a contrapuntal rather than a harmonic pattern? One of partiality not totality? Multiplicity not unity? Quantification not fusion? I believe that we find in Froissart the central learning and focusing consciousness and an obsession with the authorial self comparable to what we find in Machaut's *dit amoureux*. The phenomenology may well be typical of a late medieval mind-set and style of art, a literary late Gothic or Rayonnant.

Froissart's is a world of Bachelardian hard earth, of cutting swords, knives, pikes, axes, arrows, catapults and other siege engines, of hard stone castles and soft flesh pierced, broken, or sapped, a world of chivalry and ruse, of splendour, spectacle, fine speeches, courtly *beaux gestes* and also of ruthless savage violence, of winners and losers, masters and slaves; glory and death are inevitable and no one weeps over the losers and the slaves.

Froissart writes to entertain, of course, and also to provide information on current events as a journalist should. In part, he writes in a mode of encomium or celebration for the glorification of chivalry. His is a conservative ideology, corresponding to the mentalities of his age, exalting the aristocratic, chivalric, 'romantic' ideal of the warrior caste. He confirms the values present in the group, appealing to collective memory and unifying group consciousness; as an author he speaks to and for his public, granting it a consensus concerning its own past and recording for memory what its historical consciousness deems important to be remembered. And, as we have seen, the chronicler also enriches the romantic ideal with a deeper vision of fatality, tragic loss, and the passing of generations.

Froissart, along with Machaut, is a luminary in this century of Rayonnant mannerism. He explores new possibilities of narrative technique. He manifests extraordinary self-consciousness concerning his function as artist and a sense of the dignity of his vocation, as he makes the craft of writing verse or being an historian the subject of poetry and history. His literary masterpieces perpetuate the great myths of the past, give them new life, and transmit them to their followers in the manner of *translatio studii*, or in what Curtius called the tradition of true *aristoi*, who pass the flame of culture over the centuries. Froissart inherited a notion of heroism and chivalry from three centuries of *chanson de geste* and *roman courtois*, and invested them with the reality of his own age. Or, if you prefer, he took the crass reality of his day and ennobled, dignified, and poeticized it with panache from the old books. The result is history, to be sure, but also epic, romance, tragedy, and even, as we have seen, pseudo-autobiography; his work of creative literature has a legendary quality and becomes legend. The new legend of English and French chivalry during the great wars would endure until Flaubert. Froissart's myths became a mythical project for Frédéric Moreau and his comrade Deslauriers, and then they were lived frighteningly one last time by comrades and enemies in the Great War. This, the greatest 'Grande Illusion,' was to be enshrined and demystified in another medium in our age; our time of myth and mannerism, and of artistic and historical self-consciousness enables us perhaps better to understand and appreciate the late Middle Ages and Froissart.

7. Chartier

Charles d'Orléans and François Villon are generally recognized to have been France's greatest poets of the fifteenth century. Few would challenge the modern consensus. However, the fifteenth-century public envisaged matters quite differently. Leaving out of account the grands rhétoriqueurs, the late medieval and Renaissance public would no doubt have claimed that the premier writer of the century was Alain Chartier (c. 1385–1430). Chartier, who served as secretary, notary, and ambassador to the exiled Dauphin who became Charles VII, cultivated two modes of expression. One is moral and political, embodied in prose treatises in Latin and French pleading for reform of the kingdom and for peace. Such texts include *Le Quadrilogue invectif, Dialogus familiaris amici et sodalis, Ad detestationem belli gallici*, and *Traité de l'Espérance ou consolation des trois vertus*. In this category can also be ranged his satire on the court, *De vita curiali*. The other mode includes specifically courtly texts, in French, the subject of which is love. They include a number of *ballades* and *rondeaux*, and a number of debate or judgment poems – *dits amoureux* – in the tradition of Machaut, Froissart, and Christine de Pizan. The most important of these are *Le Lay de Plaisance, Le Livre des Quatre Dames, Le Débat du Réveille matin, Le Débat des Deux Fortunés d'amour*, and *La Belle Dame sans mercy*.

This latter piece, *La Belle Dame sans mercy* (1424), is the most important single poem of its century in terms of literary history, and one of the finest in aesthetic terms as well. It launched a famous literary quarrel, the second in French literature after 'la querelle du *Roman de la Rose*' and equally important. And it launched a veritable school of writers and writing. At least twenty texts in French derive directly from Chartier, and a number are immediate, conscious sequels or responses to *La Belle Dame* (Piaget 1901–5).

Chartier's works have survived in almost two hundred manuscripts, and his masterpiece in forty-four, with at least six separate early printed editions. *La Belle Dame sans mercy* was translated into Italian by Carlo del Nero in 1471 and into Catalan by Francesch Oliver in 1460. Two other Catalan poets, Pere Torella and Fra Rocaberti, quote from the poem in French; Chartier is praised by the Marqués de Santillana and known to at least two other Castillian poets; and *La Belle Dame*, perhaps performed on the stage, was adapted by Anne de Graville into French *rondeaux*, c. 1524, and cited twice in the *Heptameron*.

In addition, few if any French writers of the Middle Ages received as much attention from Great Britain. Chartier enjoyed seven translations into English and one into Scots. The *Quadrilogue*, the *Curial*, and the *Traité de l'Espérance* were taken over into English prose. One author – possibly Sir John Fortescue – late in the century Englished the two French treatises and the Latin *Dialogus familiaris*. Either the original or the Fortescue version influenced Cantos 9 and 10 of Book I of *The Faerie Queene*. Meanwhile, the author of the *Complaynt of Scotlande*, 1549, adopted the idea and general plan of his book from the *Quadrilogue* and included in it extensive passages taken directly from the *Quadrilogue* and the *Espérance*. Last but not least, Sir Richard Roos translated *La Belle Dame sans mercy* into English verse (six manuscripts); this very important poem in time was attributed to Chaucer. It is from an edition of Chaucer, containing the Roos translation, that Keats took perhaps the idea, and certainly the title, for his great *La Belle Dame Sans Merci*.

The plot of Chartier's original poem is simplicity itself. A melancholic, unhappy Narrator, mourning the death of his own beloved, overhears a conversation between a man and woman, the Lover and the Lovely Lady. Over and over again, the Lover tells her of his passion and tries to convince her to reciprocate it or at least to permit him to 'serve' her. The Lady refuses adamantly, refuting each of his arguments in turn. In the end they separate; she returns to the dance and he goes off in despair. According to the Narrator, it is reputed that he since has died.

Modern scholars have naturally asked the question: In this debate or judgment poem, who is 'in the right,' the Lover or the Lovely Lady? Whose arguments does Chartier support, and with whom does he have greater sympathy? And what does he think of *fin' amor*? Most of the moderns, though not all, side with the Lady (a perceptive exception, Kibler 1978–9); whereas the Lover appears to mouth courtly clichés, she appears to embody a 'modern,' bourgeois demystification of the clichés and a no less modern statement of woman's rights. The medieval public – Chartier's friends and enemies at court, his poetic disciples, and his rivals – asked the same questions; however, they came up with strikingly different answers.

How serious and how playful, how literary and how ideological, was the contemporary response to *La Belle Dame sans mercy*? Although the issue is complex, it would appear that the contemporary writers reacted to the Lady as if she were a monster – an inhuman, cruel, destructive coquette, who, in their poems, is indicted before a Court of Love, humiliated, reduced to begging and weeping, and finally condemned to death, to be drowned in a well full with tears of sorrow. It is certainly true that the statutes of the *Court amoureuse* of 1400 required that all speech attacking ladies be condemned. Since any man or woman who refuses to love is deemed to be bereft of humanity, then the Lovely Lady and/or her creator, Alain Chartier, are to be presumed guilty of inhumanity and treachery vis-à-vis the God of Love. Indeed, they are condemned for this crime in two of the sequels. On the other hand, we know, from our reading of Machaut, how flimsy and artificial such judgments could be. Also, Martin le Franc, Pierre Michault, and Jean Marot speak of Chartier as a great love poet and defender of women. Of course, they may be alluding to his other works.

As Poirion (1973) has observed, none of the contemporary poets, with one possible exception, allows or even recognizes the Lady's potentiality to be free from and indifferent to the call of love (her right to control her mind and her body). I believe that their refusal to discuss what to the moderns is the central issue raised by the text may well be a void or absence, which veils yet also reveals their central concern, indeed obsession – the potential freedom and indifference of women in the face of *fin' amor.* The poetic sequels were written by men. Although one prose summons and one prose judgment are ascribed to ladies, what the ladies really thought remains an enigma. Like the Lovely Lady, they may not all have envisaged *fin' amor* as profeminine; these ladies may have been more receptive to at least some of Chartier's points than the men were. Jean de Meun and Machaut may not have taken into account all implications of the *fin' amor* debate.

This said, in my opinion both the contemporaries and the moderns have largely misinterpreted Chartier's text by assuming that the central demand it makes on the reader is to choose between the Lover and the Lady, or between love and non-love. It is a tribute to Chartier's genius that contemporary poets and modern scholars take the formal, legal issues posed by his text so seriously, and that they take the characters so seriously (at least in the fifteenth century) as to have endowed them with a biography independent from the textual one recounted in the eight hundred lines of *La Belle Dame sans mercy.*

This is Alain Chartier's first triumph; he took archetypes become stereotypes three centuries old – *l'amant martyr; la dame cruelle* – and infused such life and imaginative power into them that we *do* take them seriously. We side for or against them. We are moved by them. At the same time they are such complex, ambivalent figures with their respective strengths and weaknesses that a sophisticated reader ought to find it difficult to take sides.

The Lover is a failure (Kay 1964–5); having grounded his life in the conventions and clichés of *fin' amor*, he is defeated before he begins. He lacks introspection or any recognition of the Lady's position. He is a grand romantic, a devotee of *fin' amor* in the old style, and as far as we can tell, truly and passionately in love. Also as far as we can tell, he is a worthy man, as loyal, discreet, and respectful of the Lady's honour and reputation as Tristan or Lancelot would be. His tragedy is to be Lancelot or Tristan three centuries too late and to have fallen on the wrong woman. We can approve or disapprove the conventional diction and stylized rhetoric the Lover employs to pursue his suit. We cannot doubt his sincerity or fail to sympathize with his youth, élan, and devotion to the old ideals, and we pity his wretchedness in defeat.

The Lady, perhaps for the first time in Western literature, speaks on equal terms with her suitor; she dares to say 'No!' to the very end. Of the two characters, she is the lucid, articulate one, who sees through clichés and refutes arguments based on convention and rhetoric. Full of life, she stands on her own and makes a claim for freedom from man's domination and from love. Yet she also embodies contradictions; we do not know, perhaps she does not know, whether her desire is simply to be free from love or whether she would return the Lover's suit were it possible for him to prove his sincerity and fidelity. Secondly, by being beautiful, by gazing with her magnificent eyes (Doulx Regard), is she to be held partially responsible for having attracted the Lover? Is it not possible that her indifference and her absolute intellectual rationalizations seem to reveal rock-like, unwomanly, inhuman coldness? For both good and ill, is not Chartier's Lovely Lady, in speech and in behaviour, the revenge of Guillaume de Lorris's and Jean de Meun's Rose on an army of male rose-pluckers?

Ultimately what counts most in *La Belle Dame sans mercy* is the confrontation between two such characters. Theirs is a war of the sexes – a war because they cannot agree, because they are so different, and because, although they converse for some five hundred and seventy-four lines, they fail to communicate. There is never an instant of mutual understanding. This is because the Lover commits himself utterly to the code of *fin' amor* but the Lady rejects it in its entirety. He seeks to impose on her the feudal contract based upon fidelity, service, and the sacredness of the oath but she will hear nothing of these three. For the Lover, allegorical entities such as Amour, Mort, Danger, Pitié, Doux Regard, and Courtoisie are numinous, semidivine forces that dominate his life and must have an impact on hers. For the Lady, the same entities are mere metaphor, clichés of style and tools of rhetoric that men use to seduce women – nothing more. The Lover insists that he is worthy, loving, faithful, and sincere; the Lady declines to judge him one way or the other, or to discuss the issue of his character or any other issue he raises.

The topic of illusion versus reality contributes to misunderstanding and obstacle. The conventions of *fin' amor* that the Lover takes literally – these the Lady refuses to believe in. He is convinced that he is compelled to love her, that she is the cause of his enamourment, and that, because of his merit, she will be obliged to love him in return. She, on the contrary, declares that all this is nonsense, that the Lover can cure himself or love another if he chooses, and that no one dies from love. A crucial point they debate concerns whether or not it is possible to distinguish true lovers from false. Now it is the Lover who perceives a clear distinction between illusion and reality and proclaims that people can make this distinction; the Lady denies it. The Lady insists upon her freedom: 'Je suis france et france vueil estre' (286) [I am free, and I will to remain free]; the Lover agrees yet maintains that in *fin' amor* the Lady will always be the master. 'No,' she replies, 'once I yield to you my mastery becomes an illusion; you are the master.' Here the female voice echoes a point enunciated by Christine de Pizan concerning woman's right to conserve her freedom and her good reputation, both to be placed ahead of Eros.

The Narrator leaves these questions unanswered. In the end the readers are free to answer each in his own way. Each reader is even free to speculate whether the Lover indeed perished from unrequited desire. In Machaut's debate poems, judgment is provided; here it is not. In Machaut's poems of complaint, comfort is provided; here, it is not. In both doctrinal and narrative terms, *La Belle Dame sans mercy* is inconclusive, intentionally I believe; it is a poem of deferral and disjunction in which decisions in favour of closure, if any, are relegated to the implied reader-audience.

Leaving doctrine aside, in strictly literary terms the text is dramatic not lyric in tone and mode. The silent *domna* of the *canso* here speaks. The courtly male Speaker has to face a competing, answering, arguing female voice. Song is transformed into dialogue, and the hypothetical, provisional refusal of the lyric lady becomes actual and real. The situation is one of utter tragedy, the tragedy of unrequited love, not provisional but definitive. Because the Lover is a lover and has grounded his being in *fin' amor* for this particular Lady, for him there is no hope; his is a story of failure, ending perhaps in death. And because the fictional world in which they dwell is also grounded in *fin' amor*, the Lady's estrangement, although she does not consciously recognize the fact, is no less definitive.

The tragedy is depicted in something approaching classical or Racinian terms. Chartier offers his readers no progression, suspense, or logical evolution in argument or in statement of character. All is known from the beginning. Furthermore, the action, concentrated as it is, takes place in a single locus, a grove or garden spot – an ironic *hortus conclusus* set apart from the social world of the court. The court is a place of bustle, movement, feasting, dancing, and song, of musical, social, and sexual harmony in which couples pair off two by two. The solitude of the grove, on the contrary, is symbolized by the odd number three: the Lover and the Lady, each separated from the other by a metaphoric wall, each incapable of communicating with the other; and the Narrator-witness, hidden behind a hedge, overhearing the two principals unbeknownst to them. The Narrator is as wretched as the Lover; presumed to be both a lover and a poet, named 'l'acteur,' he functions as a persona for the author Alain Chartier. He claims that he is miserable because his lady has died and, therefore, he can no longer be a writer. Although he is forced by friends at court to join the group and partake of the festivities, this social interaction, like the Lover's, proves to be temporary. Soon the Narrator and the Lover escape from the dance to the grove. Both Narrator and Lover, bereft of joy, fail to function in the social world; they fail to integrate into the harmonious, joyful coupling of the dance. They are kindred spirits. The Lover is, to some extent, a projection and displacement of the Narrator. In the end, the two men leave the court, one of them perhaps to die, whereas the Lady, cold or not, cruel or not, returns to the dance.

The men and the woman are utterly antithetical in nature; from a tragic or ironic perspective, they make a perfect match. The Lover and the Narrator are losers, failures, sickly, pale, and dressed in black. The Lover refers to himself as one ensnared or trapped or held captive by the God of Love; the imagery of the prison, illness, and martyrdom is assimilated to him in his own voice. For that matter, he is eager to lower himself, to 'serve,' to lose his 'franchise.' These figures of melancholia then seek out a proud, strong, independent, and verbally articulate woman. Although claiming utter indifference to the Lover and his suit (perhaps the worst insult of all), she also relishes the debate; she takes pleasure in matching wits with him and refuting his arguments, thus sapping the understructure both of his courtship and of his way of life. Her seeming coldness, cruelty, and rock-like indifference, coupled with her sharp, witty repartee signal the master vis-à-vis the slave, the torturer vis-à-vis the victim, or the sadist vis-à-vis the masochist. The Lady would then function as the Lover's (or, more likely, the implied author's) sadistic female castrating fantasm – the phallic mother in Lacanian terms, a displacement of and justification for his fear and trembling before womankind. It would appear that the fifteenth-century male public did interpret her as their nightmare archetype of the Terrible Woman – a killing, castrating creature with coldness of flesh and heat of intellect, pitiless heart and cutting tongue. Hence the poets' obsession with her, and their need, in the sequels, to humiliate and punish her even beyond the grave.

Within Chartier's text, following his diegesis, fantasm or not, sadistic master or not, the Lovely Lady is not punished. Thanatos is associated not with the torturer but with the victim, not with the loveless but with those who love. The Narrator is bereft of joy and artistic creation because his lady is dead. The Lover is obsessed with metaphors of death; he states that he is dying from love, that death permeates his life, and that, because of him, the Lady's honour will never die. In the end the circle is closed when his own demise is reported. In Chartier's text winners win, and losers die. Eros ends in Thanatos. The conventions of *fin' amor* are indeed dead if they can only result in dying.

The conventions of *fin' amor*, as of chivalry itself, make an ideological statement. They are one element of the feudal-aristocratic world-vision which, by Alain Chartier's generation, had found literary expression for some three centuries. The order and stability of the courtly ideology are mirrored in the order and stability of the literary form – an amorous debate situated within the Narrator's frame story, debate and frame constituting precisely one hundred *huitain* stanzas totaling precisely eight hundred lines. Yet the Lady's refutation of the Lover's suit, her intransigence, the deferral of judgment and closure, the failure in communication, and the tragedy of unrequited love undermine the courtly doctrine that the Lover and, it would appear, the Narrator espouse. Chartier, through the Lady, diverges from himself as Narrator; through the Lady he attacks the hypocrisy and libertinism of courtly ladies and gentlemen, and implicitly criticizes the mores of real courts in the 1420s. He calls attention to the moral deterioration of both public and private life and the gap that exists between the ideal and the real. Order and stability end in decline and collapse. Idealism ends in despair and death.

I do not, however, subscribe to the notion proffered by some that the Lovely Lady is a bourgeoise or that her rebuttal of the Lover's suit is a bourgeois reaction to aristocratic *fin' amor*. Although Alain Chartier was of humble birth, like so many of his fellow writers at the court he was by education, profession, and instinct a clerk. He moved in the same humanistic, intellectual, clerkly circles as did Machaut, Froissart, Jean de Montreuil, and Gontier Col. In the poem the Narrator's alienation from the community is that of the petty clerk, royal notary, and practising artist, seeking the integration into aristocratic circles that, on more than one level, is denied to him. He may have loved; yet, in his text (as was so often the case with Machaut and Froissart), the Narrator-implied author, learned and creative but of lower social status, serves as a witness to the love of others. Unlike Machaut and Froissart, perhaps Chartier takes out his animus by depicting true aristocratic lovers in the light of failure not success, and collapse not triumph.

One facet of clerkly revenge may derive from the fact that the aristocratic Lover and Lady are not associated with feats in arms – winning a battle or judging a tournament – nor with concrete erotic activity. The implied author permits them only to speak. Thus the traditional devotees of Venus and Mars adhere to the clerkly world of Pallas and Mercury. Theirs is a war of the sexes conducted verbally, in the form of a scholastic or legal *disputatio* reminiscent of Jean de Meun.

Not only is the aristocratic Lover reduced to wielding the arms of a clerk (his narrating witness) but he also loses, and he loses to a woman. Ladies were involved in courtly debate and judgment poems prior to Chartier, and for that matter prior to Machaut, but this is the first time that, in a courting situation – the man seducing, the woman being seduced – she responds as an equal; she speaks with equal command of language and an equal number of speeches, and she wins. Part of the scandal occasioned by *La Belle Dame sans mercy* probably came from the fact that this Lovely Lady is also a clerk and that she defends and counterattacks with masculine *parole*. She refuses to be an implied audience listening to and manipulated by a male implied author; on the contrary, she stands as an author figure, opposing and correcting his literary and erotic stance; or, if you prefer, she functions as an informed, active implied reader, who deconstructs, decentres, and denies the message the Lover offers her. After all, the Lady undercuts and ultimately destroys not only the Lover's arguments but the literary conventions, indeed the very language on which they are based. She demystifies his allegories, his metaphors, and the literary essence of his *fin' amor.* Chartier has his character turn language and art against themselves, denying one kind of language and art but offering the possibility of another kind in its place.

In terms of discourse and art, the clerkly Narrator differs strikingly from the aristocratic Lover. Both are men in love and both are unhappy. At the beginning of the diegesis, the Narrator states that, because his lady is dead, he cannot write. At the end of the diegesis the Lover goes off to die; the Narrator-witness not only lives on but he creates a new work of art, including yet surpassing the Lover's art of *fin' amor.* This will be *La Belle Dame sans mercy.* It is as if once the Witness successfully displaces his own sterility and misery onto the Lover, he is endowed with new insight and with the world-view of the Lady as well as of *fin' amor*; his lovesickness is cured and he can create anew.

What he creates, of course, is not dependant upon his alleged personal happiness. The new work of art is purportedly objective and mimetic – the reconstitution of a dramatic encounter. It contains both *fin' amor* and the demystification of *fin' amor,* the court and the demystification of the court. We find powerful psychological analysis of love, human character, and human interrelations and powerful embodiments of the archetypal *amant martyr* and *belle dame sans merci.* We find a work of literature that marks a turning point in the history of courtly love in the West and that, in Roos's translation (attributed to Chaucer), will perpetuate the archetypes and the questioning of the archetypes in England for centuries to come.

There is one additional lesson, perhaps, to be drawn from a modern reading of *La Belle Dame sans mercy.* This concerns French literary history and academic French canonicity. The canon of French poetry and the general concept of what poetry is in France are largely of Romantic and Symbolist provenance. The Middle Ages became an accepted domain in French literary history also under the impulse of Romanticism. For this reason literary historians, including medievalists, to this day have generally preferred the earlier centuries, which were presumed to be fresher, purer, and more creative, to the so-called 'Waning of the Middle Ages,' deemed to be a period of decline. Those poets of the decline accorded greatness are praised in large measure because they offer the illusion of sincerity and lyricism; they are, of course,

Charles d'Orléans and Villon. One of the achievements of criticism since the 1960s had been to demonstrate that Machaut, Froissart, Christine de Pizan, Chartier, Charles d'Orléans, and Villon are great in a quite modern, even postmodern way; in their narratology, mannerism, play of forms, and self-conscious exaltation of art they share some of our concerns more than do Marie, Chrétien, and the early *chanteurs de geste*. The entry into the new, enlarged scholarly canon of an Alain Chartier will not only enrich our notion of the Middle Ages; it can help expand our horizons concerning French literature and the nature of French poetry as a whole (cf. Calin 1987G).

Sir Richard Roos's translation of Chartier can help expand our horizons concerning English literature also. English medievalists have not had to labour under such gross distortions of the national literary canon as occurred in France. Nonetheless, the very greatness of Chaucer and the Ricardians has resulted in neglect of authors and texts from the subsequent period. Not one of the great centuries of English literature, the fifteenth does offer a number of important works and currents. One such current is a tradition of love debate – one version of *dit amoureux* in the courtly French and the Chaucerian line. These poems include, in addition to original texts such the *Flower and the Leaf* and the *Assembly of Ladies*, translations from the French – Hoccleve's *Letter of Cupid*, from Christine de Pizan; the *Eye and the Heart*, from Michault Taillevent; and Roos's *La Belle Dame sans Mercy*. These poems all testify to the vital, living legacy of French courtliness in fifteenth-century England.

Roos translated Chartier with elegance and vigour. He follows the original structure of one hundred stanzas and eight hundred lines to the letter, recapturing the form, the spirit, and the doctrine of Chartier's poem. In addition, Roos adds four rhyme royal stanzas at the beginning, and another four at the end. These are his individual creation. In the Prologue the Speaker, half-awake and half-asleep, rises from his dream all but naked; then he suddenly remembers that, 'as part of my penaunce' (9), he was ordered to translate *La Belle Dame*:

> Half in a dreme, not fully wel awaked,
> The golden sleep me wrapped under his wing;
> Yet nat for-thy I roos, and wel nigh naked,
> Al sodaynly my-selve remembring
> Of a matér, leving al other thing
> Which I shold do, with-outen more delay,
> For hem to whom I durst nat disobey. (1–7)

Humble and afraid, nevertheless he dresses and proceeds to a *locus amoenus*, where he commences his reading and writing:

> What wyse I shuld performe the sayd processe,
> Considering by good avysement
> Myn unconning and my gret simplenesse,
> And ayenward the strait commaundement
> Which that I had; and thus, in myn entent,
> I was vexed and tourned up and doun;
> And yet at last, as in conclusioun,
>
> I cast my clothes on and went my way, ...
> Til I cam to a lusty green valey
> Ful of floures, to see, a gret plesaunce;
> And so bolded, with their benygn suffraunce
> That rede this book, touching this sayd matere,
> Thus I began, if it plese you to here. (15–22, 24–8)

The Epilogue is made up of a modesty topos, the Speaker addressing his poor, little book, 'Wild as a beest, naked, without refute' (842), in hope that it will be well received, that is, have 'better aventure' in the real world than Chartier's miserable Lover had in the world of fiction.

In his own verse Roos recaptures brilliantly the spirit of the original and he adds to it. He creates his own frame narrative that encloses Chartier's frame (that encloses the narrative kernel). In a witty, sophisticated manner, the Roos Speaker, a dreamer who wakes up and proceeds to a 'gret plesaunce,' himself mirrors the traditional courtly lover; and, ordered to translate, overwhelmed by modesty yet obeying the order, he also mirrors the traditional self-conscious clerkly author figure. The barriers between Chartier's fictional universe and the purported reality of the translator are blurred; Roos's Speaker imitates the Chartier Narrator and more or less fuses with him. It is significant that a naked translator in the Prologue should, in the Epilogue, address his naked book; again the concrete and the figurative, the experiential and the literary, are juxtaposed. Roos employs Chartier's own typology – his themes and motifs, his wit and play – thereby contributing to and undermining the courtly diegesis and the courtly authorial self-consciousness.

Roos and his English contemporaries were fully at ease with the French legacy of courtly fiction, *fin' amor*, antifiction, and anti-*fin' amor*. Their mannered, refined civilization would endure to the end of the Middle Ages and beyond.

Conclusion

The seven works or groups of works examined in this section – *Huon de Bordeaux*, the *Prose Lancelot*, *Le Roman de la Rose*, Guillaume de Digulleville's sacred allegories, Guillaume de Machaut's secular tales of love, Foissart's *Chroniques*, and Chartier's *La Belle Dame sans mercy* – were all highly esteemed in the Middle Ages. They were copied, imitated, revised, rewritten, provided with sequels, and translated into foreign tongues. They had a major impact on French literature and on English literature. They form part of the French cultural legacy so important to the development of a renewed native English culture in the fourteenth, fifteenth, and sixteenth centuries; in some cases the seed would prove to be more fertile on the English side of the Channel than on the French.

Significantly, none of these books belongs to the 'classical' canon of Old French masterpieces, as it took shape in the nineteenth and early twentieth centuries. As the canon was enlarged by later generations of Romance scholars, the *Romance of the Rose* came to be treated with as much respect and authority as the twelfth-century icons; something roughly comparable is occurring today for the prose romances. Nevertheless, it remains a fact that, for the general reader or professor in French and most non-medievalist French scholars, the Middle Ages means the early period – the troubadours, the *Song of Roland*, *Tristan*, and Chrétien – and François Villon. The books which contributed most to the cultural heritage of England are far from being the best known on the Continent even in specialized circles. Many still do not receive the attention they deserve.

It is for this reason that I chose to scrutinize these texts as works of literature from a modern critical vantage point. It is crucial to discover their literary essence and to understand what makes them works of art, how they differ from the early masterpieces, and how they achieve their own unique world-vision, structure, and style. When we understand the essence of Jean de Meun and Machaut or of the *Prose Lancelot*, then it is easier to determine what Chaucer or Malory took from them and how the English writers shaped it and constructed it for their own purposes. These French books of the later Middle Ages are masterpieces in their own right. Recognizing them as masterpieces and investigating what makes them so is one way of determining how and why the great English writers who followed in their footsteps did what they did. It presents a more complex and, I believe, a more authentic vision of the creative process than the older, Whig notion of English writers improving upon their continental sources.

The French works presented above can be divided into two categories, according to the radical of presentation – third-person narratives and first-person narratives.

Huon de Bordeaux, the *Prose Lancelot*, and Froissart's *Chroniques* belong to three distinct literary kinds: *chanson de geste, roman courtois*, and chronicle or history. Whatever the genre distinctions (more a modern than a medieval problem), all three works offer English writers and an English public one great gift – heroic adventure narrative told in the third person. The *Prose Lancelot* is perhaps the archetypal story of heroism – great knights involved on their quests, performing deeds in arms, and enduring adventures, all for a lady or the king or themselves. In splendid fashion the Lancelot-Grail cycle juxtaposes love and war, exploring how courtly *fin' amor* is indispensable to the growth of heroism; however, in the last analysis, it destroys the very heroism it helps create. *Huon de Bordeaux* treats of adventure and the surpassing of human limits in an exotic oriental locale inundated with elements of the supernatural; it also explores, in comic fashion, an issue treated seriously in the *Lancelot* – the relationship between king and captain, between the (symbolic) passive ruling father and the (symbolic) active rebellious son, for the hero's prowess is essential to society yet it can also threaten society's well-being. In Froissart a non-fictional, historical narrative is filtered through the same romance prism. The result is warriors and princes attempting to live up to the heroic life and in large measure succeeding yet, for reasons other than Lancelot's and Gauvain's, causing terrible harm in their wake.

The prose cycle and Froissart also create myths of history – the rise and fall of Arthurian chivalry, bound to events dating from the Crucifixion, or indeed from the Garden of Eden; the rise and fall of

English chivalry, bound to the earthly careers of Edward III and the Black Prince in fourteenth-century Europe. The reasons for catastrophe are many: the incompatability of *fin' amor* and a well-regulated social order or the incompatability of martial heroism and the Christian call for rejection of the carnal world (*Lancelot*); the inevitable, universal change in the fortunes of war, uncontrollable by man, and the immediate, precise evolution in tactics and strategy from the old heroism to a new, modern Du Guesclin mentality (Froissart). Whatever the causes, whatever the contingencies, one result is something approaching a tragic vision of history – man finite in his striving before God and before his fellow men. The only alternative to such finiteness will be escape into a universe of wish-fulfilment, in which the hero struggles against yet also benefits from love, the supernatural, and the exotic in a fantasy world where he cannot lose (*Huon*).

Whatever the world-vision and whatever the mode, these third-person narratives revel in action. They offer the English a priceless fund of themes and motifs. They also offer a technique of story-telling, whether there be one hero or many. With numerous heroes the interlace technique becomes de rigueur. Whatever the political or even religious message, whether the mode be comic or tragic or heroic, the story is never lost sight of; action predominates and exists for its own sake. Yet despite this emphasis, or perhaps because of it, the French books offer English writers patterns of mythic power: Huon, the Saracens, the emir's daughter, and Auberon, king of the fairies; Lancelot, Guinevere, Arthur, Merlin, and the Quest of the Grail; the magnificent ideals of English chivalry and English heroism. These are among the great myths of the Middle Ages, which so many a writer did dream on.

The first-person narratives are offshoots from the daring, pioneering *Roman de la Rose* by Guillaume de Lorris and Jean de Meun. Following upon them (it) we have Guillaume de Digulleville's *Pèlerinage de la Vie humaine* and *Pèlerinage de l'Ame*, *dits amoureux* by Guillaume de Machaut, and Alain Chartier's *La Belle Dame sans mercy*.

The poetry and mystery of the dream vision genre is as archetypal as the poetry and mystery of romance and was to have as great an impact in England as in France. Nevertheless, in the hands of Guillaume de Lorris and Guillaume de Digulleville, the dream vision, for all its poetry, serves another purpose; it probes the human psyche. These two poets, one working in the secular sphere and one in the sacred, explore the workings of love (secular and sacred) and the growth of the individual. Personification allegory mirrors aspects of the individual dreamer's self; it reflects an inner psychomachia and an inner spiritual quest. Digulleville shares with Jean de Meun a concern for the macrocosm as well as the microcosm; Jean and the monk of Chaalis are vitally committed to the moral vision of life. They relate the individual to society and the myriad of forces that surrounds him. Their works become, to some extent, encyclopaedic summae, meant to reveal a total vision of the cosmos. Jean's *Roman* differs from Guillaume's *Pèlerinages*, however; one exalts the manifold splendour of the secular world and the other loathes it. Jean's is a *conflictus* in which all views are given free reign in what appears to be open debate; Guillaume's discourse is consciously moulded in a strictly didactic mode from the beginning; intellectual resolution accompanies narrative closure.

In the following centuries Guillaume de Machaut and Alain Chartier retain the debate motif but narrow it down to questions of love casuistry. The narrowing also brings about a deepening and an intensity of passion in Machaut's lyrical passages and in Chartier's entire poem. Machaut picks up on Jean de Meun's social orientation, again restricting Jean's global vision in order to focus on the bond between patron and poet. Jean and all who followed him – Digulleville, Machaut, Chartier, and so many others – raised the question of art and the artist. First-person narrative permitted deeper psychological analysis; it also encouraged the speaker (a comic, bumbling author figure) to discuss the nature of art and to relate, metatextually, how the very work he is writing comes into being. The most profound and most elegant examples of such metatextuality, along with superb *mises en abyme*, are to be found in Machaut, who included in his narrative *dits* lyrical inserts of his own composition, ascribed to the fictional narrator or to other characters in the story. The highly self-conscious stance of the implied author was a great gift to Chaucer and his circle.

Machaut especially, but also Chartier, explored Jean's notion of disjunction and deferral; they presented an open narrative which leaves judgment on intellectual matters to the implied audience, or veils the plot so that it is up to the implied audience to determine what actually occurred in the course of the narrative. The implied audience must also determine whether or not the narrator has cause to believe in his own happy (or sad) ending. These extraordinary advances in narrative technique, where narrative is indulged in from artistic posturing or for sheer play, also profited the Ricardians enormously.

The encyclopaedic, cosmic scope in late allegory corresponds to the historical, cyclical vision of romance and history. Similarly, the technical dash and brio of a self-conscious I-narrator recounting his dream vision recalls the same sort of technical virtuosity in romance or chronicle interlace. And the imago of the Lover in quest of his Rose, or the Pilgrim on the voyage of life, or the Lover in eternal debate with his Cruel Lovely Lady are great medieval myths (in Frye's sense of the term) that resemble the great myths of heroism. Subject matter, theme and motif, tragedy and comedy, narrative technique, psychological analysis, story-telling, image and symbol, disjunction, debate, the claims of high art, and the elaboration of myth and archetype – these are elements in the literary tradition that writers in English found in the French books. The French books of this period, like those in Greek and Latin, make up part of our common cultural heritage. With that heritage, the writers of English, in their cultural belatedness, were able to profit from the belatedness and to create extraordinary literary renewals and syntheses of their own.

PART THREE

English Court Poetry

Introduction

Much attention has been lavished on the social context of Chaucer and his circle. That Chaucer belonged to and epitomized a current of cultural and literary activity is certain. Associated with him are John Gower and also Clanvowe, Stury, Clifford, Strode, Scogan, Bukton, La Vache, and Usk. Later, following in the Chaucerian tradition, as disciples of the master, are to be ranged Hoccleve, Lydgate, Roos, and the authors of the *Flower and the Leaf*, the *Assembly of Ladies*, and the *Court of Sapience*, among others. These are the English Chaucerians; the Scottish Makars form another more vital and original offshoot.

The old Whig view of Chaucer torn between the backward, decadent, aristocratic, medieval culture and a more progressive, bourgeois, modern, living culture, ultimately moving from the old to the new and from the medieval to the modern (Patterson 1987), has largely disappeared from the profession. However, the old distinctions survive, under a different guise and in a much more historically accurate framework, in the effort to situate Chaucer and his circle in their social context. This change in direction can be associated both with more advanced historical studies, based upon richer documentation, and with a greater theoretical concern for the social context, derived, in part, from the new historicism. One thesis emphasizes the role of the courts, especially the royal court, as a centre of culture and the functioning professional 'home' for Chaucer and his friends, who were, after all, as Strohm (1989) tells us, 'en service,' part of the *camera regis* and belonging to the king's affinity (and/or Lancaster's). According to Green (1980), literature in the Chaucerian style would be inconceivable but for the nourishing cultural milieu of the court, which was a locus of entertainment and leisure, sociability and elegance, conversation and courtship, music, dance, and, last but not least, books treasured for what they contained and as precious objects in their own right.

The other thesis downplays the importance of the Plantagenet and Lancastrian monarchs as patrons of the arts and originators of a period style. According to this view, in contrast to the literature-patronage structures on the Continent, the history of English kings offers no evidence for original taste or leadership in the arts. Furthermore, theirs is a French-speaking milieu. The books we know to have belonged to the literate aristocracy are almost exclusively in Latin and French and reflect old-fashioned aesthetic values. Scattergood, Sherborne (*English* 1983), and the other revisionist scholars emphasize that Chaucer and his friends belong to a distinct social nexus – a stratum made up of petty gentry, royal clerks, and civil servants, of diplomats and administrators, of educated, literate men associated with the law, government, and commerce – a public that can be envisaged as receptive to books in English and in the modern style.

There is much truth in both theses. I am not convinced that they cannot be reconciled. That Richard II and John of Gaunt possessed books exclusively in French and Latin and that they both spoke French fluently does not imply that they would have disdained poetry in English or that the works of a Chaucer and a Gower would have been unwelcome at their courts. A presentation volume from Froissart or Philippe de Mézières is one thing; listening to Chaucer read aloud or someone read aloud from Chaucer is a different matter altogether. One can treasure French books and even read them, on one level, and appreciate listening to English texts, on another. Furthermore, the very society of civil servants, lawyers, chamber knights, etc., that included Chaucer, Gower, and their immediate circle, was in turn included in the king's affinity and could not have functioned outside of it. Chaucer mentions Gower, Strode, Bukton, and La Vache, among others; he also alludes, albeit indirectly, to John of Gaunt, Blanche of Lancaster, and Anne of Austria. Gower invokes Chaucer and dedicates works to Richard II and Henry IV. On into the fifteenth century, the tradition continues. The broad public of educated civil servants and gentry persisted and expanded; so did the phenomenon of royal and aristocratic patronage.

The poetry produced by this literary school can be designated court poetry, given that it is poetry of the courts, whether or not a specific earl or king was included in its audience or participated in its patronage. Similarly, the English Chaucerians created high court poetry in imitation of their French predecessors and contemporaries, who had elaborated a tradition of verse and prose of the courts over the centuries. However, the relevance of the French legacy has been called into question. Nobody denies the seminal French literary presence at the beginning of Chaucer's career. Yet the equivalent of the Whig version of literary history, as I extend the range of the term, states that Chaucer soon outgrew and surpassed the superficial, conventional courtliness of the French and proceeded to a deeper, more learned, and more complex vision of the human condition, manifest in deeper, more learned, and more complex literary texts. According to this school, Chaucer was inspired by the literature of Antiquity, and also by Dante, Petrarch, and Boccaccio as well as by writing in English. These new elements along with his own genius gave rise to the masterpieces that we associate with his name. Gower, Hoccleve, and Lydgate – to the extent that they also are deemed figures of the first rank – were inspired directly by Chaucer; they followed in his footsteps, enriching or surpassing the French courtliness of the age, by also turning to Greece, Rome, and Tuscany. Furthermore, although they differ from each other in so many other respects, the current of which I speak is, if anything, reinforced by the exegetical or Robertsonian school, which sees a powerful Christian presence – structural and doctrinal – in the masterpieces of Chaucer and his successors. This Christian essence would designate the English books as high culture in the Middle Ages and distinguish them from less 'serious' writing, including some of the continental analogues.

I wish to call into question the above theses. In my opinion, the distinction made between Chaucer and the French and between English poets and their predecessors is largely one of perception, based upon differences in modern academic critical approaches. It does not come from the original texts. The more recent criticism of medieval French books sees in these texts the same complex questioning of courtly love and courtliness that scholars found a generation ago in Middle English. We see in Guillaume de Lorris, Jean de Meun, Machaut, and Froissart the same witty, sophisticated, and problematic stance vis-à-vis court society, and the same witty, sophisticated, and problematic use of stories from classical Antiquity. And, were Old French scholars eager to do so (and some are), French books could be found to reveal the same powerfully Christian world-vision that the exegetical scholars recognize in the Ricardians. From my perspective, much in the English court school is to be found, in an advanced stage of artistic achievement, in books in French – the dream-vision frame; a complex dream psychology; the problematic treatment of Greco-Roman myth; the problematics of art and the artist; the comic, bumbling author figure; the comic and problematic bond between an author figure and the embodiment of authority; the comic frame narrative containing inserted exempla or stories; the stories wielded as rhetorical arms in a competition of voices; and the idea of the vernacular summa treating every aspect of a topic.

Chaucer, his friends, and his disciples all read French and were steeped in the tradition. As inspiration for their own texts in English and in order to write in English, they turned to the French. Furthermore, in the course of their writing lives, the poets in English did not shake off or renounce the French legacy. They read books from the Continent in the most immediate, up-to-date contemporary style; they also juxtaposed the contemporary style with other French books representative of divergent currents from the immediate or more distant past. Thus they combined models, varied inspiration, and deepened their knowledge of the elements in the legacy.

I propose to examine the works of Chaucer, Gower, and Hoccleve, keeping in mind the problem of evolution in style and taste. For Chaucer, I shall begin with two tales of love in the line of Machaut, the *Book of the Duchess* and the *Prologue to the Legend of Good Women*. Then I shall consider a number of the *Canterbury Tales*, also subject to the Machaldian example but closer to and evolving more vitally from earlier, perhaps richer French currents such as the fabliau, the Breton lay, and above all Jean de Meun's *Roman de la Rose*. With Gower also I shall proceed from the relatively early *Mirour de l'Omme*, a work in the penitential and estates satire mode, as much in the insular, Anglo-Norman style as in the continental. Then I shall go on to the later Gower, who is more of a secular poet and author of *Cinkante Balades*, a lyrical sequence very much in the continental line, exploiting not repudiating *fin' amor*. Lastly, I shall consider the English *Confessio Amantis*, a synthesis of the *dit amoureux*; it has the scope of *Le Roman de la Rose* and the *Canterbury Tales* and yet is also shaped by the contemporary Machaut-Froissart conventions. Finally, with Hoccleve we see the evolution, from relatively simple lyrics and simple sacred or *fin' amor* translations from the French (Digulleville and Christine de Pizan), to a more sophisticated, complex, and artistically masterful series of texts that combine the structure, style, narrative technique, and world-view of Jean de Meun, Machaut, and Chaucer. The French inheritance was rich and complex. The English court poets explored it in depth and used it to the full to create their own texts in their own world.

I. Chaucer

Edward III and Richard II were French-speaking monarchs, presiding over partially francophone courts, French in taste and ambition. Their courts, especially Richard's, were a focus for ceremony, pageantry, leisure, luxury, and extravagance, rivalling Paris yet always based on the Paris example and with Paris in mind. These Plantagenet kings of London (and Bordeaux) were also perfectly licit claimants to the throne of France against the Valois kings of Paris. Froissart and Granson were, for a period, honoured guests. Chandos Herald, the old Duke of Lancaster, and Gower wrote in French, and a French of distinction.

Chaucer himself married the French-speaking daughter of a knight from Hainault, served as a diplomat in France, and undoubtedly wrote daily in French and Latin in his official duties. More than any Englishman, and perhaps more than any foreigner, of his day, he was steeped in French culture, both the 'classics' from the twelfth and thirteenth centuries, and the most recent, fashionable court poetry of his own generation. It has been proposed by two distinguished scholars (Robbins 1976, 1978–9, Wimsatt 1982) that Chaucer composed his first works, perhaps lyric texts such as the *ballade*, in French, and we have been shown the sort of French that Chaucer could and might have written. Recent opinion proposes as Chaucer's audience a circle recruited from the petty gentry and educated civil servants. If this is so, and the question is far from decided, it explains why Chaucer and Gower chose finally to write in vernacular English and not French, but in no way negates the primary, fundamental Frenchness of their inspiration.

In sum, Chaucer's Frenchness transcends the question of his sources and of the literary genres and modes he chose to cultivate. Over fifty per cent of his lexicon is of French origin; profoundly, viscerally English in tone and texture, his language is also profoundly, viscerally French. With no writer, before or since, has there been so perfect a synthesis of the two languages. The same is true for questions of versification and metrics. Whatever Chaucer thought of the native English alliterative metre (it may have appeared crude, dated, and provincial), he chose to naturalize and popularize the French verse forms he knew. The octosyllabic rhyming couplet, the standard medium for narrative verse in French since the twelfth century, had long since appeared in English. Chaucer adopted it, as he did the decasyllabic couplet cultivated by Machaut and Froissart, and the favourite stanzaic form of Machaut and Deschamps, rhyme royal, used in their *ballades* but also in the *chant royal*. Wimsatt (1991) especially has explored the impact of the French *ballade* stanza and of French lyricism in general on Chaucer. Chaucer's language, diction, rhetoric, and syntax are French to the core; they mirror and transfer to the English vernacular the three centuries of French court culture of which he is the heir. Muscatine (1957) has stated rightly that Chaucer stands as the culminating artist in that centuries-old French tradition.

Chaucerians have generally been aware of these facts, although, from decade to decade, people may concentrate on the 'English Chaucer' or the 'Italian Chaucer' (both are valid concepts). The problem is that the first generation of modern Chaucer scholars, who read almost all the texts and made almost all the appropriate textual analogies, were philologists not literary critics in our sense of the term. This means that they occasionally missed major structural similarities – themes, patterns, and topoi – that were not of a textual or stylistic nature. In addition, more recent generations of scholars, trained in modern critical approaches, on occasion neglect the French tradition, or deem it unimportant, or cite Chaucer's striking originality vis-à-vis source 'A' when in fact he modelled his text closely on source 'B.' The *Man of Law's Tale* does partake of an archetypal narrative structure in the pan-European tradition; it is also an adaptation of part of one specific Anglo-Norman chronicle. The *Nun's Priest's Tale* is or is not part of a pan-European tradition of the beast fable; more specifically, it is an adaptation of one branch of *Le Roman de Renart*, embellished with elements from a fable by Marie de France and from *Renart le Nouvel*. Major books of Chaucer criticism (exemplary in all other respects) which discuss thoroughly, say, the presence of Ovid in *The Legend of Good Women* and Boccaccio in *Troilus and Criseyde*, do not treat with comparable seriousness the legacy of Guillaume de Machaut or of Froissart. Nor do they always remember that Chaucer read his Ovid, Boethius, and Boccaccio in French versions or with the help of a French 'crib,' and therefore that his transformations of Ovid, for example, may already have been present in *l'Ovide moralisé*. Even when Jean de Meun, Machaut, and Froissart are recognized, the aesthetic problem remains; there is a tendency to assume that the Frenchmen had less to contribute than did Ovid, Boccaccio, and Petrarch, and therefore that Chaucer borrowed less from them and that, whatever he took and whenever he took it, Gallic lead was automatically transmuted into the gold of Albion. It would be possible to quote a dozen books on Chaucer that allude to the alleged artificiality, formalism, exaggeration, thinness, conventionality, and artifice of the French tradition.

To be fair, to a large extent this 'great books approach,' this 'Whig literary history,' also applies to Ovid, Petrarch, and Boccaccio. Whatever the discipline, scholars investigate how their author uses, changes, or adapts his sources, with the implicit aesthetic presupposition that the result will always be better not worse. Graff (1987G) and Patterson (1987G), among others, have observed the extent to which the very discipline of positivist literary history was determined by historical conditions in the nineteenth and twentieth centuries, in conjunction with national pride. Furthermore, Chaucer scholars simply echoed the verdict on medieval French literature, especially the later Middle Ages, disseminated within French departments both in Paris and abroad. Generations of romance philologists, under the influence of German romanticism, were fascinated by the oldest, earliest texts, purportedly the 'simplest' and most 'naive,' whereas they scorned the more civilized, refined muse of the fourteenth and fifteenth centuries. Or, under the influence of French classicism or Third Republic lay militancy, they underrated the literary value of all medieval literature before the Renaissance, *en bloc*.

Even though many view the current literary-critical scene as culturally confused, chaotic, and suffering from the excesses of a theory-oriented postmodernism, I am convinced that, along with the theory, which can be liberating or restrictive depending on how one uses it, comes also a genuine liberation of the spirit in terms of the canon and its classics. Since the 1960s a revolution has occurred in Old French studies involving the introduction and practice of modern criticism, and the reception into the canon of writing from the beginnings up to Jean Lemaire de Belges, inclusively. Something roughly comparable has taken place in English studies. The new Chaucerians and *romanistes* have no superiority or inferiority complexes and are no longer enslaved to the great books approach or to questions of national pre-eminence. We can all deal with great creation in the Middle Ages and the formation of the modern vernacular traditions in both lands. This is one of the most exciting moments, a truly European moment, in the history of world culture.

1. *The Book of the Duchess*

The *Book of the Duchess* is an elegy commemorating the death in 1368 of Blanche, Duchess of Lancaster, the first wife of John of Gaunt and the daughter of Henry of Grosmont, author of the Anglo-Norman didactic treatise *Le Livre de Seyntz Medicines*. Chaucer's first extended creative work is also, aside from translations, his most derivative and most French, since from one half to two thirds of the poem is adapted textually from *Le Roman de la Rose*, Machaut, and Froissart (cf. Wimsatt 1968). The most fashionable, up-to-date writer in England succeeded brilliantly in his maiden effort in transplanting, translating, and transferring into English the most fashionable and up-to-date in French letters. In his very first poem, a text that, in terms of composition, style, and tone, stands out in the English of its day, the author made the *dits amoureux* of the continental masters come alive, in all their richness and complexity.

The story line, as in the French *dits amoureux*, is relatively simple. The Narrator, suffering from insomnia, reads in a book the myth of Ceyx and Alcyone. This enables him to fall asleep, whereupon he dreams that he wakes up, participates in a deer hunt, and meets a grieving Black Knight. The Narrator enters into a conversation with Black and eventually draws out of him the information that the cause of his misery is the death of his beloved, 'goode faire White' (948). The hunt ends; the dream is over.

A number of scholars assumed that the book that most influenced the *Duchess* was Machaut's *Jugement dou Roy de Behaingne*, and as they held a negative opinion of the quality of Machaut's and Froissart's poetry, they made claims for Chaucer's originality – in terms of dream psychology, realism, humanity, and warmth – vis-à-vis the French source and the ways he changed and improved upon it. Now it is true that more lines were translated from the *Behaingne* than from any other text; and it is in the *Behaingne* that Chaucer found a seminal cluster of motifs – a bereaved knight (and a lady) mourning the loss of their beloveds, and the knight evoking his past joy with her, all overheard by a narrator-witness. However, Chaucer had several models from Machaut and Froissart at his disposal. It is from these other texts – Machaut's *Remede de Fortune* and *Fonteinne amoureuse*, Froissart's *Paradis d'Amour* and *Bleu Chevalier*, and *Le Roman de la Rose* – that Chaucer took so much of the rest of his poem.[20] The most important of these models and the one that inspired him the most was not the *Behaingne* but *La Fonteinne amoureuse*. It is the intertextual presence of this work that dominates the *Duchess*; Chaucer faithfully imitates and responds to this text, incorporating, reshaping, and recreating it.

The *Book of the Duchess* narrative, containing three strands, is arranged in rings, as with so many Machaldian texts. The frame concerns the Narrator and his experiences in illness, insomnia, and, eventually, artistic creation. Within the frame is located the story in the book that the Narrator reads – the literary, Ovidian tale of Ceyx and Alcyone. And within this segment is to be found the Narrator's dream and the dream narrative, specifically his encounter and dialogue with the Black Knight. This is the experience-book-dream pattern that will become the hallmark of Chaucer's early works. The Narrator himself and his implied audience progress through the structure to the center, which is a level of deeper, more significant experience. There is nothing original about a love-vision frame for a story about someone else. *La Fonteinne amoureuse* provided the inspiration – a tale in which the Narrator, an unhappy lover suffering from insomnia, dreams of or overhears the Knight, a lover still more unhappy than himself and also suffering from insomnia, tell the myth of Ceyx and Alcyone, a tragic story of love and sleep. Later in Machaut the Narrator meets the Knight and seeks to console him; they fall asleep and dream together the Knight's consolation and comfort from Venus and the Knight's beloved, from whom he is separated, a radiant creature resembling Fair White.

What links the three strands in Chaucer's tale, as in Machaut's, is first of all the unifying theme of psychic disorder – melancholia, the malady of lovers and poets, those born under the sign of Saturn. The *Duchess* Narrator cannot sleep; in addition, he has been ill for eight years, and only one physician can cure him:

> I holde hit be a sicknesse
> That I have suffred this eight yeer;
> And yet my boote is never the ner,
> For there is phisicien but oon
> That may me hele ... (36–40)

In *Le Roy de Behaingne* the Knight had been ill and a servant to Bonne Amour for a good seven or eight years. Given the tradition of the French love poems, where Machaut and Froissart link insomnia and unrequited love with their narrating personae and depict themselves, in their personae, as lovers and poets of love, it is clear that the Chaucerian Narrator also is a lover as well as an insomniac, and that it is his amorous 'sorwful ymagynacioun' (14) and 'melancolye' (23) that drive him to torpor – *tristitia* and *acedia* – and almost to death: 'And drede I have for to dye' (24).

In the 'bok' that he reads, Alcyone is separated from her husband Ceyx. She suffers from intense 'sorwe,' dreading his death; like the Narrator, she is driven to wallowing in melancholia and begging for sleep (in order to dream the truth about Ceyx). She then sleeps and is indeed told the truth about Ceyx – that he *is* dead. In response she also dies three days later, crushed by 'sorwe.' Finally, in the Narrator's dream, the Black Knight speaks of dying; he endures a situation of misery and psychic depression, again one of melancholia and *tristitia*, because he is mourning the death of Fair White. The Narrator and Alcyone desperately want to sleep. Alcyone and the Black Knight mourn the deaths of their beloveds. All three are wretched because of love and/or death, and all three manifest the same symptoms.

The Narrator's sleeplessness gives way to Alcyone's insomnia and death that in turn enable the Narrator to perceive the Black Knight's misery because of death. Not only do the Narrator's melancholia and Alcyone's bereavement anticipate the Man in Black's grief, but the Narrator's obsession with sleep is surpassed by the real deaths of Ceyx and Fair White, and Black's obsession with death. Alcyone's dream and the death of Ceyx are the key to the Narrator's dream of the death of Fair White. Thus Eros is allied to Thanatos, and both Eros and Thanatos to sleep and the world of dreams, to the activities of the night under the moon in the feminine realm of Dame Fortune, and to the passions, the unconscious, and the 'lunatic.' The bond of Eros, Thanatos, melancholia, and the oneiric; love leading to melancholia or death; love, melancholia, and death made manifest through the dream vision of a poet – these are part and parcel of the French poems of complaint and comfort: *Le Jugement dou Roy de Behaingne*, *Le Jugement dou Roy de Navarre*, *La Fonteinne amoureuse*, *Le Paradis d'Amour*, and *Le Bleu Chevalier*.

Chaucer, again following Machaut, raises the social issue along with the psychic. The Narrator, in the beginning, is alone in his misery and so is Alcyone, who is incapable of functioning as a 'quene.' Then, whereas in the dream the Narrator joins the chase in an atmosphere of festivity and joy (rather like the Narrator of *Le Jugement dou Roy de Navarre* who, after participating in the hunt, is invited to the court), the Black Knight complains to Fortune and bewails his fate in solitude. He, like Alcyone, a figure of the highest status, is isolated from the community and in desperate need of consolation. All three characters are speakers without an audience, narrators lacking a narratee. All three desperately have to be reintegrated into society.

A second element of coherence, no less essential than the first, is the persona of the Narrator, present throughout his narrative, as an obtrusive, active participant; he is an actant subject in the insomnia frame, the reader of Ceyx and Alcyone, and the dreamer-witness of the Man in Black. In the dream, Chaucer displays a witty and profound command of modern dream psychology. This he also learned from Machaut and Froissart. For example, in the *Fonteinne amoureuse* dream, as we saw in the chapter on Machaut, Venus talks about Peleus and Thetis, the Apple of Discord, and the Fall of Troy. She and the Lady comfort the Knight. Manifest dream content mirrors day residue; both the Narrator and the Knight had thought endlessly of ladies and love, the Knight told and the Narrator overheard the myth of Ceyx and Alcyone, and both of them spoke of Venus, among the other gods who built the *fonteinne amoureuse*, on which are represented Paris's abduction of Helen and the subsequent history of Troy.

Similarly, in the *Book of the Duchess* a melancholic lover who has just read the classical story of Eros and Thanatos – Alcyone's bereavement because of Ceyx's death followed by her dream – has a dream; in his dream he joins a hunt led by the classical Roman emperor, Octavian, and encounters a Knight clad in black (the colour of melancholy), who bewails his wretchedness over the death of Fair White. The wildness of the chase on horseback would be the prolongation of the Narrator's frustration and anxiety in his waking state. In addition, scholars have insisted, the very structure of the dream narrative reflects the abrupt, illogical, fragmented experience of dreams as they occur – the Narrator's waking up and mounting a horse apparently before he leaves his room; the Freudian pun on 'hert' and 'herte,' the object of the chase; the brusque transition from the hunt to the encounter with Black; and the fumbling, passive, inconsequential speeches and behaviour of the Narrator when faced with the Black Knight.

Chaucer follows the pattern in Machaut and Froissart where, in the frame, a clerkly narrator figure claims to be enamoured, suffering from melancholia, and in need of consolation; in the dream he then offers consolation to a knight or prince still more wretched than himself. In the *Book of the Duchess*, as in *Le Roy de Behaingne*, *La Fonteinne amoureuse*, *La Prison amoureuse*, and *Le Bleu Chevalier*, the Knight-lover can be considered, in terms of latent dream work, the Narrator's alter ego, a surrogate figure, on whom he has displaced his own amorous failure. By displacing onto the Knight the worst of Eros and by seeking to comfort him (that part of his own psyche in need of comfort), he releases anxiety. To the extent that the Narrator and Black are both parts of the Self, the dream work (embodied in the whelp taken from *Le Jugement dou Roy de Behaingne*) brings them together. The Narrator's joy in at least having fallen asleep anticipates the Knight's joy (his happy love for White in the past and, perhaps, the eventual end of his bereavement). At the very least, the Narrator can attempt to console and to join with his alter ego. And the Knight in Black's past happiness and present command of memory is a wish-fulfilment compensation for the Narrator's wretched past and present, and his forgetfulness. The Narrator's wish-fulfilment fantasy occurs, as it should, under the sway of the unconscious, in his dream life. The power of Morpheus, god of sleep, and the power of the dream both as reverie, adventure, and initiation, and as imagination and artistic experience, grant unity to *La Fonteinne amoureuse;* Chaucer adopts them for his own book.

However, because both poets treat the dream experience in terms of mimesis they also demystify its privileged allegorical standing. The medieval audience placed little value on a *somnium animale* that recounted only the dreamer's psychology (Freud's day residue) without reference to symbolic or objective reality.[21] Machaut, Froissart, and Chaucer choose to interpret their fictional dreams objectively; in psychological, subjective, specifically human terms, they treat the dream vision seriously and poke fun at it at the same time. So Chaucer follows Froissart's *Bleu Chevalier* in not incorporating consolation from an allegorical female authority figure such as Esperence or Venus, which would transform his dream into a *visio* or *oraculum*. He also follows Machaut's *Fonteinne amoureuse,* undercutting his own Morpheus myth by having the Speaker promise comic offerings, including a glorious feather bed, if only the Greek god will answer his prayers:

> Yif he wol make me slepe a lyte,
> Of down of pure dowves white
> I wil yive hym a fether-bed,
> Rayed with gold and ryght wel cled
> In fyn blak satyn doutremer,
> And many a pilowe, and every ber
> Of cloth of Reynes, to slepe softe –
> Hym thar not nede to turnen ofte – (249–56)

The narrating persona, both as a dreamer within the diegesis and as an implied author recounting it later, accepts the objective reality of the dream. Yet the real author – Machaut, Froissart, Chaucer – remains skeptical. The real author has created fictional characters and a narrating voice that are illusion; their experience is fictional; and the author's complex, ambivalent representation of the dream calls attention to this very literariness. All three poets explore the limits of dream knowledge and dream psychology, questioning both, because they have read Macrobius and also have lived in an experiential world.

As in Machaut and Froissart, the Chaucerian Narrator observes the amorous dilemma of a prince of the highest social world, a patron figure vis-à-vis himself as author figure. Like the Machaut and Froissart 'I,' who mingles with the King of Bohemia, the King of Navarre, the Duke of Berry, the Duke of Normandy, the Duke of Anjou, and the Duke of Brabant, Chaucer's implied author pays homage to the Duke of Lancaster. Within the diegesis, he enters into social contact with a figural representation of the duke, the Black Knight. Socially inferior to him, the clerkly narrator figure becomes something akin to the Knight's friend; he plays the role of confidant (some would say, of therapist), draws Black out of himself, makes him speak, and offers him, if not consolation, at least a measure of sympathy and understanding. This highly literary, highly problematic 'friendship' between noble and clerk, or patron and poet, forms part of the French tradition that Chaucer transmits to England. Theirs is not a debate but a dialogue. Mutual respect and a growing attachment develop between the two men, presumed to be total strangers when they meet. They both manifest good manners – the plain, simple observer and the hyperbolic, courtly lover.

This distinction, between the plain and simple on the one hand, and the hyperbolic and courtly on the other, is social, psychological, and stylistic. In the French tradition, as in Chaucer, for a viable, human relationship between non-equals to function, the poet-narrator indulges in self-deprecation, adopting the middle or the low style (*genus medium* or *tenue*) and a comic persona – he depicts himself as clumsy, obtuse, a snob, a coward, an insomniac, and an unsuccessful lover – in conscious antithesis to the *genus grande* and high, heroic sentiments of the prince beloved of Venus and Mars. Grounding his 'I' in the traditional French persona, Chaucer has his Narrator play the fool. In a comic manner he is obsessed, in an almost mechanical, Bergsonian manner, with his insomnia, and he deems sleeplessness to be a mortal threat. Self-conscious yet comically unaware, he is ignorant of the significance of the Ceyx and Alcyone myth, relating it uniquely to his insomnia; to cure the insomnia, he indulges in the famous comic prayer to Morpheus for sleep. Then, inside the dream, in his dialogue with Black – either intentionally, out of an exquisite sense of tact, or unintentionally, because he is somewhat dull – he fails to understand the Black Knight's courtly rhetoric and the meaning of his bereavement; he fails to understand what the Man in Black means by having lost his 'fers,' or how serious and profound the loss is, and how deep and meaningful Black's love was in the first place. Even though he is a lover, the Narrator doesn't appear to comprehend the essence of *fin' amor.* In any case, whether as a character his behaviour is meant to be conscious or unconscious, as a literary creation the author Chaucer intentionally makes him a foil to the high, tragic lover-protagonist in mourning.

As much a subject of controversy among Chaucerians as whether the Narrator is consciously tactful or unconsciously stupid vis-à-vis the Man in Black is the question: Is the *Book of the Duchess* a poem of comfort and consolation? If so, who consoles whom? There is general agreement that, if nothing else than as an example not to be followed, Alcyone is not consoled, and Morpheus, himself originally in a state of torpor, fails to comfort her. Chaucer, following Machaut, suppressed the Ovidian transformation and the happy avian reunion of the couple *post mortem atque metamorphoses.* In the *Book of the Duchess* once Alcyone is informed of her husband's death, in sorrow and despair, refusing Ceyx's (Morpheus') good counsel, she also dies:

> With that hir eyen up she casteth
> And saw noght. 'Alas!' quod she for sorwe,
> And deyede within the thridde morwe. (212–14)

That is all.

In line with the psychological analysis and dream symbolism discussed above and in line with the French tradition, I should say that the Narrator, in contrast to Alcyone, undergoes a most successful comforting. After having read the Ovidian myth, he learns how to invoke the gods, how to sleep, and how to dream; he learns the power of imagination and of creativity. Although his own love malady is cured no more than Alcyone's, his torpor *is*, and, for a clerkly narrator, the torpor and insomnia weigh more heavily than Eros. In his dream, the Narrator awakens to a trumpet blast and sets out on the hunt. He is released from care, his *tristitia* and *acedia* evaporated. The hard riding to the hounds in quest of a 'hert' – a stag but also the human heart – (cf. Leyerle 1974, Shoaf 1979, Prior 1986) is, in Freudian terms, an image of sexual arousal; it is a desire which, although not consummated, is given free reign and expressed in an active sanguine manner, in contrast to the melancholic torpor of the frame. The hunt also symbolizes the Narrator's initiation into a new life; through his waking in springtime to the song of birds, he has a death-rebirth experience. Furthermore, although the Narrator does not capture the 'hert,' he does encounter the Man in Black, unbeknownst to himself the genuine object of his quest. The hunt and the encounter, as in Machaut's *Jugement dou Roy de Navarre*, bring a solitary, foolish, melancholic man into contact with the court and the community. Withdrawn into himself, self-absorbed, and self-centred, the Narrator learns to focus on another and to react to the Other as a subject, not an object. The bed gives way to the meadow; then the hunt gives way to speech and to genuine communication with the Other. The bookish Narrator integrates the Other's experience and the Other as a person, helping bring about his own maturation. He succeeds in a quest. And he learns that the reason for the Other's woe, and the irrefutable power of death – a grief and a reality greater than his own. This is a discovery and a recognition (redemptive knowledge from a redemptive dream) that are the subject of his dream and will become the subject of his poem.

As for the Black Knight, it has traditionally been assumed (by Bronson 1952, Lawlor 1956, Clemen 1963, Cartier 1967, Wimsatt 1968, Kean 1972) that the Chaucerian Narrator, through his sophistication and tact, does bring comfort and consolation to his noble interlocutor. He communicates with him and makes him voice his grief and ultimately recognize both the value and the inherent *consolatio* to be found in his past joy with White, his present memory of her truth, beauty, and goodness, and the future continuity of life in nature. I disagree. I follow the more recent school of critics[22] who state that Chaucer mutes the consolation and leaves the ending of his tale ambiguous, indeterminate, and unresolved. He asks questions but does not provide answers (as will so often be the case in the later books). There is no doubt that the Chaucerian Narrator's stance toward the Black Knight is derived from and corresponds to the Machaut and Froissart narrators who seek and find a relationship of warm, human interaction with their prince-patrons through the topos of consolation. I am also convinced that, as in the *dits amoureux*, the Black Knight is an eminently sympathetic figure, voicing high courtly ideology in beautiful high courtly speech. He is worthy of the Narrator's (and the implied audience's) respect and is not at all the object of satire as some scholars would have us believe. The *Book of the Duchess* is an extension of the French courtly tradition, not a rejection of it.

It is then in sympathy that the Narrator is moved by Black's pain and is eager not only to discover the truth but to offer help. After more than one false start, he succeeds in discovering the truth, and indeed in communicating with the man. He makes Black speak to another human being. However, whether or not this is successful therapy is open to question; each reader has to decide for himself. At no time are we told specifically of consolation and comfort or of any change in the Man in Black's psyche. The Knight and the Narrator together focus on the terrible, irremediable fact of death. Alcyone dies, the Knight maintains his wretchedness, and the Narrator, having learned how to sleep, now also learns the greater, more horrible mystery of death:

> 'Allas, sir, how? What may that be?'
> 'She ys ded!' 'Nay!' 'Yis, be my trouthe!'
> 'Is that youre los? Be God, hyt ys routhe!' (1308–10)

Dreams and art can order experience only up to a point. The end is stark. Death is final, Black's loss is total, and the dream is over.

Chaucer departs from the central consolation and comfort tradition in the French *dits amoureux*, as represented by his chief source, *La Fonteinne amoureuse*, and also *Le Paradis d'Amour*. However, in so doing he picks up a divergent thread also to be found in Machaut and Froissart. *Remede de Fortune* offers a comparably ambiguous ending, in which the Narrator is comforted (more or less) but the implied audience has good reason to doubt the validity of the message. In *Le Jugement dou Roy de Behaingne* the Knight seeks to console the bereaved Lady, and the King of Bohemia decides against her. She accepts the judgment (she has no choice) but evidences no acceptance whatsoever of the proffered consolation. Her misery remains absolute. Similarly, in *Le Bleu Chevalier* the Knight in Blue listens to the Narrator's good words and is grateful for them, but the extent to which he believes and is moved by them remains problematic. In the *Book of the Duchess* Chaucer adopts the structure and images of *La Fonteinne amoureuse* and *Le Bleu Chevalier* but superimposes upon them the doctrine or, if you prefer, the world-view of the two *Jugements*: death is a powerful, devastating force in the universe; death can destroy the greatest of lovers and the greatest of men;

in the face of death we can only murmur, in pity and awe: 'Be God, hyt ys routhe!'

This being the case, Chaucer creates a situation – exactly like Machaut in *Remede de Fortune, La Fonteinne amoureuse,* and *Le Voir Dit* – in which the obtuse Narrator fails to comprehend the impact of his own narrative, although the implied audience perhaps does. Machaut and Chaucer, who both follow in the steps of Jean de Meun, distance themselves from their narrating personae, thus maintaining a sense of complicity, at the Narrator's expense, between the implied author and the implied audience. The implied audience sees beyond the Narrator and comprehends the reality of an experiential situation and its implications in a way that the Narrator, living the experience, never does.

In this way, the consolation, which is refused by the Man in Black and perhaps never truly understood by the dreaming witness-observer, is made available to the implied audience. The implied audience is shown a pattern of death followed by rebirth; the melancholic Narrator finally falls asleep and awakens to a dream world of light, colour, sheen, communal activity (the hunt), and human interaction (the encounter with Black). Springtime, the song of birds, the meadow, the *locus amoenus* – all the stylized beauty from Guillaume de Lorris – offers an indirect, oblique resolution to Black's tragedy; life goes on; the world goes on, in all its beauty as well as its tragedy. That is the nature of beauty and death; they exist, and they must be accepted for the reality they are. So, one continues to live, responding to the ups and downs of Fortune's wheel with decorum and dignity.

Secondly, the audience perceives the work of memory – the process by which the Man in Black recovers the imago of Fair White and his love for her by remembering and recounting the past (how he met her, fell in love with her, courted her, and won her). Black succeeds, in spite of himself and unbeknownst to himself, in making her live anew in all her beauty and glory, and in reliving his joy in her as well. White's virtue and the memory of her are imperishable in Black, and therefore in the Narrator and in the audience. All that is good in Black came from her in the past; all that remains good in him will come from her in the present and future. Thus is posed, in pre-Proustian terms, how, to what extent, and for what purposes the past can be recaptured. Here Chaucer's classical allusions have an important function. The Narrator reads in his 'romaunce' the Ovidian myth of Ceyx and Alcyone; the story of Troy is depicted on the windows in the Narrator's chamber; the king who leads the hunt is named Octavian; Fair White is compared to the phoenix. We are made aware of the greatness of a classical Golden Age that corresponds to the Golden Age of Jean de Meun, a time of joy and contentment in love that is not entirely lost, for it can be made to live again in books, in landscape, and in the Black Knight's memory and speech.

This brings us to the fact that at the heart of the poem stands Black's praise of Fair White. In the traditional *Roman de la Rose* garden, adhering to the neo-Platonic aesthetic of his age, Black praises her as inherently beautiful, good, and true. She is like the phoenix – one, unique, and immortal. Also in neo-Platonic terms, she exists in and because of her name – White, Blanche – comparable, in her shining, radiant glory, to the shining, glorious radiance of light and the sun:

> 'For I dar swere, withoute doute,
> That as the someres sonne bryght
> Ys fairer, clerer, and hath more lyght
> Than any other planete in heven,
> The moone or the sterres seven,
> For al the world so hadde she
> Surmounted hem alle of beaute,
> Of maner, and of comlynesse, ... ' (820–7)

As such, her whiteness stands in antithesis to but also achieves a synthesis with the blackness of the melancholic Knight. Chaucer took Froissart's 'Bleu Chevalier' and clothed him in black, the colour of *acedia* and melancholia, as the mourner of Fair White, the literary representation of the deceased Duchess Blanche. In a very real sense, the *Book of the Duchess* is, as its title implies, a celebration of White more than it is a consolation of Black. As an encomium it assumes its shape and force from being ascribed to Black rather than to the Narrator. By uttering it in Black's voice, the poem celebrates both White and Black – her goodness and beauty, his greatness and love. And the praise of *fin' amor* by which he serves her is also, implicitly, a praise of the formalized, courtly, rhetorical world in which she and Black dwell. The courtliness, urbanity, and beauty of their world and world-vision, that of the French love books, is also a response to the harsh reality of experience in love or death. The world-view and the books that relate it are also part of experience and reality. White endures, like a work of art, in a work of art, as an idealized rhetorical portrait at the centre; this is Chaucer's monument to White and his gift to Black.

In his very first extended creative effort, Chaucer follows his great predecessors, Machaut and Froissart. He explores the theme of art and the artist, and creates a metatext that treats, among other things, its own creation by an implied author, a persona of Geoffrey Chaucer, who is the narrator telling the story and the observer-witness living it. The Man in Black pronounces a lyrical complaint (475–86) that expresses his sorrow and makes an unusually powerful impression on the eavesdropping Narrator, who then enters into contact with him. Later Black sings from memory his first song of love to Fair White (1175–80); the sung lyric of the past is set in antithesis to the spoken complaint of the present. As in a number of works by Machaut and Froissart, Chaucer ascribes the lyrics inserted in his text to another. Black's talents as a poet provide a link to the Narrator, a poet, just as the Narrator's love sickness and melancholia provide a link to the mourning prince. Prior to the encounter, the Narrator woke up (in his dream) in a luxurious chamber embellished with such works of art as the Fall of Troy represented on the stained glass windows and *Le Roman de la Rose* painted al fresco on the walls. These are the two traditions – the classical and the modern, the scholarly Latin and the courtly French – that comprise the Narrator's and Chaucer's cultural world. Finally, the dream itself and the encounter inside it take place because the Narrator reads the story of Ceyx and Alcyone – a classical myth from Antiquity that functions as *texte générateur*, as it was already contained in and functioned as *texte générateur* in a great modern French book, *La Fonteinne amoureuse*. The Ceyx and Alcyone story – one of love, separation, death, and dreaming – mirrors the problematic of the *Book of the Duchess* as a whole; as with Machaut, it is a work of art within a work of art, a *mise en abyme* that modulates and is set in antithesis to the misery-consolation topos of the Man in Black and of the Narrator himself. Furthermore, in Chaucer's first poem a book is connected with life experience and with the world of dreams in a pattern that he will repeat, with variations, in all his dream poems up to and including the *Prologue to the Legend of Good Women*.

The frescos from *Le Roman de la Rose* and the stained glass recounting the story of Troy correspond to and no doubt derive from the stories of Paris and Helen and of the Trojan War chiselled on the Machaldian 'Fonteinne amoureuse,' itself a beautiful artifact. It recalls the fountain of love in Guillaume de Lorris, shows Ovidian myths narrated elsewhere in the text, and serves as a *mise en abyme* that reflects, comments on, and symbolizes the narrative structure that contains it. Would it not then be a delightful touch were the 'romaunce' (48) (the 'bok' containing 'written fables' [52]) that Chaucer's Narrator reads to have been not Ovid, not even the *Ovide moralisé*, but Machaut's own *Fonteinne amoureuse* or a compendium Machaut manuscript? The written text would then have provided as much day residue for the Chaucerian Narrator's subsequent dream as the Prince's verbal, lyrical complaint (in fact by Machaut himself) did for Machaut's narrator. Machaut (and Ovid) would then offer a complete intertextual matrix for Chaucer, with his (their) book as intertext included in Chaucer's text, in dream and waking reality, in much the same way that Machaut included Ovid, or for that matter his own Ovidian complaint, in *La Fonteinne*.

The book-experience-dream sequence that some scholars have claimed to be distinctly Chaucerian is borrowed from the French, with, however, a crucial difference; Machaut's tales include as intertextual *mises en abyme* and *textes générateurs* the author's own lyrical or narrative creations (self-referential autotexts) – in *Remede de Fortune* the Narrator's *lai*; in *La Fonteinne amoureuse* the *complainte* attributed to the Knight; in *Le Jugement dou Roy de Navarre* the implied author's own previous *Jugement dou Roy de Behaingne*; in *Le Voir Dit* the implied author's entire previous corpus – whereas, until the *Legend of Good Women*, Chaucer uses books by Cicero, Virgil, Ovid, and Machaut. Writing in English not French, Chaucer adopts a modesty-topos; lacking Machaut's and Froissart's joyful self-assurance, his persona reads other people's books. In this respect, as in others, Chaucer innovates in English by partaking of a continental French convention and then shaping it to fit his own social, linguistic, and aesthetic situation in England.

Chaucer also innovates by presenting his persona (in his first book) not as a great, accomplished poet but, on the contrary, as a distraught man in the process of becoming a poet. The Ovidian-Machaldian book leads to a dream which is the embodiment of and metaphor for imagination; the dream then inspires and becomes the subject of a poem (the *Book of the Duchess*); writing and the process of creating a work of art inspires and becomes the narrative that will recount it. Alcyone and Black do not grow; they remain the same – powerful icons of unalterable grief. However, their sorrow and Fair White herself will be embellished in a work of art about sorrow. The Narrator grows and evolves; he not only sleeps and awakens but he also becomes a writer. His story began with a book – the Machaut-Ovid pre-textual *texte générateur*; it ends with a book, the devouring textual *Book of the Duchess*. The Narrator falls asleep with the 'romaunce,' the other book, under him; he awakens with it in his hand, and he proceeds presumably with his hand to compose the account of his dream, that will be his book. In a quite Bakhtinian way, dialogism comes into play as the source voices function alongside varied Chaucerian voices, contributing to the final revolved and devolved text.[23] This text is a magnificent first effort. It is the first great court poem in English and it masters the French tradition in such a natural and totally authentic way as to make it English. This text is a masterpiece of intertextuality and metatextuality, a precedent and a model for Chaucer himself and for all who will follow him.

2. *Prologue to the Legend of Good Women*

With the *Parliament of Fowls* and the *House of Fame* Chaucer continues to draw from and to branch out of the French tradition of the *dit amoureux*. The French precedents, analogues, and intertextual references are legion. However, it is in the fourth dream vision, the *Prologue to the Legend of Good Women*, that Chaucer bases a text upon, and makes creative use of, French pre-texts in the totalizing manner of the *Book of the Duchess*. Significantly, he does this in a work dating from the late 1380s and the 1390s.

The plot (I follow the 'F' version) adheres to one of the classical French *dit amoureux* patterns – vision, debate or discussion, and judgment. The Narrator is a great reader of books. However, on May Day he quits his books in order to wander out-of-doors and pay his devotions to the Daisy, whom (which) he loves. Upon returning to his chamber, he falls asleep and dreams that he wanders again into the meadow. There he is accosted by the God of Love (Cupid), accompanied by his queen and a retinue of noble ladies. Cupid denounces the Narrator for amorous heresy and crimes against him (*lèse-divinité*) and for having defamed ladies and love, because he wrote *Troilus and Criseyde* and translated *Le Roman de la Rose*. The queen intercedes on the Narrator's behalf, proclaiming his guilt but also citing attenuating circumstances. He is condemned to write a series of poems in praise of good and true women, loyal in the ways of love – legends of Venus' saints. He discovers that the lady who intercedes on his behalf is the mythological figure Alceste (Alcestis) and that she is also the Daisy he adores. The Narrator then proceeds to his task. The *Prologue* is followed by nine legends, the stories of Cleopatra, Thisbe, Dido, Hypsipyle and Medea, Lucrece, Ariadne, Philomela, Phyllis, and Hypermnestra, the last one left incomplete.

Chaucerians are universally aware of the French 'Marguerite poems.' Chaucer's Myth of the Daisy was inspired by a tradition of court encomium and court play derived from Machaut, Froissart, and Deschamps. The most important of these, from a Chaucerian perspective, would be Froissart's *Paradis d'Amour,* a text which recounts how the Narrator sins against love, is aided by the intercession of great ladies (Plaisance, Esperance), makes his peace with Cupid in a spirit of repentance, and succeeds in pleasing his Marguerite. The God of Love figure in relation to a poet-lover-singer of love also owes much to portions of Jean de Meun's *Roman de la Rose,* one of the texts that within the fiction, diegetically, provides evidence of the Narrator's guilt.

The problem of the *Prologue to the Legend of Good Women* is indeed complex. Here is a poem that mocks *fin' amor* and its conventions and ideology. A number of specialists claim that this text reveals ways in which Chaucer repudiates or surpasses the French courtly tradition. However, when they say this the specialists are less conscious of the fact that the core, the very structure of the *Prologue,* is taken from Machaut's *Jugement dou Roy de Navarre.* The question in both of Machaut's Judgment poems – who loves better, man or woman – provides the crucial subtext for Chaucer's poem (in both his *Prologue* and the legends). Machaut's Narrator tells how he is tried before a court of love (the authority figures are one man and one woman – the King of Navarre and the allegorical Dame Bonneürté) for having spoken ill of ladies and *fin' amor* in *Le Jugement dou Roy de Behaingne,* one of his earlier books. After a mock defence in a mock trial, in which the hero appears to have the worst of it but which in fact shows the plaintiff's charges to be absurd, he is condemned – to write more poetry of love. All this is taken over into Chaucer's *Prologue,* in which the charges are the same; he substitutes for Guillaume's *Behaingne,* as the incriminating antifeminist and anticourtly subtext, his own *Troilus* and also his version of the *Rose,* and instead of courtly lyric poems his persona is condemned to relate myths from Antiquity in the narrative mode. Avis's counsel to the King of Navarre is paralleled by Alceste's counsel to Cupid, and both culminate in anagnorisis – the recognition by the Narrator of the great lady before him, Bonneürté (Happiness or Good Fortune) in Machaut, and Alceste the Daisy in Chaucer. Furthermore, four of the five exempla recounted by the Machaut Narrator's accusers, stories from Antiquity told by feminine allegories in defence of women, reappear among Chaucer's legends in defence of 'wommen trewe in lovyng' (438). They are the myths of Dido, Ariadne, Medea, and Thisbe. It is by no means improbable that the impulse for the legends came from Machaut and that the reference to 'olde bokes' (25), 'olde stories' (98), and 'these olde appreved stories' (21) concern Machaut's *Jugement* as much as they do Virgil and Ovid.

That Machaut's or Chaucer's persona in a work of fiction defends himself badly or fails to defend himself at all does not necessarily incriminate his case. Theirs is a complex, ironic palinode. It is Guillaume de Machaut or Geoffrey Chaucer as author who is responsible for constructing the work of fiction. It is the author who decides that the persona will lose; he shapes the speeches and action with that end in view. The trial, the judgment, and the punishment are meant to be interpreted ironically. And, while ironically having his Narrator lose, the author also has him tell the truth and justify his telling it. Even the Chaucerian persona, who assumes a more passive role than his predecessor, protests:

> 'Ne a trewe lover oght me not to blame
> Thogh that I speke a fals lovere som shame.
> They oghte rather with me for to holde
> For that I of Creseyde wroot or tolde,
> Or of the Rose; what so myn auctour mente,
> Algate, God woot, yt was myn entente
> To forthren trouthe in love and yt cheryce,
> And to ben war fro falsnesse and fro vice
> By swich ensample; this was my menynge.' (F466–74)

Alceste points out that if there be error in the Narrator's works, it is due to the authors he translated. The translator is less guilty than if he were the original 'auctour':

> 'He ne hath nat doon so grevously amys
> To translaten that olde clerkes writen,
> As thogh that he of malice wolde enditen
> Despit of love, and had himself yt wroght.' (F369–72)

Chaucer tells us, adopting a defence he found in Jean de Meun (one of his authors), that (1) I only attack bad lovers not good ones; and (2) if I am wrong, so are the great 'olde clerkes.' On the one hand, the future creator of the Wife of Bath plays with the idea of 'auctour,' reversing our expectation that the 'olde clerkes' are automatically to be cited, glossed, and revered. On the other hand, he also intimates that they and I, *we*, are not so wrong after all. The poet, while he gives the superficial impression of recanting his earlier works, in fact defends them and his own function as artist with brio.

One means of generating irony and winning the reader's approbation is to make the trial machinery and the accusing personage appear ridiculous. Machaut did it in *Le Roy de Navarre;* Chaucer follows in the *Prologue*. After all, their Narrators are author figures; the accusers are reader figures. We the extradiegetic implied audience have the right to judge the critical capacities of readers-become-accusers such as Paix and Franchise, or Cupid and Alceste. Cupid is presented as a tyrant, totally irrational and not very clever; he is a simple-minded, literalist reader who imposes (as was the case in Machaut) guilt based upon tautology: if the books you translated speak ill of ladies and of love, then you are guilty of speaking ill of ladies and of love, and these are crimes from my perspective as the god of *fin' amor;* there is one Truth only – mine – and you shall conform. It is manifestly unfair to condemn a translator for what he translates and bad criticism to confuse the subject matter or the story of a text and its ethical import. In the 'G' version dating from 1394, Cupid makes himself even more ridiculous by citing authors and books favourable to love that the Narrator could have imitated, in a tradition he could have partaken of. Unwittingly he ignorantly includes in his list texts by Saint Jerome and/or Walter Map, classics of misogyny which were among Jean de Meun's sources and were used by Chaucer in the very books for which he is being incriminated. Chaucer takes splendid advantage of the fact that his accuser and judge is the God of Love, in order to inject into his text layers of sacred parody — a god accusing the Narrator, a mere mortal, not only of bad writing but of sin and heresy, which, due to the intercession of a sacred *mediatrix,* he is obliged to recant; as penance, he must write saints' lives, *vitae,* of ladies martyred in the cause of true love. The naive, obtuse Narrator is willing to do it because he already has been performing devotions to a sacred relic, the Daisy. Finally, Alceste's intercession casts discredit on Cupid and the values he represents; while dismissing the Narrator as naive and condemning his *auctores,* she also points out that it behooves a god to manifest mercy not sternness and that the god may have been misled by slander from malicious accusers. Alceste intimates, among other things, the presence of anticourtly 'losengeours' in the God of Love's own court of *fin' amor* and that Cupid's judgment is as frail as anyone else's.

Much of the comedy and the irony are generated by the fact that Machaut, Froissart, and Chaucer create distance between themselves as implied authors and their fumbling, inept, literary characters – their own personae as Narrators and, in this case, protagonists. The Chaucerian Narrator is undermined in that (1) he is depicted as a courtly lover who performs excessive devotions to the Daisy, an allegory but also a mere plant, and who fails to recognize the object of his devotion, the real woman Alceste, when she appears; and (2) he defends himself in such an inept manner; he is inarticulate and self-effacing, accepts the verdict of the court, and will obey it. Furthermore, Alceste defends him in a patronizing way, suggesting, among other things, that he didn't know what he was doing, and that he may have been too stupid to recognize the real import of the books he translated (also perhaps a self-conscious, ironic reflection on how the French sources are/have to be transformed):

> 'And eke, peraunter, for this man ys nyce,
> He myghte doon yt, gessyng no malice,
> But for he useth thynges for to make;
> Hym rekketh noght of what matere he take.' (F362–5)

As with Machaut, the point of view is largely external; it is limited to the Narrator's recounting in the present his speeches and actions in the past. His inner sentiments, if he has any, remain hidden. Therefore, mistakenly or not, we assume that he is obtuse and unaware of the complexities and ironies in his own situation and in himself. This is the case because, although the narrating voice is reliable in that the story he tells is presumed to be factually true (he is not a liar, nor a schizophrenic, nor a protagonist of *nouveau roman*), he is not reliable given that the implied audience interprets the situation in ways that the persona could not have intended or understood. Look at his defence of the artist and the mockery of *fin' amor* and the rigid, artificial courts in which it flourishes. The Narrator's authoritative voice and the authoritative voices of Cupid and Alceste recounted by him and filtered through his consciousness all prove to be inadequate; they are refuted by the very text that he makes.

Generations of scholars assumed that the Chaucerian persona – the naive, inept, timid, cowardly witness-narrator and naive, inept, timid, cowardly lover who is also a highly self-conscious, bookish, clerkly, author figure – is a Chaucerian creation and thus one mark of his originality. In fact, it was largely invented by Machaut, who took some hints from Jean de Meun; then it was elaborated by Froissart. The nature of the persona also tells us something about the alleged restraints imposed upon Chaucer by oral performance. The 'modern,' 'new critical' analyses of the persona have been challenged by Bronson (1960) and others on the grounds that, because Chaucer himself read his texts to the court, the likeness between the persona and Chaucer the writer had to be close and any divergence relatively minor. In my opinion, it is the revisionist view which errs. True, all medieval literature was meant to be delivered orally, to be sung, chanted, or read aloud. Yet most medieval texts, whether heterodiegetic (*chansons de geste*, romances, and fabliaux) or homodiegetic (courtly lyrics and the *dit amoureux*), are largely conventional in mode and told by a conventional, archetypal narrator. Furthermore, the fact of Chaucer's semiretirement away from London in his later years indicates that he could not habitually have recited his own works at court, in his circle of the lower gentry (also London-based), or anywhere else and that, more often than not, others read the master's texts. Finally, since the persona is conventional and of French origin, the extent to which it corresponds to the historical London government functionary had to be to a large extent fortuitous. Less fortuitous was the comic tension perceived between the persona and the real Chaucer or between both of them and the reciter. Although this is an aspect of medieval audience response which we will never be able to capture in its essence, we can take it for granted that the more cultivated among the audience were aware of the nature of the Chaucerian speaker. Ever since the dissemination of the first Machaldian texts (in the 1330s), the horizon of expectations of the courtly public had been enlarged to include the new persona. Hearing him speak English and hearing him designated as 'Geoffrey' would presumably have ellicited a shock of recognition and of pleasure from those who, indeed, had ears to hear.

The persona is, above all, a maker of texts. The greatest gift Machaut offers Chaucer is the notion of a poet writing poetry about the writing of poetry by a poet. In both the *Roy de Navarre* and the *Legend of Good Women* the defendant is tried, judged, and punished not as a courtier or a lover but as a writer who has written books in the past and will compose others in the future. The Narrator begins with praise of 'olde bokes' (25) and of those who have gone before; he later confesses that he comes late, after the others, that he can glean only the remains, and that (his) English is not good enough:

> Allas, that I ne had Englyssh, rhyme or prose,
> Suffisant this flour to preyse aryght! ...
> For wel I wot that ye han her-biforn
> Of makyng ropen, and lad awey the corn,
> And I come after, glenyng here and there,
> And am ful glad yf I may fynde an ere
> Of any goodly word that ye han left. (F66–7, 73–7)

This is a standard modesty topos in medieval rhetoric, functioning as *captatio benevolentiae*. It is especially appropriate to a 'maker' in the English vernacular, but also is a tribute to the French courtly makers, already known as 'poëtes,' Guillaume de Lorris, Jean de Meun, Machaut, and Froissart, from whom Geoffrey will gather not just the leftovers but the essence and kernel of his new book. However, ironically belying the alleged modesty, for the first time in his career Chaucer now has the confidence of a Jean de Meun or a Machaut; for the first time he employs the Machaut practice of autotextuality; the *texte générateur*, the book which launches the dream and the experience, is an autotext, his own earlier books, the *Troilus* and *his* version of the *Rose*.

The point is that like Machaut, Chaucer has his Narrator accused of having done badly as a writer, but then he is ordered to continue writing and to make up for alleged bad verse by composing good verse. The dream vision convention leads not to a love debate but to the discussion of literature, specifically the material Chaucer ought to work on. Although the conclusion apparently is for him to work within the *fin' amor* tradition he supposedly broke, in fact he will continue doing what he wants, inventing and imagining and practising, as he always has, *inventio* and the creation of *imagines*. In the frame the Narrator abandons his books to serve the Daisy and observe the May; but then he returns to the same old books – Ovid, Jean de Meun, Machaut, Boccaccio – to find the stories and the style in which to obey Cupid and to exalt the Daisy and, with the Daisy, Alceste. Alceste is, in any case, the muse and inspiration for all the implied author's verse, including the *Rose*, *Troilus*, and the *Legend of Good Women*. Furthermore, just as Machaut deftly praised his own verse by ascribing it to characters in his *dits*, here Chaucer turns the process around and has Alceste praise her author (Chaucer); he has her cite his 'good books,' those favourable to love and ladies, in the course of her intercession. As author, Chaucer includes his bibliography in this book on the making of his own books. Chaucer's books – the *Troilus* and the *Rose* – give rise to the *Prologue*, in which he names his other books, which then gives rise to his next book, the *Legend*. The dream vision is framed by the Narrator's bookish and amorous experience; the *Prologue* as a whole is framed by the implied author's earlier books, which it questions, and his next book, which it launches. In the beginning, the middle, and the end, the writer is vindicated. As with Jean de Meun and Machaut, for the clerkly narrator figure, service in art equals love service. The only way for such men to obey the

God of Love is to practise their craft and 'make' their art. Such poets, in this case Chaucer, choose as the true subject of their verse its own textuality: how it comes into being, how it functions, and how it questions itself and its essence as artifice and art.

The Chaucerian persona is ordered to write anew and to become a poet again. As in *Le Jugement dou Roy de Navarre,* the action occurs in springtime (in Machaut after the rigours of the Plague winter), and specifically on May Day, a time when little birds sing joyfully of love. The Daisy opens her petals to the sun every morning and closes them at night (a motif taken from the Machaut-Froissart Marguerite poems). The Daisy undergoes a death-rebirth experience; so did Alceste; so do the Narrator and mankind as a whole, who celebrate the coming of spring and the new year, the time of love. Like Machaut's persona, Chaucer's Narrator had been alone with his books. In his dream he enters into contact with the community, joins the court, and, for good or ill, is brought into contact with the vital forces that stand behind the death-rebirth experience and the change of the seasons – Eros, envisaged as *fin' amor* but also as the divine creative impulse that gives birth to life and restores the cosmos. The contact and the communion occur in an atmosphere of court ceremonial. Cupid and Alceste are the King and Queen of the May, the *imagines* of restorative fertility and rebirth. And the Narrator, the bookish outsider, plays the role of scapegoat but then is accepted into the festive society and permitted to benefit from its renewal in his artistic renewal.

Chaucer differs from Machaut by making his anticourtly defendant a truly courtly lover, who reveres the Daisy and conforms to the dictates of *fin' amor.* He also reverses the Machaut pattern, in which Boneürté and her female retinue accuse the male Narrator before a male judge who obviously sympathizes with him; in the *Prologue* the male God of Love accuses the male Narrator, who is defended and interceded for by a female authority figure, Alceste. Thus Chaucer has his persona appear to be less guilty than Machaut's because, whatever they say about him, he adheres to ladies and true love and because it is not the ladies who accuse him of misogyny, but a man. In fact, the woman is more sympathetic and humane than the man (the opposite is the case in Machaut). Thus the irony of his condemnation becomes all the greater, and the play with ideology and literary structure more complex, as Chaucer comments intertextually on Machaut's *Jugement.*

As Knopp (1973) has demonstrated, he also indulges in intertextual play with Jean de Meun's *Roman de la Rose.* In the *Rose* the implied author defends himself from (eventual) criticism on the grounds that he is but a translator citing old books – just as Chaucer's Narrator will do. Jean de Meun also has Cupid praise *him* by name as the greatest poet in France of his time. How deliciously ironic then for Chaucer to have the very same God of Love attack him for translating Jean de Meun, now considered an author of old books in turn, and for the Narrator to defend himself (to appear modest and self-effaced in antithesis to Jean) by saying that all he did was to translate Jean!

Finally, we see a new classicism in Chaucer. Machaut's *Jugement* recounts a number of Greco-Roman myths in the course of the trial. Chaucer's *Prologue* will launch an entire legendary of classical stories; it serves metatextually to tell us how and why the myths are being retold. But within the *Prologue*, as Kiser (1983) has shown, Chaucer creates his own, new classical myth. He introduces the Greek Alcestis, imago of true married love, in place of the allegorical Bonneürté, and he assimilates her to the Daisy of the Marguerite poems (we are told that after Alceste's death she was transformed into a daisy). Just as *Le Roman de la Rose* culminates in the Ovidian myth of Pygmalion, so the *Prologue to the Legend of Good Women* culminates in the Chaucerian myth of Alceste the Daisy – Alceste from Ovid and the Daisy from Machaut, Froissart, and Deschamps. Chaucer fuses the classical and the contemporary French worlds (the French also containing the classical) with Alceste the Daisy, the metaphor for his muse – his creative, inventive powers. We ought not, in my opinion, to posit Chaucer's repudiating the French tradition in favour of the classical or Christian. Machaut and Froissart, and for that matter Guillaume de Lorris, associated the ancient gods with *fin' amor.* Froissart, preceding Chaucer, invented a series of Ovidian myths, one of which, in his *Dit de la Margheritte*, concerns the origin of the Daisy. In this Chaucer probably imitates him.

Alceste the muse and Alceste the judge and counsellor to a god inspires, indeed orders, the Narrator to compose

> 'a glorious legende
> Of goode wymmen, maydenes and wyves,
> That weren trewe in lovyng all hyre lyves.' (F483–5)

The nine legends that he recounts are his punishment and penance, the direct outcome of his trial in the *Prologue*. Thus, the book comes after the experience and the dream; it is created by the experience and the dream rather than preceding and creating them, as in Chaucer's earlier vision poems. The legends indeed serve to counter *Troilus and*

Criseyde, where a woman betrayed a man, and *Le Roman de la Rose*, where Ami, Le Jaloux, and la Vieille expound at length on how women do or ought to do wicked things to their men. They correspond to the penance in Machaut's *Roy de Navarre* (*Le lay de Plour*), where the Narrator also had to write manifestly about and in the voice of a woman who loves better than men do.

In Machaut's case the Greco-Roman myths are integrated into the frame narrative and become part of the pleading during the trial, evidence for or against the defendant; the Narrator only writes in penance one lyric *lai*. Chaucer, perhaps in intertextual homage to his French predecessors, includes a French-style *ballade* in the dream (adapted from Froissart) which cites the great ladies of Antiquity about whom he will write. The *ballade* is a *mise en abyme* and a *texte générateur*. However, the nine legends are then removed from the trial narrative and separated from the *Prologue*; they follow it sequentially.

The legends have been criticized, especially by an earlier generation of Chaucerians, who find them dull, boring, repetitive, and absurd in their reduction of great classical myths to the simplistic antithesis of good women and bad men. According to this theory, Chaucer's first effort at a story collection is a failure; England's greatest writer of the Middle Ages fails here to properly translate and transmit the classical culture he so loved. This is because he chose to elaborate an unfortunate structural cohesive pattern demanding a single topic and a single attitude toward that topic.

Most recent scholars, however, defend the *Legend* as a total work of art. One position, argued convincingly by Frank (1972), holds that the stories, taken from Ovid's *Heroides*, from the *Metamorphoses* (and the *Ovide moralisé*, cf. Delany 1987), and from Boccaccio's *De claris mulieribus*, are not as bad as some would have us think. Like other medieval story collections, including Gower's *Confessio Amantis*, they have a single, unimpeded narrative line; they recount momentous events in the world of myth; and they make a point, a moral. These tales, treating the most important concerns of mankind (love, honour, and death), are memorable and deserve to be remembered; they are links to the past and even a meaningful guide for the living. Furthermore, they represent a new departure in Chaucer's career; they are his first efforts in brief fiction (a successful striving toward brevity) and his first effort, after *Troilus and Criseyde*, to work directly in the classical tradition and to explore a new range of human experience – tragic or pathetic, non-Christian and, ultimately, non-courtly. For a number of critics, the tragedy and pathos are genuine and aesthetically valid on their own terms; they tell movingly of fidelity and betrayal; they even capture some of the *tremendum* (the religious aura) that should emanate from *legenda aurea*. The *Legend*, which is a superb preparation for the *Canterbury Tales*, also bears witness to Chaucer's will to innovate.

The other position states that the legends are to be interpreted ironically and that Chaucer wrote them as an extension and culmination of the comedy in the *Prologue*. The Narrator is condemned for having translated *Le Roman de la Rose*; he then composes nine classical tales, four of which already appeared as exempla in the *Rose* – the stories of Lucretia, Dido, Phyllis, and Medea. The legends indeed open up a new world of experience; they are dark and tragic. With their villainous men and gullible women they no more uphold the ideals of *fin' amor* than did *Troilus and Criseyde*, perhaps less. With them love leads to disaster. Ostensibly they present a favourable picture of woman but they treat legendary figures some of whom (Cleopatra, Dido, Medea) were generally considered in pejorative terms during the medieval period. And, favourable or not, these classical figures are impulsive, irrational, libidinal, and tyrannical, scarcely an ideal in any society. Furthermore, according to the fiction of the *Prologue*, the Narrator writes these stories uniquely because he is forced to do so by a court order. Therefore, whatever in Virgil, Ovid, Jean de Meun, Machaut, and Boccaccio that runs counter to Cupid's thesis (wicked women and good men) is simply altered or suppressed. Those members of the audience with the slightest literary culture would be aware of the distortion and would call into question the principles of *fin' amor* and the functioning of the trial machinery already mocked in the *Prologue*. They would enjoy the comedy of the Narrator's dishonest selectivity. (The exempla cited by the ladies in *Le Roy de Navarre* are not always apt, either, and for the same reasons.) Chaucer also, following upon the *Prologue*, indulges in religious parody. This 'Seintes Legende of Cupide' is, structurally, a parody on the *Legenda Aurea* yet and, as parody, it tells of pagan figures, all of whom are guilty of lechery and a number of whom commit suicide. Inappropriate, incongruous imagery is used to transform unredeemed sinners into hagiographic martyrs. To the extent that the legends are dull and repetitive, this is the Narrator's failure not Chaucer's, for Chaucer wills the repetitions and the dullness, to force his artistic penance on a court of love that dared make him (his persona) do penance.

Which position was Chaucer's? We can perhaps answer this question by referring back to Machaut's *Roy de Navarre*. There the Narrator is condemned to write a *lai*, a *virelai*, and a *ballade* in praise of women and of love. Only the *lai* is extant in the manuscript tradition, a *Lay de Plour.* It is a highly successful, beautifully composed, rhetorical, and sonorous plaint of bereavement and mourning, in a female voice, a woman suffering over her recently deceased male beloved; thus Machaut yields to the 'Judgment' and composes a poem supportive of the Lady in *Le Jugement dou Roy de Behaingne,* placing the poem implicitly in her mouth. On its own terms, the *lai* ought to be 'taken straight,' as a monument to *fin' amor* as serious and as moving as any of Machaut's other lyrics. On the other hand, given its place in the manuscript tradition, directly after *Le Jugement dou Roy de Navarre,* and given the comic, ironic context of *Le Roy de Navarre,* the sophisticated reader, conceived of as an 'ideal reader,' will also respond to the *Lay de Plour* as comedy and irony.

Such a double vision surely ought to be possible with Chaucer as well. It is by no means unlikely that he leaves his legends to the audience's judgment. Those who believe in *fin' amor* (those who identify with Cupid and Alceste) will take the legends 'straight.' Those who share Machaut's and Chaucer's own ambivalent position toward *fin'amor,* who share their rich literary culture, and who are aware of the distortions of Virgil, Ovid, and Boccaccio in the legends will recognize the art of the poem as comic and ironic. Both responses are acceptable in and for this great poet of 'sceptical fideism' (Delany's term 1972), who, in the *Parliament of Fowls,* the *House of Fame,* and the *Canterbury Tales* asks questions but does not provide answers; to the illusion of a single, authoritative meaning, he prefers an ideological and literary structure of deferral, decentring, and inconclusiveness.

This does not imply, however, as some scholars would have us believe, that in the *Legend of Good Women,* any more than in the *Book of the Duchess* or his other works, Chaucer repudiates the French heritage. He questions and undermines *fin' amor;* so did Jean de Meun and Machaut. He praises it; so did Machaut and Froissart. He cultivates the myths of classical antiquity; so did Guillaume de Lorris, Jean de Meun, Machaut, and Froissart. He invents a new myth of the Daisy; so did Froissart. To the extent that he mocks and undermines *fin' amor,* Chaucer does so from within, as a court poet of *fin' amor.* Like his French predecessors and because of them, he playfully questions courtly conventions, his own role as an artist within the conventional universe, and the textual and intertextual functioning of a conventional and self-conscious book, his own. His *Prologue* and his *Legend* build upon the textual and intertextual foundation of *Le Roman de la Rose, Le Jugement dou Roy de Navarre,* and *Le Paradis d'Amour.* They are the end result of the best in the French tradition; two centuries of this tradition reaches one of its culminations in the intertextual masterpiece that is the *Legend of Good Women*.

3. *The Canterbury Tales*

The old cliché of Chaucer drifting away from French influence in his later 'periods' is now fortunately defunct. Wimsatt (1976) has shown the pervasive textual presence of Machaut, as an authority on *fin' amor* and on Boethian *fortuna*, where we would ordinarily least expect it – in *Troilus and Criseyde*. It is possible that Chaucer adapted a *Roman de Troyle* in conjunction with Boccaccio's *Filostrato* (Pratt 1956); *Troilus* can also be thought of, in C.S. Lewis's words, as Boccaccio medievalized – specifically by being filtered through Machaut. In addition, Nolan (1992) relates *Troilus* to the tradition of the *roman antique*, which is of French origin and as much French as it is Italian. Then, after the *Troilus*, we find Chaucer's first effort at a tale collection – the *Legend of Good Women* – grounded in and based upon the convention of a mock trial and mock condemnation taken directly from Machaut's *Jugement dou Roy de Navarre*. Never has the French presence been so precise, so immediate, and so intertextually vital as in the *Legend of Good Women*.

The *Canterbury Tales* (c. 1386–1400) is a very different kind of text. Here it must be said that the story collection, as a genre or mode, is less specifically French than the dream vision or *dit amoureux*. The 'Italian Chaucer' is rightly assumed to play an important role. However, there is some doubt as to whether Chaucer actually read the *Decameron* or Sercambi's *Novellino*. Most likely, the 'Latin Chaucer' was inspired by Ovid's *Metamorphoses*, a unified narrative structure including a number of individual tales, a common theme, links between the tales, a framing device, on two occasions a story-telling contest, and finally interaction, both psychological and moral, between the tale and its teller. It is also true that, as was so often the case in England, French may have been the vehicle through which Latin and/or Italian culture reached English vernacular writers. Chaucer may have read his Ovid primarily in the *Ovide moralisé*. For that matter, other collections of tales – the *Disciplina clericalis* or the *Septem sapientes* – also, as likely as not, would have reached him in a French translation or adaptation. And some other tale collections that could have inspired or influenced him are also French – the *Ysopet* fable compendium, *Le Livre du chevalier de la Tour Landry*, and William of Waddington's *Manuel des Pechiés*.

For the spirit of Chaucer's book, there are two major French analogues. Chaucer, like Langland, found in Guillaume de Digulleville's sacred allegory, *Pèlerinage de la Vie humaine*, the idea of a great pilgrimage poem in the vernacular, with the crucial motifs of quest, transformation, true and false seekers, edifying and satirical discourse, the growth of the individual, and the judgment of Christian society as a whole. From the great secular allegory, *Le Roman de la Rose*, Chaucer took more. In Guillaume de Lorris he found the structure of his *General Prologue* – evocation of spring, followed by a static list of beings, followed by the active participation of people and the Narrator. Far more significant is the example of Jean de Meun's *Rose* – a Menippean satire of cosmic proportions, a total poem of love and society, presenting a world of carnival burlesque through a sequence of delegated voices engaged in exhortation, debate, and competition, and closed by no one clear-cut, explicit doctrinal line.

From Jean de Meun and also from Machaut and Froissart, Chaucer was inspired in the realm of narrative technique, for he imagined a work of art focused on a community of unself-conscious narrators, including himself, each with his own narrow vision, totally lacking introspection, and telling stories whose interest for us derives in part from the fact that they reflect their tellers' limited insight and imperfect self-knowledge. For such a conception of narrative, one inspiration would be Jean de Meun's *Rose*; another would be Machaut's masterpiece, *Le Voir Dit*, the first I-narrative in modern literature grounded in the limited, restricted point of view of the narrator-hero.

Meanwhile, the Machaldian, Froissardian persona – the inept, comic, narrating author figure – is maintained; indeed he is raised to new heights of brilliance. On one level, the entire *Canterbury Tales*, including but not limited to the *General Prologue*, is filtered through the consciousness of the Narrator, an author figure closely associated with Geoffrey Chaucer. The tales are (re)told in his voice and mirror his powers of style and rhetoric. On another level, the diegetic level of the frame narrative, this author figure is merely one of the pilgrims on the road – an eye-witness observer and an occasional participant. From this perspective, all the pilgrims are author figures as well as reader figures, and so is the Narrator; the controlling literary presence is not Geoffrey Chaucer but Harry Bailey, the innkeeper.

Generations of scholars have debated how we should interpret the narrating persona. This observer who praises to the heights and accepts at face value the Prioress's worldliness, the Monk's virility, the Franklin's good fellowship, the Man of Law's and the Physician's wealth – is he naive and innocent? Is he knowledgeable and sarcastic? Or is 'it' a conventional, rhetorical, and textual voice mirroring no character and no psychology whatsoever?

One thing is certain. Chaucer carries the French persona one step further by having the narrating author figure participate in the story-telling contest on an equal footing with the others and by having him perform far from the best. The Narrator is the only pilgrim to deliver two stories. He tells *Melibee* because the Host interrupted his tale of *Sir Thopas* and wouldn't let him go on because it was so bad. Is the persona a naive, inept, and, above all, bad author figure, who bungles his job with a miserable version of tail-rhyme romance (a genre that the courtly master Geoffrey Chaucer himself despised) and then bungles it even more with a miserably dull moral treatise? Has Chaucer chosen to have himself (his persona) literally tell the worst tales in the entire book? Or, on the contrary, are we witnessing a witty, urbane, sophisticated author figure who plays a joke on the Host and on the other pilgrims, first with a delightful, brilliant parody on contemporary romance that the Host fails to appreciate, and then with a dull, absurd parody on moral treatises (or a 'straight' moral treatise) that the Host has to accept but also misreads as badly as he did the mock romance? In the first case, Chaucer establishes complicity with his audience by distancing himself and them from his persona; in the second case, he establishes complicity by distancing both his persona and the audience from the Host and the other pilgrims. Both techniques have multiple precedents in French courtly *dits amoureux*. What is certain is that Chaucer uses his own presence as an implied author in the narrative to develop the theme of story-telling and of literature and to create a 'Literature Group' of no less significance than the 'Marriage Group.' The Host and the Man of Law – the latter compares the works of Chaucer and Gower, unaware that 'Chaucer' is one of his fellows on the road – are miserable critics and miserable readers of literature. The Narrator, a version of 'Chaucer,' proves to be far from the best of author figures. The complexity, variety, and richness of literary texts and the complexity, variety, and richness of responses to literary texts become a major element in the frame and in the kernel of the *Canterbury Tales*, a metatext in the metatextual tradition of French courtly verse going back directly to *Le Roman de la Rose* and indirectly to the first troubadours.

Finally, in the tales themselves, the French presence is enormous and pervasive. At least twenty-one out of twenty-four have marked literary association with France (cf. Braddy 1979). It is true that, in his masterpiece, Chaucer primarily looks elsewhere than in the direction of the 'advanced' contemporary French courtly mode embodied in Machaut and Froissart. For the extraordinary range of style and subject matter in the *Tales*, Chaucer sought inspiration in fabliaux, *Le Roman de Renart*, satirical texts by Deschamps, and in the more satirical, earthy portions of *Le Roman de la Rose*. He was also inspired by chronicles, saints' lives, romances, and moral and penitential treatises. As Muscatine (1957) has shown, Chaucer derived the range and register of styles, and the notion of a mixed style, from the French legacy. For the first time we find an English author in full command of, and profiting to the utmost from, the entire French literary tradition, in its three golden centuries; this is the intertextual matrix from which Chaucer constructs his *Canterbury Tales*.

The Reeve's Tale

The *Canterbury Tales* mix or juxtapose styles – high, middle, and low; *genus grande*, *genus medium*, and *genus tenue* – all three taken from the Latin and French tradition. The low style is not (as it was once and often still is thought) of bourgeois origin but an habitual, authentic, authorized element of classical rhetoric. It is present in a number of French literary works or modes – *Le Roman de la Rose*, *Le Roman de Renart*, and the fabliaux. In contrast to the dream visions, Chaucer is fascinated by the low in the *Canterbury Tales*, and he adopts extensively from the three French works mentioned above.

There are approximatively one hundred and sixty French fabliaux extant. The fabliau is a brief narrative in verse, often but not always of an erotic nature; the principal characters are the husband, the wife, and the lover, the latter often a priest. The plot concerns the seduction, manipulation, or coercion of one of the three by the other two.

Fabliaux are works of comedy, their principal function being to please and amuse the public. Therefore, the climax is a comic climax, and the comedy is often grounded in repetition or reversal of the initial situation. Action takes precedence over psychology or doctrine or symbolism; descriptions and character analysis contribute to the functioning of the plot.

Although fabliaux generally treat in a naturalistic manner the concrete life of the lower orders, they are not 'realistic' in any modern sense of the term. And, although some are frankly obscene, an equal number are not. The genre ought to be considered consciously and wilfully anticourtly; it is an anticourtly, anti-*fin' amor* response to high romance and the *grand chant courtois* and composed for roughly the same audience as the romance and the courtly lyric. As anticourtly texts, fabliaux revel in what Bakhtin has called the material bodily lower stratum – sex, food, excretion. They also revel in violence and greed. In a conflict between the deceiver and the deceived, the loser is subject to deception (lying, cheating, disguise) and to outright victimization at the hands of the winner. This conflict generally takes place on sexual grounds, is a contest over sexual prerogatives, and is resolved through quick wits – intelligence and ruse – not force. It is a disordered world without ideals, values, or moral law. Instead of raising man to heroic, chivalric heights, the fabliau drags him down to animal depths, but always in a literary, textual context. Although one cannot assimilate this genre to the *chanson de geste* or *roman courtois* as a major contribution to the heritage of Western civilization, the best fabliaux are works of art and very good ones at that.[24]

Chaucer alone, like the greatest French and Italian writers of his age, mastered high culture in all its subtlety and its totality. This includes modes of undermining and demystification. Therefore, the *Canterbury Tales* contain, depending on one's definition of the genre, from four to six fabliaux: the *Miller's Tale*, the *Reeve's Tale*, the *Merchant's Tale*, the *Shipman's Tale*, and, if you will, the *Summoner's Tale* and the incomplete *Cook's Tale*.

Scholars are in agreement that the fabliau gave to Chaucer – not limited to the four, five, or six tales listed above – one among a number of models for the brief narrative, emphasizing neatness and coherence of structure and for that matter unity of time, place, and action. From fabliaux he learned how to portray in literary terms small town or rural life, humdrum detail, and the everyday, authentic, concrete life of the lower classes. The fabliau encouraged his desire to emulate in English the French mixture of styles, especially in the use of authentic spoken idiom, non-courtly familiar dialogue, and dialect. Last but not least, he learned how to portray the broad comedy of sex and deceit in a cruel world of dupers and dupes, of aggression and retaliation. The reader discovers an ironic undermining of literature and life.

Many analogues have been proposed for Chaucer's fabliau texts in the *Canterbury Tales*; a number, in some cases a preponderant majority, of these are French. However, and this is surely a testimony to Geoffrey's originality, in only one case do we have a concrete, identifiable source. Although even here, influenced by the 'great books approach,' some scholars allude only to the analogues or to an international popular comic tale tradition, it has nonetheless been recognized by Olson

(1969), Burbridge (1971), and Goodall (1980), among others, that for the *Reeve's Tale* Chaucer was inspired by the French fabliau 'Le Meunier et les ii clers,' and perhaps also by Jean Bodel's variation on 'Le Meunier,' 'Gombert et les ii clercs.'

A number of Anglicists, in comparing 'Le Meunier' and the *Reeve's Tale*, assume and hope to demonstrate that Chaucer always and in every detail improves on his source. Here the nationalism that influenced an earlier generation of literary scholars is to be found. True, the *Reeve's Tale* is itself a masterpiece, superbly integrated into the total masterpiece, the *Canterbury Tales*. 'Le Meunier et les ii clers' inevitably proves to be a less rich and complex text than its English adaptation. Nonetheless, it is a very good fabliau, excellent on its own terms. And, especially in terms of narrative, it can hold its own in the inevitable comparison with the *Reeve's Tale*.

The plot, in both 'Le Meunier' and the *Reeve's Tale*, concerns two clerks who bring grain to be ground at the mill. The miller tricks the boys, stealing from them, and then allows them to spend the night in a bed in his family's room. In the dark the first clerk succeeds in deflowering the miller's daughter. The second, by moving a cradle (containing the miller's baby) from next to the miller's bed to alongside his own, causes the miller's wife to enter his bed by mistake; he pounces on her, cuckolding the miller. However, the first clerk, returning from the daughter, because of the cradle also mistakes beds; he enters the miller's and boasts to his bedmate about his sexual conquest. A brawl ensues. The miller is beaten, and the clerks make off, having recovered their stolen goods.

In contrast to the Chaucerian treatment, 'Le Meunier' tells of two young men who initially are unaware that they have been robbed. Thus, they enjoy the women of the house not out of competition or revenge vis-à-vis the miller but simply driven by animal instinct. The animal instinct is 'natural,' perhaps, but, above all, obscene and antifeminist; for example, in the recounting of his night's exploits the first clerk boasts:

> 'et si fait trop bon foutre en huche!
> Conpeignon, car va, si t'i muce
> et si pran do bacon ta part:
> assez en a jusq'a la hart.
> Par .VII. foiz l'ai anuit corbee ... ' (279–83)

'Fucking is great in a *huche*. Old buddy, now go, hide in there and take your share of the meat; there is plenty still up to the rope. I screwed her seven times in this one night.'

Here we see literary anti-*fin' amor* and literary sarcasm. Vile animal desire and mockery in the fabliau correspond to a no less vile sense of revenge in Chaucer. The one is not necessarily superior to the other. Furthermore, it is perhaps still more humiliating for the miller to be punished by accident (by coincidence so to speak) than by conscious intent; an ironic 'poetic justice' occurs here, absent in the *Reeve's Tale*. It is perhaps a still more ironic commentary on the human condition that the two poor clerks prove to be 'naturally' as vicious and as nasty vis-à-vis their host as he was to them; human nature is as defiled in the clerks as in the miller.

At the end, of course, the clerks do discover that they have been robbed, and they recover their losses. In Chaucer, Aleyn is informed by the daughter. In 'Le Meunier,' in an unusually deft touch, after the miller realizes that both his daughter and his wife have dishonoured him, he quarrels with the wife, unjustly beating her for being a whore. She then responds, quite justly accusing him of being a thief. It is an excellent ironic twist of the plot that the miller himself brings about the boys' discovery of his knavery and, therefore, the financial as well as sexual reversal. Furthermore, in 'Le Meunier' the miller is punished in his knowledge; this is the only version in which he *sees*, and we know that he sees, the evidence of his cuckolding.

In the French fabliau the miller steals the clerks' mare; in Chaucer, Symkin releases Aleyn's and John's stallion. The stallion symbolism is excellent, as scholars have noted; however, the mare has a valid symbolic function in the fabliau. The miller thought he would appropriate permanently the clerks' female horse, of no sexual interest to him. The clerks see to it that the appropriation is only provisional; in the meantime, they appropriate the miller's wife and daughter provisionally, of great sexual interest to all. A neat ironic parallelism is established, obviously to the miller's detriment. And the imagery of reification of female bodies, and of their possession, expropriation, and exploitation by men, is powerful and graphic.

Finally, there is the question of an episode in the fabliau that Chaucer suppressed, one that many find superfluous and unrealistic. In 'Le Meunier' the daughter is locked up in a 'huche.' The first clerk takes a useless ring from the andiron on the hearth and tells her that it is gold and that it will restore her virginity. An exchange is made. The girl gives him the key and he enters the 'huche' and deflowers her. The incident is not especially realistic (although until recently Breton peasants slept in a *lit clos* or placard bed). The point, of course, is to demonstrate that the girl is unusually stupid and greedy, and that she is seduced not raped; also that she is hoarded as a commodity by her father and literally locked up in a coffer, much as he would lock up gold and jewels or for that matter the clerks' wheat. Once again, parallelism is established for, later in the night, the second clerk, like the first, uses his wits to attain his ends, and has his way with a stupid, greedy woman, the miller's wife, who participated in the theft and who is not perceptive enough to distinguish one man from another in the dark.

The incident of the key, ring, and placard bed reinforces a pattern of exchange, of reification, and of low phallic imagery. Keys open locks and placard-coffers; rings prove to be of little value, whether made of gold, iron, or vaginal flesh. But above all, 'Le Meunier' and its French analogue 'Gombert' use this episode to increase the action. Bergson insists upon the element of repetition inherent in comedy. In a genre such as the fabliau, repetition contributes to the comic structure, and the piling up of incident and the acceleration of action are essential aspects of the genre. Chaucer recognizes this, for he does the same, accelerating the action with unlikely plot increments in the *Miller's Tale*, the text that precedes the Reeve's performance.

This said, like the French texts but with more detail and greater depth, Chaucer emphasizes his fabliau's 'rustic naturalism' and its functioning as literature, especially anticourtly literature. In imitation of other fabliaux, where languages, including French spoken by an Englishman, are mocked, Chaucer has Aleyn and John speak in an unfashionable, uncourtly North English dialect. Transplanted from a French 'bochage' to the Cambridgeshire fens, the locus is the one-room peasant home, with emphasis on drinking, snoring, making water, and horse and pig imagery. In a delightful touch Chaucer has Aleyn part from Maline in the morning with a parody on the Occitan *alba* (cf. Kaske 1959), only, as in the fabliau, to boast vulgarly of his conquest twenty-five lines further on:

'Fare weel, Malyne, sweete wight!
The day is come; I may no lenger byde;
But everemo, wher so I go or ryde,
I is thyn awen clerk, swa have I seel!' (I 4236–9)

'Thou John, thou swynes-heed, awak,
For Cristes saule, and heer a noble game.

> For by that lord that called is Seint Jame,
> As I have thries in this shorte nyght
> Swyved the milleres doghter bolt upright,
> Whil thow hast, as a coward, been agast.' (I 4262–7)

It is also clear that Symkin himself is a parody of the *gilos* in *fin' amor* texts – a husband fiercely jealous of his wife, who insists she be treated like a lady and called a 'dame.' Both Aleyn and John are parodies of the courtly knight lover but, of course, play the role of clerical trickster or peasant rapist instead.

It is well known that the major difference between the *Reeve's Tale* and its sources lies in the fact that Chaucer's is a world not of animal appetite but one of competition and vengeance. From the beginning the clerks and Symkin engage in a battle of wits; there is a contest in which the body is used as a weapon. Aleyn and John know that Symkin is a thief, who has been robbing their college for years. They pretend to be stupid in order to monitor the grinding of the grain, and catch Symkin in the act. The latter, aware of the ruse, deceives them by releasing their horse, causing the 'sely clerkes' to abandon their watch and tire themselves running over the fens in search of poor Bayard. They return worn out, robbed, and knowing they have been robbed:

> 'Allas,' quod John, 'the day that I was born!
> Now are we dryve til hethyng and til scorn.
> Oure corn is stoln; men wil us fooles calle,
> Bathe the wardeyn and oure felawes alle,
> And namely the millere, weylaway!' (I 4109–13)

At this point Symkin proves to be overcomplacent. Moved by greed, with silver dazzling before his eyes, he agrees to keep the clerks in his house for the night. Moved by pride, he mocks them for their clerical knowledge. Moved by gluttony, he and his family eat and drink too much. In more or less a drunken stupor, father, mother, and daughter snore away. As Brown (1979-80) and Kolve (1984) have indicated, in the cramped, restricted space of the dark room, five people share three beds. Then, inevitably, hostility is unleashed, taking the form of libido and violence. The stallion – Aleyn and John's horse released by Symkin – symbolizes the boys' libido. Because Symkin keeps the clerks awake with his snoring like a horse they become animals in turn. In competition with Symkin, Aleyn 'releves' himself by all but raping Maline, taking her flower in exchange for his stolen flour at the mill. Then, in competition with Aleyn, John moves the cradle and takes Symkin's wife. 'He priketh harde and depe' (I 4231), as he would a horse. As in the French source, Aleyn's false promise of love and John's silence retaliate for Symkin's false promise of grain and his wife's silence. And, as in the French, Aleyn's healthy, 'productive' fatigue (three acts of intercourse) retaliates for the negative fatigue to which Symkin had subjected him earlier.

Like the French fabliau miller, Symkin is proud of his shrewdness. In addition, the Reeve endows him with brute strength and inappropriate snobbery; he is proud of his wife and of her pedigree and the daughter's (his wife is the bastard daughter of the village priest). Aleyn and John defeat him on all three levels. He is outsmarted, for the boys recover the stolen wheat in the form of a loaf and make off with it. Symkin is beaten physically by them with the unwitting help of the wife who strikes him on his bald pate in error. And he is humiliated sexually, as the clerks enjoy his wife and his daughter. According to the mill-imagery in the tale, also taken from 'Le Meunier,'[25] Symkin the man is the natural grinder and feeder into the female mill. But, asleep and impotent, others grind in his mill and run off with his (their) loaf. The deflowering of Maline also makes her eventual marriage to a man of higher class unlikely, thereby dashing Symkin's social pretentions.

Class conflict, endemic in the fabliau tradition, comes to the forefront in this tale. Symkin is depicted as a parvenu, a mere peasant with ridiculous social pretentions. He believes he is superior to the other peasants in the village and superior to Aleyn and John, stronger, shrewder, wealthier, and more successful than they are. It is true, the students are 'sely,' and their Northern accent situates them in a different world from the narrator of the *Clerk's Tale*. Nonetheless, low-class, provincial, and 'sely' as they are, they prove to be higher and better than their adversary. As in the French fabliaux, the courtly audience and clerkly author instinctively prefer clerks to peasants. The peasant family is the collective scapegoat.

Although Aleyn and John 'releve' themselves motivated by competition and vengeance (not love or even healthy libido), the *Reeve's Tale* does partake of the standard fabliau ethos, also shared by Roman comedy: the triumph of young men over old, of the id over the superego, of freedom over the perverted social order imposed by a bully and a tyrant, and, perhaps most of all, the triumph of flexibilty over rigidity. Symkin is guilty of the Bergsonian comic flaw; 'du mécanique plaqué sur du vivant,' he is rigid in his snobbery, his greed, his animality, and his insufferable self-assurance.

The paradox in the *Reeve's Tale* centres on Symkin's reversal of fortune. The self-assured master proves to be a slave and the torturer a victim, whereas the slaves and victims end as masters. Or, to use the terminology of New Comedy popularized by Frye, a self-assured *eiron* discovers that he is the *alazon* and a *miles gloriosus* to boot, this brought about because the two seeming *agroikoi* prove to be victorious *juvenes* with a touch of *dolosi servi* in their makeup.

The conscious, wilful destruction of Symkin in so absolute a manner by the inscribed narrator, the Reeve, and by the implied author, Geoffrey Chaucer, brings us to the relationship between the teller and the tale. This sort of question, endemic to Chaucer studies, is not valid for the French fabliau world; among other things, it indicates the extent to which the *Reeve's Tale*, in the context of the *Canterbury Tales* as a whole, inevitably manifests a degree of complexity not to be found in 'Le Meunier et les ii clers.' The traditional position, dominant from Kittredge (1915) to Lumiansky (1955), that the tale does indeed reveal the psychology of the teller, is currently out of fashion. Recent studies often dismiss with scorn the once-honoured term 'roadside drama.' Today's scholars[26] are right to point out the distortion involved in determining artificially the character or psychology of the teller based upon evidence from the ideal type-figure of the *General Prologue* and the comic interaction (the link) between tales, and then to reduce the tale to functioning as a manifestation or a symptom of that psychology. Such an approach can detract from truly great tales and, especially with the allegorical or typological approach, impose ironic condemnation, from an Augustinian Christian perspective, on tellers and tales when both are in fact innocent and the tale ought to be 'taken straight'; such would be the case, I believe, for the *Man of Law's Tale*, the *Franklin's Tale*, the *Monk's Tale*, and the *Prioress's Tale*, among others. According to Rogers (1986), each tale is a world-view that Geoffrey the witness, Chaucer the implied author, and we the implied audience share for the duration of the telling; each such world-view then proves to be unsatisfactory and gives way to another. The *Canterbury Tales* are a sequence of world-visions as well as a sequence of tales. Furthermore, literary genre and level of style play as important a role in determining the mood and the world-view of a tale as does the psychology of the teller. The literary reality of any one tale comprises a synthesis of elements that is finally manifest in a voice, the voice of the text and tale. It is this voice and this textuality that create the teller, not the contrary.

All this is true. Nonetheless, Chaucer's tales do not exist alone, as discrete diegetic entities, but within a frame, and the Chaucerian frame is more important than in any other medieval story collection. The frame is also diegetic; it tells the story of a series of confrontations between the tellers, mimetic characters who are engaged in a story-telling contest while on a pilgrimage from Southwark to Canterbury. From an extradiegetic perspective Geoffrey Chaucer is the omniscient creator of his characters and text, and we the implied readers are his implied audience and also the judges of his characters and his text. On the other hand, within the frame diegesis, the pilgrims are, in turn, authors and audience, the Host is the judge, and Geoffrey is, in the Machaut-Froissart tradition, for the most part simply a witness and observer to these events, except for the period when he becomes a comic participant – the worst of the author figures – in his turn.

In a good number of cases the tale is, to some degree, characteristic of the teller or, at least, of his 'type' or 'estate'; it mirrors and therefore helps reveal his social class, aesthetic taste, moral or religious stance, and, sometimes, his personal or caste obsessions. In the pilgrimage narrative, each tale is a monologue pronounced by its teller. Why should it not contribute to our understanding of him or her and, from time to time, to the inner drama that *is* him or her?

Sometimes, according to the frame diegesis, the tale comes into being as one result of an outer drama, the competition or quarreling or emulation or flattery between the tellers. Not only because of the spatial ordering in the Ellesmere manuscript (subject to caution) but also because of the chronological sequence of telling within each of the extant groupings of tales, most tales do comment on the preceding tale or tales. The stories form an intertextual chain, each link of which 'contains' textually one or more of the preceding links.

Therefore, it is not wrong to posit that our understanding of both the tale and the teller can benefit from a sympathetic and sensitive analysis of the relationship between them, and of both the inner and the outer drama, when they in fact do exist. The links and even the *General Prologue* can deepen our appreciation of the tales, the total human experience, and the total work of art. To refuse such analysis a priori can impoverish our reading of Chaucer in both the short and the long run.

A number of scholars have suggested that the modifications Chaucer brings to 'Le meunier et les ii clers' are oriented toward and shaped by the narrative situation of the *Reeve's Tale* in the total *Canterbury Tales* diegesis; the Reeve, an active, intrusive narrator, directs his story against the Miller, his immediate predecessor in the story-telling contest. Therefore, I believe the traditional consensus is correct when it observes, from the *Reeve's Prologue* and the last line of his tale, 'Thus have I quyt the Millere in my tale' (I 4324), that Oswald the Reeve is furious at his immediate predecessor in the Canterbury narrations, Robin the Miller. The *Miller's Tale* is a fabliau, the victim and scapegoat of which is an old fool, cuckold, and carpenter by trade. Now the Reeve tells us he is old and used to be a carpenter; he also states openly that the *Miller's Tale* is directed against him personally. Given the context, we have reason to believe that Oswald is mistaken. We can conclude, given the Miller's temperament and his drunken state, that, despite Oswald's intervention, he scarcely took into account the Reeve's existence at the time of his performance. Thus the Reeve is guilty of confusing illusion with reality and determining that Robin's story was meant to be historical or doctrinal when, in fact, it is not; in other words, Oswald takes the game of the story-telling contest too seriously, making excessive earnest out of the game.

Why should he do so? Why this error in communication? In part, because millers and reeves represent two competing professional trades; theirs is an example of craft conflict within the lower classes, the sort of conflict that, like the narrative content of both fabliaux, would amuse the upper-class Chaucerian implied audience. Thus would be extended to the tales themselves the estates satire that Mann (1973) has shown to be so prominent a structuring device in the *General Prologue*. Even more, Chaucer has created a situation in which the two characters embody divergent temperaments; Robin is a bluff, brash, hearty extrovert, the man who heads the pilgrimage procession playing his bagpipes, whereas Oswald is an old, puritanical, gloomy, hypersensitive introvert and outsider, who brings up the rear. We can presume that antipathy exists between them, expecially on Oswald's side, comparable to the antipathy between Roland and Ganelon, Tristan and the felons, or Lancelot and Agravain. The key image from the *General Prologue* is the rusty sword that Oswald bears, an image of phallic decay corroborated by the obsessive meditation on phallic decline in old age that constitutes the prologue to his tale. Such a man would instinctively loathe the seemingly potent Miller and the joyful life-exalting, Rabelaisian quality of the *Miller's Tale*.

As a result, the Reeve does precisely what the Miller did not do; he denounces the morality of his predecessor's tale and directs his own performance against Robin, *ad hominem*. Symkin, as the Reeve portrays him, is a bluff, hearty, swaggering caricature of Robin. And the *Reeve's Tale*, as a tale, parallels and seeks both to undermine and to surpass the *Miller's Tale*, with Cambridge substituted for Oxford, two women seduced instead of one, two seducers successful instead of one, and the victim a knave as well as a fool and punished on three or four levels not just one. Furthermore, the Miller's Rabelaisian joy in earthy sensuality is undercut by a text in which the motivating forces are greed and competition, a world-view in which people such as Robin prove to be fools.

To what extent the *Reeve's Tale* reveals Oswald's psychology, and to what extent Oswald's psychology ought to colour our reading of the *Tale* is a more delicate matter. The Reeve announces, 'I shal hym quite anoon; / Right in his cherles termes wol I speke' (I 3916–17) which means that he will tell a churl's story in a churl's style, a fabliau against a fabliau, for his revenge. The fabliau of Symkin the miller does not, therefore, necessarily correspond to Oswald the Reeve's personal literary taste or register of speech. Furthermore, in my opinion, some scholars have overemphasized what they deem to be the mean, dirty, base, nasty qualities of the *Reeve's Tale*. From a continental perspective, the tale itself is no more mean, dirty, nasty, and base than *Le Roman de Renart*, *Le Roman de la Rose*, and most fabliaux. Like them it presents a powerful existential world-view in which mankind is driven by competition, greed, and violence – by the inherent will to dominate and not be dominated, and to be a master not a slave, a knave not a fool – and in which love, compassion, and Christian faith are largely absent. Although Oswald's is not the only world-view in the *Canterbury Tales*, nor the most complete, it is a legitimate one, in human as well as in textual terms, and I do not believe we are meant to reject it, either because of some secret self-revelation on his part or because of some abstract philosophy of Augustinian Christianity on Chaucer's.

Finally, both the *Miller's Tale* and the *Reeve's Tale*, both Robin the Miller and Oswald the Reeve, form part of a grander literary design (cf. Kolve 1984). Fragment I includes them as well as the *Knight's Tale* and the extant fragment of the *Cook's Tale*, a literary design in which order progressively gives way to disorder, harmony to disharmony, high to low, and idealism to demystification. The fabliaux provide Chaucer with a register of low style (the North English dialect, the snoring and pig imagery, 'swyved,' etc.) and low subject matter. Deception, aggression, and sexual domination, a cruel world of competition, violence, and ruse on the one hand, and a concrete, material world of bread, ale, homes, hearths, and beds, on the other hand – these form a striking social, psychological, literary, and textual contrast to the high world and high texts of the Knight and the Man of Law. The low world and the low texts that create it can contribute magnificently to a total work of high art. Chaucer has learned the supreme lesson from Jean de Meun, for the fabliaux in the *Canterbury Tales* contribute to the psychological and intertextual agon and to the author's total, complex *oeuvre*.

The Merchant's Tale

The *Merchant's Tale* is often considered to be Chaucer's greatest fabliau. A fabliau it is, in the central narrative and the ending. The ending tells how a blind old man (January) is jealous of his young wife (May). She cuckolds him with a young bachelor (Damian), in her husband's pleasure garden, in the branches of a pear tree. When January's sight is miraculously restored and he actually sees the guilty couple *in flagrante delicto*, May convinces him (1) that she has discovered a magical means to cure her husband's blindness which involves a 'struggle' with a man in a tree; (2) that they were struggling, not making love; and (3) that January suffers from an optical illusion, for it takes time to recover from blindness. The fabliau situation is repeated and reinforced on another level; Pluto and Proserpina enter the garden. The god takes the husband's side, and the goddess the wife's. It is Pluto who ends January's blindness and Proserpina who grants to May (and to all women) the wit to talk her way out of such predicaments. Thus the comic domestic quarrel of the gods reflects and shapes the comic agon between the human couple, with the identical outcome; in both cases the female triumphs over the male. We find in the denouement of the *Merchant's Tale* comic fabliau elements at their best: rapidly expanding action, a double surprise (intercourse in the pear tree, the interaction of the gods) and therefore a double, repeated comic climax, and one recognition and reversal of fortune (January's discovery) followed by escape and a second reversal of fortune (May's speech of self-justification).

Like the French fabliaux and like the *Reeve's Tale*, the *Merchant's Tale* contains a powerful satire on *fin' amor*. We are told that January is a knight and Damian is his squire. January refers to his squire as a 'gentil man,' and 'gentil May' refers to herself as a 'gentil womman.' We hear of Damian's love sickness and of May's eventual cure of the sickness with her 'franchise' and 'pitee.' In fact, January is a disgusting, senile fool, a *senex amans* of the worst sort become the traditional *gilos*, who will literally not allow his wife out of reach. Damian is a servant in the house, fawning like a spaniel to attain his ends; he pays court to May after only four days of love sickness, and she accepts his love after only four days of marriage. She maintains courtly discretion (*mezura*) by reading and then dropping the boy's love letter into the privy. All Damian wants is sex, and the promise of sex suffices to end his pain. Indeed, their *fin' amor* results in one brief act of copulation, in the branches of a tree, into which May climbs on her husband's back. Hence the sardonic, powerful irony of the Merchant's commentary on their relationship, pronouncing *in sensu malo* the Chaucerian courtly line, 'Lo, pitee renneth soone in gentil herte!' (IV 1986).

At the same time, unlike the *Reeve's Tale*, the *Merchant's Tale* is much more than a fabliau. Damian and May embody a travesty of *fin' amor* and January and May embody a travesty of marriage. The real subject of the tale is not love; it is marriage. The entire first half recounts January's decision to wed, his deliberations with Justinus and Placebo on marriage, his choice of a bride, the wedding itself, and the disastrous wedding night. Justinus, Placebo, and January indulge in an 'altercacioun,' a 'disputisoun,' itself a comic verbal agon on the nature of marriage. The *Merchant's Tale* thus enters into the tradition of intellectual debate and satire associated with allegories, the high point of which is Jean de Meun's *Roman de la Rose*.

Although among the analogues to the tale are to be found a number of French fabliaux, two fables by Marie de France, a Latin *comoedia Lydiae*, and a story by Boccaccio, there is no direct source for the pear tree denouement. Still, three fabliaux develop the theme of a wife and her lover copulating before the husband's eyes and convincing him that his eyes lie; others contain the motif of the stolen key. More important for our purposes, perhaps, the marriage debate is of immediate French provenance. Economou (1965) and Calabrese (1990) examine echoes from *Le Roman de la Rose*. Chaucer was also influenced, perhaps by Jehan le Fèvre's 1371–2 translation of Matheolus' antifeminist *Lamentationes* and by *Le Livre du chevalier de la Tour Landry*, and most probably by Eustache Deschamps' *Miroir de mariage*.[27] In Deschamps' book – a satirical *disputatio* influenced by Matheolus and, above all, by Jean de Meun – Franc Vouloir considers whether or not to get married. Désir, Folie, Servitude, and Faintise speak in favour of the institution; Répertoire de Science sends him an epistle adopting the opposite stance. In the end, Franc Vouloir decides against marriage, opting instead for the spiritual life.

The fundamental structure of *Le Miroir de mariage*, the counsel of true and false friends, the main arguments for and against, and the use of allegorical names are taken over into the *Merchant's Tale*. A psychomachia through debate and discussion, in which a man of middle years makes up his mind and grows in maturity, is transformed into a farce in which an old man, his mind already made up, scarcely listens to his brothers, and the ideas are never really debated at all. In Deschamps the protagonist makes the right choice, in Chaucer he makes the wrong one. The spiritual life and a reasonable hope for paradise become the farcical conjugal paradise of a cuckolded, semi-impotent fool. Themes and motifs highlighted in Chaucer – the difficulty of satisfying a young wife, the danger of jealousy, the bizarre food appetites of pregnant women, woman's infinite capacity for verbal deceit, and the imagery of paradise, birds, and fruit – also appear in Deschamps. What Chaucer has done, in brilliant fashion, is to adapt the *Miroir de mariage* scenario to a fabliau context – mimetic fiction – and to reduce it to a mimesis of some 1200 lines.

January's flaw, of course, is to be sixty years old and to seek and find a bride of twenty. According to any medieval system of *gradus vitae hominis* – the four or five or seven ages of man – he has now reached *senectus*, the winter of life symbolized by his hoary locks. Unfit for the game of love, according to Andreas Capellanus and Eustache Deschamps, he should turn his thoughts from the world and the flesh to the attainment of wisdom. *Sagesse*, however, is the last of January's concerns; on the contrary, he is obsessed with the world and the flesh. In this, and in his inappropriate marriage, he wilfully transgresses the laws of Nature. May and Damian, both in the flower of youth, follow natural law in their mutual attraction. Their victory over January is the same comic victory as in the *Reeve's Tale*, that of youth over age, life over death, and freedom over tyranny.

It is also the Bergsonian comic triumph of flexibility over rigidity. January is the Bergsonian comic character par excellence, a fanatic, obsessed in his commitment to marriage, to marrying a young girl, and to doing it quickly. He has several fixations, won't listen to reason, and can't be budged. In his praise of marriage he exalts it in the wrong terms and cites the wrong authorities. Justinus and Placebo serve as excellent foils to convince the implied reader of January's folly, indeed his madness, because Justinus' arguments are so superior to Placebo's that one has to be obsessed to continue as January does, on the path that he takes.

Furthermore, our *senex amans* is sincere but guilty of the most revolting Sartrean bad faith. A bachelor who has actively been cuckolding husbands for most of his sixty years now wants to take a wife; he wants to have an heir, he says, and to merit salvation by avoiding the capital sin of lechery. He is, alas, utterly sincere. However, in point of fact he simply wishes to satisfy *luxuria* within marriage; hence his insistence upon a young girl, tender veal not old beef, as he puts it:

'But o thyng warne I yow, my freendes deere,
I wol noon oold wyf han in no manere.
She shal nat passe twenty yeer, certayn;
Oold fissh and yong flessh wolde I have fayn.
Bet is,' quod he, 'a pyk than a pykerel,
And bet than old boef is the tendre veel.' (IV 1415–20)

And January's justification for having a young bride – to be certain she is fertile and to be able to mould her character and therefore not be deceived by her – fools no one. On the contrary, these arguments merely testify to his bad faith and to his weakness.

A major theme of the poem is January's self-delusion. Although lacking introspection, the man is nonetheless totally self-centred. He fails to know himself and his wife; hence the farce of the wedding night. January boasts of his sexual powers, makes much of his 'greenness' and 'corage,' even pities May for the virile performance she, as a bride, will have to endure. Well he might pity her, but for the opposite reason. In spite of the aphrodisiacs he imbibes, the wedding night proves to be a catastrophe, with January all but impotent yet gleeful in whatever he has been able to do after hours of labour. The Merchant shows us May's apparent goodness, innocence, and very real passivity, from January's point of view, and then January's senescent ugliness from May's point of view. May says nothing; we can only guess what she really thinks of her groom, until the omniscient, intrusive Narrator for one line states the truth:

The slakke skyn aboute his nekke shaketh
Whil that he sang, so chaunteth he and craketh.
But God woot what that May thoughte in hir herte,
Whan she hym saugh up sittynge in his sherte,
In his nyght-cappe, and with his nekke lene;
She preyseth nat his pleyyng worth a bene. (IV 1849–54)

That January should refer to his future bride as tender veal not old beef, that he should seek a young bride in order to mould her like wax, is significant. He treats May like a thing, not a person. She is literally the fruit of his treasure and, after he is struck by blindness, he keeps his hand on her at all times. He touches her the way a miser touches coin; he keeps her in the house or in the pleasure garden as a miser locks his treasure in a box or a room. The relationship of January to May (for that matter the relationship between all three characters) is one of reification, in which, despite the courtly speeches, all three treat each other as objects and as commodities, and where the unique human rapport is one of exchange: money for sex, sex for money, or sex for sex.

In the beginning, Justinus warns that love is blind; toward the end, January becomes physically blind. This is, on one level, sexual punishment (the oedipal punishment, as it turns out) for sins against law of kind, i.e., for indulging in *amor* during the age of *senectus*; the blindness is a reinforcement of *senectus* and symbolic castration or impotence. Also, it is obvious that the poor creature has been morally, intellectually, and spiritually blind throughout; he has never looked at May the person and he has never seen the real Damian. Then, at the denouement, with his vision restored, January remains sightless; he will not accept the evidence of his eyes and, blinded by May's rhetoric, leaves the garden stroking her belly, *cocu et content*. His blindness is one of the dominant Chaucerian images in this text so rich in imagery.

Another pattern of imagery in the *Merchant's Tale*, the one most dependent on the French, is composed of gardens, trees, and fruit. The pleasure garden that January constructs in order to make love to his wife alone in the daytime, in order for 'thynges whiche that were nat doon abedde, / He in the gardyn parfourned hem and spedde' (IV 2051–2), is derived from *Le Roman de la Rose*. Employing the common *impossibilia* topic of rhetoric, the Merchant says:

> For, out of doute, I verraily suppose
> That he that wroot the Romance of the Rose
> Ne koude of it the beautee wel devyse. (IV 2031–3)

Like Guillaume de Lorris's Garden of Delight, January's garden is a *locus amoenus* of great beauty, enclosed by walls, with a narrow wicket, the only key of which is jealously kept by January. As in Guillaume de Lorris, the situation is Freudian. The garden is enclosed, a *hortus conclusus* redolent with vaginal imagery, through whose narrow entrance January penetrates with his phallic key. However, in contrast to Lorris, where, by the way, Vieillesse is excluded, Chaucer makes of his garden a mock *locus amoenus*, in which Lorris's delicate allegorical equilibrium is consciously debased, for the garden is used for overtly sexual purposes, just as May's young body is salaciously desecrated by contact with her senile husband. How ironic, and symbolic, that May, whom January expected to mould like wax, makes a wax imprint of the key and gives it to Damian. Damian now has the same phallic power and prerogatives as January. In a similar, ironic vein, January claimed, in defence of marriage, that a man cannot be wounded by his own knife; as it turns out, he will be erotically bested by the squire who carves meat at his own table.

Earlier in the tale January imagined in the mirror of his mind which girl of his acquaintance he ought to marry. Gazing into the mirror of the Fountain of Love prior to choosing a rose is again one of the central elements in Guillaume de Lorris. Lorris's mirror-fountain in the garden, where the gatekeeper is Oiseuse, is the source for Chaucer's ironic 'mirour ... in a commune market-place' (IV 1582–3). Whereas gazing into the crystals of the Fountain of Love opens up an entire world for Lorris's protagonist, January dreams away in idleness, denying reality. It is as if, in January's narcissism, Chaucer reverses Guillaume de Lorris, yet also reverts to Lorris's original conception of the mirror, the Ovidian Fountain of Narcissus. Furthermore (here Chaucer perhaps remembered Jean de Meun's skeptical analysis of optics), mirrors can reflect accurately and they can distort; poor January's imagination is hardly the most dependable of mirrors. He chooses the wrong rose bud, and she ceases to be a love object. She becomes an active human being, and a subject, on her own.

Both Guillaume de Lorris and Jean de Meun concentrate on flower imagery; their narratives tell of courting and seduction. Although Jean de Meun's characters praise reproduction and fecundity, the relationships portrayed in his section of the *Rose* are located outside of marriage. Having scattered pollen inside the petals, it is possible but by no means certain that Jean's Lover has become a father. To put it bluntly, in *Le Roman de la Rose* flowers are plucked; they do not become fruit.

Chaucer takes off from his French predecessors by bringing his lovers together in marriage and by raising the question of issue. Hence he substitutes fruit imagery for the flower imagery of the *Rose*. January states that one of the reasons for his decision to wed is to have an heir. The eventual mother of his heir will be the fruit of his treasure. Hoary he may be on the outside, he claims, but he is green within. Yet, as we know, May will seek other fruit from another plant. As an excuse for climbing the pear tree in the garden (substituted for Guillaume de Lorris's pine tree), May intimates that she is pregnant and that green pears are the gustatory caprice of an expectant mother:

> 'I moste han of the peres that I see,
> Or I moot dye, so soore longeth me
> To eten of the smale peres grene.
> Help, for hir love that is of hevene queene!
> I telle yow wel, a womman in my plit
> May han to fruyt so greet an appetit
> That she may dyen but she of it have.' (IV 2331–7)

Pears are a traditional phallic image in folklore, and the implied audience knows that Damian is the fruit waiting for her in the branches of the tree. January salaciously assimilated his sexual desires for a young bride to his culinary preferences for fish and flesh; May does the same, associating Damian's body with the green pears she claims to desire. So, in the end, May satisfies her lust (for Damian) just as January did (for May), and she, having given her vaginal fruit, receives a hard pear in exchange. Ultimately, the green January, grasping the pear tree, can only assist his wife in her coupling with another man; and his only fruit proves to be the branches of the tree he grasps, symbolic horns sprouting from his own cuckolded head. May hints that she is pregnant, telling January precisely what he wants to hear. She thus manoeuvres him into allowing her to climb the tree, the one place where he believes she cannot deceive him. Is she pregnant, from January? Is she lying? Is she telling the truth, about to be impregnated by the more virile Damian? The Merchant does not say; nor does Chaucer. We are meant to speculate on the indeterminate, deferred answer to this question as January leaves the garden fondly stroking his wife's belly: 'He kisseth hire and clippeth hire ful ofte, / And on hire wombe he stroketh hire ful softe' (IV 2413–14).

With the exception of the pear tree episode, once January has gone blind he never takes his hand off May and never allows her out of arm's reach. Thus, from a literary parody on Guillaume's and Jean's Lover, he becomes the embodiment of Jean's Jealous Husband. Unlike le Jaloux's wife, May is willing to disrobe and allow January his conjugal rights. Also, although she offers herself to Damian, it is for love not money. Money she gets from January. She fleeces her husband, convincing him of her innocence and good reputation and proclaiming that she keeps his honour; then immediately thereafter she betrays him. She proves Jean de Meun's Jaloux to be accurate in his analysis of women and marriage – le Jaloux is wiser than January – and she follows the advice of Jean's la Vieille perfectly; she fleeces an old man and enjoys a young one, using both and used by none.

Chaucer also expanded on Guillaume de Lorris by placing classical gods – the greatest of the gods – in his garden. In my opinion, here, above all, he was influenced by Machaut; Machaut's presence is felt precisely where Chaucer alludes to *Le Roman de la Rose. La Fonteinne amoureuse*, the most important source for the *Book of the Duchess*, will account alone for why the gods are associated with the fairies in January's grove. In *La Fonteinne* Machaut's Narrator says that his garden was Cupid's 'demours' (1381), and that Venus, Jupiter, nymphs, and fays came there regularly to take their pleasure. The garden, and more particularly the Fountain of Love at its center (the artistic *mise en abyme* for the book in its entirety) were constructed by Cupid and by Pygmalion, under Venus' orders and at Jupiter's instigation. The Machaldian Narrator and his Knight fall asleep and dream of a visit from Venus, who provides consolation and comfort to the victimized Knight and who, in recounting the Wedding of Peleus and Thetis, to which she and Bacchus were invited, recalls her interest in the figure of Priapus.

Chaucer's Merchant also tells of a garden and a well, made by January, whose wedding Venus and Bacchus attended. It is so beautiful that neither the author of *Le Roman de la Rose* nor Priapus could describe its beauty; Pluto, Proserpina, and 'al hire fayerye' come to take their pleasure there:

> Ful ofte tyme he Pluto and his queene,
> Proserpina, and al hire fayerye,
> Disporten hem and maken melodye
> Aboute that welle, and daunced, as men tolde. (IV 2038–41)

Like Machaut's Venus, Pluto and Proserpina intervene in the narrative, Pluto to provide consolation, comfort, and hard truth to January, and Proserpina to nullify his efforts by granting lying, hard wit to May that will comfort her husband and exculpate herself. Chaucer's mastery of intertextuality is supreme; he incorporates elements from Machaut's *dit* in his own text and he undermines Machaut's characters and his own characters. On the one hand, Machaut's 'fonteinne delitable' (422) is a work of high art, situated in a locus of high courtly love which used to be ruled by celestial deities and was created by Pygmalion. On the other hand, referring back to and mocking it (and Guillaume de Lorris's fountain as well), Chaucer's Merchant's phallic pear tree is planted in a plot of degenerate lust; it was created by the wealthy, aesthetically sterile and senile January and is presided over by the lord and lady of Hades. Since Machaut had invoked Jupiter,

Juno, Venus, and Cupid, and associated them with fairies, and a laughing Venus associated with Priapus, it is an elegant touch on Chaucer's part to have Venus laugh at January's wedding and to introduce the gods of the nether world, promoted to king and queen of the fairies and mentioned in the same breath with Priapus, in this anticourtly text redolent of a Priapian 'material bodily lower stratum.' And what a contrast between Venus and the Lady's *Confort* to the Knight and Pluto's gift to January. One is pure and idealized and transmitted through a universe of Machaldian dream (as well as the pure, idealized dream fantasies in Guillaume de Lorris); the other calls forth corrosive, cynical, demystifying truth and countertruth à la Jean de Meun, in concrete actuality, which leads to January's befuddlement in a private, subjective fantasy existence. Now the disciple of Jean de Meun, Chaucer undercuts and demystifies the second Guillaume (de Machaut) in the same vein exploiting the same processes as Jean used when he undercut and demystified the first Guillaume (de Lorris).

Although I disagree with the scholars who consider that the *Canterbury Tales* as a whole, and the *Merchant's Tale* in particular, have to be read uniquely from a typological perspective, as works preaching *caritas* and castigating *cupiditas*, I agree that Chaucer has added a sacred dimension (although treated ironically) that we do not find in Guillaume de Lorris, Jean de Meun, or Machaut. January himself raises the issue of sin and salvation; he weds, partaking of a sacrament, in order to eschew sin and attain salvation. He even proclaims that marriage is heaven on earth and wonders, at the height of folly, whether too much heaven now will not endanger his passage to the other paradise later.

Then, in language parodying the Song of Songs, the blind husband invites his bride to his pleasure garden. He is sincere, and his *hortus conclusus* is a sort of paradise. However, the Merchant makes it clear to us that it is a fool's paradise to January and hell to May. Pluto and Proserpina do rule over Hades and, in terms of Christian typology, embody the lechery and avarice endemic to January.

Furthermore, the garden contains overtones from the Garden of Eden. January proceeds backwards, as it were, from the Canticles to Eden, reversing the usual chronological and ontological journey from Eva to Ave, and thus recommits the Fall. The paradise-like garden contains a laurel and a pear tree. The phallic pear tree functions as an ironic parody of the Tree of the Knowledge of Good and Evil, and Damian, squatting in the garden and then coupling with May in the tree, recalls Satan corrupting Eve. However, here Eve is as guilty as

Satan. Although January's eyes are open, this *vetus homo* (*senex amans*) does not comprehend the Fall as a sin of the flesh. Thus his knowledge proves to be as evanescent as his wife's innocence. She deceives him as Satan deceived Eve, and he leaves the garden as intellectually blind as when he entered it – a fool fooled by yet another lie.

Whether true or false, speech plays a comical role in the narrative. Burger (1977–8) argues that out of the 1174 lines that make up the tale, more than a third – 444 lines – constitute monologue or dialogue. Justinus and Placebo debate marriage, to no avail, since January has already made up his mind. January talks and talks, in a fantasy world, justifying his obsession to himself and to others. He exaggerates, he cites inappropriate biblical exempla, and his reasoning is warped from beginning to end. Meanwhile, May says nothing. Youth and presumed innocence are symbolized by acquiescent silence in response to the husband's silly speeches and vile behaviour. However, if the girl ever were innocent, she soon learns otherwise, and May's mastery in corruption is made manifest by her new-found mastery in language. She delivers one discourse to proclaim her fidelity to January and her respect for him and his honour at the very moment she intends to betray him; her second discourse is the brilliant denial (prompted by Proserpina) of her act of betrayal when she is caught *in flagrante delicto*. January's endless tirades prove to be nonsense leading nowhere; his self-delusion hurts only himself. May learns to trick and deceive and to employ wickedly deft speech that deludes and hurts the Other. Thus the twenty-year-old masters the sixty-year-old; the wife becomes a master, and the husband a slave. The Merchant indulges in satire, courtly and religious alike, on false speech and the false ideas it expresses. He also demonstrates how the Eternal Woman uses her tongue to manipulate poor, wretched Man. Women are inherently faithless and men are fools to believe in them.

Even more than for the *Reeve's Tale*, enormous scholarly discussion has been expended concerning the relationship of the *Merchant's Tale* to the link and the *General Prologue*. It concerns the appropriateness of the tale to its teller and whether the appropriateness or inappropriateness is relevant to our reading of the tale. I side with those Chaucerians who observe the importance of the link. We are told that the *texte générateur* for the *Merchant's Tale* is the *Clerk's Tale*. In the *Merchant's Prologue* the narrator, reacting against the idealized Griselda of the *Clerk's Tale*, confesses that he is a bitter, unhappy man, unhappy in marriage because his wife is a shrew and full of malice:

'I have a wyf, the worste that may be;
For thogh the feend to hire ycoupled were,
She wolde hym overmacche, I dar wel swere.
What sholde I yow reherce in special
Hir hye malice? She is a shrewe at al.' (IV 1218–22)

A case has been made, by many a scholar, among others Olson (1961), Harrington (1971), Brown (1978–9), and Edwards (1991), that the Merchant projects his own animus onto the tale, and that his bitterness and hatred provide and are manifest in a consistent narrative voice and a particular point of view. From this perspective, we see that January is a projection of the Merchant. Both have failed marriages. The presumed difference between them (the crucial difference from the Merchant's perspective) lies in the fact that the Merchant knows the truth about the wedded state; he can see. January cannot; he remains blind.

Also, the tale is appropriate to a merchant in that it is located in Lombardy, the archetypal land of commerce, and Janus is the patron of merchants; January is guilty throughout of avarice, and the characters treat each other like commodities or objects of exchange. There is, of course, specifically Chaucerian irony in the fact that, for this portion of the 'Marriage Group,' a typically clerical denigration of woman and marriage should be placed in the mouth of the bourgeoisie. From a clerical and aristocratic perspective, the irony is delicious in that it is burghers, not clerks, who will know the hard facts of marriage from experience and that the burgher, not the aristocrat, will enter into the state with fond expectancy.

I am also convinced that, as was the case for the *Reeve's Tale*, from a continental perspective there is no reason to consider the Merchant's voice and the atmosphere of his tale to be nasty, unpleasant, rank, sniggering, disgusting, or dirty. Nor is the tale simple animal comedy. Like the *Reeve's Tale*, but to a greater degree and on more complex levels, the *Merchant's Tale* is a powerful, serious text offering a powerful, serious vision of life, legitimate on its own terms, corrosive, satirical, and brilliantly, painfully lucid. It again resembles Jean de Meun's world and the world-view of the fabliaux and *Le Roman de Renart*. Life is made up of conflicting elements of lust, greed, deceit, and the desire for domination. People exploit and reify each other: January and Damian seek May's body; May and, presumably, Damian seek January's money. The world is unfair and unjust. The classical gods don't help; they only confirm the reality of existence. As for the Christian God, he is remarkable by his absence; and imagery of the sacred – allusions to the Song of Songs and the Garden of Eden – not only underscore the degradation of the century but are degraded in turn. That is all. This is the Merchant's world-vision and Chaucer's vision at this point in the *Canterbury Tales*; it is one of his visions of life, one that he found in the French tradition and made his own.

The Wife of Bath's Prologue and Tale

With the Wife of Bath and the Pardoner, however beautiful and meaningful the tales themselves may be, ultimately they are dwarfed vis-à-vis the prologues that frame them. They are also to some extent of interest because they are told by a specific teller, forming part of that teller's performance and contributing to the revelation of the teller's human condition. Often called confessions or sermons and assimilated to medieval pulpit oratory, I prefer to think of these performances as pleas or debates. The Wife of Bath is derived from la Vieille (and le Jaloux's wife) in Jean de Meun's *Roman de la Rose* and the Pardoner is derived from Faux Semblant in the same work. Allegorical entities in *Le Roman de la Rose*, who deliver long dramatic monologues, who embody philosophical attitudes, and who seek to teach the Lover or the God of Love or Bel Accueil, are metamorphosed by Chaucer into pilgrims, like the others, on the road to Canterbury.

Alice of Bath, undoubtedly the best-known single character in all of medieval English literature, plays a crucial role in the *Canterbury Tales*. She launches a discussion of marriage and of the relationship between man and woman; hers is the first segment in the 'Marriage Group,' including the *Merchant's Tale* which mentions the Wife of Bath by name. Alice starts the debate by enunciating a fascinating yet extreme position. She, a woman speaking as a woman, defends sex and sexual pleasure within marriage, indeed within serial marriages (she has had five husbands). She does this in a medieval context in which the clergy exalted ascetic celibacy, and the aristocracy, at least in books, exalted *fin' amor*. And, as a woman, she proposes the dominance of the wife over the husband within marriage, in a medieval context where both clergy and feudal aristocracy assumed the sovereignty of the husband over the wife.

As with the *Merchant's Tale*, scholars have proposed as sources for the Wife of Bath's discussion of marriage Deschamps and Jehan le Fèvre, Gautier le Leu's fabliau 'La Veuve' and, for the classical exempla, *l'Ovide moralisé*. However, the main source is Jean de Meun's *Roman de la Rose*. For the *Wife of Bath's Prologue*, as for the *Pardoner's Prologue*, the intertextual presence of Jean de Meun is pervasive and all-encompassing, and Chaucer's use and refashioning of Jean are absolutely brilliant.

In the person of la Vieille, Jean de Meun took the archetypal Old Bawd, the *vetula* of Roman comedy, and placed her in a new context as a debater in his grand symposium on love. La Vieille, if not a rounded person, becomes a vibrant, living, dynamic persona, in a philosophical and satirical genre wherein ideas contribute to psychology, and psychology shapes and gives expression to ideas. In her long dramatic monologue, speaking of her past, la Vieille's discourse takes on an autobiographical dimension; she is a human being existing in time and adopting the stance of nostalgia vis-à-vis her lost youth and beauty in the past, compared to her present poverty in old age. In what is, after all, naturalistic discourse, the poor creature employs imagery of money, sex, and concrete domestic realia. She also displays more than a little of Jean de Meun's own classical learning – erudition that can be justified in mimetic terms by the years she has spent as a prostitute or kept mistress in the company of clerks. La Vieille expresses herself uniquely through first-person direct discourse to her pupil, Bel Accueil. She seeks to instil in Bel Accueil theoretical and practical precepts for the deception of lovers so that he may exert mastery over them.

In the person and performance of Alice of Bath, Chaucer adopts the character, ideas, imagery, and speech of la Vieille. Like la Vieille, Alice delivers a long, rambling autobiographical monologue; she reveals her own career of duplicity and manipulation of men; she pleads for woman's freedom and the right to mastery in the sexual domain; she also regrets her lost youth and beauty –

> But – Lord Crist! – whan that it remembreth me
> Upon my yowthe, and on my jolitee,
> It tikleth me aboute myn herte roote.
> Unto this day it dooth myn herte boote
> That I have had my world as in my tyme.
> But age, allas, that al wole envenyme,
> Hath me biraft my beautee and my pith.
> Lat go. Farewel! The devel go therwith!
> The flour is goon; ther is namoore to telle;
> The bren, as I best kan, now moste I selle ... (III 469–78)

and confesses how deeply she was hurt when she herself fell in love and was deceived and mastered in turn; and she buttresses her discourse with a fund of ill-digested classical lore and scholastic argumentation, presumably derived from contact with clerks, especially her fifth husband, Jankyn.

Initially Chaucer transforms Jean de Meun from the need to take an allegory, however vital, and shape it, in a work of mimetic fiction, into (1) a total human being and (2) one of the Canterbury pilgrims. Therefore, the relatively abstract Old Bawd becomes Alice of Bath, a clothmaker by trade; she has concrete, precise, human experience, including her husbands, to talk about. La Vieille's theories become Alice's practice. Furthermore, whereas la Vieille's purpose in speaking was to teach Bel Accueil the ways of the world and enable Bel Accueil to succeed where she had failed, therefore to take vengeance on men, the Wife of Bath, placed in a different context, speaks with a different view in mind. Except for nuns, there are no other women on the pilgrimage. Alice's goal, although she manifests aggression toward the clergy in general and the Friar in particular, is to win the approval of her fellow pilgrims and to entertain them as part of the storytelling contest. In other words, to play. As she says, in response to the Pardoner:

> But yet I praye to al this compaignye,
> If that I speke after my fantasye,
> As taketh not agrief of that I seye,
> For myn entente nys but for to pleye. (III 189–92)

In addition, Alice of Bath's doctrine differs from la Vieille's. Jean de Meun's character urges on her pupil the right to sexual freedom and the practice of deceit, for the purpose of economic survival; Bel Accueil is being taught how to use her mind and body in order to become affluent and to remain so in her declining years. Similarly, Dame Alice is conscious of the fact that she is (was) a commodity and that marriage is commerce. She trades herself, multiplying profit not children; she sold herself to her first three husbands, and then reached a position of affluence where she could dominate the market and purchase her fourth and fifth marriages. However, for this very reason we are made aware that she urges sexual freedom and the practice of deceit in the name of a different cause. Whereas la Vieille emphasizes lucre, the Wife of Bath emphasizes sex, and sex in the name of love. Unlike her source, she is capable of affection and of giving; indeed she desperately wants to give in order to receive.

Finally – and this is Chaucer's major transformation of *Le Roman de la Rose* – whereas la Vieille is of uncertain social class and by profession a prostitute or kept mistress become, in old age, a combination duenna and go-between, Dame Alice is a respectable bourgeoise and a married woman. Several of Jean de Meun's speakers, including la Vieille, observe that prior to marriage, in a state of *fin' amor,* the woman dominates; after the ceremony the man dominates. Jean's discoursers prefer free love, wherein both partners are equal. Chaucer picks up on Jean's argument. He has Alice propose another solution – marriage in which the woman exerts mastery, in harmony with premarital courting, where the woman also exerts mastery. The irony of the situation is derived largely from the imposition of marriage upon Jean's old bawd and one-time whore. It is quite different to proclaim the exercise of manipulation and deceit in an Ovidian universe of free love (Jean) than to do so in the sacramental institution of Christian marriage (Chaucer). The practice of free love within marriage leads either to frequent adultery or, as in the Wife of Bath's case, to a number of sequential marriages. Chaucer also comically dislocates the traditional, literary *fin' amor* ideal of the lady's (*domna*'s) dominance prior to marriage or in a marriage-free, timeless, eternal present by thrusting it into a novelistic setting of duration and wedlock.

Just as la Vieille presents in a positive light practices and a way of life that le Jaloux condemned so vociferously, Alice not only functions as a transmutation of la Vieille but also as a reincarnation of le Jaloux's wife. Chaucer reveals to us the wife's version of their story, so to speak. Furthermore, whereas Jean de Meun has le Jaloux attack his wife, delivering a tirade of misogynistic precepts and anecdotes in his own voice, from a male perspective, Chaucer picks up on Jean's narrative technique and does him one better. He has Alice attack her first three husbands for delivering antifeminist speeches attacking her from a male perspective, but her words are used to crush her husbands, not to vindicate them, just as, later, he has her recount, again in her own voice, a resumé of the antifeminist material contained in Jankyn's book. In so doing the Wife of Bath assimilates both the old husbands and the young Jankyn to le Jaloux and mocks them in their own words. It is perhaps more than a coincidence that the young clerk with a misogynistic book should be named Jankyn, Little John, the English equivalent of Petit Jean. Does not Alice, metaphorically and ironically, rip three pages out of Jean de Meun's book, *Le Roman de la Rose,* and then burn it in the fireplace, converting her Jean de Meun from a misogynistic clerk into a docile, obedient husband? Just so Geoffrey Chaucer converts, translates, and reduces Jean's book into English and transmutes his Old French vision into an equally complex and doubly or triply ironic Middle English one.

A central preoccupation of Chaucer scholars, over the decades, has been to interpret the Wife of Bath as a literary character and in a sense to 'judge' her, and then to determine Chaucer's intentions vis-à-vis her and her ideas. The most recent current of Chaucerians (including Leicester 1990, among many) rejects this approach; they deem it all but a critical heresy to treat Alice as a person and not uniquely as a subject, a vector or focus of forces, a literary construct, and a textual artifact. In one sense, of course, this is right for all literature, not just the medieval. It is no doubt an error for critics to speculate on alleged activities outside the text, such as whether or not Alice murdered her fourth husband, or for that matter her fifth. On the other hand, it is clear to me that Chaucer took Jean de Meun's old bawd – already a humanized vector or focus of forces, with life experience in her past, and emotions and desire in her present – and then humanized and individualized her still more. He transformed a perorating, fascinatingly ambiguous voice into a no less passionate and magnificent mimetic person, a product of mimesis due to a process of mimesis. The result is the best-remembered character from the entire English Middle Ages, a novelistic character in the century of the *novella*. Since the inscribed audience within the *Canterbury Tales* frame reacted to her as a person in their world, it is only to be expected that the implied historical audience in Chaucer's day did the same, as have readers and scholars ever since. The divergence of opinion concerning the Wife of Bath stands as testimony to Chaucer's success in creating a novelistic character in his imaginary narrative, and also to the perennial, universal impact of the ideas she debates and the world-view she embodies.[28]

On the one hand, there are those who deem Alice, as a character in Chaucer's fictional world, to be a fool and a laughing-stock, both for the other pilgrims (her narratees on the pilgrimage) and for us (the extradiegetic implied audience). After all, she does argue badly, misinterpreting and misquoting Scripture, unaware, as Jean de Meun's Genius is unaware, of the spiritual sense of 'increase and multiply.' She has no notion whatever of the meaning of Christian marriage. And for all her talk of 'engendrure,' she herself, probably, is physically and, no doubt intellectually, barren. La Vieille's life of *fornicatio* is bad enough, but when the Old Law of carnality – *luxuria* and *cupiditas* – undermines a sacrament, the situation worsens; to argue for the domination of woman over man, and therefore of the flesh over the spirit, within the sacrament would be not only absurd but also blasphemy.

Secondly, for all her talk of giving and loving, it can be said that Alice is not a good person; in addition to sexual infidelity, she indulges in cruelty and sadism as she browbeats her first three old husbands and, in the long run, her last two young ones. This is true in the telling (recollection) as well as, presumably, in the original behaviour. Curiously, the male public may well have felt more sympathy for la Vieille, who after all suffered in life and ended in an impoverished, miserable old age, than for this vulgar, all too successful and happy virago. Alice of Bath embodies all the misogynistic clichés in Jankyn's book and in Jean's *Roman*: she is shrewish, nagging, tricky, deceitful, unfaithful, carnal, conniving, loud, and vulgar, and she never stops talking. She condemns her husband's book and denigrates his views on women and yet her every speech and act prove them right.

The Wife of Bath then would have been a living, walking self-contradiction; she contradicts and denies herself at every turn in both behaviour and speech. In her latest marriage she plays precisely the same role that her husbands played in the first three, that of a wealthy, relatively old, unattractive creature who purchases the body of the spouse yet seeks desperately also to win the spouse's affection, all the while maintaining dominance over him/her; although she wants dominance at all cost, she is happiest, in the last two marriages, when her husband does the dominating. Although Alice claims to uphold woman and woman's rights to pleasure and power, she attacks women, mouthing in her own voice the misogynistic clichés of her age; by repeating to the pilgrims in extenso the antifeminist charges she accuses her husbands of planning to make against her and revealing to them the contents of Jankyn's book, her *Prologue* becomes as much an anthology of misogyny as *Le Roman de la Rose* taken as a whole. Whatever her conscious intent, Alice not only acts but speaks against womankind and against herself.

The issue of speech is crucial. This garrulous, unstoppable discourser is a woman discussing theology, upholding doctrine, exposing ideas, seeking to convince the pilgrims of her way of thought, and to some extent indeed delivering a sermon. Although a woman, she employs man's reason and rhetoric, and by so doing she ceases to be a woman. Following the same line of argument, Alice hates clerks and clerkly wisdom, which is antifeminist, antisexual, and antimatrimonial:

> For trusteth wel, it is an impossible
> That any clerk wol speke good of wyves,
> But if it be of hooly seintes lyves,
> Ne of noon oother womman never the mo ...

The children of Mercurie and of Venus
Been in hir wirkyng ful contrarius; ...
Therfore no womman of no clerk is preysed.
The clerk, whan he is oold, and may noght do
Of Venus werkes worth his olde sho,
Thanne sit he doun, and writ in his dotage
That wommen kan nat kepe hir mariage! (III 688–91, 697–8, 706–10)

Yet she is obsessed with theology and theological disputation. It is as if, driven by her obsessions, she wishes to become a clerk and, in attacking women, attacks her own self in the name of *clergie*. Yet the Wife of Bath cannot be a man or a clerk. She can only rip out the pages of a book and eventually burn it. She can deny 'clerkness' and maleness, just as she denies her own feminine subordination, and yet existentially, she is riddled with bad faith, for she neither changes herself nor the world she lives in. For all intents and purposes she reinforces the masculine, clerical world-vision in that she exists only within the parameters assigned to her in it; she is a married woman and a creature of the flesh, obsessed by her body and its 'bele chose.' If proof were needed, we are reminded that, whereas Jean de Meun's Vieille does mould Bel Accueil and presumably contributes to the Rose's seduction, an act of pleasure in the present and, no doubt, more pleasure in the future, poor Alice perorates before an audience made up uniquely of men and nuns, none of whom will be convinced by her. Her failure to communicate would be presumably as absolute as her failure to understand herself, or her failure in life, or her failure in thought, and her failure to understand that everyone is laughing at her. It is for these reasons that Rowland (1972) called her a sociopath, within either a medieval or a modern context.

Finally, this comically incoherent and deranged character can be thought of as an unreliable narrator. Leicester (1990) observes that her story has to be considered, at best, retrospective revision. Critics less sympathetic to this particular Subject, including Shapiro (1971–2), state that, as she has lied consistently and wilfully to all of her husbands, how can we presume she is telling the truth to the pilgrims? Is it likely that this sexual devourer was truly chaste after discovering that her fourth husband, the 'lechour,' deceived her with his mistress? Is it likely that this unattractive, unloved creature was capable of making him jealous in turn? Should we believe her when she claims that she and Jankyn have lived happily ever after, once she burned his book and became the master? Are not her stories of sexual escapades and her proclamation of sexual appetite mere bravado? We will never know, any more than we will know what the Wife really wants: sovereignty? the illusion of sovereignty? equality? freedom? happiness? love? How can we know when she, with her befuddled intellect and lack of introspection, appears to be incapable of knowing? Nowhere in medieval literature would an author surpass Chaucer in the strategy of narrative technique used to unmask and undermine a literary character in a work of fiction. This would also be the opinion of a number of feminist critics who designate Alice as the ultimate vision of woman, as Other, focalized through and invented by the male literary ego. Thus is she read by one major tendency in the profession.

On the other hand, there are those who defend the Wife of Bath as a character and admire her as a person. They point out that, if she is strident and aggressive and manifests contradictions, she has been forced into such a state by medieval marriage and by having been forced to live up to or to rebel against male stereotypes, the only models for existence that her era allowed her. Nonetheless, Alice is more than the product or the victim of clerical misogyny. For example, resembling la Vieille, she calls for sexual indulgence, freedom of movement, and self-expression for woman as well as for man; she likes money and what money can purchase; and she assaults hierarchy and bookish authority in the name of experience. She embodies practical common sense and the reality of life in the secular world. Jankyn's misogynistic book is a compendium of clerical argument against marriage. Even were one to agree with its ideas, it is clear that such books were written to dissuade clerks from marrying. Now Jankyn is a clerk who has wed. It is too late for him to profit from his *florilegium* and it is cruel of him to humiliate his wife by insistently reading aloud to her from it. In her act of protest, is Alice necessarily wrong?

Perhaps more to the point, it can be claimed that the Wife of Bath is more intelligent and more articulate than her husbands. She defeats the three old men by attacking them before they can attack her; she crushes them with wit and verbal brio. As for Jankyn, she outwits him also; she pretends to be dying and to die willingly, with only thoughts of love for him. We discover that in Bath a woman outsmarts and out-talks a series of men, and that on the road to Canterbury the same woman employs scholastic reason to discredit scholasticism; a master of speech, she compels her largely male audience to give heed to what she says, silencing the Friar in the process. Oberembt

(1975–6) maintains that, rather than embody the triumph of flesh over spirit, Alice herself is more a creature of reason than the men around her and that, on their own terms, she, not they, deserves to rule.

Whereas the three old men were selfish and impotent, the fourth husband a cold adulterer, and the fifth a selfish misogynist, Alice says she is willing to give as well as to take. She is never frigid and, for a modicum of affection and respect, offers much in return. She renews herself as she renews her husbands; she grows and learns to live, love, and survive. And to win. For the Wife of Bath is a winner; she obtains wealth from the first group of husbands and sex from the second. In her *Prologue* she defeats a clerk; in her tale the hag defeats a knight. Unlike la Vieille, she will not endure poverty and disgrace in old age. She may well regret her lost youth; yet she perseveres, holding her own in the fray, and her life apparently has a happy ending. She proves to be la Vieille's best pupil, having learned her lesson to the utmost and having surpassed her teacher. (The Wife refers to another Alisoun, 'my gossib, dwellynge in oure toun' [III 529], who taught her and from whom she learned much; is not this mirror image of herself also a reflection of and allusion to Jean's Vieille?)

Medieval misogynists and twentieth-century scholars will claim that all this is wrong in a woman; it is absurd and to be condemned because Dame Alice is a woman. But that is the point; Alice dares to claim certain rights, including power in and out of marriage for women, and her speech launches a debate on her terms. The Middle Ages, no more than the twentieth century, did not have a single world-view, or one sole position on marriage or sex or the war of the sexes. There were feminists and antifeminists, secularists and ascetics, then as today. Alice's position, like the Reeve's and the Merchant's, is a valid one, powerful, imaginative, and convincing; Chaucer the author makes it his own, at least for the telling of her tale.

Finally, even if one disagrees with Alice's ideas, reasoning, or rhetoric, one has to admit her power as a literary creation; joy and fulness of life emanate from her. Whatever her ideas, whatever her character, she is unforgettable. As I said before, she bursts forth from the pages of the *Canterbury Tales* as a living person, a mimetic novelistic personage, with a force and vitality comparable to but greater than Jean de Meun's Vieille.

The same dichotomy in critical response – approval or non-approval, admiration or condemnation – of the Wife of Bath is to be observed when we consider the story Alice tells, the *Wife of Bath's Tale*. The tale is a story of folkloric origin, which, however, concerns a point of love casuistry typical of French and Occitan lyric debate poems and a common motif in the antifeminist texts of Jean de Meun and Eustache Deschamps. It tells of a knight who commits rape and is condemned to discover within one year's time what women most want or to endure the death penalty. Informed by a hag, the knight makes the correct response – women seek mastery – but he must then marry the hag. In the face of the man's repugnance on their wedding night, the hag lectures him on true nobility. When she finally offers him the choice between an old wife who will be faithful or a young bride who may deceive him, the knight leaves the decision to her:

> 'My lady and my love, and wyf so deere,
> I put me in youre wise governance; ...
> For as yow liketh, it suffiseth me.'
> 'Thanne have I gete of yow maistrie,' quod she,
> 'Syn I may chese and governe as me lest?'
> 'Ye, certes, wyf,' quod he, 'I holde it best.' (III 1230–1, 1235–8)

Because he has granted her mastery, she is transformed into a youthful beauty who will also be faithful and make him happy.

Critics' responses to the tale are divided. Some underscore the Wife of Bath's triumph – a story recounting the education and reformation of a brutal male rapist who learns to be governed by wise ladies. Others see the bad faith and the inauthenticity in the Wife's wish-fulfilment fantasy narrative. Most important perhaps is Chaucer's skill in ascribing to the Wife a Breton lay that ironically undercuts masculine prowess and chivalry, preaching in its stead a lesson of inner nobility – 'gentillesse' to be found in the heart and in a person's behaviour – taken from Jean de Meun, of all people.

What are we then to conclude? In my opinion, Jean de Meun created, in la Vieille, an intentionally ambiguous 'entity' offering ideas and a world-view in competition with other allegorical entities offering ideas and world-views. I am convinced that Jean de Meun leaves his book open to interpretation from the implied audience and implied reader, and that the public is free to side with Raison, Ami, le Jaloux, Faux Semblant, la Vieille, Nature, Genius, none of the above, and all of the above. His is the first great medieval book grounded in inconclusiveness and deferral. We have some evidence that the majority of medieval authorities (important readers) reacted negatively to la Vieille and then either praised or blamed Jean for having unmasked the negative Old Bawd. Nevertheless, in the Middle Ages and today one is not obliged to condemn this spokesman for deceit and manipulation and also for free love, woman's liberty, and equality between the sexes.

I suggest that, like Jean de Meun with la Vieille, Chaucer leaves the options and the response of the implied audience open. Whatever judgment he personally has concerning the Wife of Bath is deferred and inconclusive. The implied audience outside the text and the inscribed audience of pilgrims within the diegesis are free to agree or disagree with her, and to admire or scorn her. In the last analysis, as with Jean de Meun's Vieille, nothing prevents us from doing both; we can recognize the fascinating issues raised by an absurd argument, and the exciting, controversial debating points made in an atmosphere of comedy and farce. Nothing prevents us from recognizing Alice as a laughing-stock, loud, vulgar, and self-contradictory; she is a feminist who fulfills every misogynist's expectations of the *vagina dentata*, the figure of the bossy woman who nonetheless wants to be mastered in bed. And nothing prevents us, at the same time, from admiring her pluck and courage, or from being moved by her vitality and her unforgettable élan.

Dynamism, spark of life, vitality, and élan – such traits remind us of the spirit of carnival claimed for the later Middle Ages by Bakhtin. A number of recent studies locate Chaucer and the Wife of Bath in this tradition. While I agree with those specialists (such as Berrong 1986G) who criticize Bakhtin for gross errors in the use of sources and in the writing of what he thought was History, I also believe the Bakhtinian carnival can be a useful approach to certain medieval texts. Both *Le Roman de la Rose* and certain of the *Canterbury Tales* mock official court and church doctrine with laughter, satire, and a joyful will to life. Both of them revel in the body and the grotesque. Both revel in heteroglossia and the irreverent, inebriating, overpowering flow of discourse.

It is surely in discourse, its textuality and its intertextuality, that la Vieille and Alice of Bath stand out. La Vieille participates as a full equal in Jean de Meun's grand symposium on love and the war of the sexes. She herself cites Ovid and other authors, and implicitly responds to previous discoursers in the *Rose* such as the speeches by Ami and le Jaloux. The Wife of Bath also quotes and misquotes her classical sources, including Jean de Meun. As we have seen, she perhaps introduces into her own world Jean and the *Rose* as Jankyn and his book. A number of critics, for example Patterson (1983), Hanning (1985), and Leicester (1990), have remarked that she glosses, argues against, and ultimately harasses men's texts as much as she does mere men. Furthermore, in a sense, unlike la Vieille who speaks against earlier allegorical voices, Alice herself launches the marriage debate. Later discussion will have to respond to her. Just as Chrétien reformulated *fin' amor* in terms of marriage, Chaucer reformulates Jean de Meun's war of the sexes in terms of marriage. With the *Wife of Bath's Prologue and Tale* he brings Jean de Meun's ideas, people, and worldview into his book. He devours Jean as Jean had devoured Guillaume de Lorris. The ideas and the texts will live on in a new life.

The Pardoner's Prologue and Tale

The Pardoner's confession-sermon-plea is derived from Faux Semblant's in *Le Roman de la Rose*. The Pardoner is a textual, psychological, and archetypal reworking of Faux Semblant. Now Faux Semblant is one of the most interesting and disturbing of Jean de Meun's allegories, and his speech is located at the midpoint of the *Rose*. The embodiment of hypocrisy, clad in the garb of a Dominican friar, Faux Semblant offers his services to Cupid with the purpose of helping the Lover win the Rose. In order to convince the others to accept his offer, this worthy makes a public confession, revealing the truth about himself. He boasts of his capacities for evil; yet also he denounces what he does and what the friars do in his name. By unmasking himself, confessing his secrets, and denouncing his own practices even when boasting of them, the imago of hypocrisy ceases to be himself. In effect he denies his own essence and yet, in another sense, by so doing he becomes most truly himself. Although The God of Love deems this unsavoury personage to be more than a little dubious, he does enrol him in his army; from a true Ovidian perspective, without the manipulation and deceit that he represents, success in the erotic sphere will be impossible. Once enrolled, Faux Semblant proceeds to act. Having reverted to his original nature (pure hypocrisy), with his friend Abstinence Contrainte disguised as a Béguine, he approaches the castle where Bel Accueil is sequestered. They wheedle and flatter and smooth-talk Male Bouche into confessing himself to them, and then slit his throat and sever his tongue, thereby securing one of the gates and permitting the Lover to enter the castle and have an interview with Bel Accueil.

Faux Semblant's appearance in the narrative and his discourse function on several levels: they further the plot; they inform us cynically à la Ovid of one crucial aspect of courting and of the nature of love; they deliver a magnificent satire on the Church in general and on the mendicant orders in particular; and they underscore the role of greed, disguise, and manipulation in life. It is also true that to have the embodiment of hypocrisy boast of his deeds and then unmask, revealing the truth about himself, and to have him, dressed as a Dominican, denounce the friars, from within as it were, is a brilliant comic invention on Jean de Meun's part. It is no less true that Jean de Meun's, and Faux Semblant's, comic brio are not naturalistic in psychological terms, nor, since we are dealing with allegories in the satirical mode, is there any particular reason why they should be.

How does Chaucer adapt Faux Semblant to the *Canterbury Tales*? He transforms the personification of hypocrisy into a character like the Wife of Bath, in the novelistic or mimetic mode; he becomes one of the pilgrims on the road to Canterbury. And he chooses character traits and a profession that will, from his perspective, approximate Faux Semblant in the real world. Faux Semblant's double is also of the Church, a *quaestor* who seeks charitable gifts to the Church and who issues indulgences in the Church's name. This trickster-villain reveals to the pilgrims his tricks, boasting how, out of greed, he cheats the peasants by selling or offering them the benefits of patently false relics. He also denounces the same sins in others, in a sermon supposedly delivered to his peasant victims. Finally, he blesses the pilgrims but then, imitating Faux Semblant, reverts to his true nature of deceit. However, instead of deceiving others (Male Bouche in the *Roman de la Rose*), the Pardoner tries to deceive the very pilgrims to whom he had previously told the truth. That is, he tries to hoodwink them into paying him for the use of the relics they and he know to be false. And he commits the imprudence of calling upon the Host to be the first to open his purse and kiss the relics. The Host reacts violently, insulting the Pardoner. The latter has failed. Peace is restored by the Knight.

As a personification Faux Semblant manifests the same brio, the same rhetorical flair, and the same intellectual passion we find in all of Jean de Meun's characters. As an allegorical abstraction, both satirical and comic, he calls forth our laughter and our admiration. Transforming him into the equivalent of a person, interacting with other people in a concretely human and community-oriented context, Chaucer paints his Pardoner in much darker colours. There is something demonic about this money-oriented, cash-obsessed individual who is aggressive, assertive, and ruled by his own 'coveitise':

For myn entente is nat but for to wynne,
And nothyng for correccioun of synne ...
But shortly myn entente I wol devyse:
I preche of no thyng but for coveityse ...
I preche nothyng but for coveitise. (VI 403–4, 423–4, 433)

Furthermore, not only is the Pardoner himself guilty of sin, but he instils it in his uneducated, lower-class victims; by according indulgences without proper contrition on their part, he gives them, with his false relics and forged papal bulls, the false, forged, and improper presumption of remission of sin. Resembling Jean de Meun's friars, this 'ful vicious man,' indifferent to the spiritual health of 'lewed peple,' in fact actively contributes to their damnation. Instead of loving his fellow man, created in the image of God, he holds him in contempt. Endowed with the gift of grace and misusing it by knowing the truth and yet committing and recommitting sin, he sins against the Holy Ghost.

It is normal for a figure of allegory – la Vieille or Faux Semblant – to perorate about himself in his own voice for thousands of lines. When the Wife of Bath or the Pardoner does it, even if for only a few hundred lines, we are made aware of human egocentrism. And, as Manning (1974, 1979) has so well observed, the Pardoner is a rhetor, a man of speech. The rhetorical repetition of 'I wol' and 'I wol nat' underscores the Pardoner's obsession with himself and his pride and self-satisfaction in what he does.[29] Significantly, whereas Faux Semblant condemns himself, the Pardoner cannot. He only condemns his sins when committed by others. Utterly unselfconscious and lacking in introspection and lucidity, the Pardoner blabs on and on about his deeds but not his inner self, about what he does but not what he is; either he is ignorant or he desperately wishes us to remain ignorant of his inner self.

For all that, as a preacher he also manifests an extreme distaste vis-à-vis the physical – food, drink, sex, and the body – a distaste which scholars have rightly interpreted as inhuman and unchristian. This probably reflects the ultimate stage in his own immersion in sin; as a sinner who mocks his fellow men he therefore mocks God, and his hatred for others ultimately turns against himself. This is his inner destitution, the void that he cannot face in himself much less reveal to others.

Whereas Faux Semblant, like Ami and la Vieille, cites classical authorities, alludes to myth, and occasionally relates exempla to reinforce his message, he is not a pilgrim engaged in a story-telling contest. The Pardoner is. He relates to the pilgrims the kind of sermon he uses to manipulate the 'lewed peple'; his tale proper forms part of the sermon and is contained in it. Chaucer uses the *Pardoner's Tale* as a whole, among many other things, to reveal the man's character and to show the extent to which he is indeed the son of Faux Semblant. As the scholars have pointed out, the *Pardoner's Tale* itself reinforces what we come to know about the Pardoner. The story is of three young drunken 'riotoures' who wish to find and slay Death; they are directed to a treasure of gold where, indeed, they find death in that they slay each other while trying to keep the treasure each for himself. Just as Faux Semblant delivers a good and true speech concerning corruption in the Church, and just as Faux Semblant does contribute to the winning of the Rose and therefore to the furthering of the life force, so too Chaucer has his Pardoner deliver a powerful, magnificent, truly Christian story: 'A moral tale yet I yow telle kan' (VI 460). In him also good comes out of evil. Whether the tale grows out of the sermon, as appears to be the case in terms of narrative logic, or the sermon grows out of the tale, as may well be the case in terms of artistic composition – which of the two has psychological or ontological priority – is irrelevant. The Pardoner's discourse – prologue, sermon, tale, and epilogue – forms a totality that is his essence as one of the pilgrims.

In addition, like Faux Semblant, the Pardoner is an outsider seeking to become a member of the community and to be accepted by the others; as in the case of Faux Semblant, the central issue in the diegesis is his contact with others and his ultimate acceptance or rejection by them. Here a problem arises that has bothered and inspired generations of Chaucerians. Why does the Pardoner, the embodiment of hypocrisy, confess his hypocrisy to the pilgrims, and then bless them, and then turn around and try to sell them his false relics? Chaucer has adapted his character's fixed essence and his active behaviour from Faux Semblant in the *Rose*: sincerity from a hypocrite and sudden reversals in attitude and behaviour are not shocking in a comic allegorical personification. The problem is, none of Chaucer's pilgrims is a comic allegorical personification; all of them, including the Pardoner, are mimetic representations of people, and therefore their comportment is subject to the laws of people and, from more than one critical perspective, has to be justified also in psychological terms.

Among the theories proposed to justify his behaviour are the following: (1) the Pardoner acts with sincerity throughout but goes too far, making a fool of himself under the influence of alcohol because he drank too much ale at the beginning; (2) the Pardoner is sincere in his confession, because he wishes desperately to win the pilgrims' approbation (hence his blessing) but in the end he reverts to his true nature, driven by 'coveitise'; (3) throughout he is insincere, for he confesses to the pilgrims in mockery, with the aim of cheating them, by appealing to their superiority over the peasants and then, in the end, he simply overreaches himself and commits an error in tactics by turning to the Host; or (4) the Pardoner throughout is having a joke, entertaining the pilgrims with his humourous alleged confession; however the Host, less intelligent and sophisticated than his adversary, fails to understand the joke, makes earnest out of game and foolishly loses his temper.

These are four among a larger number of hypotheses concerning the Pardoner. A range of these readings is to be found in good articles by Beichner (1963), Calderwood (1964), Halverson (1969–70), Rhodes (1982–3), Glasser (1983–4), Fritz (1986–7), Bowers (1990), and Dillon (1991). I believe that the key to unlocking this secret lies in another one, the secret of the Pardoner's 'nature,' the secret this imago of deceit carefully avoids revealing in the course of his sermon-confession-tale. What does Chaucer tell about his nature? In the *General Prologue* the narrator-witness-implied author informs us that the Pardoner has a smooth, hairless face, beautifully long yellow but thin hair, a high-pitched voice like a goat, and protruding eyes like a hare. In conclusion, 'I trowe he were a geldyng or a mare' (I 691). Furthermore, the Pardoner rides in company with the Summoner, one of the most disreputable characters on the pilgrimage. The Pardoner sings 'Com hider, love, to me!' (I 672), and the Summoner accompanies him; the accompaniment can also be interpreted as phallic innuendo: 'This Somonour bar to hym a stif burdoun' (I 673).

When the Host requests a story from the Pardoner, addressing him condescendingly or sarcastically as 'Thou beel amy,' the 'gentils' protest: 'Nay, lat hym telle us of no ribaudye!' (VI 324). Although the Pardoner had spoken of getting married (interrupting the Wife of Bath in her Prologue) and brags of having a wench in every town, in his sermon he excoriates the physical aspect of mankind, expressing disgust with the material bodily lower stratum, the sexual as well as the digestive tract:

O wombe! O bely! O stynkyng cod,
Fulfilled of dong and of corrupcioun!
At either ende of thee foul is the soun. (VI 534–6)

In the end, he asks the Host to open his purse and kiss the relics. It is this discourse, whether in earnest or in game, which causes the Host to lose his temper and respond with violence. The Host denounces the Pardoner in scatological terms, with allusion to the Pardoner's anus and to his castratable testicles:

'Thou woldest make me kisse thyn olde breech,
And swere it were a relyk of a seint,
Though it were with thy fundement depeint!
But, by the croys which that Seint Eleyne fond,
I wolde I hadde thy coillons in myn hond
In stide of relikes or of seintuarie.
Lat kutte hem of, I wol thee helpe hem carie;
They shul be shryned in an hogges toord!' (VI 948–55)

An early generation of scholars designated the Pardoner as a *eunuchus ex nativitate* (Curry 1926); this gave rise to decades of studies on the spiritual as opposed to the physical eunuch. More recently he has been identified as a 'testicular pseudo-hermaphrodite of the feminine type' (Rowland 1964). Only since 1980 have a number of critics, starting with McAlpine (1980), been willing to say the unsayable – that the Pardoner is simply a male homosexual, that is, the caricature of the male homosexual from a traditional heterosexual perspective. This is my conviction also. I arrive at it from the background of Jean de Meun's use of phallic and scatological imagery and from his statements on homosexuality. Only the homosexual thesis makes sense of Jean de Meun. In *Le Roman de La Rose* Faux Semblant himself is actively heterosexual; he has even fathered a son on Abstinence Contrainte, who will become the Antichrist. However, Nature denounces those who commit sodomy and unnatural acts that impede the reproduction of the species. Later in the poem, in powerful, sublime, apocalyptic terms, Genius excoriates the sodomites to be found in the Church, especially in monastic orders; they fail to reproduce, and he threatens all non-reproducers with castration, just as the Host, in essence, threatens the Pardoner with castration.

Earlier in the *Rose* Lady Reason informs the Lover that Venus was born from the castrated 'coilles' of Saturn. This statement gives rise to a delightfully comic scene in which the Lover attacks her for using filthy words 'unseemly in the mouth of a courtly damsel' and yet, in attacking her, he utters no less obscene speech himself. Reason defends her lexicon and her level of discourse by the argument: What if balls were called relics and relics were called balls? Which then would be the dirty word? 'Coilles' and 'reliques' are assimilated in her speech, as they will be in the denouement when the Narrator tells us how, as Lover, he pried open the door to the reliquary with his pilgrim's purse and staff (his 'bourdon'), and deflowered the Rose ('relique') with his 'coilles' and 'vit.'

It was a stroke of genius on Chaucer's part to transform Jean's Faux Semblant into a clerical homosexual, a type that the clerical Genius and Jean denounced with such passion. In Chaucer's reading of Jean, Genius attacks sodomy in creatures such as Faux Semblant, who claim to be great seducers of women. Has Genius discovered the one secret vice that Faux Semblant cannot confess? Chaucer at any rate makes this statement about his Faux Semblant. Chaucer adapts the persona of ecclesiastical greed, hypocrisy, and deceit into one who boasts of his female conquests but is also an ecclesiastical sodomite, yet he avoids the subject altogether. If we envisage the Pardoner as a homosexual, it becomes obvious why the Host addresses him contemptuously as 'beel amy,' why the gentles dread the 'ribaudye' he is likely to tell, and why in the end the Host reacts to him with violence. But there is more. As Chaucer portrays him, the Pardoner is the alienated outsider in this community, the marginal man, the outcast. Obsessed with the body and its sins, he is in fact obsessed with *his* body and, by denouncing the body, he denounces himself in a verbal outburst of self-hate. He appears to confess all and yet he never reaches the point of revealing his only real secret, the essential secret of his sexuality, which, given his overt physical characteristics, the Narrator, the Host, and most if not all the pilgrims know anyway. He transfers his frustrated libidinal drive into avarice, rhetoric, the will to mastery (over peasants and pilgrims), and an obsession with death; his Eros is transformed into Thanatos from beginning to end.

I follow Howard (1976) and others, also profiting from the theory of self-hate, in speculating that the Pardoner has ambivalent feelings toward the other pilgrims. On the one hand, he is desperate to belong. On the other hand, he hates and despises them as he despises the peasants because, although he is their verbal and intellectual superior, they have not accepted him. Therefore, perhaps he also wishes to be rejected by them in order to continue to hate them and to take revenge on them. Hence the apparent inconsistency in his behaviour. Furthermore, the charisma, energy, and frenzy of his speech are not those of an evangelical preacher but the symptoms of a man possessed, a man not physically drunk but manic in his alienation and despair. In the end, the Pardoner simply loses control and, by challenging the pilgrims in general and the Host in particular, he self-destructs; he is carried along by the rhythm of his discourse and the telling of his tale to Thanatos, the death instinct that results in metaphorical castration and verbal silence.

Why choose the Host? In terms of psychology, we can extract from Chaucer's text traces of a largely unspoken antipathy between the Host and the Pardoner, comparable to the more overt antipathy between the Miller and the Reeve or between the Friar and the Summoner. The Host is a large, burly, coarse, virile, masterful man, the sort who in our culture most loathes and feels threatened by homosexuals; the Pardoner is a young, delicate, sensitive, fastidious intellectual, who senses in the Host his most dangerous foe. Challenged to tell a story, 'beel amy' directs it implicitly against the Host; he satirizes sins – gluttony, drunkenness, avarice, gambling, profanity – endemic to taverns and locates his tale of 'riotoures' and 'hasardours' in 'that develes temple,' a tavern. All this is done in the presence of the story-telling contest judge, who is an innkeeper and who, in the course of the Canterbury frame narrative, shows himself to be guilty of all the tavern sins. The Pardoner then concludes by inviting the very same innkeeper and judge to be the first to kiss the relics and unbuckle his purse.

On one level, this is a challenge to the *magister ludi* in his *magisterium*. The Pardoner, the most intelligent and articulate of the pilgrims, threatens the Host in his seat of authority, for he wishes to master all on the road, as he masters the peasants on Sundays. He is also challenging him, so to speak, in his seat of virility. The Pardoner, who apparently has read or heard about Jean de Meun, knows that a purse equals testicles and that relics equal testicles or a penis. His invitation is a mocking parody of *Le Roman de la Rose* and a mock invitation, scarcely veiled, to a homosexual act. Though presumably not especially familiar with belles-lettres in French, the Host nonetheless understands full well the innuendo. His decorum outraged (even the Host has a level of decorum), and his sexuality threatened, he responds like the Lover vis-à-vis Reason in the *Rose*, with irrationality and with even coarser speech. Furious with the Pardoner, he alludes still more directly to the forbidden topic, assimilating the relics to be kissed with the Pardoner's fecal matter, and therefore with the offending orifice, and in the traditional masculine reaction of outrage in sexual matters he threatens him with castration. Chaucer, in the Host's voice, reproduces the metaphor of *Le Roman de la Rose*. Instead of *relics* the host prefers to have the Pardoner's *balls*, to cut them off (as Saturn's were) and enshrine them not in the sea but in porcine excrement; his bogus testicles would accompany porcine bones, the Pardoner's other bogus relics. The scatology is Chaucer's contribution, going beyond Jean de Meun and repudiating stylistic decorum even more than Jean did, assimilating (in the Host's mind) sodomy with animality and the super-low, the material bodily lower stratum that the Pardoner claims to despise. The poor Pardoner, who had declined the Host's invitation to tell a fabliau ('a myrie tale ... som myrthe or japes,' VI 316, 319), finds himself and the Host to be characters in a fabliau situation, with one of them – not the Host – the victim.

The Pardoner's strength is derived from his brains and his tongue. He is a preacher and an actor, an author figure who performs before his audience (his inscribed readers) and creates for and with them a work of art. It is their response that determines the outcome (a happy or sad ending) of his total performance. The man's genius lies in his wager to perform before two publics – the intradiegetic public of pilgrims and the metadiegetic public of peasants – shifting from one to the other at will. In the end he fuses them (intentionally? by accident? as I believe, out of frenzy?), seeking to make the pilgrims of the frame enter his fictional world and accept his mastery in it.

On the one hand, Chaucer, by having him fail, wants us to recognize that the Pardoner is a brilliant but corrupt manipulator of language; Chaucer also shows that art cannot be separated from moral and civic concerns. In addition, he shows us that, in strictly human terms, speech is the only medium for expressing virility that society allows the Pardoner; for him the tongue replaces the penis. With his tongue, full of 'venym,' this alleged snake in the garden attacks the peasants and the pilgrims and forces them to submit to metaphoric rape. When the Host scathingly refers to the Pardoner's 'fundement' and 'coillons' and would have the latter 'kutte ... of,' the Pardoner is reduced to silence: 'This Pardoner answerde nat a word; / So wrooth he was, no word ne wolde he seye' (VI 956–7). The Host does not castrate the man's testicles; he has no need to. He castrates his tongue in a gesture that recalls Faux Semblant who, more fortunate than the Pardoner, severed the tongue of Male Bouche. Faux Semblant, speaking and cutting, is a winner; the wretched Pardoner, truly a Male Bouche among the pilgrims, reduced to silence, is made doubly sterile and robbed of the only virility and identity he is allowed to have.

One can say that Chaucer, imitating Jean de Meun's achievement with Faux Semblant, has created a ferocious satire on hypocrisy, on the Church, and on sodomy. In his agon with the community, the liar and hypocrite loses; from a self-designated *eiron* he is transformed into a pitiable *alazon* and still more pitiable *pharmakos*. Still worse, generations of critics have held the belief that the Pardoner is the one lost soul on the pilgrimage, and that he is to be damned. Perhaps. Yet reader response is more complex than many scholars recognize; as always with Chaucer (and Jean de Meun) other things remain to be said. First of all, some of the implied audience outside the text as well as some of the inscribed narratees on the road to Canterbury are caught up in the spell of the Pardoner's rhetoric and surely admire the man for his supreme brilliance as an artist. The brilliance of the tale itself, one of the finest brief narratives in world literature, testifies to that. As an author figure, the Pardoner is the best. Secondly, some of us, especially those familiar with French literature, can hold other values than those of Kittredge and Robertson. We may like Faux Semblant and la Vieille; we may prefer Renard to Isengrin and fabliau wives to fabliau husbands. It is possible to admire wit, rhetoric, discourse, and, yes, intensity of deceit and desire. Note also that the narrative does not end with the Pardoner's discomfiture and silence. Chaucer has the Knight make peace between the Pardoner and the Host and urge upon them the kiss of peace. The Pardoner is restored to the community. Given the Host's implied feelings toward homosexuals, the kiss has to be a vindication for the victim and more than a little humiliating for the victor. The Pardoner gets his kiss after all. And the Host is forced to give it. Against the exegetical rigorists, I agree with those who point out that no soul is lost by judgment of man; only God judges and only he knows. There is hope for all, including the 'pervert' with the poisoned tongue. This kiss of peace with the Host, the symbol ending the Pardoner's episode, redeems his obscene song of love with the Summoner, the sign at its beginning. Although the Pardoner and the Summoner corrupt love and justice, for them and all the others there remains a higher Justice and a higher Love. This is because *Amor vincit omnia*, the doctrine that the Prioress carries with her everywhere, is a conquering Love open to all, whether they be conscious of it or not.

The Franklin's Tale

Chaucer's comic mode of fabliau and satire is not the only register in the *Canterbury Tales*. Far from it. The *Canterbury Tales* is a unique masterpiece in part because of the extraordinary range of modes and styles that are juxtaposed. If I have concentrated on the comic and satirical, it is because this mode demonstrates Chaucer's evolution from and contrast to the earlier love-vision poetry of Machaut and Froissart. It is perhaps, from a modern perspective, Chaucer at his best, and in it the French presence is pervasive.

Romance or high courtly narrative is as important as the comic-satirical. Chaucer's treatment of the tradition is complex and ambivalent. No doubt familiar with and influenced by alliterative and metrical English romance (the only vernacular genre to have attained a coherent literary identity prior to his own contribution), Chaucer nonetheless seems to have held the native romance tradition in little esteem. The elegant London court poet parodies English romance in *Sir Thopas* and the *Squire's Tale*. On the other hand, the same elegant London court poet aims at establishing a high courtly romance standard, something approaching the *genus grande* of epic. To do so, in this domain he turns to Italy. *Troilus and Criseyde*, the *Knight's Tale*, the *Clerk's Tale*, and the *Franklin's Tale* are all derived from texts by Boccaccio, and the *Clerk's Tale* comes from Petrarch's Latin version of Boccaccio's story of Griseldis. The *Man of Law's Tale*, which some scholars associate more closely with hagiography than romance, is the free reworking of a section of Nicolas Trevet's fourteenth-century Anglo-Norman chronicle. Otherwise, French prose versions of Boccaccio serve as 'cribs' for the English poet, who was relatively insecure in both Latin and Italian. However, there is an additional indirect French presence in the Italianate high romances. For example, when Chaucer 'medievalizes' Boccaccio's *Filostrato* in the *Troilus*, he does so under French influence, introducing from French courtly authors – specifically Guillaume de Machaut – a vocabulary, mood, and tone of traditional aristocratic *fin' amor* and of traditional clerical Boethian philosophy. *Troilus and Criseyde* reveals the pervasive textual presence of Machaut; it can be thought of as Boccaccio filtered through Machaut (Wimsatt 1976). Something even more striking occurs in the *Franklin's Tale*. Borrowing a *questione d'amore* from the *Filocolo*, Chaucer recreates the spirit, mood, tone, and structure of a true Breton lay in the French style, in the manner of Marie de France or, as romance, in the manner of Chrétien de Troyes, as well as Machaut (for the Machaldian component, Wimsatt 1991). Familiar with the latest, most fashionable literature on the Continent and with 'classics' such as *Le Roman de la Rose*, Chaucer also knows, respects, and borrows from still older traditions, the Reynard beast epic integrated into the *Nun's Priest's Tale*, and early Breton lay and romance resurrected in the *Franklin's Tale*. The *Franklin's Tale* represents one of his most subtle intertextual and intercultural literary creations.

Here I wish to raise again the problem of readings based upon the assumption of irony – Chaucerian irony vis-à-vis the tale and the teller. I believe such readings are valid in the case of texts that are, in and of themselves, comic and satirical and where the ironic presence of the teller or link enriches the over-all comedy and satire. It is, however, a very different matter when we deal with serious, beautiful stories in the high style such as the *Knight's Tale*, the *Clerk's Tale*, the *Man of Law's Tale*, the *Franklin's Tale*, and the *Prioress's Tale*. A number of scholars, by over-emphasizing a few light humorous remarks concerning the tellers in the *General Prologue* and by measuring both tellers and tales against the strictest Christian morality of an Augustinian bent, arrive at the conclusion that all tales and tellers have to be viewed in the same way that we view the Wife of Bath, the Merchant, and the Pardoner. In my opinion, this hermeneutic operation is one of reductionism; it not only distorts the best of Chaucerian romance and hagiography but it also impoverishes our appreciation of Chaucer, taking from us so much of his literary variety and complexity.

The *Franklin's Tale* is a perfect case in point. The plot, simply told, concerns a Breton knight, Arveragus, who weds his beloved, Dorigen, offers her freedom and equality in marriage – the ideal sequel to *fin' amor* – and then sets off to do deeds of prowess in England. A squire, Aurelius, pays court to Dorigen, in his own version of *fin' amor*. She spurns his suit, nonetheless promising him her love if he can remove the chain of rocks in the sea that poses a threat to her husband's ship when he returns. Arveragus returns. Meanwhile, Aurelius suffers. Then the man's brother helps him discover a magician in Orleans who will remove the rocks (by covering them with the sea). This he does. Aurelius appeals to Dorigen for his reward. Out of generosity and inherent nobility Arveragus sends her to Aurelius, lest she break her 'trouthe'. No less generous, Aurelius renounces a love that would disturb so noble and loving a couple; and the magician declines to claim his fee, proving that he too, a clerk, can possess 'gentillesse.'

In brief, the ironic, 'Robertsonian' reading of the *Franklin's Tale*, elaborated by Gaylord (1964, 1991), Peck (1966–7), Robertson himself

(1974), Miller (1980), and others, runs something like this. Dorigen is an emotional, irrational female who (1) foolishly accuses the rocks of manifesting disorder in the divine scheme of things and (2) adopts the principles of *fin' amor* 'in pley' (V 988) that allow Aurelius to perform deception on her and threaten her marriage vows. Still more guilty is Arveragus; he is wrong to abandon just sovereignty over his wife in Christian marriage in the name of *fin' amor*, a form of idolatry; he is wrong to leave home and abandon his responsibilities for two years; above all, he is wrong to order his wife to yield her body to another man. No one can be made to break a sacrament or to commit a capital sin, and no one is obliged to keep one's word if it covers a lie and undermines *caritas*. Arveragus is uxorious, a bad husband, and a bad Christian. Furthermore, given that the Franklin approves of the husband, the lover, and the magician, and their purported generosity and nobility, he also has to be viewed ironically. From this perspective, Chaucer undermines him as an authoritative and reliable narrator in the *General Prologue* and in the link. Both the teller and the tale therefore manifest a secular, bourgeois, modern sentimentalism that any true medieval Christian, especially Geoffrey Chaucer, would find odious and riotously, ridiculously funny.

I agree, instead, with those scholars who believe that Chaucer and his Franklin take the tale and the idea of virtue it illustrates seriously, and so should we.

Concerning the Franklin's moral character, an excellent case can be made that he is an ethically reliable narrator. The humorous remarks in the *General Prologue* concerning his propensity to food and drink (that he is, among other things, a man of pleasure) in no way incriminate the man or his tale. As with the Reeve and the Merchant, these are clichés from medieval estates satire; in addition, for the secular courts it was no more a fault to hold a good table and give good cheer in Chaucer's century than in Dickens's. The Franklin's largesse embodies the secular, aristocratic virtue of his class. We are probably expected to consider this 'vavasour' as a substantial, reputable freeholder, an esteemed member of the country gentry (cf. Specht 1981), an admirable figure in French romance (cf. Pearcy 1973–4 and Carruthers 1981) and, in late medieval England, a member of roughly the same social class as Geoffrey Chaucer the author and his immediate intended audience.

The gracious, worldly, tactful Franklin then tells a gracious, worldly, tactful tale. As a member of the gentry, he narrates an old story, a Breton lay, à la Française. Finally, his claim to be ignorant of rhetoric:

> But, sires, by cause I am a burel man,
> At my bigynnyng first I yow biseche,
> Have me excused of my rude speche.
> I lerned nevere rethorik, certeyn;
> Thyng that I speke, it moot be bare and pleyn.
> I sleep nevere on the Mount of Pernaso,
> Ne lerned Marcus Tullius Scithero. (V 716–22)

is simply an example of mock humility, itself a topos of rhetoric, the *captatio benevolentiae* appropriate to the beginning of his tale. With it he makes claim for a plain style akin to *genus medium*. It has also been observed that the Franklin's frequency of French and Latin loan words – 13.5 per cent – is among the highest in the *Canterbury Tales*, and is at its highest in the very passage where the man denies that he ever learned Cicero or slept on Mount Parnassus!

I am convinced that it is neither strikingly original nor strikingly heretical for the Franklin (and Chaucer) to speculate on the functioning of *fin' amor* within marriage or on the sort of marriage that could be grounded in *fin' amor*; they confront the ideal of *fin' amor* with the reality of marrying in the secular world. Chrétien de Troyes and Gautier d'Arras asked the same questions and arrived at roughly comparable answers in twelfth-century France as Chaucer's Franklin was to do in fourteenth-century England. Furthermore, in *Le Roman de la Rose* Jean de Meun has Raison propose 'amisté,' Ciceronian friendship between equals, as 'good love,' in contrast to the slavery of passion; also he has Ami (and la Vieille) insist that love can only flourish when both partners are free and therefore equal; and Ami counsels the equivalent of Arveragus' 'pacience' as the only attitude for a sensible man to hold vis-à-vis the woman he loves. All of Jean's characters consider empowerment to be anathema. Therefore, in a sense the Franklin is synthesizing Chrétien de Troyes and Jean de Meun, assimilating Jean's ideas on love to the institution of marriage in the same way Chrétien assimilated the *fin' amor* and chivalry of his epoch to the same institution.

In the courtly French tradition it is natural for Dorigen to commit an act of imprudence for the man she loves; she makes a rash promise in order to wish away the rocks that pose a threat to her love. Chrétien's Enide and several of Marie's heroines did comparable things, not to speak of the entire careers of Isolt and Guinevere. Such imprudence, especially in a woman, is a sign of her nobility and also of her 'womanness.' The result may be (provisionally) unfortunate; the motivation is admirable. It is no less admirable, indeed it is necessary, for Arveragus to leave his wife:

> to goon and dwelle a yeer or tweyne
> In Engelond, that cleped was eek Briteyne,
> To seke in armes worshipe and honour –
> For al his lust he sette in swich labour – (V 809–12)

Chrétien's Erec and Yvain, Gautier's Ille, and Marie's Eliduc do the same. If they did not, they and Arveragus would be dishonoured or 'recreant,' each unworthy of his wife's love and doomed to lose it.

Upon hearing Dorigen's story, Arveragus responds 'with glad chiere, in freendly wyse ... : "Is ther oght elles, Dorigen, but this? ... Ye shul youre trouthe holden, by my fay!"' (V 1467, 1469, 1474). This is the most noble, generous, and forebearing response a medieval husband can make. Those modern scholars who condemn him do so either from a nostalgic rigorist ultra-Christian perspective (à la St Augustine or St Bernard) or from a twentieth-century bourgeois world-view obsessed with fidelity in marriage. It is they who are anachronistic, projecting their own postromantic prejudices onto a fourteenth-century tale set in pagan Antiquity. There was a variety of ecclesiastical mentalities in the late Middle Ages, one of which indeed is represented by Chaucer's Parson. There was also a powerful feudal-aristocratic mentality, which, in its 'idealized style of life,' assumed courtly and chivalric archetypes. For the feudal aristocracy, marriage (which had become a sacrament only in the thirteenth century) was first and foremost a civil contract, crucial for the distribution of the patrimony. One's wife was not a possession, a body, or a thing to be hoarded or owned. Love – *fin' amor* – was one of the mainsprings of prowess and chivalric honour. Love could occur in marriage and outside of marriage, and although this was never the ideal, bodies could be shared. Lancelot and Guinevere, Tristan and Isolt, Guilhem de Nevers and Flamenca, the duke and the Châtelaine de Vergy make up a small number of the famous adulterous couples. In such cases the husband can be deemed odious, as in Marie's *Yonec* and *Laüstic* or the *Prose Tristan;* or he can be treated with sympathy and respect, as in *Amadas et Ydoine* and the *Prose Lancelot*.

Arveragus is a knight, Dorigen a lady, and Aurelius a squire. Chaucer manifests sympathy for the courtly aristocracy in the *Franklin's Tale* as in the *Knight's Tale* and *Troilus and Criseyde*. Arveragus, a noble, treats his wife as a noble person, a subject not an object:

> 'Ye shul youre trouthe holden, by my fay!
> For God so wisly have mercy upon me,
> I hadde wel levere ystiked for to be
> For verray love which that I to yow have,
> But if ye sholde youre trouthe kepe and save.
> Trouthe is the hyeste thyng that man may kepe.' (V 1474–9)

Her 'trouthe' and honour come first, because they are also his 'trouthe' and honour, and because, ever since *La Chanson de Roland*, the epic that invokes a God who never lies, keeping one's word was the first duty of the nobility and the first trait of 'gentillesse.' For Arveragus, freedom and trust come before domination and before physical possession; marital love, as in Chrétien and Marie, requires trust and forebearance, responsibility and sacrifice.

Furthermore, Arveragus' generosity extends outward to the community; it is contagious and he knows it. This is why he says, 'It may be wel, paraventure, yet to day' (V 1473). Arveragus is right. His nobility brings out the best in Aurelius, an aristocrat who makes songs and assumes the role of the courtly artist and poet. And their nobility brings out the best in the magician, a 'clerk' or 'philosophre,' the embodiment of *clergie* and the life of the intellect. Well it might, for, as Jean de Meun said, true nobility is defined by good deeds and virtue in the heart, and these are encouraged by the reading of books. The denouement of the *Franklin's Tale* is an exercise and a contest in grandeur as in a play by Corneille. Corneille's sense of what it means to be *généreux* (that is generous, free, and noble) is the late Baroque equivalent of the Old French *franc* and *franchise* – the quality of largesse, freedom, and nobility – that is the early medieval equivalent of the Franklin's 'gentillesse' and of his adjective 'fre.' This is a human grandeur that the Parson would treat with contempt but which Chaucer and his pilgrims can offer as one ideal for the human condition.

However, we should not make the error of attributing to Chaucer and his Franklin, as their contribution to the marriage debate, a modern bourgeois ideal of equality or identity between the sexes. Although Chaucer scrutinizes the notion of love and equality in marriage, to scrutinize and to proclaim are quite different matters. With the best of intentions, Dorigen does overreact, emotionally and irrationally, both with regard to the threat of the rocks to her absent husband,

and then to the threat of Aurelius holding her to her pledge. (In defence of Dorigen, see Morgan 1977 and Lee 1984–5, among others.) In her emotional, irrational shifting back and forth, Dorigen resembles the sea, the feminine element upon which she gazes, looking for Arveragus' ship – the sea of illusion that will indeed cover the rocks. The feminine sea, subject to the moon, 'lunatic' in its essence, is the objective correlative and the symbolic projection of Dorigen. Arveragus then returns over the sea, mastering the waters, and later, perceiving that chaos has invaded his household, proceeds to re-establish order. He also re-establishes the reign of masculine reason over passion (in Aurelius) and of generosity over greed (in the clerk). By correcting his wife and upholding her 'trouthe' and honour as well as his own, he upholds his sovereignty – the rightful sovereignty of husband over wife, reason over passion, order over disorder, and spirit over the flesh. Interestingly, this is the identical solution to the marriage problem offered by Chrétien de Troyes in *Erec et Enide* and *Le Chevalier au lion*, where, in the end, Erec and Yvain also attain sovereignty over land, their people, and their wives. Good sovereignty is one of the central themes in medieval secular literature. The Franklin's, therefore, is indeed one solution to the marriage debate, no doubt superior to the Wife of Bath's and the Merchant's, and yet not necessarily Chaucer's final solution, for the *Second Nun's Tale* will follow. Unlike Chrétien, Chaucer does not propose *the* answer to any problem. He continually juxtaposes instead of superimposing and, like Jean de Meun, defers his own response indefinitely, in a state of permanent inconclusiveness.

The Franklin's answer is the least clerical and the most aristocratic. Such is to be expected from an idealistic, committed member of the lesser gentry, who told a Breton lay in the French courtly style. Chaucer's idea, in the late 1390s, to recreate in English the great short fiction of twelfth- and thirteenth-century France is a stroke of genius.

It is generally agreed that Chaucer was familiar with metrical and alliterative romance in England. It has been proposed that he knew the Auchinleck manuscript which contained a number of vernacular romances and three Breton lays in English: *Lai le Freine*, *Sir Degaré*, and *Sir Orfeo*. From them Chaucer could have obtained the topoi developed in the Franklin's exordium, and from the lay of *Orfeo* the structure of marriage, separation, and reunion (cf. Loomis 1941).

Donovan (1969), however, points out that Chaucer could equally well have been familiar with Breton lays in French. After all, there were five manuscripts containing French lays available to him as opposed to the one English Auchinleck text. Furthermore, Chaucer formed part of a French-speaking and French-reading circle connected with the royal court, possessing an aristocratic, international culture that was strongly French-oriented. My own feelings support the second view, especially since critics who emphasize Chaucer the Englishman sometimes blur, in their account of vernacular romance, the French, Anglo-Norman, and English traditions. The stylistic features Chaucer is alleged to have borrowed from romance – a neutral, plain style, a vivid, concrete sense of realia, naturalistic dialogue, and a more formal rhetoric – would be more likely of French than of English provenance. The *Franklin's Tale*, in its idealized, conventional formalism enhanced by lyrical and rhetorical *amplificatio*, especially in the monologues, and the no less stylized, conventional behaviour on the part of the characters, is French in essence, and closer to Marie de France and Chrétien de Troyes than to the Auchinleck narratives. If ever anyone in English took a 'conte' and made of it a 'molt bele conjointure,' it is Chaucer in the *Franklin's Tale*.

The *Franklin's Tale* is truly a Breton lay: in the prologue, it has the authenticity and modesty topoi; the tale itself has a Breton locus, the port town of Penmarc'h; in the time frame it happens in a vague but distant past; in the love story, a triangle – husband, wife, and suitor – is grounded in *fin' amor* and lived by the nobility. We find additional courtly Arthurian motifs: the suitor makes songs of love wooing his lady in a *locus amoenus*; the clerk provides the element of magic and the supernatural with his enchantments; and the Arthurian 'rash boon,' committed by Dorigen, proves to be the structural kernel of the narrative.

Most of all, Chaucer has recaptured the flavour of Marie's *lais*. What dominates is not heroism or feats in arms but sentiment and inner feeling. Like Marie, Chrétien, and Thomas, Chaucer's Franklin is concerned with the ethical problems raised by love and marriage; he scrutinizes the implications of freedom, nobility, love, and 'trouthe.' Like his French forebears, the implied author seeks and finds the essence of idealism, courtliness, and gentle behaviour, the generosity of love and of 'gentillesse.'

Finally and perhaps most important of all, Chaucer, like Marie in so many of her lays, chooses one image that will play an archetypal role in the narrative and, as *mise en abyme*, itself mirror the problematic of the narrative and the proposed solutions to it. This is the chain of rocks, 'the grisly rokkes blake' that terrorize Dorigen and are the immediate cause of her rash boon:

> But whan she saugh the grisly rokkes blake,
> For verray feere so wolde hir herte quake
> That on hire feet she myghte hire noght sustene ...
> 'But, Lord, thise grisly feendly rokkes blake, ...
> An hundred thousand bodyes of mankynde
> Han rokkes slayn ...
> But wolde God that alle thise rokkes blake
> Were sonken into helle for his sake!
> Thise rokkes sleen myn herte for the feere.'
>
> (V 859–61, 868, 877–8, 891–3)

She projects onto the rocks her passions and fears, her love for Arveragus, her resentment at Arveragus' absence, her doubt of God's providence, and her horror at having to submit to Aurelius. Aurelius and his clerk create the illusion that the rocks have disappeared. The rocks become the focal point for the play of illusion and reality and of order and disorder that lies at the heart of Chaucer's tale. Harsh, cutting, black, Bachelardian hard earth of the will (cf. Bachelard 1948aG), the rocks give the impression of threatening both Arveragus and Dorigen. In fact, however, they also function as the image of her love and of his steadfastness. Although Aurelius' clerk will make them appear to go away – 'It semed that alle the rokkes were aweye ... "But wel I woot the rokkes been aweye"' (V 1296, 1338) – they do not go away. They are there, and Arveragus and Dorigen, as lovers and as a couple, survive in spite of them and because of them. Arveragus completes his quest – his martial withdrawal and return from Brittany; Dorigen completes her quest – her withdrawal and return from Aurelius' garden. Man and wife, singly and as a couple, grow in the course of the narrative, test their marriage on stone, and 'In sovereyn blisse leden forth hir lyf' (V 1552), as they deserve. The rocks and the sea, Arveragus and Dorigen, reason and passion, male and female, animus and anima, are integrated, a maturation process whereby a couple is formed and bound in the state of marriage and the exercise of sovereignty.

Nevertheless, we are never allowed to forget that life is harsh, people make mistakes, and desire is not always satisfied nor is fidelity automatically rewarded. The rocks symbolize the power of the unknown and the dread that the unknown rightly instils in us. Life is threatening; so is Nature; so is the cosmos. The *Franklin's Tale* is not a poem of bourgeois sentiment and bourgeois optimism. On the contrary,

Chaucer captures, and recreates, along with the ideals of marital 'pacience' and marital sovereignty, a quality we find in Marie de France and Thomas: poignancy of dread and loss, of suffering and sacrifice. Tragedy also forms part of the human condition.

The Manciple's Tale

Not all the stories included in the *Canterbury Tales* are masterpieces like the *Reeve's Tale*, the *Merchant's Tale*, the *Wife of Bath's Tale*, and the *Pardoner's Tale*. Some were considered dull or insignificant and were passed over in early studies on Chaucer. In more recent times the non-masterpieces have been studied seriously and with sympathy. We now take into account divergences in taste between the Middle Ages and our twentieth century. We also recognize that a tale apparently insignificant on its own terms can receive enhanced value either in relationship to its teller and the pilgrimage frame or in the total structure of the *Canterbury Tales*. Such is the case for the *Monk's Tale*, *Melibee*, *Sir Thopas*, the *Squire's Tale*, and the *Manciple's Tale*. The *Manciple's Tale* is of special interest in relation to the French tradition. It is a fascinating example of Chaucer's intertextual practice.

One of the least elaborate of the Canterbury stories, the *Manciple's Tale* is a brief, simple retelling of one episode in Ovid's *Metamorphoses* – the myth of how the Crow (in Ovid, the raven)[30] came to have black colouring, told in Chaucer as an exemplum against 'jangling,' i.e., being a tattletale. The Manciple says that the Crow, beloved of his master Phoebus Apollo, sees Phoebus' wife (in Ovid, Coronis of Larissa) commit adultery. He informs Phoebus of the adultery. Phoebus, in a rage, slays his wife, and then, equally in a rage, turns upon the Crow, changing his feathers from white to black and taking away his beautiful voice.

Chaucer knew his Ovid well. However, he knew Ovid partly in the original and partly through the fourteenth-century *l'Ovide moralisé*. For the story of the Crow, he was inspired by *l'Ovide moralisé* and by Guillaume de Machaut's *Voir Dit*, which also contains a version of the myth. Both works stimulated Chaucer's imagination and directed his creative powers into new directions.

The *Ovide moralisé* offers an accurate and vigorous French translation of the *Metamorphoses* interspersed with allegorical commentary of an historical, typological, and moral nature. Machaut and Chaucer never reproduce the *moralitas* typology. Given that for the moralist, Phoebus is a figure for God, Coronis for mankind, and the raven for the devil, and given that both Machaut and Chaucer modify the story in order to make Phoebus appear more guilty (or at least more foolish) and the Crow-raven more innocent, it is obvious that they disregard the typology and/or treat it with humorous disrespect. This should be a warning to Chaucerians and Old French scholars to beware of imposing allegorical or typological readings, in the Augustinian mode, on secular texts.

However, Chaucer does follow *l'Ovide moralisé* in the 'secular' moral – the danger of jangling. The fourteenth-century French poet is the first who denounces, with rhetorical and sententious invective, 'jenglerie,' 'jengles,' 'jenglerres,' and 'jengleours.' Like the Manciple he draws the conclusion:

> Mieux doit mentir,
> Ou taire soi, pour pais avoir,
> Que mal souffrir pour dire voir. (2546–8)

It is better to lie or to keep silent for the sake of peace, than to suffer harm for telling the truth.

The rhetorical invective and the down-to-earth, almost cynical moral lesson are taken over, in toto, by the Manciple. Indeed, Chaucer expresses in the Manciple's voice the ideas, the spirit, and even the wording of the French text.

The *Ovide moralisé* and Machaut are both closer to Ovid than Chaucer is. Machaut begins to simplify the Ovidian narrative, and Chaucer, following his example, simplifies it a great deal more. The *Metamorphoses* and *l'Ovide moralisé* contain an important episode. On the way to inform Phoebus of his cuckolding, the raven meets a crow who seeks to dissuade him by recounting her own comparable experience. The Ovidian crow, a beautiful girl transformed into a bird by Pallas to escape the lust of Neptune, told 'jengles' to her benefactress, and Pallas, in anger, transformed her feathers from white to black. Machaut includes the crow's story and her warnings but deletes the near-rape and the metamorphosis, perhaps for reasons of decorum as the seamier side of classical mythology would be inappropriate in his courtly *dit amoureux*. Following Machaut's lead but in more radical fashion, Chaucer suppresses the entire crow-Pallas narrative. The myth becomes in his hands a simpler, more stark tale, appropriate to the voice of the Manciple and his traveling companions. Yet it inevitably loses the structural complexity and the *mise en abyme* effect – a story within a story – to be found in both Machaut and *l'Ovide moralisé*. On the other hand, perhaps in compensation, Chaucer has the Manciple introduce into the tale his mother, who, he tells us, warned *him* about jangling in much the same manner and language that the crow warned the raven.

The chief effect of the deletion is to make the Crow (raven) appear less guilty. In the Manciple's hands, the Crow tells Phoebus of his wife's philandering out of idealism, in pure innocence, without having been warned in advance against jangling and without expecting a reward. Other changes in the narrative contribute to the Crow's increased innocence and Phoebus' and his wife's increased guilt. For Chaucer also suppresses the key element, in Ovid, *l'Ovide moralisé*, and Machaut – the girl (Coronis) was pregnant with Phoebus' child, the great physician Aesculapius.

Furthermore, whereas in *l'Ovide moralisé* Coronis confesses her guilt and Phoebus, about to punish the raven, merely states that the girl didn't deserve to die, in *Le Voir Dit* Machaut has Coronis keep silent concerning her guilt or innocence and has Phoebus speculate that perhaps she was innocent. In Chaucer, of course, Phoebus swears irrationally that the girl *was* and *is* innocent. Also, perhaps influenced by the metaphorical adultery ('avoutre' and 'avoutire') in the French, Chaucer transforms Coronis of Larissa, Phoebus' 'amie,' into an anonymous 'wyf' with the result that in the English the Manciple recounts a literal, canonical adultery and cuckolding. Also, in Chaucer, the level of discourse is lowered to reflect the greater offence on the part of the woman. The French words, in themselves quite un-Ovidian – 'lecherie,' 'vileynie,' 'avouture' – in the Manciple's voice become the Crow's triumphant and brutal 'Cokkow!' (IX 243) shrieked three times, followed by a brief account culminating in the line 'For on thy bed thy wyf I saugh hym swyve' (IX 256). The Manciple alludes to Phoebus' cuckolder as a 'lemman' and implicitly to the wife also as a 'lemman' and, cynically, a 'wenche'; he then defends his use of language, maintaining that the distinction between a 'lady' and a 'lemman' or 'wenche' is based upon artificial class etiquette not concrete physical reality. In the meantime he has delivered a series of misogynistic remarks directed against womankind as a whole, borrowing three passages from Jean de Meun that compare woman in animal terms to a bird, a cat, and a she-wolf.

In Chaucer's hands, the myth has been shifted to proclaim the guilt of Coronis, the guilt and stupidity of Phoebus, and the innocence of the Crow, while at the same time Chaucer retains the message of *l'Ovide moralisé* and *Le Voir Dit* – do not jangle! As a result, some scholars have protested that the genuine subject matter of the tale has to be justice and injustice, not loose talk, and that an inappropriate and foolish moral (do not jangle) has been tacked onto an inappropriate and foolish tale which recounts the punishment of innocence. Or, from a more modern critical perspective, other scholars observe the paradox of a torrent of discourse condemning discourse and urging silence; often they plead in favour of indeterminacy and against any coherent, univocal reading of the Manciple and his tale.

Before pursuing this subject further, it is important to see what Machaut, Chaucer's immediate predecessor, does in roughly the same situation, where he inserts the Coronis of Larissa myth into *Le Voir Dit*. In the second half of *Le Voir Dit*, the relationship between the Narrator and Toute-belle disintegrates and the jealous Narrator has difficulties in communicating with Toute-belle; here some exempla from classical myth are introduced. These stories – Semiramis, Hebe and Iolaus, Picus and Canens, Polyphemus and Galatea, Coronis, and, finally, an elaborate discussion of Fortuna – give Machaut an opportunity to enrich his narrative with all the subtlety and complexity of intertextual gloss and *mise en abyme*.

In the course of the unravelling of the love bond, twice the Narrator takes Toute-belle's 'image' (her portrait or sculpture) off the wall and locks it in a chest. Twice the 'image' appears to him in a dream, berating him for mistreating it and for his unwarranted suspicion of Toute-belle. During the second dream the 'image' tells the Narrator the story of the raven.

In Machaut's hands, the incident achieves full comic status. Irony is generated because of the incongruity of the Ovidian myth when applied to the story of *Le Voir Dit*, and the incongruity of both Coronis of Larissa and Toute-belle vis-à-vis the ideals of *fin' amor* that *Le Voir Dit* purportedly upholds. The Ovidian myths (both the raven's story and the crow's) are anticourtly in the extreme: the one is an account of cheap adultery and cuckolding; the other emphasizes the crow's spite at having been supplanted in Pallas's eyes by the owl. Meanwhile the love affair between the Narrator and Toute-belle also turns courtly ideals upside down. Talebearers, instead of slandering the lover to the lady, slander the lady's reputation to the lover-narrator. And he believes them. Similarly, it is Toute-belle who, defying the courtly precept of secrecy, wishes their affair to be known to the court. The court does know about it and presumably has a right to comment, for or against.

The 'image' recounts the myth to the Narrator so that he will cease believing gossip that sullies Toute-belle. Metaphorically, Coronis represents Toute-belle, and Phoebus Apollo the lover. The analogy is uproariously comic because, first of all, although the Narrator is a great poet (the persona of Guillaume de Machaut), otherwise he fails to resemble Apollo in any way. In contrast to the Greek god, he is aging, ill, unattractive, one-eyed, and a coward. When the 'image' refers to Coronis and her 'damoisel,' joined by nature, it evokes ironically the natural union of young bodies that the Narrator and Toute-belle cannot attain. Even more ironic is the fact that, gossip or no gossip, talebearing or no talebearing, in the myth Coronis *is* guilty of being unfaithful to Apollo; in the myth the story is true! This is hardly the most skillful approach to convincing the Narrator to cease being jealous. The 'image' all but admits as much when it asks: 'And *if* it is true, if Toute-belle is guilty, why do you punish *me*? Why should I pay for her?' 'Le doi-je pour ce compere? ... Convient-il que je le compere?' Again, this is hardly an argument to allay the Narrator's suspicions, but it is a splendid comic response to his frustration; he punishes Toute-belle by punishing her portrait, and it is the portrait that protests!

In what follows, although the Narrator takes the 'image' out of the chest and replaces it on the wall, he is not convinced by the dream, for he later curses Amour and Fortune for his having lost Toute-belle and for the evil reports about her. As in Machaut's other texts, we see the ambiguous use of dream material, which grants authenticity, connects with the day residue, and creates distance, all at the same time. The dream, like the exchange of letters and like lyric verse, does not ensure communication or truth. Toute-belle's 'truth' is presented ambiguously, purportedly from her point of view (that of her 'image') but in fact it is told by her 'image' in the Narrator's consciousness through his wish-fulfilment dream. What we see is a tormented lover, in the throes of jealousy, not knowing the truth and not knowing that he can never know the truth. We also see the transmutation of failure and non-truth into 'The True Story,' *Le Voir Dit*, which captures the failure of love and the failure of truth in the magisterial success of art. And in *Le Voir Dit*, a total work of art, the raven-Coronis exemplum, as a classical story from Ovid inserted into the narrative and as the imago of truth told by an 'image' inserted into a dream, mirrors the hermeneutic and psychological problematic of *Le Voir Dit* structurally as a double *mise en abyme*.

It is significant then that Machaut, in the dream exemplum, underscores the thematics of beauty and art, developing these themes far beyond his sources. He tells us (the 'image' tells us) that the raven is beautiful, whiter than milk, and more beloved of Phoebus than his harp and his musical bow. When the raven appears before Phoebus, the latter is playing his harp, making beautiful music in an ornate palace embellished in gold, silver, and precious stones. The raven's denunciation is compared to a swan's song – the swan who sings beautifully prior to dying. Phoebus in consternation lets the harp fall from his hands and the crown from his brow. Instead of cremating Coronis' body (as in Ovid and *l'Ovide moralisé*), he embalms and preserves it in the temple of Venus, like a work of art. Finally, in his act of vengeance Phoebus not only turns the raven black, but he makes sure that the raven will never speak intelligibly again. The bird's voice is destroyed. Forever after, instead of speech or song, 'Jamais ne feras que jangler.' Machaut's hidden message is that both Phoebus and the raven are artists: the one fails as a lover; they both fail to communicate and to function in society. Speech harms as much as it helps. Such is, presumably, also the case for the Narrator-lover of *Le Voir Dit*.

Following Machaut, Chaucer elaborates the myth still further as a commentary on art and the artist. Phoebus is praised as an artist:

> Pleyen he koude on every mynstralcie,
> And syngen that it was a melodie
> To heeren of his cleere voys the soun.
> Certes the kyng of Thebes, Amphioun,
> That with his syngyng walled that citee,
> Koude nevere syngen half so wel as hee. (IX 113–18)

Phoebus himself taught the Crow how to speak, to tell tales in performance (like the tellers on the pilgrimage), and to sing beautifully:

> Whit was this crowe as is a snow-whit swan,
> And countrefete the speche of every man
> He koude, whan he sholde telle a tale.
> Therwith in al this world no nyghtyngale
> Ne koude, by an hondred thousand deel,
> Syngen so wonder myrily and weel. (IX 133–8)

Upon receipt of the bad news, Phoebus breaks his martial arms and his musical instruments – 'For sorwe of which he brak his mynstralcie, / Bothe harpe, and lute, and gyterne, and sautrie;' (IX 267–8) – and he punishes the *losengier* Crow in his quality of speaker and singer:

'Thou songe whilom lyk a nyghtyngale;
Now shaltow, false theef, thy song forgon,
And eek thy white fetheres everichon,
Ne nevere in al thy lif ne shaltou speke.
Thus shal men on a traytour been awreke;
Thou and thyn ofspryng evere shul be blake,
Ne nevere sweete noyse shul ye make,
But evere crie agayn tempest and rayn,
In tokenynge that thurgh thee my wyf is slayn.' (IX 294–302)

Like Machaut, Chaucer's Manciple tells us that artists are no better than other men and that they make mistakes in their use of speech. The Crow's 'janglerie,' after all, does incite to wrath and to murder. Speech disrupts the social and the private order. The Crow in a sense tells the truth, and yet in a sense he does not, for he fails to recognize the 'truth of the heart' – that Phoebus' love for his wife is the only truth and that his passion will nullify whatever empirical evidence is brought against it. Although Phoebus lies to himself and to the Crow concerning the girl's innocence, at the same time he does not lie, for his sentiments remain firm; he loves her still, and this experience of love proves more vital than the experience of adultery. The Manciple's digressions on the nature of speech, based on comparable digressions in Jean de Meun, also prove that verbal distinctions – between 'lady' and 'lemman' or 'wenche' – are artificial and culturally determined; they fail to account for life in its totality, in this case wifely adultery and husbandly affection. A disjunction is revealed between language and life; the incapacity of discourse to encompass reality is also revealed.

Phoebus can control neither his wife's fidelity nor his Crow's tongue. The Crow succeeds in communicating with Phoebus, and Phoebus with the Crow, to the discomfiture and misery of both. Communication is shown to be a positive evil, which causes harm and ought to be avoided. Phoebus, forced to choose between, on the one hand, his pride and self-deception based upon appearances and, on the other hand, whatever reality is embodied in the Crow's speech, chooses self-deception and illusion; therefore he deprives the Crow of his song and destroys his own song-producing instruments. He succeeds in deceiving himself and in maintaining his love by speaking to his dead wife and to the Crow and by imposing on the speechless Crow his own language. The wife is made to live again, remade, in his speech (not unlike White in the *Book of the Duchess*) and on his terms. And the tale itself ends in a flurry of language – discourse by Phoebus, by the Manciple as narrator, and by the Manciple's mother. (For different views on speech in the tale, see Harwood 1971–2, Wood 1980, Fradenburg 1985, McGavin 1986–7, Grudin 1990–1, Pelen 1990–1.)

Like Machaut's exemplum, Chaucer's tale forms part of a larger continuum. On the surface, Chaucer's frame, the *Manciple's Prologue*, concerns only jangling. In this text the Host indulges in play, mocking the Cook, who ought to tell the next story but is too sleepy or too drunk to do so. The Manciple jumps in, insulting the cook more virulently than the Host did:

> 'And, wel I wott, thy breeth ful soure stynketh ...
> See how he ganeth, lo, this dronken wight,
> As though he wolde swolwe us anonright.
> Hoold cloos thy mouth, man, by thy fader kyn!
> The devel of helle sette his foot therin!
> Thy cursed breeth infecte wole us alle.
> Fy, stynkyng swyn! Fy, foule moote thee falle!' (IX 32, 35–40)

When the Cook takes umbrage at the Manciple, the Host warns the triumphant insulter that cooks and manciples are professional enemies (like millers and reeves or friars and summoners) and know each others' professional secrets. The Cook can, if he wants, tell more about the Manciple's dealings than the Manciple would like. The Manciple responds by agreeing with the Host. He mollifies the Cook and tells a tale that apparently reinforces the Host's warning and does penance for his own social offence.

One key to the puzzle lies in the fact that the tale is told in the Manciple's voice, not the implied author's. When Geoffrey Chaucer ascribes a tale to a teller, the presence or absence of centring and determinacy becomes the teller's responsibility and presumably will contribute to the phenomenon of reader-audience identification or distancing.

Such a lesson of cynicism and expediency is appropriate from the Manciple, who also, in typically Chaucerian fashion, betrays himself to the implied audience, and perhaps even to the pilgrims on the road, in both his prologue and his tale. Whatever we think of his philosophy, being an inveterate babbler, he cannot himself live up to it. After having lost control of his tongue by insulting the Cook, he loses control of his tale with witty but uncalled-for digressions insulting women. The man who preaches silence in order to avoid making enemies has risked turning against him the Cook, the Host, the Wife of Bath, the Prioress, and the First and Second Nuns, not to speak of those others, 'gentils' or not, who don't fancy crooks. Each in his own way, Trask (1977), Wood (1980), and Burrow (1986) underscore the Manciple's failing. The Manciple betrays his failings and the inappropriateness of his social sense in much the same way, although at a lower level, as the Lover in *Le Voir Dit*.

Why does he tell his tale? Is the story merely an apology for having babbled against the Cook, because he is afraid of the Cook's babbling against him in turn? Surely Chaucer is more complex than that. Following the Host's example, the Manciple loves to 'jape.' He claims to be deathly afraid of the Cook and would do anything in the world to keep the latter quiet (IX 76–81). This is probably not to be taken seriously because, in fact, the Cook is speechless, out of either anger or drunkenness. The wily Manciple then ensures his adversary's silence by offering him still more to drink! The Host and the Manciple are both having 'pleye' with the Cook, who presumably poses a threat to no one. Why then the Ovidian myth and its *Ovide moralisé* and *Voir Dit moralitas*? Perhaps it is a warning to the Host, that *he* had better not meddle in the Manciple's affairs, and neither ask questions nor offer answers, whether in game or in earnest, concerning the man's business dealings. Perhaps cynical expediency and voiceless prudence are the Manciple's way of life, one however that he is incapable of living up to and that unmasks him at his worst. Perhaps, as Davidson (1979) has ingeniously proposed, the Manciple wishes to appear dull and stupid, telling an inconsequential and apparently modestly self-incriminating tale in order to avoid the far more serious unmasking and self-destruction that befell his predecessors in the story-telling contest. Finally, I think, perhaps it is a joke. He jokingly pretends to be afraid of the Cook. He jokingly gives way to the Host (the *magister ludi*) and his warning. He jokingly reaffirms his fear and his giving way in an Ovidian exemplum. In so doing, he jokingly mocks an empowered tyrant and unhappy husband who can be recognized as *his* parody of the Host. He and Chaucer mock proverbial wisdom – in fables and in social intercourse; and Chaucer mocks once again the simplistic morals that the naive inscribed tellers or inscribed listeners (the Man of Law, the Host) derive from their, his *Canterbury Tales*.

While undercutting the characters in his Ovidian *mise en abyme* and undercutting the Narrator (his own persona as lover and artist), Guillaume de Machaut always exalts the work of art, his *Voir Dit*; it will succeed as art in spite of the Narrator's and Phoebus' failures in love, and everyone's failure to communicate with and understand the other. Although speech does not lead to understanding, it does lead to and is the prime material for poetry that includes and recounts the failures in love and understanding.

While emphasizing more than Machaut did how Phoebus and the Crow function as artists, Chaucer on one level removes his fable from the Machaldian framework of a commentary on, and contribution to, the exaltation of literature. In the context of the diegesis, the Manciple, the Cook, and the Host are neither lovers nor poets. However, on the level of the ordering of the *Canterbury Tales* as a whole, Chaucer does make a statement on art and the artist. In fact, he refutes the high idealism of Machaut in its essence. From Fragment VII on, one of the themes of Chaucer's opus is the nature and functioning of literature. Recent scholarly opinion, for example Cooper (1984), Dean (1985), and Rogers (1986), emphasizes that the last four tales – the *Second Nun's Tale*, the *Canon's Yeoman's Tale*, the *Manciple's Tale*, and the *Parson's Tale* – form a coherent structure of decline and disintegration that ends however in new hope; thus they parallel the pattern of Chaucer's first four (or five) tales: the *Knight's Tale*, the *Miller's Tale*, the *Reeve's Tale*, the fragmentary *Cook's Tale*, and the *Man of Law's Tale*. The splendid but impossible ideal of the *Second Nun's Tale* gives way to the failed ideal – the perversion of art and intellect – in the *Canon's Yeoman's Tale*, which gives way to the impossibility of idealism and the failure of speech in the *Manciple's Tale*, which then gives way to the uniquely didactic functioning of sacred speech and art (non-art) in the *Parson's Tale*. Both the Manciple and the Parson undermine and ultimately destroy belief in imaginative literature, rhetoric, and the very taletelling that makes up the *Canterbury Tales*. The second half of Chaucer's masterpiece then presides over a disintegration in the aesthetic sphere that matches the erotic disintegration in the second half of the *Le Voir Dit*. The Parson answers the Manciple and all who preceded him, not only surpassing the Manciple's pitiful, cynical sense of justice and injustice but also his use of speech and of art:

> 'Thou getest fable noon ytoold for me,
> For Paul, that writeth unto Thymothee,
> Repreveth hem that weyven soothfastnesse
> And tellen fables and swich wrecchednesse.' (X 31–4)

The Parson, from an orthodox Christian perspective, considers all secular taletelling and all art that aims at 'solaas' to be dangerous.

He will not indulge. His 'myrie tale in prose / To knytte up al this feeste and make an ende' (X 46–7) is a penitential treatise treating God's justice and mercy. It disdains the secular erotic concerns of Jean de Meun and Machaut, the Wife of Bath, and the Franklin; it disdains the literary elegance of Jean de Meun and Machaut, the Knight, and the Nun's Priest. It urges the pilgrims to abandon their desire for profit, pleasure, art, and play, and to undertake, under his direction, 'thilke parfit glorious pilgrymage / That highte Jerusalem celestial' (X 50–1). In his ending, Chaucer enters a dimension all but foreign to Machaut and Jean de Meun. Just as Guillaume de Digulleville renounced Jean de Meun and hoped to surpass him with a nobler, better pilgrimage, so Chaucer in the voice of the Parson appears to renounce and surpass himself, with his own text in his own text, *in nomine Patris et Filii et Spiritus sancti.*

Whether, in fact, the Parson's voice reflects Geoffrey Chaucer's last words and last ideas is open to question. In the *Manciple's Tale*, however, we do find an exciting and, ultimately, coherent work of art that contributes to the total *Canterbury Tales* structure. Greatly influenced by Machaut's reading of the Ovidian myth, Chaucer includes the tale in his discussion of love and communication, and of art and the artist. At the same time, equally influenced by Jean de Meun, Chaucer degrades the courtly and artistic aspects of the myth, underscoring the low, and underscoring failure in all aspects of life. He then precedes it with a 'low' *Prologue* rich in medieval kitchen humour. The end result contributes brilliantly to what Dean (1985) and Allen (1987) have called the dismantling of the Canterbury Book, the thematic disintegration in the later tales that paves the way for closure. The end result also shows Chaucer reconstructing and bringing to a close the dialectic inherent in all of French medieval narrative in the preceding centuries.

Conclusion

The structure and meaning of the *Canterbury Tales* have become perhaps the greatest single subject of controversy on a single text in world literature. Chaucer's masterpiece is a story-telling contest, with all the passionate, human interest of the stories themselves, and the psychological, social, and ethical interaction among the story-tellers. It is also, as so many critics have emphasized, a pilgrimage. In the form that it has come down to us, the narrative begins at the Tabard Inn in Southwark; it ends as the pilgrims approach Canterbury. It begins in springtime, in April, and ends with the setting of the sun. It begins with the magnificently secular, courtly, and classicizing *Knight's Tale*, told by the leader of the secular world under the aegis of the Host as judge, and ends with the *Parson's Tale*, told by the humble parish priest, *pauperus pauperorum*, under his clerical aegis with God as judge. Given this structure, it is understandable that a generation and more of scholars are committed to the belief that Chaucer does propose to his implied audience an ideal of pilgrimage, quest, and purgatorial growth; and that, whether conscious of it or not (most are not), the pilgrims and tellers are on a spiritual journey from a spiritual tavern to a spiritual shrine. In terms of typological Christian analysis, they wend their way from Babylon to Jerusalem, from birth to death, from *cupiditas* to *caritas*, and from Creation to Doomsday. Given that the *Parson's Tale* and the *Retraction* appear to be Chaucer's last words, certainly his last words in the text, it is not outlandish to assert that the *Parson's Tale* does embody the author's final vision and personal judgment. The *Parson's Tale* is a penitential treatise on the seven deadly sins, probably translated from the French. Its position as the culminating tale would call upon the implied audience to reconsider all the preceding tales and their tellers in terms of the capital vices, and to distinguish true from false tellers, stories, relics, pilgrims, and lovers, and especially, to distinguish the devotees of Saint Venus à la Jean de Meun from the few who truly revere Saint Thomas, whose shrine is the ostensible goal of everyone on the road. Chaucer then would be portraying in microcosm the ills of a flawed Christian community and offering a spiritual healing process – the possibility of recovery of Christian law and Christian order through repentance, growth, and the realization of *peregrinatio*. From this vantage point, the fictional view of man in festivity on earth gives way to a non-fictional vision of God's creation seeking virtue in heaven (or vice in hell), and Chaucer's own voice would be found in the 'prose of reason' – the *Melibee*, the *Parson's Tale*, and the *Retraction*. Therefore, Chaucer's most important French predecessor and major French inspiration would have to be the Digulleville of *Pèlerinage de la Vie humaine*, and Chaucer's greatness would lie in his transformation of Digulleville's relatively static personal allegory into a more vital allegory of the entire teller-and-tale community.

I must admit that I give more credence to an alternative reading of the *Canterbury Tales*. I prefer to endorse the position that since Chaucer's masterpiece has come down to us unfinished and incomplete – a series of ten fragments in more than one state of disorder – we cannot be certain of the author's final intentions concerning his text.

We should be wary of attributing to him a rigorous Christian world-vision based largely upon the fact that the last tale of the last fragment, as the fragments have come down to us, happens to be the Parson's. An excellent case can be made that the Parson, who exceeds the conventional ecclesiastical doctrine of his age in his condemnation of love, sex, and marriage, proves to be not only a bore but a fanatic. His tale, like the others, can be interpreted ironically; like the others, it can be seen as casting aspersions on its teller and contributing to the 'roadside drama.' It is late in the day, the pilgrims are weary, and the Host is as condescending and vulgar as ever. Everyone wants a short, merry tale. So the Parson regales them with the longest, dullest, least aesthetic, least plausibly literary piece in the corpus. Furthermore, whether the implied extradiegetic audience agrees with the Parson or not, his is only one voice and one world-vision – like the others and comparable to them. We have no reason to assume that his voice – any more than Dame Raison's in *Le Roman de la Rose* – should be normative, whereas all the others are not, or that this voice is meant to negate the others. As for the *Retraction*, a case has been made that it is uttered by the naive, gullible, relatively unintelligent Narrator, who, under the Parson's influence, does repent; and that, once more, we ought not to confuse this Narrator's voice with that of the author Geoffrey Chaucer. In addition, like the palinode in the *Legend of Good Women*, the *Retraction* is a rhetorical commonplace, a topos of aesthetic not doctrinal import; it does not and cannot express Geoffrey Chaucer's personal credo. *Conclusio* topoi can include elements of prayer, intercession, confession, and, above all, pretended modesty, which allows the author to list his *opera omnia*. Such palinodes are frequent in the medieval French canon, which Chaucer knew and from which he probably borrowed the idea.

Although Chaucer may have been inspired to write a pilgrimage book by Guillaume de Digulleville, I am convinced that, in spirit, it adheres more closely to the secular *Roman de la Rose* than to Digulleville's sacred *Pèlerinages*. From Jean de Meun Chaucer took the ironical vision of man, a vision that, in a number of the best tales, is powerfully cynical and existentially stripped of illusion. Life on the road does take precedence over *caritas* and *cupiditas*. Like Jean, Chaucer asks questions but declines to offer answers. He juxtaposes rather than superimposes; he is conscious of conflicting alternatives and contradictory truths, and he suspends his own authorial, normative judgment. Issues are raised but not resolved. Each tale evokes one voice and embodies one world-vision, valid on its own terms but fragile, provisional, and undermined by the succeeding tale(s) and world-vision(s). Like Jean de Meun, Chaucer is a master of Gothic pluralism. Indeed, more than was the case for Jean, the fragmented form in which the *Tales* have come down to us and Chaucer's method of composition – working from and within fragments, and creating the fragments first with the idea of linking them later – testify to a highly problematic aesthetic reflecting a problematic attitude toward the universe – one that reveals the medieval equivalent of Bakhtin's heteroglossia.

This textual situation gives credence to the opinion, derived in part from a currently fashionable hermeneutic allegedly of continental origin, that the subject and message of the *Canterbury Tales* is its own textuality. According to this view, rather than preach truths, Chaucer discusses the discourse of those who discourse on truth. The *Tales*, in play and in earnest, focus on the functioning of language, the narrative fragmentation, and the disjunction exemplifying and contributing to the discourse debate problematic. From this perspective, Chaucer gathers together and juxtaposes diverse materials, aiming at multiplicity not unity, and generic and stylistic contrast, not drama or mimesis.

There is much truth and insight in this position. Nonetheless, I do not believe that the 'textual Chaucer' necessarily has to negate the 'comic Chaucer' and the 'mimetic Chaucer.' Like Jean de Meun, Geoffrey Chaucer is a master of variety and complexity. We find in his text almost all literary genres and modes that the Middle Ages offered; we find the most complex manipulation of voice and point of view, of narrative technique and of stylistic register, that the Middle Ages had seen. The *Canterbury Tales*, like Jean's *Rose*, is a supreme example of Menippean satire and, as such, a summa of medieval kinds and genres, but also of people, tellers, and listeners. Much of the best and the most dynamic work in the *Canterbury Tales* is secular, satirical, and powerfully, sensuously human. Chaucer's cutting edge is sharper, more powerful, more existentially disillusioning, and more French than the warm, wise, humane Geoffrey of Lowes' and Kittredge's generation. Yet they saw in Chaucer a truth that some of us have forgotten; he is the creator of a poetic universe, an imaginative universe of extraordinary power and vitality. I should say, following Muscatine (1957), that, in so doing, he did for English what great poets two centuries earlier had done for French. Under the aegis of the Latin classics and of two or three centuries of contemporary French classics, he created a vernacular standard, a *Hofsprache* and *Hochsprache*. His elegant, vital, and witty texts are comparable to those of the French masters, extending from Marie and Chrétien to Froissart and Deschamps. Like them, under their aegis, he treats the classics of Antiquity with urbanity and humour. Like them, he revels in psychology, satire, human interaction, the social world, and the sheer pleasure of story-telling. Like them, he varies the high and the low, juxtaposes stylistic registers, and plays with convention and discourse. Like them, he speaks out for freedom, responsibility, and 'gentillesse': His is a medieval, late Gothic humanism comparable to their medieval Gothic humanism. Like them, he grants to his vernacular speech and his vernacular-speaking people the sense of a tradition that bears authority, that can be imitated, and that will endure – a monument to the sophistication and maturity of his age and of himself. He remains England's greatest medieval creator and, in so many ways, with all caveats respected, still the father of his nation's literature.

II. Gower

John Gower is the second most important court poet of the Ricardian Age. In some ways he epitomizes the age more than Chaucer does; he certainly epitomizes the theme of this book. Gower is notable, over all other authors of the century, for trilingual achievement in the world of letters. In French he wrote *Mirour de l'Omme, Cinkante Balades,* and *Traitié pour essampler les Amantz marietz;* in Latin *Vox Clamantis* and *Cronica tripertita;* in English *Confessio Amantis* and *To Henry IV, in Praise of Peace.* In addition to the Latin opus – a significant accomplishment even though not in the same category with the Latin of Dante, Petrarch, and Boccaccio – Gower illustrates in his own person the bicultural, bilingual reality of his land and his age. Along with Chaucer, Langland, and the *Pearl*-poet he embodies the Ricardian Renaissance. He is also a major French poet, comparable to his brothers across the Channel, the last Englishman to compose a significant corpus in what was not yet entirely a foreign tongue. Furthermore, the notion of the three periods – French yielding to Latin yielding to English, accompanied by the notion of progress as the author moves from one period to another – is no more valid in Gower's case than in Chaucer's. The chronology of Gower's opus remains problematic. However, we have reason to believe that he composed in all three languages throughout his career, and in all three at the end of it. Rather than a 'progressive Gower' or a 'conservative Gower,' let us deem him the archetypal medieval Englishman in all his medieval Latinate and Frenchified Englishness.

1. *Mirour de l'Omme*

Mirour de l'Omme is an imposing didactic summa, composed in the 1370s. It contains a penitential treatise on the virtues and vices, estates satire, and a life of the Virgin and of Christ. Gower's chief source appears to have been Frère Laurent's *Somme le roi* of 1279. He also consulted William of Waddington's *Manuel des pechiés* and poems by Hélinand de Froidmont. Hélinand is quoted and cited by name (11404–9). Gower uses throughout the 30,000-line text a difficult twelve-line octosyllabic stanzaic form – aab aab ccb ccb – called the Hélinand strophe for the French poet who marked it with his stamp. Although the *Mirour* is extant in only one manuscript, it was known in Gower's day. It served as a major source for Gower's later work – the *Vox Clamantis* and *Confessio Amantis* – and, according to Lowes (1914), inspired parts of Books I, IV, and V of the *Faerie Queene*.

Like Victor Hugo with his great cosmic trilogy *La Légende des siècles*, *La Fin de Satan*, and *Dieu*, Gower conceived of his three long poems, to which he gave similar Latin titles – *Mirour de l'Omme* is renamed *Speculum Hominis* and then *Speculum Meditantis* – as a unity. The *Mirour*, the *Vox*, and the *Confessio* do treat similar problems and develop a similar thematic. Gower's vision concerns the individual and social ethics of mankind in a fallen world. Man has fallen but remains free. He has the choice between good and evil, reason and madness, God and Satan, and 'miseria' and 'dignitas.' Because of the fall, the order of nature is disturbed, as is the hierarchical *ordo* of society in its estates. Order in society and salvation in the individual ('commun proufit' from a 'homo justus') can only be attained through individual virtue, that is, personal morality, grounded in 'bone resoun.' Personal repentance and the personal choice of virtue over vice will then lead to social reform, public ethics, and legal justice in a proper hierarchical community; this can lead in turn to the universal victory of the spirit over flesh and of God over Satan.

Didactic literature, especially when it adopts the form of a summa, does not readily find a place in the modern canon. Since Romanticism the term 'literature' has been generally restricted to 'works of the imagination.' As we have seen in the course of this book, it is only since the 1950s that Jean de Meun's section of *Le Roman de la Rose* has been recognized as a masterpiece. The same can be said for Gower's major achievement in English, *Confessio Amantis*. And Guillaume de Digulleville still awaits reception into the cursus. It will surprise no one that more than one scholar has referred to Gower in general, and *Mirour de l'Omme* especially, as being pedantic, mediocre, marginal, and, above all, dull.

I contest this stance. Some of Gower's sources may indeed be so; however, *Mirour de l'Omme* is a true work of art, in the medieval and modern senses of the term, and worthy of our scrutiny and esteem. From the perspective of medieval aesthetics, Gower, like Jean de Meun and Guillaume de Digulleville, or for that matter like Dante, conceives of poetry as ethical instruction that combines *dulce* and *utile*, game and earnest. From the perspective of modern aesthetics, his 'mirour' or 'speculum' adheres to the literary category Frye calls an anatomy – a total, inclusive, encyclopaedic work of art with a strong intellectual and satirical thrust. Gower's mode is satire, his style is invective, and his tone is one of passion. Since Horace and Juvenal, satire has continually been deemed one of the great modes in world literature, as literary and as artistic as any other. Gower establishes a speaking voice and a speaking persona – a witness, guide, and teacher who denounces vice and pleads for virtue, who excoriates sin and sinners, who pleads with the implied audience to mend its way and lead a good life, and who finally enters directly into the fabric of his book, telling the Life of our Lady as an act of penance that will help bring about his own salvation. The speaking voice-implied author does this in a magnificent flow of Anglo-Norman French, vehement and highly rhetorical and yet at the same time fluent and organic. *Confessio Amantis* is a masterpiece in the plain style, the vernacular 'middel weie'; *Mirour de l'Omme* is a masterpiece in the flowing, rhetorical, passionately lofty register of the vernacular literature of ideas.

Unlike Digulleville, who concentrated on the voyage, Gower adheres to the combat. His theme is the war between virtue and vice, reason and passion, light and darkness, and God and Satan. He himself wages verbal war as narrating voice and implied author. *Mirour de l'Omme* is divided into four sections. In Part 1 Omme is assaulted by Pecché and her daughters, the seven capital sins; although saved by appeals from l'Alme and the assistance of Resoun and Paour, the seven vices wed Siecle, the World. Gower describes the vices in detail. Because of the vices, Omme is taken captive. In Part 2, to counter Siecle's wicked marriage and the proliferation of evil in the world, Resoun weds the seven Virtues, daughters of God. The virtues counter the vices, good counters evil, and the narrating voice continues to excoriate and to denounce. However, whatever may happen to Omme as an individual, Siecle, wedded to the vices and the sire of their progeniture, is doomed. The world is bound to the flesh and the devil; good fails to win out over evil. In Part 3 Gower turns to the World, to the condition of the estates in contemporary England. Here follows a denunciation of vice in social and historical terms comparable to the moral, ethical denunciation of vice in Part 1. When he has finished, the Speaker tells us that the only hope for man is as an individual, a soul to be saved through the mediation of the Blessed Virgin Mary and Our Lord. He then, in Part 4, proceeds to tell the lives of Mary and Jesus as an historical and individual response to the historical and social errors of the world. Although Siecle is lost, Alme and, therefore, Omme can be saved. In a structure of psychomachia, the virtues are set off against the vices, and our spiritual mediators and saviours are set against the corruption of a fallen world. Evil yields to good that yields to evil that finally will be conquered by the only Good – Christ the son of Mary, the Incarnation that redeems man and the world.

The antithesis between good and evil and God and Satan that constitutes the 'inner form' of Gower's anatomy is reflected in a pattern of antithetical imagery – demonic imagery employed to characterize the vices and the estates, and apocalyptic or pastoral imagery to characterize the virtues and the Holy Family. The seven sins correspond to, and are in part derived from, the seven heads of the beast of the Apocalypse. Pecché herself is that seven-headed monster:

L'apocalips q'est tout celeste
Reconte d'un horrible beste,
Q'issoit de la parfonde mer:
Corps leopart, ce dist la geste,
Mais du leoun ot geule et teste,
Des piés fuist urce a resembler,
Sept chief portoit cil adversier,
Si ot disz corns pour fort hurter,
Ove disz couronnes du conqueste ...
C'estoit le monstre a qui donné
Fuist plain poair et plain congié,
Au fin qu'il duist contre les seintz
Combatre et veintre du pecché. (9889–97, 9913–16)

The heavenly Apocalypse tells of a horrible beast that arose from the depths of the sea: the book says it had the body of a leopard, but the snout and head of a lion, and its feet resembled a bear's. This devil had seven heads and ten horns with which to strike, with ten crowns of conquest ... This was the monster to which was granted plenary power and authority to combat the saints and overcome them with sin.

Her seven daughters, corresponding to Digulleville's seven monstrous hags, ride to their wedding feast each mounted on the appropriate emblematic beast, with the appropriate emblematic bird perched on her fist. From the medieval bestiaries, the creatures are to be interpreted *in sensu malo*: the lion and the eagle are aligned with pride, the dog with envy, the boar and the cock with wrath, the ass and the owl with sloth, the wolf and the kite with gluttony, and the goat and the dove with lust. In addition, the wolf in lamb's clothing serves as a metaphor for hypocrisy and for the friars; the camel, dog, and snake for hatred; devouring beasts of prey and the owl for 'covoitise'; the lion and tiger, kite and hawk for 'ravyne' (abduction); the dog, kite, and crow for excess; and the salamander for 'foldelit.' In the estates satire, the papacy is a monster, bishops are stinging bees, lords are peacocks, parish priests are birds of carrion, and friars are wolves. These animal images underscore the fact that sin dehumanizes mankind, dragging men to the level of bodily instinct so that he is no longer subject to reason.

The material bodily lower stratum is also symbolized by imagery of rot, corruption, ordure, and physical decomposition. Ipocresie and a number of judges in their estate are shown to be whited sepulchres, beautiful on the outside with rot and filth within (1117–26). Tençoun manifests herself in the pus of a bursting wound or vomit from the mouth; Superfluité is like a bursting inflated belly, with accompanying rot, ordure, and vomit; and Leccherie embodies the stench and texture of leprosy. Religious orders and secular lords are associated with corruption, corpses, and butchery. Sompnolence and Peresce are depicted in images of softness and effeminacy.

At the worst, corruption and decomposition end in poison. Poison is secreted by serpents; the serpent is the emblem of Satan, the snake in the Garden of Eden. Therefore Fals semblant and Envye are assimilated to serpents and dragons; Tençoun is ill with poison; Avarice grants fever.

The serpent's venom originates in his forked tongue. Detraccioun, Fals semblant, and Tençoun are characterized by sins of the mouth, double-tongued, distorted discourse. Meanwhile, the essence of evil in the social world is shown to be 'triche' – trickery, cheating, prevarication, hypocrisy, deceit, lying speech – especially prevalent in the merchant classes but not unknown to the clergy. Thus, as in *Le Roman de la Rose*, illusion triumphs over reality and the mask becomes the image of life.

False speech serves as the foundation for false institutions, social bonds that turn the world upside-down. One arena of corruption in the social domain is Parliament and the court. Men of the law are to be found among the worst of the evil-doers; they are creatures who cheat the poor for lucre, whose golden tongues are activated only by gold, and who function as traps and glue to capture innocent birds:

> O comme le siecle ad poesté,
> Qant tiel miracle ad demoustré
> Sur son sergant q'ensi l'orr donne:
> Car meintenant q'il l'ad donnée,
> Sa langue en ce devient dorré,
> Qe jammais puis sanz orr ne sonne.
>
> Sicomme les reetz et les engins
> Soubz les buissons en ces gardins
> Hom tent as petitz oisealx prendre,
> Ensi fait il de ses voisins
> Qui sciet pleder ... (24433–8, 24505–9)

Oh, how mighty is the world when it can manifest a miracle such as the one that gold gives to its sergeant of law: for, once it has been given, his tongue becomes gilded in such a way that ever since it cannot speak without gold ... Just as one lays nets and traps under the bushes in gardens to seize little birds, in like manner he who knows the law does unto his neighbours.

Equally significant is the fact that Pecché and her seven daughters hold a parliament to seduce Omme; Pecché will become his companion, Siecle grants him material goods, and Temptacioun preaches to him, with the result that Char (the Flesh) does offer homage. Although Omme and Char escape from the first assembly, a second, the Devil's Parliament (a 'court pleniere'), is held in the presence of Pecché, Siecle, his seven wives, and their thirty-five daughters. On this occasion, after a violent onslaught, Omme does yield and is enclosed in the prison of Accidie, Siecle serving as jailer.

If Omme succumbs to temptation and loses the battle, it is because, *allegorice*, Satan has brought into the world such variety and complexity of sin. *Literaliter*, it is because so many adversaries – seven mothers and thirty-five daughters – assault him. On one level, these are personifications of vices and subvices; on another, strictly diegetic level, they are forty-two threatening women. The process of multiplication and division is presented in terms of marriage, engendering, and the family. Satan couples with his daughter, Sin, and Sin gives birth to Death. Death couples with his mother to give birth to the seven Vices. They couple with the World to engender the thirty-five hermaphroditic subvices. Sin and vice are thus associated with woman and the body; with copulating, engendering, and giving birth; with incest; with perversion; and with marriage. Avarice and man stand at the centre of estates satire, and Lust and woman at the centre of the diegetic tale of the vices. At fault are 'Amour seculer' and a twisted, corrupt version of the marriage rite. The corrupt marriage and corrupt court then give rise to a world out of joint, full of strife and disorder. The imagery, including sex and procreation, recalls the demonic pattern in Digulleville's *Pèlerinage de la Vie humaine*, a probable source for Gower.

However, in antithesis to the demonic imagery, Gower establishes a pattern of positive, Christian imagery. According to Olsson (1977), it is grounded in the four cardinal virtues. Conscience and Resoun appeal to God, supported by the advocacy of Mercy and as a result the Lord offers his seven daughters, all seven Virtues, to Resoun. Resoun wears to his wedding the blue robe of fidelity with a white band of purity. Gracedieu performs the ceremony. The virtues and their progeny represent Christian womanhood, Christian marriage as sacrament, and Christian life under the guidance of grace and reason. Good speech, by Debonaireté and Loenge, negates the discourse of sin. In addition, Gower encourages his audience to listen to good sermons, to avoid 'fol parler,' to keep silent in good shame (Vergoigne), and to pray silently in the heart, as true Devocioun is better than words.

In contrast to the softness, rot, and corruption of the world, and for that matter in contrast to the fires of passion, six of God's daughters are evoked metaphorically with imagery of stone: Humility is depicted as a diamond, Virginity as a pearl, Charity as the portal and road to heaven, Magnanimity as allegorical armour, Constancy as a tower built on rock, and Patience as precious metals hammered and burnished into a chalice. This is Bachelard's hard earth of the will conceived in medieval terms, grounded in a medieval aesthetic that exalts light and sheen; it allies aesthetic beauty with moral goodness and epistemological truth. No less significant is the function of water – Devocioun's tears and Pités' sea water extinguish evil fire.

Furthermore, the wicked animal imagery of the vices and the estates is countered in two ways. Good animals, *in sensu bono*, replace the beastly, subhuman creatures of evil, *in sensu malo*: the eagle of devotion, the lamb of humility, bees of praise, the dove of modesty, the ant of solicitude, the cock of wakefulness, and the eagle and lamb now assimilated to Saint John the Apostle's virginity. These animals, which partake of a tradition of Christian iconography, grant biblical and typological overtones to Gower's text. The same is true for his plant imagery. *Mirour de l'Omme* tells of the daisy, lily, palm tree, cedar, flowers and trees in general, and the Parable of the Sower. These trees and flowers have biblical, typological connotations. In addition, archetypally, they evoke the green world, the pastoral vision of beneficent nature, Eden before the Fall, and the *civitas Dei*, that respond to and negate the violent, bestial manifestations of Satan in his 'siecle.'

For human beings two patterns of behaviour are counselled. On the one hand, vigilance, control, and the domination of reason and will over the passions is urged. Paour appears as a sentinel or gatekeeper, Vigile protects her flock of sheep and the citadel, and Bonnegarde and Discrecioun (the latter with four eyes) guard the five senses. Secondly, ever in antithesis to the softness and sloth of Siecle's women, humans, like Resoun's wives and daughters, should live the active life of hard work and liberality; Almosne is presented as the active chambermaid, and Sollicitude imitates Martha not Mary. Such power, control, and activity result in a truly spiritual existence – one of humility and modesty (Vergoigne), of forty days fasting to resist Satan in the desert (Sobreté), of slimness and asceticism (Aspre vie). Spirit triumphs over the flesh, and will and reason both over the sensual appetite. The Christian enjoys freedom and mastery (Franchise) in place of slavery to the world, the flesh, and the devil.

In the end, however, Gower tells the story of Mary and Jesus. Sacred history and imagery and the divine world of the Holy Family alone can master the tyranny of Satan and his minions. The Blessed Virgin Mary and the Living Christ embody, literally incarnate, those positive images that Gower had expounded earlier in his discussion of the virtues. Jesus is the Lion of Judah and his word the Eagle and Dove of the Spirit, while he remains the Agnus Dei who offers his flesh and blood as nourishing bread and wine for all men. He is the Temple of Jerusalem, the road to salvation, the gate to heaven. His mother is the Rose of Sharon, the Lily of the Field, and the gem of gems.

Jesus and Mary embody chaste, unselfish, generous, total love – *caritas* – to each other and mankind. Christ multiplies the loaves and feeds the multitudes; he heals illness and brings Lazarus back from death. Joachim and Anna give away their riches, offering even their child to God. Mary, the image of humility and chastity, is purified in the temple, as is the infant Christ, born in a manger with the ox and the ass. Christ, like Mary, stands for non-violence. He preaches the Good Word, using speech for good purposes, counselling justice and love, offering his body and blood to mankind, and then his Word, in tongues of fire, to the fledgling Church at Pentecost. Gower tells of Mary's joys and her sorrows. Life is both harsh and beautiful, wicked and ecstatic, even for the Mother of God.

Gower tells of Mary and Jesus because their story is his answer to the problem of evil in the individual and in society. Nature and the four elements, created by God, are good. The Fall is man's responsibility, for Omme alone is at fault; he stands both free and responsible. Because the estates are corrupt and out of joint, Omme is guilty in the social context. The only hope is for individual Man and men to free themselves and to attain salvation. Salvation can only be had through Jesus Christ, the Son of God, and through the intercession of the Mother of God. In this way do slaves resist masters; indeed they triumph over masters. In this way is the bodily function of engendering and giving birth redeemed, as is the spiritual use of speech and of the mind. Here only are men and women made whole, as complete human beings.

Mirour de l'Omme begins with the beginning of time – with Creation, the fall of Satan, and his engendering Sin and Death. It ends with a series of events turning around the greatest historical event of all, Advent – the revolution in time, with God the Father through the Holy Ghost engendering God the Son of Mary. Death gives way to eternal life, and sin to salvation. The history of Jesus and Mary is recounted by an I-narrator, an author figure who chooses to tell a happier, better story. The Narrator says: 'All seven sins are present and eager to claim me. What can I do? I can appeal to Mary to heal and to save me. I speak in French, to instruct lay people and for remembrance by clerks' (27361–480 passim).

The individual to be saved is the implied author. 'Omme' represents Every Man, and the particular man who speaks and prays, who ends his book by naming Mary's Holy Names. The actant – Siecle or Omme – is male, and the Speaker as observer and, in the end, as actant is male. The adversaries and adjuvants are female. Phenomenologically, the Self is a man and is passively subject to onslaught or to succour, to being dragged down or pulled up, by woman as the Other. The women, eighty-four of them, act on him, for and against, in rot and in stone, in poison and in speech. In the end, the Speaker is saved (or hopes to be saved) by a man, Jesus, but also, and emotionally more so, by still another mother, the greatest of all.

Mirour de l'Omme is, in macrocosm, a *speculum* that contains a totality of ethical thought. As a microcosm, it bares the soul of one thinking and suffering man; he understands good and evil, he is eager to teach others and transmit wisdom from Latin to Romance, and he also seeks to imitate Christ and Mary in their humility, in his own lone, humble, forlorn quest for the good life and for eternal life.

2. *Cinkante Balades*

Gower's remaining French works – *Cinkante Balades* and the *Traitié pour essampler les Amantz marietz* – are of a mode and style different from *Mirour de l'Omme*, so passionate, satirical, vehement, and sublime in its rhetoric, and so grandiose in its scope. The *Balades* and the *Traitié* are *ballade* sequences – fifty-two and eighteen respectively – composed in the most contemporary, Parisian court style and displaying all the rigour of composition demanded by the lyrical fixed form.[31] Gower does a splendid job with rhyme royal, which he may well have borrowed from Chaucer (Itô 1976, Dean 1991). Although they have a doctrinal core, these texts are at least as lyrical as they are didactic, and their subject matter is high courtly love, in and out of marriage.

Partly because Gower condemns his own 'fols ditz d'amours' (27340) [lewd poems of love] in the *Mirour* and also in *Confessio Amantis* (I: 2708 ff.), and partly because of the assumption that Gower's 'French period' was abandoned for a more rewarding career in Latin and English, scholars (including Fisher 1965) generally ascribed these texts, especially *Cinkante Balades*, to the author's youth. More recently it has been recognized (by Itô 1976) that the *Balades* are extant in a manuscript containing also the *Traitié* and a number of other works in Latin and English, and that this manuscript constitutes a trilingual medley dedicated to King Henry IV, perhaps presented to him at his coronation. The dedication Envoy ending the *Balades* provides a link with the *Traitié* and functions organically in both sequences. The *Traitié* can also be considered a sequel to and semi-palinode for *Confessio Amantis*. It is probable then that most if not all of these lyrics were composed in the late 1390s, with Henry in mind, and the theme of marriage meant to reflect on the order and harmony presumed to emanate from the great Lancastrian prince.

Marriage is one theme that distinguishes Gower's *ballade* sequences from those composed in France. *Cinkante Balades* begins with six pieces treating love that will end in marriage, continues with forty-five lyrics more 'universal' in application (for all lovers whatever their situation in 'la fortune d'amour'), and ends with a palinode in which the Speaker abandons all other loves for the Virgin Mary, Mother of God. The *Traitié* then contains eighteen *ballades*, all in praise of marriage. It has been proposed that Gower's exaltation of licit, conjugal love, here as in *Confessio Amantis*, relates to his personal life (he wed Agnes Groundolf in 1398) or to his supposed class ideology (that of the bourgeoisie) or to the Christian philosophical world-view of 'moral Gower.' Yeager (1990) also has proposed that Gower's exaltation of wedlock implies repudiation or sabotage of the preceding French tradition of *fin' amor*. Although Yeager's argument is most persuasive, I envisage the marriage-topos from a different perspective. The marriage metaphor is especially appropriate in a collection offered at the moment of coronation to a new monarch, the lord and master of his realm and the bridegroom of his people. Furthermore, there is a long tradition of writers seeking to harmonize *fin' amor* and marriage and legitimize and socialize the dominant literary passion of the age and thus bring a literary ideal into congruence with man's social aspirations. What Chrétien de Troyes and Gautier d'Arras did in the twelfth century, and what Chaucer did in the 'Marriage Group' of the *Canterbury Tales* (especially the *Franklin's Tale*), Gower was to do in his courtly lyrical sequences. Gower's originality and his contribution to the centuries' old debate on love is to juxtapose the two loves – frustrated and unhappy, consummated and happy; he exalts both *fin' amor* and marriage in lyrical poetry, the mode that gave birth to *fin' amor* and was always its most striking generic vehicle.

I imagine John Gower integrating *fin' amor* and marriage rather than repudiating *fin' amor* because, first of all, the two 'states' are depicted in almost identical terms. The first six *ballades* portray licit love as passion and as *fin' amor*. Topoi endemic to the courtly tradition and that Gower will employ in his 'universal' *ballades* are developed here: the coming of spring, the lovers' separation, the growth of desire, and the lyrical text itself functioning as messenger and go-between. These poems differ from the rest of the sequence only in two themes: fidelity, and shared, satisfied desire. The refrain of *ballade* 4 is: 'Vostre amant sui et vous serrez m'amie' [I am your lover and you will be my beloved]. In the culminating *ballade* the Speaker declares:

> Jeo me doi bien a tiele consentir,
> Et faire honour a trestout moun pooir,

> Q'elle est tout humble a faire mon voloir:
> Jeo sui tout soen et elle est toute moie,
> Jeo l'ai et elle auci me voet avoir. (5: 3–7)

I must agree to such a person as she and honour her with all my might, for she is completely submissive to do my will. I am all hers and she is all mine; I have her and she wishes also to have me.

It is as if, in his century and in his land, marriage has to be proclaimed for the Speaker to give literary expression to happy, shared, sensual, successful passion. Perhaps Gower exalts marriage simply because he wishes to explore the literary vein of happy love. He speaks of fidelity and joy, not the sacraments. The *Traitié*, it is true, expounds conjugal love in terms ideologically appropriate to Christian wedlock – the dominance of reason over the flesh, of the soul over the senses, and of the values inherent in chastity and fidelity. These poems denounce 'foldelit' and 'fole amie'; they proclaim 'Horribles sont les mals d'avolterie' (9: refrain) [horrible are the evils of adultery]. It is also true that, of the eighteen *ballades*, a good ten repeat *ad nauseam* the same message, citing *ad nauseam* classical examples. John Gower would not be the first or the last writer whose most exciting, most beautiful poems treat unfulfilled desire, and who then ran out of inspiration concerning 'Honest amour.'

Gower is at his best in his lyric mode as a poet of *fin' amor*. The best of *Cinkante Balades* depicts *fin' amor* in all its power and passion. There is nothing strikingly original in Gower's treatment of the subject, as critics have noticed. Nor should there be. *Fin' amor*, especially in the fourteenth century, was a conventional literary, rhetorical stance expressed in literary, rhetorical texts. Gower had before his eyes a legacy of two centuries of great lyric verse; this includes the troubadours and trouvères as well as Machaut and Froissart. In Gower, as in the troubadours, the trouvères, and the Minnesänger, the poem is situated chronologically in springtime; the month of May is the time of renewal for the seasons, the liturgical year, nature, and love. The Lady's beauty equals the month of May, says the Speaker (10); although flowers and birds rejoice in the new season, he is miserable from love (36). The Lady stands supreme, much higher, better, and nobler, than he. She is the sun (21), a diamond and a crystal (38, 45), the phoenix (35), the flower of flowers (6), and the physician who can heal the Speaker's illness (6, 27, 45). The Lover indulges to the full the religion of love, venerating his Lady and honouring and adoring her in the secular parody of Christianity that *fin' amor* came to be. The adoration and the veneration, the distance separating lover and lady, testify to the Speaker's state of unsatisfied desire. The great courtly theme of obstacle is explored in over a half-dozen *ballades* (2, 7, 8, 9, 25, 29, 39); obstacle is depicted as separation both physical (in space) and symbolic (in spirit or sentiment). The Speaker gazed upon the Lady and fell in love, 'A bone houre est qe jeo vi celle ymage' (23: refrain) [it was my good fortune when I saw her likeness]. He is eager to behold her again and does so in his mind's eye, and yet she will not gaze on him. Danger turns her eyes elsewhere. Nor does he dare speak to her; if and when he can make a plea, it is to no avail: 'Com plus la prie, et meinz m'ad entendu' (18: refrain; also 14) [the more I beg her, the less she believes me]. If that were not enough, the Speaker also suffers from the 'fals jangle,' the 'male langue' of 'mesdisantz,' the traditional tattletales and sowers of discord who slander the courtly lover in his beloved's eyes and function as obstacle figures – *opposants* – in the archetypal structure of courtly love.

As a result of this, the Speaker suffers. He endures the wound of love from Cupid's dart (27) and love madness. Love is 'sotie.' Love and the Lover are mad in a world upside-down, a *confusio oppositorum* subject to the turn of Fortune's wheel. The Speaker is a ship at sea; storms oppress him for the Lady's mouth blows forth destructive winds (30). Indeed, more often than is generally the case with the trouvères or Machaut and Froissart but not more often than with Occitan troubadours, Gower reverses the seasons; in four texts he evokes January or March, not sweet spring. His heart and his erotic mood are centred in winter, in the cold, in the old year, or shifting back and forth from winter to spring, never in repose.

More than his French predecessors and contemporaries, the Speaker dares to complain out of misery and frustrated desire; he protests, and he reacts to his situation with wit and humour. He calls upon the Lady to respond; after all, a good servant has to be paid (28). Praise is mitigated:

> Car pour sercher le monde, a moun avis
> Vous estes la plus belle et graciouse,
> Si vous fuissetz un poi plus amerouse. (11: 5–7)

For, even were I to search the entire world, I still would believe you are the most beautiful and full of grace – if only you were a little more loving.

The Speaker doesn't wish to blame anyone; still he gets nothing for his troubles (17). In *ballade* 40 he accuses the beloved of being fickle, 'changables,' and of loving more than one, like Helen of Troy. Words differ from deeds, he says, and 'Loials amours se provont a l'essai' (refrain) [loyalty in love is put to the test through experience].

Significantly, five *ballades* are composed in a woman's voice, from the point of view of the woman as lover (41, 42, 43, 44, 46). No less significantly, the structures of desire are altered by gender. Sometimes the female Speaker praises her beloved, affirming her passion for him and offering herself to him; if not that, she keeps the bounds of her honor (46: 5–6) for the sake of reputation. Sometimes she denounces her lover, 'Cil tricheour' (41: 18), for deceit on his part, falseness that originates in his crude animal nature:

> Unqes Ector, q'ama Pantasilée,
> En tiele haste a Troie ne s'armoit,
> Qe tu tout nud n'es deinz le lit couché,
> Amis as toutes, quelqe venir doit,
> Ne poet chaloir, mais q'une femne y soit. (43: 9–13)

Never did Hector of Troy, beloved of Penthesileia, put on his armour with such haste as you, naked, go to bed; lover to all, you don't care whoever turns up, provided it be a woman.

The obstacle persists, not from the man's refusal – this presumably is inconceivable – but from the woman's discretion or from the man's promiscuity. A generation before Chartier, Gower, along with Christine de Pizan, explores the woman's perspective on *fin' amor*. He allows the lady to utter reproaches, to denounce her suitor (in three of the five poems), and to make the audience see how a woman can suffer from *fin' amor* as a man does (in four of the five poems). In Gower the Narrator-lover, regardless of gender, is the victim in *fin' amor* poems vis-à-vis the Narratee-beloved; the act of speaking and making poetic discourse is assimilated to suffering and thwarted desire, independent of gender. Perhaps the act of speaking creates thwarted desire.

Still, as in the earlier tradition, *fin' amor* is a literature of hope as well as of frustration. The Narrator-lover hopes to move the Narratee-beloved to love him in turn. He does so through discourse, through the very language of the poem. Therefore, Gower, inspired perhaps by Machaut's and Froissart's *dits*, or perhaps by the early trouvère lyric, exploits the motif of the *ballade* itself serving as messenger – a go-between that can unite the lover and beloved in the very fiction it recounts. The Speaker dares not speak to his Lady; however, as he is a writer and author figure, perhaps his text will convince her. The text plays a functional role in the fiction it itself recounts; it becomes a *mise en abyme* of itself in itself.

Art can be good. Love can be good when it is shared, when the lovers are faithful, and when 'honest amour' triumphs over 'foldelit.' It is not inappropriate that the author figure, an implied author learned in three languages, should display learning and multiply classical allusions in praise of good love and in denigration of fornication and adultery. Nor is it inappropriate that this poet of *fin' amor* and of 'honest amour' should take pride in his own work; flowery writing and perfect language are or ought to be the hallmarks of the good lover, the good wooer, and the good writer. For two centuries the trouvères insisted (and Machaut reiterated) that art is bound to Eros, and Eros to art; the good, sincere lover will sing, and the true singer has to be good and sincere.

In *Mirour de l'Omme* salvation and wisdom are attained through a fusion or synthesis of the masculine and the feminine – the intercession of Christ and the Virgin Mary brought about by telling the lives of Christ and the Virgin – leading to the integration of feminine personifications of virtue in the male thinking and creating consciousness. So also in the realm of 'seculer amour' the happy ending is the fusion or integration of the male and female principles through marriage, marriage and the female cultivated as the subject of poetry by a great male thinking and creating consciousness, that of John Gower the poet. Sexual integration, the assimilation of learning, and the attainment of wisdom are combined in the world-view of this Londoner who, like Chaucer, had a total vision of life and a total mastery of art.

3. *Confessio Amantis*

John Gower's masterwork, the text that crowns his career and makes him one of the leading figures in English literature of the Middle Ages, is *Confessio Amantis*, preserved in some forty-nine extant manuscripts. The first, most important version was composed from approximately 1385 or 1386 to 1390. A revised dedication in both the Introduction and the Conclusion can be ascribed to 1392 or 1393; Latin hexameter headings and prose glosses were added still later.[32]

Confessio Amantis combines the intellectual orientation of *Mirour de l'Omme* and the courtly mode of *Cinkante Balades*. Unhappy in love, the Narrator (Amans) sets out to a grassy meadow in the month of May. There he encounters Venus and Cupid. Cupid shoots fiery darts into Amans' heart. Venus asks why the man is so ill. Amans replies that he is miserable due to failure in love. Although Venus promises to cure this illness, first he must confess himself and receive absolution from her priest, Genius. After his 'shriving,' Amans makes a formal appeal (supplication, complaint) to Venus. The goddess responds that Amans is too old for love. She will indeed heal him, not by satisfying his desire but by removing it. Cupid withdraws the arrows from Amans' heart; Venus provides an ointment to close the wound. Now recognized to be an old man, Amans will return to his books and to the cultivation of a more fitting bond with Reason. He will aim for a higher, better love than that of Cupid and Venus – *caritas*.

So much for the frame. The kernel of the narrative, occupying some 31,000 lines, recounts the shriving. It records the extended dialogue between Genius and Amans. Genius questions Amans as to the seven deadly sins and the subsins within each category (a structure taken over from *Mirour de l'Omme*), each one interpreted as an aspect of or an affront to *fin' amor*. Genius discovers whether or not Amans has been guilty of committing the sin in question, he explains its nature, and exhorts his penitent to do good. The structure of the confession allows Gower to add an important dimension to his work – the telling of stories. Genius recounts one hundred and forty-seven tales (a number from Ovid), all purportedly told as exempla of the vices or of their contrary virtues in order to dissuade Amans from sin in love and to encourage him to lead a better amorous life. Thus *Confessio Amantis* functions as a story collection resembling the *Canterbury Tales*, the other English book of the century comparable in scope and artistic range.

Up until quite recent times the scholarly community envisaged *Confessio Amantis* much as they still envisage *Mirour de l'Omme*, as a long, rather dull book not in the same canonical register with Chaucer. For a good twenty years and more, the wind has changed. However, although the more recent school of critics recognizes Gower's English magnum opus to be a magnum opus, with some exceptions it is still interpreted in much the same terms as *Mirour de l'Omme* and *Vox Clamantis*. The consensus – and to a very real extent there is one – judges *Confessio Amantis* to be a major poem in the Christian tradition – serious, ethical, didactic, and truly the work of 'moral Gower.' According to this view, the poet repudiates 'love seculer' (*fin' amor*); in its place he proclaims Christian marriage. This 'love honeste' also has an ethical and political dimension, concerning 'jus naturae' and common profit, the duties of a just ruler in his commonwealth. And whereas courtly discourse corrupts, good speech reflects the *verbum Dei* and contributes to the didactic goal of instilling wisdom grounded in *caritas*.[33]

The standard reading is consistent and intelligent; it has a great deal to tell us about *Confessio Amantis.* It may well encompass Gower's intentions in writing the work and the reaction of a good portion of his audience. However, from a French courtly perspective other interpretations can parallel or supplement the standard reading.

Gower is, along with Chaucer, one of the English poets of the Ricardian era most oriented toward France, and most French in his reading and his personal aesthetic. The English *Confessio* is composed largely in 'French' octosyllabic rhyming couplets with lyrical segments in 'French' rhyme royal. The language contains word and rhyme play, rhetorical figures and colours, and an expanded, French lexicon – all typical of the French-oriented court style. Like Chaucer, Gower introduces into the English vernacular French literary and social ideas and French stylistic devices; he defends and illustrates English, standardizing the vernacular and enlarging its horizons by transmitting to it all that three centuries had already brought to the French *volgare illustre.*

French sources abound. For the central structural device of the seven vices, we need only list again Laurent d'Orléans' *Somme le roi,* the main source for *Mirour de l'Omme,* as well as *Mirour de l'Omme* itself. Gower evidently is exploiting his own earlier French text, and recasting it in English in a different guise and for a different purpose. The expository material in Book 7 – Aristotle's education of Alexander – comes directly from Brunetto Latini's *Livre dou Tresor* and from the *Secreta secretorum* – perhaps the French version by Jofroi de Waterford and Servais Copale. The framing device for Book 7 – the story of Nectanabus – is taken in part from Thomas of Kent's *Roman de toute chevalerie.* As for the exempla recounted by Genius to Amans, the Ovidian myths, as in Chaucer, are derived as much from *l'Ovide moralisé* as from the original *Metamorphoses.* For the non-Ovidian tales, a number of French sources have been cited: Benoît's *Roman de Troie, Le Roman de Marques de Rome,* Trevet's *Cronicle,* and French translations of the *Septem sapientes, Barlaam and Josaphat,* and Livy. Others, no doubt, are yet to be identified.

The listing of Gower's sources from whatever provenance pales in importance vis-à-vis the French courtly and anticourtly tradition embodied in Jean de Meun and Guillaume de Machaut – the tradition that had so dominant an impact on Chaucer. The diegesis of *Confessio Amantis* and the two principal characters are taken directly from *Le Roman de la Rose.* Jean de Meun and Guillaume de Lorris provide a naive, obsessed, somewhat innocent courtly lover, eager to please, eager to learn, and desperately eager to win his lady. Jean de Meun also provides the ultimate teacher and confessor, the priest of love,

Genius. The third figure in the frame, Venus, is a conflation of Venus and Nature in the *Rose*. Certain of Jean's personification characters and his themes reappear in John Gower's book – Faux Semblant, Danger, Male Bouche; the encyclopaedic ideal of a summa, the value of hard work, the functioning of good and bad speech, the necessity to replenish the species, the evil of homosexuality, the role of money in amorous affairs, the conflict of love and reason, and the metaphorical assimilation of sex to growth in nature and to writing. Jean de Meun's allegories are retained by Gower as a structure for his own story collection; the stories are always related to and set off by it.

From Machaut and earlier tales of love, Gower took the frame narrative; a love-lorn Speaker on a spring morning wanders into a *locus amoenus*, perceives divine authority figures, appeals to and is advised by them in a pattern of complaint and comfort, and finally is judged before a court of love. Also, in *Le Jugement dou Roy de Navarre* and, more particularly, *Le Voir Dit*, Gower found the notion of a Narrator-protagonist unfit for love because he is too clerkly, too much a man of books, and, above all, too old. Two Machaldian motifs among many exploited by Gower are the jealous, unattractive suitor assimilated to Polyphemus, and the inappropriateness of a suitor paying court to his lady or indulging in amorous devotions in church.

Instead of seeing Gower as a repudiator of the French courtly vision, I see him as a disciple of Jean de Meun, Machaut, and Froissart; he is also in his English text a disciple of Chaucer's *Book of the Duchess*, *Parliament of Fowls*, *House of Fame*, and the first redaction of the *Legend of Good Women*. The French authors, like Chaucer and influencing Chaucer, came to treat *fin' amor* in a complex, sophisticated, individual way, for courtly literature implies its own scrutiny. In this line, I believe that Gower indeed mocks *fin' amor*, laughing at it but also with it from within the tradition, and that he laughs at the more serious moral, Christian world-vision too. He indulges in what Wetherbee (1986) calls the comedy of high prosaic seriousness. Humour and wit are their own rewards, exploited not necessarily for a ponderous ethical goal but simply for themselves; they create a comic world and please the implied audience.

Gower's Prologue has been interpreted in many ways. I envisage it as a defence of the English vernacular using the state of that vernacular as a justification for a different kind of writing. A learned, scholarly man, proficient in three languages and a reader of Brunetto Latini's *Tresor*, Gower exploits the traditional categorization of literary discourse into the three registers: *genus grande*, *genus medium*, and *genus humile*. Renouncing at this point, for this book, the *genus grande* of Latin and French, the implied author stakes out his claim for a 'middel weie,' because the less exalted, mixed style permits 'Somwhat of lust, somewhat of lore' (19). 'Lust' is set off against 'lore,' and 'lore' against 'lust.' The lower register allows for, indeed encourages wit, amusement, and pleasure. Like Dante in his Italian, the use of the vernacular is itself a rhetorical stance that makes a rhetorical statement. The 'middel weie,' the *genus medium*, will not say the same things as *genus grande*; *Confessio Amantis* will not be the same book as *Mirour de l'Omme* and *Vox Clamantis*.

Humour is generated, first of all, by the juxtaposition of two independent, discrete, and divergent systems, the penitential and the erotic (cf. McNally 1964 and Burrow [*Gower's* Confessio Amantis] 1983, among others). Capital sins are confused with sins against the god of love or against the precepts of *fin' amor*. Desire, longing, obstacle, illness, healing, and salvation form a comic counterpoint on two levels, the erotic-secular and the confessional-sacred. Both levels are mocked, in themselves of course, but above all as a tandem, because of their juxtaposition. The juxtaposition of the two structures makes us aware of the extent to which each alone is rigid, mechanical, and, compared to the dynamic reality of life, artificial. It is the Bergsonian rigidity of both systems which is held up to laughter as they are juxtaposed to each other and to the down-to-earth, common sense reality of life.

There are many examples. Pride: Amans admits vainglory, for he is inordinately proud of his Lady's beauty and reputation; he normally obeys her but is disobedient in that he cannot cease loving her or telling her of his love even when she forbids him to do so. Envy: Amans, normally the most charitable of mortals, loses charity in the domain of Eros, where he joys in his rivals' sorrows, commits 'detraccioun,' and becomes 'Falssemblant' (Jean de Meun's Faux Semblant) in order to slander them in the Lady's eyes. Wrath: Amans never hates his Lady per se but does loathe her cruel words to him; also he loathes his fellow suitors. Gluttony: food imagery is applied to infidelity and adultery – a lover's unfaithfulness is likened to 'delicacy' in his eating habits – and love gluttony is likened to witchcraft. Also Amans often falls into a trance and is hypnotized in his Lady's presence; therefore he is 'lovedrunke.' Avarice: if Amans ever possessed his Lady, he would be guilty of this sin and keep her only to himself. As it turns out, since she has never given herself to him, he remains innocent. From these few instances, we see that the penitential system can be applied to the conventions of *fin' amor*, and the conventions of *fin' amor* are susceptible to analysis in terms of virtue and vice. However, the process proves to be humorous or ironic, and the validity of the operation superficial and contradictory.

The same is true concerning the stories told by Genius. Often his stories do, indeed, exemplify the aspect or situation of love which the context demands; often they appeal to virtue and dissuade from vice. On the other hand, no less often the stories, Ovidian and non-Ovidian, appear to be told for their own sake, as good stories. They have no immediate discernable rapport with the penitential context; or they are wrenched out of context to bear on the scheme of things Genius is preaching at the moment; or, indeed, they contradict his context and his scheme of things.

More than once, Amans quite properly observes that Genius' exempla, treating a particular vice, have nothing whatever to do with love; they do not speak to Amans as a lover or as a penitent confessing to the priest of Venus. This is the case for the first two stories on 'surquiderie,' *Capaneus* and *The Trump of Death*, and also for *King Namplus of Troy* as an exemplum of hatred. Other stories are told exemplifying a sin of which Amans is totally innocent; their didactic value to him is nil. Both he and the implied audience realize that the call of narrativity takes precedence over and enters into a state of tension with the purported call to virtue. This is the case for the tales about boasting and about idleness – *Capaneus*, for example, and *Rosiphelee*. From the perspective of narrative technique, it is obvious that, in very long stories, like *Jason and Medea* (1000 lines) or *Apollonius of Tyre* (1800 lines), the supposed moral of the story is lost sight of in the process of the telling, and that both Amans and the implied audience become engrossed in the superb telling of superb stories, to the detriment of moral exhortation. We temporarily 'forget' that Genius is the narrator and that a specific sin – false witness or incest – is being castigated.

Finally, as scholars have observed, it is inappropriate that *Pyramus and Thisbe* be cited as an example of haste; *Canace and Machaire* as an example of anger; or *Paris and Helen* as an example of sacrilege. These magnificent tales refer more naturally and immediately to other faults – suicide, incest, and adultery. To be cited for haste, anger, and sacrilege wrenches them out of context and undermines the very process of exemplifying that they are supposed to represent. In addition, if 'supplantacioun' is a sin, then why tell the story of *The False Bachelor*, who succeeds in 'supplantacioun'? If hatred is a sin, why tell of *Namplus of Troy*, whose hatred is successful? In Book 4, Philemenis is rewarded by a glut of fornication; in Book 5, Viola leaves Babio for Croesus (adultery? bigamy?), and the King of Apulia weds his steward's wife (more adultery? more bigamy?).

Humorous incongruity, visible at the level of the microtale, also pervades the macrostructure, even in its most serious manifestations. It is delightfully ironic to examine the frame for Book 7, Alexander's education, the text taken so seriously by Christian exegetical scholars. Amans requests the information (what Aristotle taught Alexander) as a digression to divert him for a while from the misery of unrequited love:

For be reson I wolde wene
That if I herde of thinges strange,
Yit for a time it scholde change
Mi peine, and lisse me somdiel. (6: 2416–19)

Genius replies that, as Venus' priest, he is ignorant in such matters; and since Alexander's education does not concern love, he hesitates launching on it. However, he has heard of it and, like Amans, is eager to know. Once the interminable digression is over, Amans quite appropriately comments that Genius' discourse is indeed interesting but that he, Amans, can still think only of his love and is eager to return to it:

Do wey, mi fader, I you preie:
Of that ye have unto me told
I thonke you a thousendfold.
The tales sounen in myn Ere,
Bot yit myn herte is elleswhere,
I mai miselve noght restreigne,
That I nam evere in loves peine:
Such lore couthe I nevere gete,
Which myhte make me foryete
O point, bot if so were I slepte,
That I my tydes ay ne kepte
To thenke of love and of his lawe;
That herte can I noght withdrawe.
Forthi, my goode fader diere,
Lef al and speke of my matiere
Touchende of love, as we begonne. (7: 5408–23)

Genius' diversion – his therapy, like Reason's in *Le Roman de la Rose* – proves to be an amusing failure.

Comic tension also exists on the level of character and psychology. The 33,444 lines of *Confessio Amantis* are story-telling, confession, and moral discourse; they also are conversation. Two figures take part in the conversation, Amans and Genius, each taken from *Le Roman de la Rose*. Each, as an allegory, is divided in himself, on the horns of a dilemma, in a state of comic tension. Together, they interact in a state of tension, forming a magnificent comic pair – priest and lay, father and son, reason and the flesh.

More than one scholar deems Genius to be the ideal Christian confessor, mild and just, who ferrets out Amans' sins and leads him along the path of salvation. I am not convinced. With other scholars, I believe the inherent contradiction in Genius' character derives from the fact that he is the priest of Venus, who is pagan goddess of love and metaphoric queen of the court of *fin' amor*, and, at the same time, he is an ordained priest in the Christian Church. The same contradiction played in Gower's source, the Genius of *Le Roman de la Rose* (where he was Nature's chaplain); in Jean de Meun, as in John Gower, the contradiction opens up a magnificent arena for comedy.

The tension between Genius' divided state, or between the two elements that constitute his state, recurs throughout the poem. The Christian priest excuses passion and incest in the story of Canace and Machaire, and he excuses crimes committed in the name of passion by Mundus. On the other hand, the priest of Venus lauds virginity, condemns adultery, and even is shamefaced when, in his account of the history of comparative religions (Book 5), he has to admit that Cupid and Venus are false gods like the others: 'Mi Sone, I have it left for schame, / Be cause I am here oghne Prest' (5: 1382–3).

As priest of either Venus or Christ, Genius often gives superficial, inappropriate, cynical, or just silly answers to Amans' questions and he fails to respond adequately to the penitent's situation. Concerning detraction, for example, instead of pointing out that scandalmongering is evil, Genius exhorts Amans to cease backbiting because (1) the Lady is so clever that she herself will discover whatever faults the other suitors may have, and (2) she is also clever enough to be aware of Amans' petty spite:

> For as thou saist thiselven here,
> Thi ladi is of such manere,
> So wys, so war in alle thinge,
> It nedeth of no bakbitinge
> That thou thi ladi mis enforme:
> For whan sche knoweth al the forme,

How that thiself art envious,
Thou schalt noght be so gracious
As thou peraunter scholdest elles. (2: 555–63)

Concerning 'cheste,' Genius urges the Lover to be 'debonnair,' not angry, when it is obvious that Amans is already debonair and has no need of this counsel. When faced with challenging or embarrassing questions on avarice or on the dangers of virginity (Jean de Meun's point, that the race will die out), Genius avoids responding altogether. On other matters, such as sloth, he simply counsels Amans to abstain. Furthermore, he always grants absolution, even when the penitent persists in his sin and adamantly refuses to mend his ways.

In spite of the superficiality and even downright silliness in his behaviour (or, some might say, because of them), Genius takes his mock task of mock confession too seriously. Deficient in imagination and sensitivity, he tells inappropriate stories to exemplify very real vices or appropriate stories vis-à-vis artificial, non-existent ones. He draws earnest morals from absurd or simply pleasant tales, and pleasant morals from serious tales. Above all, resembling most of Jean de Meun's characters, he is garrulous. He goes on and on, telling stories, dispensing morality, and proffering advice, whether appropriate or inappropriate, valid or invalid, whether Amans is listening or not. He pontificates, digresses, babbles, and muddles his way through, obsessed by his own scholastic notion of vice and virtue; he imposes his structure, his fund of stories, and his vision on Amans and on the reader. John's Genius is very different from Jean's Genius – the cynical embodiment of comic fecundity and life force – but equally funny. In his own way and on his own terms he is a superb comic creation, one of the great allegorical figures in medieval literature.

More than a little complexity appears in the character of Amans. On the one hand, this allegorical entity and voice can be seen as a man of good will, eager to be confessed properly and candid in his speeches to Genius. On the other hand, Amans inevitably responds as a courtly lover who subverts all morality to the ends of his courtly love. He is guilty of some sins and promises to avoid them in the future – because they hinder his winning the Lady. He is not guilty of others, because she has never given him the chance – fornication, possessiveness – but he would if he could and will if he can. Still other sins he commits and will continue to commit, whatever Genius says, for such is the nature of love and 'omnia vincit Amor.' We recognize Amans' natural and very believable human failings as the victim of frustrated libido, self-torment, and depression. We also recognize the Bergsonian topos of the comic, 'du mécanique plaqué sur du vivant.' Amans, like Genius, babbles on and on. He reduces every topic to his obsession – himself and the Lady. He persists in disobeying her and Genius whenever his passion is thwarted. He will continue to love her, to speak to her of love, and to suffer in the throes of melancholia, regardless of how hopeless the situation is or of what Genius and the Lady say.

Mechanical obsessions lead to foolish behaviour. Amans reveals in himself the flaws and contradictions inherent in *fin' amor*: he becomes a slanderer in response to the other slanderers; he runs and fetches and jumps and dances to please the Lady, at her beck and call, like a little boy, a pet, or a slave. Furthermore, as we have seen, whatever innocence from vice he is willing to avow derives largely from the fact that the Lady never permitted him to sin. Also, however, the sin would not have been very grave; at most Amans would have obtained a private audience or stolen a kiss or a caress. Sad to say, that is all. We have to conclude that, although Amans *is* guilty in his heart, even here his guilt is trivial; obsessed with *fin' amor*, the vices in which he would like to indulge are hardly serious; they are literary or societal conventions that a real, functioning priest would dismiss out of hand.

It is not surprising, therefore, that our foolish penitent manifests, from time to time, more than a little ignorance. In Book 1, he asks what hypocrisy means; in Book 3, wrath and hate (the French word 'ire' bothers him):

> Mi goode fader, tell me this:
> What thing is Ire?
> Sone, it is
> That in oure englissh Wrathe is hote ... (3: 19–21)

In Book 4, he queries sorcery and witchcraft; in Book 5, jealousy. He naively asks Genius how he can believe the latter's story of Venus, Vulcan, and Mars, if there is only one God. And, near the denouement, at the end of his tether, Amans begs Genius, 'a clerk / Of love,' to help him, for he (Amans) is but a 'lewed man' (8: 2052–4).

Tension is generated by the fact that this naive, foolish, ignorant, and obsessed lover is also a scholar and a learned man, that is, the clerkly narrator figure in the French tradition, typical of Machaut and Froissart but also going back to Chrétien and Thomas, indeed to the earliest saints' lives. He and Genius are brothers as well as adversaries. In Book 4, Genius urges Amans to find good examples of love in books, to learn from the Ancients, especially Ovid, and to work hard, using his mind, in the ways of love (another theme from *Le Roman de la Rose*). In the same book Amans adopts a strongly clerical stand against martial prowess. Like Machaut's persona in *Le Voir Dit*, Gower's narrator declares he is not adept in arms; furthermore, he argues, it is morally wrong to slay anyone, even Saracens, because of the threat to their souls (and to one's own). Significantly speech – rhetoric, *persuasio* – plays an important role in the love stories either as negative seduction (Mundus, Paris, Nectanabus) or as positive devotion (Pygmalion). In addition, the frame narrative of *Confessio Amantis* consists almost uniquely of discourse between Genius and Amans. In this action, this grand *conflictus*, the narrator-protagonist does not emerge as a loser vis-à-vis his clerical confessor; in the realm of discourse, in contrast to that of desire, Amans is a winner.

In the realm of desire, on the contrary, he loses. In the end Venus refuses his plaint and denies him his request on the grounds that he is too old. Like the narrating lover in Machaut's *Voir Dit*, Gower's narrating Amans is told that his green grass has turned to hay and that he is incapable of plowing his field and paying his debt:

> 'I wot and have it wel conceived,
> Hou that thi will is good ynowh;
> Bot mor behoveth to the plowh,
> Wherof the lacketh, as I trowe:
> So sitte it wel that thou beknowe
> Thi fieble astat, er thou beginne
> Thing wher thou miht non ende winne.
> What bargain scholde a man assaie,
> Whan that him lacketh forto paie?
> Mi Sone, if thou be wel bethoght,
> This toucheth thee; foryet it noght:
> The thing is torned into was;
> That which was whilom grene gras,
> Is welked hey at time now.
> Forthi mi conseil is that thou
> Remembre wel hou thou art old.' (8: 2424–39)

Whereas the goddess of love had responded favourably to a young lover's desire in *Le Roman de la Rose*, here, using Jean de Meun's phallic imagery of fecundity and reproduction – the plow, the field, fruit, trees, and grass – Gower turns the narrative upside-down by having Venus banish Amans from the realm because of his physical incapacity to reproduce the species (cf. White 1987 and Dean 1989). In the end, the clerkly narrator, inept for love in the tradition of Machaut, Froissart, and Chaucer, returns to his books. There is irony in this supposedly learned man being so ignorant in matters of love and so blind to his own failings that he realizes the truth only at the end. The unmasking that pervades Jean de Meun's and Machaut's texts is taken up with a vengeance by Gower at the moment of his striking, astonishing denouement. The theme of the denouement is the contrast between illusion and reality, between the romantic, *fin' amor* illusion of an Amans embodying only desire and the reality of an aging narrator, who has wasted his life in a fruitless quest for the Other because of a no less fruitless obsession with his libido. The denouement reveals an all-too-human, confused, and defeated mortal man, caught up in passion, and then forced to recognize, too late, his failure in passion and in life. In the end Amans learns from Venus what he had failed to know all along (and what Genius had failed to teach him); he learns the reality of *fin' amor* and his own reality as a human being, that the two realities are disjunctive, incongruous, impossible to fuse, and that to imagine their conjunction is only illusion.

In the end Venus takes Amans at his word and cures him by revealing the truth and making him lucid. Are we to assume that, unlike Amans, the goddess of love did not suddenly discover the truth of her supplicant's ineptness for love but knew all along? that Amans was an old man and therefore an absurdly inappropriate courtly lover from the beginning? and that we the implied reader-audience should also have been aware of this truth and should have relished the irony of the blind *senex amans*, wallowing in passion and in bookish convention, making an utter fool out of himself?

One current of recent Gower studies, begun by Schueler (1967), takes this stand, responding in the affirmative. To do so, the critics of this school emphasize the scholarly, learned nature of Amans' persona and the factor of time and distance as Amans, in the present, recounts to Genius his activities in the past as an addle-brained youth and a lusty suitor in competition with other lusty suitors. The sense of decay and of a world grown old (*être*) posited in the Prologue would then be exemplified by the old, decaying Amans (*agir*) acting or, rather, failing to act in the course of the metadiegesis.

I believe these scholars are partially in the right. In terms of narrative technique, we have seen that the narrator-lover or narrator-witness in the *dit amoureux* – in Machaut, Froissart, and Chaucer – is a conventional figure, a literary persona not to be confused with the historical implied author; however, by ostentatiously naming the figure 'Guillaumes,' 'Jehan,' and 'Geffrey,' the historical author does call attention to himself and establish a bond, however artificial, between himself and the lover-narrator he has created in the work of fiction. The audience cannot help but observe the similarities and dissimilarities between the two; presumably such observation constitutes a significant feature of humour and irony in the reader-audience response to the text.

As this narrative convention of French origin was known to the cultivated Ricardian audience, it is probable that some of Gower's public would inevitably compare the fictional Amans to the historical John Gower and perhaps identify one with the other, making ironic commentaries about the identification. However, *Confessio Amantis* differs from texts such as *Le Jugement dou Roy de Navarre*, *Le Voir Dit*, *The House of Fame*, and *The Legend of Good Women* in that the identification of the lover-narrator (his naming as John Gower) is withheld until the denouement; it occurs at the end of the narrative and constitutes, so to speak, the climax. Gower thus plays upon, and adds his own variation to, a time-honoured French conventional practice. The sudden recognition that Amans is, in fact, (also) the implied author John Gower should, for its full effect, come to the implied reader-audience as a pleasant shock. Prior knowledge or recognition or anticipation of Gower's variation on the theme would diminish the literary effect and reduce its power and immediacy. Indeed, except for the convention, there is no particular reason to make the identification earlier. I am convinced that Amans is presented to us much more as a naive young lover and a naive young clerkly narrator than as a wise old clerkly narrator, and that his passion for the Lady is meant to have taken place over an indefinite period of time – long enough for him to be considered faithful and unhappy but not at all (given the conventions of *fin' amor*) so long that he be deemed an old man. If I am right, the effect of the discovery and the identification in narrative terms would be the following: to the extent that Amans is part of Gower and Gower part of Amans, in the course of his confession, Amans lives an ironic parody of the love experience; he experiences, as he reveals them, all the stages of love; he evolves through the psychology of love; and he grows into an artist and, to some extent, a sage; he also grows old. Or perhaps, on an even more comic level, we can deduce that the confession, absurd in terms of confession and in terms of Eros, takes up such a long time – an inflated *Erzählte Zeit* justifying an inflated *Erzählzeit* – that, in the course of the 30,000 lines, the poor penitent ages and, because of Genius' loquacity, is removed from the sphere of Eros.

Confessio Amantis is a rich, dense, complex, many-faceted work. It contains over one hundred well-told, meaningful stories, many of them myths from Antiquity. Like Jean de Meun's *Rose*, it is a summa, an encyclopedia of life, and, in its way, a grand *conflictus amoris*. It is also a comic masterpiece, focused on two magnificent comic figures – Genius and Amans – and their interaction. And it sums up intertextually two centuries of courtly debate on man, woman, and desire. Like Jean de Meun and Chaucer, Gower emphasizes discrepancies for he is also a writer of deferral and indeterminacy, who asks questions and who makes the answers be ambiguous and tenuous.

Gower's major English text is a masterpiece, as are his French texts. It is a rare individual who can achieve supremacy as one of the leading poets of his age in his own tongue – inferior to Chaucer, of course, but in the same class, I submit, with Langland and the *Gawain*-poet – and also prove to be one of the leading writers of his century in French – not the equal, perhaps, but in the same class with Machaut, Froissart, Deschamps, and Christine; at the same time, although not the equal of Dante, Petrarch, and Boccaccio, he is an important, significant writer in Latin. John Gower, in his own way, is as protean as Dante and Boccaccio, Machaut, Froissart, and Chaucer. No one, not even Chaucer himself, is more representative of the Franco-English court culture of the fourteenth century.

III. Hoccleve

Thomas Hoccleve and John Lydgate were the self-proclaimed disciples of Chaucer and Gower, especially Chaucer; they belonged to the same courtly school. Active writers from 1411 to 1422 (and Lydgate for long after that), they had similar noble patrons and similar literary concerns, and may have been rivals. For a brief period Hoccleve propagated in verse the court position on a number of issues; he was a sort of unofficial poet laureate and his *Regement of Princes*, extant in forty-four manuscripts, proved to be one of the six most popular poems of the fifteenth century. However, he never came close to attaining the prestige of a Lydgate in his lifetime and, despite a regain of favour in Anglicist circles, does not today command the respect granted to Gower, Langland, Henryson, and Dunbar, not to speak of Chaucer and the *Gawain*-poet. I am convinced, however, that Hoccleve is an exciting and creative poet in the secular courtly tradition (more exciting and creative than Lydgate); therefore, I close this section on English court poetry with him.

Despite the regain of favour, a number of people, including Mitchell (1968), still prize Hoccleve most for the purportedly autobiographical element in his verse and for its purported realism, that is, the information it reveals on fifteenth-century society and politics, and the life of a writer and civil servant.

The alleged autobiographical authenticity is, in my opinion, based upon a misconception of the nature of medieval poetry, a misconception largely abandoned in Chaucer studies but still prevalent in work on the lesser figures. I agree with Doob (1974) that what the Hoccleve texts reveal concerning the narrating persona – marriage, poverty, insanity, and vice – is not validated in contemporary historical documentation of the Privy Seal or elsewhere. The fact that a pseudo-autobiographical stance is rare in Middle English proves nothing. It is quite common in the French tradition, and Hoccleve partakes of that tradition to the same extent as do Chaucer and Gower. The notion that Hoccleve's inner self gives rise to, and in some way creates, the poetic texts that recount the inner self is a tribute to the author's skill at creating a fictional universe justifying itself through the illusion of truth and authenticity (not the truth and authenticity themselves, about which we know nothing). Similarly, it is an error to attribute veracity to the events recounted by Hoccleve because of the concrete physical detail and the humour manifest in his poems, or because of the aura of sincerity, realism, individuality, and unconventionality that emanates from the same texts. These are literary qualities, derived from a number of century-old French conventions, conventional especially when they appear to be unconventional, and literary especially when they appear to be realistic. With his pseudo-autobiography, Hoccleve stands chronologically and in artistic terms between Machaut, Froissart, Deschamps, and Christine de Pizan on the one hand, and Jean Regnier, Pierre Michault, and François Villon on the other.

It is much more reasonable to situate Hoccleve in the conventional world of a story-teller who constructs stories in a first-person narrative frame. The frame, whether or not it recounts a dream-vision experience, is fictional; the narrating persona, whether protagonist or witness, is a fictional character. Madness is a metaphor for sin and/or love and/or the melancholia of the artist born under the sign of Saturn; poverty is the result of sin and/or love and is a standard attribute of the artist not born under the sign of Jupiter or Sol. Madness is a literary pretext for confession; poverty is the necessary literary pretext for asking for money. Hoccleve uses love-vision experience in a diegetic frame or in metadiegetic inserts; a narrating poet as lover and as artist suffering from madness; the need for money and the asking of it from a prince, thereby establishing the bond of *amicitia* between prince and poet; and the confession of poverty, sin, and worldy ineptness as clerkly *captatio benevolentiae*. There are themes, motifs, conventions, and modes that derive from and constitute the Franco-English court tradition of the late Middle Ages.

To sum up, Hoccleve is an artist and a government official, like Machaut, Froissart, and Chartier, like Chaucer and Gower. He forms part of the clerkly inheritance, both social and artistic. His apparent self-denigration is derived from the rhetorical and social constraints of his clerkly estate. The very last thing a sophisticated reader ought to do is to take the artist at his word, that is, be taken in by the illusion, and separate Hoccleve from the court tradition he mastered so well.

As part of the tradition, Hoccleve's verse forms, themes, and diction all come from Chaucer and from the French. The Frenchness of Hoccleve's talent is especially striking in the line extending from Machaut to Villon. This should be scarcely surprising, given that, during his years of public service, every day Hoccleve wrote in French as a clerk of the Privy Seal. The intellectual clerk that he was drafted an all-inclusive, well-organized Formulary for the use of his department (edited by Bentley 1965); most of the model documents are in French (the others are in Latin), and Hoccleve's marginal notes are uniquely in French. Finally, like Chaucer, Hoccleve began his career as a translator from the French, Englishing a narrative text by Christine de Pizan and lyrics from Guillaume de Digulleville, before he presumed to soar on his own wings.

1. *The Letter of Cupid*

The *Letter of Cupid* (476 ll., 1402) is a free translation – an adaptation if you prefer – of Christine de Pizan's *L'Epistre au dieu d'Amours*. It testifies to Hoccleve's fluency as a versifier in his first major 'public poem,' and to his familiarity with the latest literary trends in Paris, specifically Christine's contribution to the 'Querelle du *Roman de la Rose*.' In Christine's *Epistre*, as in Hoccleve's *Letter*, Cupid, god of love (and of *fin' amor*), delivers a speech defending ladies. In women are to be found constancy and virtue, he says. Men, on the contrary, seduce and abandon ladies and then boast of their exploits; and clerks, the old as well as the young, defame women when they ought not to. Cupid observes that he is capable of making clerks yearn after a hussy and of giving women the arms to resist men's advances and/or to deceive them in turn. Cupid ends by declaring that he will expel such evil men from his court.

Bornstein (1981–2) has suggested that Hoccleve, in adapting Christine's text to an English audience, subtly introduces an antifeminist tone by modifying both the original subject matter and its style. According to this view, whereas Christine's speech is that of the French court, Hoccleve's derives from an English tavern. Detailed descriptions in French are transformed into proverbial expressions, the proverbs existing for their own sake rather than to defend women; also, when Cupid is made to speak Hoccleve's English, the stylistic register is lowered and Cupid's defence of ladies now appears exaggerated, untrustworthy, and even comic. Furthermore, following this line of argument, Hoccleve reduced or omitted entirely elements of Christine's feminist vision – praise of women, attacks on men, depiction of proper courtly behaviour – while expanding the statements made by the bad clerics. Thus, while ostensibly transmitting Christine's poem and her message, Hoccleve was intentionally involved in undermining and parodying it.

I do not agree. In my opinion, Fleming (1971) is correct. He points out that Hoccleve simply 'adapts' the text while translating it, retaining the spirit of the original. It is true, the author rearranges a number of sections and shortens the original by almost one-half; however, he also adds some eighteen stanzas, including, in praise of woman, Saint Mary's mercy and Saint Margaret's constancy. It is normal in medieval translation-adaptation either to expand (*amplificatio*) or to reduce (*abbreviatio*) the original.[34] Hoccleve's deletions and his additions, if anything, tighten up Cupid-Christine's argument, making it more logical and rigorous and perhaps improving it as rhetoric. Inevitably, a translator's additions or deletions will alter the total literary reality of the original text, just as the translation of courtly French into a less courtly, less cultivated Germanic vernacular will also bring about a change in tone. Such was the case when Hartmann and Wolfram translated Chrétien, or for that matter when Malory translated the *Prose Lancelot*. However, we have no evidence for a radical shift in argument, that is, a denial or distortion of Christine's ostensible and ostentatiously didactic message. To find such a shift in argument is, on the one hand, to fall into the same error that Machaut's, Chaucer's, and Hoccleve's own fictional inscribed audiences did in *Le Jugement dou Roy de Navarre*, the *Prologue to the Legend of Good Women*, and Hoccleve's *Series*.[35] It is also, I believe, a subjective twentieth-century response, derived from one twentieth-century ideology.

What Hoccleve *has* done in his first work is to substitute for Christine's allusion to Medea one of his own to Chaucer. The god of love, who just condemned Jean de Meun and Ovid, alludes to Chaucer's *Legend of Good Women*: 'In our legende of martirs may men fynde, / who-so þat lykith ther-in for to rede ... ' (*Minor Poems*, p. 303: 316–17). Furthermore, imitating Genius in *Confessio Amantis*, Hoccleve has Cupid, in his function as the god of *fin' amor*, praise Saint Margaret as a woman but then condemn her chastity, in his function as the god of Eros:

> But vndirstondith / We commende hir noght
> By encheson of hir virginitee:
> Trustith right wel / it cam nat in our thoght,

For ay We werreie ageyn chastitee,
And euere shal / but this leeueth wel yee:
Hir louyng herte / and constant to hir lay,
Dryue out of remembrance we nat may.

(*Minor Poems*, pp. 306–7: 428–34)

In this we find Hoccleve aware of and grounded in the metatextual Machaldian-Chaucerian tradition of artistic self-consciousness; he is aware that a literary character does not automatically reflect his author's ideas or persona and that, when he is a semi-allegorical character such as Cupid, he can embody divergent, indeed contradictory philosophies. I do not believe that, by having Cupid allude to and implicitly praise Chaucer, Hoccleve creates a situation in which the god of love undercuts his own denunciation of Ovid's and Jean de Meun's antifeminism; Chaucer, in the *Prologue to the Legend of Good Women*, was accused by the same Cupid of the same crime, but then the Chaucerian persona exonerated himself, and neither Hoccleve nor his audience would presume to hold Chaucer guilty. These intertextual references are brief. They indicate Hoccleve's sophistication, his urbane distancing from some aspects of the text. Nevertheless, they do not repudiate the text, its narrator (Cupid), or its original author (Christine). With more urbanity and literary self-consciousness than Christine had, Hoccleve reproduces her poem, Englishes it, and transmits it with elegance, brio, and charm. His is an example of *translatio* at its best, the transmission not only of a book but, with it, of a literary mode and a way of viewing both books and life. None of this will be forgotten in the succeeding years.

2. Lyrics

A number of Hoccleve's lyrics can be ascribed to a period from the beginning of the fifteenth century to 1415. These texts, for the most part *ballades* stanzaic in form and of indeterminate length and composed in the fashionable Franco-Chaucerian style, partake of two currents – the sacred, and the social or occasional.

Hoccleve's most powerful sacred text is a 245-line *Complaint of the Virgin*, translated from Guillaume de Digulleville. This is one of fourteen lyrics embedded in the 1413 prose translation of *Pèlerinage de l'Ame*. All fourteen have been attributed to Hoccleve. It has even been suggested that he is responsible for the entire Englished *Pèlerinage*. Hoccleve displays a gift for sacred poetry in this version of the *stabat mater* theme. With the first-person, dramatic intensity of an eyewitness, Mary bewails the crucifixion of her son by means of a lamentation directed in turn to God the Father, the Holy Ghost, Gabriel, Elizabeth, Simeon, Joachim and Anne, Christ himself, death, the moon, stars, the firmament, the sun, the earth, Jesus again, John the Apostle, the angels, Mary herself, and the sons of Adam. Blood imagery is prominent as is the play on words 'Mary'-'Mara'-'amère'-'marred.' As the Speaker points out, Maria minus 'i' [Iesus] equals Mara. The Virgin speaks as an historical person (a mother lamenting the death of her only son) and as a type for humanity, suffering the loss of the redeemer and the death of the messiah come to save mankind.

In another lyric, a 140-line prayer to Saint Mary and Saint John entitled the *Mother of God* or *Ad beatam virginem*, also probably following a French source, the Speaker begs that his lechery be forgiven and redeemed, and that, a sinner, he be sustained in holiness. In this text cleanness and purification imagery dominates. Also significant is the situation; a poet, the narrating Speaker, begs the Mother of God to speak on his behalf to the Son. Just as Christ mediated between Mary and Saint John, bringing them together, they can bring the Speaker to God. Verbal communication and the clerkly privilege of the *verbum* are used to form a bond between the humble yet eloquent Speaker, the Virgin Mary, and Christ.

A moving prayer in alternate stanzas to the Virgin and to Christ (160 ll.) was thought to be original with Hoccleve. We now know that he translated an Anglo-Norman poem for the first one hundred and twenty lines. The *Ballade* to the Virgin or *Miracle*, recounting the legend of the monk who clad the Mother of God by saying his Ave's and Pater's (126 ll.), is also a French translation.

The secular, occasional verse, although of less aesthetic value, is quite varied in subject matter. We find a number of *ballades* that commemorate social events. One *ballade*, addressed to Sir Henry Somer, purportedly forms part of an epistolary exchange concerning the annual feast of the 'Court de Bone Compaignie,' like the Puis devoted to good fellowship and to the cultivation of verse. The best of the secular texts are begging poems, bewailing the Speaker's alleged predicament of 'coynes scarsetee.' The Begging Poem is a conventional genre embodying a conventional topos. Although analogous to some verses in Anglo-Saxon, in my opinion the Middle English probably is a direct transplant of a French form which goes back at least to Machaut. The most notable texts in the tradition are a forty-four-line *Complainte* and a poem entitled 'A toi Henri' by Machaut, Froissart's *Dit dou Florin*, *ballades* by Deschamps, and Chaucer's 'Complaint to his Purse.' Later examples include texts by Villon and Marot. *Le Dit dou*

Florin (492 ll.) recounts a dialogue between the Speaker and the last florin in his purse, the one wedged in the bottom after the others ran away. The florin urges the Speaker to seek help from his good patrons. Hoccleve's achievement in this vein is a series of roundels addressed 'a la dame monnoie.' In this delightful parody of *fin' amor* and pastiche of the French erotic *rondeau,* the Speaker begs his lady – Money, coin – to return to him. Although she imprisoned him – his heart – he never kept her captive. However, Lady Money scorns the Speaker and his plaint. In the final roundel, he raises his voice to deliver a mock encomium of her beauty, alluding to her sheen and gold, adroitly juxtaposing the categories of womanhood and of money and intentionally confusing the kind of beauty appropriate to each. Given the anticourtly genre of the *sotte chanson,* which counters *fin' amor* in poems that are, nonetheless, intertextually grounded in the *fin' amor* tradition, Hoccleve's mock dialogue with Lady Money occurs in texts that can be designated as *sots rondeaux* – a witty, urbane, eminently sophisticated and eminently conventional creative reworking of the tradition.

3. *La Male Regle*

The begging motif functions as one of the central elements in *La Male Regle* (448 ll., 1405), the first major text from Hoccleve's maturity and his first major original work. The Narrator confesses to the god Health; guided by Misrule, he committed excess in his youth, excess with women but above all in the realm of food and drink. As a result, he succumbed to illness and lost his money. Since, as a prisoner of Sickness, he is ill in body and purse, he prays to Health to replenish the body, and to Lord Fournival to replenish the purse.

Thornley (1967) has pointed out that *La Male Regle* parodies the Middle English penitential lyric and that Hoccleve adheres to and transcends the genre of the sacred lyric in his own secular text. The penitential lyric calls attention to the mortality of life and calls for penance – contrition, confession, and satisfaction. It also can recount an anecdote as an exemplum for homiletic purposes. *La Male Regle,* in telling the Narrator's past history and present condition, offers more than one such exemplum. In a first-person stance, the Narrator-protagonist addresses the god of health as the penitential speaker would address God, the Virgin Mary, and the communion of saints. Like his spiritual counterpart, the Hocclevian persona openly confesses the folly he committed and the physical and spiritual sickness that has overcome him.

He alludes to all seven of the capital sins, especially gluttony. And he prays to be healed. All this, of course, is treated in the ironic, parodic mode: Health is not God, the Narrator's life of sin is comic not apocalyptic, and the purpose of the confession is not salvation but a very different cure – to extract money from the king's treasurer.

La Male Regle is also a parody on *fin' amor* and on the *dit amoureux* genre, the court mode that speaks of fine love, fine poetry, and fine poets. The Narrator's illness, melancholia, and obsession with death recall the state of the Machaut Narrator in *Le Jugement dou Roy de Navarre*. The *Male Regle* Narrator does have erotic commerce with women; he flirts and expresses desire, and yet does not proceed very far on the *gradus amoris*. His desire and his restraint mirror behaviour associated with *fin' amor*. Comedy arises from the fact that the objects of his libido are no ladies. They are prostitutes encountered in a tavern, and the Narrator indulges in no more than kissing:

> Of loues aart / yit touchid I no deel;
> I cowde nat / & eek it was no neede:
> Had I a kus / I was content ful weel,
> Bettre than I wolde han be *with* the deede:
> Ther-on can I but smal; it is no dreede:
> Whan þ*a*t men speke of it in my p*re*sence,
> For shame I wexe as reed as is the gleede. (*Minor Poems*, p. 30: 153–9)

His cowardice in matters of the heart recalls the timidity and ineptness of the clerkly narrator figure in Machaut, Froissart, Chaucer, and Gower. The Hoccleve Narrator, like Machaut and like Christine de Pizan, evokes Lady Fortune; he adores the god Health and seeks his intercession much as the Machaut-Froissart-Gower protagonist invoked Lady Hope, the god of love, or Venus. The worship of Health is a neat parody on *fin' amor* as well as on Christian *caritas*:

> O god! o helthe! vn-to thyn ordenance,
> Weleful lord / meekly submitte I me.
> I am contryt / & of ful repentance
> þ*a*t eu*er*e I swymmed in swich nycetee
> As was displesaunt to thy deitee.
> Now kythe on me thy mercy & thy grace!
> It sit a god, been of his grace free;
> Foryeue / & neu*er*e wole I eft trespace! (*Minor Poems*, pp. 37–8: 401–8)

It is then especially appropriate that the Narrator suffers from *acedia* and melancholia – the sloth and the black bile of the poet and lover, born under the sign of Saturn; in this case the imbalance is comically derived from *gula* in the tavern, not from ascetic meditation on the Lady in a *locus amoenus*. His illness is concrete, not a metaphoric Malady of Heroes.

Finally, the comic, cowardly, sexually innocent penitent is, from beginning to end, involved in the use of discourse, as to be expected from a clerkly poet figure. On the one hand, he is deceived in speech; he is tricked by flatterers in the tavern. It is significant that these deceivers are 'losengeour,' the archetypal talebearer and sower of discord in *fin' amor*, and that they are compared to sirens, and the Narrator himself to Ulysses. The Narrator has erred by listening to Misrule not Reason, entrusting his body, his mind, and his health to the fluctuating waters of Dame Fortune (he is ferried over the Thames) in a realm of appearance and illusion instead of the *terra firma* of faith and reason. However, now that he has learned and been chastened, the very same Narrator employs discourse to warn others, specifically the lords of the earth, to avoid his fate. The clerkly author figure speaks to, instructs, and consoles the knightly, princely reader figures in his implied audience, as Machaut did in *La Fonteinne amoureuse* and *Confort d'ami* and as Froissart did in *Le Bleu Chevalier* and *La Prison amoureuse*. The clerkly voice confesses his sins and mocks himself; yet he also speaks of himself as a subject of discourse and the protagonist of verse, and he requests payment, a mock cure for a mock illness and a mock reward for a mock confession. This is also legitimate subsidation for legitimate service – the creation of a work of art.

4. *Regement of Princes*

Regement of Princes (5439 ll., 1411), like *La Male Regle*, is grounded in the begging poem format (although it is much more than that) and contains passages of regret over a lost youth wasted in poverty, vice, and ill health. Above all, Hoccleve takes one small element of *La Male Regle* – advice to noblemen – and makes this the central theme of his text. The major part of *Regement of Princes* (some 3000 lines) is just that – a moral treatise devised to assist rulers in the process of ruling. Hoccleve names his sources for the *Regement*: the *Secreta secretorum*; Aegidius Romanus, *De regimine principum*; and Jacobus de Cessolis, *De ludo scaccorum*. Hoccleve may have been drawn to the *Secreta secretorum* and to the idea of a mirror for princes by Book 7 of *Confessio Amantis*. Gower probably consulted the *Secreta* in a French version, as Hoccleve may also have done. Another analogue and possible inspiration not recognized heretofore is Machaut's *Confort d'Ami*. Machaut's *speculum*, addressed to Charles the Bad, King of Navarre, resembles Hoccleve's *Regement* in an extraordinary way. Both Machaut and Hoccleve underscore the king's dignity and the need for justice, law, pity, mercy, patience, chastity, largesse, prudence, good counsel, and peace. (I follow the general order of topics in Hoccleve.) Since Machaut is writing for a captive, he particularly emphasizes patience in the face of adversity. He and Hoccleve converge in several areas: the concern for an ordered family life and also for the prince to keep his word and manifest correct social behaviour while avoiding excess; the appeal to the prince's generosity and pity; and, finally, the near-obsession that the prince should choose good counsellors, tried and proven older men, while avoiding at all cost flattery from inexperienced or wicked parvenu youths. Two of Machaut's other near-obsessions appear in Hoccleve's frame: contemporary decadence mirrored in and caused by effete new fashions in dress; and the fall from riches to poverty as a manifestation of Dame Fortune, punishment however that leads to wisdom. Both Machaut and Hoccleve warn against playing for money and against debasing the coin of the realm. Machaut elaborates a Boethian-type monologue, himself playing the role of Lady Philosophy, in which he consoles and comforts a Boethian prince figure. It is quite possible that Hoccleve was then inspired by his French predecessor to compose a Mirror for Princes on the same line, but framed by a Boethian dream-vision dialogue (also in the Machaut-Chaucer style) in which he the implied author is consoled and comforted by someone else, who proves to be his own alter ego.

Hoccleve's major innovation, in addition to launching the Mirror for Princes in English, is to precede his Mirror with this two-thousand-line frame in the Boethian and *dit amoureux* tradition. As in *Le Jugement dou Roy de Navarre*, a lengthy preamble concerning the Narrator's illness paves the way and functions as a frame for the central literary structure. As in Machaut's *Fonteinne amoureuse*, Froissart's *Paradis d'Amour*, and the first three of Chaucer's dream-vision poems, the Narrator suffers from insomnia:

> Thus ilkë nyught I walwyd to and fro,
> Sekyng restë; but, certeynly sche
> Appeerid noght, for þoght, my crewel fo,
> Chaced hadde hir & slepe a-way fro me;

And for I schuldë not a-lonë be,
Agayn my luste, Wach profrid his seruise,
And I admittid hym in heuy wyse.

So long a nyught ne felde I neuer non ... (*Reg*: 71–8)

As in the tradition, he wends his way in solitude to a field or meadow, a version of *locus amoenus*, where he will undergo a complaint and comfort experience with an authority figure, a Giver of Discourse. The Narrator's insomnia, and his wanderings, are caused by deep melancholia, the same excess of black bile that causes illness – anxiety, chills, fever, delirium, yearning for death – leading to insanity. The *Regement of Princes* Narrator is an older version of the Narrator in *La Male Regle*; the cause of his melancholia is not love but poverty. In place of the female allegories – Reason, Hope, Venus – typical of the tradition, Hoccleve subtitutes a miserable old beggar who, for all his poverty (greater than the Narrator's), is capable of imparting wisdom. The inscrutably wise Old Man may have been derived from Genius in *Confessio Amantis* or from the enigmatic figure of age in the *Pardoner's Tale*. Also, Machaut as a wise, old author figure appears as his own Narrator in *Le Jugement dou Roy de Navarre*, *Confort d'Ami*, and *La Fonteinne amoureuse*. Most important of all, the Old Man, who is poor, was in the past a young man who suffered from illness and vice (*gula*, *luxuria*, *ira*) just as the Narrator does in the present, and from poverty which the Narrator expects in the future. Just as, in *Le Roman de la Rose*, Raison, Ami, Faux Semblant, Nature, and Genius can be considered external universals but also aspects of the Lover's own psyche, so, here also, the Old Man functions as a projection and an alter ego of the Narrator. And, as in the Machaut-Froissart-Chaucer tradition of wish-fulfilment, the Hoccleve Narrator, suffering from poverty, illness, and vice, desperately in need of consolation and comfort, discovers a living Old Man, still poor, but who has overcome his illness and vice and who has attained consolation and comfort, which he now is capable of dispensing in turn.

As in the *Book of the Duchess* and *Remede de Fortune*, the Dispenser of Discourse teaches the suffering Narrator and cures him of his melancholia by speaking to him but also by making him speak in turn. Furthermore, the Old Man addresses the Narrator as a clerk and appeals to him in his clerkly function. He makes the Narrator recount the miseries of his life as a scrivener. He discusses with him the pros and cons of marriage for a clerk. He urges him to avoid a clerk's errors and, as a man of learning, to heal himself through faith and reason.

Finally, the Old Man offers the Narrator a solution and a cure. When he discovers that the person he is addressing is Hoccleve the Writer, he insists that the Narrator can snap out of his misery and be comforted, and rewarded financially by writing a book for Prince Henry:

'What schal I callë þe? what is þi name?'
'Hoccleuë, fadir myn, men clepen me.'
'Hoccleuë, sone?' 'I-wis, fadir, þat same.'
'Sone, I haue herd, or this, men speke of þe; ...

Al-thogh þ*o*u seyë þat þ*o*u in latyn,
Ne in frenssh nowther, canst but smal endite,
In englyssh tongë canst þ*o*u wel afyn ...

Syn þ*o*u maist nat be paied in thescheqer,
Vnto my lord þe princë make instance
þat þi patent in-to þe hanaper
May chaunged be.

... now, syn þ*o*u me toldist
My lord þe princë is good lord þe to,
No maistri is it for þe, if þ*o*u woldist
To be releeuëd; wost þ*o*u what to do?
Writtë to hym a goodly tale or two,
On which he may desporten hym by nyghte,
And his fre gracë schal vp-on þe lighte.'
(*Reg*: 1863–6, 1870–2, 1877–80, 1898–1904)

In Machaut, Froissart, Chaucer, and even Jean de Meun, the speaking narrators, whether they be lovers or witnesses, are author figures who attain fulfilment as authors by writing the very text that recounts their plight; they are even (in *Le Jugement dou Roy de Navarre* and the *Legend of Good Women*) condemned to write verse and then do so. As with Machaut, Froissart, and Chaucer, Hoccleve composes an eminently self-referential and metatextual work of art in the mode of the poetic pseudo-autobiography. The frame of *Regement of Princes* recounts how and why the implied author wrote *Regement of Princes*. It is a didactic *speculum* but also a courtly, clerkly late medieval metatext concerned with its own creation and functioning as art.

Also, as in Machaut and Chaucer, the frame narrative and the Mirror proper cohere because of thematics and imagery common to the two sections. Hasler (1990) and Scanlon (1990) discuss the theme of empowerment and the imagery of bodies (the Narrator's body, the King's Two Bodies). In addition to these, we can underscore the thematics of communication and discourse. The Old Man warns the Narrator against the dangers of solitude, saying that it is bad for his health to be alone. The Narrator later instructs princes in relating to the community they are called upon to govern. A central concern in the Mirror is that princes should seek good counsel from proved, older retainers and eschew the flattery of inexperienced or ill-intentioned younger men. By so addressing Prince Henry, the Narrator demonstrates that he has accepted the good Old Man's counsel to write a serious book for Henry and not to resort to flattery in it.

A pattern emerges; as the Old Man offers wise counsel to the Narrator, the Narrator will offer wise counsel to his prince. The Old Man is a father figure and teacher to his symbolic son and pupil, who aspires to play the same role vis-à-vis Prince Henry; he derives much of his argument from the *Secreta* formula of Aristotle instructing Alexander the Great. (Hoccleve invokes the textual authority of another 'father' – Geoffrey Chaucer – prior to his own empowerment as a writer.) Just as Aristotle is portrayed as a clerk teaching the princely Alexander, disciple of Venus and Mars, with wisdom worthy of Pallas Athena, so too the Speaker endows himself and the Old Man, his double, with traits appropriate to *clergie* vis-à-vis the eminently chivalric Henry. The frame addresses the problems of clerks; the Mirror addresses the problems of rulers. In both sections wisdom is provided by clerk figures, through speech and art. The rhetoric of the Old Man and the rhetoric of the Narrator are contained in a rhetorical structure meant to instruct and to please the intradiegetic inscribed audience, Prince Henry, and the extradiegetic implied audience, Thomas Hoccleve's medieval public. The result is a resounding success.

5. *The Remonstrance against Oldcastle*

The *Remonstrance against Oldcastle* (1512 ll., 1415), an anti-Lollard tract purportedly designed to convince a leading heretical baron to end his rebellion and return to King and Church, does not enter directly into the purview of this chapter. It is nonetheless significant that, throughout the text, Hoccleve's Narrator adopts the stance of a clerk remonstrating with a lay aristocrat. On the one hand, the Narrator himself ostentatiously invokes scholarly authorities, especially Saint Augustine, as well as secular rulers from a classical-Christian pantheon, such as Constantine, Theodosius, and Justinian. On the other hand, with more than a little condescension, he urges his inscribed narratee, Oldcastle, to leave theology to the clerks. If you must read, he tells Oldcastle, plunge into *Lancelot* or stories of war in the Old Testament. Popes take precedence over kings, Hoccleve reminds him, and priests over knights; Christ's disciples did not rebel against their master. Last of all, Oldcastle is repeatedly exhorted to obey Holy Church. Now it is obvious that Holy Church's spokesman within the context of this poem is its Narrator, the implied author Thomas Hoccleve. He adopts the voice of a good, 'concerned' subject of the realm; with deft use of the modesty-topos, he avows his own weakness while claiming the right, in spite of his weakness, to preach to Oldcastle. It is the Narrator who, moved by charity, contrasts Oldcastle's madness to reason (his own) and who, at the midpoint, prays to God on Oldcastle's behalf. The *Remonstrance against Oldcastle* offers the most pertinent example in English of the clerkly narrator figure staking a claim to a place in public and intellectual life vis-à-vis the secular aristocracy, and establishing a bond with the aristocracy on *his* terms, a bond in which deference and *captatio benevolentiae* play the least possible, least ostentatious of roles.

6. *The Series*

The *Series* (3829 ll., 1421–2) represents Hoccleve in his full maturity. It is his most varied and complex effort in the court tradition, his masterwork. The *Series* carries the frame-kernel structure to another level of sophistication. Here, in conscious imitation of Chaucer and Gower, Hoccleve embeds a number of briefer texts – two narrative, one didactic – inside a frame narrative which contains equivalents of the Chaucerian prologues, epilogues, and links. The frame is the central narrative structure; it exists, as in the French *dit amoureux*, in order to recount how the inserted texts came into being. As with Chaucer, although the frame and the texts are named independently in the manuscript tradition and can be studied in isolation, they in fact form a coherent totality. There are several major elements in the *Series*: *Hoccleve's Complaint*, *Dialogue with a Friend*, *Jereslaus' Wife*, *Learn to Die*, and *Jonathas*. *Jereslaus' Wife* and *Jonathas* are stories taken from the *Gesta Romanorum*; *Learn to Die* is a didactic work in dialogue form taken from Henry of Suso's *Horologium Sapientiae*.

Jereslaus' Wife develops the calumnied wife motif. The Empress of Rome is persecuted, harassed, and abused by four men in sequence: her brother-in-law, an earl's steward, a thieving servant, and a shipman. Reduced to life in a convent healing the sick, the lady, in her husband's presence, draws confessions from all four of her persecutors, who now suffer from severe illness. She is reunited with the emperor, and they live happily ever after.

Jonathas tells of a man who loses station because of his mistress. Jonathas possesses three magic treasures – a ring, a brooch, and a piece of cloth – that make him all but omnipotent. Fellicula succeeds in sequestering all three items and then abandons her lover in a distant exile. He succeeds in returning, however, and becomes a physician; when Fellicula falls ill he makes her confess, recovers the three treasures, and causes her to die.

Learn to Die takes the form of a dialogue between Sapientia and Discipulus. Wisdom bids the Disciple to imagine a dialogue between himself and a Dying Man. In this dialogue within a dialogue, the Disciple urges the Dying Man to repent of his sins. However, the Dying Man, having wasted too much of his youth, cannot rid his mind of the picture of hell and passes away in despair. Before expiring, he warns the Disciple. 'Live a pure life and prepare to die now,' he says. 'Don't be like me.' The Disciple takes to heart the Dying Man's words, turns to Wisdom, and does repent. The first stage of Sapientia proves to be Timor Domini.

Hoccleve, from a book provided by the Friend or in his own voice as Narrator-implied author, offers an allegorical gloss on the two fictional tales. Although the allegory is simplistic and reductionist, it does create a link between the *Gesta Romanorum* material and Henry of Suso's *Ars moriendi*. All three texts are treated seriously as works with a moral message. All three develop the theme of illusion and reality: the empress and Jonathas suffer from illusion imposed upon them by tricksters; the Dying Man creates his own illusion. Jereslaus' Wife, Jonathas, the Disciple, and Wisdom attain fulfilment only when they recognize and/or reveal to others the reality that lies behind illusion. With this, justice is served for justice cannot exist otherwise. Although people are persecuted and/or suffer from their own misdeeds, the persecution and the suffering function as tests from God. Justice comes about because of God and because of man's free will, when men choose to reject the world, the flesh, and the devil in favour of a life of repentance and virtue. When people act wisely, they will be rewarded in this world and the next.

The *Series* frame – especially the *Complaint* and *Dialogue with a Friend*

– amplifies this thematic in the context of the French and English court poem, the mode Hoccleve cultivated so well in *La Male Regle* and *Regement of Princes*. Once again the Narrator complains of his treatment at the hands of Dame Fortune. Once again he is comforted by an external male figure, the Friend who comes knocking at his door. According to Hoccleve, the Narrator went mad some five years previously – a nervous breakdown or onset of melancholia that perhaps refers intertextually to the Narrator's state of mind in *Regement of Princes* and *La Male Regle*. The *Series* therefore continues the fictional pattern elaborated in those earlier works. The Narrator's problem, one that drives him to despair, is that, although God cured him in the past, in the present people do not perceive him to be sane; they do not trust him. Furthermore, in the course of his labour as a writer, he may well display the symptoms of madness; thus people are likely to deduce that his cure was only temporary and that he has suffered a relapse. The Narrator, however, is consoled and reassured, in part by Friend but much more by a book he read in the recent past:

> This othar day / a lamentacion
> of a wofull man / in a boke I sye,
> to whome word[e]s / of consolation
> Reason gave / spekynge effectually;
> and well easyd / myn herte was ther-by;
> for when I had a while / in the boke red,
> with the speche of Reason / was I well fed.

(*Minor Poems*, p. 106: 309–15)

This volume, which we know (from Rigg 1970) to have been Isidore of Seville's *Synonyma: De Lamentatione animae dolentis*, is a consolation book in which Reason consoles an afflicted soul; Isidore of Seville himself claims he was moved to write it after having read a treatise by Cicero. Therefore, as Cicero moves Isidore, Isidore now moves Hoccleve's Narrator. As a result, the Narrator declares he will circulate the *Complaint* and translate *Learn to Die* for the honour of God, as reparation for his previous life of sin, to prove he is now permanently sane, and to convince others to avoid his plight.

The thematic ties between the frame narrative and the inserted texts are obvious. The Narrator also suffers from the disparity between appearance and reality; although he really is sane, people will interpret his appearance falsely and be deluded by it into deeming him mad. Like Jonathas, he has lost his friends; like Jonathas and Jereslaus' Wife, he is about to lose status and become an outlaw in a community where possession of reason is one element in the definition of humanness. Like the others, especially Jonathas, the Dying Man, and the Disciple, the Narrator suffers from sins committed in the past. Nonetheless, all will end for the best. Like the others (Jonathas, the Wife, and the Disciple) the Narrator is patient. Like them he trusts in God. Like them, either allegorically or on the literal level, he is aided by penance, reason, and the Church. As the Disciple learned to follow the dictates of Wisdom, the Narrator learns to follow the dictates of Reason. Through speech – the confessions of Feliculla, the four villains, the Dying Man, the Disciple, and the Narrator himself – will come a new resolve, in favour of the good life and the laws of God.

Once again a distraught Narrator suffers from insomnia and the onslaught of melancholia. The *Series* frame narrative occurs not in spring but in November, a time of decline corresponding to the decline and possible end of the Narrator's own life, and a period of excess in black bile, especially in author figures born under the sign of Saturn. Hoccleve's situation appears to be based on that recounted in Machaut's *Jugement dou Roy de Navarre*, a frame also situated in the fall and winter, telling of an ill, melancholic Narrator who spends the winter separated from the community, alone and indoors, and who delivers a moving complaint. Unlike *Le Roy de Navarre*, in *Dialogue with a Friend* the Narrator is visited by Friend, who contributes to his rehabilitation. I believe that the idea for Friend, an alter ego projection of the Narrator, may have come from Machaut's *Confort d'Ami*, where the Machaldian speaker and author figure comforts King Charles of Navarre, the judge of the preceding *Jugement*. As I have suggested, *Confort d'Ami* may also have been a source for Hoccleve's *Regement of Princes*. In addition, Friend was based on Ami in Jean de Meun's *Roman de la Rose*. Like Jean de Meun's Ami, Hoccleve's Friend is witty and urbane, a man of the world who embodies so well the opinions of society at large. Like Ami, Hoccleve's Friend is by no means an undisputed authority figure and giver of discourse. On the contrary, he discourages the Narrator from publishing his *Complaint* and from composing *Learn to Die*. Fortunately (we are led to believe) the Narrator does not heed his advice. Furthermore, just as in *Le Roman de la Rose* where first Raison and then Ami counsel the Lover, in Hoccleve the despairing Narrator is comforted first by the discourse of Reason in a book and then by the concrete, personal intervention of Friend. It is a particularly deft touch that the Narrator runs to a mirror to study his features:

And in my chamber at home when I was
my selfe alone / I in this wyse wrowght:
I streite vnto my myrrowr / and my glas,
to loke how that me / of my chere thowght[e],
yf any [other] were it / than it owght[e];
for fayne wolde I / yf it had not be right,
amendyd it / to my kunynge and myght.

Many a sawte made I to this myrrowre ...

(*Minor Poems*, p. 101: 155–62)

Surely this is intertextual allusion to the most famous of medieval courtly mirrors, the Fountain of Narcissus in the *Rose*, Guillaume de Lorris's narcissistic mirror that Jean de Meun condemns.

The *Series* is the most literary and intertextual of Hoccleve's books. We have seen the allusions to a thematic derived from tradition. We have seen that the Narrator, who five years earlier was cured of insanity by God, now is cured of melancholia by a book authored by Isidore of Seville in which an author figure is cured by still another book authored by Cicero. Hoccleve's mastery of the medieval version of *mise en abyme* is total. In addition, the discussion between the Narrator and Friend concerns literature every bit as much as it does madness and melancholia. The two clerkly figures debate the relationship between writing and madness and the implications of loss of wit in a cleric. Study and the making of books can give rise to an imbalance in the humours and, eventually, to insanity. Will the Narrator's current writing projects cause him to have another breakdown? In response to Friend's counsel to lie to others and to cease his life's work, the Narrator insists that his mind is strong, that truth is better than a lie, and that he shall both write and publish.

More than Hoccleve's earlier works, the *Series* is metatextual. It recounts not just any writer's anxiety, but the anxiety of the implied author who created it. It treats not just any literary reception, but its own reception at the hands of Hoccleve's contemporary implied audience (Burrow 1984). Self-consciously, the implied author of the *Series* uses the *Series* to tell how the various increments of the *Series* came into being. Indeed, resembling Machaut's *Voir Dit*, the *Series* is a pseudo-autobiographical text that recounts its own composition as it is being composed; it is a book whose subject is its own elaboration as a book as it is being elaborated.

Finally, two of the insertions – *Jereslaus' Wife* and *Jonathas* – are linked to the courtly palinode theme launched by Machaut and Chaucer, in *Le Jugement dou Roy de Navarre* and in the *Legend of Good Women*. Friend tells the Narrator that, because of complaints by ladies concerning the antifeminist *Letter of Cupid*, he ought, as reparation, to compose a profeminine book for the great warrior and lover, Duke Humphrey of Gloucester (*Minor Poems*, p. 133: 659–79). In Hoccleve's sophisticated reworking of the palinode topos, Duke Humphrey would play roughly the same role in the *Series* that King Charles of Navarre did in Machaut, and Cupid in Chaucer. Irony springs from the fact that, in the very text allegedly cited, Hoccleve had Cupid speak in praise of the purportedly antifeminist Chaucer. Now, imitating Chaucer, he has the Cupid figure, speaking for Duke Humphrey, rebuke Hoccleve (or permit him to be rebuked) for his own purportedly antifeminist discourse.

Hoccleve follows Machaut's structure beautifully. Machaut's *Jugement dou Roy de Behaingne* was not in the least uncourtly or antifeminist. Accused of antifeminism, Machaut then wrote the truly uncourtly and antifeminist *Jugement dou Roy de Navarre*. The *Letter of Cupid*, based on Christine de Pizan, is a book authentically in defence of ladies and in defence of *fin' amor*. It is absurd for anyone to attack it. The Narrator defends his work with the traditional Jean de Meun-Machaut-Chaucer arguments: what I wrote was favourable to women; also I told the truth; also I only translated what others have said. In a delightful touch, Hoccleve even has Friend admit that he personally has not read the book to the end and can't offer an opinion either way:

> 'The book concludith for hem / is no nay,
> Vertuously / my good freend / dooth it nat?'
> 'Thomas, I noot / for neu*ere* it yit I say.'
> 'No, freend?' 'no, Thomas' / 'Wel trowe I, in fay;
> ffor had yee red it fully to the ende,
> yee wolde seyn / it is nat as yee wende.'
>
> (*Minor Poems*, p. 138: 779–84)

And, while accusing the Narrator of antifeminism, Friend lets go a number of misogynistic remarks himself. Then, Hoccleve does compose the profemale *Jereslaus' Wife*, the story of a good woman persecuted by bad men, but he also composes the misogynistic *Jonathas*, where a good man is almost destroyed by a very bad woman. When the Narrator hesitates to tell the story, because Friend had commanded him only to say nice things about ladies, the Friend offers Jean de Meun's retort: since you are criticizing only an evil woman, only evil ones can possibly object. Thus Hoccleve undercuts the arguments purportedly made against him as well as those made against Jean de Meun, Machaut, and Chaucer.

The circle is complete. Hoccleve completes his own, most ambitious text, a Chaucerian, Goweresque medley, granting it coherence and unity through the elaboration of traditional themes and also through the metatextual process of elaborating how the various increments in the work came into being. By so doing, he alludes, directly or indirectly, to the rest of his opus, including texts which treat the same intellectual problems raised in the *Series* or which recount earlier stages in the Narrator's illness, and one text which the Narrator-implied author both defends and illustrates. Hoccleve also renews his bond with his great predecessors and with the tradition from which he comes and of which he is one of the last great masters.

There are those who speak of Hoccleve's narrow range as a writer. Nothing could be further from the truth. Chaucer's most fervent disciple illustrates any number of themes and modes. He introduces into vernacular English the genres of Mirror to Princes, *ars moriendi*, and mock panegyric. He is a master of sacred verse, public verse, the didactic, and the courtly. It matters little to what extent, if any, the troubles the Hoccleve Narrator encounters in his poetic career are real or fabricated. Sin, poverty, illness, melancholia, and madness are the standard attributes of the clerkly narrator figure in the Anglo-French tradition. Within the tradition, the narrating persona adopts a number of distinct voices: the wretch, the sinner, the petitioner, the scourge of heresy, the wise cleric, the urbane man of the world, the friend and adviser to princes. Most of all, this Narrator is a writer. As much as in Machaut, Froissart, Christine de Pizan, and Chaucer, the Hoccleve persona assumes the stance of an author figure, a potential or actual creator in the process of creating, anxious over the question of audience reception, doubtful of his vocation, suffering from a writer's ills and benefiting from a writer's counsel. Such is an appropriate subject matter for one of the last great English poets in the line of Chaucer, one of the last flowerings of the Chaucerian, courtly, French literary revolution.

Conclusion

Chaucer, his friends, and his disciples form a distinct current in the literature of the English Middle Ages. For quality and lasting achievement, their current is rightly considered to be the dominant one. To a greater or lesser extent, Gower, Hoccleve, Lydgate, and a number of others are Chaucerians, influenced by the precept and example of Geoffrey Chaucer and writing in conjunction with him or in his wake. It is the claim of this book that the shape of English poetry in this line is determined also by literature from France, more particularly by a tradition of lyrical, narrative, and allegorical verse in the high courtly mode that achieves its greatest impact (from an English perpective) with *Le Roman de la Rose* and the more recent writers who perpetuate the ideas and registers launched by the *Rose*, Guillaume de Machaut and Jean Froissart. For this reason, as much as for questions of literary public and the sociology of texts, the English current can be called high court poetry.

Chaucer himself, who translated books from the French, was solidly grounded in a centuries-old French tradition of writing. I am convinced it was the dominant influence on him throughout his career. Chaucer's friends and disciples, simply by reading and imitating him, would have assimilated much of the French legacy. In addition, Gower, Hoccleve, and Lydgate were widely read in French themselves. Gower wrote as much and as well in Anglo-Norman as he did in English; Hoccleve and Lydgate translated a number of French works. All three followed Chaucer in going directly to the French and thus elaborating theme and variation from the international style that they all were in the process of transmitting to their own tongue.

One relatively minor aspect of the tradition is the lyrical, the introduction into England of fixed-form verse, especially *ballades*. Chaucer and Hoccleve composed a number of such *ballades* as occasional verse; among their most successful are 'begging poems,' a subgenre launched by Machaut and Froissart. The wit, the sophisticated repartee, and the assumption of an urbane community of connoisseurs, endemic to the French texts, are impeccably reproduced in English. Chaucer and Hoccleve also translated sacred verse; both men Englished prayers to the Virgin by Guillaume de Digulleville. Chaucer's 'An ABC' is especially noteworthy for its technical skill and emotional range. However, the lyrical high point in the Chaucerian line would have to be Gower's *Cinkante Ballades*, a sequence treating secular *fin' amor*, composed not only in the French style but also in French. Gower understands perfectly the thematics and the rhetorical stance available to the courtly love lyric. He develops them with power and verve. He also contributes his own, exciting variation on the courtly typology; Gower proposes marriage as the outcome of or the alternative to *fin' amor*, as a state in which *fin' amor* can be perceived both as licit and as successful and happy. Until the end of the Middle Ages, the only comparable English *fin' amor* sequence will be the work of the Harley Poet, translating and expanding the French verse of Charles d'Orléans.

Perhaps the central element in the French legacy is constituted by the tale of love (*dit amoureux*), launched by Guillaume de Lorris and illustrated by Machaut and Froissart. Chaucer's *Book of the Duchess, House of Fame, Parliament of Fowls*, and *Prologue to the Legend of Good Women* are the most notable English contributions to the genre. After Chaucer, the English Chaucerians composed a number of texts we can call *dits amoureux*. Among these are direct translations from the French: Hoccleve's *Letter of Cupid*, from Christine de Pizan; Lydgate's *Reason and Sensuality*, from *Les Echecs amoureux*; Roos's *La Belle Dame sans Mercy*, from Alain Chartier; the *Eye and the Heart*, from Michault Taillevent; and, to the extent that it constitutes a narrative sequence, the Harley corpus, from Charles d'Orléans.

The *Book of the Duchess* is an elegy which adopts the form of the French poem of complaint and comfort. The *Prologue to the Legend of Good Women*, based on Machaut's *Jugement dou Roy de Navarre*, adopts the form of the French judgment poem. Gower's *Confessio Amantis* and Hoccleve's *La Male Regle, Regement of Princes*, and *Series* are delightful parodies on the poem of complaint and comfort, centred on the appeal to an authority figure. The frame structure for all of these works is a version of the dream vision. As in Lorris, Machaut, and Froissart, an I-narrator recounts his falling asleep or falling into a trance, an event which occurs either in a *locus amoenus* or in bed at home. These texts explore with deftness and urbane wit the complex, ambiguously conflicting claims of dream psychology: dreams can be objective and supernaturally valid on the one hand, and yet subjective and derived from the dreamer's day residue on the other hand. In a state of misery, due to the catastrophic downturn of Dame Fortune – amorous misery in Chaucer and Gower and financial misery in Hoccleve, both leading to illness – the narrating dreamer or his alter ego appeals for assistance to a Granter of Discourse, who may or may not provide comfort and who may or may not judge the petitioner.

Originating in Machaut and Froissart, and for that matter in Jean de Meun and Guillaume de Digulleville, is a crucial literary element; the bond between dreaming and experience and between seeking comfort or authority and finding them must be mirrored in the problematics of the work of art (a book, song, or sculpted artifact) that launches the protagonist into the dream experience. In Machaut the work of art is generally autotextual, by Guillaume de Machaut himself; in the English poets, as in Jean de Meun and Digulleville, it is the work of someone else, an earlier authority figure. The work of art functions both as *mise en abyme* and as *texte générateur*; it begins the action and develops or comments on the themes, concerns, motifs, and imagery that the total structure will exemplify as a totality. The book or work of art also contributes to a structure of metanarrative, specifically of pseudo-autobiography; in the French writers, as in Chaucer, Gower, and Hoccleve, one central function of the story is to recount the circumstances under which it came into being. Finally, the Narrator as author figure addresses the question of the artist in society, specifically the social bond (ideally one of Horatian *amicitia*) between prince and poet. A variation on this theme, adopted by Machaut, Hoccleve, and Gower is the Mirror of Princes, in which the Narrator, as an implied author and a clerk, dares to offer advice to the Prince, his inscribed patron and narratee.

The didactic centre in these courtly or mock-courtly texts can be identified with an older, more predominantly clerkly tradition, that of Jean de Meun's *Roman de la Rose* and its great sacred analogue, Digulleville's *Pèlerinage de la Vie humaine*. The English poets Chaucer and Hoccleve and, to some extent, Gower, conceived of creating in English longer, more complex, and more problematic works of art than the *dit amoureux* or the lyric sequence. As one model for the more secular and problematic art of maturity, they turned backwards in time to the earlier French style of Jean de Meun. It is Jean's *Rose* that offered so much to the *Canterbury Tales, Confessio Amantis*, and the *Series*.

In Jean de Meun, as in Guillaume de Digulleville, the English poets found didacticism concretized in imaginative literature and an imaginative work of art functioning partially in order to give expression to ideas, and indeed to formulate a complete world-vision. In the sacred realm, one of the great French books, powerfully didactic though not a work of fiction, remains Gower's *Mirour de l'Omme*. To return to the secular, the competing voices in Jean, each appealing to the Lover and to the implied audience, are mirrored in the Canterbury pilgrims; they are also mirrored in the competing dialogues of Genius and Amans, and of the Hoccleve Narrator and Old Man or Friend. The Wife of Bath, the Pardoner, Genius, Amans, and Friend are all taken from characters in the *Rose*. The vast number of stories, mostly from classical Antiquity, that serve as exempla in the ebb and flow of debate, are adopted by Chaucer and Hoccleve and become the central focus of narrative in Gower. In one respect, however, the English masters go beyond Jean de Meun, Machaut, and Froissart, in that they expand the element of story-telling; in their works the stories occupy the centre stage and the circumstance of their telling functions only as a frame.

One of Jean de Meun's contributions is the notion that high satire and social commentary can be voiced in the vernacular, in a line of argument and registers of style more varied and more universal than those to be found in the tradition of *fin' amor*. The *Canterbury Tales* captures best the essence of Jean's text in its variety and complexity of language, style, and a world-view which is envisaged in terms of money, lust, deceit, manipulation, and social conflict. Though not to the same extent, much of this societal scrutiny is maintained in *Confessio Amantis, La Male Regle, Regement of Princes*, and the *Series*. All three authors create masterpieces in the secular mode, concerned with the secular world, transcending the court of love, and also transcending the more rigid, ecclesiastical stance of Digulleville and Gower's own *Mirour de l'Omme*.

Finally, from Jean de Meun the English authors receive the notion of inconclusion, of a work of art that can, while adhering to the comic mode, in some sense refuse narrative closure and doctrinal resolution. I believe that the comedy and the deferral of closure, in a fictional world conceived largely in secular terms, inform the *Canterbury Tales, Confessio Amantis*, and the *Series*.

Much in the fourteenth- and early fifteenth-century English masterpieces is of French inspiration. Stories from Antiquity, a renewed interest in questions of love, a multiplicity of narrative or didactic voices interacting in a nexus of conflict, satire on contemporary social phenomena, exploration of individual and societal problems in the secular world, the implied author conceived as a bumbling figure of fun, and the problem of art and the artist - these are not manifestations of a Renaissance, although Italian impact there is, but simply the transmission and recreation in English of centuries of French literary achievement.

Such transmission and recreation occurred because of the prestige of writing in French; in addition, the various modes for writing already existed in French, and the English, coming after, inevitably would adopt them. Coming after, the cultural belatedness of the late medieval English vernacular proved to be advantageous. Chaucer and the others were able to draw from several different currents and centuries of the French tradition (as well as Latin and Italian, of course). Their 'translacioun' would approximate, in certain respects, the process of *imitatio* in a later Renaissance. Chaucer, for one, would juxtapose and sometimes fuse elements from Jean de Meun, Digulleville, Machaut, Froissart, Marie de France, and the fabliaux. Gower and Hoccleve, in a more narrow register, would reformulate elements in Jean de Meun and Machaut. The end product would be literature of vast complexity and exciting ambiguity, working on multiple levels, asking questions, telling stories, and offering so much in addition to the story. High art is always a product of high civilization; in that, the English participated and achieved the highest.

PART FOUR

Middle English Romance

I. Verse Romance

The question of Middle English romance is one of the most discussed and most controversial in all of medieval studies. Widely divergent, highly challenging theses have been offered concerning the nature of the genre, its origins, its constituent traits, and its public. Therefore, prior to literary analysis of seven romances – *Ywain and Gawain, Sir Degaré, The Earl of Toulouse, Floris and Blauncheflur, William of Palerne, Amis and Amiloun*, and *Athelston* – I shall reconsider the romance genre as a whole, focusing on the comparison with Old French romance, the generic and textual model for the English writers of chivalric narrative.

Theoretical Introduction

Romance constitutes a vast corpus of narrative, the most important genre in Middle English after the court poem. According to the scholars, there are now ninety-five to one hundred and fifteen verse romance texts extant, contained in some ninety or so manuscripts. The oldest romances, *King Horn* and *Floris and Blauncheflur*, date from the early thirteenth century. The vast majority of romances date from 1350 to 1450. Also generally included in this corpus is a group of eight or nine briefer narratives, the 'Breton lays.' Finally, to be distinguished from verse romance are romances in prose. These, derived from the Burgundian tradition, appeared in significant quantity after 1450 and continued to flower well into the sixteenth century.

The great majority of Middle English romances are translations or adaptations from the French, with only a few texts that can be deemed original creations in the modern sense. Indeed, the term 'romance' had for the contemporary public a number of generic expectations, one of which (based upon etymology) assumed that a romance is a French book, or the French source of an English book, or an English book adapted from a French book.

English writers naturally turned to France for inspiration. Four romances are derived from a French translation of the *Pseudo-Turpin* and three others from the *Fierabras* story in *chanson de geste. Kyng Alisaunder* is derived from Thomas of Kent's *Roman de toute chevalerie*, the *Seege of Troye* from Wace's *Roman de Brut*, and the *Siege of Jerusalem* from Roger d'Argenteuil's *Bible en françois*. Finally, a number of romances in the courtly tradition are direct translations or adaptations: *Floris and Blauncheflur, Amis and Amiloun, Ipomadon, William of Palerne, Le Bone Florence of Rome, Partonope of Blois*, the *Romance of Partenay*, the *Knight of Courtesy*, and *Chevalere Assigne*, to cite the most important.

However, French also inspired the most significant works dealing with the Matter of England and the Matter of Britain. English heroes were among the favourite subjects of Anglo-Norman romancers writing for a Francophone public dwelling in England. Four among the more notable protagonists of these ancestral or baronial romances became popular heroes in Middle English romance: Horn, Havelok, Guy of Warwick, and Bevis of Hampton. The English text concerning a fifth worthy, Fulk Fitz-Warren, is not extant. This continuity in local subject matter and romance manner, within the province of insular story-telling, from Anglo-Norman to Middle English, is one of the more fascinating phenomena in the literary history of the age.

The English poets also celebrated the Matter of Britain, that is, narrative material about the British Isles or Brittany located in the pre-Anglo-Saxon period. Here they also turned to literature in French, but to continental as well as Anglo-Norman texts. Marie de France inspired three brief narratives: *Sir Landevale* (extant in several versions), *Sir Launfal*, and *Lai le Freine*. Chrétien inspired two fine romances: *Ywain and Gawain* and *Sir Perceval of Galles*. Thomas's *Roman de Tristan* was adapted into a *Sir Tristrem*. From Wace we have a fifteenth-century verse *Arthur*. From the *Perceval Continuations* we have the *Gest of Sir Gawain* and *Golagrus and Gawain*; these *Perceval Continuations* also had a significant impact on *Sir Gawain and the Green Knight*. Most influential of all was the *Prose Lancelot*, especially the first, second, and last sections. The *Estoire* and *Merlin* gave rise to *Arthour and Merlin, Joseph of Arimathie*, Lovelich's *Merlin*, and the prose *Merlin. La Mort le roi Artu* gave rise to the stanzaic *Morte Arthur* and the alliterative *Morte Arthure*. And, of course, the *Prose Lancelot* and the *Prose Tristan* were Englished by Malory. The French presence thus is pervasive and total throughout the corpus.

Occasionally a new French source is discovered. In general, however, the filiation between Old French and Middle English is transparent, the French book known and recognized. Despite this apparently settled state of affairs, problems arise concerning the French sources, and even the nature of the relationship between an original text and its translation-adaptation. Up to approximately a generation ago, some scholars treated English romance texts as if they were independent works of art or, after admitting the French source in a footnote, devoted the rest of their studies to a strictly ontological analysis as if, for all practical purposes, the French did not exist. Other scholars denied the relationship between the extant Old French and Middle English texts, positing instead the existence of a lost English original and/or a lost French one. Philologists assumed that it was possible to reconstitute the lost original (*Urtext*) of a story, which, because it was the earliest, ought to be more pure, simple, and primitive than what had survived. It no doubt appealed to nineteenth-century national sentiment to posit, behind the earliest French sources, an even better lost English or Celtic prototype; or, if the lost *Urtext* was French, to claim that the surviving English version was closer to the *Urtext* than the surviving French one and, therefore, superior to it. Given the preference of the Romantics for folk literature over art literature and for the oral over the written, the *Urtext* could be considered not a text at all but oral tradition and folktale.

At one time it was widely assumed (and is still believed by some scholars) that *King Horn* and *Havelok the Dane* are not derived from the preceding Anglo-Norman *Roman de Horn*, *Lai de Haveloc*, and the Havelok section of Gaimar's *Estorie des Engleis*: this belief arose because of some variation in names, because the English romances allegedly manifest greater freshness and realism, and because the material is deemed to be concretely, authentically English. At one time it was assumed that *Sir Perceval of Galles* is not derived from Chrétien's *Conte du Graal* because the Middle English does not allude at all to the Holy Grail, because the tone of the English *Perceval* is strident, burlesque, and uncourtly, and because certain elements of the plot adhere more closely to what scholars consider to be Welsh myth than to Chrétien. Finally, it was widely assumed, and still is – for those who believe that the theme of friendship is older and more authentic than the Christian elements –

that the Middle English *Amis and Amiloun* and its Anglo-Norman source *Amis e Amilun* are more primitive and closer to the lost *Urtext* than any of the other extant French and Latin versions; indeed, in a number of ways, the English *Amis and Amiloun* would be the most primitive and authentic of all.

Following this line of reasoning, scholars posited a lost French *Horn, Haveloc, Perceval,* and *Ami et Amile* close to the surviving Middle English versions, that would have given rise to the entire succeeding tradition; or an independent English or Celtic native tradition – folktales, legends, oral sources – close to the Middle English versions, that would have given rise to all the subsequent texts.

Nowadays, the majority of scholars realize that concreteness or primitiveness or realism or authenticity are literary characteristics assigned to a text by subjective judgment and that the presence or absence of such traits tells us little about the text's origins. We have no reason to believe that a simpler or more coherent narrative necessarily precedes a more complicated or less coherent one. We also can never be certain that any medieval romance – in French or English – is derived from a particular folk-tale, or that an hypothetical lost oral tradition ought to be preferred to a known literary source.

Approximately one half of the extant Anglo-Norman romances have English heroes. All but two of the extant Middle English romances with English heroes go back to preceding Anglo-Norman romances. Crane (1986) has shown that just about all Anglo-Norman romances were Englished, sooner or later, although not all of the English versions have survived. The celebration of native insular heroes was a particular, significant preoccupation of Anglo-Norman poets, subsidized and rewarded by the Anglo-Norman aristocracy. Most if not all of these stories were invented; we have no evidence of interest in or knowledge of local insular heroes the likes of Havelok, Horn, Bevis, and Guy before they became the subjects of Anglo-Norman romance. In my opinion, to posit the existence of local, English, folkloric legends about any of these characters would be gratuitous. In other words, there is every reason to believe that *Horn* and *Havelok* were derived from their French analogues, and very little reason not to.

In the case of *Amis and Amiloun*, we have an Anglo-Norman and a Middle English romance concentrating on the theme of friendship between the two protagonists, whereas the Old French *chanson de geste* is more elaborate in structure and more overtly Christian in ideology. Whether or not the Amis and Amiloun story is ultimately derived from international folk-tale types or from history tells us little about the relative authenticity of the various literary versions. The Christian *chanson de geste* may have been a reworking of an earlier *chanson* more folkloric in character; or the insular tradition may have been a romancing of the *chanson de geste*, dampening its more prominent martial and clerical traits. We have little reason to credit a thirteenth-century Anglo-Norman romance and a fourteenth-century English one for being more authentic or more primitive than the French *chanson de geste* composed c. 1200, especially since we know the story first came into being as a *chanson de geste*.

Concerning *Sir Perceval of Galles*, the most recent scholars (Fowler 1975 and Busby 1978, 1987) recognize in this fascinating text a creative response to Chrétien and the *Perceval Continuations*, a rich comic work of artistic merit that conflates a number of previous romances, secularizes the originally Christian orientation of the Perceval story, and underscores the comic and violent elements, not out of primitiveness but as a conscious literary choice.

One outcome of the hunt for lost sources has been to diminish the parameters for literary creativity on the part of the English romancers, attributing divergences from the French not to them but uniquely to the ontological state of the *Urtext*. The same is true in those cases where, even though there is no French source extant, scholars posit one anyway. We have been told the *Earl of Toulouse* was quite likely modelled after a lost French romance, because the hero is French and the subject is courtly; that *Sir Degaré* was quite likely modelled after a lost French *lai d'Esgaré* because of the name; and that *Sir Orfeo* was modelled after a lost French *lai d'Orphey* because the latter is alluded to twice elsewhere in the French corpus.

There is no reason why a Middle English poet could not invent a courtly narrative about French characters with symbolic French names. Lists of authentic and also of non-existent texts crop up all the time in Old French. The most famous bogus texts in Middle English are cited by the Narrator in Chaucer's *Sir Thopas* – purported romances singing the feats of Ypotys and Pleyndamour. Whether in fact there ever was an Anglo-Norman *lai d'Orphey* is problematic. Assuming that the text did exist, we have no certainty that it was the immediate source for *Sir Orfeo* or that it resembled *Sir Orfeo* in a determining way. The 'invention' of lost sources would remove from the annals of English literature the original creation of two charming and one great brief narrative. None of this is necessary. It is always preferable to work with the texts we have than the ones we would like to have.

More central to the problematic of English verse romance than the question of sources is the definition and categorization of the genre. What is a medieval romance? The generally accepted types of definition run something like this. A romance is a narrative that recounts the fortunes of a simple, noble, active hero. It tells his deeds of love and prowess, a story of adventure located in a supernatural setting or with supernatural elements. The hero's career mirrors a pattern of test and ordeal and of initiation and establishment in the world of the court. This narrative pattern is not meant to be mimetic. It is highly idealized, concerned with revealing a symbolic structure of archetypal quest, voyage, combat, and marriage, grounded in convention. As a result, good defeats evil, chivalry and moral elevation are upheld, and society's values are reinforced in a denouement of joy.

I believe that such definitions are, on the whole, accurate and that they aid in the critical analysis of texts. A problem does arise, however, when this or any other generic structure assumes a prescriptive instead of a descriptive function vis-à-vis works of art from the past. It is obvious that the general romance categorization cannot encompass and account for all ninety to one hundred and fifteen extant Middle English romances, works as diverse as *Sir Gawain and the Green Knight, Guy of Warwick, Sir Launfal, Morte Arthure, Destruction of Troy, Siege of Thebes, Titus and Vespasian, Joseph of Arimathie,* and *Sir Isumbras.* The issue of definition and distinction, one of the major endeavors of English romance scholarship, requires additional scrutiny.

Mehl's (1967) approach is to categorize the narratives according to length: to distinguish between shorter romances, longer romances, and biographies in verse. The majority of shorter and longer romances would concentrate on a selection of episodes; and the novel in verse would treat the hero's entire life. The problem posed by this schema lies in the fact that narrative structure or function does not always correspond to length. A number of shorter or longer romances tell the protagonist's life story, from birth to death: *Amis and Amiloun* and *Sir Tristrem,* for example. And a number of novels in verse choose a limited number of episodes and end with the hero's marriage: *William of Palerne* and *Partonope of Blois;* or they recount one person's biography yet only a partial life of the second: *Arthour and Merlin.* It is sometimes said that all traditional fiction seeks closure, finality exemplified in the hero's marriage or his death. In any case, no major effort has been made in French studies to subdivide the genre of romance according to length.

French studies do distinguish one kind of brief narrative from the *roman courtois* taken in its entirety, the *lai breton*. In the Middle English canon less than a dozen texts have been assimilated to the French genre and entitled Breton lays. Among them are *Sir Orfeo, Sir Degaré,* and the *Earl of Toulouse,* and also perhaps Chaucer's *Wife of Bath's Tale* and *Franklin's Tale*. Recently, however, scholars have questioned whether the English texts do correspond to Marie de France's *lais*. Are they perhaps brief narrative versions of material purportedly taken from a Celtic lyric lay recounting, generally in one episode, a story of *fin' amor* situated in the legendary Celtic past?

Three of the English Breton lays are versions of Marie: *Lai le Freine, Sir Landevale,* and *Sir Launfal*. However, only *Sir Orfeo, Emaré,* and the *Franklin's Tale* designate themselves as 'Breton.' In most of the English lays the action includes a sequence of episodes: such is the case in *Sir Degaré,* the *Earl of Toulouse, Sir Launfal, Sir Orfeo, Emaré, Sir Gowther,* and for that matter the two Chaucerian tales. The supernatural plays a relatively restrained role in narratives that are often quite 'realistic' in essence. Therefore, Finlayson (1984–5) has proposed that the Middle English Breton lay be considered a brief romance.

I agree, for the same situation exists in Old French. Following upon Marie, a number of poems were composed that do not conform to her literary practice, a practice that never was prescriptive or genre-determined. There is nothing Breton, Arthurian, fairy-like, or even courtly about the *Lai de Haveloc;* its English analogue, *Havelok the Dane,* is treated as pure romance. Jean Renart's *Lai de l'ombre* is an elegant, courtly masterpiece situated in a contemporary setting, with no supernatural at all. *Le Lai du lecheor* is a sarcastic parody. *Le Lai du cor, Le Lai du mantel,* and *Le Lai de l'épervier* are elevated fabliaux. Also fabliau-like is the famous *Lai d'Aristote,* which offers no hint of the supernatural and is located in classical Antiquity. Old French scholars will often consider Marie de France when discussing romance narrative as a whole. Whether they are right or wrong to do so, the great danger to avoid is the presumption that Marie embodies the French Breton lay and that one then should exclude, condemn, or otherwise judge the rest of French or English narrative using her as a touchstone.

Another approach to categorization treats the thematics or subject matter of romance. In French departments the term 'romance' is more restricted than in English departments. If one were to assume a definition of the genre corresponding roughly to the one used by Old

French scholars, based on Chrétien de Troyes, it would be possible to concentrate on Chrétien-like romances in Middle English and to remove from the canon one half of the corpus, not to condemn these texts but to ascribe them to other genres, such as history, *vita*, folktale, and epic. A number of scholars have made just this suggestion.

An obvious distinction has been made in terms of epic. Old French scholars regularly separate romance from epic, *roman* from *chanson de geste*. Whereas *roman* is said to be a secular narrative genre treating love, private adventure, and the quest (that is, the growth of the private individual in prowess and courtesy), *chanson de geste* is seen as a more specifically Christian genre treating war, the crusade, politics, and history (the celebration of public individuals and the community as a whole). In English a number of Fierabras and Otinel narratives are adaptations of *chanson de geste* material. Devoid of Chrétien-like characteristics, they have been called Charlemagne romances and included in the romance corpus. Kossick (1979) and Finlayson (1980–1) propose that it would be generically more logical and more coherent to remove such texts from romance; indeed they would remove all Middle English works that are truly epic in nature: not only *Otuel and Roland* or *Sir Isumbras* but also *Morte Arthure*, the *Destruction of Troy*, and the Alexander poems.

Given the continental and insular heritage of books in French, such a generic stance does pose problems. Some of the more 'epic' English romances are derived from Old French narratives habitually considered *romans* not *chansons de geste*. *Kyng Alisaunder* is based on Thomas of Kent's *Roman de toute chevalerie*, and the alliterative *Morte Arthure* is based on Wace's *Roman de Brut* (a chronicle with romance elements) and the *Prose Lancelot*, especially *Merlin*, *Suite du Merlin*, and *Mort Artu*. If these English texts display 'epic traits,' the same epic traits are to be found in French romance. The problems come from the juxtaposition of categories derived from world literature taken as a whole – epic as mode, romance as mode – vis-à-vis medieval texts that do not necessarily correspond to the abstract generic or modal categories.

From another perspective, I think it would be a mistake to take Chrétien de Troyes as one's model and to distil from his opus a list of characteristics and a definition of the romance genre by which to measure the Middle English romance corpus, thereby excluding or condemning one half of the extant texts. This practice not only distorts the English literary reality, but it also distorts the French reality. For, as we have seen in the domain of Anglo-Norman (the same is true for continental French), romance evolved in fascinating directions after

Chrétien, and an abstract Chrétien-oriented conception of romance does as much injury to the total Old French corpus as it does to the Middle English one.

It would be no less an error to take *La Chanson de Roland* as one's model for epic and to distil from it a list of characteristics and a definition of *chanson de geste* as a genre or the epic mode by which to measure the Old French or Middle English romance corpus. Just as there are one hundred French romances that diverge widely from Chrétien, there are one hundred *chansons de geste* that diverge widely from the *Roland*. In the course of the thirteenth century *chanson de geste* and *roman courtois* evolve in the same direction, with a tendency to coincide if not to fuse as literary entities. The epic now includes a powerful love interest, wildly improbable or supernatural episodes, a version of the quest, and court refinement and elegance. Romance includes greater historical and geographic realism and a concern for politics and history. Both genres often concentrate on telling a good story, which takes precedence over all other demands.

To take two examples, the *Prose Lancelot* manifests an interest in feudal politics, an obsession with history, a tragic Christian world-vision, and more than one protagonist. *Gui de Warewic* tells of Saracen wars and a lifetime of fighting, often in pitched battles; its heroes are two comrades in arms, its villains a lineage of traitors, its climaxes the defense of the homeland against pagan invaders. These two romances in French, which had so great an impact in England, can be deemed, following the standard generic formulation, more epic than romance. Earlier in this book I offered the theory that it is anachronistic to distinguish sharply between the medieval narrative genres; in a sense, they were to some extent based upon and measured against classical epic (Virgil and Ovid) and, along with Ariosto and Spenser, ought to be included in the world category of epic. Just as good a case can be made for their being included in the world category of romance. Anglicists may well have been right not to separate out the various strands of Middle English verse romance, and their theoretical laxness may well be more prudent and more accurate than the categorical rigour emanating from French critics.

A second distinction within the romance corpus has been made in terms of religion. Schelp (1967) proposes a category of 'exemplarische Romanzen,' to account for those Middle English romances that point a moral, teach Christian doctrine, and depict a protagonist who is either a positive or negative embodiment of the moral or doctrine. Other scholars, for example Childress (1978) and Finlayson (1980–1), go further to suggest that religious tales traditionally designated as romances, that present a passive hero or repentant sinner who achieves a happy ending through God's intervention, are in fact *vitae* or legends and ought not to be assigned to the corpus.

As with the example of epic, I remain skeptical. Many works are included, by one scholar or another, under the rubric 'legend' or 'exemplary romance': *Havelok the Dane, Amis and Amiloun, Guy of Warwick, Athelston, Sir Gowther, Le Bone Florence, Emaré, Chevalere Assigne, Morte Arthure, Joseph of Arimathie,* and the pseudo-Turpin derivations. Are not the new categories so general that almost all Middle English narrative would adhere to them? When would medieval fiction not be exemplary? When would heroes not be models of conduct? When are they not, in one form or another, succoured by the divinity?

A number of the texts cited – *Joseph of Arimathie*, the alliterative *Morte, Florence, Guy,* and *Amis* – are derived from French sources that obviously are romances and have always been so considered. Others are derived from *chansons de geste.* Since the Old French epic is frankly Christian in origin and its exemplars often display a powerful Christian message, are we to separate these works from the epic genre or mode and refer to them also as legends?

There is nothing in the romance tradition that would make sacred works or works simply containing sacred elements incompatible with it. Chrétien probably meant his own *Perceval ou le conte du Graal* to be interpreted in Christian terms; contemporary with the *Perceval*, often ascribed to the same Chrétien de Troyes, is the avowedly Christian *Guillaume d'Angleterre.* Following upon Chrétien we find a number of *Perceval Continuations*, then Robert de Boron's first Christian synthesis of Arthurian world history, to be followed by *Perlesvaus* and the *Prose Lancelot*. A number of French romances develop the *Emaré* or persecuted wife theme; quite a few have a Christian aura. *Emaré* adheres to the French romance (not hagiographic) tradition, as does Chaucer's *Man of Law's Tale*. In the thirteenth century, one orientation, common to both *chanson de geste* and *roman courtois*, is a degree of exemplarity, with absolute good set off against absolute evil in a melodramatic mode of persecution, suffering, and miraculous recovery.

The Anglo-Norman *Gui de Warewic* and the English *Guy of Warwick* devote the second half of the narrative to episodes of holy war conducted by a Christian hermit. I personally believe the Christian motif is secondary to the primary concern of the text which is to tell a good story full of incident and adventure. I can be wrong, however, and, in any case, a portion of the medieval audience may have lauded these texts as much for their Christian exemplarity as for their rapidly paced narrative. The Christian Guy is also a romance Guy, as he is an epic Guy, with little tension and no incoherence at all.

The same is true for Amis and Amiloun. The original *chanson de geste* gave rise to a *vita* (c. 1150) and to the extant *chanson, Ami et Amile* (c. 1200). It also gave rise to the Anglo-Norman *Amis e Amilun*, which gave rise to *Amis and Amiloun*. All these works – *chanson, vita*, and romance – exalt friendship, and all are Christian. The insular tradition somewhat downgrades the sacred, as it downgrades Carolingian allusions; however the story it tells is consciously, wilfully Christian, and it is a romance. The Ami and Amile story was portrayed in epic, in romance, and in hagiography, with little tension and no incoherence.

It is, therefore, wrong to adopt early French romance texts – Chrétien or the *Tristan* poems or Marie – as a prescriptive classical norm and, using this norm, to denigrate or to eliminate from the corpus one half of the Middle English romances. Using the same norm, one would have to denigrate or eliminate one half of the Old French romances as well. French romance evolves over a period of at least two centuries, perhaps three. Middle English poets had the entire gamut of the tradition to work with, and they did. They inherited and exploited the three centuries of French romance without discriminating between early and late, perhaps unaware of or unconcerned with distinction between early and late. As Reiss (1985) has said, instead of narrowing down, refining, and distinguishing our notion of romance, it will be more accurate historically and more respectful of medieval textuality to show how the romance genre (or mode) encompasses and includes so many disparate elements, derived often from other genres and modes.

A third series of categorizations within Middle English romance has been based on metrical form, associated in turn with geographical region. With the exception of a limited number of texts composed in *chanson de geste laisses*, French verse romance comes down to us almost exclusively in octosyllabic rhyming couplets, but the English tradition displays greater formal diversity. Approximately one third of the English poems are written in the equivalent of French couplets, composed largely in the South and/or in the London dialect that was most subject to French influence. Approximately one third are written in the alliterative long line of Anglo-Saxon origin, and composed for the most part in the West and North-West Midlands. Approximately one third are written in the twelve-line tail-rhyme stanza, a metrical form perhaps of Latin, and yet more likely of French origin, and these texts are composed largely in the East Midlands, East Anglia, or London.

Over the years much scholarly discussion has been devoted to the 'Alliterative Revival.' One school of thought, represented by Moorman (1968–9, 1981–2), states that alliterative texts in general, and romances in particular, are more aristocratic and more English than the rest of Middle English romance. These romances would have been composed for an aristocratic public in a region farthest from France and the francophile culture of London. They would treat English subject matter, different from that of the Frenchified court, in a non-London, traditionally and historically English verse form (Anglo-Saxon) that would reproduce the orality of Anglo-Saxon. Their tone would be specifically English; that is, epic, non-courtly, rural, oriented toward nature, primitive, violent, martial, historical, serious, and, according to some, neopagan. Finally, these romances would have given voice to unrest and rebellion and to baronial opposition vis-à-vis the court, king, and capital.

Elements of this stance have come under attack in recent years (cf. Salter 1966–7, Turville-Petre 1977, and Pearsall 1981, 1982, among others); some scholars repudiate the orthodoxy in its entirety. Far be it for me to emit an opinion whether the alliterative verse dating from 1350 on manifests and is to be accounted for by oral continuity from Anglo-Saxon times, or literary continuity, perhaps in the monasteries, or indirect literary continuity through the medium of alliterative prose, or the conscious literary revival of a dormant tradition. From the perspective of the French heritage, I suggest that the alliterative romances are no more aristocratic or oral or non-French or non-courtly than the rest of the corpus. We know now that magnates of the West and North-West Midlands – the Mortimers, Bohuns, Beauchamps, and Marches – were not in a state of discontent or rebellion during the second half of the fourteenth century. Furthermore, these princes all read and spoke French; some of them had rich libraries, most of the books being in French. Henry of Grosmont, Earl of Derby, later first Duke of Lancaster, composed the great *Livre de Seyntz Medicines*.

A significant number of the alliterative works are too long to have been memorized for oral delivery without a text and too bookish, too finished, and too 'classical' to have been composed orally. Quite a few, including Layamon's *Brut*, *William of Palerne*, *Morte Arthure*, *Destruction of Troy*, *Wars of Alexander*, *Joseph of Arimathie*, and *Siege of Jerusalem*, are translations or adaptations of long books in French or Latin. Also from the French are *Chevalere Assigne* and *Golagrus and Gawain*. Field (1982) has made an excellent case that the alliterative long line was chosen by poets (and patrons) as an English equivalent of the French Alexandrine used in epic *laisses*, especially prevalent in Anglo-Norman. Among the works composed in this metrical form are *Le Roman de Horn*, *Boeve de Haumtone*, Thomas of Kent's *Roman de toute chevalerie*, and chronicles by Jordan Fantosme and Peter Langtoft. This Alexandrine line is also to be found in religious literature and hagiography, and for all sorts of grave and sublime subject matter.

Presumably alliterative romance, like other romance in English, was composed not uniquely for the great barons (who knew and read French) but for a wider, more general public, perhaps centred in the country gentry; these readers perhaps knew no French, or were not entirely comfortable with French whatever their linguistic skills, or for whatever reason could find a place for story-telling in their native tongue. This would be a North or North-West regional variety of the general provincial public for which was composed all Middle English romance. It is hard to deem as peculiarly English, epic, and non-courtly a genre in which so many texts were translated from French courtly romance. French romance can be thought of as epic or as chronicle; so can English romance. However, there is little point in trying to separate the English spirit from the French when the two spirits appear to be identical. What does need to be distinguished is the historical literary genre and the universal literary mode. If Layamon's *Brut* and *Morte Arthure* are epic in mode, so are their sources: Geoffrey, Wace, and the *Prose Lancelot*. The epicness and the Englishness of such texts derive not from Anglo-Saxon continuity but, I should say, from the epicness and the pervasively medieval universality of the French. One can hardly deem non-courtly a tradition that contains the greatest courtly romance in English – *Sir Gawain and the Green Knight* – based on French sources, and *William of Palerne*, an elegant translation from the French that retains so much of the texture and 'feel' of the original.

In sum, it is my conviction that alliterative romance continues Anglo-Norman romance and forms the logical sequel to Anglo-Norman romance. Both traditions – the one dating from the twelfth and thirteenth centuries, the other from the fourteenth and fifteenth – are manifestations of a provincial or insular culture; they exalt local heroes, treat of local English or British subjects, and rely upon aristocratic or gentry patronage for texts in a bilingual land composed by bilingual authors for a bilingual public. During the first two centuries French was a *Hochsprache*, and English a *Volksprache* lacking a viable literary background and tradition. Later, English acquired the background and tradition and became a viable medium for literary endeavour, whereas French, still read, was spoken much less and ceased to be a medium for communication with a large, varied public.

We have no reason to isolate alliterative texts from the rest of English literature that employed metrics of French or Franco-Latin origin. Similarly, we have no reason to separate the authors of these texts from the cosmopolitan, cultured milieu of the South, including the royal court and London. The alliterative school and the Chaucerian school both use rhyme and stanzaic division. They both adopt French loan words and courtly themes; they translate or adapt the same French books; they share the same rhetoric, world-view, and even lexicon. Verse form is an important variable; however, by itself it ought not to be deemed *the* cause or effect of differentiation in romance because it is questionable whether such differentiation mirrors the reality of Middle English literature.

I believe the same situation exists for the thirty-five-odd romances composed in tail-rhyme stanzas. Traditional scholarly opinion adopts a stance similar to the one concerning the alliterative revival: that tail-rhyme romances, composed in the North-East, are a specific, definable entity within the total romance corpus. However, whereas nobility, artistry, and Englishness are projected onto the alliterative texts, it was for a long time assumed that narratives in tail-rhyme are less aristocratic and artistic, that they are more 'popular' than other romances, the creation of minstrels, their form determined by the oral tradition.

French courtly literature stands behind tail-rhyme romance in the same measure as it does elsewhere. Some narratives in tail-rhyme – *Lybeaus Desconus* for instance – reduce the French source to a skeletal frame. However, the same is true for a number of poems in couplets and in the alliterative long line. On the other hand, the tail-rhyme *Guy of Warwick* and *Ipomadon* are accurate, faithful translations from Old French, more accurate and faithful than versions of the same works in couplets. *Sir Perceval of Galles* is a brilliant, witty, literary transformation of *Le Conte du Graal*. *Athelston* and *The Earl of Toulouse* are first-rate original creations in the brief mode. And *Amis and Amiloun* and *Sir Launfal* expand upon their sources with more than a little inventiveness and style.

Recent scholars, especially Dürmüller (1975) and Fewster (1987), have made the point that the composers of tail-rhyme consciously employ a conventional, indeed archetypal style and diction and thus constitute a school of writing. According to this thesis, conventional metre and diction ought not to be condemned; they are inherently no better and no worse than other sorts of metre and diction. This formulaic, stylized, distinctive style is formed by and appeals to pre-established audience expectations. It appeals to generic awareness and is, to some extent, self-referential as a code signalling archaic authenticity, narrative pleasure, and the actual presence of romance.

I agree. I am also convinced that stanzaic tail-rhyme metre and diction have an analogue in Old French literature, not in romance but in *chanson de geste*. The *laisse* in a *chanson de geste*, like the tail-rhyme stanza and the tail-line itself, functions as a narrative and formal unit with linking devices; the *laisse* is constituted by verse that is formulaic and conventional, made up of stock phrases. *Chanson de geste*, like tail-rhyme romance, has been condemned by scholars for being ridden with clichés and fillers; like tail-rhyme romance, it has been defended (or simply represented) as a product of oral creation, not to be studied like 'other literature.'

The point is that *chanson de geste* and tail-rhyme romance may well owe some constitutive stylistic features to a pre-literary oral tradition. However, by the twelfth century in France and the fourteenth in England, we are dealing with literary texts – good and occasionally great works of literature – that exploit a highly conventional, traditional, archetypal style. The style is as literary and as artistic as any other. It will have upon its audience an impact different in degree but of the same essence as the Spenserian stanza or Corneille's Alexandrine. As romance, tail-rhyme texts are similar to those in couplets or in non-rhyming alliteratives.

It has been proposed in the past, and is accepted by many today, that Middle English romance differs in essence from Old French romance. According to this view, *grosso modo*, English poets were not interested in the depiction of courtly manners (descriptions of tourneys, feasting, and the chase, for that matter all descriptions), the discussion of courtly ideas (psychology, *fin' amor*, ethical dilemmas), and literary subtlety in general (especially irony). The romances were significantly shortened thereby. English poets concentrated on the story (action, incident) and on moral values. Hence a tighter, simpler narrative line. Hence an increased concern for prowess and valour, and also for concrete problems of kingship. Hence a distaste both for *fin' amor* adultery and for *fin' amor* sublimation and obstacle. English heroes were brave, valourous, chaste, and, in the end, they married the girl and (re)gained their inheritance. In the process, the romance genre was simplified, arriving at or reduced to a quality we can term melodramatic with good heroes opposed to evil villains, the good threatened at every turn but triumphing over evil in the end.

A significant number of the English metrical romances adhere to the pattern. *Ywain and Gawain* shortens Chrétien's *Chevalier au lion* by approximately one-third. Reduced or deleted are concrete scenes of combat, including gory details; courtly depictions of ceremony and dress; analysis of motivation for behaviour, *fin' amor*, and lovesickness; above all, ironic, witty dialogues that expose the excesses of *fin' amor* and the conflict between *fin' amor* and contemporary reality. The English poet, by deleting, sacrifices wit, elegance, passion, complexity, subtlety, and indirection. In their place, the English poem retains, and therefore emphasizes, action and the poetry of archetypal narrative plus the relationship of the individual to society grounded in knightly service and the knightly concept of 'trowthe.'

The stanzaic *Morte Arthur* reduces the prose *Mort Artu* by four fifths. The author suppresses psychological analysis, philosophical analysis (the idea of tragedy caused by Lady Fortune), and a number of interior monologues uttered by both Lancelot and Guinevere. Whereas the *Ywain and Gawain* poet respected Chrétien's narrative, here a number of incidents are cut. The slow, complex, contradictory build-up of jealousy in Arthur is drastically simplified with the reduction in Agravain's and Morgan la Fay's machinations, including the story of Lancelot's imprisonment. Political questions are simplified by the removal of Arthur's Roman campaign and by the 'melodramatization' of Guinevere's trial and of Mordred's assumption of the kingship. In general, the English poet blackens Gawain and Arthur (by making him appear weak), and whitewashes Lancelot and Guinevere (by making her appear pitiful). His book functions as a defence of Lancelot in which the latter ceases to be guilty of anything. Therefore, according to Wertime (1972), the story becomes not a tragedy of destiny or character or political institutions but simply one of 'consequence,' a chronicle of unfortunate circumstance.

A translation of the twelfth-century *Floire et Blancheflor*, *Floris and Blauncheflur* reduces the Old French by approximately two thirds. The deletions, almost without exception, fall into the category of courtly manners and rhetoric. Severely reduced or eliminated altogether are descriptions of people, places, and objects; depiction of court activities; dialogue; and interior monologue expressing love and personal sentiment. The flower symbolism (the hero and heroine both have floral names) remains, although a number of allusions to flowers have disappeared. On the other hand, the evocation of wit and deceit ('gyn' and 'ginour') has increased.

So far, so good. However, although the shortening of the French source, with the deletion of courtly materials and subsequent emphasis on the story line, occurs in a number of cases, in a number of others the transformation from French to English takes a different form. For example, the Middle English poet can, when he wants, translate accurately and faithfully from the French, constructing a native text of approximately the same dimensions as the foreign one. An excellent example of this would be *Guy of Warwick*, the most popular romance. The three major versions in verse are all, given medieval practice, accurate, authentic recensions that neither leave out nor add significant material. In only one of them do we find a major structural emendation: the Reinbrun material separated from the romance proper and reserved to the end as if it were a distinct, third division of the plot. This is an example of the dismantling of the interlace technique, a process that will reach its culmination in Malory.

It can be objected that *Gui de Warewic* is a non-courtly adventure romance concerned exclusively with narrative incident. Therefore, the English poets could follow their natural bent without having to rewrite. However, it turns out that they also translate accurately other, far more courtly texts.

Ipomadon A, 8890 lines in tail-rhyme, is almost as long as the Anglo-Norman original. The English does suppress much of the prologue and epilogue and a number of authorial interventions, places where Hue de Rotelande in his narrating persona indulges in antifeminist and obscene innuendo. 'Engin' and 'art' play a less significant role in the English than in the French. However, the translator retains all the rest: court scenes, tourneys, hunts, processions, monologues, and dialogues. He retains not only the courtly exemplariness of the original but also most of the courtly wit, the irony concerning Ipomadon as hunter of game and of ladies or Ipomadon as a fool of love yet less foolish than the ladies enamoured of him. The translation is so courtly and so sophisticated that Mehl (1967) claims it is not typically English.

William of Palerne, in 5540 alliterative long lines, occupies quantitatively approximately the same ground as *Guillaume de Palerne*, composed in 9663 brief French octosyllables. The English poet does suppress or condense geographical and historical detail, battle scenes, and the usual descriptions and psychological and moral reflections. He adds or amplifies the concrete evocation of everyday life, dialogue, recognition scenes, and reflections on kingship. Above all, he reproduces in the alliterative metre the courtly spirit of the original: court ceremonial, etiquette, splendour, the scrutiny of *fin' amor*, and rhetorical *amplificatio*. By medieval standards his is a very good translation and an artful transmission of French courtliness to the north-west Midlands.

As a last example, consider *Sir Landevale*, the first and most faithful English version of Marie's *Lanval*. The translator deletes allusions to Landevale's parentage and to his alienation at court, and he minimizes King Arthur's neglect. The trial machinary is telescoped. On the other hand, he clarifies the psychology of Landevale's judges, amplifies descriptions of the fay, her handmaidens, and her pavilion, adds some direct discourse, and has Landevale beg the fay's pardon. Marie's text has been slightly compressed, from 646 to 538 couplet lines. All in all, the courtly, chivalric spirit is the same.

It is also possible to cite texts that the English expand from the French, elaborating them according to the colours of rhetoric endemic to French romance that the English are alleged to dislike. *Sir Launfal* (1044 ll.) expands on *Sir Landevale* and perhaps on a version of Marie. The author, Thomas Chestre, adds description and direct discourse; he also 'invents' new scenes (borrowing from the French lay *Graelent*) that recount how Launfal became impoverished and that recount a tourney and a single combat in which, after Tryamour rewards him with her love, he displays courtly prowess. At one time scholars condemned Thomas Chestre for purported one-dimensional, surface, non-courtly bourgeoisie. More recent critics rightly see in him an artist eager to accentuate themes present in Marie's text and in the Lanval tradition: betrayal, pride, honour, prowess, manhood.[36]

Havelok the Dane both conflates and expands *Le Lai de Haveloc* and Gaimar's *Estorie des Engleis*. Significantly, the features he adds to or amplifies in the French – monlogues, dialogues, descriptions, narrative intervention, and rhetorical embellishment in general – are the very elements scholars elsewhere deem un-English, the features other romancers delete from their sources. In addition, the purportedly English features of the romance – concrete detail, especially depicting the activities of the lower classes: ship-building, fishing, trading, wrestling, and scullery life – are all to be found, in one form or another, in the French sources.

The insular romance versions of the Ami and Amile legend represent a simplification of the original *chanson de geste* material. The romancers romanticize the epic plot by deleting Carolingian background (*cum tradi-*

toribus) and by compressing some of the Christian imagery. This work of reduction is due to the Anglo-Norman author of *Amis e Amilun*, not his English adapter. Furthermore, in what is often designated as the didactic, exemplary, and Christian Middle English romance genre, this story proves to be less didactic and less Christian than the original *chanson de geste*. However, the Middle English poet, while adhering to the style and spirit of his Anglo-Norman source, once again elaborates and expands. He alters the plot in one important area, the question of why Amiloun is condemned to be a leper. Otherwise, he amplifies feasts, speeches, descriptions; he clarifies bits and pieces of plot, character, and motivation. His text is no more and no less courtly, chivalric, Christian, and romance-like than *Amis e Amilun*. It is expanded, amplified, and rhetorical – in the French manner.

In conclusion, it may be true in a number of cases that the English romancers were interested in French story and English morality; that they cut their sources, especially whatever is courtly (descriptions, psychology, character); that they added concrete realia; and that they were insensitive to subtlety, complexity and formal refinement. However, it is problematic whether the pattern is sufficiently universal to be valid for isolating the Englishness of English romances.

A number of English romances are accurate, faithful translations of the French; a number expand upon and amplify the French. Among those that abbreviate, some, such as *Floris and Blauncheflur*, retain the courtly flavour of the original; some, such as *King Horn*, delete concrete realistic detail found in the source. Some delete or dampen deeds of prowess (*William of Palerne*). Some add elements of courtliness and romance trappings (*Havelok the Dane*). The greatest of the English romances – *Sir Gawain and the Green Knight* – is as complex, as ironic, and as brilliant in its scrutiny of chivalry and *fin' amor* as any text in French. *Sir Gawain* is totally in the 'French spirit,' if there be such a thing as the French spirit. As for the question of French courtly adultery corrected by English Christian marriage, let us not forget a number of romances treating the great French myths of adulterous *fin' amor*, which are direct adaptations from the French: *Le Morte Arthur, Lancelot of the Laik, Sir Tristrem, The Knight of Courtesy*. One innovation common to all four of these works is the presentation of adultery in a more favourable light than the French source does.

I am not convinced that when insular poets adapt continental or Anglo-Norman models, the changes are all that significant. When the Englishman reduces or alters a French text, the orientation he gives the romance emphasizes a trait already present in the French. 'Treuthe' in *Ywain and Gawain* or in *Sir Launfal*; 'gyn' in *Floris and Blauncheflur*; governance in *William of Palerne*; upward social mobility in *Havelok the Dane*; the fall of chivalry in *Morte Arthur* – these are present, active, vital elements in the respective French sources. By deleting or dampening other elements, the English poets bring these to the fore but do not invent or discover them.

Furthermore, whatever the transformation an English poet brings to a particular French text, his state of mind does not run counter to French romance taken as a whole, especially French romance in the thirteenth century. Later French romance evolved in many directions, some of which anticipated the evolution of English romance. French romances also concentrate on the story, on incident and adventure. French romances also manifest tendencies toward melodrama and didacticism (pure good vs. pure evil). French romances also are not all masterpieces. It is unfair aesthetically and inaccurate historically to set off the Middle English verse romance tradition against Chrétien de Troyes. We also have the *Perceval Continuations*; the long verse adventure romances such as *Durmart, Yder, Claris et Laris*, and *Les Merveilles de Rigomer*; the *Prose Lancelot* and *Prose Tristan*; and so much more. The total picture explains and justifies all.

The older generation of scholars was wrong to denigrate Middle English romance for not being like the French, that is, for not being Chrétien de Troyes and Marie de France. A newer generation sometimes praises English romancers for the ways they have transmitted French sources, for their alleged artistry and conscious aesthetic design. Here also, to some extent, I am not convinced. That *Ywain and Gawain, Sir Launfal*, and the stanzaic *Morte Arthur* differ from the French is irrefutable; it is equally irrefutable that the English versions underscore elements in the French, those they have not altered or deleted, vis-à-vis those that they have. That the final result is due to a conscious, wilful aesthetic design, or an individual artistic consciousness giving expression to a unique individual world-view is more problematic.

Here I am reminded of Huby's now classic analysis (1968, 1984) of the thirteenth-century Hofenstaufen masters such as Henrik van Veldeken, Hartmann von Aue, Gottfried von Strassburg, and Wolfram von Eschenbach, German court poets who translated/adapted early French romances. Analysing the process of 'adaptation courtoise,' Huby arrives at the following conclusions. First, it is methodologically unsound to concentrate on the relatively few serious divergences between a French and a German romance while neglecting the identical passages and the passages of paraphrase and synopsis. Considering the romances in their totality, it becomes evident that the German court poets in no way sought to create an original structure, world-view, or aesthetic whole or to impose a Christian message on purportedly non-Christian source material. For the most part, they wrote on orders from a patron who gave them the text to be translated, perhaps the only French book in his possession. We cannot assume personal choice or a sentiment of personal affinity when a German poet works from a French model.

As a general rule, the adapter follows the Old French narrative, and he follows the ordering of episodes in the French. He will augment or reduce narrative increments; he will occasionally add or drop. However, the fundamental structure remains the same. When he does add or augment, it will be to attain greater formal symmetry or to elaborate the French plot in a more articulated way. Acting on rhetorical, formal grounds, he is not moved by moral or psychological considerations. If a 'moral heightening' does occur, it has the effect of heightening or deepening an attitude or judgment already manifest in the French.

Above all, the courtly adapter works on details, as often as not line by line. The end result varies from pure translation to a very free adaptation. Free adaptation implies variation on themes present in the original and amplification close to and inspired by the original. The German poet will reduce or omit here but then augment or amplify elsewhere; similarly, he will transpose from indirect to direct speech in one spot only to transpose from direct to indirect in another. The point appears to be that the adapter develops where he has an opportunity – where, in his opinion, the French did not exploit the inherent potentiality for rhetorical elaboration. On the contrary, where the French did exploit these possibilities, there is no place for him, and so he withdraws. This practice leads to apparent inconsistencies in treatment that can best be explained by the 'aesthetics' outlined above. The German poets, therefore, treat French sources as a sequence of rhetorical topoi, not a coherent aesthetic totality. The changes they introduce are almost without exception minor, concerning local incidents and not the romance taken as a whole. These changes, when they occur, are external manifestations of rhetorical, formal embellishment; they may explain or clarify strands in the diegesis or exalt the French ideal of courtliness already present in the text. The German romance becomes a social code, a guide to correct behaviour; it serves to propagate a highly stylized, exemplary ideal of courtliness and chivalry. By so doing, the adapter inevitably sacrifices some of the complexity and richness in the original, a complexity and richness of which he is perhaps unaware.

I should only wish to add to Huby's analysis the notion that French texts are chosen for translation because they offer an image of chivalry and courtliness articulated through rhetoric, and that the ethical and social message is deemed at least as important as the stylistic medium. Secondly, surely what he calls 'courtly adaptation' can also be termed 'courtly translation.'[37] The observations he makes concerning Henrik and Hartmann are also valid for much of the corpus of medieval translation, whether from Latin to French or from French to other vernaculars. Medieval translators are conscious of the problem of fidelity or authenticity. However, their claim to fidelity often means faithfulness to the sense of the original, not to its form. Or, despite elaborate protestations to the contrary, they change a great deal. In this latter case the protestations become a literary topos, perhaps exploited intentionally to veil the changes. Other translators proclaim that they amplify or modify the source for didactic purposes or for elucidation. Some medieval translations are accurate in the modern sense. Others avoid 'word for word,' sometimes adding, sometimes deleting, and often embellishing. In the case of verse translation, it is often stated that change occurs because of the demands of rhyme and metre. Even in biblical translation, and certainly in non-sacred *translatio*, it is acceptable to introduce new characters and/or subplots and to fill out the story line, provided the fundamental narrative and the spirit of the original are respected. Although admittedly a *compilator* not an *inventor*, the translator is free to exploit the veins of rhetoric, including *amplificatio* and *expolitio*, the latter implying interpretation and gloss.

In my opinion, the Huby analysis of 'courtly adaptation' can be applied fruitfully to the great majority of Middle English romances that have a French source. It is only necessary to add rhetorical *abbreviatio*, especially prevalent in the late Middle Ages, to the well-represented rhetorical *amplificatio* of the thirteenth century in order to comprehend the functioning of romance transmission. Let us consider a few examples, to which I have already alluded in this chapter.

Sir Landevale is an authentic, well-written, reasonably accurate version of Marie de France. It also corresponds to Huby's vision of courtly adaptation. Examples of expansion and reduction – condensing Landevale's prenuptial dialogue with the fay; condensing the trial machinery; amplifying conventional motifs concerning Landevale's ride, the description of the pavilion, Landevale's distribution of gifts, dialogue with the fay's messenger, and the beauty of the messengers – all can be accounted for as formal, rhetorical *mise en oeuvre* of detail, at the level of local incident; the translator amplifies when he has an opportunity and withdraws when he does not. The same is true for the translator's shifting Landevale's laments over being neglected from indirect to direct discourse, for attributing two instances of direct discourse to Guinevere, but then for shifting a speech by one of the messengers from direct to indirect. The few changes in the narrative, none of them substantive, occur either from the need to clarify or the need to render the narrative still more courtly and ensure its exemplariness. In this line Sir Landevale's largesse is emphasized as the cause of his misery, replacing Marie's sense of alienation; the fay announces early that she is a king's daughter from the Isle of Avalon; their lovemaking is shifted from preprandial afternoon to postprandial evening; Guinevere's accusing Sir Laundevale of pederasty is veiled; in the trial the courtiers immediately side with the hero and blacken Guinevere; and the hero does formally beg the fay's pardon.

The technique of courtly adaptation, natural enough in *Sir Landevale*, is also to be found in Thomas Chestre's *Sir Launfal*, often assumed to be a superficial, popular, bourgeois lowering of the original high-culture myth. Chestre proceeds along the same path as the *Sir Landevale* translator, amplifying where the latter amplified, suppressing where he suppressed. We find, still more than in *Sir Landevale*, direct discourse replacing indirect; emphasis on Tryamour's wealth; suppression of all references to homosexuality; Guinevere blackened as the cause of Sir Launfal's ills; and Launfal absolved of any and all guilt. The addition of the new episodes at Carlisle and in Italy serve two purposes. One is structural; Thomas Chestre strives for a sense of formal symmetry whereby the plot is carefully and ostentatiously articulated so that love episodes alternate with scenes of prowess, and the first half of the story – Sir Launfal and Tryamour – is set off against the second half – Sir Launfal and Guinevere. The other is courtly-chivalric; the tournament and scenes of poverty emphasize two aspects of Sir Launfal's character – prowess and largesse – stated but intentionally left in the background by Marie. Thomas Chestre, eager to make his hero an exemplar of courtliness, will enhance everything.

A case can be made that much the same concern for exemplary courtliness and exemplary chivalry motivated the *Ipomadon* translator. For propriety: Ymayne is the Fere's sister, not her maid-in-waiting; Ipomadon offers to make Tholomew a knight, however the latter declines; Ipomadon doesn't complain of fatigue when awakened, even in jest.

For propriety and for courtliness, the translator deletes a number of cynical, antifeminist or obscene interventions by the narrator-implied author, but not all. As I see it, he is translating as he goes along and has no rigid preconceptions governing the text. On the contrary, his intentions were probably of utmost fidelity both to the text and to what he considered to be its spirit. According to Meale (1984), all three Middle English writers took the original Anglo-Norman book and their own versions as exemplars of courtesy, nurture, and service, with emphasis on didactic exemplarity; the audience was to be instructed in courtesy by the protagonist's behaviour and the implied author's commentary.

The fact that *The Lyfe of Ipomydon* is a greatly reduced rendering of the original in no way modifies the above contention. The poets of *abbreviatio* had, it is my contention, the same aims and goals as the poets of *amplificatio*. Although the *Ywain and Gawain* poet was more interested in Chrétien's story than delving into psychology and character, most of his deletions can be explained by the principles of courtly adaptation, more cogently, I believe, than by alleged non-courtliness. To delete the evocation in Chrétien of Esclados's bleeding, gaping wounds and Laudine's passionate, irrational weeping over the corpse serves the interests of courtesy; the gaping wounds are unseemly and violate literary decorum; Laudine's weeping violates literary and social decorum. It also calls the audience's attention to her bad faith, to Yvain's folly in loving such a woman, and to the artificiality of the *fin' amor* code. Yvain's rhetorical monologues and Laudine's witty, precious dialogues with Lunette and with Yvain – these all call into question, scrutinize, and undermine the ideals of *fin' amor* and of chivalry, contrasting an artificial literary code with concrete reality, underscoring the literariness, indeed the comic absurdity, of the Esclados-Yvain-Laudine triangle and all it represents. By his other deletions the English adapter removes the indirection and the self-referentiality of Chrétien's text. In his hands, Ywain and Alundyne cease to bear guilt, cease to be problematic, and cease to make us laugh. They become exemplars of courtesy, an exquisite couple whose words and deeds entertain and instruct in the ways of chivalry.

From a somewhat different perspective, the same is true for the stanzaic *Morte Arthur*. Deletion of a number of scenes concerning Agravain's early plotting against Lancelot and Morgan's role in the story lightens the weight of destiny that hangs over the kingdom and reduces the importance both of Arthur's jealousy and of the theme of illusion versus reality. The story becomes less the tragedy of the fall of the Arthurian world and more the enactment of magnificent, exemplary deeds. Again, for the purposes of exemplary courtliness, Lancelot is absolved of guilt, and Guinevere also; responsibility for the collapse is placed firmly on Gawain's shoulders. Instead of a tale of adultery, we are told of armed conflict, Lancelot versus Gawain. The adultery is depicted in as favourable terms as possible, as if it were thrust upon the characters and not wilfully chosen by them (no allusion to *fol' amor*). Arthur is made weak, in order to enhance Lancelot, Guinevere's insane jealousy is reduced, and Lancelot does not go mad. Instead of a problematic world, in which all characters share in good and evil, we find a universe of melodrama, in which good opposes evil. The public, of course, is encouraged to imitate the good and eschew the bad.

Last of all, I should like to address two final questions. How were romances created? What was the nature of the public in which they were disseminated? For a long time the dominant theory held that French romances could be distinguished from English ones on the grounds that, whereas the French were literary works of art, composed by trouvères, the English were oral creations, composed and performed by minstrels ('disours'), much closer than the French to traditional oral narrative. Indeed, so the theory went, the English romances may have been recreated during each oral performance and/or the text that has come down to us reflects minstrel performance.

This minstrel theory is based upon the alleged poor quality (hack-work) of the romances, the poor quality of the manuscripts that preserve them, the alleged low class of people that listened to them, the frequent reference in the texts to oral presentation or performance, and, most important, the patently formulaic style and diction of the language in which they are composed. It has been observed that, in any specific romance, from 10 per cent to 42 per cent of the lines are formulaic, made up of stock tags and clichés. Although this diction is especially prevalent, as we have seen, in the alliterative and tail-rhyme romances, it is also to be found in narratives composed in rhyming couplets. The pervasiveness of formulicity, compared to the more individualized style of the court poets, has caused a number of scholars to posit oral construction in the romances and an oral tradition behind them. However literary the romances are recognized to be, a number of scholars, including Mehl (1967) and Rosenberg (1985), still speculate on which texts are the work of minstrels or, in analyzing the romances, use an oral-formulaic approach (cf. Wittig 1978) that, admitted or not, belies the texts' literariness.

The texts have to be literary, given that the vast majority are direct translations or free but careful adaptations from the French, or occasionally from the Latin. These translations-adaptations had to be written down at a table or lectern, with the learned (French, Latin) source before the poet's eyes. Most are far too long for even a minstrel to learn by heart. Furthermore, the prologues and epilogues that allude to oral delivery are grounded in rhetoric, with rhetorical topoi. The didactic, Christian thrust of so many romances provides still more evidence for their clerical origin.

Secondly, critics nowadays recognize that the romances are not hackwork. Texts concerned with the larger interests of narrative and doctrine and with a larger archetypal structure than the individual word or line can manifest pattern and order and can attain a high level of art. A popular, archetypal style and structure implies neither aesthetic deficiency nor non-literariness.

Deluxe manuscripts dated prior to 1400 with texts in English have not survived at any level for any genre. Since the flowering of literature and the development of respect for a vernacular culture occurred earlier in French than in English, we find elegant presentation copies of French epic, romance, and allegory at a time when nothing comparable exists in English. On the other hand, going back to the twelfth century, early *chansons de geste* and a number of early romances from that period survive in modest manuscripts that the French call *manuscrits de jongleur.* During these early years elegant, deluxe manuscripts were reserved for works in Latin. This does not mean that the aristocracy spurned the vernacular in twelfth-century France or fourteenth-century England or that these texts were not literary; they simply did not enjoy the same prestige as literature in the *Hochsprache*: Latin in early France; Latin and French in England somewhat later.

There is confusion in some Anglicist circles as to the precise nature and functioning of Old French romance. One scholar has the impression that the French romances were read privately and silently by individuals; another, on the contrary, assumes that they were composed orally by minstrels (Fichte 1981, Rumble 1965). The quasi-universal belief, in French studies, is that romances were written by trouvères as works of literature with a view, however, to be read aloud (by jongleurs and by others) as part of a more or less public performance. The majority of scholars believe the same to be true for *chansons de geste*. It is not surprising that both genres – *chansons* and *romans* – should be studded with motifs alluding to oral delivery by jongleurs. That the English romances display precisely the same oral-performance motifs as the French means probably (1) that, in this particular domain, the English again copied the French, and (2) that the English texts, like the French, were written literature meant to be read aloud.

It is true that French romances are not formulaic in diction; however, Old French epics are. *Chansons de geste* reveal roughly the same sort of highly traditional, highly conventional, repetitive style as do English romances. The majority of Old French scholars account for this formulicity in style as a residue from a preliterary period when the *chansons* or their oral-legendary predecessors may indeed have been composed orally by jongleurs. The traditional style was then maintained in works of literature by trouvères familiar with the corpus of formulae and of traditional themes and motifs, for an audience equally familiar with and sympathetic to the tradition. That the same formulaic style with its allusions to oral delivery persists, indeed increases, in *chansons de geste* of the thirteenth and fourteenth centuries indicates that they function as generic markers, not that these late texts or the earlier ones were all composed orally.

It appears most reasonable that the same is true for English romance. There also, as Fewster (1987) has said, the formulaic style and the allusions to oral delivery would appear to function largely as generic markers and as a form of self-referentiality. The 'romance style' would coincide with and reinforce pre-existing audience expectations as to the nature of romance; it would function as the only appropriate style for romance narrative. In fact, like *chanson de geste*, a highly conventional, artificial, formulaic language does mirror and reinforce a no less conventional, artificial, and archetypal narrative. It is romance style; it contributes to generic awareness because it is indissolubly fused with the genre. It *is* the genre, and the genre is inconceivable without it.

The preceding remarks are not meant to oppose a current hypothesis (cf. Quinn and Hall 1982, McGillivray 1990, and others) that the versions of certain romances that have come down to us, such as *King Horn* and *Floris and Blauncheflur*, may well not inscribe the original literary creation or translation. Instead, they would be late versions of texts that, originally literary, were performed by minstrels and underwent minstrel improvisation or, at the least, memorial transmission. In a few cases they might even be a version copied from memory; that is, the faulty memorized redaction of an earlier literary work, for memorization in transmission can occur in scribal recasting as well as in performance. The chain of composition would then be this: a French or Anglo-Norman romance, literature; adapted into English, literature; performed by minstrels, orality; copied down in manuscript, literature – in sum, it is literature but literature which has been influenced by oral performance and improvisation. At this point, the evidence is still not conclusive, and the question remains open.

What was the public for which English romances were composed? Here again scholars have long distinguished English from French romance on the basis of the social class ascribed to the public. The early view, still held by some, maintains that, whereas French literature, both in France and in England, was composed for the aristocratic, courtly, upper reaches of society, the public for English romance was non-Francophone, popular, and undiscriminating, the lower orders, as it were.

A first 'revisionist' theory, from Mehl (1967), Crane (1986), Barron (1987), and others, proposes a broad public for Middle English narrative, an audience larger and more varied than for the French. This public would not be limited to the 'lewed.' It would include the small provincial nobility and the urban bourgeoisie, merchants and gentry from both London and the counties. The public would also include members of the high aristocracy, those who didn't read or care for French, those with literary interests but whose French was weak, or those who did read French and who also encouraged versions in the spoken vernacular. The English romances would then reflect the ideology of this broad, enlarged public – with English heroes and narratives treating English history, concerned with the rights of inheritance and sovereignty but less specifically feudal and socially hierarchical than the French. Pearsall's (1985) variation on this theory proposes a shift in the public over time, English romance catering at first to the needs of the middle strata in society, and then, after 1400, attaining a wider audience, appealing to the aristocracy and to county families now that the English vernacular had achieved a measure of respect, but also appealing to less refined people, a *profanum vulgus* that sought in books only entertainment and wish-fulfilment fantasy.

A second revisionist theory, from Hudson (1984), Coss (1985), and others, takes into account the fact that the high aristocracy possessed books only in French and Latin and that the urban merchant class had the same tastes as the aristocracy, aping the nobility in culture as in everything else. According to this view, the audience for metrical romance should be limited to the local provincial gentry and clergy, which, some would say, includes courtiers, civil servants, and other professional men. The imago for the gentry theory is the Thornton family of the Thornton manuscript. In the fourteenth and, especially, fifteenth centuries the county minor gentry was rising but separated from the true nobility, and therefore threatened in its legitimacy. The aspirations of this class would be mirrored in the romances – a hierarchical but fluid social order in which deserving heroes could rise to the top. We also find, in a number of texts, the humorous or problematic scrutiny of the ideals of chivalry, the presumed ideology of the high nobility.

Comparison with writings in French can only reinforce the revisionist theories. Once again, it is similarities not differences between the two literatures that stand out. Anglo-Norman literature was destined for a broad public of provincial nobility and gentry that felt, to some extent, isolated and insular with regard to the Continent. The shift from French to English in the fourteenth century may have implied no shift at all in the audience; on the contrary, it may have functioned as language functioned in the society taken as a whole. It is quite likely that the same audience patronized Anglo-Norman and English books, at the same time.

Something roughly similar can be said for continental literary culture as well. It is true that Marie, Chrétien, Gautier d'Arras, and Jean Renart, to cite the most eminent, dedicated their major works to members of the high aristocracy. What does this mean? Either that a Countess of Champagne and a Count of Flanders appreciated, even subsidized, the new vernacular high culture; and/or that the new vernacular narrative poets – clerkly author figures – sought to win the graces of the aristocracy and/or to impress the public with their apparent connections to the aristocracy. It does not mean, however, that the French magnates were the only public for romance or that romance could only speak, ideologically and aesthetically, to them. On the contrary, it would appear that the new lyric and narrative genres reflect the aspirations of the *juvenes*, the *bachelers* – young, landless warriors in search of a place in society. This would be the audience for which romances were written; the texts offer the wish-fulfilment fantasy of a new order based upon gentle birth but above all based upon the inner qualities of courage, fidelity, enthusiasm, élan, and *fin' amor* that permit the deserving youth to win a bride and a kingdom. The theme of the *juvenis* and the qualities he embodies are central to French romance throughout its evolution. Now the *juvenes* of early medieval France resemble remarkably the gentry of late medieval England; they have the same social status, the same aspirations, and the same alienation. In France, and in England, romance appealed to a relatively broad-based, gentle public. The nobility determined taste; the other classes followed its lead.[38]

In sum, I believe that Middle English romance resembles closely its Old French generic source and model. Both genres comprise artistic, literary works of art, not the haphazard transcriptions of oral performance; both were composed for a broad-based public with aristocratic aspirations, eager to espouse an ideology oriented toward the nobility. Both genres contain elements of epic and of Christian apologetic, as they do of quest-heroism and *fin' amor.* The shift from an early French to a later English romance tradition can be accounted for in two ways. One is evolution from the dense, complex, symbolic texts of Chrétien, Beroul, Thomas, and Marie, to a more consciously didactic narrative that is more concerned with rapidity of incident and adventure and the sheer pleasure of telling a good story. However, the same evolution occurs in French. It is one of the roads taken by both continental French and Anglo-Norman narrative in the thirteenth century, as well as by romance in English in the thirteenth, fourteenth, and fifteenth centuries. A second way is constituted by the process of courtly translation or adaptation. The English translator-adapter is eager to amplify or to abbreviate his French book, according to the principles of rhetoric, and to make the English a perfect exemplar of chivalry. Lacking some of the complexity and irony in the French, English romance will evidence doctrinal correctness and archetypal power.

In line with these considerations, I propose now to examine seven romances: *Ywain and Gawain, Sir Degaré, The Earl of Toulouse, Floris and Blauncheflur, William of Palerne, Amis and Amiloun,* and *Athelston*. I have chosen these seven because I believe they are worthy representatives of the Middle English corpus. They manifest a variety of metrical forms; they are in the 'French style,' some direct translations or adaptations, and others independent creations. They are all, in my opinion, aesthetically of the first class. And they embody the phenomenon of courtliness. With regret, I do not include a chapter on *Sir Gawain and the Green Knight*. This masterpiece is truly unique, and the problems it poses are not typical of Middle English romance in the way that the others are; besides scholars have written so much and so well on it, and to accord *Sir Gawain* anything like the scrutiny it deserves would exaggerate the length of this volume.

Ywain and Gawain

Something like a scholarly consensus exists concerning the fourteenth-century *Ywain and Gawain* expounded elegantly by Harrington (1970) and Busby (1987): this translation-adaptation of Chrétien de Troyes' *Chevalier au lion* deletes material concerning love, ladies, courtesy, psychology, and the emotions; with the loss of passion and depth (or 'roundness'), characterization suffers; and, as Hunt (1984) observes, the poet is unaware of or he relentlessly suppresses all in Chrétien that is irony, self-referentiality, indirection, and burlesque. We are left with a text concentrating primarily on the story and its telling, treating secondarily the protagonist's evolution in the course of the narrative and his exemplification of loyalty and 'trowthe.' The modifications introduced by the adapter would then reflect the concerns of his English audience, which was less sophisticated and less aristocratic than Chrétien's.

I believe that the divergences between the French and the English versions can be accounted for otherwise. As I see it, the Middle English poet was not necessarily writing for a different public than Chrétien did. *Ywain and Gawain* is shaped in a certain way not because the author repudiates chivalry and courtesy but because, on the contrary, he wishes to render Chrétien's characters perfect exemplars of courtliness as he sees it. He makes more explicit what is subtle and indirect in Chrétien, and he corrects speech and behaviour that do not conform to his own sense of what Ywain and Alundyne ought to be as models of conduct. In the end he inevitably smooths over the delicate irony, complexity, and questioning of the courtly in Chrétien. And, of course, he does concentrate on the story. The reader of *Ywain and Gawain* is moved especially by the aspect of Chrétien that the Englishman retains in toto – the archetypal power of the narrative. The poetry of the story (which may have originated in popular traditions and/or memories of Celtic myth) in *Le Chevalier au lion* and in *Ywain and Gawain* is transformed by a highly complex literary imagination that works upon the conventional themes and structures of romance.

Sir Ywain is immersed in a stylized, poetic world where knights submit to ordeals which test their valour and the other classes in society live only to serve brave warriors or to be rescued by them. Adventures come as if miraculously to a tiny elite, and events in the external world are interpreted symbolically as a representation of inner struggle and initiation. Adventure, which lies in a realm beyond history and above mundane contingencies, gives meaning to life; it is the essence of life. The chivalric-courtly society alone is worthy of such an experience.

On at least two occasions Ywain finds himself in predicaments that can only occur in the Other World. First his cousin Colgrevance, and later the protagonist, undergo the ordeal of the fountain. A knight traverses a Waste Land (the barrier to the Other World), encounters a Hospitable Host and a Giant Herdsman (guardians of the threshold), and finally arrives at a *locus amoenus* containing a well (fountain) where a tempest is unleashed and birds sing for joy. The custom demands that the intruder give battle to Salados, the master of the place. Then, when Ywain succeeds in slaying Salados, he marries Alundyne, the widow. This episode probably results from a fusion by Chrétien of Celtic myths recounting the testing of warriors by a god of storms, the luring of a mortal to the Other World by an aquatic fay, and a rain-making cult in the forest of Brocéliande.

Sir Gawain then convinces Ywain to leave his bride and join him in quest of martial exploits. When the knight overstays his leave, Alundyne repudiates him, causing him to go insane. However, through a long process of struggle Ywain regains respectability. His exploits include, among others, the rescue of Lunet, Alundyne's servant (who had previously helped him to win her mistress's hand), and the rescue of three hundred captive maidens from a pair of gruesome sons of a demon. Ywain succeeds in these battles with the aid of a lion, who befriends him after Ywain took his side in a fight with a serpent. Then, following a trial by battle with Gawain at court, Ywain returns to the well in order to recover Alundyne.

Ywain's story, which includes a solitary journey, adventures, rites of passage, withdrawal and return, marriage, and the attainment of sovereignty, corresponds to the traditional structure of quest romance. Chrétien and, following him, the English adapter have given an original direction to the plot, for the fairy bride is a widow not a maiden, and the hero, before winning her, slays her husband. It is one way of 'co-opting' adulterous *fin' amor* into a romance setting. Also, this basic increment in *Ywain and Gawain* contains the death and rebirth archetype that early scholars associated with the *rex Nemorensis*, a priest-king who defends the sanctuary and is succeeded only by a newcomer who slays him in battle. The priest-king of the grove or the knight of the fountain is regularly replaced and as regularly wed to a goddess-fay who endures. However, Ywain refuses to become like Salados, to perish and be replaced by another Ywain. Instead, Sir Ywain dies and is reborn as the Knight with the Lion in order to win back ('remarry') the divine lady. Yet, before so doing he violates a tabu, falls from grace, and is expelled from her presence; this is another form of death. His experience in the world, naked, mad, and devouring the raw flesh of beasts is a form of spiritual death, the degradation of his rational and social being. Ywain's fall corresponds to Adam's, both men driven naked from their paradise. Then a lady and her maidens cure the knight with an ointment that symbolizes baptism or provenient grace or the anointment of Christ. He then is given new clothes (*nova vestimenta* for a *homo novus*) and acquires a new name – the Knight with the Lion. Although Ywain talks of dying, after the symbolic death-rebirth experience he proceeds to live in the world with his new name and to conquer the supernatural bride a second time.

I have no doubt that Ywain's battle with the stranger knight, whom he slays, and his subsequent marriage to Salados's widow, the semi-divine Lady of the Fountain, is a version of unconscious oedipal wish-fulfilment, especially since one source for the twelfth-century *Yvain* was the Oedipus-Jocasta story in *Le Roman de Thèbes*. Although the young knight's virility is threatened by the Giant Herdsman, tamer of beasts, and the giant Salados, a sun-storm figure whose spear and horse are larger than Ywain's, he nonetheless succeeds in defeating the father figure and penetrating into an enclosed, feminine Other World where the id rebels and the ego is awakened. The *durus pater* is displaced from King Arthur onto Sir Kay and Sir Salados. Youth conquers age and creates a new, festively congenial society in its image, successfully enacting the oedipal fantasy. The protagonist nonetheless endures symbolic guilt; he slays Salados but is himself wounded in the process. A second wound, amorous this time, occurs when the hero beholds the weeping mistress of the castle. Alundyne proves to be a Terrible Mother as well as a good one, a phallic mother who replaces the dead phallic father. The well produces a tempest and Alundyne's palace, with its falling portcullis, is a castrating trap as well as a refuge. Within, the victor of the fountain is rendered timid and passive, whereas the active roles are assumed by Alundyne and Lunet. For whatever conscious reasons, Ywain consents to escape the well and its mistress as soon as he can. Only with the denouement do we find a mature, socially acceptable male desire that breaks the tabu and brings about reconciliation.

Although the English adapter whitens Sir Ywain's conduct and speeches throughout the narrative, it is still valid to state that, as in Chrétien's text, the protagonist grows in the course of the narrative.

The diegesis begins with Ywain brave, impetuous, and enthusiastic, full of romantic brio but not yet secure in a state of perfection. His comportment in the Other World marks him as lacking measure in love and in war, too weak before Alundyne and too strong before her husband, whose lands he invades and whom he slays uniquely in order to avenge Colgrevance. After the wedding and during the probationary year he is guilty of a form of *acedia*, that is, neglect of marital and professional obligations. The appropriate punishment for *acedia* is its medical, physiological consequence, *tristitia* or *melancholia*, an insane, frenetic despair. Our protagonist literally goes mad after having committed a crime against his lady, the god of love, and the code of chivalry:

Sir Ywayn, when he þis gan here,
Murned and made simpil chere;
In sorow þan so was he stad,
þat nere for murni[n]g wex he mad ...
An evyl toke him als he stode;
For wa he wex al wilde and wode. (1637–40, 1649–50)

He hates himself and wishes to perish; bereft of reason he wanders naked in a Waste Land, hunting wild animals and devouring their flesh. Ywain has become a beast, punishment for the beastly way he treated Alundyne; he failed to respect her as a human being and, according to Hamilton (1976), to respect the human 'trowthe' he pledged to her.

Yet the knight's mad state is also endemic to good lovers and therefore it is to be pitied and regarded with wonder. The Savage Man can be a positive as well as a negative icon. At any rate, Ywain returns to the threshold of social intercourse through the mediation of a hermit; this first human contact is grounded in barter and in the juxtaposition of nature and culture, the raw and the cooked. Then, as Ywain was formerly saved from physical death by Lunet, now three ladies save him from the death of the spirit; they are images of the beneficent feminine principle inherent in society. For the rest of his career, the Knight with the Lion will struggle to merit reconciliation with Alundyne, not by proving himself in frivolous, show tournaments but by serving others; this is a public function of ridding society of ogres who threaten the common weal. In each case he rescues damsels in distress: Sir Alers's victim, Sir Gawain's niece, Lunet herself, the three hundred prisoners in the Castle of the Heavy Sorrow, and the disinherited younger sister. This madman, who formerly was assisted by ladies and then was scorned by his wife and a Loathly Damsel, is redeemed by service to womankind. Thus he integrates into himself the feminine principle, without which he and his society are imperfect; he becomes a whole, adult human being.

Directly after the first altruistic deed, Ywain, having acted like a lion, encounters a lion giving battle to a serpent; he takes the lion's side and wins him as pet and ally. In this 'adventure' the lion chooses to follow Ywain:

> When Syr Ywayne þat sight gan se,
> Of þe beste him thoght pete,
> And on his way forth gan he ride;
> þe lyown folowd by hys syde.
> In þe forest al þat day
> þe lyoun mekely foloud ay,
> And never for wele ne for wa
> Wald he part Sir Ywayn fra. (2009–16)

Like Husdent in Beroul's *Tristan*, he hunts for his master and also assists him three times in battle. At the centre of the narrative Sir Ywain earns a friend. Whatever symbolic interpretations we give the animal (Christ, the Spirit, God's grace, *fortitudo*, sovereignty), there is no doubt that he represents the natural or supernatural forces that grant Ywain special aid, prove his heroic virtue and his election to greatness, and sanction his quest.

In the course of the narrative a number of individuals are compared to or associated with animals – the Giant Herdsman, who resembles savage beasts and who holds lordship over bulls, bears, lions, and leopards; Harpyns of Mowntain; the demons; and Salados. Ywain also, after he goes insane, descends to an animal level, lower than that of the Herdsman and Harpyns. He had hunted Salados, hunter of men; now he tracks wild game for a hermit and is transformed himself into a grateful beast. Then, in his adventures with the lion, he respects a grateful animal in turn, masters a creature like the Herdsman, and is aided by one far more loyal to him than he was to Alundyne.

Finally, the lion gives the romance hero his name and helps resolve his identity crisis. Sir Ywain's name is an honoured one, announced with pride by him to Lunet and by Lunet to Alundyne. Alundyne is especially eager to marry the son of King Uriene. However, after his fall, symbolically the knight has lost the right to bear a name and, in disarray or as evidence of newly acquired humility, he insists on fighting incognito. On the road to regeneration, however, Ywain chooses to be known as the Knight with the Lion:

> Sho said, 'Sir, sen þou wyl wend,
> Sai us þi name, so God þe mend.'
> 'Madame,' he said, 'bi Saint Symoun,
> I hat þe knight with þe lyoun.' (2659–62)

This new identity reveals the break in Ywain's consciousness; it is an integral step in his initiation experience, a recognition of the fall and the need to rise. The lion, become part of Ywain's title, also shares his identity. The good beast sanctions Ywain's quest and lends him its name and its honour – as king of the animal world – until the *homo novus* has won such glory that he can, first at Arthur's court and later in Alundyne's castle, unlace his helmet and reveal that the Knight with the Lion and the son of King Uriene are one:

> þus þe knyght with þe liown
> Es turned now to Syr Ywayn
> And has his lordship al ogayn;
> And so Sir Ywain and his wive
> In joy and blis þai led þaire live. (4020–4)

For the medieval public the Arthurian world and the court of King Arthur and his knights are a manifestation of paradise lost; the court represents an ideal of social decorum and moral judgment against which Ywain must be measured. However, the romance's attitude toward the court is ambivalent. It contains witty, gracious people – Guinevere, Gawain, Colgrevance, and Arthur himself – but also Kay the Steward, who is a *miles gloriosus* acting in an absurd, inconsequential, and insulting manner. Even Sir Gawain, the 'observed of all the observers,' is guilty of having seduced Sir Ywain into quitting his bride immediately after their honeymoon. It is Ywain who protects Lunet and delivers members of Gawain's own family, during a time when King Arthur's nephew is nowhere to be found. Finally, when Gawain does reappear, he promises to support the older sister without inquiring into the justness of her cause and thus situates himself on the wrong side of a *judicium Dei*. Ywain does not physically defeat him; their duel ends in a draw. But morally he has surpassed his companion and alter ego; he has gone beyond him in service to the community, and in so doing has learned to cope with that part of himself responsible for negligence. Indeed, halfway through the story he changes companions. In Gawain's stead he substitutes the lion, who proves to be of more help to him than any man. For the norms of the court he substitutes a more elemental, more spiritual entity, a finer, higher, nobler *fortitudo et sapientia*.

The court legitimizes Ywain and embodies the values that Ywain struggles to embrace. However, he does not win his 'essence' there. He acts and changes; his ordeals take place in other settings, especially the well. A typological reading can be made of the pine tree (*arbor vitae* or Tree of Jesse), the spring (*fons vitae*), and the baptism of fire and love that takes place there. Three times Ywain undergoes an adventure at the source; three times he rescues or conquers a fair lady: Alundyne, Lunet, Alundyne. The first ordeal brings Ywain status; the second grants him inner worth, responsibility, and self-awareness; the third consecrates his worth, restores status, and offers the right to sovereignty. In the end, Ywain leaves the king and queen to return – alone, with the lion – to his spouse. The climax of his career is consecrated not in acceptance at court but in reconciliation at home. He will devote the rest of his life to defending the fountain, maintaining a reputation for prowess away from King Arthur. From one perspective, the public and private worlds of action are dissociated, and, to some extent, the private is given value over the public. On the other hand, the poem also recounts the triumph of another kind of life, that of the couple; the protagonist chooses a kingdom with his wife over the Arthurian kingdom of the fathers. Ywain decides in favour of existence over essence, of an eternal becoming over stasis. The structure of *Ywain and Gawain* is in large measure determined by the opposition of these two symbolic décors, the court and the well, and voyages by the hero and others from one to the other.

It is possible to speak of competing masculine and feminine 'worlds' in *Ywain and Gawain*. The masculine universe is embodied in King Arthur's court, in the rule and functioning of the law, and in the persons of the ruling, reasoning king and his warrior nephew. The feminine is manifest in the fountain of storms and fertility, and the labyrinthine castle with its secret chambers; this strange, magical realm is under the sway of the passionate, capricious Alundyne and her servant, Ywain's second friend, the moon figure Lunet. The light and the dark compete for Ywain's loyalty. Lunet is the embodiment of ruse as opposed to Gawain's force, and of love as opposed to his comradeship and honour. Only by integrating both of them, the masculine and feminine aspects of his self and of the universe (mind and heart, reason and passion, the conscious and the unconscious, responsibility and self-indulgence, animus and anima, reality and faerie, the real and the supernatural), can Ywain become a total adult being, capable of serving others and of wielding sovereignty – in marriage and in his new kingdom, which he shall defend and where he shall reign.

Sir Degaré

Sir Degaré is a brief romance, some 1076 lines in couplets, of the Breton lay type. Like *Ywain and Gawain*, it treats of quest, growth, and discovery in an exotic, Other World locus. Like Marie de France's *Yonec* and *Milun*, it recounts the family romance careers of the protagonist's parents. Less subtle than Marie and less complex than Chrétien and his adapter, the *Degaré* poet exploits an all but inexhaustible fund of traditional romance themes and motifs. *Sir Degaré* can be considered the exemplar of the romance archetype.

The story tells of a king who will permit his daughter to marry only if the suitor can vanquish him in a joust. The princess remains unwed. However, she is raped and impregnated by a fairy knight. Fearful of the consequences, the new mother conceals her pregnancy and sends her baby away. The foundling, Degaré, is raised by humble folk. Then, armed with recognition tokens (a pair of gloves and a broken sword), he sets out to find his parents. He delivers an earl from a dragon. Then he defeats the king in jousting and weds his mother, but happily avoids incest when he discovers her identity in time. Degaré then proceeds to deliver a maiden in a fairy castle from a giant. Before marrying her, however, he endures further adventures that include battle with his father, recognition, and bringing the parents together in wedlock.

Rosenberg (1975) underscores the folkloric aspects of *Sir Degaré*, proposing that the Middle English romance or its putative French source represents the fusion of three folk-tales and testifies to the oral mentality that would have shaped medieval romance. I disagree. Whatever the ultimate origins of the archetypal patterns of romance narrative and whatever the rapport between high culture and low culture in the Middle Ages, Middle English romance is a literary genre. The English poets express the *Volksgeist* and speak to the masses of the people no more and no less than Chrétien de Troyes and Thomas do in twelfth-century French. I also see no reason to posit the existence of a lost Old French *Lai d'Esgaré*. The English poet, like so many others, was capable of shaping and adapting French sources by himself. In fact, we know the French books that would have provided the relevant narrative material: one romance, *Richars li biaus*, and any one version of the legend of Pope Gregory the Great. This said, the French legacy provides the determining generic structure for romance in English, even when there is no French original; hence the symbolic import of the French echo in the hero's name. In spite of the criticisms by Slover (1931) and Kane (1951), we have here a gifted story-teller who, in his work, epitomizes romance structure and the very essence of romance.

This essence of romance concerns how a youth grows to manhood, freeing himself from the constraints of the adult world embodied in his real or putative parents. He discovers and attains his true nature, personal and sexual, and becomes a Self integrated into society. To do so, he undertakes a journey, symbolically to the Other World. There he submits to ordeals, gives battle to adversaries, is aided by magic tokens, and, in the end, wins a bride and a kingdom. The episodes in sequence either point to the hero's evolution or are simply progressive revelations of the greatness inherent in him from the beginning.

In *Sir Degaré* this structure is grounded in the family romance pattern we found in Marie's *Yonec*. The protagonist's early alienation and later rise to legitimacy are seconded by a series of incidents explaining that the boy's putative parents, of humble circumstance, are not the real parents; the real parents, an earthly princess and a fairy prince, are also alienated or otherwise victims of circumstance; and the youth will not only emerge to his own wish-fulfilment regal and semi-divine state, he will also set to right the injustice committed against his parents and restore them to their state.

Three events or situations account for the blocking, tyrannical society and the hero's personal degradation; this 'lack' will launch a second series of events to liquidate the lack.

The king will not allow his daughter to wed in the usual manner. He sets an 'impossible task' in the way of prospective suitors. The task – to defeat him in a joust (he is a furiously successful jouster) – recalls the *rex Nemorensis* motif in *Ywain and Gawain*. In *Sir Degaré* the motif is more overtly oedipal; the struggle is between a father figure and a son figure who must defeat the father in order to win his bride and attain sexual maturity. The incest motif between father and daughter is not stated directly; however, the princess does confess later that she especially dreads public revelation of her pregnancy for people will assume that her father was the man responsible:

'ȝif ani man hit underȝete,
Men wolde sai bi sti and strete,
That mi fader, þe king, hit wan.' (167–9)

In response to paternal tyranny and the thwarting law, the princess wanders into a deep forest where she undergoes a Pluto-Proserpine experience. Plucking flowers, she is plucked and ravished by a supernatural prince; her retainers are powerless to aid her. This is the first encounter with the Other World. Standard Celtic motifs are the forest, the deep sleep of the retainers, the fairy prince, the prince's prophecy, and the magic tokens he bestows on the princess. The scene can be envisaged as the princess's wish-fulfilment fantasy; she escapes into the realm of the passions and the unconscious, where, in a world of dreams, she integrates her animus. However, as in Marie's lay, the first experience is not entirely successful; although the princess will have a son, her thwarting of the law is illegitimate. She remains bound to her father, and she must wait a good two decades for deliverance. Similarly, the fairy prince has no identity and fails to legitimize his presence and his behaviour in the courtly world.

The illegitimate son is exposed. Raised by a hermit and his entourage, the boy is a misfit, suffering from confusion, alienation, and loss of identity. The author, grounded in the French tradition and using French litarary sources, names his protagonist Degaré, presumably from the French 'd'esgaré,' the lost one:

He hit nemnede Degarre:
Degarre nowt elles nis
But þing, þat not neuer, whar it is,
Or þing, þat is negȝ forlorn, also;
Forþi þi child he nemnede þous þo. (254–8)

The broken sword his mother left to him is the appropriate symbol for Degaré's broken identity and impotent social Self at this stage in his development.

On his road of trials, in quest of his identity, Degaré endures a number of successive ordeals. He sets out on foot, armed only with a stake. Lacking traditional knightly accoutrements and weaponry, he stands as a Perceval figure, resembling a number of youths in epic and romance in French (Perceval himself, of course, Rainouard, Fergus, and Havelok, among others), who, of noble birth yet raised in humble surroundings, wish to obtain renown in martial feats but do not know how to go about it. Degaré's first feat is to defeat a dragon, thereby rescuing an earl. The dragon can be perceived as an image of the castrating mother or father or as a natural adversary representing societal injustice. Because of this first victory the protagonist is granted a horse, an attendant, and the arms of war. Metaphorically, he has already risen in the hierarchy and is deemed worthy to partake of chivalric doings.

In the next ordeal Degaré jousts with the man who, unbeknownst to him, is his grandfather, the chief blocking figure of parental law. Despite the king's larger, more powerful lance ('þe king haþ wel þe gretter schaft,' 511), Degaré defeats him, bests the father figure, ends his tyranny over the princess, and weds her. Indeed, the youth is about to commit incest when he remembers the first recognition token and, because of the gloves, is reunited with his mother and his family. Does Degaré conquer the father and wed the mother without sin? Or rather, is he not so great a hero that he can almost violate the tabu and risk incest of the worst sort, reserved for elect victims of Fortune, and still escape?

At any rate, having conquered a father figure and having found his mother with the feminine token of the gloves prove to be insufficient. Since external conquest also is required, Degaré sets out to the Other World. Here he discovers one better than the mother, a licit bride, and his victory over the amorous giant who had slain her men is as outstandingly oedipal as his previous exploit, and more licit. Degaré will not make the same mistakes as his father and grandfather; he surpasses them in law as well as in arms. Also, he surpasses his mother for he succeeds in the Other World where the princess had failed. The empty castle (containing only women and a dwarf), a world without speech in which Degaré is put to sleep, is a feminine décor in the style of Ywain's kingdom of the fountain – a feminine world of passion, dreams, darkness, and the unconscious. Like his mother, Degaré sleeps, awakens, and communes. In contrast to her he triumphs. He has successfully assimilated the anima and is ready for the ultimate passage.

That passage is perceived as struggle and atonement with the father. It is not the defeat of a wicked father figure in innocence (the king), nor the slaying of a neutral father figure (Salados), but a ritual act of hostility transformed into mutual recognition and reconciliation. The evil paternal imago is displaced onto the king, the giant, and the dragon; the good one onto the fay. Still, the fay did rape the princess. He broke but did not end the bad father's injunction. This triumph is reserved to his son, Degaré, who, provided with the gloves and the sword, fulfils the tasks his father left him; he fulfils the archetypal deeds begun and prefigured by the father. Just as the vaginal gloves reveal the mother, the phallic sword reveals the father. To the extent that we can envisage this ultimate adversary as a Jungian Shadow, the Shadow is integrated as the youth's own flesh and blood, his Self. Master of both masculine and feminine and master of the Other World and of ours, Degaré reunites his mother and father, and the action culminates in a double wedding.

Threatened by hostile female and male sexuality (the dragon, the giant) and by incest, the predestined hero overcomes all obstacles. He wins a princess associated with the Other World, performing successful exogamy as he conquers a supernatural realm. Whereas the mother and father only half succeed, their son Degaré wins on all fronts; he masters the Other World and his own and he masters male and female. He integrates the anima and the Shadow and is ready to become a king, a husband, and a father in turn. After multiple withdrawal and return and after metaphoric death and rebirth, the Lost One ceases to be lost; Degaré finds his identity – lineal, social, and sexual. Wickedness is forgiven and forgotten, and both worlds are joined in festivity.

The Earl of Toulouse

The *Earl of Toulouse* is another brief romance, somewhat longer (1224 lines in tail-rhyme stanzas) than *Sir Degaré*. Although located in a near contemporary setting, without faerie and the supernatural, like *Sir Degaré* and *Ywain and Gawain* it treats the perennial themes of growth, struggle, and the attainment of sovereignty. Again love is at the centre; the protagonist wins a kingdom and a bride. As in the two previous romances, the obstacle to growth is also an obstacle to love.

Sir Bernard, Earl of Toulouse, is persecuted by his lord, the German emperor. He successfully resists the emperor in battle. Told of the empress's extraordinary beauty, the earl goes to Germany in disguise in order to behold her. The empress, Beulybon, resists the suggestion of Tralabas, a steward, to betray Sir Bernard, and she chastely sends him a ring. On his way home, Bernard escapes an ambush prepared by Tralabas. Then two knights endeavour to seduce Beulybon; failing to do so, they accuse her of adultery. Again Bernard hastens to Germany and, in the guise of a monk, first confesses Beulybon and then defeats the treacherous knights in a trial by battle. Three years after the subsequent reconciliation, the emperor dies and Bernard succeeds to his throne and his wife.

In the *Earl of Toulouse* we find a plot incorporating traditional *fin' amor* – deep, true love between a bachelor knight and a great married lady. Bernard is first attracted to Beulybon by reports of her beauty (*amor de lonh*):

> 'To seek the worlde more or less,
> Crystendom and hethynness,
> Ys none so bryght of blee.
> Whyte, as snow, ys hur colour,
> Hur rud radder, þen þe rose flour,
> Yn syght who may hur see.' (196–201)

At that point in the narrative, and up to the denouement, he is content to gaze upon her radiant, shining face and he is overjoyed to be rewarded by the gift of a ring (to be interpreted as an avowal of deep but blameless affection). The poet shows skill in integrating the Gyges motif (originally in Herodotus) into a *fin' amor* romance and having it symbolize *fin' amor.*

Paradoxically, this romance of high courtliness is, in my opinion, closely akin to, and probably derived from, elements of French *chanson de geste*. Cabaniss (1969) claims that a plausible, distant historical source for the *Earl of Toulouse* was the love affair between the ninth-century Count Bernard of Barcelona and Judith, second wife of the emperor Louis the Debonair. This Bernard was the son of the historical Count William, after whom were based the epics of the Guillaume d'Orange cycle. I am convinced that other elements in the English poem – a rebel in the right persecuted by an unjust king; his chaste love for the empress who gives him a ring and intercedes on his behalf; his disguise as a monk and a merchant; his southern French name and fief – recall poems in the Guillaume cycle and, even more, the Occitan epic *Girart de Roussillon* (1953–5G), extant only in an English manuscript. This 'epic quality' in the *Earl of Toulouse* is due, in large measure, to the French sources and the general French ambiance of medieval narrative, where *chanson* and *roman* intersected in the thirteenth century, each contributing to a total structure of narrativity.

From its epic-romance origins, the *Earl of Toulouse* is, first of all, a poem of persecution and betrayal. The emperor makes war unjustly on his loyal vassal, the earl. Sir Bernard defends himself by overcoming the persecutor on the field of battle. Later, two knights attack Beulybon's chastity. She withstands their assault verbally; her defence, through *sapientia*, is as effective as Bernard's deeds in *fortitudo*.

However, once the good people have succeeded in resisting a direct assault, they then must cope with acts of treachery. Tralabas, Bernard's prisoner, first betrays the emperor his lord (and the empress) by intriguing with Bernard how to behold Beulybon in secret. Then, after the crucial scene when he gazes at her, he commits a second act of betrayal; acting against courtesy, he arranges for the ambush of the beholder, his new benefactor. Bernard survives the ambush as he survived the emperor's army, by defeating his adversaries in blood. It is more difficult for the empress to defend herself when the accusation is sexual and the victim has no ready means of proving her innocence. After betraying a youth and slaying him in her chambers, the treacherous knights accuse the lady of adultery:

> 'We are here, thou false hore,
> Thy deds we have aspyedd!
> Thou hast betrayed my lord,
> Thou schalt have wonduryng in þys word,
> Thy loos schall sprynge wyde!' (788–92)

Twice she is assaulted as Bernard was assaulted. The second time, she would have been burned at the stake had Sir Bernard not come to wage combat on her behalf.

Because of the omnipresence of treachery in this fictional world (as in *chansons de geste*, in Beroul, and in *La Mort Artu*), it is natural for the characters, good and bad, to distrust those about them. The emperor distrusts the earl and his own wife; each traitor knight distrusts the other, and both distrust Beulybon; even Sir Bernard, trusting and loving Beulybon, ensures he is defending the right when he confesses her to discover the truth before enduring battle.

Nonetheless, in antithesis to behaviour of treachery and ill will, the good people exemplify throughout a proper sense of 'rycht,' 'tryste,' and 'trowthe' (cf. Dürmüller 1975 and Reilly 1975). It can be maintained that the author indulges in melodramatic fireworks in order to demonstrate the highest effects of loyalty and trust. Thus, Bernard is a true vassal, even though the emperor betrays his side of the feudal contract. Beulybon, aware of the truth, is loyal to her husband especially when she defends the earl and blames the emperor for having made war on him:

> 'Syr, y red, be seynte John,
> Of warre that ye hoo;

> Ye have the wrong and he þe ry3t,
> And that ye may see in sy3t
> Be thys and othyr moo.' (152–6)

Both Bernard and the empress keep their trust and act in the right vis-à-vis their betrayors. Beulybon, loyal to her promise, does not reveal the knights' attempts to seduce her. Finally, the Earl of Toulouse is loyal to the emperor by not trying to seduce the empress (in contrast to the knights' lust), and she is loyal in that she never betrays her husband in word or deed – with men she does not love or with the one man she does. Bernard and Beulybon are exemplars of selfless self-control, in contrast to egotistical self-indulgence in others – lust in the knights and greed in the emperor.

A central concern is the pledged word as one manifestation of duty – a personal and a social feudal obligation. 'Rycht,' 'tryste,' and 'trowthe' ensure order in society, manifested by the capacity of man to withstand anarchy and evil. Bernard's testing of Beulybon in the confessional constitutes a first climax in the romance, followed directly by the earl's victory over the knights. Both *fortitudo* and *sapientia* play a role in determining the truth and in upholding honour.

Determining the truth is not an easy matter. Although the principles of feudal order are simple enough, their application in the immediate, ephemeral world of appearance is another matter. A reality of treachery in Tralabas and the knights is veiled behind the illusion of normative courtly trust. The appearance of martial hostility in the earl belies a fund of heart-felt feudal loyalty to the emperor and all he possesses. A façade of indifference, indeed of total ignorance, between Bernard and Beulybon masks the reality of loyal, chaste affection that, were it to be made public, would be misread by the courtiers as something vile.

Therefore, one manifestation of *sapientia* in combating treachery is to turn the arms of treachery against itself. The empress will never openly admit that she knows the identity of the beggar in her court, that is, that she both knows and cares for Bernard. She employs secrecy to protect herself, her husband, and the earl. Passive behaviour from the empress corresponds to more active deeds from the earl. Sir Bernard three times resorts to disguise in order to have his way. He actively deceives others but in a good cause.

However, wisdom does not suffice. In this harsh, brutal world of war, ultimately the separation of right from wrong is determined by physical contest. A number of agons play a role in the narrative both concrete and symbolic. In the beginning Bernard with his army defeats the emperor in battle. At the end Bernard slays the wicked knights in a judicial duel. In between occur the disguises, temptations, and betrayals, including the murder of a youth by the knights and Bernard's victory when ambushed by Tralabas and his men. All three villains are slain; they are punished by death for their betrayal of the code that alone preserves life in the community. Also, Bernard earns Beulybon's love by besting the emperor in war and by defending her life and honour in law; both times the husband either stood on the wrong side or failed to commit himself. Having overcome the emperor in war and love (*militia et amor*), the earl deserves to reign and love in turn. And he shall.

This highly stylized narrative is granted sacred overtones. Sir Bernard, master of *fortitudo* and *sapientia* (arms and letters), dons disguises in the religious, clerkly mode. He appears before Beulybon first as a hermit beggar and then as a monk confessor. Admittedly such disguises are common in French epic and romance, where they draw a comic, even anticlerical reaction from the audience. Here the disguise functions on a different level. The clerkly garb serves as a symbolic guarantee of Bernard's intentions and the chasteness of his love. As we have seen, a first climax to the action occurs when the earl, in his second clerkly disguise, confesses the empress to ensure, for himself (and for the audience), that she is guiltless. Beulybon's testing is then followed by Bernard's testing. After swearing on holy relics, the earl confounds the lying knights in a formal *judicium Dei*. God intervenes in this narrative of deception and violence. Invoked by the good and dreaded by the wicked, he ensures that 'rycht' and order shall prevail.

The Earl of Toulouse undertakes two quests from his home in France to the seat of the German empire. The first voyage is one of love; at the centre is to be found communion with the beloved. This adventure ends with escape from an ambush. The second voyage is also one of love; Bernard will confess his beloved and, later, wed her. At the centre is to be found struggle with the enemy. The first series of actions concern Bernard as a lover; he survives simple betrayal of the Self. The second series of actions concern Bernard as lover and judge; now he confounds a complex betrayal of the Other. This symbolic road of ascension leads inevitably to the protagonist's ascension in society. With reconciliation to his lord ('My frend so free, / My wrathe here y the forgyve,' 1197–8), he is named steward of the empire.

Three years later, when the lord dies, Bernard is named emperor and he weds his beloved.

The emperor functions as a blocking, tyrannical father figure, the embodiment of unjust law, and lord and master of the lady. The young earl undergoes a period of disarray when he and the beloved are subject to persecution and betrayal, to violence and falsehood. Although never sinking as low as Ywain and Degaré, Sir Bernard resorts to disguises that lower him in status and temporarily deprive him of identity. Also, he cannot satisfy his desires. However, due to his right arm and the beloved's innocence, a wicked society is reformed and the father figure himself converted. After a series of ordeals and a sacred judgment, justice triumphs, to be followed by the father's death and the hero's wedding and coronation. The generations pass, and goodness prevails.

Floris and Blauncheflur

In English as in French, alongside the tradition of Arthurian romance with its symbolism and road of trials, we find a different kind of narrative – Byzantine or Oriental or contemporary adventure romance, one current of which is the extremely popular 'idyllic romance.'

The relatively early English text, *Floris and Blauncheflur,* corresponds to the Anglo-Norman idyllic romance, *Amadas et Ydoine.* These works do not display rounded characters, growth, the Arthurian Other World, and arcane symbolism. Love predominates over valour and war. Love conquers all.

Floris and Blauncheflur tells of children – a Saracen prince and a captive Christian maiden – who are born the same day, are raised together and, of course, fall in love. Dreading misalliance, the king sells Blauncheflur to travelling merchants, who sell her in turn to the Emir of Babylon. Floris follows his beloved's traces and arranges to be admitted secretly into the harem, where they are reunited. The emir is furious but eventually forgives the lovers, who wed.

The English romance is a 'courtly adaptation' of the twelfth-century French *Floire et Blancheflor* (aristocratic version). The adapter reduces his source by two-thirds, suppressing descriptions and psychological analysis. However, he adds and transforms nothing, following the French to the letter in terms of plot and style, often keeping the same rhymes. Of the numerous foreign versions of *Floire et Blancheflor,* his is the most faithful and the most courtly in atmosphere and tone.

A number of scholars have posited that, because of the plethora of Oriental motifs in the Floris and Blauncheflur story, there must have been a true, complete Oriental tale (in Greek, Arabic, Persian, or an Indian language) behind the first French recension. A number of stories from the *Arabian Nights* have been proposed. I prefer, on the contrary, Reinhold's (1906) hypothesis that the first French poet created an original poem of love, working from within the Western, learned tradition, that is, contemporary French versions of the stories of Aeneas, Pyramus, Alexander, and the family of Thebes. This is not to say that the Orient played no role in *Floire et Blancheflor.* On the contrary. The forbidden exotic, Saracen East is essential to the French and English romances because it is exotic and because it is Other. The authors project onto the Orient both nightmare dread and wish-fulfilment desire, their fantasies of Eros and Thanatos.

Structurally, *Floris and Blauncheflur* is markedly simpler than the romances considered above. *Ywain and Gawain, Sir Degaré* and the *Earl of Toulouse* all present a complex pattern: crisis, road of trials, success, second crisis, second road of trials, second success. The double crisis-quest-victory pattern allows for backsliding, self-criticism, self-exploration, and growth. A first victory with happiness is shown to be insufficient. The protagonist will instead suffer defeat and fall into misery until he perseveres to acquire a newer, better victory and happiness on a higher level.

Floris and Blauncheflur, on the other hand, adheres to a much simpler schema: union (misalliance), separation, and reunion (legitimacy) or presence, absence (lack), and presence (liquidation of lack). It is as if the *Floire-Floris* poets took the first half of a Chrétien-type romance and stopped there, content with the first happy ending. In the idyllic romance there is no place for faults, growth, repentance, or expiation. Struggle occurs uniquely on a physical plane between good and evil, between good people whose happiness is given and those who threaten the happiness.

In this stylized, archetypal world, more explicitly than in other romances, youth is pitted against age and innocent children against wicked fathers. The two blocking figures are Floris's father the king and the Emir of Babylon. The king thwarts his son's hopes for love and marriage for reasons of propriety; Blauncheflur is not of a suitable social class or religion. He separates the young people in sundry ways, finally selling the girl to merchants in exchange for a rare, beautifully carved golden cup. He thus embodies the adult world's principles of law, social constraint, and business (he barters a human being as if she were a commodity). The emir intends to wed Blauncheflur. Even more, he holds in thrall a harem of maidens (destined against their will for him alone), blocking them from natural union with youths of their own age. His is the city of Babylon, the castle with its walls and towers, and the harem with its eunuchs; it is an adult world of force, command, and wonder, inhibiting desire and change.

The fathers wield death in order to resist life. Death and the threat of death are arms in their arsenal. The king twice threatens to have Blauncheflur slain, and when he does send her away, he builds a tomb and the queen informs Floris that she has died:

> 'Dame', he seide, 'y tel þe my reed:
> I wyl þat Blauncheflour be do to deed.'
>
> 'Let do bryng forþ þat mayde!
> From þe body þe heued shal goo.'
>
> Al wepyng seide þenne shee:
> 'Sir', shee seide, 'deed'. 'Deed!' seide he.
> 'Sir', she seide, 'forsothe, ȝee!' (E45–6, 140–1, 238–40)

The emir, who each year slays his wife and replaces her with a new one, threatens the children with summary execution when they are discovered.

To this, the children remain impotent and passive, willing to die rather than live without the beloved. Twice Floris suffers from an almost fatal bout of love sickness; once he does attempt suicide. When they are discovered, in the face of the emir's wrath Floris and Blauncheflur plead each to die if only the other will be spared:

> 'Sire', quaþ Floriz, 'forsoþ ihc telle,
> þu noȝtest noȝt þat maide quelle.
> Of al þis gilt ihc am to wite;
> Ihc oȝte deie] he go quite.'
> Quaþ Blauncheflur: 'Aquel þu me,
> And let Floriz aliue be.
> ȝet hit nere for mi luue,
> He nere noȝt fram his londe icome.' (C721–8)

Nevertheless, although they are willing to face death, Floris and Blauncheflur do not perish; they live on, and their love triumphs. Both children, but especially Floris, possess the élan, enthusiasm, and generosity endemic to the young that constitute the trait of *joven* in *fin' amor*. Because of their *joven* and because they live only for love and each other, the adults are moved to pity and, from pity, to complicity. Because of *joven*, Floris does not hesitate to cross the seas to Babylon and go into the emir's forbidden tower. He symbolically dies and is reborn inside a basket of flowers, inside a room in the harem – reborn in a paradise of pure love. He and Blauncheflur subvert or undermine the emir's soldiers, eunuchs, towers, and gardens. Their seemingly prelapsarian *amor* subverts his *militia*; their flowers defy his walls in a burst of innocence and joy.

That flowers prevail over sword and stone reveals a femininity capable of resisting the law of the fathers. It is the queen, Floris's mother, who first dissuades her husband from slaying Blauncheflur; she then gives her son a magic ring to protect him on his quest. She is one adjuvant and mediator who aids the couple. Blauncheflur's friend and confidante Claris is another. Most of all, Floris himself, beautiful, emotive, and with no martial qualities whatsoever, perfectly resembles his spiritual twin, the girl Blauncheflur. It is not surprising that we find in the romance a structure of positive feminine imagery. This pattern includes flowers, the cup, the tomb, the basket, and the garden.

Although the Middle English text omits a number of floral allusions in the Old French original, a significant pattern of recurrence remains. The children are born on Palm Sunday, the feast of flowers (*Pascha floridum*). They both are given floral names. The emir chooses a new wife by sending to her a flower from a magic Tree of Love that has designated her. To counter this practice, Floris arranges to be carried to his beloved in a basket of flowers. Claris alludes to the butterfly (Floris) that frightened her upon darting out of the basket. She repeatedly teases Blauncheflur concerning the flower in her basket. And the children do refer to each other as flowers.

Both Floris and Blauncheflur are presumed to partake of those qualities thought peculiar to flowers: youth, freshness, purity, beauty. Flowers are symbolic of the passion they bear; they evoke the goddess Flora, the power of Eros, and even Ovidian heroes transformed into flowers. The floral world also brings to mind visions of springtime. The protagonists' tenderness appears in its first bloom, indifferent to the ravages of age and death; theirs is the most powerful and natural of forces, which acts in harmony with nature. More than most medieval narratives, this poem adheres to a 'myth of spring.' Following the dictates of the heart, the children discover a fresher, purer, more authentic world than that of the fathers. The 'analogy of innocence' does create a new order, an earthly paradise of love.

Equally feminine, from a medieval perspective, would be the tactics of ruse whereby Floris wins back his beloved. Perhaps because he studies together with Blauncheflur, the youth evidences a very real command of practical *sapientia*, in contrast to *fortitudo*. After having been deceived by his mother into believing Blauncheflur dead and counselled by an innkeeper, he deceives a porter; then, counselled by the porter, he deceives the emir. In the end, the emir spares the children not primarily because of their beauty or his pity but in order to discover how he was tricked. Whereas allusions to flowers are reduced in the English version, the adapter augments references to 'gyn,' 'ginour,' and 'council' (Barnes 1984). The skill in the mind associated with love in the early romances of Beroul and Hue de Rotelande is retained in *Floris and Blauncheflur*.

'Gyn' also is associated with works of art. Floris is advised to proceed to the castle walls and launch a conversation with the porter on the pretext that he is a 'ginnur,' an engineer come to study works of fortification. As the porter will discover, the youth is more ingenious in the pursuits of love than in those of war. However, he would never have arrived in Babylon at all had he not possessed and then traded the precious goblet, a work of art for which Blauncheflur was herself traded in the first place. The cup is a vaginal image that symbolizes Blauncheflur's own precious beauty. It also functions as a *mise en abyme* for the Floris and Blauncheflur narrative in which it plays a role. For on it is carved the story of Paris and Helen, and it belonged to Aeneas, who took it with him to Rome:

> þer was purtrayd on, y weene,
> How Paryse ledde awey þe Queene;
> And on þe couercle aboue
> Purtrayde was þer both her loue ...
> Enneas þe King, þat nobel man,
> At Troye in batayle he it wan,
> And brouȝt it into Lumbardy. (E167–70, 177–9)

This tale of a great but catastrophic passion compares unfavourably with Floris's pure, happy love, just as the early travels of the chalice, from East to West (the old *translatio imperii*) contrast with the movement of the children and, eventually, Blauncheflur's Christian faith, from West to East (a new *translatio studii* and *translatio amoris*). On the other hand, that Aeneas gave the cup to Lavinia, 'his lemman, his amy' (E 180), in happy, licit love, encourages Floris to give it away in order to establish his recovery of and marriage to Blauncheflur. 'Gyn,' artifice, and art – these are the human devices, the workings of the mind that enable lovers to triumph in the world and create their own world of joy and art. This includes, of course, the Floris and Blauncheflur story, itself grounded in true love and based on tales of love from the *auctores* of Rome.

In a romance which recalls Roman New Comedy, youth triumphs over age, and love over law. In the end two couples are wed, and the fathers themselves come to accept the new law of the children. Floris acts as his own *dolosus servus* to win over and convert the *duri patres*. The aged spirit of Babylon dies and is reborn in the youth of a Western, Christian, idyllic *gaudium* symbolized by children and flowers.

Blauncheflur's mother was taken captive on a pilgrimage. The children, spiritual twins, were born on Palm Sunday, benefiting from the equivalent of a miracle. Their travails in the East can be deemed, on a metaphoric or symbolic level, a lifetime of pain crowned by judgment and rebirth – a happy end in the flowering of Easter Sunday (Reiss 1971). As in a number of courtly works, the Christian analogy and Christian imagery are employed for secular purposes to enhance (without irony or blasphemy) the secular message of faith, hope, and love according to the dictates of *fin' amor*, in a world of flowers and recovered innocence.

William of Palerne

William of Palerne, written sometime before 1361, was commissioned by Humphrey de Bohun, Earl of Hereford and Essex. One of the first important late medieval works composed in the alliterative long line, it is a quite accurate translation of the Old French romance *Guillaume de Palerne* that dates from c. 1194–7.

The story tells of a foundling raised at the court of the Roman emperor. William and Melior, the emperor's daughter, fall in love and then flee, clad in the skins of animals. They are aided by a wolf, in fact a werewolf – Alphouns, the prince of Spain, enchanted by his stepmother. After multiple adventures the three arrive in Sicily where William defeats the King of Spain, who had been ravaging the land. William is recognized as the long-lost heir to the crown, abducted in infancy by a wolf. Alphouns, who committed the abduction in order to rescue the baby from a conspiracy, is reunited with his father and freed from enchantment by his stepmother.

A number of scholars, especially Dunn (1960), subscribe to the hypothesis that the William story is close to folklore and that the first extant text, the French *Guillaume de Palerne*, was derived from a Sicilian folk legend. It is true that *William* and *Guillaume* contain folkloric elements, as do most medieval romances. Whether the folklore preceded literature or literature gave rise to folklore is open to question. However, as with *Floris and Blauncheflur*, we have no evidence concerning the earlier, preliterary stages of the romance, if indeed there were any. The Old French poet could have composed his text with no other materials than a version of the Eustachius legend and Marie de France's *Bisclavret*. For fourteenth-century England as for twelfth-century France, the texts we have are beautifully and conventionally literary in their courtly, conventional, high-culture essence.

William of Palerne, like *Floris and Blauncheflur*, adheres to the category of idyllic romance. The children are raised together, fall in love, and escape to the woods where they endure their fate passively. They survive and triumph due to the support of others, not their own exertions. Also, Melior falls in love first, adoring William for traits other than valour. Stronger in character, she directs the action; Melior comes to William, and it is she who urges flight:

> 'Whi so, mi dere hert?
> Forwardes þat I have fest ful wel schal I hold,
> I hope to þe heiȝh King þat al heven weldes.
> þerfor stint of þi striif, and stodie we anoþer,
> what wise we mow best buske of þis lond.' (1649–53)

Structurally, *William of Palerne* develops the union, separation, restoration pattern. In this poem the lovers are not separated; they go into exile together, but they do endure lack of status and identity. Melior is threatened by a bad marriage, escapes from it, and in the end enjoys the reality of a good marriage. This idyllic romance structure is conflated with the family romance. William is the Fair Unknown, a foundling recognized in the end to be a prince, the son of great parents and the beneficiary of all-but-supernatural protection; he weds the emperor's daughter and becomes an emperor. However, their story is complicated by the career of the all-but-supernatural protector, Alphouns, who also proves to be a king's son and heir. Alphouns suffers from enchantment as William suffers from abduction; in the end both lacks are liquidated, and the heroes are recognized in their legitimate identity and sovereignty.

The blocking paternal figures are of two sorts. On the one hand, we have fathers who wish to marry girls off against their will: the emperor intends Melior to wed the son of the Emperor of Constantinople; the King of Spain intends his second son, Braundis – the prince who 'replaced' Alphouns – to wed the daughter of the Queen of Sicily, William's long-lost sister. A displaced oedipal rivalry is apparent, as the old authority figures dispose of the girls, preventing them from choosing and being chosen in a more natural fashion. These fathers are as much at fault as their generic forbears, the *duri patres* of Roman comedy.

More dangerous still is the uncle, who plotted William's death as an infant, an act which lead to his abduction by the werewolf, and the stepmother who created the werewolf, removing the young prince Alphouns. Real or symbolic step-parents, they dispose of innocent boys out of greed and will to power. The Queen of Spain is particularly nefarious in that she employs the black arts to cast a spell on the prince, thereby depriving him of both his identity and his humanity.

More so than in most romances, even those of the idyllic sort, the protagonists remain largely passive in the face of destiny. They are enabled to overcome by adjuvants, helpful figures who counter the hostility and the enchantments. In Rome the children are succoured by Alisaundrine, Melior's confidante (Kooper 1984). This Brangain figure (as in *Le Roman de Tristan*), a medieval *dolosa serva*, brings the lovers together in a garden, helps them to communicate by voicing their secret passion, and assists them in their flight. It is she who conceives the notion of disguise in animal pelts. It is she also who, in the English version, employs magic (good magic in antithesis to the stepmother's wicked magic) to cause William to return Melior's love:

> Alisandrine algate þan after [þat] þrowe
> biþouȝt hire ful busily howe best were to werche
> to do William to wite þe wille of hire lady
> properly unparceyved for reprove after.
> Ful conyng was sche and coynt, and couþe fele þinges
> of charmes and of chantemens to schewe harde castis.
> So þurȝh þe craft þat sche couþe, to carpp þe soþe. (649–55)

On the road, away from Rome, first William, and then the children together, are aided by Alphouns. The latter, in his lupine form, serves as food-provider, guide, and protector to his human charges. He saves William from certain death by abducting him. He leads the emperor to the young boy in order that he be raised at court. Then, when the children flee, Alphouns more than once creates a diversion by drawing pursuers away on another scent – himself.

On the one hand, we see in Alphouns a male adjuvant, a *dolosus servus* who serves William in the same way and to a greater extent than Alisaundrine served Melior. However, he is, like William, of royal extraction. Even before the Spanish prince reverts to human form, he and William share the same bedchamber:

> þe werwolf þat ȝe witen of was in Williams chaumber,
> and hade be þere in blis bi niȝtes and daies. (4328–9)

After the disenchantment, the two become true friends, in the epic-romance tradition of Roland and Oliver, Garin and Bègue, Girart and Fouque, Erec and Guivret, and Lancelot or Yvain and Gauvain. William is shown to be a great hero because he can command the loyalty and affection of such a beast and such a friend. In contrast to the treachery of kin, the children count on the service of extrafamilial adjuvants.

Most importantly, in response to the stepmother who transformed Alphouns into a beast, the werewolf uses all his animal-like traits to aid William and to restore himself. In literary terms, Alphouns functions as the helpful spirit of nature, who, like Ywain's lion, provides the hero with natural and supernatural aid. Normally wolves are viewed with dread; they embody the lowest, bestial qualities and they symbolize a number of the capital sins including *superbia*, *invidia*, and *ira*. Here, in this nature figure, the wolflike traits are turned around; in this werewolf, they are humanized. The animal's physical strength, quickness, and ruse act on man's behalf; serving William, the werewolf proves to be a creature of *humilitas*, *caritas*, and *dulcedo*. In war William bears a shield emblazoned with a wolf:

> 'Bi Crist, madame,' sede þe kniȝt, 'I coveyte nouȝt elles
> but þat I have a god schel of gold graiþed clene,
> and wel and faire wiþinne a werwolf depeynted,
> þat be hidous and huge, to have alle his riȝtes ... ' (3215–18)

The wolf is his good-luck charm and his first statement of identity.

The children disguised themselves in the skins of bears, and then as a stag and doe. The Queen of Sicily comes to them in the skin of a doe. They are aided by a wolf. Twice Melior and once the queen dream of heroes and villains in animal guise. In the guise of beasts, good people retain their deepest humanity. The wicked, empowered by society, live and act like beasts (Simms 1977). The poem tells us about the human condition and its closeness to the animal and to the divine, as people pray to a God incarnate, who also was subject to metamorphosis, resembling his creatures in their contingent world of fantasy.

Countering the contingent and the hostile empowerment of parents and step-parents, we find, in addition to the assistance of companions, the hero's own sterling inner nature that acts in congruence with a beautiful external nature. Whatever William's putative origins, everyone at court is certain of his inherent nobility. Nature is shown to be superior to nurture. Good nature takes precedence over bad culture. In line with this, William, like so many other Fair Unknown types, instantly demonstrates his skills in the chase, at table, and in war.

Although in the conduct of their amours William is as passive as Melior and more passive, if possible, in their escape from Rome and flight over the countryside, on two occasions he is transformed into another person altogether. Serving the emperor in Rome, he defeats the invading Duke of Saxony; serving his mother in Sicily, he defeats the invading King of Spain. Even though the details of these martial campaigns are reduced in the English version, enough remains to distinguish William from Floris, for example. William of Palerne is a leader in war as well as a lover in peace. He embodies the masculine as well as the feminine. Also it is presumably because of his martial accomplishments that he deserves not only to wed Melior but to succeed to the imperial crown as the best, ahead of Alphouns and everyone else in the hierarchy. This concern for status and power will also explain a number of speeches (a thematic augmented in the English) concerning behaviour at court, feudal duty, and the exercise of kingship.

Before exercising kingship the hero and his adjuvant-companion undergo a number of rites of passage. A first withdrawal or exile from Spain by the enchanted Alphouns coincides with William's first withdrawal and exile from Sicily. What would appear to be William's second exile, from Rome (and the second stage in Alphouns's permanent life of exile), proves instead to be a return to the Mother; William in Sicily attains communion with his mother and, at precisely the same time, Alphouns attains communion with his father and stepmother. Recognition by the mother restores William to legitimacy; recognition and disenchantment by the stepmother restore Alphouns to legitimacy and humanity. Both heroes rise from apparent bestiality to their full humanness; both symbolically die and are reborn. The rebirth of a prince also requires establishment in his estate. The quasi-ritual of Alphouns's passage is especially significant; the poet tells how he is metamorphosed from a beast into a man, and then how the man, ashamed of his nudity, is offered a bath. Afterwards, he retires to a bed where he is discovered and identified by the others. He insists upon being clad as a knight only by William.

Social death and physical animality are not portrayed as tragedy, with demonic imagery. Despite hardship, in this idyllic romance the protagonists and their werewolf lead lives of comradeship and love in the forest, a green world of innocence more natural and humane than courtly society with its onus of power and treachery. Then, when good people do return to the court, it is transformed. As the young are restored, the old are converted. The King of Spain and Braundis abandon at once their campaign of violence in Sicily; the Queen of Spain willingly restores Alphouns to his human state and is reconciled with him. Even the despised Byzantines arrive in time to share in the rejoicing. *William of Palerne*, like its French source, ends in a slow, measured pace of solemn festivity. One character after another is reunited with his father or mother; one after another is granted a noble spouse. The emperors of Greece and of Rome appear. The story is told and retold. A triple wedding takes place followed by a double coronation. Then, in time, the fathers die and the sons become monarchs in turn, the last reunion and celebration consecrating William's coronation as emperor. His two sons will continue the line and perpetuate the harmony that is the denouement of his story.

Amis and Amiloun

Amis and Amiloun is a fourteenth-century Middle English tail-rhyme version of one of the great literary legends of the Middle Ages, the story of Ami and Amile. According to the English romance, Amis and Amiloun are Lombard nobles, born the same day and resembling each other so closely that no one can tell them apart. They serve the Duke of Pavia. Amiloun leaves the court to get married. The duke's daughter Belisaunt falls in love with Amis and coerces him into granting her his troth and sleeping with her. The couple is denounced by a felonious steward. A judicial duel is arranged between accuser and accused. Finding himself in a desperate position, Amis sets out to take counsel of Amiloun, who offers to change places and fight in his stead. The judgment is in Amis's (Amiloun's) favour; the steward falls; Amis weds Belisaunt. However, because he perjured himself in a judicial duel, Amiloun is stricken with leprosy. Persecuted by his wife, the leper leaves home, begging his sorry way, assisted by his faithful nephew Amaurant. Amiloun is reunited by chance with Amis, who welcomes the leper with joy. When an angel announces that Amiloun can only be cured by having his body smeared with the blood of children, Amis insists on beheading his own young sons. By a miracle, Amiloun is healed and the two boys are restored to life. The poem ends when Amis and Amiloun found an abbey in Lombardy and die the same day.

There are four versions earlier than the English text: an Anglo-Norman romance, *Amis e Amilun*, which can be dated c. 1200; a French *chanson de geste* from that same time span; a twelfth-century *Vita* in Latin; and the *Epistola ad Bernardum* by Radulfus Tortarius, 1108. I see no reason whatsoever to credit the hypothesis that the insular romances preserve a more primitive or authentic version of the legend than the continental narratives and/or that *Amis and Amiloun* itself must have been derived from a lost Anglo-Norman model and would represent the oldest, most authentic stage. It is much more likely that the Middle English poet adapted the Anglo-Norman romance and that the Anglo-Norman romancer adapted a *chanson de geste*, perhaps the very one that is extant.

Differences between *La Chanson d'Ami et Amile* and *Amis e Amilun* or *Amis and Amiloun* can be explained almost exclusively by the demands of literary genre. Authors of romance, especially insular authors of romance, will suppress Charlemagne, Charlemagne's wars, pilgrimage roads, and the lineage of traitors. Authors of romance will introduce or amplify the love motifs: Belisaunt wooing Amis in a *locus amoenus*, the Potiphar's Wife tactic, the active role Belisaunt and her mother assume defending Amiloun's honour, and the extraordinary physical beauty of the two men.

As with *Sir Degaré* and *William of Palerne*, it has been posited by Leach (*Amis* 1937) that *Amis and Amiloun*, in its literary form, came into being as the conflation of a number of traditional folk-tales and, therefore, that the medieval versions of the Ami and Amile legend are representative of a specifically medieval type of narrative, produced and disseminated by oral transmission and close to the popular culture that nourished it. It can be argued that certain facets of *Amis and Amiloun*, as of *Sir Degaré* and *William of Palerne*, and even of *Floris and Blauncheflur*, are reminiscent of *Märchen* and partake of their aura. This is because the aura of a folk-tale can exist in a *chanson de geste* or *roman courtois* as well as in supposed oral tradition. As for the tradition, concerning its nature in the twelfth, thirteenth, and fourteenth centuries we know little if anything at all. A situation of tautology is created when literary texts, specifically Middle English romances, are combed to contribute retroactively and anachronistically to the standard motif index of folk literature, and then the presence of such elements in the motif index 'proves' the folkloric origins of the medieval text. Aspects of one poem, which scholars would like to explain in terms of folklore, can be accounted for equally well by literary analysis; *Ami et Amile* is a *chanson de geste* and its creator was influenced by a *Roman de Tristan*. Whatever may have been the origins and genesis of that *chanson*, the English *Amis and Amiloun* is the adaptation of an adaptation – literature twice removed from other literature.

The English romance contains epic and sacred elements derived from the Old French *chanson de geste*. It can also be envisaged as a new, anticourtly variation on the idyllic romance theme. Amis and Amiloun are conceived and born on the same day; radiating beauty, they appear to be identical twins. They are given similar names. They swear an all-encompassing friendship. They willingly choose temporary loss of identity. Upon separation each retains a precious, identical cup as a token of the friendship, the equivalent of a lover's ring. The steward and Amiloun's wife are jealous, as well they might be, given that Amiloun cares for Amis more than for his wife and that Amis declines the steward's offer of comradeship. In the end, each of the protagonists leaves his spouse to set out with the other on a life of religion. They found an abbey and pass away together.

It is as if the themes and motifs appropriate to *fin' amor* in romance, especially idyllic romance, have been subverted in order to proclaim, against the courtly, secular love of man and woman, a heroic, Christian love between man and man. This notion is reinforced by the treatment of women in the text. Although in some ways it is a masculine wish-fulfilment fantasy – it is the duke's daughter who offers herself and who seduces Amis – Belisaunt employs underhand methods to attain her ends and puts Amis's and Amiloun's lives in jeopardy. She is redeemed in the end only by denying her womanhood and accepting the sacrifice of her children in order to heal her husband's beloved friend:

> 'O lef liif,' sche seyd þo,
> 'God may sende ous childer mo,
> Of hem haue þou no care.
> ȝif it ware at min hert rote,
> For to bring þi broþer bote,

My lyf y wold not spare.
Shal noman oure children see,
To-morrow shal þey beryed bee
As þey faire ded ware!' (2392–400)

Amiloun's spouse does not benefit from the redemption. Cruel and selfish, she begrudges her husband's act of charity to save his friend's life, and she hounds him unmercifully when the leprosy strikes.

The problematic, questionable behaviour of both ladies is contrasted to noble, self-sacrificing deeds by Amis and Amiloun, each on behalf of the other. To exalt 'compagnonage' is by no means rare in medieval letters. The warmth, devotion, and love evidenced by any number of heroic masculine 'couples' constitute a recurring theme of *chanson de geste;* the breaking of 'compagnonage' contributes more than one nobly pathetic scene to *La Chanson de Roland* and *La Mort Artu*. However, the Ami and Amile poems are unique. Here alone the companions are social equals and of equal personal worth, not hero and follower as is the case with Achilles and Patroclus, Orestes and Pylades, Aeneas and Pallas or Achates, and their medieval progeny. This means that the *Amis and Amiloun* poet and his sources, using traditional materials, go beyond the tradition to arrive at a new concept in human relations. Furthermore, the friendship they posit is capable of imitation; it is contagious. Amiloun's nephew Amaurant serves him with as much devotion and sacrifice as Amiloun had served Amis. The notion of manly love – hero and companion, uncle and nephew, friend and friend – provides a sacred-oriented alternative to the more common courtly, heterosexual passion which dominates the secular books of the period.

On one level, the mode of friendship is a touchstone for the working of good and evil in the secular world. Amis, Amiloun, and Amaurant are good in that they follow the dictates first of affection and secondly of their pledged word, 'treuthe' (Baldwin 1980). In honour of 'treuthe,' the truth and troth of both friendship and kin-loyalty, each does the right thing, sacrificing his health, possessions, and life if necessary. As Amiloun proclaims to himself prior to the judicial combat:

He þouȝt, 'ȝif y beknowe mi name,
þan schal mi broþer go to schame,
Wiþ sorwe þai schul him spille.
Certes,' he seyd, 'for drede of care
To hold mi treuþe schal y nouȝt spare,
Lete god don alle his wille.' (1279–84)

A contrario, the steward and Amiloun's wife act against 'treuthe' and their social duty out of egotism and spite. Society and the individual function because the world is not made up only of stewards and wives; it also contains great, true knights and nephew squires.

On another level, this spirit of loyalty, abnegation, and sacrifice ought to be envisaged as sacred – a working out of the Christian life in a Christian-inspired narrative. Granted, the insular romances – *Amis e Amilun* and *Amis and Amiloun* – delete a number of Christian allusions to be found in the *chanson*, especially to the pilgrimage roads and to Rome. This is the case, I believe, primarily because such *chanson de geste* imagery would have appeared generically incongruous in a *roman courtois*. Nevertheless, the fundamental structure of the story stands unchanged. There is no need whatsoever to distinguish between romance and hagiographic elements. Our romance contains and embodies the sacred without tension and without incoherence.

Among the Christian elements retained in the plot are the following: Amiloun and the steward engage in a *judicium Dei* preceded by the swearing of oaths; Amiloun is warned by an angel of his transgression and its punishment; he is punished by the holy illness, leprosy; Amaurant first conducts the leper into exile on the back of an ass and later carries him on his own back; an angel comes a second time to announce how Amiloun can be healed; after Amis slays the sons and prays in a chapel, on Christmas day Amiloun is cured and the children are restored to life; quitting their wives, the two comrades found an abbey in Lombardy.

Specifically Christian images abound: the sword of chastity, separating Amis from his companion's wife; the cups that serve as tokens of friendship and recognition but also recall the chalice of the Mass; and the blood sacrificed by the slaying of innocent children on Christmas that restores health to the leper. Amiloun, who offers himself in abnegation and willingly sacrifices himself for his friend, becomes a figure of Christ. Stricken with leprosy, driven from his own people in hatred, riding on the back of an ass, he bears on his tortured shoulders his suffering and the suffering of others. Amaurant, by serving his uncle in peace and loyalty and by bearing Amiloun on his back, also partakes of the archetype:

> þus Amoraunt, as y ȝou say,
> Serued his lord boþe niȝt & day
> & at his rigge him bare.
> Oft his song was, 'Waileway!'

So depe was þat cuntray,
His bones wex ful sare. (1849–54)

Christ-like abnegation is then completed by Amis who, to rescue his sworn brother from the hell of pain, offers the blood of his own children. Just as Longinus recovered his sight by applying to his eyes Christ's blood, and just as Perceval's sister offered her life's blood to heal a maiden's leprosy in *La Queste del saint Graal*, here Amis's children are decapitated so that their blood may cure Amiloun. Typologically, the blood of the Lamb was shed for all men. He died that we may live. Amiloun, like Longinus and the maiden in the *Queste*, is saved through Christian sacrifice. The children, slain on Christmas day, are assimilated to the Innocents slaughtered by Herod and to the Agnus Dei; they figuratively give Christ's blood. Amiloun, annointed by the blood, represents the human aspect of Christ; he becomes one with God. Red is the colour of divine love and of martyrdom. Archetype of the water of life, the blood evokes the new existence that the companions and the children attain. As a reminder of the heroes' blood brotherhood and spiritual twinship, it serves as a final bond between them. The blood offered by Amiloun for his friend in the duel is returned. Both companions, by shedding their own and the children's blood, will live on in the *civitas Dei*.

The ultimate analogy between the Longinus story and the medieval romance is that in both tales the sacrificial victim – provider of blood – dies but then returns to a new life. In *Amis and Amiloun* two miracles occur in the last section of the narrative; both are resurrections. After having been decapitated, Amis's sons are discovered to be alive and well:

As ȝe mow listen and lyth,
Into a chamber þey went swyþ,
þer þe children lay;
With-out wemme and wound
Hool and sound þe children found,
And layen to-geder and play.
For ioye þey wept, þere þey stood,
And þanked god with myld mood,
Her care was al [away]. (2416–24)

Their sacrifice ensures that Amiloun, a leper to the world and thus in a state of social death, will return to society. Then the companions will pass away together, presumably to be reborn in the afterlife on the right hand of God.

For Amis and Amiloun the answer to their problem and the secret of their existence is abnegation. The theme of renunciation is interwoven with the heroes' destiny from the beginning. Amiloun leaves wife and home to risk fighting for Amis. He accepts sickness, poverty, and banishment. Amis then sacrifices his children and risks his life to heal Amiloun. They both renounce family and inheritance in favour of the monastic life and they both perish in the endeavour. Each sacrifice parallels the one that has gone before and anticipates the one to come. The sacrifices become more and more difficult, building up to a magnificent climax.

Amis and Amiloun sacrifice all worldly concerns: wife, children, material comfort, service, and position in the hierarchy. In the end they sacrifice the entire feudal and material world. This human world and the loves connected with it must not be considered bad in themselves. They have a place in the universe. Yet other, higher values will prevail: humaneness, forgiveness, and Christian love. The hero is offered a choice, roughly between flesh and the spirit or prowess and charity. He is expected to decide what he shall love most of all.

Man must learn to suffer and by suffering to merit grace. Without knowledge of what is expected, even the best intentioned stray from the right path. Amis lets himself be induced into *luxuria* by Belisaunt. Amiloun, having wed a moral leper quickly, has leisure to devote to the repenting. Amis fails to recognize the leper begging at his door and almost slays his companion in error. An angel has to inform Amiloun of the measures necessary for his cure. Yet the young men finally comprehend the reality of existence. Having discovered the necessity and the virtue of sacrifice and the goodness of suffering, they know more in the end than at the beginning. They have achieved lucidity, vision, and a kind of anagnorisis.

For both protagonists life at court gives way to Eros, which in turn gives way to God. Or, in different terms, love of the feudal is transformed into love of family, only to become *caritas*. Before the end the companions have developed a sense of Christian virtue and have actualized their potential for *humilitas, sapientia*, and *caritas*. Their final stage is the life of religion. By renouncing the pleasures of the world (*contemptus mundi*), they demonstrate Christian perfection to the extent of following Christ (*imitatio Dei*) in his crucifixion. By renouncing sovereignty over women and land, they achieve control of self (*ascesio*). By renouncing glory at court, they attain a place among the elect.

The two friends have sought for the best throughout their lives. God's miracles prove that they have found it and that their message of sacrifice and charity is valid for all men.

Athelston

The relatively brief (812 ll.) tail-rhyme romance, *Athelston*, tells of four messengers who meet on the road and swear brotherhood. One of them, the title figure, becomes king; the others are elevated in kind. Egeland, who weds Athelston's sister Edyff, is named Earl of Stone; Wymound becomes Earl of Dover; Alryke becomes Archbishop of Canterbury. Wymound, however, betrays Egeland, falsely denouncing him to the king. Athelston condemns Egeland, spurning appeals by Edyff and by his own wife. Fortunately, Alryke is sent for and forces the king to allow trial by ordeal. Thus Alryke succeeds in defending the victims and later unmasks the traitor. Since Athelston had struck his pregnant wife, causing her to abort their son and heir, it is Egeland's and Edyff's son who will in time succeed to the crown; he will be the future Saint Edmund of England.

Hibbard (1921) proposed that *Athelston*, the story of which is ultimately derived from the folk legend of Queen Emma and the Ploughshares, is a typically, specifically English-type romance; there is no French source. The names and places are English; the narrative treats pre-Conquest history; the tone is pious and exemplary; and the text contains no French chivalry or courtly love.

This notion, I am convinced, is misguided. The four most important romances treating the Matter of England – *Horn*, *Havelok*, *Guy*, and *Bevis* – are all translations or adaptations of Anglo-Norman romances composed in French. They also treat legendary figures of pre-Conquest English history. They also do not emphasize chivalry and courtly love. There are any number of other French romances that prove to be pious and edifying, concerned with both telling a good story and reinforcing established feudal virtues, not *fin' amor*. There are any number of French epics and romances that exploit the theme of treachery and persecution of the innocent. *Athelston*, an excellent, independent English romance, adheres to the tradition of Matter of England tales in both French and English, and to other narratives in the French and English romance mode.

Whether or not the author had in mind *Amis and Amiloun* or one of the earlier French versions of the legend, *Athelston* can be envisaged as a counterexample to the *Amis* story. In *Athelston* four, not two, knights swear blood brotherhood and unending loyalty:

For loue of here metyng þare,
þey swoor hem weddyd breþeryn for euermare,
In trewþe trewely dede hem bynde. (22–4)

Then their 'treuthe' is undercut not by villain figures from the outside – a steward, a wife, or a mistress – but by one of their own. Wymound denounces Egeland and Edyff to the king out of envy. Then without demanding corroborating evidence, Athelston condemns his symbolic brother and his biological sister.

The psychology of betrayal is explored in a deft manner. Wymound approaches the king. Instead of words to the Earl of Dover concerning himself, Athelston can only ask about the bishop, Egeland, and Edyff (97–108). Athelston is tactless in his love for his sister and her husband. He is obsessed and this obsession presumably infuriates Wymound; it is the cause for his rage but it also plays into his hand. The king's question enables the traitor to claim he has just seen Egeland and Edyff and to broach his act of treachery in a natural manner. In addition, once the venom has seeped into Athelston's consciousness, he reacts with as much emotional, irrational excess against the faithful couple as he had manifested previously on their behalf:

'Meete ne drynk schal do me goode,
Tyl þat he be dede;
Boþe he and hys wyff, hys soones twoo,
Schole þey neuere be no moo
In Yngelond on þat stede.' (170–4)

As in *Amis and Amiloun*, the resolution to the problem will be clerical and Christian. However, in *Athelston*, Christian power acts entirely in the secular world. It is the fourth 'brother,' Alryke the archbishop, who intervenes to set matters right. If we envisage the diegesis as one where Egeland is the hero, a passive victim persecuted by the villainous Wymound and the credulous Athelston, then Alryke functions as an adjuvant, an all-but-supernatural figure who steps in from outside the court to rescue the protagonist in much the same way that Auberon, king of the fairies, rescues Huon de Bordeaux. We can also envisage the diegesis from another perspective, with Alryke himself as the actant subject, righting wrongs and combating evil in the name of God for the kingdom of England.

Either way, once he is summoned and enters the story, the bishop dominates it, employing all his powers to bring about his desired ends.

He calls for justice; when the call is denied, he excommunicates the king and reduces the kingdom to interdiction. This is a powerful spiritual statement and a shrewd political move, in that the people subsequently force the king to withdraw the sentence of exile and to heed Alryke's words. Alryke imposes judgment by ordeal on Egeland and his family. Their innocence proclaimed, the bishop uses the secret of the confessional to force the truth out of Athelston. He then tricks Wymound into riding to court, forces the same judgment by ordeal on him, and attends to his death.

In antithesis to Wymound's ruse, Alryke employs ruse and a half; his wisdom counters and ultimately frustrates the distorted, corrupt mental calculations of the earl. He uses deception in a good cause, to nullify Wymound's shameless deception. The result is justice, human and divine, expedited in the name of the living Christ, son of God, judge of the quick and the dead, the person of the Trinity associated with wisdom. The dominant image in *Athelston*, evoking God's wisdom and justice, is fire; the ordeal is imposed four times in order to test Egeland, Edyff, their children, and, finally, the perpetrator Wymound. It is divine justice, beyond Alryke's power in the world, that ensures the innocent pass the test unscathed and the guilty do not. Finally, divine justice also punishes the credulous monarch. His son and heir perishes in the womb when Athelston stikes the queen. As a result, Egeland's son will succeed to the crown and become, in Egeland's line, one of England's greatest, most Christian monarchs, Saint Edmund.

Only Alryke and God are capable of stemming the tide of wickedness and reversing archetypal evil with archetypal good. In *Athelston*, more than in most romances, the villain's presence is felt throughout, and the narrative is focused on reversing the action rather than on the hero's growth or recognition. However, reversing the action implies the need to strip off masks and to recognize that Egeland is innocent and Wymound is guilty. Therefore, we can envisage the romance as structured in two major sections. Part 1 tells of Wymound's manipulation of Athelston and his request for secrecy; this leads to the messenger's summoning Egeland to London to a first, provisional condemnation. Part 2 then tells of Alryke's manipulation of both Athelston and Wymound and his successful discovery of the secret; this leads to the messenger's summoning Wymound to London to his definitive condemnation. Separating the two is a central section in which the women plead in vain on Egeland's behalf (cf. Kiernan 1975). The queen, however, failing to manipulate anyone, does succeed in sending a messenger to summon Alryke, who will act against the king and the earl and impose justice on both of them.

The presence of the queen (Ellzey 1992) and the countess, the roles played thus by Athelston's wife and sister, are crucial to the action. Wymound is jealous because of Edyff; Edyff and her children are enticed to court on the promise of knighthood. Both women plead, in vain, on Egeland's behalf. Both are pregnant. Athelston beats his wife, slaying their unborn child. Edyff's children pass the ordeal of fire successfully. The child to whom she gives birth on the spot will become the new king:

> And whanne þis chyld iborn was,
> It was brouȝt into þe plas;
> It was boþe hool and sound.
> Boþe þe kyng and bysschop free
> þey crystnyd þe chyld, þat men myȝt see,
> And callyd it Edemound.
> 'Halff my land,' he sayde, 'I þe geue,
> Also longe as I may leue,
> Wiþ markys and with pounde,
> And al afftyr my dede –
> Yngelond to wysse and rede.'
> Now iblessyd be þat stounde! (651–62)

On the one hand, we perceive a pattern of birth and death that pervades the narrative. People are threatened with death; eventually one adult villain and one innocent baby in the womb do perish. However, life triumphs over death just as the spiritual power of women and clerks proves to be greater than the physical might of earls and kings. Because of women and clerks, one baby in the womb shall survive and prevail, as a king and a clerk, as a heroic martyr, and as the imago of *sapientia*. The pattern of the *Athelston* narrative is melodramatic in nature as women and children play central roles, women and children are threatened with death, and women and children triumph in the end.

Juxtaposed to this woman-child-clerk melodrama is another pattern of motifs, treating what Dickerson (1976) calls the subplot of the messenger. A curiously important role is assigned to the messenger who carries out three crucial summonses: he brings to court Egeland and his family at the behest of the king, Alryke at the behest of the queen, and Wymound at the behest of the bishop. These three journeys occur at the beginning, middle, and end of the poem; they account for 216 of the total 812 lines of verse. The messenger apes in the minor key the doings of the principal characters in the major: they were messengers when they swore brotherhood; he is a messenger. The king's name is Athelston; our messenger (also) is named Athelstone. The man's activity and his career are exalted and granted some of the dignity and prestige emanating from the great ones at court. Furthermore, Athelstone the messenger believes in the good and reacts with courage and generosity to the events. At first, against his will, he serves the king; then, with enthusiasm, he serves the queen and the bishop. Athelstone, functioning as a *mise en abyme*, mirrors the thematics and the reversal of action inherent in the narrative as a whole.

The messenger is also a comic figure; he insists on food (Curtius's Kitchen Humour), recounts his own story at length, and whines over the loss of his horse. In all of this Athelstone radiates humour; he also is, on his own, a trickster hero who deceives Wymound into his fatal voyage to London and into replacing the lost horse. On their own distinct levels of *sapientia*, the messenger takes Wymound's steed and the bishop takes his life.

Does this then mean, as Dickerson (1976) proposed, that *Athelston*, in contrast to the French romances, appeals to a middle-class English public with lowered bourgeois tastes and values? In my opinion, not at all. Messengers (ambassadors) proliferate as important functioning adjuvants in early and late *chansons de geste*. They develop the narrative, launching epic action on their own initiative; they can be thought of in a negative light (Ganelon in *Roland*) or in a very positive one (Naimes in *Aspremont*). These are properly aristocratic 'functions' in an aristocratic genre. Similarly, in late *chanson* and *roman* and in late medieval letters generally, one trend lies in the direction of melodrama and sentiment, with women and children in the forefront. This is Auerbach's (1946G) notion of the *Kreatürlich*, which he extracted from the fifteenth-century prose of Antoine de la Sale, a late medieval manifestation not limited to one public or social class.

Conclusion

The seven texts studied above illustrate, I believe, the variety to be found in the Middle English verse romance corpus. Four are relatively extended narratives; three are brief. Three are composed in couplets, three in tail-rhyme stanzas, and one in the alliterative long line. Four of the seven are translations or adaptations from the French; three are independent creations in the French style. All seven are structural, cohesive works of art that tell a good story, offer a message, and appeal to the audience's aesthetic sensibilities. The seven romances uphold an ideal of chivalry and noble conduct, emphasizing manly virtue (sometimes in arms, sometimes in love) and the ethical qualities deemed endemic to the gentle life – a proper sense of 'rycht' and 'trowthe.'

All seven, to a greater or lesser extent, adhere to the archetypal structures of romance – a quest from the point of departure to the court and/or to the Other World followed by return to the point of departure, enabling the hero to grow into adulthood, to commit great deeds, and to win his identity as well as sovereignty and a bride. This structure of initiation can also be understood as a succession of union, separation, and reunion; of false or incomplete identity, loss of identity, and new, complete identity; of balance, struggle, and new balance and harmony; or of plenitude, lack, liquidation of lack, and new plenitude. In general terms, we almost always uncover an oedipal pattern whereby the young hero struggles against and liberates himself from the law of the fathers; his rebellion and his triumph are of the young over the old; the old are generally *duri patres* but occassionally, as in *William of Palerne,* the phallic mother. In this process a mother figure (the wife or the widow of a great prince) or a virgin bride joins the hero, functioning as his adjuvant and as his 'object' or reward.

Given the crucial importance granted to the feminine adjuvant role, one variation on the standard quest pattern involves the idyllic romance, in which the couple (a boy and a girl) together are the focus of the action, and passive submission to love is opposed to active heroism in arms. Here the girl often assumes the role of actant subject. Still another variation substitutes *amicitia* between male comrades for the more common, erotic *amor* between boy and girl. Given the clerical world-view allied to and evoked by the suppression of the female, the romances of comradeship almost always involve strong Christian overtones of renunciation and the ascetic.

Within these parameters, the romancers are free to explore and to elaborate, to play with theme and motif, and to comment intertextually on earlier works in the tradition. The English texts admittedly lack some of the tension, irony, and complexity to be found in a number of the French originals. On their own terms, however, as late romances in a tradition of European dimensions, they stand up well, as the epitome of story-telling and as powerful, exciting works of art.

It is clear that the earlier generations of scholars were wrong to condemn the romances for lack of elegance and polish, or for stock tags, prolixity, and facility. They were wrong to dismiss the romancers as literary hacks who made uncritical use of whatever material was available, who mixed things up, and who at best failed to preserve the beauty and complexity of the French sources and at worst introduced their own contradictions and misreadings.

More recent scholars, including Richmond (1975) and Brewer (1980, 1988), have quite properly observed that, in literature, one has the right to concentrate on the story (on adventure and archetype) or on moral values and ideals of behaviour in society. Archetypal structures and high moral ideals are valid components of art and valid standards according to which art can be judged. That the verse romances are, in some sense of the term, more 'popular' than both Chrétien and Chaucer does not mean that they are inferior works of art. Popular, archetypal narrative can appeal to a sophisticated audience; it can be aesthetically satisfying and attain a high level of structure, order, power, and emotional impact.

The thrust of this argument derives, in part, from the realization that medieval romance is not the same genre or mode as the modern novel and that the traits endemic to nineteenth- and twentieth-century fiction are not endemic to the Middle Ages. Therefore, it is methodologically inappropriate to set up these modern traits or qualities as a norm against which to measure medieval romance, the absence of which in medieval texts would serve to condemn them.

I have also sought to prove, for different reasons perhaps, that to condemn English romance in the name of French romance, because the English texts differ from French ones, is equally invalid. This is the case, in part, because it is methodologically an error to take as one's model a limited twelfth-century corpus – say Chrétien de Troyes – and then to downgrade the one hundred or so English romances that do not resemble Chrétien. Classical prescriptive norms are as unacceptable when derived from a medieval classic (Chrétien) as from a classic of Antiquity (Virgil) or a modern classic (Flaubert). This is also the case because, in fact, when one takes into account the entire corpus, English romance does not differ as much from the French as some scholars say. French narrative also evolved over the centuries, following the same paths that English romance would follow. Many French romances, like the English ones, concentrate on the story, on adventure and archetype, and/or on moral values and ideals for behaviour in society. Many French romances are also more 'popular' than Chrétien and Chaucer. Well they might be, given that a number of the archetypal, moral-type English romances are accurate, faithful translations from the French.

I am also convinced, like Michel Huby, that the purpose of the medieval adapter or translator was not to create an original work of art or state an original world-vision but simply to reproduce the source text in another language, clarifying the original where necessary, making it acceptable in moral terms, and providing the audience with impeccable didactic models of courtesy. In so doing, although the archetypal power of the narrative and the ideology of courtliness inherent in the French will be preserved, other elements in the original such as irony, humour, and a problematic world-view are diminished. The translation often will be less complex than the source.

This combination of archetypal power - including the growth and integration of the hero, the family romance structure, the analogy of innocence, and the conversion of parents to a new order embodied in the children - along with the ideology of courtliness and chivalry, gives rise to manifold works of art that possess their own tone and texture and their own generic expectations. They are legitimate works of art on their own terms. They introduced into the language and the culture dozens of magnificent stories of love and adventure, of prowess and rule. They introduced into the language and the culture the ethos of chivalry and courtesy, of manhood and sovereignty. They set patterns of archetypal narrative for centuries. This is an achievement of the very first order. It is one of which we can be proud, that need never again be disdained.

II. Prose Romance

Since English prose romance exceeds the chronological parameters of my book – from the twelfth century to *c.* 1420 – this chapter shall be brief. Caxton and Malory are, however, of great importance to my theme: Malory's *Morte Darthur* is a supreme aesthetic accomplishment; and the French connection of both men represents one more, and by no means the least significant, literary current from the Continent transmitted to England. The mode of transmission shows remarkable affinities with the phenomenon of courtly adaptation in verse romance and with the adaptation of the French court poem by Chaucer and his school. The late medieval Burgundian vogue repeats the earlier French vogues; it constitutes the final impact of French literature in medieval England.

Prose romance in English came two centuries after verse romance and two centuries after the flowering of secular literary prose in French such as the historical writings of Villehardouin and Robert de Clari, and the various books of the *Perlesvaus, Prose Lancelot,* and *Prose Tristan.* One reason for the belatedness lies in the fact that, from 1066 to 1417, all official writing was in Latin or French. Fisher (1977, 1984) proposes that the rise of an English prose standard coincides with and follows upon the coming into existence, in the fifteenth century, of the new Chancery English.

Prior to Caxton we know of eight extant romances in prose, all dating from the fifteenth century, the earliest a *Life of Alexander, c.* 1430. These texts, directly or indirectly dependent on the French, reflect continental trends. In the form of family chronicle or pseudo-history, they claim greater authenticity and historicity than what is to be found in verse. Prose romance clarifies incident, tightens motivation, and aims at concrete representation of reality through documentation and detail. Chivalry, religion, and the didactic are stressed, as well as the marvellous and the sensational.

The phenomenon of narrative fiction in prose, from the 1460s on, coincides with the vogue of things Burgundian. Commercial, diplomatic, and cultural relations between the Kingdom of England and the Grand Duchy were close. Edward IV assembled a collection of ornate, lavish manuscripts in French, on the Burgundian model, largely as a result of his exile in Bruges as the guest of Louis de Gruthuyse; seventeen items in Edward's library prove to be identical with books owned by Gruthuyse. King Edward and the English aristocracy in general were eager to assimilate all aspects of Burgundian culture: pageantry, luxury, and romantic, chivalrous books including prose reworkings of epic, romance, history, and sacred biography.

Caxton

William Caxton, successful cloth merchant and Governor of the English Nation in Bruges, bought and sold manuscripts and then diversified his business by printing and selling books. He became a translator as one link in the process of becoming a printer and of exploiting the English market. His translation of Raoul Lefèvre's *History of Troy* was the first printed book in English (published in Bruges in 1473 or 1474). In Bruges Caxton published six items in all: four in French and two of his own translations into English. He then settled in Westminster, published the first book in England in 1476, and pursued an active commercial and scholarly existence until his death in 1491.

With an interest in Burgundian-style books and a commitment to didacticism and to perpetuating the ideals of chivalry, Caxton was totally 'modern' in taste. He chose to translate and to disseminate books appreciated by the high European nobility and written in fashionable aureate high style. This was the appeal to his readers – the prestige of Burgundian culture, as sanctioned first by the continental and then by the English highest circles, who delighted in the new courtly fashion. The only caveat to the above, made by Veyrin-Forrer (1976–7) and Blake (1982), is that Caxton chose to translate and print books that were read in the Low Countries and in France generally (not limited to the Burgundian ducal library); in addition to the Burgundian connection, he also had commercial relations with France and imported, indeed translated, a number of texts printed in France. We can retain the notion of a Burgundian period and style, however, recognizing that the mode was cultivated in Paris and Lyon as well as in Dijon and Bruges.

The question of Caxton's patronage has been debated. Did he write specifically for and was he subsidized by the exalted personages whom he mentions in his prologues and epilogues – Edward IV, Richard III, Margaret of York, Henry VII's mother and wife, two princes of Wales, etc.? Or (Belyea 1981–2, Rutter 1987), did he allude to the exalted personages in order to manipulate his real public, the urban merchant class, a relatively broad public subject to and determined by Caxton's expertise in marketing, merchandising, and distribution? In either case, whether Caxton translated and published under patronage or on his own initiative, whether he sought to please a court circle or to attract an outside market, it is clear that he did adhere to the taste of the age. Caxton was at the same time a scholar-translator and a very successful businessman. However, a number of scholars, including Sands (1957), Markland (1960), Montgomery (1972–3), and Yeager (1984), have also insisted that because the former Governor of the English Nation chose the books that constituted his business, translated so many himself, and composed his own prologues and epilogues, we should recognize and celebrate his achievements as a writer, editor, critic, and translator.

Leaving aside the recent emphasis on Caxton's ties to France in a strictly commercial sense, what is of particular concern to me in this chapter is Caxton the translator and transmitter of French prose, especially prose romance. Of the one hundred and seven books published by Caxton, four are in French and thirty are English translations from the French. Of the thirty translations, twenty-two were Englished by Caxton himself; we know of two additional translations by him, one published by Wynkyn de Worde after the master's death, the other an *Ovide moralisé* left in manuscript. Of the twenty-four volumes taken from the French, seven can be considered books of romance in the broad Anglicist use of the term: *Blanchardin and Eglantine, Charles the Great, Four Sons of Aymon, History of Troy, Jason, Paris and Vienne,* and *Siege of Jerusalem*.

Just as Chaucer, Gower, and Lydgate broke away from an earlier native tradition in verse, Caxton does the same in prose. Among his achievements as critic and creator is to have turned to *translatio* – translation and transmission – as his way of appealing to a new English public, and to have illustrated a new English prose style grounded in the French-Burgundian model, enriching and illustrating it much as Chaucer did English verse. As a translator, Caxton was reasonably accurate and faithful to his sources. However, he probably acted from habit and convenience, not conviction; therefore, as he worked phrase by phrase and in haste, errors inevitably slipped through. In this he was typical of his age. No less typically, Caxton's English is shaped by French syntax, and he does not hesitate to drink deeply from the well of the French-Latin lexicon.

Caxton's most important romance is his version of Malory's *Morte Darthur*, printed in 1485. The famous Winchester manuscript of the works of Sir Thomas Malory, now B.L. Additional 59678, was in Caxton's shop from perhaps as early as 1480 until 1489. According to Blake (1982), the generally accepted view nowadays states that the Winchester manuscript was not the immediate source for Caxton's *Morte*, and certainly not the printer's copytext; Caxton may well have had two manuscripts to work from. In any event, Blake (1969) has emphasized that Caxton did not respect Malory as he did an English 'classic' such as Chaucer. He acted quickly, and the *Morte* was treated the same as any book in need of editing prior to publication. Caxton modernized and regularized Malory's Book 2 (Caxton 5), the most archaic in style, both in word order and vocabulary. The rest of the *Morte* he treated more casually, subjecting Malory's text to routine, non-systematic emendation. On the one hand, he directed Malory towards what was to become modern English linguistic consistency and clarity, while at the same time retaining numerous Middle English features of the text. He also continued Malory's work, so to speak, following his example vis-à-vis the French sources, by reducing or deleting some battle scenes, minor characters, and speeches. Above all, he treated the *Morte* as a single Arthurian summa, which he proceeded to divide into twenty-two books and five hundred and seven chapters, emphasizing, in his divisions, the moral and the didactic.

It has been said that Caxton's introduction of the printing press was the most important single historical event of the century. It has also been said that his greatest contribution to English literature, by far, was to have published *Le Morte Darthur*. Prior to Vinaver's edition of the Winchester manuscript, for centuries everyone – the scholar and the average reader – read Malory through Caxton. Many still do. For this reason, because the first great writer of English prose was and is 'Caxton's Malory,' we ought not to neglect Caxton's achievement as a writer, one who, along with Malory, contributed powerfully to the elaboration of English prose and the elaboration of an English standard.

The translation of French texts and the elaboration of romance in prose continued well into the following century. The ideals of chivalry, nobility, and Christian conduct endured, along with a literature that upheld the ideals. Wynkyn de Worde followed Caxton's precedent by publishing nine new prose romances. He commissioned translations of *Valentine and Orson, Olyver of Castille,* and *King Ponthus*. Robert Copland translated Helyas' *Knight of the Swan*. Above all, Lord Berners translated *Arthur of Lytell Brytayne, Huon of Burdeux,* and Froissart. These are the last books of medieval England.

Malory

In 1929 Vinaver observed that, in the popular mind (that is, among non-specialists), Sir Thomas Malory is given credit for old Arthurian romance. What was true in 1929 is only a little less true today, six decades later. Medievalists, on the contrary, know that Malory, more than any other major English writer of the Middle Ages, is a translator, and *Le Morte Darthur* is first and foremost a translation and reduction from what he consistently refers to as the 'Frensshe booke.'

Vinaver himself, an Anglicist of French background, is chiefly responsible for calling attention to the French sources and to their implications for the study of Malory. Vinaver edited the Winchester manuscript, offering scholars for the first time a text close to the original Malory before he was regularized and modernized by Caxton. According to Vinaver's thesis, exposed in the Introduction, Vol. 1, and the Commentary, Vol. 3, of his edition, whereas Caxton wanted *Le Morte Darthur* to be a unified, coherent story of King Arthur and his knights, and consistently modified the text with this in mind, such was not Malory's intent. Because of perceived chronological and structural contradictions within the Malory corpus as well as a number of *explicit* which separate the various sections, Vinaver posits that Malory composed eight distinct Arthurian romances. Instead of assuming that Malory granted unity to incoherent, disunified French sources, Vinaver all but proclaims the contrary – that Malory unravelled the careful interlace pattern of the French romance cycles, suppressing and condensing, telescoping and deleting, both material within a section and strands connecting one section to other sections. The result was a series of continuous but non-integrated individual *nouvelles*. In some ways the result was to be unfortunate because of the loss of interlace and structural unity and because, according to Vinaver, Malory did not understand the spiritual message of *La Queste del saint Graal;* in addition he also devoted one half of the corpus to extraneous, digressive insertions: the *Tale of Sir Gareth of Orkney* and the *Book of Sir Tristram de Lyones*. The one mark of excellence Vinaver (1925, 1929) does grant Malory unconditionally is stylistic; Vinaver claims that, in style, the French is inferior to the English text he calls *The Works of Sir Thomas Malory* (1947).

For a good twenty years after the publication of Vinaver's edition, scholars argued the merits and demerits of the Vinaver thesis. The argument was passionate because a number of the contestants may have felt that something akin to the honour of English literature was at stake. Only with the 1970s did critics proclaim that they had done with sources and the 'unity question' and that they would now engage in more immediate, intrinsic criticism.

In a very real sense the critics are right. Yet, as with Chaucer and with verse romance, I am convinced that the issue of the French literary heritage may occasionally have been looked at in a distorted way from a distorted perspective, and therefore that light can still be shed on the Middle English Arthuriad considered alongside the French.

One view, expressed by a number of critics, and quite convincing in my opinion, responds to Vinaver in general terms. According to Brewer (*Essays* 1963), Moorman (1965), and others, we can distinguish between 'historical' unity in a work of art (when the writer consciously intended it) and 'critical' or 'organic' unity (when it is unconscious or unintentional). Whatever Thomas Malory's intentions, and as a medieval writer he may not have given the matter much thought, it can be maintained that *Le Morte Darthur* achieves an organic structure and a cohesiveness that would be the medieval equivalent of unity because it does recount a single story or sequence of stories – the rise and fall of the Arthurian world. In the process, it displays continuity of atmosphere, tone, characterization, and style. Such unity does not cease to function when and if we find discrepancies – in a medieval book that was read aloud to a listening audience – and when and if the cohesion exists first of all and to a greater extent in Malory's sources. According to Brewer and his colleagues, questions such as originality and imitativeness are not relevant to the study of traditional stories, told in many versions by many writers, where the story exists in something like archetypal form and where the specific contributions of specific creators cannot be determined with precision.

Equally convincing, in my opinion, is Benson's (1976) argument that Malory adheres to fifteenth-century practice on the Continent. A mass of prose epics, romances, and chronicles, including some of the books translated and printed by Caxton, came into being, responding to their sources, in the same way as the *Morte*. A number of authors, including presumably Thomas Malory, wished to create a compendium volume of some great historical or pseudo-historical subject matter: the history of Jason or Troy or Alexander or Charlemagne or Guillaume d'Orange or Lancelot. They all did the same thing, choosing, combining, condensing, telescoping, and smoothening a French prose cycle from the earlier centuries. Thus, Malory was in no way unique in his century nor was he unique in relation to his sources for all the sources of the various compendia were cycles with their idea of history and their sense of totality and unity. Within England alone, and with reference to earlier texts, at least two of Malory's presumed English models – *Of Arthour and Merlin* and the stanzaic *Morte Arthur* – themselves reduced and simplified sections of the *Prose Lancelot* as Malory was to do with the *Prose Lancelot* and the *Prose Tristan* on a larger scale.

A third approach, launched by Lumiansky (*Malory's Originality* 1964), Moorman (1965), and their colleagues, consists in the careful scrutiny of the entire Malory corpus compared to the sources, looking for what Malory retained, altered, omitted, or added, and why. This work leads to quite interesting and, I believe, valid conclusions concerning the linkage, foreshadowing, and retrospection between Vinaver's eight tales. Ultimately it refutes Vinaver's argument that each of the eight tales was written independently from the others. What concerns me is the methodology of the source study and the other conclusions drawn from it, i.e., that in all cases and for all the tales, and on almost every page, Malory improves on his sources, for he is a superb, conscious artist, and their authors are not. Thus is 'proved' not only the unity of the *Morte* but also its author's greatness and originality as a writer.

This current of Malory scholarship did for its author what Chaucerians had been doing for theirs for half a century. The methodology was roughly the same and so were the results; only the Malory people did it with total concentration and all at once. I find the method subject to reservation because, however apt and sensitive the readings of individual passages, it can lead, in my opinion, to a distorted picture overall. The approach takes those parts of the French prose cycles used by Malory and then, isolating them from their context and disregarding their literary value and their standing in French and European literature, judges them against Malory's intentions, what Malory did to them, or, to put it more accurately, against a modern-critical, 'great books' reading of Malory, stressing his strengths and ignoring his failings. The method combines positivist scholarship, critical interpretation, and national pride – both for good and, as I believe, for ill. Although the approach has been abandoned by recent scholars, some of its conclusions have endured as common wisdom in the profession.

One drawback of this scholarship is that it displaces any number of failings onto the French romances that then are contrasted to the sterling success of the *Morte*. We read, from a number of critics, that the *Prose Lancelot* (including the *Queste* and *Mort Artu*) and the *Prose Tristan* are concerned with plot alone; that their narrative structure is entangled, disunified, and incoherent, without design and purpose; that they lack precise, coherent chronology, or for that matter any sense of the passage of time; that they reveal no awareness of political or social questions and are impervious to history and human tragedy; finally, that their style is cumbersome and confused. Much of this is, in my opinion, subjective and ill-informed. What may be partially true of one romance is certainly not true for another. So often a new-criticism Malory is contrasted to an old-fashioned, philological *Lancelot* or *Tristan*, viewed, at best, through the prism of the 1920s' Eugene Vinaver. Works, now accorded the same status in France as Malory has in England, are all but dismissed out of hand.

Scholars of the 1960s but also the 1970s and 1980s ascribe, and rightly so, a number of qualities to *Le Morte Darthur*. They suggest that the *Morte* is a high tragedy of history and of the human condition; that Malory both praises chivalry and demonstrates how the chivalric ideal can disrupt society; that love and chivalry give rise to and are undermined by family feuds; that divided loyalties and a divided sense of responsibility contribute to social decline; that Lancelot is the central figure of the corpus, the touchstone of chivalry against whom the other characters are judged; that the *Morte* recounts the rise and fall of the Arthurian world, a world glorious yet doomed to destruction because of the violence and incest which accompanied its inception and because, in the end, the secular must give way to the sacred and the human to the divine.

These notions are all valid concerning *Le Morte Darthur*. They also are valid as critical commentary on the *Lancelot* proper, the *Queste*, and the *Mort Artu*. This was my position in the chapter on the *Prose Lancelot*; a number of critical studies on the French prose cycles state basically the same premise. Therefore, to affirm that these traits constitute Malory's originality, either because he shaped the French in such directions or without reference to the French at all, is to consider only part of the data and only part of the literary essence of the *Morte*.

Another misconception concerning Malory's originality can occur when scholars apply to *Le Morte Darthur* a sociological approach, assimilating Malory's text to late medieval historical conditions and the late medieval mind-set. A number of studies, some of book length, have taken this approach, in one form or another. Kennedy (1985) contrasts the heroic knight and the worshipful knight, taken presumably in chronological order from earlier traditions (the feudal and the courtly), with the 'true knight,' Malory's own contribution from his era – an ideal that is feudal, courtly, and religious, socially responsible and spiritually transcendant. Other books (Pochoda 1971, Merrill 1987) relate the *Morte* specifically to the cultural crisis of the late fifteenth century. One assumption is that the original Arthurian 'myth' is idealized and unproblematic, lacking time, duration, and social and political commentary. According to this view, Malory then adopted the myth in all its splendour, as nostalgia, but also exposed the inner contradictions in it, the painful truths that the myth occults. Malory uncovered the temporal, the historical, and the political, those social concerns that relate to the fifteenth century. He demonstrated the inadequacy of the Arthurian ideal. His concern and his demonstration then reflected and responded to the crisis of both the monarchy and the nobility, for these institutions ground their existence in traditions and conventions bequeathed from the past but no longer meaningful in a changing age, the beginnings of the modern world.

One problem here concerns the fact that scholars do not always distinguish between the two principal French sources. *Grosso modo*, the *Prose Tristan* idealizes courtly chivalry largely without social and sacred overtones; the *Prose Tristan* mirrors an unproblematic, atemporal Arthurian mythical past. However, the *Prose Lancelot*, including *Le Lancelot propre*, *La Queste*, and *La Mort Artu*, is a different work altogether. The *Lancelot* cycle in its entirety does perform, in historical and political terms, precisely the role that scholars attribute to Malory. In the *Lancelot* we find a socially and religiously conscious, worshipful knighthood, a sense of time and history, the unmasking of contradictions inherent in the Arthurian world-vision, and the unbridgeable conflict between kin loyalty, feudal duty, *fin' amor*, kingship right, and the good of the realm. It is not Malory but Malory's French predecessors who first question and undermine the Arthurian myth.

All these political contradictions, inadequacies, and unmaskings occur first in a work composed during the early decades of the thirteenth century. The cultural crisis of the fifteenth century exemplified in *Le Morte Darthur* proves also to be a cultural crisis of the thirteenth century. Admittedly, Malory may have chosen his texts in part because they did respond to socio-political concerns in his own age. However, we cannot ascribe to the end of the Middle Ages (assuming there was one) and to the cultural crisis brought about because of it (assuming there was one) the central motivating force that gives rise to *Le Morte Darthur*, given that, for such matters, the *Morte* is a translation, and the original socio-political vision, world-view, and crisis date from two and a half centuries earlier in another land.

This said, I do not wish to make the counterclaim that the French prose cycles are superior to *Le Morte Darthur.* That would go against the spirit and intention of this book. Nonetheless, it should be pointed out that to compare Malory with his sources one ought to consider the Englishman's choice of his French books in addition to what he did to them. This assumes that Malory did indeed choose his sources and not that he found them chosen for him, so to speak, in one composite, non-extant, manuscript. Both positions have their defenders (cf. Meale 1985).

I have in mind, especially, Vinaver's Tale 5 (Caxton 8–12), *The Book of Sir Tristram de Lyones.* A problem is posed when Malory inserts into his Arthuriad a largely extraneous rendering of portions of the French *Prose Tristan* that takes up one third of the total corpus. For most Old French scholars, the *Prose Tristan*, given its virtues as a thirteenth-century adventure romance, differs strikingly from the *Prose Lancelot* and *Perlesvaus*, or for that matter from the early *Roman de Tristan* by Beroul and Thomas. The prose version has extreme melodrama: Tristan and Isolt are all good and King Mark is all bad; the enmity between Tristan and Mark is vulgarly derived from a previous sexual rivalry: they both (Tristan *after* he had met Isolt) were competitors for Sir Segwardys' wife; there is the double vulgarity of having the Tristan and Isolt adventures and their affair continue after Tristan weds Isolt of Brittany; the adultery of Tristan and Isolt 'living together' in a castle provided for them by Lancelot is too easy and comfortable. All this contrasts with the complex, anxiety-ridden, tragic human situation in Beroul, Thomas, the *Prose Lancelot*, and so much of the rest of Malory. On the contrary, in this section of the *Morte*, adventure is performed for its own sake, without psychological, social, or metaphysical depth; and the mood is one of sentimental melodrama, with the all-good, all-powerful Tristan and Isolt, exemplars of courtly behaviour and of pure, idealized chivalry, arrayed against and always triumphing over the weak, wicked King Mark. A major incoherence then disrupts the fabric of the *Morte*.

Some very distinguished Malory critics, including Moorman (1965) and Rumble (*Malory's Originality* 1964), have made valiant efforts to justify the *Tristram* insertion. Among the arguments are that Tristan functions as an antihero or counterhero to Lancelot – his is private heroism as a free agent in contrast to Lancelot's public heroism grounded in the Round Table, or his is a flawed adultery compared to Lancelot's supremely courtly adultery – and that Tristan's adventures comprise a middle section of narrative on the testing of chivalry, which Malory otherwise would have lacked. I beg to disagree. The problem with a sentimental, melodramatic *Tristram* inserted into a tragic *Morte* is that Tristan does not function as an antihero or counterhero vis-à-vis Lancelot. Whatever the narrator says concerning Lancelot being Number One and Tristan Number Two, in the narrative space of the total book more attention is paid to Tristan, he commits more and greater deeds of prowess, he is defeated less often, and, unlike Lancelot, nothing ever clouds his *liaison* with a wedded queen. In the narrative space of the *Morte,* Tristan eclipses Lancelot in *militia* and in *amor.*

A narrative middle exists in the *Prose Lancelot;* it concerns the feats and testing of Lancelot. By substituting a Tristan centre for the Lancelot centre, or for that matter by substituting a Tristan *enfances* for the Lancelot *enfances,* Lancelot as protagonist and as the central narrative focus is effectively decentred. Yet, because the Tristan section is abruptly terminated before Tristan's own decline and fall, he never has the occasion to supplant Guinevere's lover in depth and emotional intensity. Since we are to envisage *Le Morte Darthur* as a coherent, unified telling of the rise and fall of the Arthurian world, we can deduce that one third of the total corpus is too much to devote to the all-triumphant adventures, in love and war, of this second, non-Lancelot Lancelot.

The Tristan material contributes one important element to the *Morte* structure and that is the slowly developing, inevitable, and catastrophic enmity between the Orkney lineage – Sir Gawain, Sir Gareth, and the other brothers – and the Pellinore lineage. This feud between kin groups, carried out over a period of decades, makes a major contribution to the dramatic tension and ultimate collapse of the Arthurian world.

On the other hand, it is also true that, with the middle or centre of the *Morte Darthur* narrative occupied by the *Tristram* insertion, the purportedly central Lancelot story loses weight and inevitably contributes less to the total opus. Perhaps it is intentional. One of Malory's consistent changes to the Lancelot-Grail source is to downgrade, veil, and occasionally delete the *fin' amor* between Lancelot and Guinevere.

Generally hostile to 'paramours,' Malory celebrates in their stead the adventure and prowess inherent in the fellowship of the Round Table. One result of this stance is that we are told much less of Lancelot's early feats and of his growth as a knight under Guinevere's inspiration and tutelage, the youth owing all to her and doing all for her. Specifically, the *Knight of the Cart* (Caxton 18 and 19) is shifted from its position in the French cycle, relatively early in Lancelot's career and in his and Guinevere's amours, to the end and inserted after material (the *Poisoned Apple*, the *Fair Maid of Astolat*) taken from *La Mort le roi Artu*. Instead of forming part of a long, coherent, carefully orchestrated narrative of the rise and fall of Lancelot as the imago of Arthurian chivalry, the *Knight of the Cart* and the *Healing of Sir Urry* become distinct episodes fitted into the story just before its end. The narrative is as exciting as in the *Prose Lancelot* and even more so; these episodes are isolated from their context and stand alone as the epitome of adventure; because they stand alone, their symbolism stands out. Yet they also contribute less to the unified, coherent presentation of the rise and fall of a world. Separating out blocks from the original romance cycle and unravelling the interlace creates a different work of art. With difference there is inevitably loss as well as gain.

I am convinced that Malory in prose does basically the same things regarding his sources as the English verse romancers did in the two previous centuries. Malory participates in the centuries-old English tradition of what I have called courtly translation and courtly adaptation. Like so many others, he practices rhetorical *abbreviatio* in contrast to *amplificatio* (Ihle 1983). Like them, Malory is a courtly translator-adapter. He concentrates on the story and on ethical matters. He adheres to the plot, characterization, and ideas of his sources. What he retains is infinitely more important than what he adds or discards. When he does add or discard, it is not to create his own personal conception of unity or sense of history or vision of man. Malory modifies the French in order to make the courtly and chivalrous in his source more explicit, to make the exemplary more exemplary, to veil or delete what he deems unseemly, to underscore and to specify, to simplify and to make melodramatic. The very same procedures that are blamed when an anonymous trouvère adapts a great name in the canon (Chrétien, Marie, Thomas) are praised when a great name in the canon (Chaucer, Malory) adapts the work of anonymous trouvères. Both the blame and the praise are, I venture to say, excessive.

It can be maintained that part of Malory's *abbreviatio* includes the processes by which he diminishes analysis of feeling and of inner states, smooths over complexity and ambiguity, and shies away from questions of attitude and motivation (cf. Lambert 1975, Benson 1976, Brewer 1981). His is a shame not a guilt culture; if anything, he reverts from and counteracts complexities of guilt in the *Prose Lancelot* in favour of his own, external, shame mentality. Furthermore, as Mann (1981) has observed, because Malory suppresses explanations and elucidations and eliminates logical and causal relations, the resultant discrete sequence of tales offers uniquely aesthetic and symbolic connections. *Le Morte Darthur* becomes a sequence of adventures dominated by a sense of fatality; this sense of fatality grants the text its sombre tone and texture. It is a world of force and violence, of fate and destiny, to be accepted by the characters and then narrated by the author. Therefore, the author, with his comprehension of its tragic flaws, stands far from the nostalgia and dream-like, romantic evocation of the past that some have seen in him and that we do find in later Arthurian writers (Spenser, Tennyson) subject to the phenomenon of Medievalism. Malory's chivalry is contemporary; he wishes people to take the good and leave the bad and to live as best they can - which was precisely the attitude two and a half centuries earlier in France at the time of the *Prose Lancelot*.

We find in Malory and his book a sense of specifically English history; the deeds of the past and the glory of chivalry are part of the life of England directed to English readers. As much as Chaucer, and in some ways more than Chaucer, Sir Thomas Malory functions as the mediator between two languages and two cultures. He transmits to English the didactic and historical ideals as well as the tragic insights of the French *Prose Lancelot*, as he transmits to English the potentiality and the realization of prose narrative at its greatest. He recreates the old myths and the old archetypes in his age and for his people, appropriately for his people since the myths concern them.

The birth of prose romance in the latter half of the fifteenth century is in many ways a less significant phenomenon for the history of English literature than the consistent and continual flowering of romance in verse, over the entire medieval span. That belief has determined the structure and format of this study. Most of the books in prose pale beside the verse romances. Yet Malory and Lord Berners alone validate the new movement and grant it importance. This last wave of Frenchness follows in the wake of earlier ones. In his method of composition, Malory adheres to the precept and example of his forebears when faced with French texts; he translates and adapts as they did. The result, however, rightly has been recognized to be one of the masterpieces of English literature. Preserving much of the literary reality of the *Prose Lancelot* in terms of time, tragedy, and history, and preserving much of the mythical quality because of the very work of translation-adaptation, *Le Morte Darthur* also projects its own sense of violence, fate, and symbolic action. It is in Malory's remaking of the French books (including myths, structure, and a sense of symbolic action) that King Arthur and his knights and the matter of medieval romance as a whole will survive for future centuries in England and become history in turn.

Conclusion

The record of vernacular literature in England extends through the entire Middle Ages; it forms a continuum, from the Anglo-Saxon period to the time of Humanism and the Reform. During the first three centuries after the Conquest most of the vernacular literature is composed in French, not English. Two languages were spoken. In addition to the native English, Anglo-Norman French served the upper classes, clerks, merchants, and the civil service. It enjoyed class prestige, embodying the discourse of the masters; with a European vogue, permitting England to benefit from and participate in European culture as a whole, it came to have something akin to the authority of Latin. The French literature written in England or for English patrons and/or an English public proves to be rich and complex, and to have made a major contribution to the culture and literary history of England as well as of France; the great Anglo-Norman texts form one element in that enormous, seminal French literature of the Middle Ages in its European dimension.

Some Anglo-Norman pioneering ventures are in the domain of the sacred: saints' lives, miracles, translation of scripture, and sacred drama. It would be a mistake, however, to characterize the Anglo-Norman temperament (if there is such a thing) as being especially pious, sober, and didactic. There are concrete sociological reasons why the francophone masters of England would have pioneered employing the vernacular in spheres previously reserved to Latin. The continental French soon followed and then surpassed their insular cousins in learned, ecclesiastical writing. Furthermore, Anglo-Norman 'précocité' surfaced in profane as well as in sacred letters. Indeed, the number of outstanding achievements in secular narrative, specifically romances and lays of chivalry, adventure, and *fin' amor*, preclude hasty assessments of the Anglo-Norman character. From my perspective, the major Anglo-Norman achievement is to be found in the domain of narrative, both secular and sacred. Romance, hagiography, and chronicle are the three most important genres.

The tradition of writing that recounts heroism and adventure coincides with a peculiarly Anglo-Norman phenomenon, the ancestral or baronial romance, which exalts the feats of the forebears of great contemporary Anglo-French magnates. Romances such as *Gui de Warewic* and *Boeve de Haumtone* manifest a deep concern for establishing roots and continuity from the English past to the present, and also for questions of legitimacy, family, inheritance, land, and justice that together contribute to the formation of a baronial ideology. Other romances from an earlier generation manifest quite different qualities. Marie and Beroul, writing most probably for an insular audience, compose works that display, from the one, consummate psychological insight into the yearnings of love, and, from the other, equally lucid portrayals of savagery, violence, and deceit. Thomas offers Racine-like probings of jealousy, passion, and love-death; Hue de Rotelande offers Voltaire-like mockery of love, ladies, and courtesy; the anonymous creator of *Amadas et Ydoine* explores to the fullest, in seriousness and in play, the casuistry of *fin' amor.* The romances and the saints' lives share a taste for imagery and symbolism, one or a number of 'arch-images' dominating the narrative structure and granting it meaning. Both genres work from conventional themes and motifs, elaborating conventional structures of narrative. They include the active quest for good by male-oriented heroes and the passive endurance of evil by female-oriented heroes. These powerfully archetypal structures, functioning much the same as on the Continent, gave rise to great new myths such as Tristan, Isolt, and Mark; Arthur and Guinevere; Lanval and the Fay; Guy of Warwick; and Bevis of Hampton. Although sacred biography, translated from Latin, cannot create myths, it can transmit them to the lay world and thus recreate them in a new context; hence the vogue in the British Isles of Saint Margaret, Saint Catherine, and Saint Giles, as well as specifically English figures such as Saint Edmund and Saint Edward the Confessor.

As Anglo-Norman gave way to English in the public sphere and as English replaced Anglo-Norman for a wider variety of literary uses both secular and sacred, English poets turned to writings in French as their models for translation and imitation. At different times, for different reasons, and concerning different literary registers, the English would imitate French books of insular or of continental origin, books from both the past and the present.

Of interest to the historian are genres from the French corpus that were not cultivated with success; some of them were neglected in Anglo-Norman as well as in Middle English. Among the more noteworthy omissions are the *chanson de geste*, the fabliau, the Reynard the Fox cycle, and the courtly lyric. The question of the Old French epic is probably the most easily resolved. Insular audiences and, more to the point, insular patrons undoubtedly saw in *chansons de geste* a defence and illustration of the Capetian line and its claims for suzerainty in the West. It was in reaction to these claims and to this literature that the Norman-Angevin monarchs themselves encouraged the growth of an Arthurian narrative genre that would compete with the Carolingian poems of *geste*. It was also perhaps in reaction to *chansons de geste* that Anglo-Norman poets composed the ancestral romances that function, in England, as an Anglo-Norman epic, playing much the same role as the *chansons* in France.

Fabliaux and the beast epic pose a different problem. Chaucer recognized the extraordinary possibilities inherent in these genres and made the most of them. Otherwise these comic forms, which had so great an impact in Germany and the Low Countries, are largely absent from the English scene. For example, aside from the Chaucerian corpus, only one fabliau, *Dame Sirith*, and one animal fable, *Of the Vox and of the Wolf*, have survived from before 1400. Furrow (1989) opposes the idea that a list of fabliaux ought to be included in the 'lost literature of medieval England.' The fabliau and the beast epic apparently did not appeal to the taste and sensibility of the English reading public. The old thesis states that the English (and Anglo-Normans) were too sober and inherently moral a race to appreciate 'low' subject matter or genres that would have struck them as immoral and obscene. I believe this concept is based on fragile, subjective value-judgments that no longer carry weight. More plausible is the argument that, although the subject matter is low, it is treated with great subtlety and sophistication; the fabliau and the beast epic are as much literature of the court as *chanson de geste* and *roman courtois*. In fact, to savour a fabliau or a branch of the *Roman de Renart* to the fullest, the audience has to be grounded in courtly literature and aware of courtly conventions. Insular readers, grounded and aware to that extent, would have savoured the texts in French and might even have assumed that the experience could be had only in French. After all, the courtly texts that were mocked or parodied in a fabliau or a beast epic, prior to

Chaucer's day, flourished in French and not yet in English. Therefore, those unable to understand French might not have been interested.

The same argument, *mutatis mutandis,* would seem to hold for the courtly lyric. Secular song, with Eros as its theme, is one of the glories of Old French literature: the Occitan *canso* and the French *grand chant courtois* in the thirteenth century; the *ballade, virelai,* and *rondeau* in the fourteenth and fifteenth centuries. Here again, we find in Middle English a relatively insignificant corpus of fixed form amorous lyrics based on the French model, although it is probable that the French lyric had a much greater impact on Chaucer than has previously been recognized (Wimsatt 1991). Boffey (1985) argues convincingly that throughout the late Middle Ages the literate English public, especially the aristocratic public, savoured courtly song in French and indeed collected and exchanged compendium manuscripts of French lyric verse. Perhaps for that reason there was no need for comparable lyrics in English; those that did come into being did not and could not benefit from literary reception analogous to the French. Once again, it is possible that, as in the case of the fabliau, to appreciate a courtly lyric one had to be familiar with the store of courtly conventions, not to speak of the subtleties of metrics and song. Such awareness and such subtlety may not yet have reached the sphere of writing in English.

These hypotheses, excellent as they are, do not help explain the analogous phenomenon where we find little production of fabliaux, Reynard stories, and courtly lyrics in the Anglo-Norman corpus either.[39] One accounting for the choice of genre, in addition to these others, can be derived from literary chronology. In the twelfth century the Anglo-Normans themselves pioneered the creation of literature in the vernacular. By the thirteenth and fourteenth centuries French-speaking Englishmen, still writing in French and producing excellent works in a number of literary kinds, may have become solidly anchored in their own tradition and consequently become less innovative. Perhaps for reasons of aesthetic propriety, they did not adopt relatively new, recent genres inaugurated on the Continent for a continental audience. Later writers in English would then not have adopted them either because there was no precedent for such texts in Anglo-Norman and because, by 1350, a number of these genres were no longer in fashion. As far as England is concerned, the *grand chant courtois* and the fabliau, literary forms from the thirteenth century, may well have slipped through the chronological net as it were; they were too recent and too foreign for the Anglo-Normans and they were too ancient and too foreign for the English.

The preceding considerations lead me to claim that substantive differences between the peoples of England and France in the Middle Ages, if there were any, have to be justified on other than literary grounds. This refers to the French-speaking inhabitants of England as well as to the English people as a whole. Throughout this book I have argued that literature in English is not more heroic or epic than literature in French, nor is it (including literature in Anglo-Norman) more pious, moral, didactic, and Christian. A heroic or epic tradition exists in English romance, specifically in alliterative romances; these texts, however, are analogous to, or direct translations from, French texts which are just as heroic or epic. A number of English romancers elaborate structures of quest and adventure that lead to the recovery of inheritance and attainment of sovereignty, including Christian marriage; or they exploit a thematic of renunciation leading to Christian abnegation and triumph in another, sacred realm. Yet these romances, both the Christian and the marriage-oriented, are also often direct translations of Anglo-Norman or continental French texts, and they correspond to a tradition of later, thirteenth-century insular and continental romance in French that reveals the same ideology and contains identical narrative structures. The French tradition exhibits wide diversity in its modes of narrative; so does the English corpus derived from it. Finally, the divergences between a French text and its English version can best be explained by the workings of courtly adaptation, a rhetorical process grounded in similarity and sympathy rather than in the conscious efforts of Englishmen to alter their models.

A different literary school came into being, centred in London, working from different French models. Chaucer and the Chaucerians exploited a more recent French tradition – courtly literature such as the *dit amoureux* and secular and sacred allegory. They treated French *fin' amor* with humorous, ironic detachment; they exalted it and undermined it at the same time. This complex, ambivalent attitude toward courtly love and courtesy corresponds precisely to what was being done by the French masters of the courtly school – writers who also probed, analyzed, scrutinized, and synthesized courtly doctrine and a courtly world-view with the same sympathy and detachment.

That this should be the case appears natural, given that I see no major divergence in social class between the anglophone and francophone publics. The old distinction between a learned, aristocratic public for books in French and a much lower, 'lewed' public for books in English no longer holds for most literary historians.

Much less work has been done in French studies than by Anglicists on the sociology of literature in the Middle Ages. One school of romance philology, derived from Köhler (1956G), insists on the role of the *juvenes* – young, landless *bachelers* – as an ideological centre and idealized public for the twelfth-century French and Occitan classics. This petty nobility would inevitably share the public function with members of the higher nobility to whom works of literature are so often dedicated and with the educated, secular-oriented clergy, whose ranks contain a number of the writers who wrote not only for the petty and high nobility but also for each other. We can, therefore, posit for books in French, both on the Continent and in England, a relatively broad public that includes the high aristocracy, the petty nobility, a section of the Third Estate (bourgeoisie) that frequented the courts and aped aristocratic manners, and a section of the clergy that also served and found its place at the courts. Recent investigations into the social context of English literature arrive, with greater complexity and nuance, at similar results – a broad public of civil servants and gentry, lawyers and chamber knights, associated with or allied to the courts, in the circle and influence of monarchs and magnates. Rather than a dramatic shift from a French-speaking high-culture public to an English-speaking low-culture public, England offers a picture of continuity; there is essentially one public evolving in time, which first enjoyed literature in French and then, in a later period, literature in both French and English. The choice of language, just as the choice of literary genre, was based primarily upon considerations of decorum and rhetoric, and not of national difference.

If this is so, a fruitful avenue for criticism in the coming years would be to investigate both the social context and literary structures from a broader, more universal, 'comparative' perspective.[40] One could examine the royal clerk and secretary as author or the prince of the blood as patron, from a transnational perspective; similarly, one could attempt a typology of sacred romance or the mirror of princes or the judgment poem, in more than one language. Such investigations could be focused rigorously in time (from 1330 to 1380, for example, or from 1380 to 1430) or could aim at an all-but-panoramic sweep over the centuries. In the long run, one might aim at a universal history of medieval literature in French, concentrating on the contributions from each region, or an all-but-universal history of the medieval literature of England, in English, French, and Latin.

Overall, the English were most intensely attracted to two major French modes of imaginative literature, which correspond to the two currents or schools sketched above. The first is romance. Throughout the Middle Ages and throughout the domain of writing in English,

Englishmen turned to the French for stories of heroism, love, and adventure. Some romances were historical, celebrating English heroes derived from the Anglo-Norman ancestral or baronial romance; some developed the matter of King Arthur and his knights in a legendary British past or one fraught with the aura of tragedy; some treated contemporary material. A number elaborated themes of active heroism, a number idyllic stories of passive love. Some celebrated forbidden *fin' amor*; others led the reader to Christian abnegation and *caritas*. The French romance corpus offered English readers an all-but-infinite fund of exciting stories; it also offered English writers a fund of conventional themes, motifs, and archetypal narrative patterns. The active quest romance, the passive idyllic romance, the interlace romance with multiple strands and multiple protagonists – these are three among a number of competing structures. The result was the translation and also the free invention of dozens of texts that helped recreate in English the historic past and make vital the living present.

The second mode is, in the broadest sense of the term, allegory. English writers connected with courts and centred in the general area of London took to a more recent style of French writing; their contribution begins roughly in the 1360s. They borrowed from *Le Roman de la Rose* and Digulleville's *Pèlerinages* the idea of psychological processes expressed through the speech and behaviour of allegorical personifications. From the French they also borrowed the idea of a passionate, intensive scrutiny of the individual's moral nature and how the individual functions in a social nexus. They also aim at a total presentation of the topic, the universe conveyed in a summa. From these texts, and from *dits amoureux* by Machaut and Froissart, and later by Christine de Pizan and Chartier, English court poets derived a fund of courtly themes and motifs, the structure of the dream vision and the poetic pseudo-autobiography, a complex dream psychology, the dialogue between author figure and authority figure, and the notion of a metatextual work of art recounting its own creation as art and treating the theme of the social relationship between its author and the aristocratic world in which he functions. From them, English poets derived the rivalry of voices and authorities, the deferral of closure, and the example of narrative heteroglossia and stylistic mannerism. Like the romances, these texts juxtapose the sacred and the secular, relating the individual lover or poet to his lady and his prince, or to the Virgin Mary and God, alternatively and in different registers.

The two modes extend over much of the time frame of Middle English literature in its full maturity: the fourteenth and fifteenth centuries. They also seem to have appealed to much the same public, or at least relatively similar publics, running the gamut from petty gentry to high aristocracy; and they express a roughly similar aristocratic ideology of arms and love, *militia et amor.* I think it would be a mistake to posit a radical shift in taste, created by or exemplified in Chaucer and the Chaucerians. On the other hand, Chaucer and his circle do expand the parameters of English literature by seeking out and imitating new models in a new aesthetic. Compared to the romance models, these new models are more modern and, specifically, continental. There is a direct correlation between the adoption of a more contemporary courtly mode by the Ricardians and a turn to contemporary central French writing. The older French literature was both insular and continental; the new was almost uniquely continental because, by the year 1350, Anglo-Norman had ceased to be a viable, dynamic source of inspiration. This inevitably would also be the case a century later when the circle turned and a new romance mode became fashionable. This time it was the Burgundian-French prose summa – a return to romance (prowess, adventure, and history), the romance models being exclusively continental in origin. We must emphasize, however, the extent to which, given these shifts in fashion and in inspiration, the various modes did coexist in time. It is the factor of coexistence, with cross-fertilization between modes, that helps explain the character of later English writing and the opportunities that belatedness brought to English writers. We see in Chaucer an heir to romance and Breton lay as well as to Jean de Meun and Machaut; in Gower an heir to the devotional tradition, Digulleville, Jean de Meun, and Machaut; and Malory recaptures the spirit of the *Prose Lancelot* in addition to the Burgundian compedia of his own time.

Medieval literature in England forms a continuum. The literature of France, or for that matter of Europe in its entirety, forms a continuum. It is quite exciting to see the medieval foundations of the modern English-speaking world built, first in French and then in English, and to see formulated specific medieval ideas that are also universal Western ones – ideas such as chivalry, courtesy, *fin' amor,* the quest, debate, confession, pilgrimage, and any number of others. I subscribe to Curtius's (1950G) ideal of cultural continuity as the *exempla maiorum,* a perpetual celebration, preservation, rediscovery, and restoration of our culture. The true *aristoi* are kindred spirits who give the lie to barbarism and pass along the torch of civilization. The process began long ago. Our Western culture is a common culture, with common origins. It came into being, with many roots in the past. Threatened today, it shall survive because of its centuries-old roots and because it has grown and flourished so widely, in so many lands.

Notes

1 The later 1980s have seen thought-provoking revisionist analyses of the evolution of English studies in their social and political context. Among the best are Graff (1987G) and Patterson (1987G).

Following a system of author-date citation linked to the Bibliography, one version of the MLA Style Sheet, I reduce endnotes to the minimum and encourage the reader to consult the Bibliography, subdivided according to categories that follow the divisions of this study. Works of a general critical nature or which otherwise would be inappropriate under a given category are placed at the beginning of the Bibliography under the heading General; a reference in the text to Auerbach's *Mimesis* would then be: Auerbach (1946G). I endeavour to include those books and articles that I consider particularly important and/or that have helped shape my thinking on the subject, and I hope the Bibliography will be of use in itself. I apologize for the numerous works that, for reasons of space, I have not been able to include.

2 I use the standard, readily available English versions of Old French texts, citing them by page number and including them in the Bibliography. When no page number is cited, the translation is my own. When I have paraphrased the Old French in the immediately preceding lines, a translation would be redundant and therefore is not given.

3 The literature on *mise en abyme* and its function in narratology is immense. Dällenbach (1977G) remains fundamental.

4 This is a standard topos in Old French romance, and the central structuring device in Renaut de Beaujeu's *Le Bel Inconnu* and its fourteenth-century English adaptation, *Lybeaus Desconus*.

5 For the actantial model in narratology, see Greimas (1966G).

6 In Calin (1983G) I discuss this question, arguing that in French literature we find a steady and continuous evolution of verse narrative – the long poem – from the Middle Ages to the twentieth century. We can understand this tradition only by treating it as a whole; specifically, we must avoid prescriptive definitions of the epic, based on classical precept, that would diminish the scope of the corpus. The same, of course, is true for literature in English. This also means that rigid, conceptual definitions of medieval genres, *chanson de geste* or *roman courtois*, are also to be avoided. See Part 4 for my analysis of Middle English verse romance.

7 For this phenomenological approach to literature, the reader should consult Bachelard (1948aG).

8 What constitutes Anglo-Norman is subject to controversy. As stated in the Preface, I include Marie, Beroul, and Wace, following the precept and example of M. Dominica Legge. The most recent edition of Wace, by Hans-Erich Keller (*La Vie* 1990), is a splendid work of philology and textual history. However, given that Keller offers a diplomatic edition of the Wace manuscripts, for the purpose of this book I feel it is best to cite MS A from the older, Francis edition (*La Vie* 1932).

9 Bec (1977–8G) has formulated, for the lyric, the concept of 'texte popularisant' (text in the popular style) as opposed to 'texte aristocratisant' (text in the aristocratic style). I believe that the distinction is equally valid for the narrative and dramatic modes. It goes without saying, whether in the popular or aristocratic style, that these are works of art composed by conscious artists.

10 Stylized theme and register, archetype and convention, are scarcely unique to the Middle Ages. On the contrary, they contribute to an aesthetic of world-wide proportions – the classical literatures of India, China, Japan, Arabia, Persia, and of the West prior to, say, 1770 or 1780. The appreciation of French poetry, from the *Song of Roland* to Chénier and Lamartine, has especially suffered from the imposition of a narrow Romantic or Symbolist aesthetic. See Calin (1987G).

11 Following Lot (1918), I prefer to name the entire cycle the *Prose Lancelot* by analogy with the *Prose Tristan*. Other titles to be found in English are the *Vulgate Cycle* (because of a false claim in the text that it is a translation from Latin) and the *Lancelot-Grail (Prose) Cycle*. The equivalents in French are *Le Lancelot en prose*, *Le cycle de la Vulgate*, and *Le (grand) Lancelot-Graal*.

12 This view is not meant to oppose Kennedy's (1986) challenging thesis that the cyclical *Lancelot* was preceded by a shorter, non-cyclical romance subsequently expanded and rewritten.

13 A central section of the *Prose Lancelot* incorporates and remodels the narrative of Chrétien's *Chevalier de la Charrete.*

14 The specific number of lines varies according to which manuscript or which critical edition is consulted.

15 This case has been made by Lejeune (1973) and Hult (1986), among others. In addition, Hult offers a challenging reading of the text as a whole.

16 He has traditionally been called Guillaume de Deguileville. Faral (1962) established the new name and spelling, with reference to the native village of Digulleville in Normandy.

17 See note 7 above. In addition, Bachelard (1938G, 1948bG).

18 Kibler and Wimsatt (1987) modify the extreme formulation of this thesis. They demonstrate that although Machaut was surely involved with the later compendium manuscripts – in the arrangement of his works and the illuminations – he did not provide close personal authorial supervision of the copying.

19 Another *mise en abyme*, concerning Gaston Phoebus' brother, Pierre de Béarn – his sleepwalking and hallucinations – has psychoanalytical and folkloric overtones: see Zink (1980), Grisward (1986), Ainsworth (1990), and Harf-Lancner (1990).

20 Wimsatt (1968) argues convincingly that Chaucer's *Book of the Duchess* influenced *Le Dit du Bleu Chevalier.* In this one instance I disagree. Philological and historical evidence place the composition of *Le Bleu Chevalier* before 1365 when Froissart himself dwelt in England and before Blanche's death. The author of *Les Chroniques* is highly sensitive to language; he often alludes to the languages people speak, and to his own practice as an interviewer of participants and eye-witnesses. He appears to have relied on, and to have been limited by recourse to, French-speaking informants. We have no data in *Les Chroniques* or the poetic corpus to indicate that Froissart learned to speak and read English.

21 For this and other aspects of medieval dream theory (and Chaucer's practice), consult Curry (1926: chap. 8) and the books in the Bibliography under The Dream Poems.

22 Among others, see articles by Palmer (1980), Walker (1983-4), Donnelly (1987), Martin (1987), and Anderson (1992). Under Chaucer, see books by Sklute (1984), Ferster (1985), and Lawton (1985).

23 Consult Bakhtin (1981G, 1984G). Chaucerians have paid greater attention to Bakhtin than French scholars have. Among a number of studies, in addition to Ganim on the *Canterbury Tales* (1990, under Canterbury Tales), see the fall 1989 issue of *Exemplaria*, with bibliography.

24 Much has been written on the fabliau genre. I recommend Cooke

(1978), Muscatine (1986), and Schenck (1987). On the question why, outside Chaucer, there was so limited a fabliau tradition in English, see below, pp. 515–16.

25 'Tant l'ont folé et debatu, / par po qu'il ne l'ont tot molu; / puis vont modre a autre molin' (317–19).

26 Cf. Sklute (1984), Ferster (1985), Lawton (1985), and Jordan (1987) under Chaucer; Cooper (1984), Benson (1986), Rogers (1986), and Leicester (1990) under Canterbury Tales.

27 Lowes (1910–11), McGalliard (1946), and Altman (1975–6) make a most convincing case. However, Thundy (1979, under Wife of Bath's Tale) argues that Deschamps' *Miroir* was not available for public dissemination until 1406. Thundy's stance is weakened, in my opinion, by the belief that Deschamps was influenced by Chaucer. I am convinced that Deschamps would have had no occasion to learn English and, given the mind-set of the age, no reason to do so either. The famous 'Ballade to Chaucer' is fulsome, conventional rhetoric that recalls earlier texts by a number of figures including Deschamps himself. It indicates no more than that Sir Lewis Clifford, an eminent habitué of French and English court circles, must have spoken to Deschamps on Chaucer's behalf, and Deschamps (1) was flattered and (2) wanted to please Clifford.

28 Despite allusions to Derridean textuality, much recent feminist criticism also scrutinizes Alice as a character in a book of fiction.

29 Fritz (1986–7) points out that, in 133 lines, the 'I' appears fifty-two times.

30 Ovid, the *Ovide moralisé*, and Machaut tell the tale of Apollo and the raven. Inserted in this story is a similar story of Pallas and the crow. In Chaucer, the raven becomes a crow, and the inserted tale of the crow is deleted. I try to distinguish between Chaucer's Crow (capitalized) and the raven and crow in the sources.

31 *Cinkante Balades* contain, in fact, fifty-two fixed-form texts. Macaulay, following his manuscript, numbers them from one to fifty, allotting number four twice. He also designates the closing religious leave-taking as number fifty-one. These are *ballades* in the English sense of the term, comprising, in addition to regular *ballades*, a number of what the French call *chansons royales*.

32 Pearsall (1989) argues convincingly that the Latin rubrics offer a reading of *Confessio Amantis*, perhaps by Gower himself, deserving of consideration; however, we ought not to allow it to impose constraints on our own critical interpretation of the text.

33 The standard reading includes the major full-length studies: books by Fisher (1965), Schmitz (1974), Gallacher (1975), Peck (1978), Olsen

(1990), Yeager (1990), and Olsson (1992); and important articles by Minnis (1980 and *Gower's* Confessio Amantis 1983).

34 See my discussion of these conventions in the section on verse romance in Part 4.

35 In the *Series* Friend states that the public thinks the *Letter of Cupid* is antifeminist. This is a Machaldian-Chaucerian literary device, not evidence for the history of literary reception in the fifteenth century. See my analysis, below.

36 On Marie's relationship to *Sir Landevale* and *Sir Launfal*, I recommend Stemmler (1962), Williams (1969), and Spearing (1990).

37 The bibliography on medieval translation is immense. I find especially pertinent Buridant (1983G), Copeland (1991G), and Morse (1991G).

38 In addition the most recent investigators (for example, Hudson 1984, 1989, Reiss 1985, Reichle 1991) relate popularity to social class and the radical of expression, carefully avoiding the privileging of the nonliterary and the folk.

39 The lyric, in its amorous, sacred, and satirical modes, deserves more scholarly attention. See, for example, *Anglo-Norman Political Songs* (1953), the recent anthology, *Anglo-Norman Lyric* (1990), and articles by Harvey (1978, 1989).

40 We can envisage the past from new perspectives, employing divergent approaches, and at the same time use the historical otherness of the past to test the validity of these approaches. We also ought to be able to demystify the prevalent myth, shared by a number of medievalists, that subjectivity, modernity, and man as we know him began only with the Renaissance. Patterson (1990) is most persuasive in this domain.

Bibliography

General

Auerbach, Erich. *Mimesis: dargestellte Wirklichkeit in der abendländischen Literatur.* Bern: Francke, 1946.

Bachelard, Gaston. *La Psychanalyse du feu.* Paris: Gallimard, 1938.

– *La Terre et les rêveries de la volonté.* Paris: Corti, 1948a.

– *La Terre et les rêveries du repos.* Paris: Corti, 1948b.

Bakhtin, Mikhail. *Rabelais and His World.* Cambridge: MIT Press, 1968.

– *The Dialogic Imagination: Four Essays.* Austin: University of Texas Press, 1981.

– *Problems of Dostoevsky's Poetics.* Minneapolis: University of Minnesota Press, 1984.

Bec, Pierre. *La Lyrique française au Moyen Age (XIIe–XIIIe siècles): Contribution à une typologie des genres poétiques médiévaux.* 2 vols. Paris: Picard, 1977–8.

Bergson, Henri. *Le Rire: Essai sur la signification du comique.* 97th ed. Paris: Presses Universitaires de France, 1950.

Berrong, Richard M. *Rabelais and Bakhtin: Popular Culture in* Gargantua and Pantagruel. Lincoln: University of Nebraska Press, 1986.

Buridant, Claude. 'Translatio medievalis: Théorie et pratique de la traduction médiévale.' *Travaux de Linguistique et de Littérature* 21:1 (1983): 81–136.

Calin, William. *A Muse for Heroes: Nine Centuries of the Epic in France.* Toronto: University of Toronto Press, 1983.

– *In Defense of French Poetry: An Essay in Revaluation.* University Park: Pennsylvania State University Press, 1987.

Copeland, Rita. *Rhetoric, Hermeneutics and Translation in the Middle Ages: Academic Traditions and Vernacular Texts.* Cambridge: Cambridge University Press, 1991.

Curtius, Ernst Robert. *Europäische Literatur und lateinisches Mittelalter.* Bern: Francke, 1948.

– *Kritische Essays zur europäischen Literatur.* Bern: Francke, 1950.

– 'Über die altfranzösische Epik.' In his *Gesammelte Aufsätze zur romanischen Philologie.* Bern: Francke, 1960: 106–304.

Dällenbach, Lucien. *Le Récit spéculaire: Essai sur la mise en abyme.* Paris: Seuil, 1977.

Duby, Georges. 'Dans la France du Nord-Ouest au XIIe siècle: Les *jeunes* dans la société aristocratique.' *Annales. E.S.C.* 19 (1964): 835–46.

Elias, Norbert. *Über den Prozess der Zivilisation.* 2 vols. Basel: Haus zum Falken, 1939.

– *Die höfische Gesellschaft.* Darmstadt: Luchterhand, 1969.

Frye, Northrop. *Anatomy of Criticism: Four Essays.* Princeton: Princeton University Press, 1957.

Girard, René. *La Violence et le sacré.* Paris: Grasset, 1972.

– *Des choses cachées depuis la fondation du monde.* Paris: Grasset, 1978.

Girart de Roussillon, chanson de geste. Ed. W. Mary Hackett. 3 vols. Paris: Picard, 1953–5.

Graff, Gerald. *Professing Literature: An Institutional History.* Chicago: University of Chicago Press, 1987.

Greimas, A. J. *Sémantique structurale: Recherche de méthode.* Paris: Larousse, 1966.

Köhler, Erich. *Ideal und Wirklichkeit in der höfischen Epik: Studien zur Form der frühen Artus- und Graldichtung.* Tübingen: Niemeyer, 1956.

Morse, Ruth. *Truth and Convention in the Middle Ages: Rhetoric, Representation, and Reality.* Cambridge: Cambridge University Press, 1991.

Patterson, Lee. *Negotiating the Past: The Historical Understanding of Medieval Literature.* Madison: University of Wisconsin Press, 1987.

Stanzel, Franz. *Die typischen Erzählsituationen im Roman.* Wien: Braumüller, 1955.

Walsh, P.G., ed. and tr. *Andreas Capellanus on Love.* London: Duckworth, 1982.

Preface

Benson, Larry D. *Malory's* Morte Darthur. Cambridge: Harvard University Press, 1976.

Crane, Susan. *Insular Romance: Politics, Faith, and Culture in Anglo-Norman and Middle English Literature.* Berkeley: University of California Press, 1986.

Huby, Michel. *L'Adaptation des romans courtois en Allemagne au XIIe et au XIIIe siècle.* Paris: Klincksieck, 1968.

– *Prolegomena zu einer Untersuchung von Gottfrieds* Tristan. 2 vols. Göppingen: Kümmerle, 1984.

Huizinga, Johan. *The Waning of the Middle Ages: A Study of the Forms of Life, Thought and Art in France and the Netherlands in the XIVth and XVth Centuries.* London: Arnold, 1924.

Legge, M. Dominica. *Anglo-Norman Literature and Its Background.* Oxford: Clarendon Press, 1963.

Muscatine, Charles. *Chaucer and the French Tradition: A Study in Style and Meaning.* Berkeley: University of California Press, 1957.
Vinaver, Eugène, ed. *The Works of Sir Thomas Malory.* 3 vols. Oxford: Clarendon Press, 1947.
Wimsatt, James I. *Chaucer and the French Love Poets: The Literary Background of the* Book of the Duchess. Chapel Hill: University of North Carolina Press, 1968.
– *Chaucer and His French Contemporaries: Natural Music in the Fourteenth Century.* Toronto: University of Toronto Press, 1991.

Introduction

Bezzola, Reto R. *Les Origines et la formation de la littérature courtoise en Occident (500–1200).* Vols. 2, 3. Paris: Champion, 1960–3.
Blaess, Madeleine. 'L'abbaye de Bordesley et les livres de Guy de Beauchamp.' *Romania* 78 (1957): 511–18.
– 'Les manuscrits français dans les monastères anglais au Moyen Age.' *Romania* 94 (1973): 321–58.
Blake, Norman. *The English Language in Medieval Literature.* London: Dent, 1977.
Boffey, Julia. *Manuscripts of English Courtly Love Lyrics in the Later Middle Ages.* Cambridge: Brewer, 1985.
Book Production and Publishing in Britain, 1375–1475. Ed. Jeremy Griffiths and Derek Pearsall. Cambridge: Cambridge University Press, 1989. Articles by Edwards and Pearsall, Gillespie, Harris, Meale, and Voigts.
Burrow, J. A. *Ricardian Poetry: Chaucer, Gower, Langland and the Gawain Poet.* London: Routledge and Kegan Paul, 1971.
– *Medieval Writers and Their Work: Middle English Literature and Its Background, 1100–1500.* Oxford: Oxford University Press, 1982.
England in the Fifteenth Century: Proceedings of the 1986 Harlaxton Symposium. Ed. Daniel Williams. Woodbridge: Boydell Press, 1987. Articles by Backhouse, Fleming, and Stratford.
Green, Richard F. 'King Richard II's Books Revisited.' *The Library* 5th ser. 31 (1976): 235–9.
Hunt, Tony. *Popular Medicine in Thirteenth-Century England: Introduction and Texts.* Cambridge: Brewer, 1990.
Kekewich, Margaret. 'Edward IV, William Caxton, and Literary Patronage in Yorkist England.' *Modern Language Review* 66 (1971): 481–7.
Krochalis, Jeanne E. 'The Books and Reading of Henry V and His Circle.' *Chaucer Review* 23 (1988–9): 50–77.
Lambley, Kathleen. *The Teaching and Cultivation of the French Language in England during Tudor and Stuart Times.* Manchester: Manchester University Press, 1920.

Legge, M. Dominica. 'Anglo-Norman and the Historian.' *History* ns 26 (1941–2): 163–75.
– 'The French Language and the English Cloister.' *Medieval Studies Presented to Rose Graham*. Ed. Veronica Ruffer and A. J. Taylor. Oxford: Oxford University Press, 1950: 146–62.
– 'Anglo-Norman as a Spoken Language.' *Proceedings of the Battle Conference on Anglo-Norman Studies: II, 1979*. Suffolk: Boydell Press, 1980: 108–17.
– Also see under Anglo-Norman Narrative.
Orr, John. *Old French and Modern English Idiom*. Oxford: Blackwell, 1962.
Petit, Herbert H. 'A Wood Needing – Clearing: Desiderata in Anglo-Norman-English Linguistics.' *Annuale Mediaevale* 1 (1960): 102–7.
Pope, M.K. *From Latin to Modern French, with Especial Consideration of Anglo-Norman*. Manchester: Manchester University Press, 1934.
Richter, Michael. *Sprache und Gesellschaft im Mittelalter: Untersuchungen zur mündlichen Kommunikation in England von der Mitte des elften bis zum Beginn des vierzehnten Jahrhunderts*. Stuttgart: Hiersemann, 1979.
Rickard, P. *Britain in Medieval French Literature: 1100–1500*. Cambridge: Cambridge University Press, 1956.
Rosenthal, Joel T. 'Aristocratic Cultural Patronage and Book Bequests, 1350–1500.' *Bulletin of the John Rylands Library* 64 (1981–2): 522–48.
Rothwell, William. 'The Teaching of French in Medieval England.' *Modern Language Review* 63 (1968): 37–46.
– 'The Role of French in Thirteenth-Century England.' *Bulletin of the John Rylands Library* 58 (1975–6): 445–66.
– 'Language and Government in Medieval England.' *Zeitschrift für Französische Sprache und Literatur* 93 (1983): 258–70.
– 'Stratford atte Bowe and Paris.' *Modern Language Review* 80 (1985): 39–54.
– 'From Latin to Modern French: Fifty Years On.' *Bulletin of the John Rylands Library* 68 (1985–6): 179–209.
Salter, Elizabeth. *English and International: Studies in the Literature, Art and Patronage of Medieval England*. Cambridge: Cambridge University Press, 1988.
Schirmer, Walter F. and Ulrich Broich. *Studien zum literarischen Patronat im England des 12. Jahrhunderts*. Köln: Westdeutscher Verlag, 1962.
Short, Ian. 'On Bilingualism in Anglo-Norman England.' *Romance Philology* 33 (1979–80): 467–79.
Vale, Juliet. *Edward III and Chivalry: Chivalric Society and Its Context, 1270–1350*. Woodbridge: Boydell Press, 1982.
Whitehead, F. 'Norman French: The Linguistic Consequences of the Conquest.' *Manchester Literary and Philosophical Society: Memoirs and Proceedings* 109 (1966–7): 78–83.
Wilkins, Nigel. 'Music and Poetry at Court: England and France in the Late

Middle Ages.' *English Court Culture in the Later Middle Ages*. Ed. V. J. Scattergood and J. W. Sherborne. New York: St Martin's Press, 1983: 183–204.
Wilson, R.M. 'The Contents of the Mediaeval Library.' *The English Library before 1700: Studies in Its History*. Ed. Francis Wormald and C. E. Wright. London: Athlone Press, 1958: 85–111.
Women and Literature in Britain, 1150–1500. Ed. Carol M. Meale. Cambridge: Cambridge University Press, 1993. Articles by Boffey, Meale, Millett, and Riddy.

Anglo-Norman Narrative

Crane, Susan. *Insular Romance: Politics, Faith, and Culture in Anglo-Norman and Middle English Literature*. Berkeley: University of California Press, 1986.
Legge, M. Dominica. *Anglo-Norman in the Cloisters: The Influence of the Orders upon Anglo-Norman Literature*. Edinburgh: Edinburgh University Press, 1950.
– *Anglo-Norman Literature and Its Background*. Oxford: Clarendon Press, 1963.
– 'La précocité de la littérature anglo-normande.' *Cahiers de Civilisation Médiévale* 8 (1965): 327–49.
Vising, Johan. *Anglo-Norman Language and Literature*. London: Oxford University Press, 1923.
Walberg, E. *Quelques Aspects de la littérature anglo-normande: Leçons faites à l'Ecole des Chartes*. Paris: Droz, 1936.

Marie de France

Marie de France. *Lais*. Ed. Alfred Ewert. Oxford: Blackwell, 1960.
Aubailly, Jean-Claude. *La Fée et le chevalier: Essai de mythanalyse de quelques lais féeriques des XIIe et XIIIe siècles*. Paris: Champion, 1986.
Baader, Horst. *Die Lais: Zur Geschichte einer Gattung der altfranzösischen Kurzerzählungen*. Frankfurt: Klostermann, 1966.
Bruckner, Matilda Tomaryn. 'Strategies of Naming in Marie de France's *Lais*: At the Crossroads of Gender and Genre.' *Neophilologus* 75 (1991): 31–40.
Burgess, Glyn S. *The Lais of Marie de France: Text and Context*. Athens: University of Georgia Press, 1987.
– and Keith Busby, tr. *The Lais of Marie de France*. Harmondsworth: Penguin Books, 1986.
Dragonetti, Roger. *'La Musique et les lettres': Etudes de littérature médiévale*. Genève: Droz, 1986: 99–121.
Fitz, Brewster E. 'Desire and Interpretation: Marie de France's *Chievrefoil*.' *Yale French Studies* 58 (1979): 182–9.
Freeman, Michelle A. 'Marie de France's Poetics of Silence: The Implications

for a Feminine *Translatio*.' *PMLA* 99 (1984): 860–83.
Hunt, Tony. 'Glossing Marie de France.' *Romanische Forschungen* 86 (1974): 396–418.
Koubichkine, Michèle. 'A propos du Lai de Lanval.' *Moyen Age* 78 (1972): 467–88.
Kroll, Renate. *Der narrative Lai als eigenständige Gattung in der Literatur des Mittelalters: Zum Strukturprinzip der 'Aventure' in den Lais*. Tübingen: Niemeyer, 1984.
Ménard, Philippe. *Les Lais de Marie de France: Contes d'amour et d'aventure du Moyen Age*. Paris: Presses Universitaires de France, 1984.
Pickens, Rupert T. 'La poétique de Marie de France d'après les Prologues des *Lais*.' *Lettres Romanes* 32 (1978): 367–84.
Ribard, Jacques. 'Le lai du *Laostic*: Structure et signification.' *Moyen Age* 76 (1970): 263-74.
– 'Le *Lai de Lanval*: Essai d'interprétation polysémique.' *Mélanges de philologie et de littératures romanes offerts à Jeanne Wathelet-Willem*. Liège: Marche Romane, 1978: 529–44.
Rieger, Dietmar. 'Evasion et conscience des problèmes dans les *Lais* de Marie de France.' *Spicilegio Moderno* 12 (1979): 49-69.
Ringger, Kurt. *Die Lais: Zur Struktur der dichterischen Einbildungskraft der Marie de France*. Tübingen: Niemeyer, 1973.
Sienaert, Edgard. *Les Lais de Marie de France: Du conte merveilleux à la nouvelle psychologique*. Paris: Champion, 1978.
Spitzer, Leo. 'Marie de France – Dichterin von Problem-Märchen.' *Zeitschrift für Romanische Philologie* 50 (1930): 29–67.
– 'La "lettre sur la baguette de coudrier" dans le lai du *Chievrefueil*.' *Romania* 69 (1946–7): 80–90.
Sturges, Robert. *Medieval Interpretation: Models of Reading in Literary Narrative, 1100–1500*. Carbondale: Southern Illinois University Press, 1991: chap. 3.
Verhuyck, Paul. 'Marie de France, le chèvrefeuille et le coudrier.' *Mélanges de linguistique, de littérature et de philolgie médiévales offerts à J.R. Smeets*. Ed. Q.I.M. Mok et al. Leiden: 1982: 317–26.
Vitz, Evelyn Birge. *Medieval Narrative and Modern Narratology: Subjects and Objects of Desire*. New York: New York University Press, 1989: chap 6.

Le Roman de Tristan

The Romance of Tristran by Beroul: A Poem of the Twelfth Century. Ed. Alfred Ewert. 2 vols. Oxford: Blackwell, 1939–70.
Le Roman de Tristan par Thomas. Ed. Félix Lecoy. Paris: Champion, 1991.
Barteau, Françoise. *Les Romans de Tristan et Iseut: Introduction à une lecture plurielle*. Paris: Larousse, 1972.

Baumgartner, Emmanuèle. *Tristan et Iseut: De la légende aux récits en vers*. Paris: Presses Universitaires de France, 1987.

Blakeslee, Meritt R. *Love's Masks: Identity, Intertextuality, and Meaning in the Old French Tristan Poems*. Cambridge: Brewer, 1989.

Bruckner, Matilda Tomaryn. 'The Representation of the Lovers' Death: Thomas' *Tristan* as Open Text.' *Tristania* 9 (1983–4): 49–61.

Burns, E. Jane. 'How Lovers Lie Together: Infidelity and Fictive Discourse in the *Roman de Tristan*.' *Tristania* 8:2 (Spring 1983): 15–30.

Caulkins, Janet Hillier. 'The Meaning of "pechié" in the *Romance of Tristran* by Béroul.' *Romance Notes* 13 (1971–2): 545–9.

Fedrick, Alan S., tr. *The Romance of Tristan by Beroul*. Harmondsworth: Penguin Books, 1970.

Ferrante, Joan M. 'Artist Figures in the Tristan Stories.' *Tristania* 4:2 (May 1979): 25–35.

Gregory, Stewart, tr. Thomas of Britain, *Tristran*. New York: Garland, 1991.

Grigsby, John L. 'L'empire des signes chez Béroul et Thomas: "Le sigle est tut neir."' *Marche Romane* 30: 3–4 (1980): 115–25.

Huchet, Jean-Charles. *Tristan et le sang de l'écriture*. Paris: Presses Universitaires de France, 1990.

Hunt, Tony. 'Abelardian Ethics and Beroul's *Tristran*.' *Romania* 98 (1977): 501–40.

Jonin, Pierre. *Les Personnages féminins dans les romans français de Tristan au XIIe siècle: Etude des influences contemporaines*. Gap: Ophrys, 1958a.

– 'Le songe d'Iseut dans la forêt du Morois.' *Moyen Age* 64 (1958b): 103–13.

Lacy, Norris J. 'Irony and Distance in Béroul's *Tristan*.' *French Review* Special Issue No. 3 (Fall 1971): 21–9.

Larmat, Jean. 'La souffrance dans le *Tristan* de Thomas.' *Mélanges de langue et littérature françaises du Moyen-Age offerts à Pierre Jonin*. Aix-en-Provence: CUER MA, 1979: 369–85.

Ollier, Marie-Louise. 'Le péché selon Yseut dans le *Tristan* de Béroul.' *Courtly Literature: Culture and Context*. Ed. Keith Busby and Erik Kooper. Amsterdam: Benjamins, 1990: 465–82.

Payen, Jean-Charles. 'Lancelot contre Tristan: La conjuration d'un mythe subversif (Réflexions sur l'idéologie romanesque au Moyen Age.)' *Mélanges de langue et de littérature médiévales offerts à Pierre Le Gentil*. Paris: Société d'Edition d'Enseignement Supérieur, 1973: 617–32.

Pensom, Roger. 'Rhetoric and Psychology in Thomas's *Tristan*.' *Modern Language Review* 78 (1983): 285–97.

Pitts, Brent A. 'Absence, Memory, and the Ritual of Love in Thomas's *Roman de Tristan*.' *French Review* 63 (1989–90): 790–9.

Polak, L. 'The Two Caves of Love in the *Tristan* by Thomas.' *Journal of the War-*

burg and Courtauld Institutes 33 (1970): 52–69.

Regalado, Nancy Freeman. 'Tristan and Renart: Two Tricksters.' *L'Esprit Créateur* 16 (1976): 30–8.

Ribard, Jacques. 'Le *Tristan* de Béroul, un monde de l'illusion?' *Bulletin Bibliographique de la Société Internationale Arthurienne* 31 (1979): 229–44.

Rigolot, François. 'Valeur figurative du vêtement dans le *Tristan* de Béroul.' *Cahiers de Civilisation Médiévale* 10 (1967): 447–53.

Trindade, W. Ann. 'Time, Space, and Narrative Focus in the Fragments of Thomas's *Tristan*.' *Romance Philology* 32 (1978–9): 387–96.

Tristan et Iseut, mythe européen et mondial. Ed. Danielle Buschinger. Göppingen: Kümmerle, 1987. Articles by Batany, Gouttebroze, Martineau-Genieys, and Ollier.

Vàrvaro, Alberto. *Il* Roman de Tristran *di Béroul*. Torino: Bottega d'Erasmo, 1963.

Ipomedon

Ipomedon, poème de Hue de Rotelande (fin du XIIe siècle). Ed. A.J. Holden. Paris: Klincksieck, 1979.

Hanning, Robert W. '*Engin* in Twelfth-Century Romance: An Examination of the *Roman d'Enéas* and Hue de Rotelande's *Ipomedon*.' *Yale French Studies* 51 (1974): 82–101.

Krueger, Roberta L. 'Misogyny, Manipulation, and the Female Reader in Hue de Rotelande's *Ipomedon*.' *Courtly Literature: Culture and Context*. Ed. Keith Busby and Erik Kooper. Amsterdam: Benjamins, 1990: 395–409.

Spensley, Ronald M. 'The Structure of Hue de Rotelande's *Ipomedon*.' *Romania* 95 (1974): 341–51.

Amadas et Ydoine

Amadas et Ydoine, roman du XIIIe siècle. Ed. John R. Reinhard. Paris: Champion, 1974.

Arthur, Ross G., tr. *Amadas and Ydoine*. New York: Garland, 1993.

Aubailly, Jean-Claude, tr. *Amadas et Ydoine, roman du XIIIe siècle*. Paris: Champion, 1986. 'Préface': 9–18.

Le Gentil, Pierre. 'A propos d'*Amadas et Ydoine* (Version continentale et version insulaire).' *Romania* 71 (1950): 359–73.

Lyons, Faith. *Les Eléments descriptifs dans le roman d'aventure au XIIIe siècle*. Genève: Droz, 1965: chap. 1.

Reinhard, John Revell. *The Old French Romance of* Amadas et Ydoine: *An Historical Study*. Durham: Duke University Press, 1927.

Gui de Warewic

Gui de Warewic, roman du XIIIe siècle. Ed. Alfred Ewert. 2 vols. Paris: Champion, 1932–3.

Crane, Ronald S. 'The Vogue of *Guy of Warwick* from the Close of the Middle Ages to the Romantic Revival.' *PMLA* 30 (1915): 125–94.

Crane, Susan. See under Anglo-Norman Narrative.

Hopkins, Andrea. *The Sinful Knights: A Study of Middle English Penitential Romance*. Oxford: Clarendon Press, 1990.

Legge, M. Dominica. See under Anglo-Norman Narrative.

Richmond, Velma Bourgeois. *The Popularity of Middle English Romance*. Bowling Green: Bowling Green University Popular Press, 1975.

Schelp, Hanspeter. *Exemplarische Romanzen im Mittelenglischen*. Göttingen: Vandenhoeck and Ruprecht, 1967.

Wolfzettel, Friedrich. 'Cavalleria esemplare o cavalleria problematica? Il caso del *Gui de Warewic*.' *L'Imagine Riflessa* 12 (1989): 91–108.

Vitae

La Vie de saint Laurent: An Anglo-Norman Poem of the Twelfth Century. Ed. D.W. Russell. London: Anglo-Norman Text Society, 1976.

Wace. *La Vie de sainte Marguerite*. Ed. Elizabeth A. Francis. Paris: Champion, 1932.

Wace. *La Vie de sainte Marguerite*. Ed. Hans-Erich Keller. Tübingen: Niemeyer, 1990.

The Life of St Catherine by Clemence of Barking. Ed. William Macbain. Oxford: Blackwell, 1964.

La Vie de saint Gilles par Guillaume de Berneville, poème du XIIe siècle. Ed. Gaston Paris and Alphonse Bos. Paris: Didot, 1881.

La Vie de sainte Marie l'Egyptienne: Versions en Ancien et Moyen Français. Ed. Peter F. Dembowski. Genève: Droz, 1977.

Baker, A.T. 'Saints' Lives Written in Anglo-French: Their Historical, Social and Literary Importance.' *Transactions of the Royal Society of Literature of the United Kingdom* n.s. 4 (1924): 119–56.

Bambeck, Manfred. 'Das Credo des Eremiten in der *Vie de S. Gile* des Guillaume de Berneville.' *Neuphilologische Mitteilungen* 76 (1975): 372–88.

Cazelles, Brigitte. 'Modèle ou mirage: *Marie l'Egyptienne*.' *French Review* 53 (1979–80): 13–22.

– *Le Corps de sainteté, d'après Jehan Bouche d'Or, Jehan Paulus et quelques vies des XIIe et XIIIe siècles*. Genève: Droz, 1982.

Dembowski, Peter F. 'Literary Problems of Hagiography in Old French.'

Medievalia et Humanistica n.s. 7 (1976): 117–30.

– 'Le poème anonyme sur Sainte Marie l'Egyptienne est-il anglo-normand?' *XIV Congresso internazionale di linguistica e filologia romanza*. Vol. 5. Napoli: Macchiaroli, 1981: 445–61.

– 'Traits essentiels des récits hagiographiques.' *La Nouvelle: Formation, codification et rayonnement d'un genre médiéval*. Ed. Michelangelo Picone et al. Montreal: Plato Academic Press, 1983: 80–8.

Elliott, Alison Goddard. *Roads to Paradise: Reading the Lives of the Early Saints*. Hanover: University Press of New England, 1987.

Ernst, Ursula. *Studien zur altfranzösischen Verslegende (10.–Anfang 13. Jahrhundert): Die Legende im Spannungsfeld von Chanson de geste und Roman*. Frankfurt: Lang, 1989.

Gnädinger, Louise. *Eremitica: Studien zur altfranzösischen Heiligenvita des 12. und 13. Jahrhunderts*. Tübingen: Niemeyer, 1972.

Heffernan, Thomas J. *Sacred Biography: Saints and Their Biographers in the Middle Ages*. New York: Oxford University Press, 1988.

Hurley, Margaret. 'Saints' Legends and Romance Again: Secularization of Structure and Motif.' *Genre* 8 (1975): 60–73.

Hyun, Theresa M. 'Dualistic Narrative in the Old French Martyr Poems.' *Romance Philology* 37 (1983–4): 49–56.

Images of Sainthood in Medieval Europe. Ed. Renate Blumenfeld-Kosinski and Timea Szell. Ithaca: Cornell University Press, 1991. Articles by Robertson, Uitti, and Vitz.

Johnson, Phyllis and Brigitte Cazelles. *'Le vain siecle guerpir': A Literary Approach to Sainthood through Old French Hagiography of the Twelfth Century*. Chapel Hill: University of North Carolina Department of Romance Languages, 1979.

Legge, M. Dominica. *Anglo-Norman in the Cloisters: The Influence of the Orders upon Anglo-Norman Literature*. Edinburgh: Edinburgh University Press, 1950.

– 'Anglo-Norman Hagiography and the Romances.' *Medievalia et Humanistica* n.s. 6 (1975): 41–9.

Lewes, Ülle Erika. *The Life in the Forest: The Influence of the Saint Giles Legend on the Courtly Tristan Story*. Chattanooga: Tristania Monograph Series, 1978.

Montgomery, Edward. 'Structure and Symbol in Wace's *Vie de Sainte Marguerite*.' *Kentucky Romance Quarterly* 24 (1977): 301–9.

Robertson, Duncan. 'Poem and Spirit: The Twelfth-Century French *Life* of Saint Mary the Egyptian.' *Medioevo Romanzo* 7 (1980): 305-27.

Surdel, Alain-Julien. 'Amour, mariage et ... sainteté dans les légendes et les mystères hagiographiques.' *Amour, mariage et transgressions au Moyen Age*. Ed. Danielle Buschinger and André Crépin. Göppingen: Kümmerle, 1984: 73–91.

Uitti, Karl D. 'The Clerkly Narrator Figure in Old French Hagiography and Romance,' *Medioevo Romanzo* 2 (1975): 394–408.

Vitz, Evelyn Birge. 'Vie, légende, littérature: Traditions orales et écrites dans les histoires des saints.' *Poétique* 18 (1987): 387-402.

Wogan-Browne, Jocelyn. 'Saints' Lives and the Female Reader.' *Forum for Modern Language Studies* 27 (1991): 314–32.

– '"Clerc u lai, muïne u dame": Women and Anglo-Norman Hagiography in the Twelfth and Thirteenth Centuries.' *Women and Literature in Britain, 1150–1500*. Ed. Carol M. Meale. Cambridge: Cambridge University Press, 1993: 61–85.

Huon de Bordeaux

Huon de Bordeaux. Ed. Pierre Ruelle. Bruxelles: Presses Universitaires de Bruxelles, 1960.

The Boke of Duke Huon of Burdeux, done into English by Sir John Bourchier, Lord Berners. Ed. S.L. Lee. 4 vols. EETS, es, 40, 41, 43, 50. London: Trübner, 1881–7.

Adler, Alfred. *Rückzug in epischer Parade*. Frankfurt: Klostermann, 1963.

Calin, William. *The Epic Quest: Studies in Four Old French 'Chansons de Geste.'* Baltimore: Johns Hopkins Press, 1966.

Heintze, Michael. *König, Held und Sippe: Untersuchungen zur Chanson de geste des 13. und 14. Jahrhunderts und ihrer Zyklenbildung*. Heidelberg: Winter, 1991.

Johnson, Phyllis. '*Huon de Bordeaux* et la sémantique de l'*enfes*.' *Zeitschrift für Romanische Philologie* 91 (1975): 69–78.

Lewis, C.S. *English Literature in the Sixteenth Century, Excluding Drama*. Oxford: Clarendon Press, 1954.

Rossi, Marguerite. 'Loyauté et déloyauté dans *Huon de Bordeaux*.' *Société Rencesvals: VIe Congrès International, Actes*. Aix-en-Provence: Université de Provence, 1974: 373-87.

– Huon de Bordeaux *et l'évolution du genre épique au XIIIe siècle*. Paris: Champion, 1975.

The Prose Lancelot

Lancelot, roman en prose du XIIIe siècle. Ed. Alexandre Micha. 9 vols. Genève: Droz, 1978–83.

Lancelot do Lac: The Non-Cyclical Old French Prose Romance. Ed. Elspeth Kennedy. 2 vols. Oxford: Clarendon Press, 1980.

La Queste del Saint Graal, roman du XIIIe siècle. Ed. Albert Pauphilet. Paris: Champion, 1923.

La Mort le Roi Artu, roman du XIIIe siècle. Ed. Jean Frappier. 2nd ed. Genève: Droz, 1956.

Approches du Lancelot en prose. Ed. Jean Dufournet. Paris: Champion, 1984. Articles by Chênerie, de Combarieu, Dufournet, Micha, Paradis, and Poirion.

Baumgartner, Emmanuèle. *L'Arbre et le pain: Essai sur* La Queste del Saint Graal. Paris: Société d'Edition d'Enseignement Supérieur, 1981.

– 'Géants et chevaliers.' *The Spirit of the Court: Selected Proceedings of the Fourth Congress of the International Courtly Literature Society*. Ed. Glyn S. Burgess and Robert A. Taylor. Cambridge: Brewer, 1985: 9–22.

Bourquin, Emmanuelle. 'Saint Bernard héritier du Graal: Le silence du "nice" et l'écrit du diable.' *Littérature* 41 (1981): 119–28.

Burns, E. Jane. *Arthurian Fictions: Rereading the Vulgate Cycle*. Columbus: Ohio State University Press, 1985.

Cable, James, tr. *The Death of King Arthur*. Harmondsworth: Penguin Books, 1971.

Chase, Carol J. 'Multiple Quests and the Art of Interlacing in the 13th-Century *Lancelot*.' *Romance Quarterly* 33 (1986): 407–20.

Dornbush, Jean M. *Pygmalion's Figure: Reading Old French Romance*. Lexington: French Forum, 1990: chap. 4.

Dover, Carol. 'The Split-Shield Motif in the Old French Prose *Lancelot*.' *Arthurian Yearbook* 1 (1991): 43–61.

Frappier, Jean. *Etude sur* La Mort le Roi Artu, *roman du XIIIe siècle*. 2nd ed. Genève: Droz, 1961.

Gilson, Etienne. 'La mystique de la grâce dans *La Queste del saint Graal*.' *Romania* 51 (1925): 321–47.

Harf-Lancner, Laurence. 'Le Val sans Retour ou la prise du pouvoir par les femmes.' *Amour, mariage et transgressions au Moyen Age*. Ed. Danielle Buschinger and André Crépin. Göppingen: Kümmerle, 1984: 185–93.

Kennedy, Elspeth. *Lancelot and the Grail: A Study of the Prose* Lancelot. Oxford: Clarendon Press, 1986.

Lancelot: Actes du Colloque des 14 et 15 janvier 1984. Ed. Danielle Buschinger. Göppingen: Kümmerle, 1984. Articles by Baumgartner, Harf-Lancner, Huchet, Kennedy, and Micha.

Leupin, Alexandre. *Le Graal et la littérature: Etude sur la Vulgate arthurienne en prose*. Lausanne: L'Age d'Homme, 1982.

Locke, Frederick W. *The Quest for the Holy Grail: A Literary Study of a Thirteenth-Century French Romance*. Stanford: Stanford University Press, 1960.

Looze, Laurence N. de. 'A Story of Interpretations: The *Queste del Saint Graal* as Metaliterature.' *Romanic Review* 76 (1985): 129–47.

Lot, Ferdinand. *Etude sur le Lancelot en prose*. Paris: Champion, 1918.

Matarasso, Pauline, tr. *The Quest of the Holy Grail.* Harmondsworth: Penguin Books, 1969.

– *The Redemption of Chivalry: A Study of the* Queste del Saint Graal. Genève: Droz, 1979.

Micha, Alexandre. *De la chanson de geste au roman: Etudes de littérature médiévale.* Genève: Droz, 1976.

– *Essais sur le cycle du Lancelot-Graal.* Genève: Droz, 1987.

Pauphilet, Albert. *Etudes sur la* Queste del Saint Graal *attribuée à Gautier Map.* Paris: Champion, 1921.

Pratt, Karen. 'Aristotle, Augustine or Boethius? *La Mort le roi Artu* as Tragedy.' *Nottingham French Studies* 30 (1991): 81–109.

Todorov, Tzvetan. 'La quête du récit.' *Critique* 262 (mars 1969): 195–214.

Tuve, Rosemond. *Allegorical Imagery: Some Medieval Books and Their Posterity.* Princeton: Princeton University Press, 1966: chap. 5.

Vinaver, Eugène. *The Rise of Romance.* Oxford: Clarendon Press, 1971.

Wolfzettel, Friedrich. 'Lancelot et les fées: Essai d'une lecture psychanalytique du *Lancelot en prose.*' *Marche Romane* 32:2–4 (1982): 25–42.

Le Roman de la Rose

Guillaume de Lorris et Jean de Meun. *Le Roman de la Rose.* Ed. Félix Lecoy. 3 vols. Paris: Champion, 1965–70.

Allen, Peter L. *The Art of Love: Amatory Fiction from Ovid to the* Romance of the Rose. Philadelphia: University of Pennsylvania Press, 1991.

Batany, Jean. *Approches du* Roman de la Rose. Paris: Bordas, 1973.

Baumgartner, Emmanuèle. 'De Lucrèce à Héloïse: Remarques sur deux *exemples* du *Roman de la Rose* de Jean de Meun.' *Romania* 95 (1974): 433–42.

Bouché, Thérèse. 'L'obscène et le sacré ou l'utilisation paradoxale du rire dans le *Roman de la Rose* de Jean de Meun.' *Le Rire au Moyen Age dans la littérature et dans les arts.* Ed. Thérèse Bouché and Hélène Charpentier. Bordeaux: Presses Universitaires de Bordeaux, 1990: 83–95.

Brownlee, Kevin. 'Reflections in the *Miroër aus Amoreus*: The Inscribed Reader in Jean de Meun's *Roman de la Rose.*' *Mimesis: From Mirror to Method, Augustine to Descartes.* Ed. John D. Lyons and Stephen G. Nichols, Jr. Hanover: University Press of New England, 1982: 60–70.

– 'The Problem of Faux Semblant: Language, History, and Truth in the *Roman de la Rose.*' *The New Medievalism.* Ed. Marina S. Brownlee et al. Baltimore: Johns Hopkins University Press, 1991: 253-71.

Cahoon, Leslie. 'Raping the Rose: Jean de Meun's Reading of Ovid's *Amores.*' *Classical and Modern Literature* 6 (1985–6): 261–85.

Dahlberg, Charles, tr. *The* Romance of the Rose *by Guillaume de Lorris and Jean de Meun*. Princeton: Princeton University Press, 1971.

Dornbush, Jean M. *Pygmalion's Figure: Reading Old French Romance*. Lexington: French Forum, 1990: chap. 3.

Dragonetti, Roger. *'La Musique et les lettres': Etudes de littérature médiévale*. Genève: Droz, 1986: 345–418.

Eberle, Patricia J. 'The Lovers' Glass: Nature's Discourse on Optics and the Optical Design of the *Romance of the Rose*.' *University of Toronto Quarterly* 46 (1976–7): 241–62.

Etudes sur le Roman de la Rose *de Guillaume de Lorris*. Ed. Jean Dufournet. Genève: Slatkine, 1984. Articles by Batany, Baumgartner, Kamenetz, and Payen.

Fleming, John V. *The* Roman de la Rose: *A Study in Allegory and Iconography*. Princeton: Princeton University Press, 1969.

Freeman, Michelle A. 'Problems in Romance Composition: Ovid, Chrétien de Troyes, and the *Romance of the Rose*.' *Romance Philology* 30 (1976–7): 158–68.

Friedman, Lionel J. 'Gradus Amoris.' *Romance Philology* 19 (1965–6): 167–77.

Gunn, Alan M.F. *The Mirror of Love: A Reinterpretation of* The Romance of the Rose. Lubbock: Texas Tech Press, 1952.

– 'Teacher and Student in the *Roman de la Rose*: A Study in Archetypal Figures and Patterns.' *L'Esprit Créateur* 2 (1962): 126–34.

Hill, Thomas D. 'La Vieille's Digression on Free Love: A Note on Rhetorical Structure in the *Romance of the Rose*.' *Romance Notes* 8 (1966–7): 113–15.

Hult, David F. *Self-Fulfilling Prophecies: Readership and Authority in the First* Roman de la Rose. Cambridge: Cambridge University Press, 1986.

Jung, Marc-René. *Etudes sur le poème allégorique en France au moyen âge*. Berne: Francke, 1971.

– 'Jean de Meun et l'allégorie.' *Cahiers de l'Association Internationale des Etudes Françaises* 28 (1976): 21–36.

Kessler, Joan. 'La quête amoureuse et poétique: la fontaine de Narcisse dans le *Roman de la Rose*.' *Romanic Review* 73 (1982): 133–46.

Köhler, Erich. 'Narcisse, la Fontaine d'Amour et Guillaume de Lorris.' *Journal des Savants* (1963): 86–103.

Leicester, H. Marshall, Jr. 'Ovid Enclosed: The God of Love as *Magister Amoris* in the *Roman de la Rose* of Guillaume de Lorris.' *Res Publica Litterarum* 7 (1984): 107–29.

Lejeune, Rita. 'A propos de la structure du *Roman de la Rose* de Guillaume de Lorris.' *Etudes de langue et de littérature du Moyen Age offertes à Félix Lecoy*. Paris: Champion, 1973: 315–48.

Lewis, C.S. *The Allegory of Love: A Study in Medieval Tradition*. Oxford: Clarendon Press, 1936.

Mancini, Mario. 'Servo e padrone in Jean de Meun.' *XIV Congresso internazionale di linguistica e filologia romanza: Atti*. Vol. 5. Napoli: Macchiaroli, 1981: 469–79.

Muscatine, Charles. 'The Emergence of Psychological Allegory in Old French Romance.' *PMLA* 68 (1953): 1160–82.

Payen, Jean-Charles. *La Rose et l'utopie: Révolution sexuelle et communisme nostalgique chez Jean de Meung*. Paris: Editions Sociales, 1976.

Pickens, Rupert T. '*Somnium* and Interpretation in Guillaume de Lorris.' *Symposium* 28 (1974): 175–86.

Poirion, Daniel. 'Narcisse et Pygmalion dans le *Roman de la Rose*.' *Essays in Honor of Louis Francis Solano*. Ed. Raymond J. Cormier and Urban T. Holmes. Chapel Hill: University of North Carolina Press, 1970: 153–65.

– 'Les mots et les choses selon Jean de Meun.' *Information Littéraire* 26 (1974): 7–11.

Regalado, Nancy Freeman. '"Des contraires choses": La fonction poétique de la citation et des *exempla* dans le *Roman de la Rose* de Jean de Meun.' *Littérature* 41 (1981): 62–81.

Rethinking the Romance of the Rose: *Text, Image, Reception*. Ed. Kevin Brownlee and Sylvia Huot. Philadelphia: University of Pennsylvania Press, 1992. Articles by Baumgartner, Fleming, Hult, and Uitti.

Ribard, Jacques. 'Introduction à une étude polysémique du *Roman de la Rose* de Guillaume de Lorris.' *Etudes de langue et de littérature du Moyen Age offertes à Félix Lecoy*. Paris: Champion, 1973: 519–28.

Stakel, Susan. *False Roses: Structures of Duality and Deceit in Jean de Meun's* Roman de la Rose. Saratoga: Anma Libri, 1991.

Steinle, Eric M. 'Versions of Authority in the *Roman de la Rose*: Remarks on the Use of Ovid's *Metamorphoses* by Guillaume de Lorris and Jean de Meun.' *Mediaevalia* 13 (1987): 189–206.

Uitti, Karl D. 'Understanding Guillaume de Lorris: The Truth of the Couple in Guillaume's *Romance of the Rose*.' *Michigan Romance Studies* 8 (1989): 51–70.

Vitz, Evelyn Birge. *Medieval Narrative and Modern Narratology: Subjects and Objects of Desire*. New York: New York University Press, 1989: chap. 2–3.

Wetherbee, Winthrop. 'The Literal and the Allegorical: Jean de Meun and the *de Planctu Naturae*.' *Medieval Studies* 33 (1971): 264–91.

Zumthor, Paul. *Langue, texte, énigme*. Paris: Seuil, 1975: 249–64.

Guillaume de Digulleville

Le Pèlerinage de la Vie humaine de Guillaume de Deguileville. Ed. J.J. Stürzinger. London: Nichols, 1893.

Le Pèlerinage de l'Ame de Guillaume de Deguileville. Ed. J.J. Stürzinger. London: Nichols, 1895.

The Pilgrimage of the Lyfe of the Manhode. Ed. Avril Henry. 2 vols. EETS, os, 288, 292. London: Oxford University Press, 1985–8.

The Pilgrimage of the Soul: A Critical Edition of the Middle English Dream Vision. Ed. Rosemarie Potz McGerr. New York: Garland, 1990.

Badel, Pierre-Yves. *Le Roman de la Rose au XIVe siècle: Etude de la réception de l'oeuvre*. Genève: Droz, 1980.

Bergmann, Rosemarie. *Die Pilgerfahrt zum himmlischen Jerusalem: Ein allegorisches Gedicht des Spätmittelalters ...* . Wiesbaden: Reichert, 1983.

Blythe, Joan Heiges. 'The Influence of Latin Manuals on Medieval Allegory: Deguileville's Presentation of Wrath.' *Romania* 95 (1974): 256–83.

Clasby, Eugene, tr. Guillaume de Deguilleville, *The Pilgrimage of Human Life (Le Pèlerinage de la vie humaine)*. New York: Garland, 1992.

Faral, Edmond. 'Guillaume de Digulleville, moine de Chaalis.' *Histoire Littéraire de la France*. Vol. 39 (1962): 1–132.

Hagen, Susan K. *Allegorical Remembrance: A Study of* The Pilgrimage of the Life of Man *as a Medieval Treatise on Seeing and Remembering*. Athens: University of Georgia Press, 1990.

Henry, Avril. '*þe Pilgrimage of þe Lyfe of þe Manhode*: The Large Design, with Special Reference to Books 2–4.' *Neuphilologische Mitteilungen* 87 (1986a): 229–36.

– 'The Structure of Book I of *þe Pilgrimage of þe Lyfe of þe Manhode*.' *Neuphilologische Mitteilungen* 87 (1986b): 128–41.

Lewis, C.S. See under Le Roman de la Rose above.

Subrenat, Jean. 'Lucifer et sa mesnie dans le *Pèlerinage de l'âme* de Guillaume de Digulleville.' *Le Diable au Moyen Age (Doctrine, Problèmes moraux, Représentations)*. Aix-en-Provence: CUER MA, 1979: 507–25.

Wenzel, Siegfried. 'The Pilgrimage of Life as a Late Medieval Genre.' *Mediaeval Studies* 35 (1973): 370–88.

Wright, Steven. 'Deguileville's *Pèlerinage de Vie Humaine* as "Contrepartie Edifiante" of the *Roman de la Rose*.' *Philological Quarterly* 68 (1989): 399–422.

Machaut

Oeuvres de Guillaume de Machaut. Ed. Ernest Hoepffner. 3 vols. Paris: Firmin-Didot and Champion, 1908–21.

Le Livre du Voir-Dit de Guillaume de Machaut. Ed. Paulin Paris. Paris: Société des Bibliophiles François, 1875.

Boulton, Maureen. 'The Dialogical Imagination in the Middle Ages: The Example of Guillaume de Machaut's *Voir Dit*.' *Allegorica* 10 (1989): 85–94.

– 'Guillaume de Machaut's *Voir Dit*: The Ideology of Form.' *Courtly Literature: Culture and Context*. Ed. Keith Busby and Erik Kooper. Amsterdam: Benjamins, 1990: 39–47.

Brownlee, Kevin. *Poetic Identity in Guillaume de Machaut*. Madison: University of Wisconsin Press, 1984.

– 'Guillaume de Machaut's *Remede de Fortune*: The Lyric Anthology as Narrative Progression.' *The Ladder of High Designs: Structure and Interpretation of the French Lyric Sequence*. Ed. Doranne Fenoaltea and David Lee Rubin. Charlottesville: University Press of Virginia, 1991: 1–25.

Calin, William. *A Poet at the Fountain: Essays on the Narrative Verse of Guillaume de Machaut*. Lexington: University Press of Kentucky, 1974.

– '*La Fonteinne amoureuse* de Machaut: son or, ses oeuvres d'art, ses mises en abyme.' *L'Or au Moyen Age (Monnaie–métal–objets–symbole)*. Aix-en-Provence: CUER MA, 1983: 75–87.

Cerquiglini, Jacqueline. *'Un engin si soutil': Guillaume de Machaut et l'écriture au XIVe siècle*. Genève: Slatkine, 1985.

Ehrhart, Margaret J. 'Machaut and the Duties of Rulers Tradition.' *French Forum* 17 (1992): 5–22.

Enders, Jody. 'Music, Delivery, and the Rhetoric of Memory in Guillaume de Machaut's *Remède de Fortune*.' *PMLA* 107 (1992): 450–64.

Guillaume de Machaut, poète et compositeur. Paris: Klincksieck, 1982. Articles by Cerquiglini, Ferrand, Gauvard, Planche, Poirion, and Roques.

Gybbon-Monypenny, G.B. 'Guillaume de Machaut's Erotic "Autobiography": Precedents for the Form of the *Voir-Dit*.' *Studies in Medieval Literature and Languages in Memory of Frederick Whitehead*. Ed. W. Rothwell et al. Manchester: Manchester University Press, 1973: 133–52.

Hieatt, Constance B. '*Un autre fourme*: Guillaume de Machaut and the Dream Vision Form.' *Chaucer Review* 14 (1979–80): 97–115.

Huot, Sylvia. *From Song to Book: The Poetics of Writing in Old French Lyric and Lyrical Narrative Poetry*. Ithaca: Cornell University Press, 1987: chap. 8–9.

Kelly, Douglas. *Medieval Imagination: Rhetoric and the Poetry of Courtly Love*. Madison: University of Wisconsin Press, 1978: chap. 6.

– 'The Genius of the Patron: The Prince, the Poet, and Fourteenth-Century Invention.' *Studies in the Literary Imagination* 20:1 (1987): 77–97.

Kibler, William W. and James I. Wimsatt. 'Machaut's Text and the Question of His Personal Supervision.' *Studies in the Literary Imagination* 20:1 (1987): 41–53.

Lanoue, David G. 'History as Apocalypse: The "Prologue" of Machaut's *Jugement dou roy de Navarre*.' *Philological Quarterly* 60 (1981): 1–12.

Looze, Laurence de. 'Guillaume de Machaut and the Writerly Process.' *French Forum* 9 (1984): 145–61.

Machaut's World: Science and Art in the Fourteenth Century. Ed. Madeleine Pelner Cosman and Bruce Chandler. New York: New York Academy of Sciences, 1978. Articles by Brownlee, Uitti, and Williams.

Palmer, R. Barton. 'The Metafictional Machaut: Self-Reflexivity and Self-

Mediation in the Two Judgment Poems.' *Studies in the Literary Imagination* 20:1 (1987): 23–39.
– ed. and tr. Guillaume de Machaut, *The Judgment of the King of Navarre*. New York: Garland, 1988.
Rychner, Jean. 'La flèche et l'anneau.' *Revue des Sciences Humaines* 183 (1981): 55–69.
Steinle, Eric M. '"Car tu as scens, retorique et musique": Machaut's Musical Narrative of the *Remede de Fortune*.' *Mediaevalia* 11 (1985): 63–82.
Sturges, Robert S. *Medieval Interpretation: Models of Reading in Literary Narrative, 1100–1500*. Carbondale: Southern Illinois University Press, 1991: chap. 3.
– 'The Critical Reception of Machaut's *Voir-Dit* and the History of Literary History.' *French Forum* 17 (1992): 133–51.
Williams, Sarah Jane. 'An Author's Role in Fourteenth Century Book Production: Guillaume de Machaut's "livre ou je met toutes mes choses."' *Romania* 90 (1969): 433–54.
Wimsatt, James I. and William W. Kibler, ed. and tr. Guillaume de Machaut, *Le Jugement du roy de Behaigne and Remede de Fortune*. Athens: University of Georgia Press, 1988.

Froissart

Chroniques de J. Froissart. Ed. Siméon Luce, Gaston Raynaud, Léon Mirot and Albert Mirot. 15 vols. Paris: Renouard, Champion, Klincksieck, 1869–1975.
Froissart. *Chroniques, Dernière rédaction du premier livre*. Ed. George T. Diller, Genève: Droz, 1972.
The Chronicle of Froissart Translated out of French by Sir John Bourchier, Lord Berners. 6 vols. London: David Nutt, 1901–3.
Ainsworth, Peter F. *Jean Froissart and the Fabric of History: Truth, Myth, and Fiction in the* Chroniques. Oxford: Oxford University Press, 1990.
Archambault, Paul. *Seven French Chroniclers: Witnesses to History*. Syracuse: Syracuse University Press, 1974.
Benson, L.D. 'The Use of a Physical Viewpoint in Berners' Froissart.' *Modern Language Quarterly* 20 (1959): 333–8.
Diller, George T. *Attitudes chevaleresques et réalités politiques chez Froissart: Microlectures du premier livre des* Chroniques. Genève: Droz, 1984.
Froissart: Historian. Ed. J. J. N. Palmer. Woodbridge: Boydell Press, 1981.
Grisward, Joël H. 'Froissart et la nuit du loup-garou, la "fantaisie" de Pierre de Béarn: modèle folklorique ou modèle mythique?' *Le Modèle à la Renaissance*. Ed. C. Balavoine et al. Paris: Vrin, 1986: 21–34.
Harf-Lancner, Laurence. 'Chronique et roman: les contes fantastiques de Froissart.' *Autour du roman: Etudes présentées à Nicole Cazauran*. Paris: Presses de l'Ecole Normale Supérieure, 1990: 49–65.

Jäger, Georg. *Aspekte des Krieges und der Chevalerie im XIV. Jahrhundert in Frankreich: Untersuchungen zu Jean Froissarts* Chroniques. Bern: Lang, 1981.

Medeiros, Marie-Thérèse de. *Jacques et chroniqueurs: Une étude comparée de récits contemporains relatant la Jacquerie de 1358*. Paris: Champion, 1979.

– 'Le pacte encomiastique: Froissart, ses *Chroniques* et ses mécènes.' *Moyen Age* 94 (1988): 237–55.

Shears, F.S. *Froissart: Chronicler and Poet*. London: Routledge, 1930.

Zink, Michel. 'Froissart et la nuit du chasseur.' *Poétique* 41 (1980): 60–77.

Chartier

The Poetical Works of Alain Chartier. Ed. J.C. Laidlaw. London: Cambridge University Press, 1974.

Ros, Sir Richard. *'La Belle Dame sans Mercy'*. In *Chaucerian and Other Pieces*. Ed. Walter W. Skeat. Oxford: Oxford University Press, 1897: 299–326.

Brami, Joseph. 'Un lyrisme de veuvage: Etude sur le *Je* poétique dans *La belle dame sans mercy.*' *Fifteenth-Century Studies* 15 (1989): 53–66.

Johnson, Leonard W. *Poets as Players: Theme and Variation in Late Medieval French Poetry.* Stanford: Stanford University Press, 1990.

Jonen, Gerda Anita. *Allegorie und Späthöfische Dichtung in Frankreich*. München: Fink, 1974.

Kay, W.B. '*La Belle dame sans mercy* and the Success of Failure.' *Romance Notes* 6 (1964–5): 69–73.

Kibler, William W. 'The Narrator as Key to Alain Chartier's *La Belle Dame sans mercy.*' *French Review* 52 (1978–9): 714–23.

Piaget, Arthur. '*La Belle Dame sans merci* et ses imitations.' *Romania* 30 (1901): 22–48, 317–51; 31 (1902): 315–49; 33 (1904): 179–208; 34 (1905): 375–428, 559–602.

Poirion, Daniel. 'Lectures de la *Belle Dame sans mercy.*' *Mélanges de langue et de littérature médiévales offerts à Pierre Le Gentil*. Paris: Société d'Edition d'Enseignement Supérieur, 1973: 691–705.

Rieger, Dietmar. 'Alain Chartiers *Belle Dame sans Mercy* oder der Tod des höfischen Liebhabers.' *Sprachen der Lyrik: Festschrift für Hugo Friedrich*. Ed. Erich Köhler. Frankfurt: Klostermann, 1975: 683–706.

Shapley, C.S. *Studies in French Poetry of the Fifteenth Century.* The Hague: Nijhoff, 1970.

English Court Poetry – Introduction

Coleman, Janet. *English Literature in History, 1350–1400: Medieval Readers and Writers*. London: Hutchinson, 1981.

English Court Culture in the Later Middle Ages. Ed. V.J. Scattergood and J.W. Sherborne. New York: St Martin's Press, 1983. Articles by Scattergood and Sherborne.

Green, Richard Firth. *Poets and Princepleasers: Literature and the English Court in the Late Middle Ages*. Toronto: University of Toronto Press, 1980.

Literary Practice and Social Change in Britain, 1380–1530. Ed. Lee Patterson. Berkeley: University of California Press, 1990. Articles by Patterson and Strohm.

Patterson, Lee. *Negotiating the Past: The Historical Understanding of Medieval Literature*. Madison: University of Wisconsin Press, 1987.

Salter, Elizabeth. 'Chaucer and Internationalism.' *Studies in the Age of Chaucer* 2 (1980): 71–9.

Strohm, Paul. *Social Chaucer*. Cambridge: Harvard University Press, 1989.

Chaucer

The Riverside Chaucer. 3rd ed. Gen. ed. Larry D. Benson. Boston: Houghton Mifflin, 1987.

Aers, David. *Chaucer, Langland, and the Creative Imagination*. London: Routledge and Kegan Paul, 1980.

Braddy, Haldeen. *Chaucer and the French Poet Graunson*. Baton Rouge: Louisiana State University Press, 1947.

– 'The French Influence on Chaucer.' *Companion to Chaucer Studies*. Ed. Beryl Rowland. Rev. ed. New York: Oxford University Press, 1979: 143–59.

Bronson, Bertrand H. *In Search of Chaucer*. Toronto: University of Toronto Press, 1960.

Crépin, André. 'Chaucer and the French.' *Medieval and Pseudo-Medieval Literature*. Ed. Piero Boitani and Anna Torti. Tübingen: Narr, 1984: 55–77.

David, Alfred. *The Strumpet Muse: Art and Morals in Chaucer's Poetry*. Bloomington: Indiana University Press, 1976.

Diekstra, F.N.M. 'Chaucer and the *Romance of the Rose*.' *English Studies* 69 (1988): 12–26.

Donaldson, E. Talbot. *Speaking of Chaucer*. London: Athlone Press, 1970.

Ferster, Judith. *Chaucer on Interpretation*. Cambridge: Cambridge University Press, 1985.

Fisher, John H. 'Chaucer and the French Influence.' *New Perspectives in Chaucer Criticism*. Ed. Donald M. Rose. Norman: Pilgrim Books, 1981: 177–91.

Fyler, John M. *Chaucer and Ovid*. New Haven: Yale University Press, 1979.

Geoffrey Chaucer. Ed. George D. Economou. New York: McGraw-Hill, 1975. Articles by Brown and Hanning.

Hansen, Elaine Tuttle. *Chaucer and the Fictions of Gender*. Berkeley: University of California Press, 1992.

Jordan, Robert M. *Chaucer and the Shape of Creation: The Aesthetic Possibilities of Inorganic Structure.* Cambridge: Harvard University Press, 1967.

– *Chaucer's Poetics and the Modern Reader.* Berkeley: University of California Press, 1987.

Kean, P.M. *Chaucer and the Making of English Poetry.* 2 vols. London: Routledge and Kegan Paul, 1972.

Kiser, Lisa J. *Truth and Textuality in Chaucer's Poetry.* Hanover: University Press of New England, 1991.

Knight, Stephen. *Geoffrey Chaucer.* Oxford: Blackwell, 1986.

Lawton, David. *Chaucer's Narrators.* Cambridge: Brewer, 1985.

Mann, Jill. *Geoffrey Chaucer.* Atlantic Highlands: Humanities Press International, 1991.

McCall, John P. *Chaucer among the Gods: The Poetics of Classical Myth.* University Park: Pennsylvania State University Press, 1979.

Muscatine, Charles. *Chaucer and the French Tradition: A Study in Style and Meaning.* Berkeley: University of California Press, 1957.

Nolan, Barbara. *Chaucer and the Tradition of the* Roman Antique. Cambridge: Cambridge University Press, 1992.

Patterson, Lee. *Chaucer and the Subject of History.* Madison: University of Wisconsin Press, 1991.

Pratt, Robert A. 'Chaucer and *Le Roman de Troyle et de Criseida.*' *Studies in Philology* 53 (1956): 509–39.

Robbins, Rossell Hope. 'The Vintner's Son: French Wine in English Bottles.' *Eleanor of Aquitaine: Patron and Politician.* Ed. William W. Kibler. Austin: University of Texas Press, 1976: 147–72.

– 'Geoffroi Chaucier, poète français, Father of English Poetry.' *Chaucer Review* 13 (1978–9): 93–115.

Robertson, D.W., Jr. *A Preface to Chaucer: Studies in Medieval Perspectives.* Princeton: Princeton University Press, 1962.

Shoaf, R.A. *Dante, Chaucer, and the Currency of the Word: Money, Images, and Reference in Late Medieval Poetry.* Norman: Pilgrim Books, 1983.

Sklute, Larry. *Virtue of Necessity: Inconclusiveness and Narrative Form in Chaucer's Poetry.* Columbus: Ohio State University Press, 1984.

Wimsatt, James I. 'Chaucer and French Poetry.' *Writers and Their Background: Geoffrey Chaucer.* Ed. Derek Brewer. Athens: Ohio University Press, 1975: 109–36.

– 'Guillaume de Machaut and Chaucer's *Troilus and Criseyde.*' *Medium Aevum* 45 (1976): 277–93.

– *Chaucer and the Poems of 'Ch' in University of Pennsylvania MS French 15.* Cambridge: Brewer, 1982.

– *Chaucer and His French Contemporaries: Natural Music in the Fourteenth Century.* Toronto: University of Toronto Press, 1991.

The Dream Poems

Clemen, Wolfgang. *Chaucer's Early Poetry.* London: Methuen, 1963.

Cherniss, Michael D. *Boethian Apocalypse: Studies in Middle English Vision Poetry.* Norman: Pilgrim Books, 1987.

Edwards, Robert R. *The Dream of Chaucer: Representation and Reflection in the Early Narratives.* Durham: Duke University Press, 1989.

Finlayson, John. 'The *Roman de la Rose* and Chaucer's Narrators.' *Chaucer Review* 24 (1989–90): 187–210.

Hieatt, Constance B. *The Realism of Dream Visions: The Poetic Exploitation of the Dream-Experience in Chaucer and His Contemporaries.* The Hague: Mouton, 1967.

Lynch, Kathryn L. *The High Medieval Dream Vision: Poetry, Philosophy, and Literary Form.* Stanford: Stanford University Press, 1988.

Nolan, Barbara. *The Gothic Visionary Perspective.* Princeton: Princeton University Press, 1977.

Piehler, Paul. *The Visionary Landscape: A Study in Medieval Allegory.* London: Arnold, 1971.

Russell, J. Stephen. *The English Dream Vision: Anatomy of a Form.* Columbus: Ohio State University Press, 1988.

Spearing, A.C. *Medieval Dream-Poetry.* Cambridge: Cambridge University Press, 1976.

The Book of the Duchess

Anderson, J.J. 'The Man in Black, Machaut's Knight, and Their Ladies.' *English Studies* 73 (1992): 417–30.

Bronson, Bertrand H. '*The Book of the Duchess* Re-opened.' *PMLA* 67 (1952): 863–81.

Butterfield, Ardis. 'Lyric and Elegy in *The Book of the Duchess.*' *Medium Aevum* 60 (1991): 33–60.

Cartier, Normand R. 'Le *Bleu Chevalier* de Froissart et le *Livre de la Duchesse* de Chaucer.' *Romania* 88 (1967): 232–52.

Clemen, Wolfgang. *Chaucer's Early Poetry.* London: Methuen, 1963.

Curry, Walter Clyde. *Chaucer and the Mediaeval Sciences.* London: Oxford University Press, 1926: chap. 8.

Donnelly, Colleen. 'Challenging the Conventions of Dream Vision in *The Book of the Duchess.*' *Philological Quarterly* 66 (1987): 421–35.

Hanning, Robert W. 'Chaucer's First Ovid: Metamorphosis and Poetic Tradition in the *Book of the Duchess* and the *House of Fame.' Chaucer and the Craft of Fiction*. Ed. Leigh A. Arrathoon. Rochester: Solaris Press, 1986: 121–63.

Kean, P. M. See under Chaucer.

Kiser, Lisa J. 'Sleep, Dreams, and Poetry in Chaucer's *Book of the Duchess.' Papers on Language and Literature* 19 (1983): 3–12.

Lawlor, John. 'The Pattern of Consolation in *The Book of the Duchess.' Speculum* 31 (1956): 626–48.

Leyerle, John. 'The Heart and the Chain.' *The Learned and the Lewed: Studies in Chaucer and Medieval Literature*. Ed. Larry D. Benson. Cambridge: Harvard University Press, 1974: 113–45.

Manning, Stephen. 'Chaucer's Good Fair White: Woman and Symbol.' *Comparative Literature* 10 (1958): 97–105.

Martin, Ellen E. 'Spenser, Chaucer, and the Rhetoric of Elegy.' *Journal of Medieval and Renaissance Studies* 17 (1987): 83–109.

Nolan, Barbara. 'The Art of Expropriation: Chaucer's Narrator in *The Book of the Duchess.' New Perspectives in Chaucer Criticism*. Ed. Donald M. Rose. Norman: Pilgrim Books, 1981: 203–22.

Palmer, R. Barton. '*The Book of the Duchess* and *Fonteinne Amoureuse*: Chaucer and Machaut Reconsidered.' *Canadian Review of Comparative Literature* 7 (1980): 380–93.

Prior, Sandra Pierson. '*Routhe* and *Hert-Huntyng* in the *Book of the Duchess.' Journal of English and Germanic Philology* 85 (1986): 1–19.

Rambuss, Richard. '"Processe of tyme": History, Consolation, and Apocalypse in the *Book of the Duchess.' Exemplaria* 2 (1990): 659–83.

Shoaf, R. A. 'Stalking the Sorrowful H(e)art: Penitential Lore and the Hunt Scene in Chaucer's *The Book of the Duchess.' Journal of English and Germanic Philology* 78 (1979): 313–24.

Stevenson, Kay Gilliland. 'Readers, Poets, and Poems Within the Poem.' *Chaucer Review* 24 (1989–90): 1–19.

Walker, Denis. 'Narrative Inconclusiveness and Consolatory Dialectic in the *Book of the Duchess.' Chaucer Review* 18 (1983–4): 1–17.

Wimsatt, James. *Chaucer and the French Love Poets: The Literary Background of the* Book of the Duchess. Chapel Hill: University of North Carolina Press, 1968.

Prologue to the Legend of Good Women

Allen, Peter L. 'Reading Chaucer's Good Women.' *Chaucer Review* 21 (1986–7): 419–34.

Ames, Ruth M. 'The Feminist Connections of Chaucer's *Legend of Good Women.'*

Chaucer in the Eighties. Ed. Julian N. Wasserman and Robert J. Blanch. Syracuse: Syracuse University Press, 1986: 57–74.

Bronson, Bertrand H. See under Chaucer.

Cowen, Janet M. 'Chaucer's *Legend of Good Women*: Structure and Tone.' *Studies in Philology* 82 (1985): 416–36.

Delany, Sheila. *Chaucer's* House of Fame: *The Poetics of Skeptical Fideism*. Chicago: University of Chicago Press, 1972.

– 'Rewriting Woman Good: Gender and the Anxiety of Influence in Two Late-Medieval Texts.' *Chaucer in the Eighties*. Ed. Julian N. Wasserman and Robert J. Blanch. Syracuse: Syracuse University Press, 1986: 75–92.

– 'The Naked Text: Chaucer's "Thisbe," the *Ovide moralisé*, and the Problem of *Translatio studii* in the *Legend of Good Women*.' *Medievalia* 13 (1987): 275–94.

Frank, Robert Worth, Jr. *Chaucer and* The Legend of Good Women. Cambridge: Harvard University Press, 1972.

Kiser, Lisa J. *Telling Classical Tales: Chaucer and the* Legend of Good Women. Ithaca: Cornell University Press, 1983.

Knopp, Sherron. 'Chaucer and Jean de Meun as Self-Conscious Narrators: The Prologue to the *Legend of Good Women* and the *Roman de La Rose* 10307–680.' *Comitatus* 4 (1973): 25–39.

Kolve, V.A. 'From Cleopatra to Alceste: An Iconographic Study of *The Legend of Good Women*.' *Signs and Symbols in Chaucer's Poetry*. Ed. John P. Hermann and John J. Burke, Jr. Birmingham: University of Alabama Press, 1981: 130–78.

Overbeck, Pat Trefzger. 'Chaucer's Good Woman.' *Chaucer Review* 2 (1967–8): 75–94.

Payne, Robert O. *The Key of Remembrance: A Study of Chaucer's Poetics*. New Haven: Yale University Press, 1963.

– 'Making His Own Myth: The Prologue to Chaucer's *Legend of Good Women*.' *Chaucer Review* 9 (1974–5): 197–211.

Rowe, Donald W. *Through Nature to Eternity: Chaucer's* Legend of Good Women. Lincoln: University of Nebraska Press, 1988.

Taylor, Paul B. 'Cave and Web: Vision and Poetry in Chaucer's *Legend of Good Women*.' *Poetics: Theory and Practice in Medieval English Literature*. Ed. Piero Boitani and Anna Torti. Cambridge: Brewer, 1991: 69–82.

The Canterbury Tales

Benson, C. David. *Chaucer's Drama of Style: Poetic Variety and Contrast in the* Canterbury Tales. Chapel Hill: University of North Carolina Press, 1986.

Braddy, Haldeen. 'The French Influence on Chaucer.' *Companion to Chaucer Studies*. Ed. Beryl Rowland. Rev. ed. New York: Oxford University Press, 1979: 143–59.

Cooper, Helen. *The Structure of the Canterbury Tales*. Athens: University of Georgia Press, 1984.

Craik, T.W. *The Comic Tales of Chaucer*. London: Methuen, 1964.

Ganim, John M. *Chaucerian Theatricality*. Princeton: Princeton University Press, 1990.

Gaylord, Alan T. '*Sentence* and *Solaas* in Fragment VII of the *Canterbury Tales*: Harry Bailly as Horseback Editor.' *PMLA* 82 (1967): 226–35.

Hanning, R.W. 'Roasting a Friar, Mis-taking a Wife, and Other Acts of Textual Harassment in Chaucer's *Canterbury Tales*.' *Studies in the Age of Chaucer* 7 (1985): 3–21.

Hertog, Erik. *Chaucer's Fabliaux as Analogues*. Leuven: Leuven University Press, 1991.

Howard, Donald R. *The Idea of the Canterbury Tales*. Berkeley: University of California Press, 1976.

Kendrick, Laura. *Chaucerian Play: Comedy and Control in the* Canterbury Tales. Berkeley: University of California Press, 1988.

Knapp, Peggy. *Chaucer and the Social Contest*. New York: Routledge, 1990.

Kolve, V.A. *Chaucer and the Imagery of Narrative: The First Five Canterbury Tales*. Stanford: Stanford University Press, 1984.

Lawton, David. 'Chaucer's Two Ways: The Pilgrimage Frame of *The Canterbury Tales*.' *Studies in the Age of Chaucer* 9 (1987): 3–40.

Leicester, H. Marshall, Jr. *The Disenchanted Self: Representing the Subject in the* Canterbury Tales. Berkeley: University of California Press, 1990.

Lumiansky, R.M. *Of Sondry Folk: The Dramatic Principle in the Canterbury Tales*. Austin: University of Texas Press, 1955.

Mann, Jill. *Chaucer and Medieval Estates Satire: The Literature of Social Classes and the* General Prologue *to the* Canterbury Tales. Cambridge: Cambridge University Press, 1973.

Muscatine, Charles. *Chaucer and the French Tradition: A Study in Style and Meaning*. Berkeley: University of California Press, 1957.

Nolan, Barbara. See under Chaucer.

Owen, Charles A., Jr. 'The Crucial Passages in Five of the *Canterbury Tales*: A Study in Irony and Symbol.' *Journal of English and Germanic Philology* 52 (1953): 294–311.

– *Pilgrimage and Storytelling in the Canterbury Tales: The Dialectic of 'Ernest' and 'Game'*. Norman: University of Oklahoma Press, 1977.

Pearcy, Roy J. 'The Genre of Chaucer's Fabliau-Tales.' *Chaucer and the Craft of Fiction*. Ed. Leigh A. Arrathoon. Rochester: Solaris Press, 1986: 329–84.

Pearsall, Derek. *The Canterbury Tales*. London: Allen and Unwin, 1985.

Pratt, Robert A. 'Three Old French Sources of the Nonnes Preestes Tale.' *Speculum* 47 (1972): 422–44, 646–68.

– See under Chaucer.
Richardson, Janette. *'Blameth Nat Me': A Study of Imagery in Chaucer's Fabliaux*. The Hague: Mouton, 1970.
Rogers, William E. *Upon the Ways: The Structure of* The Canterbury Tales. Victoria: University of Victoria, English Literary Studies, 1986.
Ruggiers, Paul G. *The Art of the Canterbury Tales*. Madison: University of Wisconsin Press, 1965.
Wimsatt, James I. See under Chaucer.

The Reeve's Tale

Fabliaux français du Moyen Age. Ed. Philippe Ménard. Vol. 1. Genève: Droz, 1979. 'Del munier et des .II. clers': 73–82.
Arthur, Ross G. '"Why Artow Angry": The Malice of Chaucer's Reeve.' *English Studies in Canada* 13 (1987): 1–11.
Brewer, Derek. *'The Reeve's Tale.' Chaucer's Frame Tales: The Physical and the Metaphysical*. Ed. Joerg O. Fichte. Tübingen: Narr, 1987: 67–81.
Brown, Peter. 'The Containment of Symkyn: The Function of Space in the *Reeve's Tale*.' *Chaucer Review* 14 (1979–80): 225–36.
Burbridge, Roger T. 'Chaucer's *Reeve's Tale* and the Fabliau "Le meunier et les .II. clers."' *Annuale Mediaevale* 12 (1971): 30–6.
Cooke, Thomas D. *The Old French and Chaucerian Fabliaux: A Study of Their Comic Climax*. Columbia: University of Missouri Press, 1978.
Friedman, John Block. 'A Reading of Chaucer's *Reeve's Tale*.' *Chaucer Review* 2 (1967–8): 8–19.
Goodall, Peter. 'The *Reeve's Tale, Le Meunier et les ii Clers* and the *Miller's Tale*.' *Parergon* 27 (1980): 13–16.
Kaske, R.E. 'An Aube in the *Reeve's Tale*.' *ELH* 26 (1959): 295–310.
Kittredge, George Lyman. *Chaucer and His Poetry*. Cambridge: Harvard University Press, 1915.
Kohanski, Tamarah. 'In Search of Malyne.' *Chaucer Review* 27 (1992–3): 228–38.
Kolve, V.A. *Chaucer and the Imagery of Narrative: The First Five Canterbury Tales*. Stanford: Stanford University Press, 1984.
Lancashire, Ian. 'Sexual Innuendo in the *Reeve's Tale*.' *Chaucer Review* 6 (1971–2): 159–70.
Lumiansky, R.M. *Of Sondry Folk: The Dramatic Principle in the* Canterbury Tales. Austin: University of Texas Press, 1955.
Mann, Jill. See under Canterbury Tales.
Muscatine, Charles. *The Old French Fabliaux*. New Haven: Yale University Press, 1986.

Olson, Glending. '*The Reeve's Tale* and *Gombert*.' *Modern Language Review* 64 (1969): 721–5.
– 'The *Reeve's Tale* as a Fabliau.' *Modern Language Quarterly* 35 (1974): 219–30.
Olson, Paul A. 'The *Reeve's Tale*: Chaucer's *Measure for Measure*.' *Studies in Philology* 59 (1962): 1–17.
Schenck, Mary Jane Stearns. *The Fabliaux: Tales of Wit and Deception*. Amsterdam: Benjamins, 1987.

The Merchant's Tale

Altman, Leslie J. 'January's Decision: An Example of Chaucer's Use of the *Miroir de Mariage* in the *Merchant's Tale*.' *Romance Philology* 29 (1975–6): 514–18.
Brown, Emerson, Jr. '*Hortus Inconclusus*: The Significance of Priapus and Pyramus and Thisbe in the *Merchant's Tale*.' *Chaucer Review* 4 (1969–70): 31–40.
– 'Biblical Women in the Merchant's Tale: Feminism, Antifeminism, and Beyond.' *Viator* 5 (1974): 387–412.
– 'Chaucer, the Merchant, and Their Tale: Getting Beyond Old Controversies.' *Chaucer Review* 13 (1978–9): 141–56, 247–62.
Burger, Douglas A. 'Deluding Words in the *Merchant's Tale*.' *Chaucer Review* 12 (1977–8): 103–10.
Calabrese, Michael A. 'May Devoid of All Delight: January, the *Merchant's Tale* and the *Romance of the Rose*.' *Studies in Philology* 87 (1990): 261–84.
Economou, George D. 'Januarie's Sin against Nature: The *Merchant's Tale* and the *Roman de la Rose*.' *Comparative Literature* 17 (1965): 251–7.
Edwards, Robert R. 'Narration and Doctrine in the Merchant's Tale.' *Speculum* 66 (1991): 342–67.
Griffiths, Gwen. 'Receding Images of Initiators and Recipients – Yet Another Reflection on The Merchant's Tale.' *Papers on Language and Literature* 25 (1989): 242–63.
Harrington, Norman T. 'Chaucer's Merchant's Tale: Another Swing of the Pendulum.' *PMLA* 86 (1971): 25–31.
Lowes, John Livingston. 'Chaucer and the *Miroir de Mariage*.' *Modern Philology* 8 (1910–11): 165–86, 305–34.
McGalliard, John C. 'Chaucer's *Merchant's Tale* and Deschamps' *Miroir de Mariage*.' *Philological Quarterly* 25 (1946): 193–220.
Miller, Milton. 'The Heir in the *Merchant's Tale*.' *Philological Quarterly* 29 (1950): 437–40.
Olson, Paul A. 'Chaucer's Merchant and January's "Hevene in Erthe Heere."' *ELH* 28 (1961): 203–14.

The Wife of Bath's Tale

Burton, T.L. 'The Wife of Bath's Fourth and Fifth Husbands and Her Ideal Sixth: The Growth of a Marital Philosophy.' *Chaucer Review* 13 (1978–9): 34–50.

Crane, Susan. 'Alison's Incapacity and Poetic Instability in the Wife of Bath's Tale.' *PMLA* 102 (1987): 20–8.

Delany, Sheila. 'Strategies of Silence in the Wife of Bath's Recital.' *Exemplaria* 2 (1990): 49–69.

Fradenburg, Louise O. 'The Wife of Bath's Passing Fancy.' *Studies in the Age of Chaucer* 8 (1986): 31–58.

Hanning, R.W. See under Canterbury Tales.

Harwood, Britton J. 'The Wife of Bath and the Dream of Innocence.' *Modern Language Quarterly* 33 (1972): 257–73.

Leicester, H. Marshall, Jr. *The Disenchanted Self: Representing the Subject in the* Canterbury Tales. Berkeley: University of California Press, 1990: chap. 2–5.

Oberembt, Kenneth J. 'Chaucer's Anti-Misogynist Wife of Bath.' *Chaucer Review* 10 (1975–6): 287–302.

Parker, David. 'Can We Trust the Wife of Bath?' *Chaucer Review* 4 (1969–70): 90–8.

Patterson, Lee. '"For the Wyves love of Bathe": Feminine Rhetoric and Poetic Resolution in the *Roman de la Rose* and the *Canterbury Tales*.' *Speculum* 58 (1983): 656–95.

Quinn, Esther C. 'Chaucer's Arthurian Romance.' *Chaucer Review* 18 (1983–4): 211–20.

Reid, David S. 'Crocodilian Humor: A Discussion of Chaucer's Wife of Bath.' *Chaucer Review* 4 (1969–70): 73–89.

Rowland, Beryl. 'Chaucer's Dame Alys: Critics in Blunderland?' *Neuphilologische Mitteilungen* 73 (1972): 381–95.

Shapiro, Gloria K. 'Dame Alice as Deceptive Narrator.' *Chaucer Review* 6 (1971–2): 130–41.

Slade, Tony. 'Irony in the Wife of Bath's Tale.' *Modern Language Review* 64 (1969): 241–7.

Thundy, Zacharias P. 'Matheolus, Chaucer, and the Wife of Bath.' *Chaucerian Problems and Perspectives: Essays Presented to Paul E. Beichner*. Ed. Edward Vasta and Zacharias P. Thundy. Notre Dame: University of Notre Dame Press, 1979: 24–58.

The Pardoner's Tale

Beichner, Paul E. 'Chaucer's Pardoner as Entertainer.' *Mediaeval Studies* 25 (1963): 160–72.

Bowers, John M. '"Dronkenesse is Ful of Stryvyng": Alcoholism and Ritual Violence in Chaucer's *Pardoner's Tale*.' *ELH* 57 (1990): 757–84.
Calderwood, James L. 'Parody in *The Pardoner's Tale*.' *English Studies* 45 (1964): 302–9.
Chance, Jane. '"Disfigured is thy Face": Chaucer's Pardoner and the Protean Shape-Shifter Fals-Semblant.' *Philological Quarterly* 67 (1988): 423–35.
Curry, Walter Clyde. *Chaucer and the Mediaeval Sciences*. London: Oxford University Press, 1926: chap. 3.
Dillon, Janette. 'Chaucer's Game in the *Pardoner's Tale*.' *Essays in Criticism* 41 (1991): 208–21.
Fritz, Donald W. 'Reflections in a Golden Florin: Chaucer's Narcissistic Pardoner.' *Chaucer Review* 21 (1986–7): 338–59.
Glasser, Marc. 'The Pardoner and the Host: Chaucer's Analysis of the Canterbury Game.' *CEA Critic* 46: 1–2 (1983–4): 37–45.
Halverson, John. 'Chaucer's Pardoner and the Progress of Criticism.' *Chaucer Review* 4 (1969–70): 184–202.
Harrington, David V. 'Narrative Speed in the *Pardoner's Tale*.' *Chaucer Review* 3 (1968–9): 50–9.
Howard, Donald R. See under Canterbury Tales.
Khinoy, Stephan A. 'Inside Chaucer's Pardoner?' *Chaucer Review* 6 (1971–2): 255–67.
Manning, Stephen. 'Chaucer's Pardoner: Sex and Non-Sex.' *South Atlantic Bulletin* 39 (1974): 17–26.
– 'Rhetoric, Game, Morality, and Geoffrey Chaucer.' *Studies in the Age of Chaucer* 1 (1979): 105–18.
McAlpine, Monica E. 'The Pardoner's Homosexuality and How It Matters.' *PMLA* 95 (1980): 8–22.
Miller, Robert P. 'Chaucer's Pardoner, the Scriptural Eunuch, and the Pardoner's Tale.' *Speculum* 30 (1955): 180–99.
Rhodes, James F. 'Motivation in Chaucer's *Pardoner's Tale*: Winner Take Nothing.' *Chaucer Review* 17 (1982–3): 40–61.
Rowland, Beryl. 'Animal Imagery and the Pardoner's Abnormality.' *Neophilologus* 48 (1964): 56–60.
Stevens, Martin and Kathleen Falvey. 'Substance, Accident, and Transformations: A Reading of the *Pardoner's Tale*.' *Chaucer Review* 17 (1982–3): 142–58.

The Franklin's Tale

Berger, Harry, Jr. 'The F-Fragment of the *Canterbury Tales*.' *Chaucer Review* 1 (1966–7): 88–102, 135–56.
Carruthers, Mary J. 'The Gentilesse of Chaucer's Franklin.' *Criticism* 23 (1981): 283–300.

Charnes, Linda. '"This werk unresonable": Narrative Frustration and Generic Redistribution in Chaucer's *Franklin's Tale*.' *Chaucer Review* 23 (1988–9): 300–15.

Donovan, Mortimer J. *The Breton Lay: A Guide to Varieties*. Notre Dame: University of Notre Dame Press, 1969: chap. 4.

Duncan, Charles F., Jr. '"Straw for youre gentilesse": The Gentle Franklin's Interruption of the Squire.' *Chaucer Review* 5 (1970–1): 161–4.

Gaylord, Alan T. 'The Promises in *The Franklin's Tale*.' *ELH* 31 (1964): 331–65.

– 'From Dorigen to the Vavasour: Reading Backwards.' *The Olde Daunce: Love, Friendship, Sex, and Marriage in the Medieval World*. Ed. Robert R. Edwards and Stephen Spector. Albany: State University of New York Press, 1991: 177–200.

Hamel, Mary. 'The *Franklin's Tale* and Chrétien de Troyes.' *Chaucer Review* 17 (1982–3): 316–31.

Hume, Kathryn. 'Why Chaucer Calls the *Franklin's Tale* a Breton Lai.' *Philological Quarterly* 51 (1972): 365–79.

Lee, Anne Thompson. '"A Woman True and Fair": Chaucer's Portrayal of Dorigen in the *Franklin's Tale*.' *Chaucer Review* 19 (1984–5): 169–78.

Loomis, Laura Hibbard. 'Chaucer and the Breton Lays of the Auchinleck MS.' *Studies in Philology* 38 (1941): 14–33.

Miller, Robert P. 'The Epicurean Homily on Marriage by Chaucer's Franklin.' *Mediaevalia* 6 (1980): 151–86.

Morgan, Gerald. 'A Defence of Dorigen's Complaint.' *Medium Aevum* 46 (1977): 77–97.

Pearcy, Roy J. 'Chaucer's Franklin and the Literary Vavasour.' *Chaucer Review* 8 (1973–4): 33–59.

Peck, Russell A. 'Sovereignty and the Two Worlds of the *Franklin's Tale*.' *Chaucer Review* 1 (1966–7): 253–71.

Robertson, D.W. 'Chaucer's Franklin and His Tale.' *Costerus* ns 1 (1974): 1–26.

Rogers, William Elford. 'Individualization of Language in the Canterbury Frame Story.' *Annuale Mediaevale* 15 (1974): 74–108.

Seaman, David M. '"As thynketh yow": Conflicting Evidence and the Interpretation of *The Franklin's Tale*.' *Medievalia et Humanistica* 17 (1991): 41–58.

Specht, Henrik. *Chaucer's Franklin in the Canterbury Tales: The Social and Literary Background of a Chaucerian Character*. Copenhagen: Akademisk Forlag, 1981.

Wimsatt, James I. 'Reason, Machaut, and the Franklin.' *The Olde Daunce: Love, Friendship, Sex, and Marriage in the Medieval World*. Ed. Robert R. Edwards and Stephen Spector. Albany: State University of New York Press, 1991; 201–10.

– Also see under Chaucer.

The Manciple's Tale

Allen, Mark. 'Penitential Sermons, the Manciple, and the End of *The Canterbury Tales*.' *Studies in the Age of Chaucer* 9 (1987): 77–96.

Burrow, J.A. 'Chaucer's Canterbury Pilgrimage.' *Essays in Criticism* 36 (1986): 97–119.

Cooper, Helen. 'Chaucer and Ovid: A Question of Authority.' *Ovid Renewed: Ovidian Influences on Literature and Art from the Middle Ages to the Twentieth Century.* Ed. Charles Martindale. Cambridge: Cambridge University Press, 1988: 71–81.

– Also see under Canterbury Tales.

Davidson, Arnold E. 'The Logic of Confusion in Chaucer's *Manciple's Tales*.' *Annuale Mediaevale* 19 (1979): 5–12.

Dean, James. 'Dismantling the Canterbury Book.' *PMLA* 100 (1985): 746–62.

Delany, Sheila. 'Slaying Python: Marriage and Misogyny in a Chaucerian Text.' *Writing Woman: Women Writers and Women in Literature, Medieval to Modern.* New York: Schocken Books, 1983: 47–75.

Fradenburg, Louise. 'The Manciple's Servant Tongue: Politics and Poetry in *The Canterbury Tales*.' *ELH* 52 (1985): 85–118.

Grudin, Michaela Paasche. 'Chaucer's *Manciple's Tale* and the Poetics of Guile.' *Chaucer Review* 25 (1990–1): 329–42.

Harwood, Britton J. 'Language and the Real: Chaucer's Manciple.' *Chaucer Review* 6 (1971–2): 268–79.

McGavin, John J. 'How Nasty is Phoebus's Crow?' *Chaucer Review* 21 (1986–7): 444–58.

Pelen, Marc M. 'The Manciple's "cosyn" to the "dede."' *Chaucer Review* 25 (1990–1): 343–54.

Rogers, William E. See under Canterbury Tales.

Trask, Richard M. 'The Manciple's Problem.' *Studies in Short Fiction* 14 (1977): 109–16.

Wood, Chauncey. 'Speech, the Principle of Contraries, and Chaucer's Tales of the Manciple and the Parson.' *Mediaevalia* 6 (1980): 209–29.

Gower

The Complete Works of John Gower. Ed. G.C. Macaulay. Vol. 1: *The French Works.* Vol. 2–3: *The English Works.* Vol. 4: *The Latin Works.* Oxford: Clarendon Press, 1899–1902.

Burrow, J.A. 'The Poet as Petitioner.' *Studies in the Age of Chaucer* 3 (1981): 61–75.

Chaucer and Gower: Difference, Mutuality, Exchange. Ed. R.F. Yeager. Victoria: University of Victoria, 1991. Articles by Minnis, Wetherbee, and Yeager.

Dean, James. 'Gather Ye Rosebuds: Gower's Comic Reply to Jean de Meun.' *John Gower: Recent Readings*. Ed. R. F. Yeager. Kalamazoo: Western Michigan University, 1989: 21–37.

– 'Gower, Chaucer, and Rhyme Royal.' *Studies in Philology* 88 (1991): 251–75.

Dwyer, J.B. 'Gower's *Mirour* and Its French Sources: A Reexamination of Evidence.' *Studies in Philology* 48 (1951): 482–505.

Fisher, John H. *John Gower: Moral Philosopher and Friend of Chaucer*. London: Methuen, 1965.

Gallacher, Patrick J. *Love, the Word, and Mercury: A Reading of John Gower's* Confessio Amantis. Albuquerque: University of New Mexico Press, 1975.

Gower's Confessio Amantis*: Responses and Reassessments*. Ed. A.J. Minnis. Cambridge: Brewer, 1983. Articles by Burrow, Miller, Minnis, Pearsall, Porter, and Runacres.

Hiscoe, David W. 'The Ovidian Comic Strategy of Gower's *Confessio Amantis*.' *Philological Quarterly* 64 (1985): 367–85.

– 'Heavenly Sign and Comic Design in Gower's *Confessio Amantis*.' *Sign, Sentence, Discourse: Language in Medieval Thought and Literature*. Ed. Julian N. Wasserman and Lois Roney. Syracuse: Syracuse University Press, 1989: 228–44.

Itô, Masayoshi. *John Gower: The Medieval Poet*. Tokyo: Shinozaki Shorin, 1976.

John Gower's Literary Transformations in the Confessio Amantis: *Original Articles and Translations*. Ed. Peter G. Beidler. Washington: University Press of America, 1982.

Lowes, John Livingston. 'Spenser and the *Mirour de l'Omme*.' *PMLA* 29 (1914): 388–452.

McNally, John J. 'The Penitential and Courtly Traditions in Gower's *Confessio Amantis*.' *Studies in Medieval Culture* 1 (1964): 74–94.

Minnis, A.J. 'John Gower, *Sapiens* in Ethics and Politics.' *Medium Aevum* 49 (1980): 207–29.

Olsen, Alexandra Hennessey. *'Betwene Ernest and Game': The Literary Artistry of the* Confessio Amantis. New York: Lang, 1990.

Olsson, Kurt. 'The Cardinal Virtues and the Structure of John Gower's *Speculum Meditantis*.' *Journal of Medieval and Renaissance Studies* 7 (1977): 113–48.

– *John Gower and the Structures of Conversion: A Reading of the* Confessio Amantis. Cambridge: Brewer, 1992.

Pearsall, Derek. 'Gower's Narrative Art.' *PMLA* 81 (1966): 475–84.

– 'Gower's Latin in the *Confessio Amantis*.' *Latin and Vernacular: Studies in Late-Medieval Texts and Manuscripts*. Ed. A.J. Minnis. Cambridge: Brewer, 1989: 13–25.

Peck, Russell A. *Kingship and Common Profit in Gower's* Confessio Amantis. Carbondale: Southern Illinois University Press, 1978.

Schmitz, Götz. *'The Middel Weie': Stil- und Aufbauformen in John Gowers* Confessio Amantis. Bonn: Bouvier-Verlag, 1974.

Schueler, Donald. 'The Age of the Lover in Gower's *Confessio Amantis.' Medium Aevum* 36 (1967): 152–8.

Simpson, James. 'Ironic Incongruence in the Prologue and Book I of Gower's *Confessio Amantis.' Neophilologus* 72 (1988): 617–32.

Wetherbee, Winthrop. 'Genius and Interpretation in the *Confessio Amantis.' Magister Regis: Studies in Honor of Robert Earl Kaske*. Ed. Arthur Groos et al. New York: Fordham University Press, 1986: 241–60.

White, Hugh. 'The Naturalness of Amans' Love in *Confessio Amantis.' Medium Aevum* 56 (1987): 316–22.

Wilson, William Burton, tr. John Gower, *Mirour de l'Omme (The Mirror of Mankind)*. Rev. Nancy Wilson Van Baak. East Lansing: Colleagues Press, 1992.

Yeager, R.F. *John Gower's Poetic: The Search for a New Arion*. Cambridge: Brewer, 1990.

Zeeman, Nicolette. 'The Verse of Courtly Love in the Framing Narrative of the *Confessio Amantis.' Medium Aevum* 60 (1991): 222–40.

Hoccleve

Hoccleve's Works: The Minor Poems. Ed. Frederick J. Furnivall and I. Gollancz. Rev. Jerome Mitchell and A. I. Doyle. EETS, es, 61, 73. London: Oxford University Press, 1970.

Hoccleve's Works: The Regement of Princes. Ed. Frederick J. Furnivall. EETS, es, 72. London: Kegan Paul, Trench, Trübner, 1897.

Bentley, Elna-Jean Young. 'The Formulary of Thomas Hoccleve.' PhD Diss., Emory University, 1965.

Bornstein, Diane. 'Anti-Feminism in Thomas Hoccleve's Translation of Christine de Pizan's *Epistre au dieu d'amours.' English Language Notes* 19 (1981–2): 7–14.

Burrow, J. A. 'Autobiographical Poetry in the Middle Ages: The Case of Thomas Hoccleve.' *Proceedings of the British Academy* 68 (1982): 389–412.

– 'Hoccleve's *Series*: Experience and Books.' *Fifteenth-Century Studies: Recent Essays*. Ed. Robert F. Yeager. Hamden: Archon Books, 1984: 259–73.

Doob, Penelope B.R. *Nebuchadnezzar's Children: Conventions of Madness in Middle English Literature*. New Haven: Yale University Press, 1974: chap. 5.

Fleming, John V. 'Hoccleve's "Letter of Cupid" and the "Quarrel" over the *Roman de la Rose.' Medium Aevum* 40 (1971): 21–40.

Greetham, D.C. 'Self-Referential Artifacts: Hoccleve's Persona as a Literary Device.' *Modern Philology* 86 (1988–9): 242–51.

Hagel, Günter. *Thomas Hoccleve: Leben und Werk eines Schriftstellers im England des Spätmittelalters*. Frankfurt: Lang, 1984.

Hasler, Antony J. 'Hoccleve's Unregimented Body.' *Paragraph* 13 (1990): 164–83.

Mitchell, Jerome. *Thomas Hoccleve: A Study in Early Fifteenth-Century English Poetic*. Urbana: University of Illinois Press, 1968.

Quinn, William A. 'Hoccleve's *Epistle of Cupid*.' *Explicator* 45: 1 (Fall 1986): 7–10.

Rigg, A.G. 'Hoccleve's *Complaint* and Isidore of Seville.' *Speculum* 45 (1970): 564–74.

Scanlon, Larry. 'The King's Two Voices: Narrative and Power in Hoccleve's *Regement of Princes*.' *Literary Practice and Social Change in Britain, 1380–1530*. Ed. Lee Patterson. Berkeley: University of California Press, 1990: 216–47.

Thornley, Eva M. 'The Middle English Penitential Lyric and Hoccleve's Autobiographical Poetry.' *Neuphilologische Mitteilungen* 68 (1967): 295–321.

Torti, Anna. *The Glass of Form: Mirroring Structures from Chaucer to Skelton*. Cambridge: Brewer, 1991: chap. 3.

Verse Romance

Addison, Jim. 'The Morphology of the Middle English Metrical Romance.' *Essays in Poetics* 11:1 (1986): 1–21.

Barnes, Geraldine. *Counsel and Strategy in Middle English Romance*. Cambridge: Brewer, 1993.

Barron, W.R.J. 'Alliterative Romance and the French Tradition.' *Middle English Alliterative Poetry and Its Background*. Ed. David Lawton. Cambridge: Brewer, 1982: 70–87.

– *English Medieval Romance*. London: Longman, 1987.

Baugh, Albert C. 'The Authorship of the Middle English Romances.' *M.H.R.A.* 22 (1950): 13–28.

– 'Improvisation in the Middle English Romance.' *Proceedings of the American Philosophical Society* 103 (1959): 418–54.

Brewer, Derek. *Symbolic Stories: Traditional Narratives of the Family Drama in English Literature*. Cambridge: Brewer, 1980.

– 'Escape from the Mimetic Fallacy.' *Studies in Medieval English Romances: Some New Approaches*. Ed. Derek Brewer. Cambridge: Brewer, 1988: 1–10.

Busby, Keith. '*Sir Perceval of Galles*, *Le Conte du Graal*, and *La Continuation-Gauvain*: The Methods of an English Adaptor.' *Etudes Anglaises* 31 (1978): 198–202.

– 'Chrétien de Troyes English'd.' *Neophilologus* 71 (1987): 596–613.

Childress, Diana T. 'Between Romance and Legend: "Secular Hagiography" in Middle English Literature.' *Philological Quarterly* 57 (1978): 311–22.

Companion to Middle English Romance. Ed. Henk Aertsen and Alasdair A. MacDonald. Amsterdam: VU University Press, 1990.

Coss, P. R. 'Aspects of Cultural Diffusion in Medieval England: The Early Romances, Local Society and Robin Hood.' *Past and Present* 108 (1985): 35–79.

Crane, Susan. *Insular Romance: Politics, Faith, and Culture in Anglo-Norman and Middle English Literature*. Berkeley: University of California Press, 1986.

Donovan, Mortimer J. *The Breton Lay: A Guide to Varieties*. Notre Dame: University of Notre Dame Press, 1969.

Dürmüller, Urs. *Narrative Possibilities of the Tail-Rime Romance*. Bern: Francke, 1975.

Fewster, Carol. *Traditionality and Genre in Middle English Romance*. Cambridge: Brewer, 1987.

Fichte, Joerg O. 'The Middle English Arthurian Verse Romance: Suggestions for the Development of a Literary Typology.' *Deutsche Vierteljahrsschrift für Literaturwissenschaft und Geistesgeschichte* 55 (1981): 567–90.

– 'Grappling with Arthur or Is There an English Arthurian Verse Romance?' *Poetics: Theory and Practice in Medieval English Literature*. Ed. Piero Boitani and Anna Torti. Cambridge: Brewer, 1991: 149–63.

Field, Rosalind. 'The Anglo-Norman Background to Alliterative Romance.' *Middle English Alliterative Poetry and Its Literary Background*. Ed. David Lawton. Cambridge: Brewer, 1982: 54–69.

Finlayson, John. 'Definitions of Middle English Romance.' *Chaucer Review* 15 (1980–1): 44–62, 168–81.

– 'The Form of the Middle English *Lay*.' *Chaucer Review* 19 (1984–5): 352–68.

Fowler, David C. '*Le Conte du Graal* and *Sir Perceval of Galles*.' *Comparative Literature Studies* 12 (1975): 5–20.

Ganim, John M. 'History and Consciousness in Middle English Romance.' *Literary Review* 23 (1979–80): 481–96.

Harrington, David V. 'Redefining the Middle English Breton Lay.' *Medievalia et Humanistica* ns, 16 (1988): 73–95.

Hopkins, Andrea. *The Sinful Knights: A Study of Middle English Penitential Romance*. Oxford: Clarendon Press, 1990.

Huby, Michel. *L'Adaptation des romans courtois en Allemagne au XIIe et au XIIIe siècle*. Paris: Klincksieck, 1968.

– *Prolegomena zu einer Untersuchung von Gottfrieds* Tristan. 2 vols. Göppingen: Kümmerle, 1984.

Hudson, Harriet. 'Middle English Popular Romances: The Manuscript Evidence.' *Manuscripta* 28 (1984): 67–78.

– 'Toward a Theory of Popular Literature: The Case of the Middle English Romances.' *Journal of Popular Culture* 23: 3 (Winter 1989): 31–50.

Hume, Kathryn. 'The Formal Nature of Middle English Romance.' *Philological Quarterly* 53 (1974): 158–80.

Knight, Stephen. 'The Social Function of the Middle English Romances.' *Medieval Literature: Criticism, Ideology and History*. Ed. David Aers. New York: St Martin's Press, 1986: 99–122.

Kossick, Shirley. 'Epic and the Middle English Alliterative Revival.' *English Studies in Africa* 22 (1979): 71–82.

Lawton, David A. 'The Unity of Middle English Alliterative Poetry.' *Speculum* 58 (1983): 72–94.

– 'The Diversity of Middle English Alliterative Poetry.' *Leeds Studies in English* ns 20 (1989): 143–72.

Levine, Robert. 'Who Composed *Havelok* for Whom?' *Yearbook of English Studies* 22 (1992): 95–104.

McGillivray, Murray. *Memorization in the Transmission of the Middle English Romances*. New York: Garland, 1990.

Meale, Carol M. 'The Middle English Romance of *Ipomedon*: A Late Mediaeval "Mirror" for Princes and Merchants.' *Reading Medieval Studies* 10 (1984): 136–91.

Mehl, Dieter. *Die mittelenglischen Romanzen des 13. und 14. Jahrhunderts*. Heidelberg: Winter, 1967.

Moorman, Charles. 'The Origins of the Alliterative Revival.' *Southern Quarterly* 7 (1968–9): 345–71.

– 'The English Alliterative Revival and the Literature of Defeat.' *Chaucer Review* 16 (1981–2): 85–100.

Pearsall, Derek. 'The Development of Middle English Romance.' *Mediaeval Studies* 27 (1965): 91–116.

– 'The Origins of the Alliterative Revival.' *The Alliterative Tradition in the Fourteenth Century*. Ed. Bernard S. Levy and Paul E. Szarmach. Kent: Kent State University Press, 1981: 1–24.

– 'The Alliterative Revival: Origins and Social Backgrounds.' *Middle English Alliterative Poetry and Its Literary Background*. Ed. David Lawton. Cambridge: Brewer, 1982: 34–53.

– 'Middle English Romance and Its Audiences.' *Historical and Editorial Studies in Medieval and Early Modern English for Johan Gerritsen*. Ed. Mary-Jo Arn et al. Groningen: Wolters-Noordhoff, 1985: 37–47.

Quinn, William A. and Audley S. Hall. *'Jongleur': A Modified Theory of Oral Improvisation and Its Effects on the Performance and Transmission of Middle English Romance*. Washington: University Press of America, 1982.

Ramsey, Lee C. *Chivalric Romances: Popular Literature in Medieval England*. Bloomington: Indiana University Press, 1983.

Reichl, Karl. 'The Middle English Popular Romance: Minstrel versus Hack Writer.' *The Ballad and Oral Literature*. Ed. Joseph Harris. Cambridge: Harvard University Press, 1991: 243–68.

Reiss, Edmund. 'Romance.' *The Popular Literature of Medieval England*. Ed. Thomas J. Heffernan. Knoxville: University of Tennessee Press, 1985: 108–30.

Reuters, Anna Hubertine. *Friendship and Love in the Middle English Metrical Romances*. Frankfurt am Main: Lang, 1991.

Richmond, Velma Bourgeois. *The Popularity of Middle English Romance*. Bowling Green: Bowling Green University Popular Press, 1975.

Romance in Medieval England. Ed. Maldwyn Mills et al. Cambridge: Brewer, 1991. Articles by Field, Weiss, and Williams.

Rosenberg, Bruce A. 'The Morphology of the Middle English Metrical Romances.' *Journal of Popular Culture* 1 (1967–8): 63–77.

– 'Medieval Popular Literature: Folkloric Sources.' *The Popular Literature of Medieval England*. Ed. Thomas J. Heffernan. Knoxville: University of Tennessee Press, 1985: 61–84.

Rumble, Thomas C., ed. *The Breton Lays in Middle English*. Detroit: Wayne State University Press, 1965.

Salter, Elizabeth. 'The Alliterative Revival.' *Modern Philology* 64 (1966–7): 146–50, 233–7.

Schelp, Hanspeter. *Exemplarische Romanzen im Mittelenglischen*. Göttingen: Vandenhoeck and Ruprecht, 1967.

Spearing, A.C. 'Marie de France and Her Middle English Adapters.' *Studies in the Age of Chaucer* 12 (1990): 117–56.

Staines, David. '*Havelok the Dane*: A Thirteenth-Century Handbook for Princes.' *Speculum* 51 (1976): 602–23.

Stemmler, Theo. 'Die mittelenglischen Bearbeitungen zweier Lais der Marie de France.' *Anglia* 80 (1962): 243–63.

Taylor, Andrew. 'Fragmentation, Corruption, and Minstrel Narration: The Question of the Middle English Romances.' *Yearbook of English Studies* 22 (1992): 38–62.

Turville-Petre, Thorlac. *The Alliterative Revival*. Cambridge: Brewer, 1977.

Wertime, Richard A. 'The Theme and Structure of the Stanzaic *Morte Arthur*.' *PMLA* 87 (1972): 1075–82.

Williams, Elizabeth. '*Lanval* and *Sir Landevale*: A Medieval Translator and His Methods.' *Leeds Studies in English* 3 (1969): 85–99.

Wittig, Susan. *Stylistic and Narrative Structures in the Middle English Romances*. Austin: University of Texas Press, 1978.

Women and Literature in Britain, 1150–1500. Ed. Carol M. Meale. Cambridge: Cambridge University Press, 1993. Articles by Alexander, Fellows, and Weiss.

Wurster, Jutta. 'The Audience.' *The* Alliterative Morte Arthure: *A Reassessment of the Poem*. Cambridge: Brewer, 1981: 44–56.

Ywain and Gawain

Ywain and Gawain. Ed. Albert B. Friedman and Norman T. Harrington. EETS, os, 254. London: Oxford University Press, 1964.

Busby, Keith. 'Chrétien de Troyes English'd.' *Neophilologus* 71 (1987): 596–613.

Faris, David E. 'The Art of Adventure in the Middle English Romance: *Ywain and Gawain, Eger and Grime*.' *Studia Neophilologica* 53 (1981): 91–100.

Hamilton, Gayle K. 'The Breaking of the Troth in *Ywain and Gawain*.' *Mediaevalia* 2 (1976): 111–35.

Harrington, Norman T. 'The Problem of the Lacunae in *Ywain and Gawain*.' *Journal of English and Germanic Philology* 69 (1970): 659–65.

Hunt, Tony. 'Beginnings, Middles, and Ends: Some Interpretative Problems in Chrétien's *Yvain* and Its Medieval Adaptations.' *The Craft of Fiction: Essays in Medieval Poetics*. Ed. Leigh A. Arrathoon. Rochester: Solaris Press, 1984: 83–117.

Sir Degaré

Sire Degarre. Ed. Gustav Schleich. Heidelberg: Winter, 1929.

Colopy, Cheryl. '*Sir Degaré*: A Fairy Tale Oedipus.' *Pacific Coast Philology* 17 (1982): 31–9.

Faust, George Patterson. Sir Degare: *A Study of the Texts and Narrative Structure*. Princeton: Princeton University Press, 1935.

Kane, George. *Middle English Literature: A Critical Study of the Romances, the Religious Lyrics,* Piers Plowman. London: Methuen, 1951.

Kozicki, Henry. 'Critical Methods in the Literary Evaluation of *Sir Degaré*.' *Modern Language Quarterly* 29 (1968): 3–14.

Rosenberg, Bruce A. 'The Three Tales of *Sir Degaré*.' *Neuphilologische Mitteilungen* 76 (1975): 39–51.

Slover, Clark Harris. '*Sire Degarre*: A Study of a Medieval Hack Writer's Methods.' *University of Texas Studies in English* 11 (1931): 5–23.

Stokoe, William C., Jr. 'The Double Problem of *Sir Degaré*.' *PMLA* 70 (1955): 518–34.

The Earl of Toulouse

The Erl of Tolous and the Emperes of Almayn: Eine englische Romanze aus dem Anfange des 15. Jahrhunderts. Ed. Gustav Lüdtke. Berlin: Weidmannsche Buchhandlung, 1881.

Cabaniss, Allen. 'Judith Augusta and Her Time.' *University of Mississippi Studies in English* 10 (1969): 67–109.

Dürmüller, Urs. *Narrative Possibilities of the Tail-Rime Romance*. Bern: Francke, 1975: chap. 1–6.
Reilly, Robert. '*The Earl of Toulouse*: A Structure of Honor.' *Mediaeval Studies* 37 (1975): 515–23.

Floris and Blauncheflur

Floris and Blauncheflur: A Middle English Romance. Ed. Franciscus Catharina de Vries. Groningen: Druk. V.R.B., 1966.
Barnes, Geraldine. 'Cunning and Ingenuity in the Middle English *Floris and Blauncheflur*.' *Medium Aevum* 53 (1984): 10–25.
Reinhold, Joachim. *Floire et Blancheflor: Etude de littérature comparée*. 1906. Repr. Genève: Slatkine, 1970.
Reiss, Edmund. 'Symbolic Detail in Medieval Narrative: *Floris and Blancheflour*.' *Papers on Language and Literature* 7 (1971): 339–50.
Wentersdorf, Karl P. 'Iconographic Elements in *Floris and Blancheflour*.' *Annuale Mediaevale* 20 (1980): 76–96.

William of Palerne

William of Palerne: An Alliterative Romance. Ed. G. H. V. Bunt. Groningen: Bouma's Boekhuis, 1985.
Dunn, Charles W. *The Foundling and the Werewolf: A Literary-Historical Study of* Guillaume de Palerne. Toronto: University of Toronto Press, 1960.
Kooper, Erik. '*Grace*: The Healing Herb in *William of Palerne*.' *Leeds Studies in English* ns, 15 (1984): 83–93.
Simms, Norman Toby, ed. *William of Palerne: A New Edition*. n.p.: Norwood Editions, 1977.
Turville-Petre, Thorlac. *The Alliterative Revival*. Cambridge: Brewer, 1977.

Amis and Amiloun

Amis and Amiloun. Ed. MacEdward Leach. EETS, os, 203. London: Oxford University Press, 1937.
Baldwin, Dean R. '*Amis and Amiloun*: The Testing of *Treuþe*.' *Papers on Language and Literature* 16 (1980): 353–65.
Hume, Kathryn. 'Structure and Perspective: Romance and Hagiographic Features in the Amicus and Amelius Story.' *Journal of English and Germanic Philology* 69 (1970): 89–107.
– '*Amis and Amiloun* and the Aesthetics of Middle English Romance.' *Studies in Philology* 70 (1973): 19–41.

Kratins, Ojars. 'The Middle English *Amis and Amiloun*: Chivalric Romance or Secular Hagiography?' *PMLA* 81 (1966): 347–54.

Athelston

Athelston: A Middle English Romance. Ed. A. McI. Trounce. EETS, os, 224. London: Oxford University Press, 1957.

Dickerson, A. Inskip. 'The Subplot of the Messenger in *Athelston*.' *Papers on Language and Literature* 12 (1976): 115–24.

Ellzey, Mary Housum. 'The Advice of Wives in Three Middle English Romances: *The King of Tars, Sir Cleges*, and *Athelston*.' *Medieval Perspectives* 7 (1992): 44–52.

Hibbard, Laura A. '*Athelston*, A Westminster Legend.' *PMLA* 36 (1921): 223–44.

Kiernan, Kevin S. '*Athelston* and the Rhyme of the English Romances.' *Modern Language Quarterly* 36 (1975): 339–53.

Caxton

Selections from William Caxton. Ed. N.F. Blake. Oxford: Clarendon Press, 1973.

Caxton's Malory: A New Edition of Sir Thomas Malory's Le Morte Darthur. 2 vols. Ed. James W. Spisak. Berkeley: University of California Press, 1983.

Belyea, Barbara. 'Caxton's Reading Public.' *English Language Notes* 19 (1981–2): 14–19.

Blake, N.F. *Caxton and His World*. Tonbridge: Tonbridge Printers, 1969.

– *Caxton: England's First Publisher*. London: Osprey, 1976.

– 'William Caxton Again in the Light of Recent Scholarship.' *Dutch Quarterly Review of Anglo-American Letters* 12 (1982): 162–82.

Bornstein, Diane. 'William Caxton's Chivalric Romances and the Burgundian Renaissance in England.' *English Studies* 57 (1976): 1–10.

Fisher, John H. 'Chancery and the Emergence of Standard Written English in the Fifteenth Century.' *Speculum* 52 (1977): 870–99.

– 'Caxton and Chancery English.' *Fifteenth-Century Studies: Recent Essays*. Ed. Robert F. Yeager. Hamden: Archon Books, 1984: 161–85.

Kekewich, Margaret. 'Edward IV, William Caxton, and Literary Patronage in Yorkist England.' *Modern Language Review* 66 (1971): 481–7.

Kipling, Gordon. *The Triumph of Honour: Burgundian Origins of the Elizabethan Renaissance*. The Hague: Leiden University Press, 1977.

Kretzschmar, William A., Jr. 'Caxton's Sense of History.' *Journal of English and Germanic Philology* 91 (1992): 510–28.

Markland, Murray F. 'The Role of William Caxton.' *Research Studies* 28 (1960): 47–60.

Montgomery, Robert L. 'William Caxton and the Beginnings of Tudor Critical Thought.' *Huntington Library Quarterly* 36 (1972–3): 91–103.

Pearsall, Derek. 'The English Romance in the Fifteenth Century.' *Essays and Studies* ns 29 (1976): 56–83.

Rutter, Russell. 'William Caxton and Literary Patronage.' *Studies in Philology* 84 (1987): 440–70.

Sands, Donald B. 'Caxton as a Literary Critic.' *Papers of the Bibliographical Society of America* 51 (1957): 312–18.

Sandved, Arthur O. *Studies in the Language of Caxton's Malory.* Oslo: Norwegian Universities Press, 1968.

Scanlon, Paul A. 'Pre-Elizabethan Prose Romances in English.' *Cahiers Elisabéthains* 12 (Oct. 1977): 1–20.

Simko, Ján. *Word-Order in the Winchester Manuscript and in William Caxton's Edition of Thomas Malory's Morte Darthur (1485) – A Comparison.* Halle: Niemeyer, 1957.

Veyrin-Forrer, Jeanne. 'Caxton and France.' *Journal of the Printing Historical Society* 11 (1975–6): 33–47.

Yeager, R.F. 'Literary Theory at the Close of the Middle Ages: William Caxton and William Thynne.' *Studies in the Age of Chaucer* 6 (1984): 135–64.

Malory

The Works of Sir Thomas Malory. Ed. Eugène Vinaver. 3 vols. Oxford: Clarendon Press, 1947.

Benson, C. David. 'Gawain's Defence of Lancelot in Malory's *Death of Arthur.*' *Modern Language Review* 78 (1983): 267–72.

Benson, Larry D. *Malory's* Morte Darthur. Cambridge: Harvard University Press, 1976.

Brewer, Derek. 'Malory: The Traditional Writer and the Archaic Mind.' *Arthurian Literature* 1 (1981): 94–120.

Essays on Malory. Ed. J.A.W. Bennett. Oxford: Clarendon Press, 1963. Articles by Brewer, Lewis, Tucker, and Whitehead.

Field, P.J.C. *The Life and Times of Sir Thomas Malory.* Cambridge: Brewer, 1993.

Ihle, Sandra Ness. *Malory's Grail Quest: Invention and Adaptation in Medieval Prose Romance.* Madison: University of Winsconsin Press, 1983.

Kennedy, Beverly. *Knighthood in the* Morte Darthur. Cambridge: Brewer, 1985.

Lambert, Mark. *Malory: Style and Vision in* Le Morte Darthur. New Haven: Yale University Press, 1975.

Malory's Originality: A Critical Study of Le Morte Darthur. Ed. R.M. Lumiansky. Baltimore: Johns Hopkins Press, 1964. Essays by Dichmann, Guerin, Lumiansky, Moorman, Rumble, and Wright.

Mann, Jill. '"Taking the Adventure": Malory and the *Suite du Merlin*.' *Aspects of Malory*. Ed. Toshiyuki Takamiya and Derek Brewer. Woodbridge: Brewer, 1981: 71–91.

McCarthy, Terence. *Reading the* Morte Darthur. Cambridge: Brewer, 1988.

Meale, Carol. 'Manuscripts, Readers and Patrons in Fifteenth-Century England: Sir Thomas Malory and Arthurian Romance.' *Arthurian Literature* 4 (1985): 93–126.

Merrill, Robert. *Sir Thomas Malory and the Cultural Crisis of the Late Middle Ages*. New York: Lang, 1987.

Moorman, Charles. *The Book of Kyng Arthur: The Unity of Malory's* Morte Darthur. Lexington: University of Kentucky Press, 1965.

Pochoda, Elizabeth T. *Arthurian Propaganda:* Le Morte Darthur *as an Historical Ideal of Life*. Chapel Hill: University of North Carolina Press, 1971.

Riddy, Felicity. *Sir Thomas Malory*. Leiden: Brill, 1987.

Vinaver, Eugène. *Le Roman de Tristan et Iseut dans l'oeuvre de Thomas Malory*. Paris: Champion, 1925.

– *Malory*. Oxford: Clarendon Press, 1929.

Whitaker, Muriel. *Arthur's Kingdom of Adventure: The World of Malory's* Morte Darthur. Cambridge: Brewer, 1984.

Conclusion

The Anglo-Norman Lyric: An Anthology. Ed. David L. Jeffrey and Brian J. Levy. Toronto: Pontifical Institute of Mediaeval Studies, 1990.

Anglo-Norman Political Songs. Ed. Isabel S.T. Aspin. Oxford: Blackwell, 1953.

Bec, Pierre. 'Troubadours, trouvères et espace Plantagenêt.' *Cahiers de Civilisation Médiévale* 29 (1986): 9–14.

Boffey, Julia. *Manuscripts of English Courtly Love Lyrics in the Later Middle Ages*. Cambridge: Brewer, 1985.

Busby, Keith. 'Conspicuous by Its Absence: The English *Fabliau*.' *Dutch Quarterly Review of Anglo-American Letters* 12 (1982): 30–41.

Flinn, John. *Le Roman de Renart dans la littérature française et dans les littératures étrangères au Moyen Age*. Toronto: University of Toronto Press, 1963: chap. 15.

Furrow, Melissa. 'Middle English Fabliaux and Modern Myth.' *ELH* 56 (1989): 1–18.

Goodall, Peter. 'An Outline History of the English Fabliau after Chaucer.' *AUMLA* 57 (1982): 5–23.

Harvey, Carol J. 'Macaronic Techniques in Anglo-Norman Verse.' *L'Esprit Créateur* 18:1 (1978): 70–81.

– 'Intertextuality in the Anglo-Norman Lyric.' *Journal of the Rocky Mountain Medieval and Renaissance Association* 10 (1989): 17–28.

Hines, John. *The Fabliau in English*. London: Longman, 1993.
Patterson, Lee. 'On the Margin: Postmodernism, Ironic History, and Medieval Studies.' *Speculum* 65 (1990): 87–108.
Robbins, Rossell Hope. 'The English Fabliau: Before and After Chaucer.' *Moderna Språk* 64 (1970): 231–44.
Wimsatt, James I. *Chaucer and His French Contemporaries: Natural Music in the Fourteenth Century*. Toronto: University of Toronto Press, 1991.

Index